A HISTORY OF RAILROADS IN WESTERN NEW YORK

Edward T. Dunn

Edward T. Dunn S.J.

The Heritage Press
Western New York Heritage Institute

1996

Edited by:
Edward J. Patton
and
Melinda W. Miller

For information, contact:

The Heritage Press
Western New York Heritage Institute
P. O. Box 192
Buffalo, New York 14205-0192

Dunn, Edward T., 1925-
A History Of Railroads In Western New York

Cover Photo: Exchange Street Station and yard, a view from Michigan Ave. Photo by Ernest Winter 1904-05: Will Berg Collection
Edward T. Dunn Photo: Tom Wolf
Cover design and layout: MJM Design

ISBN 1-878097-19-9
Library of Congress Catalog Card Number 96-061498
Printed in the United States of America

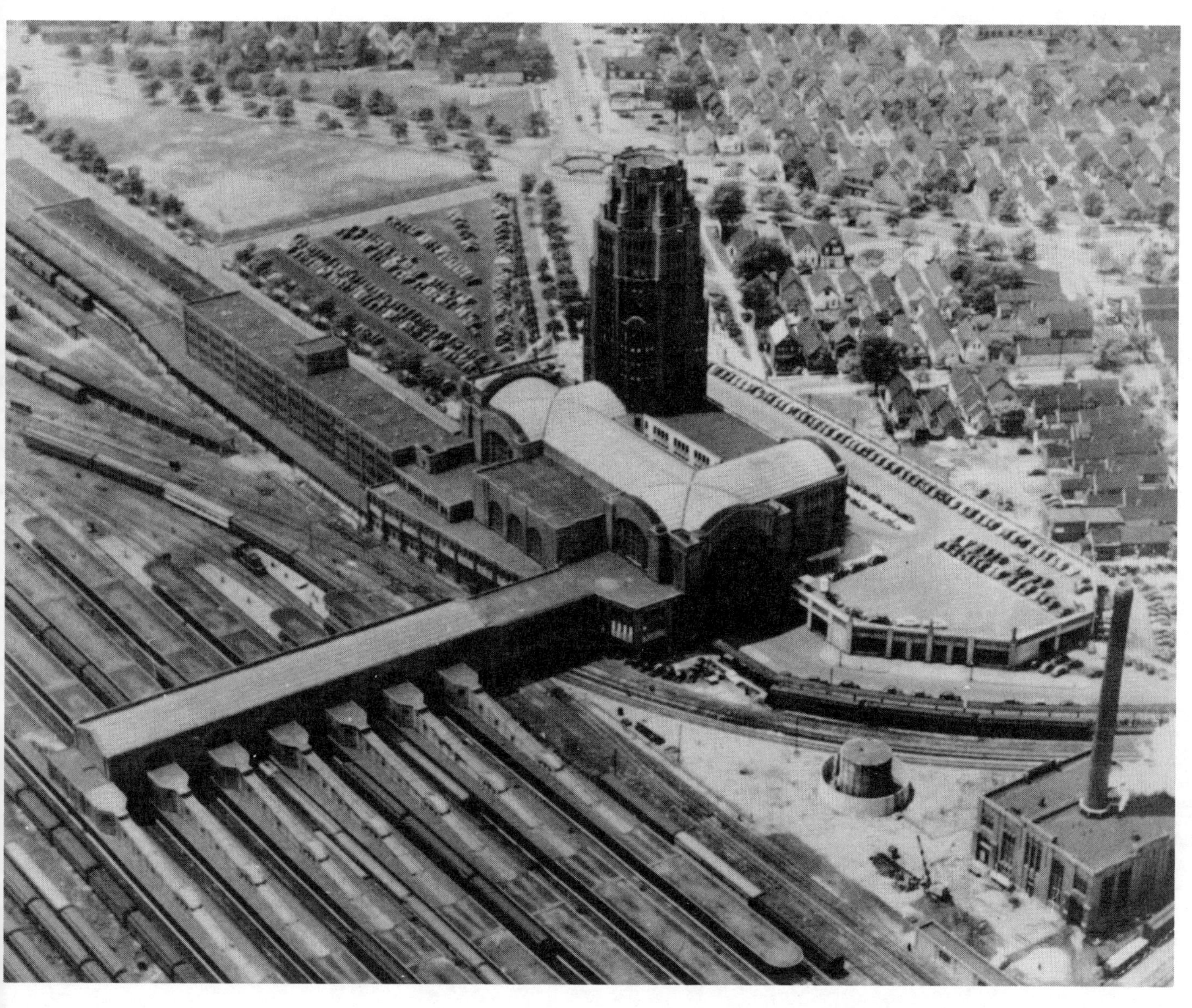

New York Central Terminal
Photo courtesy of Stanford Lipsey

To Julia Boyer Reinstein,
a historian of Western New York herself
and a loyal friend of the Western New York
Heritage Institute

ACKNOWLEDGMENTS

Several years ago, Ed Patton of the Western New York Heritage Institute suggested that I write this book. Canisius College granted me a sabbatical during 1994-1995 to research the subject on which I had already been working. The staff at the Bouwhuis Library has shown me the cooperation that seems to be the rule with librarians almost everywhere. I am especially grateful to librarians Pat McGlynn and Sandy DiCarlo, the former for providing me with easy access to Canisius's collection of local atlases, the latter for procuring from the Association of American Railroads in Washington back issues of the *Official Guide of the Railways,* which were indispensable in reconstructing over a century of Buffalo's passenger train service. Mike Vogel of the *Buffalo News*, whom I had as a student and whose wedding I performed, made available to me photographs from the paper's archives. Doug Turner, former editor of the *Courier-Express,* directed me to the library of the State University College of New York at Buffalo, where the archives of that newspaper now repose. Mary Delmont of the Butler Library there was most helpful in selecting and reproducing photographs from the *Courier* which appear in the following pages. Adele N. Frohe and Michael J. Liszewski, graduates of Canisius and up-and-coming young Buffalo attorneys, painstakingly proofread the text and made countless corrections and invaluable emendations. Kevin Mugridge, another Canisius grad and a prominent railfan, read a preliminary version and saved me from committing several serious gaffes. He also gave local habitation and a name to the unidentified pictures of several local depots. For what eluded the watchfulness of these readers I have only myself to blame. Willard Dittmar of the Historical Society of the Tonawandas instructed me in the intricacies of the 1917-1922 relocation of the New York Central Railroad through the Tonawandas, and provided me with a picture of that road's North Tonawanda depot. For many rare pictures of the local railroad scene which appear in this work I owe a debt of gratitude to Ron Dukarm, whose knowledge of Western New York railroads is encyclopedic. Al Kerr was most supportive, as was Bill Kessel, who gave me his personal copy of the *Official Guide of the Railways* for 1933. May they both rest in peace. My approach to the overall history of American railroads is that of the revisionist historian, Albro Martin, whose incisive insights into the subject enabled me to understand why what went wrong went wrong. May the renaissance of the industry, which he saw coming and proclaimed, continue *ad multos annos.*

Buffalo, New York
April 11, 1996
In Festo Sti. Leonis I

TABLE OF CONTENTS

1
Beginnings

As O. S. Noch, British railroad historian, points out:

The role played by railways in world history over the last 150 years cannot be overemphasized. In the older countries - Great Britain, France, Germany , and Austria - the railway became an indispensable tool for industrial development and the furtherance of travel. It was a predominant factor in the building of new nations like the United States and Canada, while in Europe it played an invaluable part in coalescing into new nations groups of ancient principalities and kingdoms hitherto independent. Railways began to provide cheap, reliable transport where previously there had been the hazards of long tiresome journeys by road or coastal shipping. . . . Travel between towns and cities was relatively limited for most before 1830 and for all was a hazardous undertaking. Thereafter the rapid development of railways led to immense social and economic changes. The railway offered a speed and flexibility for passengers and goods which the stagecoach and canals had never provided. Industry flourished, new towns appeared, and gradually for many a new way of life opened up. [1

With reference to America, Albro Martin, the witty, anti-progressivist, revisionist railroad historian, who has been called "the man who made deregulation academically respectable," makes this claim:

The passenger train ,which many historians have seen as "knitting together" localities into a national whole, did no such thing. It rather created these local and regional centers in the process of creating a highly vertabrate [linked together in a manner suggesting vertebrae] *nation that by the early twentieth century had achieved an efficiency and trustworthiness of travel that would not survive the emergence of the automobile and its suburbs. . . In its day the train was totally in control of national mobility as the car has been since.* [2]

Labor historian Gerald Eggert sums up the situation:

The railroads were the most important single initiator of the "take-off" stage of American industrialization. The railway network provided the transportation base upon which America's modern, specialized, interdependent, urban industrial society rested. [3]

As every schoolboy knows, the first steam railway (in the sense of a common carrier) was

England's Stockton & Darlington, completed in 1825 to carry Durham coal twenty miles to the North Sea. By 1840 this sceptered isle, the mother of railways, was crisscrossed by over 1,000 miles of iron roads. Her former American colonies were not far behind. There the first railroads originated in the contest between rival East Coast seaports to acquire tributary hinterlands to the west. It was on July 4, 1828, that Charles Carroll of Carrollton, sole surviving signer of the Declaration of Independence, turned the inaugural spadeful for the Republic's first railroad, the Baltimore & Ohio, which had been chartered the previous year. Baltimore, at the head of ocean navigation on Chesapeake Bay, an estuary of the Susquehanna River, had a population of 62,700 in 1820, which made it the third largest city in the Union after New York and Philadelphia. Also instrumental in Baltimore's rise from 6,000 at the time of Revolution was the National Road, which by 1818 linked Cumberland, Maryland, on the Potomac with Wheeling, Virginia, on the Ohio, thus joining the Atlantic coast with the Ohio and Mississippi Valleys. Ten years earlier, Maryland had updated a pre-Revolutionary Road that ran westward from Baltimore to Cumberland.

But with the opening of the Erie Canal (Figure #1) along its full length of 363 miles in 1825, Baltimore merchants realized that their National Road could not compete with Clinton's Ditch as a means of tapping the interior. Turnpikes were adequate for passengers and mail but not for carrying low revenue freight any considerable distance. After the Erie Canal went into operation, the cost per mile of transporting a ton of freight between Buffalo and New York declined from nearly twenty cents to less than two. There is extant a description of Buffalo in 1832, a decade before the arrival of the railroad from the east. The filling up of the West was in full swing:

Canal boats filled with emigrants, and covered with goods and furniture, are almost hourly arriving. The boats are discharged of their motley freight, and for the time being, natives of all climates and countries patrol our streets, either to gratify curiosity, purchase necessaries, or inquire the most favorable points for their future location. Several steamboats and vessels daily depart for the far west, literally crammed with masses of living beings to people those regions. Some days, near a thousand thus depart. As I have stood upon the wharves and seen the departure of these floating taverns, with their decks piled up in huge heaps with furniture and chattels of all descriptions, and even hoisted up and hung on to the rigging; while the whole upper deck, and benches, and railing, sustained a mass of human bodies clustering all over them like a swarming hive - and to witness this spectacle year after year, for many months of the season, I have almost wondered at the amazing increase of our population, and the inexhaustible enterprise and energy of the people! What a country must the vast border of these lakes become! And Buffalo must be the great emporium, and place of transit for their products and supplies. [4]

Despite the Erie's success, Baltimore's capitalists, in deciding on a railroad, showed more foresight than their opposite numbers in Philadelphia, who, the year after the Erie was finished, persuaded the Pennsylvania legislature to construct a 395 mile canal from Columbia on the Susquehanna to Pittsburgh on the Ohio. This Mainline Canal had to cross the Alleghenies at 2,200 feet above sea level, as opposed to a maximum of 565 feet on the Erie, and it had 174 locks (besides a portage railway at the summit) compared with the Erie's 83. (Figure VII, #2.) Completed in 1834, the Mainline Canal with its branches never covered operating costs and forced the state to default on the payment of interest on its bonds in 1840. Meanwhile, service on the B&O to Ellicott's Mills, thirteen miles west of Baltimore, began on July 1, 1831. Horses provided motive power until the introduction of steam engines in 1832. The Baltimore & Ohio reached Harpers Ferry, Virginia, in 1835, but did not justify its corporate name until New Year's Day, 1853, when its first train pulled into Wheeling on the Ohio River.

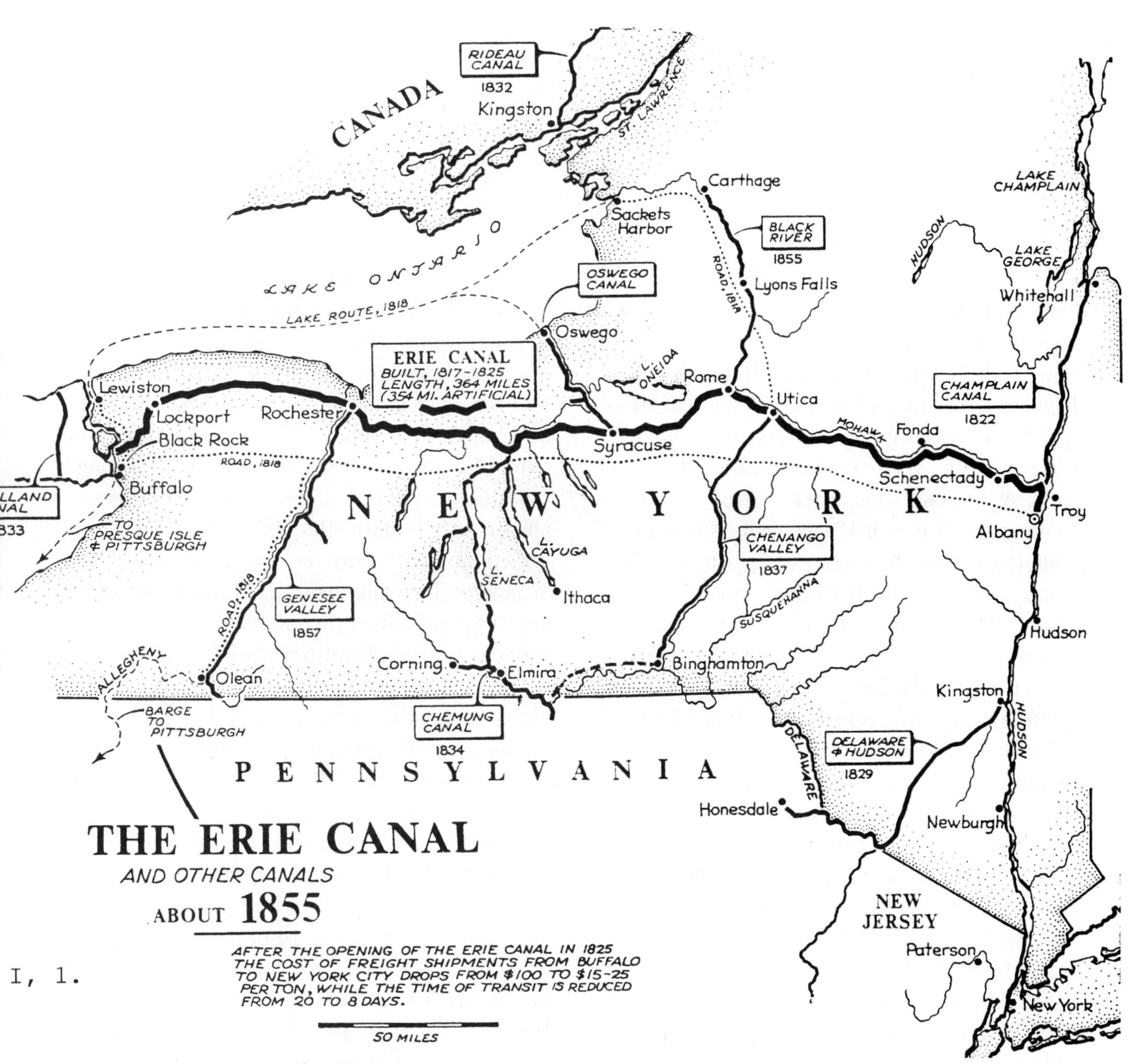

I, 1.

2
Before The Central Was

New York City was not in the vanguard of early American railroad building, since it was well supplied by waterways: Long Island Sound, the Upper and Lower Bays, the East River, and the lordly Hudson, which was navigable by ocean-going vessels for over 150 miles to Troy. A line modestly called the New York & Harlem (the Harlem River divides Manhattan from what was then Westchester County) was incorporated in 1831. It took five years to build this 6.75 mile horsecar line along 4th Avenue from City Hall to 135th Street.

Upstate, the Erie Canal had its jealous guardians in the legislature, who looked askance at proposals to build railroads that would compete with the Erie's hugely successful main artery and its less successful branches. Therefore, the first steam railroad in the state, the Mohawk & Hudson, supplemented rather than competed with the canal. Schenectady on the Mohawk is only fifteen miles from Albany, but to make the trip by canal required an ascent of 225 feet through twenty-seven locks, a day-long thirty mile ordeal for passengers, most of whom took a stagecoach over the route. The Mohawk & Hudson had been incorporated in 1826, but, because provisions in its charter made it unattractive to investors, construction did not begin until the summer of 1830, by which time the offending articles had been repealed. The first run was made on August 13, 1831, behind a locomotive named after ex-Governor De Witt Clinton. The road was 15.87 miles long with inclined planes at both ends where cars - stagecoaches with flanged wheels - were pulled up and down by cables that wound around pulleys and were drawn up by stationary engines. Since it could not compete with the canal's rock-bottom freight rates, the Mohawk & Hudson during its first decade was almost wholly a passenger hauler.

Meanwhile at the western end of the state less than a month after the De Witt Clinton's first revenue run, "at a numerous and respectable meeting of the citizens of Buffalo held at the Eagle Tavern [on the west side of Main Street south of Court] on the 6th of September for the purpose of taking into consideration the subject of railroad communication between this place and the Hudson River, Bela D. Coe was called to the chair and James Stryker was appointed secretary." [1] The proceedings consisted principally of adopting resolutions affirming the expedience of cooperating with others in central and eastern New York in constructing such a road and appointing a committee to carry out this purpose. At the time the population of Buffalo, whose northern boundary was North Street, was about 10,000. The city did not approach its present size by amalgamation with Black Rock until 1853. Nothing further is known about this project, but Coe and one of the committee members, Reuben B. Heacock, would be heard from again on railroad matters.

The success of the Mohawk & Hudson explains the chartering in 1833 of the Utica & Schenectady. Because it paralleled the Mohawk Turnpike and the canal, it was shackled with unbelievable restrictions. Carrying freight, except passengers' baggage, was forbidden, and fares were not to exceed four cents a mile. Compensating for these repudiations of free enterprise was a splendid water-level route running north of the Mohawk River seventy-eight miles to Utica. The only president of this line for its twenty years of separate existence was Erastus Corning, an Albany ironmonger and hardware dealer. Corning received no salary from the U&S but enjoyed the concession of supplying the road with all its rails, running gear, tools, and other iron and steel articles. The year the U&S was opened, 1836, also saw the chartering of the Utica & Syracuse, which commenced operations on July 3, 1839. It was no airline, since it detoured north to Rome, which accounted for six of its overall length of fifty-three miles, a maneuver designed to take advantage of easier grades and to derive traffic from Rome. It was treated more generously by the legislature than the Utica & Schenectady had been, since the U&S was permitted to carry freight as well as passengers year round, though it had to pay the canal tolls on the freight it hauled during the navigation season. Another characteristic of the Utica & Syracuse was that it ran down the middle of Washington Street, Syracuse's main thoroughfare, an inconvenience for Syracusans and the railroad for another century. The road earned ten percent on its investment in its first six months, thus giving a boost to railroad construction elsewhere.

Further to the west was an older line, the Auburn & Syracuse. Residents of this "loveliest city of the plain" were incensed that their town had been left off the course of the Erie Canal, and so began as early as 1827 to agitate for a railroad, which was finally incorporated in 1834 to link Auburn to the canal at Syracuse. Since it was not a competitor of but an adjunct to the Erie, the Auburn & Syracuse was allowed to carry freight as well as passengers, but passengers were its chief source of revenue. Construction began in 1835 and dragged along until the Panic of 1837, which led to a severe contraction of credit everywhere in the nation, further slowed recruitment of funds. Full recovery was not achieved until 1843. Nevertheless, the A&S was completed in January, 1838, though with inferior grading and trackage. Trains were pulled by horses over wooden tracks until management could afford an engine, the *Syracuse,* which hauled the first steam train into Syracuse on June 14, 1839. This jerry-built road was to prove a weak link in what was shaping up willy-nilly as a continuous string of railroads across the state.

The Auburn & Rochester was incorporated in 1836 and, at 78.5 miles, almost three times as long as the Auburn & Syracuse, was a much more ambitious venture. Its right-of-way curved to the south to reach Geneva and Canandaigua, since Canandaigua was the moving spirit behind the enterprise. It had been the most important town in Western New York at the beginning of the nineteenth century and the county seat for the entire region. As with the Auburn & Syracuse, construction was impeded by the Panic of 1837, but with the completion of a bridge over the Genesee, rails reached Canandaigua from Rochester on the Erie Canal in September, 1840, and Auburn in November, 1841. Ninety percent of the road's early revenue came from passenger service.

Indeed, the merchants of Canandaigua had to convene a public meeting in 1841 and circulate petitions to persuade the railroad to run one freight train a week.

Immediately west of the Auburn & Rochester was one of New York's first east-west railroads, the Tonawanda. It had been chartered in 1832 to run southwest 31.5 miles from Rochester to Batavia (1840 population 4,219) and from there up the valley of Tonawanda Creek to Attica (1840 population 2,710). Batavia was the headquarters of the Holland Land Company, original proprietor and developer of most of Western New York. The town was also an entrepot for the surrounding fertile countryside, which produced wheat for the mills of Rochester, then America's Flour City. Batavians had hoped that the Erie Canal would climb the Niagara Escarpment near their town. Because of water supply problems, however, the ascent was made thirty miles to the west near Eighteen Mile Creek, where constructing a double flight of five locks to carry boats up and down the sixty foot rise gave birth to Lockport.

Five years after the grant of a charter, the Tonawanda Railroad opened with two wood-burning engines brought by canal boat from the east. Unfortunately, the grand opening at Rochester was marred by reports of bank failures across the land. The reason for the road's name is somewhat mysterious, since the eleven mile extension up Tonawanda Creek to Attica was an afterthought. It was not built until 1841, and then only to link up with the Attica & Buffalo. Thomas Rogers, built the Tonawanda's third engine, the *Batavia,* (Figure #1) at his locomotive works in Paterson, New Jersey. Rogers was destined to become one of America's foremost builders of locomotives.

The Attica & Buffalo Railroad Company was incorporated May 3, 1836. Capital stock was fixed at $350,000 divided into 7,000 shares of $50 each. Ten dollars was to be paid on each $100 of stock at the time of subscription. Three cents a mile was the maximum passenger fare, but within this limitation the road was authorized to set rates "for the trans-

II, 1.

portation of property or persons," since it did not compete with the canal. Thereafter, nothing happened for several years because of the Panic of 1837. Then on September 2, 1842, the road was put into operation from Seneca Street in Buffalo to Darien in Genesee County, twenty- five miles to the east. Grading from Darien to Attica could not take place until the Tonawanda Railroad had determined the route of its extension from Batavia to Attica. With this done, the Attica & Buffalo was built on to Attica, and through service on the entire line began on November 2, 1842.

Buffalo's Common Council blocked the road from its intended terminus at Exchange Street and Michigan Avenue just north of the Hamburg Canal (an east-west extension of the Erie from just west of Main Street to Hamburg Street). As a result, for several months tracks stopped at Seneca Street, about half a mile from Michigan. The state legislature, however, overruled the Council, and during 1843 the 31.13 mile road reached its objective, where a station was erected on Exchange Street next to the Continental Hotel. In an article in *Trains,* Garnet R. Cousins writes:

In 1848 the first recorded railroad structure in Buffalo, a small brick station, was constructed on Exchange Street (once known as Old Crow Street) and became the first of several stations constructed at that site. This structure burned, (date unknown) and was replaced in 1855. . . Little is known about this second station. One account referred to it as a "grand old building."[2]

According to an article on old Buffalo railroad terminals in the September 19, 1970, *Buffalo Evening News,* "no one was quite sure how the Exchange Street Station originated. One writer said it wasn't built, it evolved." The newly organized New York Central bought land along Old Crow Street in 1853 and next year built some platforms and a shed-like structure. Cousins continued:

Railroad men took over the ballroom of the American Hotel Feb. 27, 1856, for a "dedication banquet and ball." Taking part were 20 railroads including one with the fascinating name of Mad River & Little Miami. There was dancing until dawn and newspapers of the time carried stories about the gaudy decorations, the glamorous dancers, and the profusion of both good food and good music. But not one of them got around to saying just what was being dedicated. Local historians guessed that the ball celebrated the opening of the enlarged Exchange St. passenger shed. (Figure #2.)

It may also have been in imitation of the Grand Canal Ball held in New York City on November 4, 1825, the climax of festivities marking the completion of the Erie Canal.

Promoters of the Attica & Buffalo came from the highest echelons of Buffalo's Yankee establishment. Among its directors in 1843 were Israel Hatch, Stephen G. Austin, and Walter Joy. Its first president was Oliver Lee. Two years later, Thomas T. Sherwood, Samuel Fletcher Pratt, Bella D. Coe, Reuben B. Heacock, James Osborne Putnam, Elbridge Gerry Spaulding, and Russell H. Heywood had joined the board. Hatch was a lawyer and banker who served as assemblyman, surrogate, congressman, and postmaster. He was prominently involved in dock and grain elevator enterprises. Austin was a Yale graduate and lawyer who avoided public office and became wealthy through investments. Lee was a banker and one of the city's most distinguished lawyers. Pratt was president of the Buffalo Iron and Nail Company, which boasted a blast furnace and a rolling mill. He was also engaged in the wholesale hardware business, and so may have been the Erastus Corning of the Attica & Buffalo. Coe was the proprietor of an extensive network of stagecoach lines that supplemented the Erie Canal. Heacock was a miller and grain merchant who had served in the assembly and as a director of the Buffalo branch of the Second Bank of the United States, which opened in 1829. He rose to the rank of captain during the Civil War and

II, 2.

312 FRANK LESLIE'S ILLUSTRATED NEWSPAPER. [April 26, 1856.

RAILWAY CELEBRATION, BUFFALO.

RAILWAY CELEBRATION—THE BANQUET.

ERASTUS CORNING, PRESIDENT OF THE N. Y. CENTRAL RAILROAD.

RAILWAY CELEBRATION—THE BALL.

was killed at Cold Harbor in 1864. Putnam, another Yale alumnus and lawyer, counted among his clients the Attica & Buffalo and the Buffalo & Rochester. He was a member of the American or Know-Nothing Party, a secret organization pledged to combat the growing influence in American life of the Catholic Church. When a state senator, he had secured passage of a bill forbidding bishops from holding church property. This was a transient victory for the trustees of Saint Louis's Church in their long and bitter struggle with Bishop John Timon. President Fillmore appointed Putnam postmaster at Buffalo in 1851, President Lincoln appointed him consul at Le Harve in 1861, and President Hayes named him minister to Belgium in 1880. Spaulding was a lawyer and banker. He was mayor of Buffalo in 1847, was elected to Congress as a Whig in 1848, served as state treasurer 1854-1855, and in 1858 and again in 1860 ran successfully as a Republican for Congress, where he sponsored the bill which provided for fiat money to pay for the Civil War. For this he was called "Father of the Greenbacks." Finally, Heywood, a director of the Bank of Buffalo and a prominent Episcopalian, maintained a mansion on Seneca Street much frequented by the local gentry.

There were now seven separate short lines stretching 328 miles across New York State (eight if the twenty mile Schenectady & Troy is added, which opened in 1842, an upshot of Troy's commercial rivalry with Albany). At first the harassed traveler, passing over seven different roads, had to change cars and look after his baggage six times. Therefore, it was necessary to correlate the service in the interest of through passengers. The two companies between Schenectady and Syracuse had begun the process by pooling their equipment and running trains without change of cars at Utica. But there were still too many changes, the worst - beloved of hackney cab-drivers - being that from one depot to the other at Rochester, which was not closed until March, 19, 1844. Meeting in Albany in January, 1843, representatives of the seven roads resolved to run two trains daily each way from spring to fall between Buffalo and the Hudson River, connecting with the morning and night boats out of Albany and Troy. At the time, Albany lacked railroad connections with New York City, though it had been connected with Boston via the Albany & West Stockbridge, the Western, and the Boston & Worcester since 1841. Eastbound trains left Buffalo at 6:00 A. M. and 4:00 P. M., and westbound trains left Albany and Troy at 6:00 A. M. and 7:00 P. M. A continuous trip would take twenty-five hours. Since the fastest packet boats on the Erie Canal took four to six days to go from Buffalo to Albany traveling day and night, the handwriting for them was on the wall, though cheaper if slower line boats continued for many years.

In reading the following table of time and distances in 1843, certain things should be kept in mind: the gap of several blocks on Rochester's West Side, the wooden rails plated with thin iron straps (Figure #3), lengthy stops at the more important stations for handling the train, meals for passengers in the station eating-houses, and the fact that most through passengers slept overnight at Syracuse. These trains carried no diners or sleeping cars.

Buffalo to Rochester	6 hrs.	75 mi.	12.5 mph
Rochester to Auburn	6 hrs	78 mi	13 mph
Auburn to Syracuse	2 hrs.	26 mi.	13 mph
Syracuse to Utica	4 hrs.	53 mi.	13 mph
Utica to Albany	7 hrs.	94 mi.	13.5 mph
Utica to Troy	7 hrs.	100 mi.	14 mph

During the winter there was to be one train each way daily, one leaving Albany at 9:00 A. M. and spending the night at Syracuse, the other leaving Buffalo at the same time and also spending the night at Syracuse. There was also to be an accommodation departing from each terminal at midnight and stopping everywhere, the fare on which was 2.5 cents a mile on bet-

II, 3

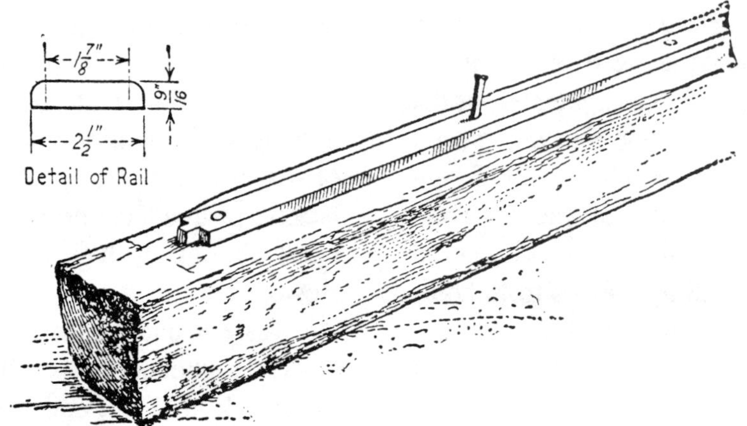

II, 4

BUFFALO & ALBANY
Rail Road.

THREE DAILY LINES.

FARE.

Rail Trains.

	1st. Class	Miles
Rochester	$2.00	75
Auburn,	5.00	153
Syracuse,	6.00	170
Utica,	8.00	232
Schenect'dy	11.00	310
Albany or Troy,	11.50	326

FARE.

Accommodation Trains.

	1st. Cl.	2d Cls.
Rochester,	$1.70	$1,00
Auburn,	3,08	2,25
Syracuse,	4,21	2,68
Utica,	5,42	3,46
Schenect'dy	7,50	4,65
Albany or Troy,	8,00	5,00

Through to Albany in 25 Hours!

Cars will leave Buffalo for Rochester and Albany, at 6 o'clock, A. M. and 4 o'clock, P. M.

Fare to Rochester,	- - - - -	**$2 00**
" Albany or Troy,	- - - -	**11 50**

THE ACCOMMODATION TRAIN.

Will leave at 12 o'clock, noon.

Fare, 1st Class Cars,			**to Rochester,** - -	**$1 50**
"	"	"	**to Albany or Troy,** -	**8 00**
"	**2d**	"	**to Rochester** - -	**1 00**
"	"	"	**to Albany or Troy,** -	**5 00**

One Train only will leave on Sundays, at 6 o'clock in the morning.

N. B.—Agents and Baggage Wagons will *always* be in attendance upon the arrival of Steam Boats to convey *Baggage* to the Depot FREE OF CHARGE.

Wm. WALLACE,
Superintendent A. & B. R. R. Co.

Buffalo, June 1, 1843.

A. M. CLAPP, PRINTER, BUFFALO.

ter cars and 1.5 cents a mile on emigrant cars. Emigrant cars at this period were broken-down coaches. Later the term was applied to meanly constructed and furnished passenger cars.

Figure #4 is a poster advertising the first through trains between Buffalo and Albany. First class or mail trains charged three cents a mile. The picture gives an idea of travel accommodations on what is presumably a first class train which made a limited number of stops. Notice the baggage car and the open carriage body on a flat car. Note also the parasols in the rear car. In the nineteenth century a tan was not looked upon as the mark of a member of the leisure class. Male, non-farm, northern laborers earned about $22 a month in 1840 (if they worked full-time.) It would cost such a Buffalo worker over half his monthly salary to ride to Albany first class and thirty-six percent for second class. (Figure #5.) Throughout the 1840s advertisements for railroads that appeared on the first page of Buffalo newspapers were lost amid announcements of departures of numerous steamboat companies that linked the city with all major ports on the lake.

The speed of trains was gradually increased after the closing of the gap at Rochester and the replacing of iron straps by solid iron rails during 1847-1849. A convention of superintendents at Syracuse in November, 1849, adopted the timetable shown in Figure #6 for the winter of 1849-1850. The *Express* took 14 hours between Buffalo and Albany, the *Mail* 17 hours and 45 minutes, and the *Night Train* 19 hours and 30 minutes. The one through freight daily was scheduled at 27 hours and it ran at first only during the winter when the canal was closed.

Although it was initially believed that railroads could carry only passengers, freight began to be carried by train in the early 1840s. "It is found that this freight will pay," observed a Rochester paper in 1843 after 200 pounds of flour and 100 barrels of pork were forwarded to Utica via the Auburn & Rochester. Moreover, and unfortunately for the Flour City, the junction of the Attica & Buffalo with the Tonawanda drained off much of the produce previously carried by the Tonawanda from Rochester to Buffalo, since the Queen City of the Lakes was better situated for further transshipment up the Lakes. The seven roads soon agreed on five cents per ton mile for merchandise and three for produce. They were hampered, however, by an 1844 law which forbade them to carry through freight except during the suspension of navigation on the canal, and even then they had to pay canal tolls to the Canal Commissioners. Not until 1851 did the state remove the tolls from the railroads altogether and leave them free to compete with the Erie Canal for the trade of the West. Indicative, however, of the growing importance of freight is the construction by the Attica & Buffalo, over the protests of the Common Council, of a spur from the mainline between Michigan Avenue and Chicago Street south to Buffalo Creek for exchanging lake borne "merchandise or other freight." This was known as the Ohio Street Branch, since it ended at Ohio Street which ran along Buffalo Creek, and since it serviced the Ohio Basin, an expansion of the Creek's wharfage.

The Ohio Basin was a 1.12 mile extension of the Main & Hamburg Canal, itself an extension of the Erie Canal from Main Street to Hamburg Street. The Main & Hamburg was begun by the city in 1836, was taken over by the state in 1848, and was completed in 1852, by which time railroads had arrived on the local transportation scene. The basin had been finished in 1851. Both projects had been slowed down by the cholera outbreak in 1849. Near Louisiana Street a branch, called the Ohio Slip, ran south from the Main & Hamburg Canal to the Ohio Basin. The basin was in turn connected to Buffalo Creek by a short channel called Dead Creek. (Figure #7.) Since neither the canal nor the slip nor the basin nor the creek had much current, the complex soon became stagnant and was declared a

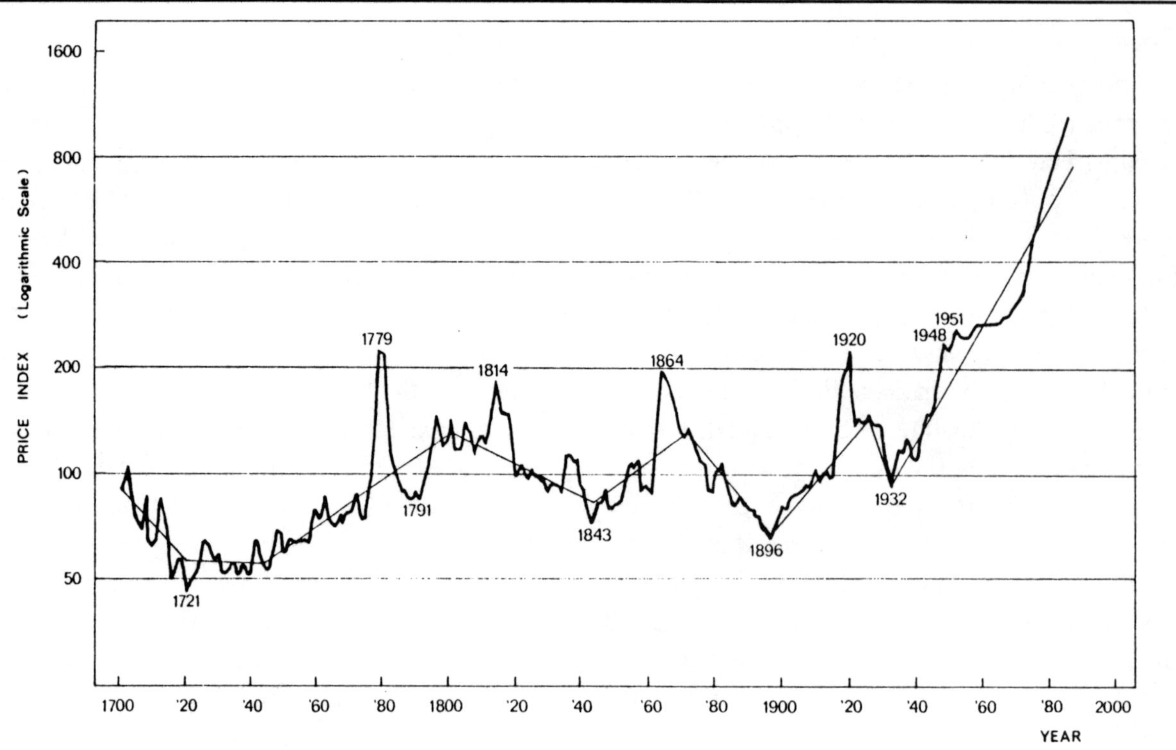 II, 5

Fig. 5 Wholesale Price Index, 1700-1985. (1910-1914 = 100)

On and After Monday, December 17, 1849—Passenger Trains

	Express	*Mail*	*Night*
Leave Albany	7 A.M.	10 A.M.	7 P.M.
Schenectady	7:45 "	11 "	8 "
Utica	11:15 "	3:30 P.M.	12 "
Syracuse	2:00 P.M.	7 "	2:30 A.M.
Auburn	3:15 "	8:45 "	4:30 "
Rochester	6:30 "	2 A.M.	9 "
Arrive Buffalo	10 "	6 "	1 P.M.
Leave Buffalo	7 A.M.	10 A.M.	7 P.M.
Rochester	10 "	2:30 P.M.	11:15 "
Auburn	1:30 P.M.	7:45 "	4:30 A.M.
Syracuse	3:15 "	9:45 "	7 "
Utica	5:45 "	1 A.M.	10 "
Schenectady	9 "	5 "	1:45 P.M.
Arrive Albany	9:45 "	6 "	2:30 "

Freight Trains

Leave Albany	2 P.M.	7 A.M.
Schenectady	3:20 "	8 "
Utica	11:00 "	1:30 P.M.
Syracuse	7 A.M.	6:30 "
Auburn	9:30 A.M.	
Rochester	4:30 P.M.	
Arrive Buffalo	10 "	
Leave Buffalo	1 P.M.	
Rochester	6 "	
Auburn	1 A.M.	
Syracuse	3:30 A.M.	6 A.M.
Utica	9 "	10:30 "
Schenectady	3 P.M.	5 P.M.
II, 6 Arrive Albany	4 "	6 "

II, 7

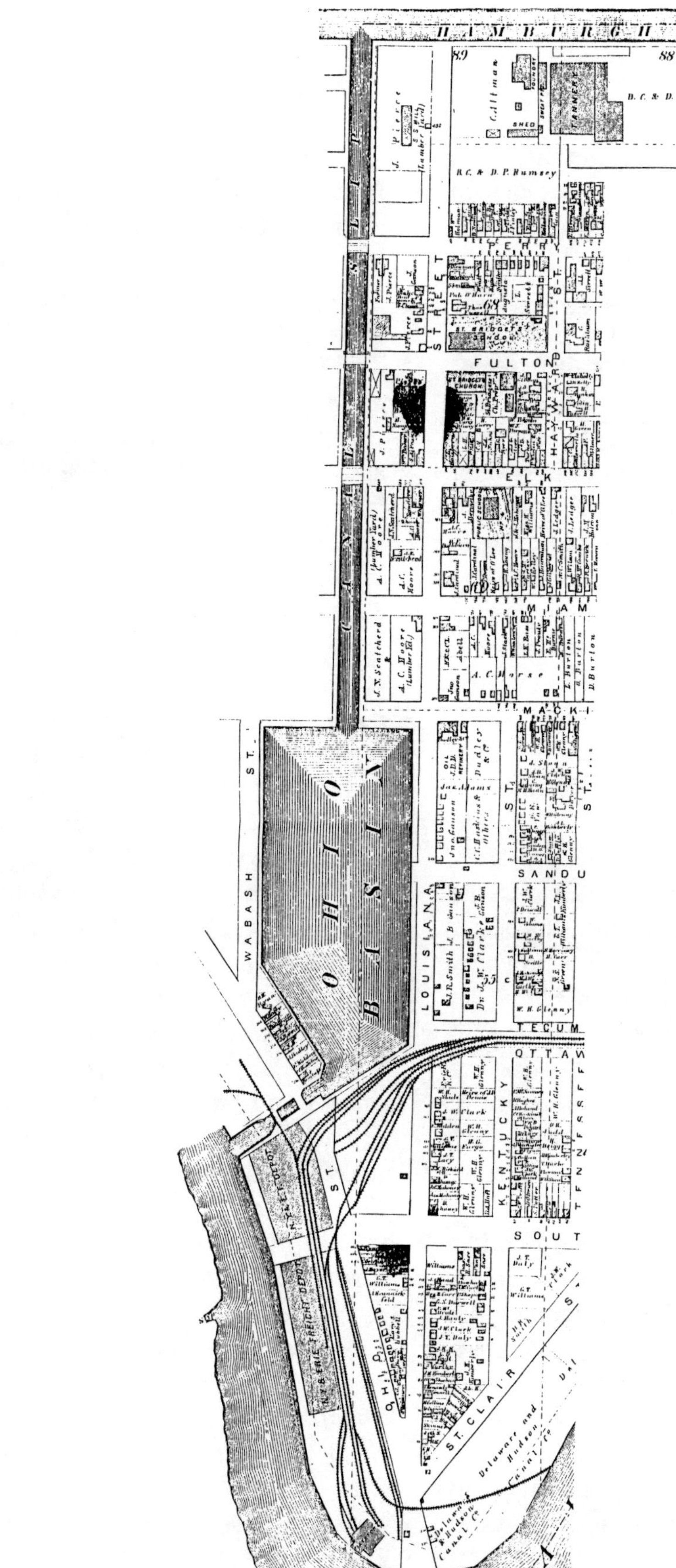
HAMBURGH
PERRY
FULTON
ELK
HAYWARD ST.
MACKI
SANDU
TECUM
OTTAW
SOUT
OHIO BASIN
WABASH ST.
LOUISIANA
KENTUCKY
ST. CLAIR
FREIGHT DEPOT
Delaware and Hudson Canal Co.

public nuisance in 1855. The canal, however, survived until the end of the century, and the basin even beyond.

Buffalo harbor in its halcyon days consisted chiefly of Buffalo Creek and the City Ship (or Blackwell's) Canal which paralleled it to the west. The canal was also built in 1850 and was extended gradually over the years. Together, creek and canal were known as the Inner Harbor and were navigable for lake sailboats and steamers. The shores of these teeming waterways sprouted grain elevators and tracks for interchange of cargo between boats and railroad cars. Figure #8 shows a passenger and a freight car of the late 1840s. Note how quickly early passenger coaches had evolved into a recognizable standard American day coach. Figure #9 reveals the road's operating statistics for its first five years. Operating ratio is the ratio of total operating expenses to gross revenue, or how much it costs to earn a dollar.

The overall route of the seven railroads had not been planned from the start but had come into existence gradually and in response to local needs. Hence it meandered. Two obvious candidates for rectification were the Buffalo-Rochester and the Syracuse-Rochester lines. The latter was the worst. It was twenty miles longer than the route followed by the Erie Canal between the two cities and it encountered heavy grades just west of Syracuse. On August 1, 1850, the Auburn & Syracuse and the Auburn & Rochester were consolidated into the Rochester & Syracuse, and construction began in the spring of 1851 of an eight-four mile (compared with 104 miles via the Auburn Road) double-track line closely paralleling the canal. The first train on the new line ran on June 1, 1853. At the western end of the state a similar arrangement was worked out. On October 8, 1850, the Tonawanda Railroad and the Attica & Buffalo were consolidated as the Rochester & Buffalo, and construction began from a point eight miles east of Buffalo on the Attica & Buffalo directly into Rochester, which resulted in the elimination of eleven miles between the two cities. The new cross-state route between Albany and Buffalo was 297.75 miles as compared with 327 via Auburn and Batavia.

The Attica & Buffalo, however, was not Buffalo's first railroad. That distinction goes to the Buffalo & Black Rock. A contemporary, Samuel M. Welch, who was to command one of Buffalo's regiments in the Civil War thus described it:

The first railway built in the town was to leave it. [Until 1853 the northern boundary of Buffalo was York Street (now Porter Avenue) and North Street.] *The depot was in the open air at the southwest corner of Pearl Street and the Terrace. (Figure #10.) The old United States Hotel had recently been built by Doctor Josiah Trowbridge; and the home station was there* [on the southwest corner]. *(Figure #11.) It was an ordinary strap road, the moving power being one horse; sometimes, when travel was heavy, another horse was added and the two tandem-driven. The rolling stock was limited to two cars, one for fair weather and the other for stormy; the first, a platform box car with two very open compartments and an outside front seat for the driver and supernumerary passengers. The two compartments and driver's seats were planed boards with straight up and down backs, painted in oak color, entirely covered by the firmament of heaven, open to the genial warmth of Old Sol in summer and the refreshing blasts of Lake Erie in winter. The other car was more elaborate; it had a flat top on stanchions, with glazed canvas curtains, buttoned on to keep out the storm, when the buttonholes were not too much worn and they didn't flap. There was no special timetable; when the car arrived at either terminus the horse turned his face to the 'right about.' The route was through the Terrace and Sixth* [later Front] *Street or thereabouts, as Sixth Street had not been opened, bearing away towards the canal, and running under bluffs at Prospect Hill, passing along nearly where the present track of the New York*

Central now is to Ferry Street, its terminal opposite Haggart's store and Ferry House. The fare was one shilling or 12 1/2 cents. [3] From there passengers took the Horse Ferry Boat, for Waterloo, Upper Canada, and there were transferred to Nelson Forsyth's or Chrysler's stagecoaches for Niagara Falls, Saint Catherines, and Little York (later Toronto). The ferry was operated by James Haggart. The Buffalo & Black Rock was begun in 1833 at a cost of $15,000, and completed in December, but the first run on this 2.5 mile line did not take place until May 16, 1834.

A French traveler, Michael Chevalier, penned a description of the Buffalo & Black Rock:

A small railroad hardly 5 kilometers long served only by horses extends along the sandy and level shore of Lake Erie from Buffalo to Black Rock. It was built by setting in the sand two rows of roughly cut trees intended to support the rails. On these trees were laid a platform composed of planks 5 centimeters wide thrown transversely from one tree to another. Above these planks are laid the rails formed of small beams 10 centimeters thick covered with a very thin strip of iron. The wooden rail is fastened to the planks by iron bolts separated 235 centimeters apart from center to center which are long enough to go through to the trees in a way to fasten also the boards onto these trees. This railroad was completed in 1835 [sic] *at very little cost, only 11,602 francs for a kilometer. It served to transport people between Buffalo and Black Rock at the rate of 133 centimes for the entire journey or 67 centimes for a kilometer. The plan of light building used by this railroad has served as a model for the one from Rochester to Batavia which, however, is served by locomotives. But on this one the longitudinal trees are held up by transverse trees in which a notch is arranged to hold the rails.* [4]

In the spring of 1836 under the name Buffalo & Niagara Falls, which had been incorporated May 3, 1834, the Black Rock line was extended north under the sponsorship of Black Rock's leading citizen, Peter B. Porter, and his nephew, William A. Bird. Bird had been closely associated with his uncle's business enterprises for years and was to become superintendent of the road. Born in Connecticut, a graduate of Yale and of Judge Tapping Reeve's famous law school in Litchfield, Connecticut, Porter came to Canandaigua in 1795, where he became clerk of Ontario County, which then embraced all Western New York. He moved on to Black Rock in 1810, where he secured a monopoly on transportation over the portage around the Falls from Lewiston to Fort Schlosser. He was a member of Congress and a prominent War Hawk from 1808 to 1813. During the War of 1812, which he had helped bring about, he rose to general of militia and saw action at Chippewa, Lundy's Lane, and Fort Erie. Reelected to Congress in 1816, he resigned to become Secretary of State of New York. In 1828 he was appointed Secretary of War by President John Quincy Adams at the urging of Porter's friend, Henry Clay.

In August, 1836, a locomotive was put on the tracks at Black Rock and ran to Tonawanda at about fifteen miles an hour, and by November 5th trains began running regularly from Buffalo to Niagara Falls. By 1847 the road ran two daily trains each way, leaving Buffalo at 9 A. M and 5 P. M. and the Falls at 6:30 A. M. and 2:30 P. M. (Figure #12.) In the course of its seventeen years as an independent line, the Buffalo & Niagara Falls had only four locomotives. The first, *Buffalo,* was a rare 2-2-0 (a two-wheel forward truck, two drivers, and no trailing truck) with drivers five feet in diameter built by the Proprietors of Locks & Canals on the Merrimack River, a water power company at Lowell, Massachusetts, which manufactured locomotives from 1835 to 1864. Next came *Niagara,* a 4-2-0 by H. R Dunham & Company of New York in 1836, and then

II, 8

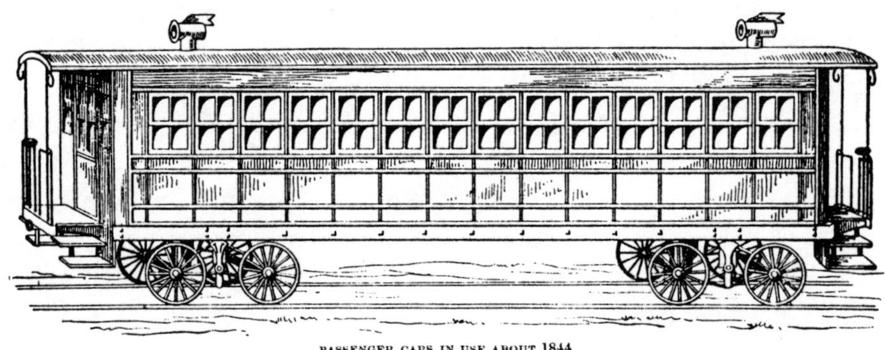

PASSENGER CARS IN USE ABOUT 1844

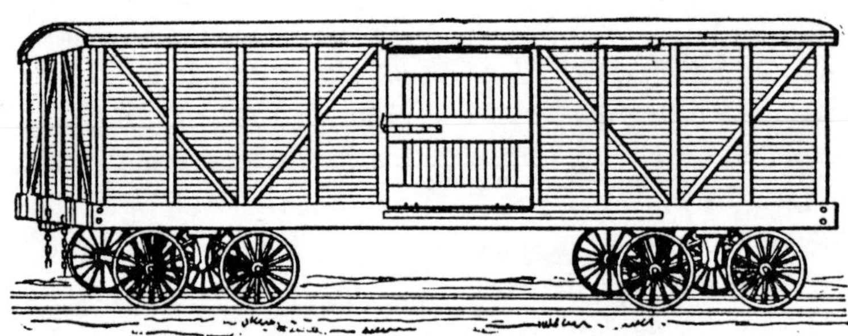

FREIGHT CARS IN USE ABOUT 1844.

II, 9

Year Ending Dec. 31	Operating Revenues				Operating Expenses	Net Income	Operating Ratio
	Passenger	Freight	Other	Total			
1842				None reported	None reported		
1843	42,836.88	3,061.67	—	45,898.55	19,149.80	26,748.75	41 72
1844	64,339.97	5,592.74	3,315.43	73,248.14	25,215.05	48,033.09	34.42
1845	58,975.93	6,602.16	4,719.45	70,297.54	30,974.67	39,322.87	44.06
1846	72,405.55	8,185.64	5,025.37	85,616.56	33,564.98	52,051.58	39.20
1847	104,010.22	15,000.00	4,800.00	123,810.22	49,000.00	74,810.22	39.58
Total for 5 Years	342,568.55	38,442.21	17,860.25	398,871.01	157,904.50	240,966.51	39.59

II, 10

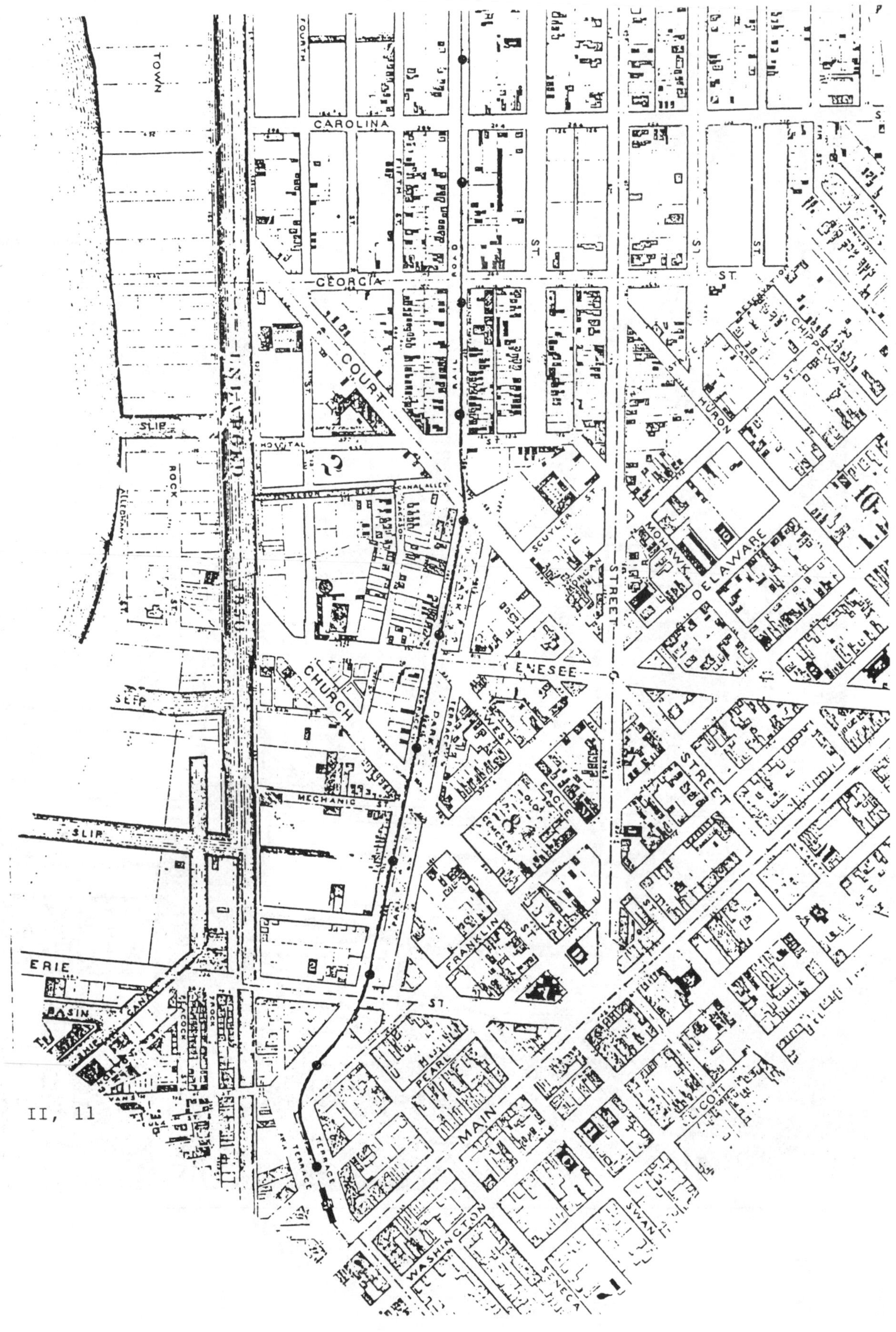
TOWN
CAROLINA
FOURTH
GEORGIA
COURT
SLIP
ROCK
ALLEGHANY
HOSPITAL
CANAL ALLEY
SCUYLER
MORGAN
STREET
MOHAWK
DELAWARE
HURON
CHIPPEWA
GENESEE
CHURCH
WEST
EAGLE
STREET
MECHANIC
SLIP
ERIE
BASIN
FRANKLIN
PEARL
MAIN
TERRACE
WASHINGTON
SWAN
SENECA

II, 11

Tonawanda, another 4-2-0 by Mathias Baldwin of Philadelphia in 1838. Finally Hinckley & Drury of Boston delivered an American, a 4-4-0, in 1845. The American was the most popular wheel arrangement for locomotives in the United States during the nineteenth century. (Figure #13 shows the spatial relationship between the Niagara River, Lake Erie vessels, the Erie Canal, and the railroad to Niagara Falls.)

Niagara Falls in 1840 was a village with a population of only 1,277 and was not located on any major artery of trade, save the portage around the Falls. Lockport was the county seat of Niagara County with a population of 9,195. Still, the Falls, abundantly supplied with waterpower, had several saw and grist mills, and of course, the matchless Cataract, much more awesome then than now. Erie Canal packet boats went directly southwest to Buffalo carrying thousands heading west. It occurred to Asher Torrance, owner of a Lockport foundry, and Washington Hunt, a lawyer who was to become governor in 1851, that many of these travelers could be induced to make a sightseeing detour to this wonder of the world only twenty-three miles away. From there they could proceed to Buffalo by stage or, as it soon turned out, by the Buffalo & Niagara Falls. Accordingly, the Lockport & Niagara Falls Railroad was incorporated on April 3, 1834. The Lockport station was to be located at the corner of Chapel and Market Streets in the lower town near the packet boat wharf, and the little locomotives would be required to pull the cars up 110 feet in less than a mile. This was a very taxing grade in excess of 2 percent. (A 1 percent grade rises 52.8 feet per mile. Anything above 1.7 percent is considered extremely steep.) Figure #14 shows the original route of the line and that of its successor.

The historian of this little road gives the following account of its construction:

In 1835 all preliminary obstacles were overcome and a hardy lot of Canadian, Scotch, and Irish workmen was brought on to begin track laying. There were 300 of them, but it took them a little more than two years to lay that 24 miles of railroad. "There wasn't no eight-hour day business about it either," said Mr. [Stephen] *Sult* [construction foreman in an 1893 interview]. *"It was the way then to work from sunrise to sunset, no matter how long the day was; and the usual pay for such a day's work was six shillings* [seventy five cents]; *while the foreman got $35 a month."*[5]

The Lockport line passed through Pekin and the Tuscarora Indian Reservation on its way to the Falls where its terminal was at the corner of Falls and Prospect Street. Indians on the reservation would occasionally race the train and more often than not win. The Lewiston Railroad in Figure #14 was a horse-car line connecting with lake boats at Lewiston. It branched off from the Lockport line just west of the reservation and was sold to the Buffalo & Niagara Falls in the early 1850s. In the summer of 1837, an eastbound passenger train left Niagara Falls at 8:00 A. M. and, returning, departed from Lockport at 10:00 A. M. The afternoon train left Niagara Falls at 2:30 and Lockport at 5:00. (Figure #15.) The Buffalo & Niagara Falls and the Lockport & Niagara Falls did not share the same station in Niagara Falls as can be seen from Figure #16.

"How many locomotives did they put on the road at first?" Mr. Sult was asked. "Locomotives!" he said and then chuckled to himself. "Why, there wasn't no locomotives. The Lockport & Niagara Railroad was a horse railroad, and it wasn't until it had been running four months that they got two engines. Maybe you wouldn't think that much of a railroad if you could see it now. The rails were what we called strap rail, made of oak scantling with a strap of iron about two and one-half inches wide and half an inch thick on top of 'em. When the track sunk, all you had to do was pull up the tie and stick it under some clay or mud or anything there was handy."

II, 12

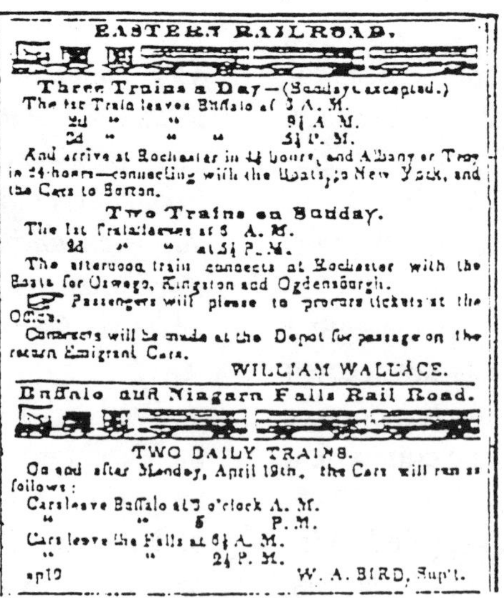

EASTERN RAILROAD.

Three Trains a Day—(Sundays excepted.)

The 1st Train leaves Buffalo at 3 A. M.
2d " " 9½ A. M.
3d " " " 5½ P. M.

And arrive at Rochester in 4½ hours, and Albany or Troy in 24 hours—connecting with the Boats, to New York, and the Cars to Boston.

Two Trains on Sunday.

The 1st Train leaves at 3 A. M.
2d " " at 5½ P. M.

The afternoon train connects at Rochester with the Boats for Oswego, Kingston and Ogdensburgh.

Passengers will please to procure tickets at the Office.

Contracts will be made at the Depot for passage on the return Emigrant Cars.

WILLIAM WALLACE.

Buffalo and Niagara Falls Rail Road.

TWO DAILY TRAINS.

On and after Monday, April 19th, the Cars will run as follows:

Cars leave Buffalo at 3 o'clock A. M.
" " 5 P. M.
Cars leave the Falls at 6½ A. M.
" " 2½ P. M.

ap19 W. A. BIRD, Sup't.

II, 13

II, 14

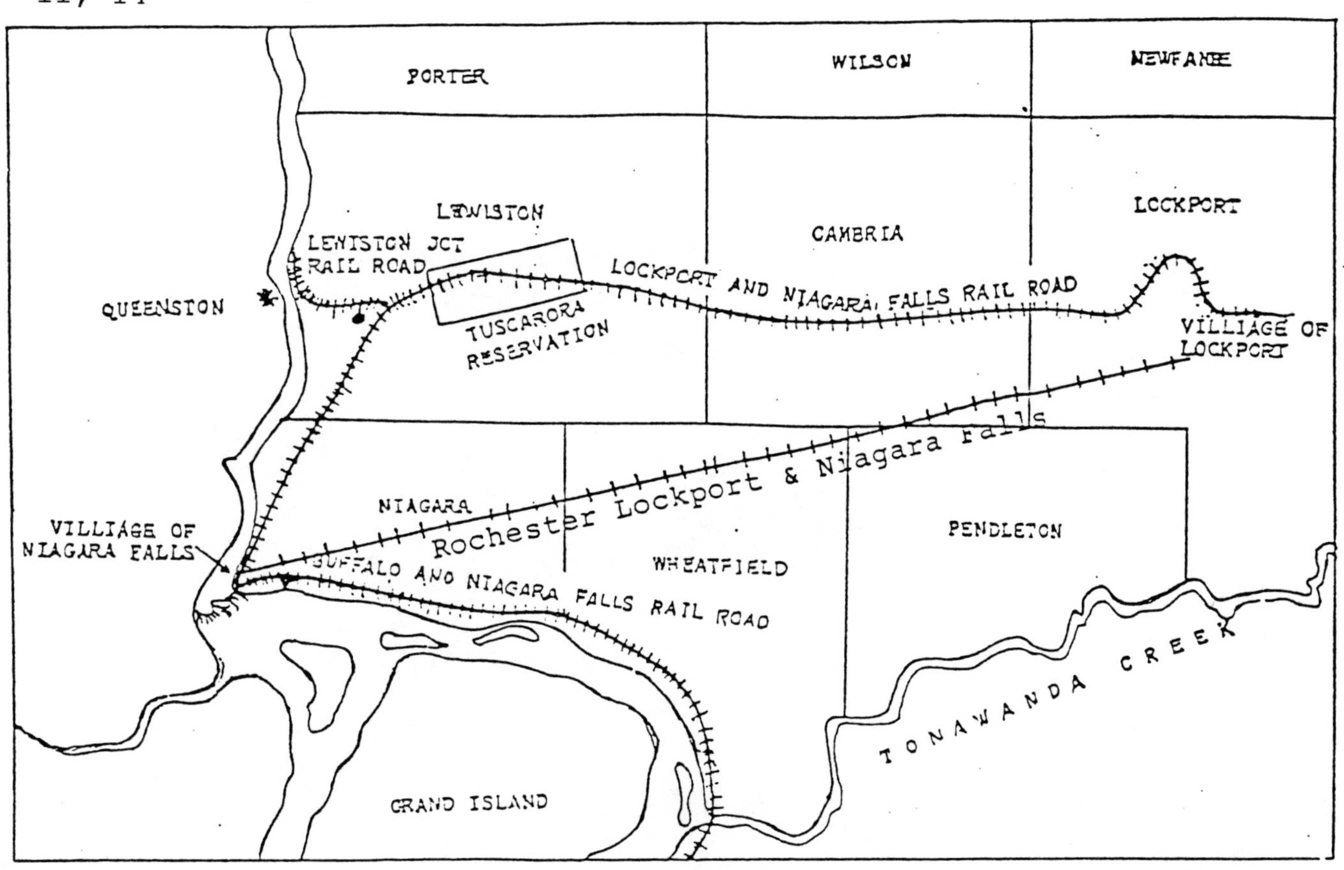

II, 15

LOCKPORT & NIAGARA FALLS RAILROAD—NEW ARRANGEMENT.—Two trips per day, by steam power, are now performed to and from Lower Lockport and Niagara Falls.

The morning train leaves Niagara Falls at 8 A. M. Lockport at 10 A. M.

The afternoon train leaves Niagara Falls at 2½ P. M., Lockport at 5 P. M.

The trips are performed in about an hour and 10 minutes, including stops, distance 24 miles.

The regular trains are intersected by cars to and from Lewiston, by the Lewiston railroad, at the junction, near the Indian Village.

In addition to the above, cars leave the Falls for Lewiston and return daily, at 12 M.

Passengers leaving Rochester by the Tonawanda railroad in the morning, reach Lockport in time to take the train to Niagara Falls the same afternoon; and the same of the reverse routes.

Passengers leaving Rochester by the packets in the afternoon or evening, reach Lockport the next morning in time for the morning train to the Falls.

A packet boat leaves Lockport for Rochester, immediately after the arrival of the afternoon train.

Stage coaches leave Lockport for Batavia and Rochester, immediately after the arrival of the morning train.

By the Buffalo and Niagara Falls railroad, passengers are taken from the Falls to Buffalo in less than two hours; distance 23 miles.

Tickets to be had at the railroad office at either termination. ASHER TORRANCE,

Lockport, Aug. 23, 1837. [52] Commissioner.

Niagara Democrat,
Aug. 25th, 1837

LOCKPORT & NIAGARA FALLS RAIL ROAD—SUMMER ARRANGEMENT.—Cars will leave Lockport for the Falls, daily, at 8½ o'clock A. M., and at 3 o'clock P. M. From the Falls to Lockport, at 6½ o'clock A. M., and at 3 o'clock, P. M.

LOCKPORT & BUFFALO.—On the arrival of the Lockport cars at the Falls, passengers can proceed to Buffalo without detention, by the Buffalo and Niagara Falls Rail Road.

Property will be transported to and from Lockport, Niagara Falls, and Pekin, at reasonable rates. Goods will be received in store at the Rail Road Warehouse, Lockport. ASHER TORRANCE,

April 26, 1837. 2tf Commissioner.

Niagara Democrat,
May 5th, 1337

II, 16

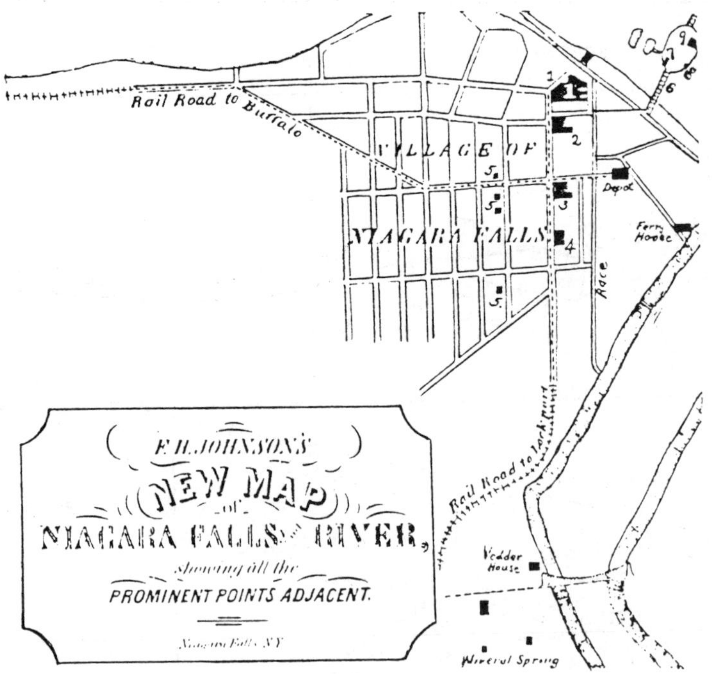

The dotted lines on this map show the routes both of the Lockport and Niagara Falls Rail Road and the Niagara Falls and Buffalo Rail Road into the village of Niagara Falls.

II, 17

A wood cut of the Dewitt Clinton locomotive, purchased by the Lockport and Niagara Falls Rail Road in 1838 and manufactured by Ketchum, Rogers and Grosvenor at Patterson, N. J. It weighed 9½ tons and was said to have been unsatisfactory in many ways. Like all locomotives of that era, it burned chunk wood carried by a small trailing car.

"At first, the new road got a pretty good business from the packet lines and the Niagara Falls tourists who were plenty even then. The line came in handy, too, in the Patriot War in 1837, when it was used to carry pork and beans for the [rebel Upper Canadian] *soldiers on Navy Island. The road had four little four-wheeled passenger cars, each divided into three compartments carrying eight passengers. They looked a good deal like the old-fashioned coach, with a seat in front for the driver and a boot behind for the baggage. Even after the engines were bought [Figure #17] and we got to be quite a modern concern, the old coaches would be put on in cold weather. Each of the two trains made two trips a day and, if I remember rightly, the fare was $1. The old stage-coach that ran to Niagara Falls before the railroad was opened charged six cents a mile* [about $1.50]. *Those old rails made us a good deal of trouble. They were forever getting loose at the ends and running up over the car wheels. I remember seeing a passenger considerable surprised once by having the end of a rail come up through the floor of the car and knock off his hat. The engine used to run out of fuel sometimes, but that wasn't anything. All the fireman had to do was to stop and take a few rails from a farm fence."*

"One time, though, we dumped out the President of the United States. It was sometime along in '37 or '38 that Martin Van Buren came up on the packet on his way to Niagara Falls, taking the train at Lockport. About a mile this side of Suspension Bridge [which did not exist then] *a spread rail ditched the train, and the car the President sat in tumbled over on its side and the passengers were pitched together in a heap. The train was going so slow that nobody was hurt. The President crawled out without a scratch, and didn't look as if he was mad any. He helped tip the car back, climbed in, and on they went just as if nothing happened."* [6]

Since its eastern terminus was a dead-end as far as railroad connections were concerned, the Lockport & Niagara Falls was authorized by the legislature in 1841 to increase its capitalization in order to finance an extension to Rochester. But the fact that its western terminus was Niagara Falls, which at that time was itself something of a dead end, meant that east-west traffic across the state would go via the Tonawanda and the Attica & Buffalo to Buffalo. Hence its new stock had few takers. The State Engineer's Report of January 11, 1849, lists three locomotives (one of which had been made in Lockport), six passenger cars, one baggage car, five freight cars, and twenty employees. The company's income in 1848 had been $13,000, "principally from way passengers . . . Freight but a trifle. No account of it kept." Yet somehow the directors eventually managed to round up $728,273 in stock subscriptions, largely from Rochestereans. Contracts were let and some grading and bridging completed. Then progress stopped. In 1850 the legislature ordered the company to sell its property and franchise, and a reorganized corporation, the Rochester Lockport & Niagara Falls took over in December, 1850. By July 1, 1852, the 54.7 mile extension into Rochester was completed. Its construction costs, $2,343,388, were very high for what was then an unimportant line. The Rochester interests, which had been the guiding spirits behind the extension, also promoted the Buffalo & Lockport Railroad, which was incorporated on April 29, 1852. It left the Rochester Lockport & Niagara Falls at a point two and a half miles west of Lockport (afterwards known as Lockport Junction) and joined the Buffalo & Niagara Falls at North Tonawanda, where its trains continued on to the Buffalo road's station, which was now located on the north side of Erie Street immediately west of the canal, following the relocation of the Buffalo & Niagara Falls westward from Sixth Street. It consisted of a headhouse and a train shed to protect arriving and departing passengers from the inclemencies of the weather, an arrangement that was becoming common for urban terminals in America, Britain, and on the continent. (Figure #18.) Meanwhile the right-of-way of the former Lockport & Niagara Falls was also relocated. With a rail connection with the east in place, it was no longer necessary to meet canal boats in the lower town, so the new Lockport station was placed above the escarpment and the new route ran in a straight line to the Falls, leaving Pekin, the Reservation, and the old junction with the Lewiston Railroad a few miles to the north. (Figure #14.)

On September 9, 1852, the Niagara Falls & Lake Ontario Railroad was incorporated to build from Niagara Falls to Youngstown. Descending the escarpment, the roadbed ran along a narrow shelf on the cliff that towers above the rapids of the Niagara River between Devil's Hole and Lewiston, which was reached in 1854. A year later a train was run over the line to Youngstown, but soon afterwards the Youngstown-Lewiston section was abandoned and Lewiston became the terminal. Here connections were made with steamers for Toronto. Figure #19 shows that in 1862 one train a day ran each way between Lewiston and Buffalo on the NF&LO, which by then had been leased by the New York Central.

II, 18

THE ERIE-STREET RAILWAY STATION AS PICTURED IN 1855.

II, 19

Buffalo to Niagara Falls, Susp'n Bridge, Lewiston & Lockport.

On and after Monday, Jan. 20th, 1861, trains will leave Buffalo, from Erie street Depot, as follows:

6 30 A. M. FOR LOCKPORT AND Way Stations to Rochester.

9 00 A. M. FOR NIAGARA FALLS, Suspension Bridge, Lewiston, Toronto, Detroit and Chicago.

1 35 P. M. FOR NIAGARA FALLS, Suspension Bridge, London and Toronto.

5 30 P. M. FOR LOCKPORT, &c.

7 00 P. M. FOR NIAGARA FALLS, Suspension Bridge, Hamilton, Detroit, and Chicago.

☞ Trains leave Niagara Falls for the East at 4-45 and 7-15 A. M., and 2-00 and 5-45 P. M., Train east from Niagara Falls on Sunday at 5-45 P. M.

These Trains connect at Rochester with Express Trains from Buffalo for the East.

☞ All of the above trains to Suspension Bridge, make close connections with trains on the Great Western Railway going West.

Trains arrive from Niagara Falls and Suspension Bridge at 10-10 A. M., 2-40 and 9-00 P. M.

Trains arrive from Lockport at 11-00 A. M., and 10-10 P. M.

☞ New York Central Railroad time is twenty minutes faster than Buffalo time.

H. W. CHITTENDEN,
Assistant Superintendent, Buffalo.

Buffalo, January 20, 1862. ja20

3
New York & Erie Railroad

Since phenomenal growth followed for towns and villages along the Erie Canal upon its completion in 1825, residents of New York's Southern Tier of counties wanted the state to create a similar thoroughfare for them. The seven little railroads were of no help to them since they more or less paralleled the canal. Topography made construction of a canal impossible, and legislators from districts along the canal balked at state support for a rival route. Nevertheless the New York & Erie Rail-road was chartered on April 24, 1832. In the best traditions of state particularism, the Erie's charter stipulated that the road remain wholly within the boundaries of the Empire State and not connect with any roads in Pennsylvania or New Jersey. Piermont, on the west bank of the Hudson, twenty-five miles from New York City and just over the New Jersey line, was to be the eastern terminus. From there passengers and freight would be taken to the city by riverboats. Since Buffalo was associated with the canal, and since the object of the New York & Erie was to benefit the Southern Tier, Dunkirk on Lake Erie was designated the road's western terminus. Eleazar Lord, the line's first president (whose estate was conveniently located at Piermont), secured adoption of a gauge of six feet between rails. What came to be regarded as standard gauge was four feet eight and a half inches. For comfort and efficiency it is unfortunate that Lord's gauge was not adopted by American railroads generally (Britain's Great Western Railway boasted a seven foot gauge), but, given that it was not, broad gauge was to prove a disaster for the Erie, since it created serious interchange problems with neighboring lines. Conversion, when it was finally completed in 1880, cost over $25 million, $3 million more than it had cost to build the line in the first place.

Failure to raise sufficient funds delayed construction, which began at Piermont, until late 1835. Wealthy New York merchants were simply not interested. Then came the Panic of 1837. However, on September 23, 1841, trains began running between Piedmont and Goshen, forty-four miles away, and by June, 1843, railhead had reached Middletown, eight miles further on. Two years of inaction followed due to financial difficulties. Eventually, with assistance from the state, construction recommenced, and Port Jervis on the Delaware at milepost seventy-four was reached the last day of 1847, Binghamton in January, 1849,

Hornellsville in September, 1850, and finally Dunkirk in April, 1851. Aboard the first two trains to traverse the entire 459 miles of mainline were President Millard Fillmore and four members of his Cabinet, including Secretary of State Daniel Webster, Governor William L. Marcy, and two ex-governors, Hamilton Fish and William H. Seward. The aging Secretary of State demanded a seat from which he would miss none of the spectacular scenery, so he was placed on a rocking chair fastened to a flatcar at the end of the second train. Wrapped in a steamer rug, the god-like Daniel had a bottle of good Medford rum for company between frequent stops for speechmaking.

Though it had two firsts to its record, the use of telegraphy to control train movement and shipping milk overnight to metropolitan centers, the early Erie had "a checkered history," as Maury Klein writes in his study of Jay Gould:

Chartered in 1832 as a grand project to connect ocean traffic at New York City with the Great Lakes, it floundered for two decades as a political football among local interests. When the road was finally completed in 1851, it ran from Piermont to the obscure village of Dunkirk on Lake Erie, without access to Buffalo at one end or New York City at the other. The interplay of local politics had forced the company to occupy a route through southern New York that had poor grades, was expensive to maintain, and could not tap rich sources of traffic in northern Pennsylvania. Botched management obscured whatever prospects the Erie had during the 1850s. The road was in such poor shape that . . . it became notorious for the insecurity of travel upon it. Thirty serious accidents occurred in 1852 alone. A succession of financial blunders saddled the road with a persistent floating debt. By August, 1859, Erie stock had plunged from 33 to 8 and the company was in receivership. [1]

The Piermont mistake was quickly rectified by the purchase in 1852 of two New Jersey railroads, the Paterson & Ramapo, which tapped the Erie near Suffern, and the Paterson & Hudson, which provided an eastern terminal on Pavonia Avenue in Jersey City across from Lower Manhattan. The mistake at the line's western end was also corrected, but more slowly. In 1850 Dunkirk had 5,616 residents, while Buffalo (together with Black Rock) had 49,769. Though poised for the take-off which would make it the hub of the nation's railroad network during the following decade, Chicago in 1850 had a population of less than 30,000. The most obvious route to Buffalo would diverge from the Erie mainline at Hornellsville. As early as 1845 when the Erie was still bogged down at Middletown, citizens of Wyoming and western Livingston Counties, along with Buffalonians eager for an alternate rail route to New York, obtained a charter for a sixty mile line to be known as the Attica & Hornellsville, since it would connect with the Attica & Buffalo at Attica and with the Erie whenever it should get to Hornellsville (For a map of the Erie lines at their fullest extent in western New York see Figure #1.) Insufficient money was raised, and so nothing was done for the next four years, at the end of which it was necessary to secure from the legislature an extension of the deadline set for completion of the road.

Meanwhile, several of the Attica & Hornellsville's Buffalo backers were induced to support instead a recently chartered line that would leave the Erie at Corning, forty miles east of Hornellsville. Farmers and merchants in Steuben and eastern Livingston Counties had hoped the Erie would abandon its plan to terminate at Dunkirk in favor of a route that would follow the Cohocton and Genesee Valleys in a roughly northwesterly direction to Avon in the Genesee Valley. From there the line would proceed west over gently rolling farmland to a rail connection at Batavia on the Tonawanda. (This connection was soon to become the Buffalo & Rochester.) The Erie,

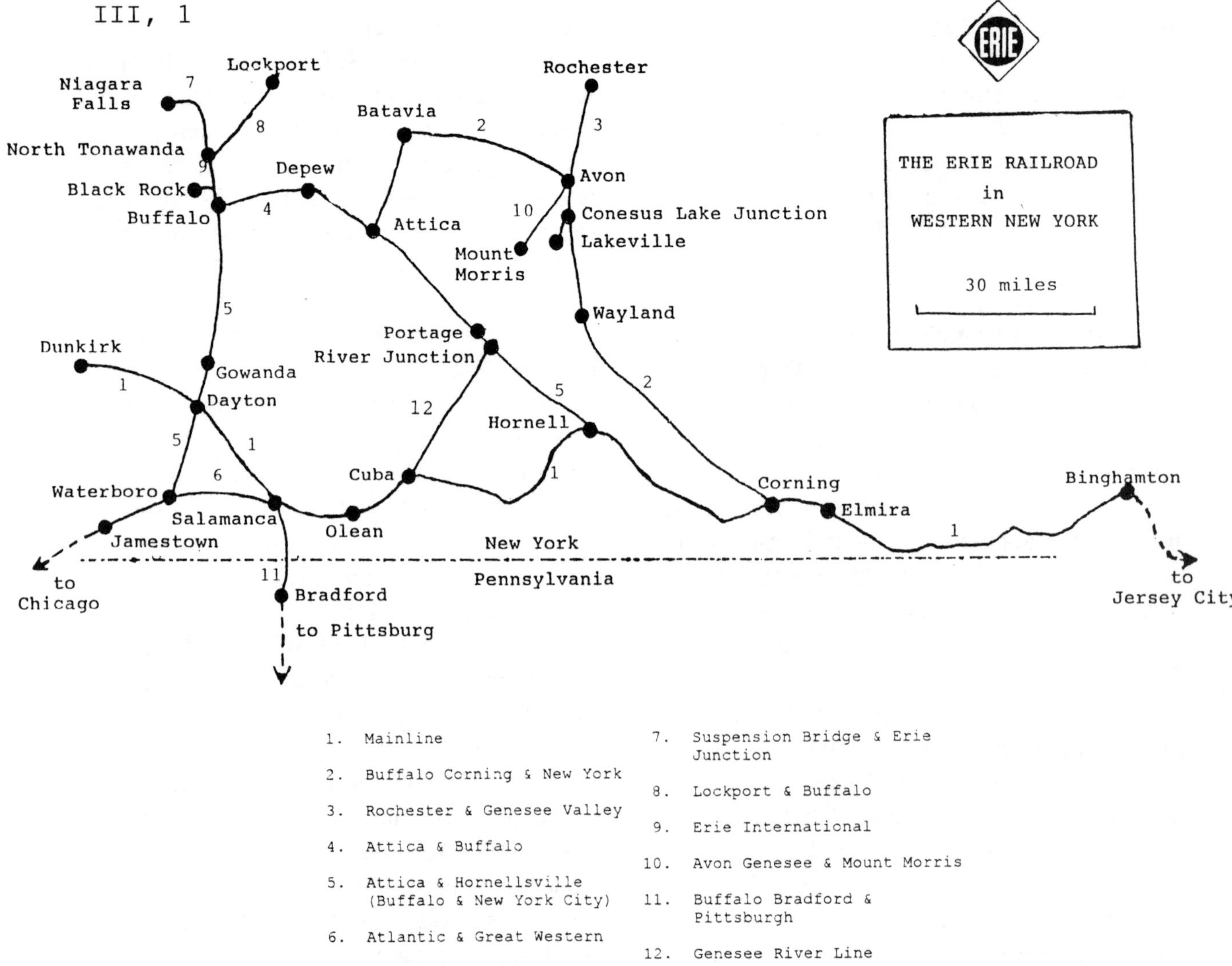

however, adhered to its originally projected route through the Tioga and Canisteo Valleys to Hornellsville and Dunkirk. Thereupon, the disappointed supporters of the Cohocton route obtained a charter on July 23, 1850, for the Buffalo & Cohocton Valley Railroad. This was to be a ninety-eight mile line from Painted Post (where, two miles west of Corning, the Tioga and the Cohocton Rivers join to form the Chemung), up the Cohocton Valley to Wayland, thence north between Hemlock and Conesus Lakes to Avon, and thence west to Batavia. Rochestereans could participate by building an eighteen mile line along the Genesee south to Avon. The organizers of the Cohocton project had checked with the directors of the Attica & Hornellsville and learned that they had abandoned the undertaking. They also discovered that some Buffalonians who had previously supported the Attica road had agreed to raise a third of the $1,950,000 estimated cost of the Cohocton line.

Two months later they changed their minds again, withdrew from the Cohocton project, and began construction of the Attica & Hornellsville, whose name was changed on April 15, 1851, to the Buffalo & New York City. The name change was made in contemplation of the forthcoming purchase from the Buffalo & Rochester of twenty-three miles of the old Attica & Buffalo from Attica to the Lancaster-Cheektowga line, which was deemed superfluous to its original owners after the opening of the direct Buffalo-Rochester line via Batavia. The sale took place on November 1, 1852, for $322,000, of which $3,000 was in cash and the balance in bonds of the Buffalo & New York City.

Thirty miles of track went into operation between Hornellsville and Portage on January 22, 1852. Daily except Sundays, a single mixed train (passengers and freight) left Hornellsville at 7 A. M., or after the arrival of the New York and Erie's westbound *Night Express,* and returned from Portage at 4 P. M. in time to connect with the Erie's eastbound Night Express to New York. Fare was three cents a mile. The timetable announced that stages would run "in connection with the train from and to the following points: Dansville, Mount Morris, Avon, Rochester, Castile, Perry, Gainsville, Warsaw, Wyoming, Pike, Arcade, Elli-cottsville, Rushford, Belfast, Cold Creek, Mixville, &c." It was a transitional period since most of these towns would soon be on a railroad. For Castile, Perry, Gainsville, Warsaw, and Wyoming that railroad would be the Buffalo & New York City. Journalist and lecturer, Benjamin F. Taylor, wrote:

There are a briskness of step and a precision of speech about people of a railway creation that you never find in a town that is accessible only to a stage-driver. . The locomotive is an accomplished educator. It teaches everybody that virtue of princes we call punctuality. It waits for nobody. It demonstrates what a useful creature a minute is in the economy of things. [2]

Albro Martin's claim that American railroads did not knit together but rather created localities needs to be qualified when applied to Northeastern United States. New England and the Middle Atlantic States had in the 1830s, besides extensive canals, a network of turnpikes over which numerous stages operated. (Figures #2 and VII, #3.) However, as has been noted, stages and wagons were useless for transporting bulk freight.

The Buffalo & New York City's first and for a time only "accomplished educator" was Erie's #4, the *Orange.* This was a 4-4-0 which had been built by the Norris Locomotive Company in Philadelphia in December, 1840, and which had pulled the first train into Goshen (the county seat of Orange County) in September, 1841. (Figure #3.) With the completion on August 9, 1852, of a bridge over the Genesee, the railroad was open from Hornellsville to Attica. (Figure #4.) The following is from Edward H. Mott, the Erie's best historian to date:

A brilliant feat of engineering was performed in carrying this railroad over the great chasm through which the Genesee River passes at Portage, a chasm 250 feet deep and 900 feet wide. How to bridge it was a puzzle to the engineering science of that day, and not until a congress of engineers was called was the definite plan of building this one-time wonder of the world in bridge architecture decided. It was built entirely of wood, in fifty-foot spans, with a height of 230 feet above the river. The bridge was nearly two years in building, and took the product of over 300 acres of closely grown pine lands amounting to 1,600,000 feet of timber, 106,280 pounds of iron, and cost $175,000 . . . the locomotive Orange, which had been used in the construction of the railroad, drew the first train across - four cars filled with people. Among them were Governor Hunt and Lieut.-Governor [George W.] *Patterson of New York; Benjamin Loder, President of the Erie; and President* [Samuel] *Heywood of Buffalo and New York City, of the Buffalo & New York City Railroad. The event was made a great celebration. This bridge was used until the spring of 1875 when it was destroyed by fire. In forty-seven days from the burning of the old bridge trains were passing over the present spiderlike structure. This bridge, 850 feet in length, is broken into spans varying from 113 to 50 feet. The Portage Bridge is one of the famous attractions to the*

III, 2

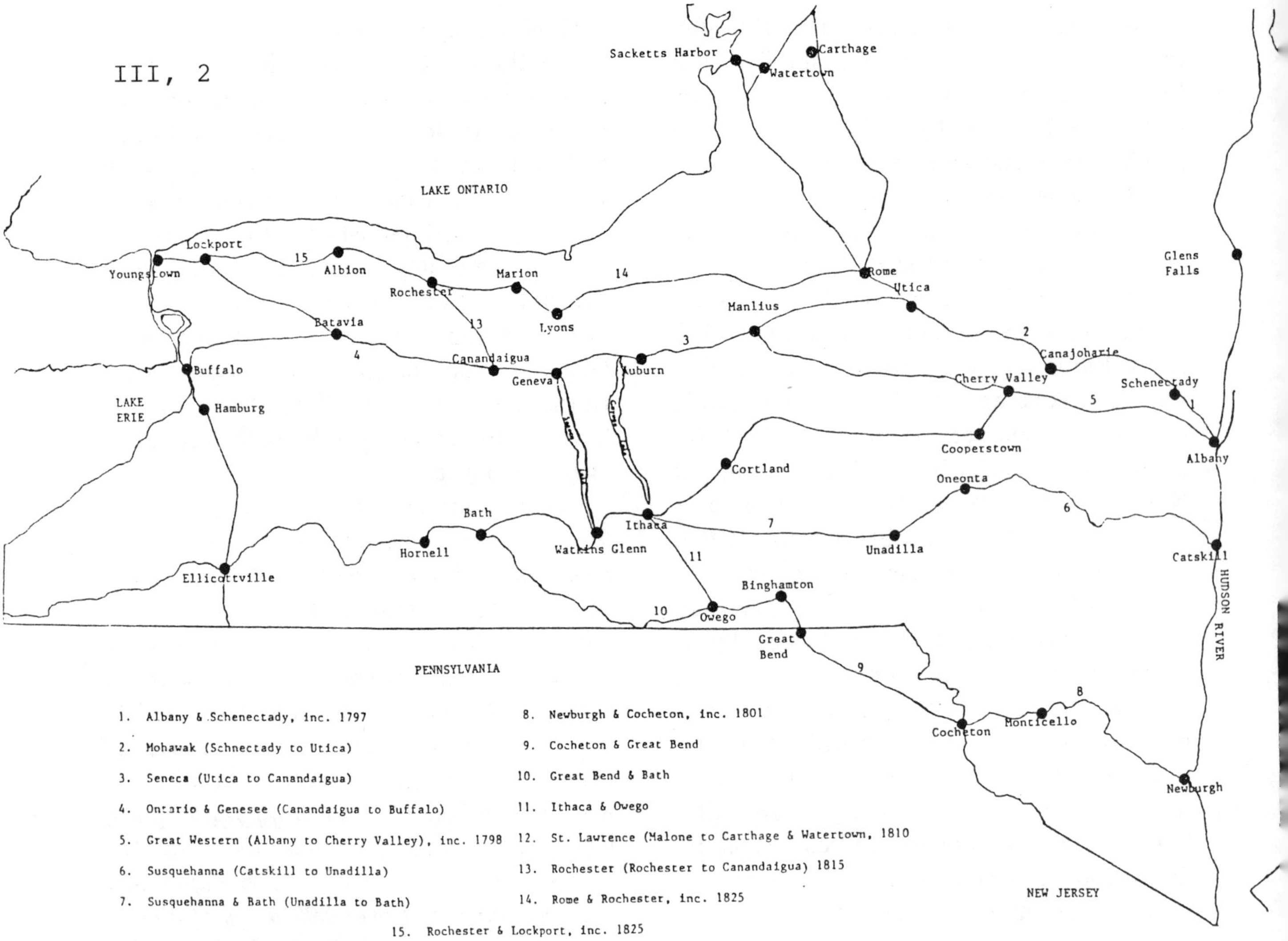

Sacketts Harbor
Carthage
Watertown
LAKE ONTARIO
Lockport
15
Albion
Youngstown
Marion
14
Rome
Utica
Glens Falls
Rochester
Lyons
Manlius
Batavia
13
3
2
4
Canandaigua
Canajoharie
Buffalo
Geneva
Auburn
Cherry Valley
Schenectady
LAKE ERIE
Hamburg
5
1
Cooperstown
Albany
Cortland
Oneonta
Bath
6
Ithaca
7
Hornell
Watkins Glenn
Unadilla
Catskill
11
Ellicottville
Binghamton
HUDSON RIVER
10
Owego
Great Bend
PENNSYLVANIA
9
8
Cocheton
Monticello
Newburgh
NEW JERSEY

1. Albany & Schenectady, inc. 1797
2. Mohawak (Schnectady to Utica)
3. Seneca (Utica to Canandaigua)
4. Ontario & Genesee (Canandaigua to Buffalo)
5. Great Western (Albany to Cherry Valley), inc. 1798
6. Susquehanna (Catskill to Unadilla)
7. Susquehanna & Bath (Unadilla to Bath)
8. Newburgh & Cocheton, inc. 1801
9. Cocheton & Great Bend
10. Great Bend & Bath
11. Ithaca & Owego
12. St. Lawrence (Malone to Carthage & Watertown, 1810
13. Rochester (Rochester to Canandaigua) 1815
14. Rome & Rochester, inc. 1825
15. Rochester & Lockport, inc. 1825

III 3

III, 4

III, 5

Buffalo & N. Y. City, and New York & Erie Railroads.

FALL ARRANGEMENT—FOUR DAILY TRAINS.

Making the Cheapest, Quickest and Most Desirable Route from

BUFFALO TO NEW YORK AND BOSTON.

This Route, extending from Buffalo direct to New York City, and passing through a beautiful panorama of the finest scenery in the world, now forms the cheapest, shortest and pleasantest route from Buffalo to New York City, Philadelphia, Baltimore and Washington; and also to Boston, Newport, Providence, Hartford, New Haven and other New England cities. The road is built and stocked in the best manner, with the WIDE TRACK or six foot guage, the cars being much wider and every way more comfortable than those upon other roads.

☞ Fare from Buffalo to New York .... $7 50.

Fare from Buffalo to New York, Second class..... 4 50.

Fare from Buffalo to N. Y. via. Newburgh and Steamboat Francis Skiddy, $6 50.

Tickets by this route to New York, can be purchased at all the principal Railroad and Steamboat offices at the west.

☞ Baggage conveyed from other roads and from steamboats to the depot, free of charge.

Passengers at Buffalo should procure Tickets to New York and Boston, and baggage checks to New York, at the Company's Depot, on Exchange street, between Michigan and Chicago streets.

Boston passengers have the choice of the Fall River or Stonington route from New York to Boston.

TRAINS RUN AS FOLLOWS:

New York Lightning Express leaves Buffalo at 6.15 A. M., stopping only at the principal stations, arrive in New York at 9.24 A. M.

Mail train leaves Buffalo at 9.35 A. M., stopping at all stations.

Passengers taking this train, can, if they prefer, stop at Portage and enjoy an excellent opportunity of seeing the magnificent Railroad Bridge and beautiful scenery at Portage Falls, take the Night Express, and still arrive in New York at 9.23 next morning.

Accommodation and Freight Train leaves Buffalo at 12.00 M., stopping at all stations.

Night Express Train leaves Buffalo at 5 P. M., stopping at the principal stations, and arriving in New York at 9.23 A. M.

One train only on Sunday, leaves Buffalo at 5 P. M.

☞ Railroad time is thirty minutes faster than Buffalo time.

N. B.—Pleasure seekers desirous of visiting Portage Falls and the High Bridge, can leave Buffalo on the Lightning train at 6.15 or Mail at 9.35 A. M., and returning, leave Portage at 5.35 and arrive in Buffalo at 9.00, giving them over nine hours at Portage for the enjoyment of scenery unsurpassed in wild and picturesque beauty and sublimity.

Excursion tickets to Portage and return.........$2.00.

This road also affords superior advantages for the shipment of all kinds of freight.

For information as to rates of freights, &c., apply to S. Drullard, Freight Agent, Buffalo, and W. C. Tallmadge, corner Broadway and Barclay sts., New York.

Buffalo, Nov. 21, 1853. oc17 J. G. HOYT, Sup't.

tourist over the Erie, and to the local pleasure excursionists. [3]

Figure #5 is a timetable for the first year of the road's completed existence, 1853. It was built to six foot gauge since one of its objectives was to connect the six foot Erie with Buffalo. There were two first class trains in each direction daily except Sunday and a mail train that stopped at all stations. Scheduled running time on the morning train for the 423 miles from Buffalo to Jersey City was 15 hours and 25 minutes and on the evening train 16 hours and 23 minutes, though how often the schedule was adhered to is not recorded. A traveler who could sleep sitting up could go all the way to Jersey City without a layover. Standard Time was thirty years in the future, hence the warning, "Railroad Time is thirty minutes faster than Buffalo time."

After acquiring the former Attica & Buffalo from the Cheektowaga-Lancaster line to Attica from the Buffalo & Rochester, the Buffalo & New York City in 1851-1853 assembled a string of properties through Cheektowaga and Buffalo to the site of its own terminal on the northwest corner of Exchange and Michigan, just east of that of the Buffalo & Rochester. Surveyor of this route and first superintendent of the road was Silas Seymour, brother of Horatio, who was to be a war-time governor of New York and Democratic candidate for president in 1868. Silas went on to dishonor as an associate of the notorious Dr. Thomas Durant in building the eastern half of the nation's first transcontinental, the Union Pacific. It was easy for railroads to string together continuous parcels of land for their right-of-ways since the state had conferred on them eminent domain, the right to expropriate private property for a public purpose *reclamante possessore.* The Buffalo & New York City's acquisitions are listed in the Erie County Clerk's office in a liber of deeds printed for that specific purpose, a practice which was repeated by later roads into the county. Actually, most western New York farmers (and the landscape then was predominantly agricultural) were only too glad to have a railroad cross their land to get their produce to market. In this they were unlike the landed gentry of England, who attempted vigorously and not always unsuccessfully to keep railroads from traversing their lands and destroying their fox covers. In imitation of the Attica & Buffalo, the Buffalo & New York City built its own spur to the Ohio Basin. It broke off from the mainline near the intersection of Exchange and Smith Streets and ran southwest to Louisiana Street, immediately west of which it crossed Ohio Street where loading tracks and a freight elevator were erected. Figure #6 shows the routes within Buffalo of its pre-Civil War railroads.

Concerning railroad building in Western New York at this time Mott writes:

The revival of the Attica & Hornellsville discouraged some of the prime movers in the Cohocton Valley route, but citizens of Livingston and Genesee counties declared at public meetings that the road from Batavia could be built independently of Buffalo and went to work to do it. Many humble citizens along the route mortgaged their homes and farms to get money to put into the stock, the mortgagees being officers or directors of the company. The work was put under contract and progressed steadily. March 5, 1852, the name of the company was changed to the Buffalo Corning & New York. The total cost of the railroad was to be $1,706,000 without equipment, or $1,950,000 with equipment. Costs were covered by stock subscriptions, of which nearly $500,000 had been paid in. Early in April, 1852, for the declared purpose of raising funds to pay for the equipment of the railroad, the directors of the company mortgaged its property and franchises for $1,000,000 to secure payment of bonds for that amount to be issued by the company. The railroad began operating between Painted Post and Kennedyville [Wayland] *on the Livingston County line, April 13, 1852, a distance of* *forty-five miles. The issuance of bonds had filled many of the stockholders along the line with apprehension. The feeling was made stronger when in March, 1853, the directors executed a second mortgage upon the franchises of the corporation for $600,000 to secure an issue of bonds to that amount. The road was completed to Batavia in 1854, when work ceased.* [4]

Land had been acquired and a survey made of a line into Buffalo from Batavia running through Newstead, Pembroke, Clarence, and Cheektowaga. (Railroads wanted their trackage so they would not be forced to split revenue with connecting lines.) For the next thirty years, nothing further was done along this route, though atlases continued to treat it as if it were an actual railroad. Since the Buffalo Corning & New York, like the Buffalo & New York City, had a six foot gauge, cars could not be interchanged at Batavia.

Figure #7 is an 1854 timetable for the Buffalo Corning & New York. It ended originally at Batavia where connections were made for Buffalo and Rochester on the former Buffalo & Rochester, which by then had become the New York Central. Connections could be made at Livonia for stages to Geneseo and at Wayland for Dansville. Liberty in the timetable is now Cohocton, and Bloods is Atlanta. Actual schedules on this 100 mile long line must have been extremely flexible since they depended on the arrival of trains from Buffalo and Rochester at Batavia and from New York at Corning. Shortly afterwards, the eleven mile gap between Batavia and Attica was bridged by a six foot gauge road that passed through Alexander.

The BC&NY's early years were unhappy ones. As Mott tells the story:

October 1, 1855, the company defaulted in the interest on its first mortgage bonds, and December 1, 1855, on the coupons of the second mortgage bonds. Proceedings in foreclosure were begun. Many of the stockholders believed that this default was utterly uncalled for, and the result of collusion, for the purpose of throwing the company into bankruptcy and giving the bondholders, chief among whom were the directors of the company, an opportunity to profit themselves by the sale of the road, regardless of the stockholders rights. [In railroad bankruptcy the bondholders succeed to the rights of the stockholders whose equity is extinguished]. *Charges to that effect were made against the managers and directors and the Board of Railroad Commissioners was petitioned to investigate them.* [5]

No report was ever made since bribery by officials of the New York Central and the Erie induced the legislature to abolish the board which had been authorized to make close inquiries into the details of railroad management in the state, a proceeding which would have made officialdom most uncomfortable. Mott continues:

On October 30, 1857, the railroad and all its franchises were sold for $3,000,000 for the benefit of the bondholders. Every dollar that had been invested along the line in the stock of the Company was swept away by that proceeding, and hosts of small subscribers to the stock were ruined - the homes of not a few being sold under mortgages that had been given to take stock in the railroad - the larger stockholders having exchanged their stock for bonds, thus not only saving themselves from loss but making money in the transaction. [6]

Often, more than trickery was involved in the bankruptcy of early railroad short lines. Robert L. Gunnarsson, the historian of the Northern Central Railroad, writes:

Although the railroad brought growth and prosperity to its territory, the same, unfortunately, was not always true for its early investors. Railroading was and still is a highly capital-intensive industry, requiring enormous investment to buy land, build a line, and equip it with locomotives, cars, and facilities.

III, 6

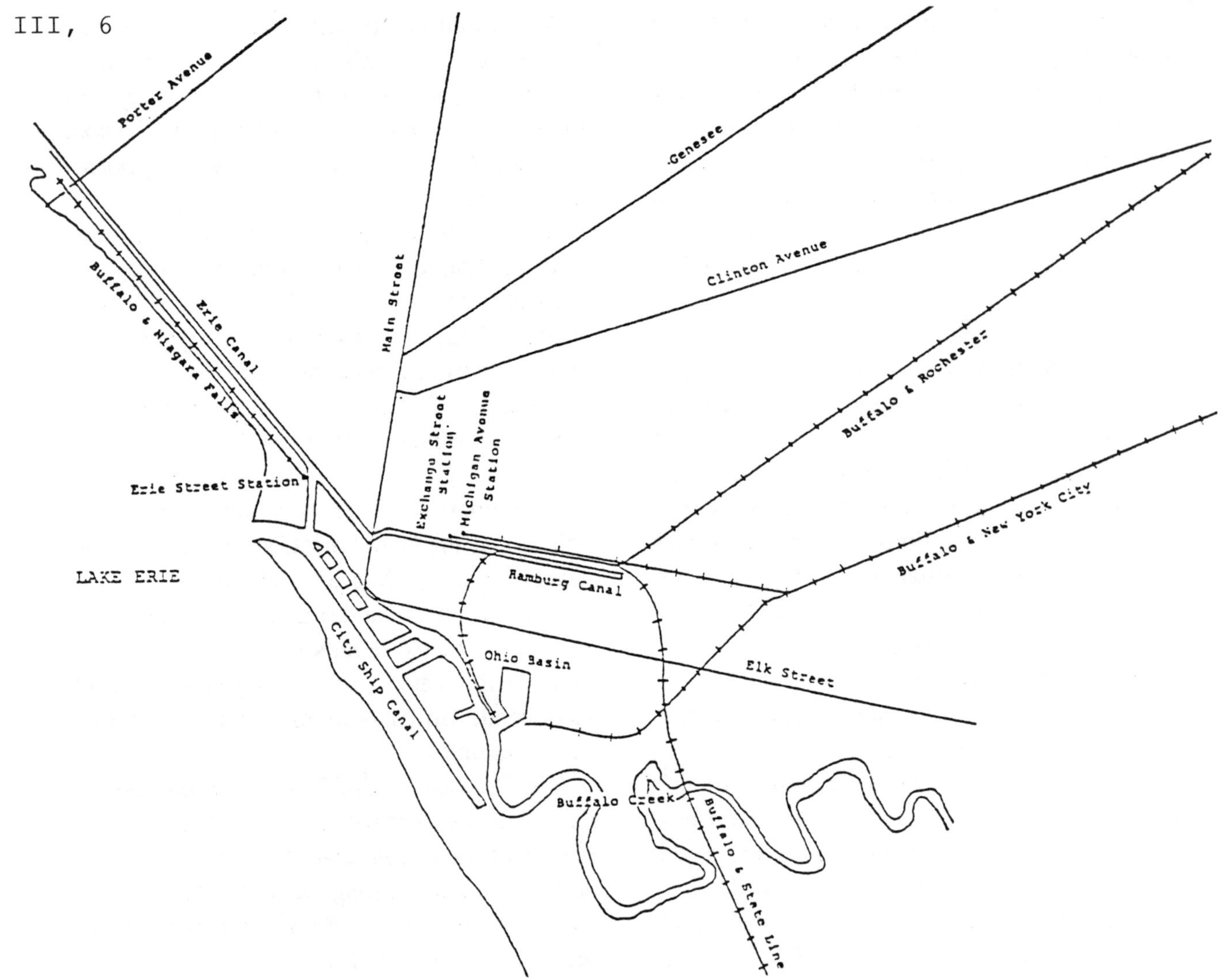

III, 7

Buffalo, Corning & New York Rail Road.

IN CONNECTION WITH THE

NEW YORK CENTRAL RAILROAD.

Trains leave Batavia every day, (Sundays excepted) as follows:

No 1, N. Y. Express, at 5 A. M., passing through Le Roy, Caledonia, Avon Springs, Livonia, (where a connection is made with stages for Geneseo, six miles distant,) Conesus, Springwater, Wayland, (stage connection to Dansville, five miles by plank road,) Bloods, Liberty, Avoca, Kanona, Bath, Savona, Campbell, Coopers, Painted Post, to Corning, connecting with the express train upon the New York and Erie Railroad, arriving in New York at 7.32 P. M.

No. 3, Freight and Accommodation, at 9.45 A. M., on arrival of Express Train from Buffalo; connects at Corning with Mail Train east and Dunkirk Express west, on New York and Erie Railroad.

No. 4, Mail, at 3 15 P. M., on arrival of Way Express from Rochester, and Emigrant Train from Buffalo on N. Y. Central Railroad; connects at Corning with Night Express on New York and Eric Railroad, arriving in N. Y. next A. M.

Trains leaving Corning will arrive at Batavia as follows: 6 40 P. M., 9.30 P. M., and 11 A. M., connecting with trains on New York Central Railroad for Buffalo and Rochester.

J. A. REDFIELD, Sup't.

SUPERINTENDENT'S OFFICE, CORNING, May 8, 1854. } my13

Yet in many cases the railroads took years to reach their intended markets and, once there, more time to build enough traffic to cover these costs. Typically, too, the early railroads aggravated their problems by underestimating their construction costs and the time it would take to get into full operation. What profits they did earn had to be quickly reinvested to keep construction moving and provide more equipment for the growing business. Thus there was little or no quick return for the investors and some became discouraged and refused further participation - causing a capital shortage when it was most needed. . . Undercapitalized, and with their costs exceeding their revenues, many of the small pioneering lines either went into receivership or sought stronger partners, and the long process of reorganization and consolidation began. [7]

The purchaser of the Cohocton Valley line was the Buffalo New York & Erie, the name assumed by the Buffalo & New York City after its own emergence from bankruptcy in 1857. The B&NYC now had two parallel branch lines about a dozen miles apart between Batavia in the west and Hornellsville on the one hand and Corning on the other in the east. On October 1, 1858, the Buffalo New York & Erie leased the Rochester & Genesee Valley, which had been opened from Rochester to Avon in 1854, the same year the Cohocton line reached Batavia. Five years later the eighteen mile long Rochester road, under the name of the Avon Genesee & Mount Morris, was extended to Mount Morris, whence stages departed for Nunda, Portage, and Perry. (Figure #1.)

The Erie had actually been maintaining and operating the Buffalo & New York City until May 20, 1854, when it was leased to its former president, Aaron Patchin. Two months earlier he had for $10,000 purchased, under foreclosure of a chattel mortgage, the road's equipment, which had cost $275,000. In December the railroad itself was sold under foreclosure to Patchin, who continued to run it during 1855. Next year the Erie was back operating it and spending $75,000 in equipment and maintenance. On New Year's Day, 1857, it was again sold under foreclosure and again purchased by Patchin.

Due to mismanagement and the lingering effects of the Panic of 1857, the New York & Erie Railroad entered bankruptcy in August, 1859. The road's finances had already been seriously weakened by two long and expensive strikes, the first in 1854 and the second in 1856, both precipitated by the engineers' refusal to abide by unrealistic work rules promulgated by Superintendent Daniel C. McCallum. Reorganized, the New York & Erie emerged as the Erie Railway Company on May 1, 1861, just after the outbreak of the Civil War. During bankruptcy the receivers had purchased in the Erie's name the former Attica & Hornellsville, and on May 1, 1862, the Erie leased the old Buffalo Corning & New York, thus finally giving the Erie direct control over alternate lines to Buffalo which converged at Attica with a branch to Rochester. (Figure #1.) The November 17, 1862, Buffalo New York & Erie timetable shown in Figure #8 is, therefore, actually an Erie Railway timetable.

This timetable shows four eastbound departures from Buffalo on the Erie, two via Attica and Hornellsville and two via Corning. The *Day Express* took 16 hours and 50 minutes to Jersey City with stops for breakfast at Hornellsville, dinner at Deposit, and supper at Turner's, for an overall average of twenty-five miles per hour, which necessitated some high stepping between stations. The Erie's huge palace cars were truly "superb" as can be seen from Figure #9. Six of these cars were constructed at the Piermont shops in the mid-1850s. They were the earliest examples of truss framing - which, next to the eight-wheel car itself (two four-wheel trucks that pivot) - was the single most important contribution of American designers to the art of car building.

III, 8

November 17, 1862.

BUFFALO, NEW YORK & ERIE

NEW YORK, PHILADELPHIA,

Boston, Baltimore and Washington.

Palace Cars by Day and Sleeping Cars at Night. Through to New York without Change of Cars.

Trains leave the Depot of Buffalo, New York & Erie Railroad, on the corner of Exchange and Michigan streets, as follows, by New York time:

3:40 A. M. BUFFALO & NEW YORK DAY EXPRESS (Via Attica and Hornellsville.) Through to New York without changing cars, in superb Palace Cars. Breakfast at Hornellsville; dinner at Deposit; supper at Turners. Arrives in New York city at 8:30 P. M.

7:00 A. M. WASHINGTON & NEW YORK EXPRESS. Dinner at Corning. Arrives at Philadelphia at 5 A. M; Baltimore 6:00 A. M.; Washington 9:00 A. M. New York passengers take supper at Deposit, and arrive at New York at 6:00 A. M. Connects at Avon for Rochester.

4:30 P. M. NEW YORK & SOUTHERN EXPRESS. (Via Corning) supper at Avon at 7:15, and connects for Mount Morris and Rochester. Arrives in Corning at 11:00 P. M.; Elmira at 12 P. M.; New York at 10:00 A. M. Leaves Elmira at 12:25 A. M., and arrives in Philadelphia at 5:00 P. M.; Baltimore at 6:00 P. M.

6:15 P. M. NEW YORK & BALTIMORE EXPRESS. (Via Hornellsville.) Though to New York without changing cars. Magnificent Sleeping Cars run on this train from Buffalo to New York. Breakfast at Port Jervis, and arrives in New York at 12:00 M. Southern passengers breakfast at Williamsport, and arrive in Philadelphia at 5:00 P. M., and Baltimore at 6:00 P. M. Sunday night express runs through to New York.

Sunday Night Express

Leaves Buffalo at 6:15 P. M.; arrives in New York at 12:00 M. Sleeping Car attached, and connecting as above.

Trains arrive in Buffalo at—

11:00 A. M., (Sundays also.) **12:30 P. M., 10:30 P. M., 11:30 P. M.**

C. G. MILLER, President.

BUFFALO, November 17, 1862. no15c

III, 9

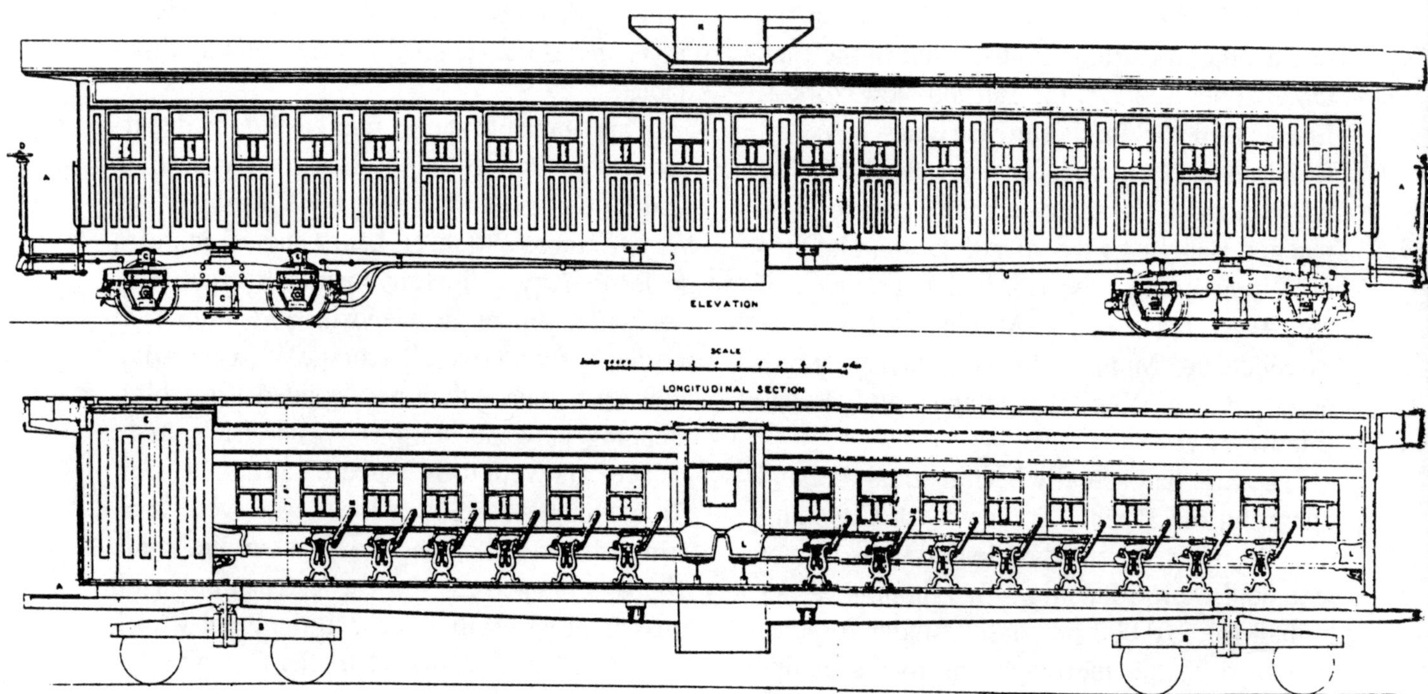

It was sixty-five feet nine inches long, ten feet nine inches wide and twelve feet, nine inches high. With twenty windows on a side each supporting a single plate of double thick French glass, it sat seventy-four passengers. (By contrast an Illinois Central standard gauge car of the same era was fifty feet long, nine feet six inches wide, ten feet six inches high, and sat sixty-five.) The night and day reclining seats were splendidly upholstered in rich velvet plush, and the gilt cornice around the inside was four inches thick. Ventilation was provided by air cooled by water and spread by fans through floor registers. Fans and water pump worked off the axle, which meant that they worked only when the train was moving. The car weighed eighteen tons, so that a trainload of these giants demanded an extremely powerful locomotive.

The Hornellsville Tribune informed its readers on September 17, 1863:

The company [sic] *have made Buffalo the permanent terminus of the Erie Railway, the passenger and freight business having increased from that point over the road. It is gratifying evidence of the growing prosperity of the Erie Railway to witness, as we frequently do, six or seven well-filled cars, with mostly through passengers, on the express trains. These palace-like sleeping cars on this road afford the night traveler a good opportunity to enjoy a comfortable lullaby repose while traveling at the rate of thirty miles an hour - finding himself at the end of his journey rested and fresh for business.*

The following is Mott's requiem on Dunkirk:

It had long been evident that the Company had handicapped itself by having its terminus at Dunkirk. There could be no escape from that place as the perpetual legal western terminus of the line, however, for it was so fixed in the Charter of the New York and Erie Railroad Company, as amended in 1838; but there was nothing to prevent the Company from regarding Buffalo as that terminus in fact. It was with that in view that the line from Hornellsville to Attica was secured and made a part of the Erie in 1861, and from that time the hopes of Dunkirk in the Erie began to fade, and since 1863 that place has been nothing more, in fact, than the terminus of a rather insignificant branch of the Erie, although it is really the termination on Lake Erie of the main line. The number of trains, either passenger or freight, running out of Dunkirk on the Erie is just the same today (1901) as it was forty years ago, and none of the palatial through drawing-room or sleeping coaches of the Erie run to or from Dunkirk. [8]

Dunkirk's claim to railroad fame was not to rest on possession of the Erie's western terminal, but on the presence of the Brooks Locomotive Company, which was incorporated in 1869 and leased the Erie's former shops. For the next half century locomotive building was the dominant industry in the city, accounting for two-thirds of the labor force. Brooks was also the largest manufacturing concern in Chautauqua County. In 1901 it merged with seven other hitherto unrelated locomotive manufacturers to form the American Locomotive Company, with headquarters and main plant at Schenectady. (For the Dunkirk plant of American Locomotive see Figure #10.)

III, 10

4

Consolidation: The Birth Of The New York Central

Ever since the last link in rail service across New York, the Attica & Buffalo, was opened in January, 1843, the seven railroads involved had to cooperate to some extent, as shown by the introduction that year of through service from Albany to Buffalo. Because of state imposed limitations on hauling freight, these lines derived most of their revenue from passenger service. Revenue from freight, however, expanded greatly when the restrictions favoring the Erie Canal were removed in the summer of 1851. The completion of the Erie to Dunkirk in May of that year and of the Hudson River Railroad from New York City to East Albany in October brought into existence two competitive all-rail routes between New York Harbor and Lake Erie. Next year, further developments to the west made consolidation to the east necessary in order to create a powerful central New York transportation organization capable of competing with these emerging transportation giants. In February, 1852, Chicago greeted its first train from the east which arrived on the Lake Shore-Michigan Southern route. Three months later, the Great Western-Michigan Central route went into service. In April the Erie reached Dunkirk, later in the same year Pennsylvania Central rails reached the Ohio River at Pittsburgh, and on New Year's Day 1853, the Baltimore & Ohio reached Wheeling. To the east, construction of Suspension Bridge below Niagara Falls was begun in 1851, which promised to the Great Western a connection with the Erie at Elmira by way of the six foot Canandaigua & Niagara Falls and the Canandaigua & Elmira.

John F. Stover describes the creation of the New York Central in his terse statistical style in Iron Horse to the West:

In the move toward a formal merger of the several railroads, Erastus Corning of the Utica & Schenectady played the dominant role. The railroads applied in 1851 to the state legislature for a law permitting the merger, and Corning asked for help from his old friend Thurlow Weed, newspaper editor and a leader of the Whigs then in power in Albany. The New York Central Consolidation Bill was enacted early in April, 1853, and in the next two months eight operating lines [Albany & Schenectady, Schenectady & Troy, Utica & Schenectady, Syracuse & Utica, Rochester & Syracuse, Buffalo & Rochester, Rochester, Lockport & Niagara Falls, and Buffalo & Lockport (Figure #1)], *plus two projected but unbuilt roads completed the formal proceed-*

ings of merger. At the stockholders meeting on July, 1853, Corning held enough proxies to have himself elected president. Dean Richmond . . . was selected vice-president. Stockholders exchanged their original stock for shares in the New York Central, with the stronger companies receiving a premium payable in thirty-year 6% bonds of the new railroad. The New York Central in 1853, with a total capital of about $23 million was reported to be one of the largest corporations in America. For a short time Corning managed to have the same cozy procurement arrangement that had been so profitable on the Utica line. These extra profits were slowed somewhat after a mildly critical report by a stockholders' committee was released in the mid-1850s. The 555-mile road prospered with each year, showing marked increases in freight traffic. By 1857 the yearly revenues were more than $8 million, twice the total of the separate roads back in 1852. In 1856 the equipment roster of Corning's line included 209 locomotives, 321 assorted passenger cars, and 2,621 freight cars. Up and down the line were 76 passenger depots, 72 freight houses, 25 engine houses with stalls for 196 engines, and 9 blacksmith shops. Dividends were paid at the normal rate of 8% per year until 1860 when they were reduced to 6%. [1]

Shortly after the consolidation, the New York Central acquired the Buffalo & Niagara Falls and the Canandaigua & Niagara Falls. The latter, contemptuously dubbed "The Peanut" by Dean Richmond, was brought into the Central family in April, 1854, in order to deprive the New York & Erie of a connection at Suspension Bridge with the Great Western. Accordingly, its gauge was changed to 4 feet 8 1/2 inches. By 1860 the NYC had completed double tracking its line with iron rail from Albany to Buffalo, a measure demanded by both safety and expeditious movement of trains.

Employing the historical present, Edward Hungerford, author of a 1938 history of the NYC, describes it shortly after consolidation:

The New York Central Railroad has become a line of consequence. Already it is a much traveled route. No longer Rochester waits for Syracuse, or Syracuse for Utica. Its through cars and its fast time are attracting many patrons. "All the Express Trains from Albany to Buffalo, and Buffalo to Albany, go through without change of cars, and all the passenger trains, during the warm weather, are abundantly supplied with good-ice-water." Express and baggage services have been introduced from one end of the line to the other. The first, the historic American Express Company, has now been in operation a decade and it helped make Buffalo history by introducing to its palate the taste of raw delicious oysters. [2]

William G. Fargo began his transportation career as freight agent at Auburn. In 1842 he became a messenger for Pomeroy & Company, pioneer expressmen, on the Albany-Buffalo route, and in 1843 he was made their agent at Buffalo. In 1844 he became messenger and co-owner of Wells & Company, which had been founded by Henry Wells, previously Pomeroy's agent at Attica. Together, Wells and Fargo founded in 1850 the first American Express Company. Wells Fargo & Company was organized in 1852 for express service to California and within three years the company controlled the Western express business, carrying gold dust, mail, packages, and passengers and conducting banking services. Though a Democrat, Fargo was wartime mayor of Buffalo for two terms, 1862-1866. His palatial half-million dollar residence with a $10,000 crystal chandelier stood on the block bounded by Fargo and West Avenues, Pennsylvania and Jersey Streets. A picture of it is reproduced here to make up for the fact that, since none of the major railroads that served Buffalo had their headquarters here, Buffalo could not boast such mansions as were built by nineteenth century railroad tycoons like Jay Gould,

Edward H. Harriman, Henry Villard, Cornelius Vanderbilt, or Jim Hill. (Figure #2.)

Cutthroat competition between the Erie and the Central was now to be expected, though it was to prove disastrous to both lines. Competitors played hard ball. A Central ad read:

Passengers taking this route can feel assured that they are with careful and experienced Engineers, the Company paying well for such, never having been obliged to use Firemen with no experience on account of strikes endangering life, and never making time as in the case on the GREAT BROAD GAUGE ROUTE. Passengers should be particular and secure tickets by this route as it is the only one having a uniform gauge from Cincinnati to Buffalo, thence to New York and Boston, saving several changes of cars and baggage and the annoyance of missing connections, which occurs so often on the New York & Erie Route. THIS IS THE ONLY ROUTE that can land Passengers by cars in New York City within a short distance of the principal Hotels. All other Routes land their Passengers in Jersey City compelling them to procure the services of porters and hacks, crossing the river, making an additional and disagreeable change, incident to the New York & Erie Road. [3]

Further cutthroat competition through rate slashing became the order of the day once the Pennsylvania and the Baltimore & Ohio had reached the Ohio Valley and the Central and the Erie had reached Lake Erie. A series of conferences of representatives of these roads was held to work out an agreement on uniform freight and passenger rates. The first of these met in Buffalo in June, 1858, and broke up in a row when the Erie refused to raise its rates to a former level. Subsequent conferences encountered a similar fate, but alarmed the shipping and traveling public and interested newspaper editors who extolled the virtues of unrestricted competition and raised the specter of monopoly.

IV, 1

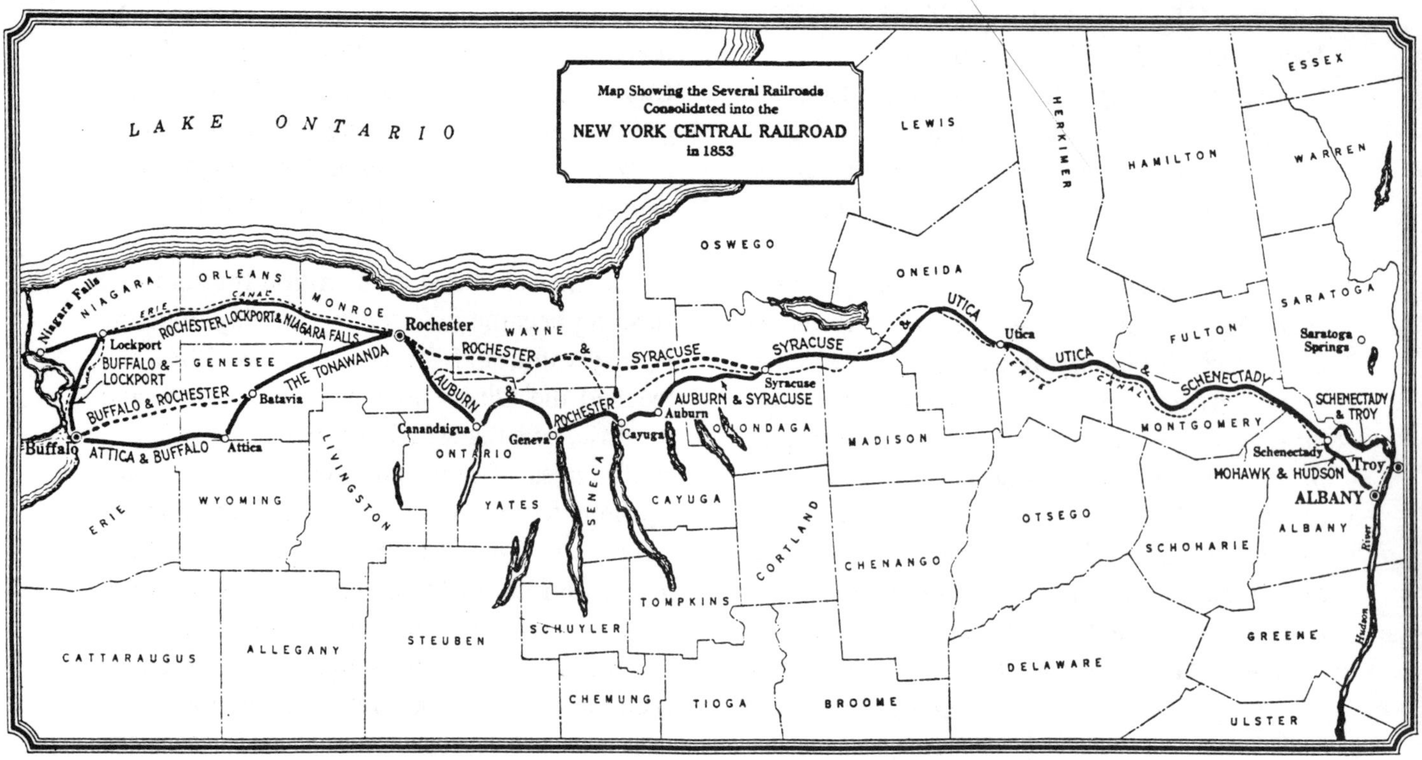
Map Showing the Several Railroads Consolidated into the
NEW YORK CENTRAL RAILROAD
in 1853
LAKE ONTARIO
Niagara Falls
NIAGARA
ORLEANS
MONROE
ERIE CANAL
Lockport
ROCHESTER, LOCKPORT & NIAGARA FALLS
Rochester
BUFFALO & LOCKPORT
GENESEE
THE TONAWANDA
Batavia
BUFFALO & ROCHESTER
Buffalo
ATTICA & BUFFALO
Attica
WAYNE
ROCHESTER & SYRACUSE
SYRACUSE
AUBURN & ROCHESTER
Canandaigua
Geneva
Cayuga
Auburn
AUBURN & SYRACUSE
Syracuse
ONONDAGA
ONTARIO
OSWEGO
LEWIS
HERKIMER
ONEIDA
UTICA & SYRACUSE
Utica
UTICA & SCHENECTADY
HAMILTON
ESSEX
WARREN
SARATOGA
Saratoga Springs
FULTON
MONTGOMERY
SCHENECTADY & TROY
Schenectady
MOHAWK & HUDSON
Troy
ALBANY
MADISON
ERIE
WYOMING
LIVINGSTON
YATES
SENECA
CAYUGA
CORTLAND
CHENANGO
OTSEGO
SCHOHARIE
TOMPKINS
CATTARAUGUS
ALLEGANY
STEUBEN
SCHUYLER
CHEMUNG
TIOGA
BROOME
DELAWARE
GREENE
ULSTER
Hudson River

IV, 2

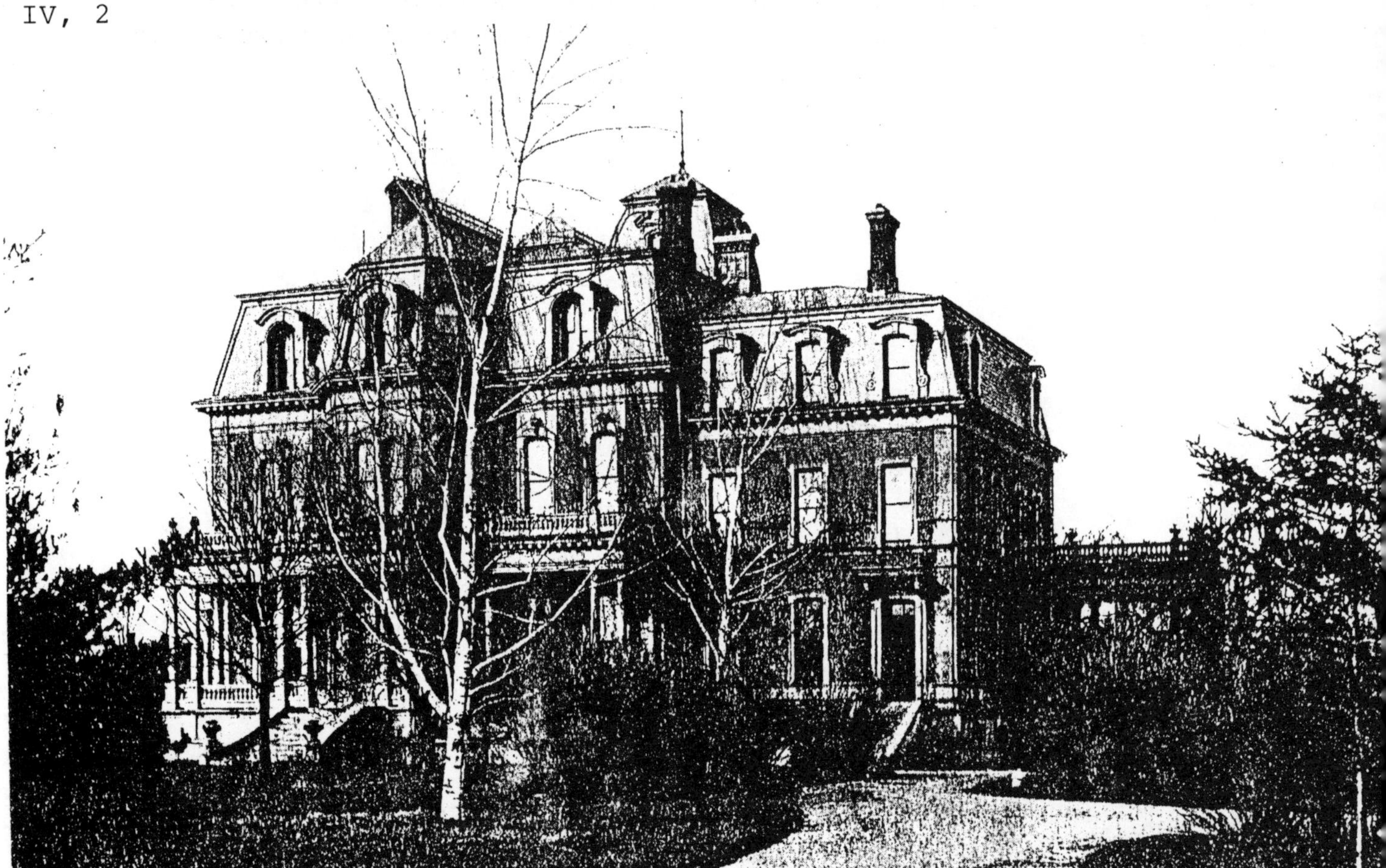

5
Rails East And West

The decade before the War Between the States was an explosive one for railroad construction. Route mileage which had been 23 in 1830 rose to 2,818 by 1840, and to 9,021 ten years later. Then during the 1850s alone 20,348 miles of railroad lines were laid down, over two and a half times the trackage that had existed when the Compromise of 1850 was being hammered out. (Figure #1.) As Stover, a bean-counter if ever there was one, writes:

In 1860, on the eve of the Civil War, each of the thirty-three states in the Union except Minnesota and Oregon had some rail mileage in operation. The westward fingers of the expanding iron network had reached La Crosse in Wisconsin, Cedar Rapids in Iowa, and Saint Joseph in Missouri. West of the Mississippi other short pieces of railway served parts of Arkansas, Louisiana, and Texas. Thus by 1860 the rail network had practically reached the nation's western frontier line. The rates at which the three regions built additional railroads in the 1850s varied. The eleven New England and mid-Atlantic states added only about 75% to their network for an 1860 total of more than 10,000 miles. The twelve southern states more than tripled their rail system to about 9,500 miles of line. The most rapid expansion was in the west, especially in the Old Northwest. The ten western states increased their rail system more than eightfold and had a network of more than 11,000 miles in 1860. As the nation faced the war in 1860, the expanded iron network fairly well covered all the states east of the Mississippi River. [1]

Most Southern lines were notoriously ramshackle, however, while the lines Northeast and Midwest were to prove indispensable in achieving a Northern victory. The two latter sections were now bound together by east-west bands of iron far stronger than the Mississippi Valley waterways, which at the time of the Louisiana Purchase had made the west look to New Orleans as the rock of its salvation. For a striking comparison between the western railroads in 1850 and 1860 see Figure #2.

The New York City Connection

Completion during 1852 of the Lake Shore and the GW-MC routes to Chicago, the PRR and the B&O to the Ohio Valley and the Erie to Dunkirk, has been noted in the previous chapter. To the east the New York & Harlem's

V, 1

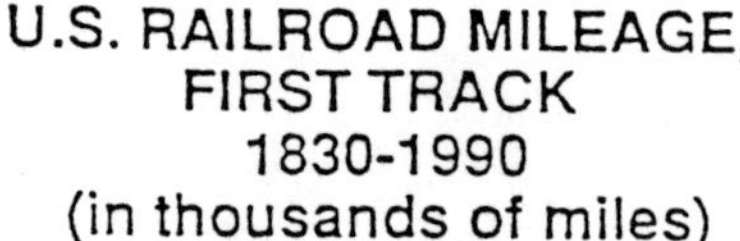
U.S. RAILROAD MILEAGE,
FIRST TRACK
1830-1990
(in thousands of miles)

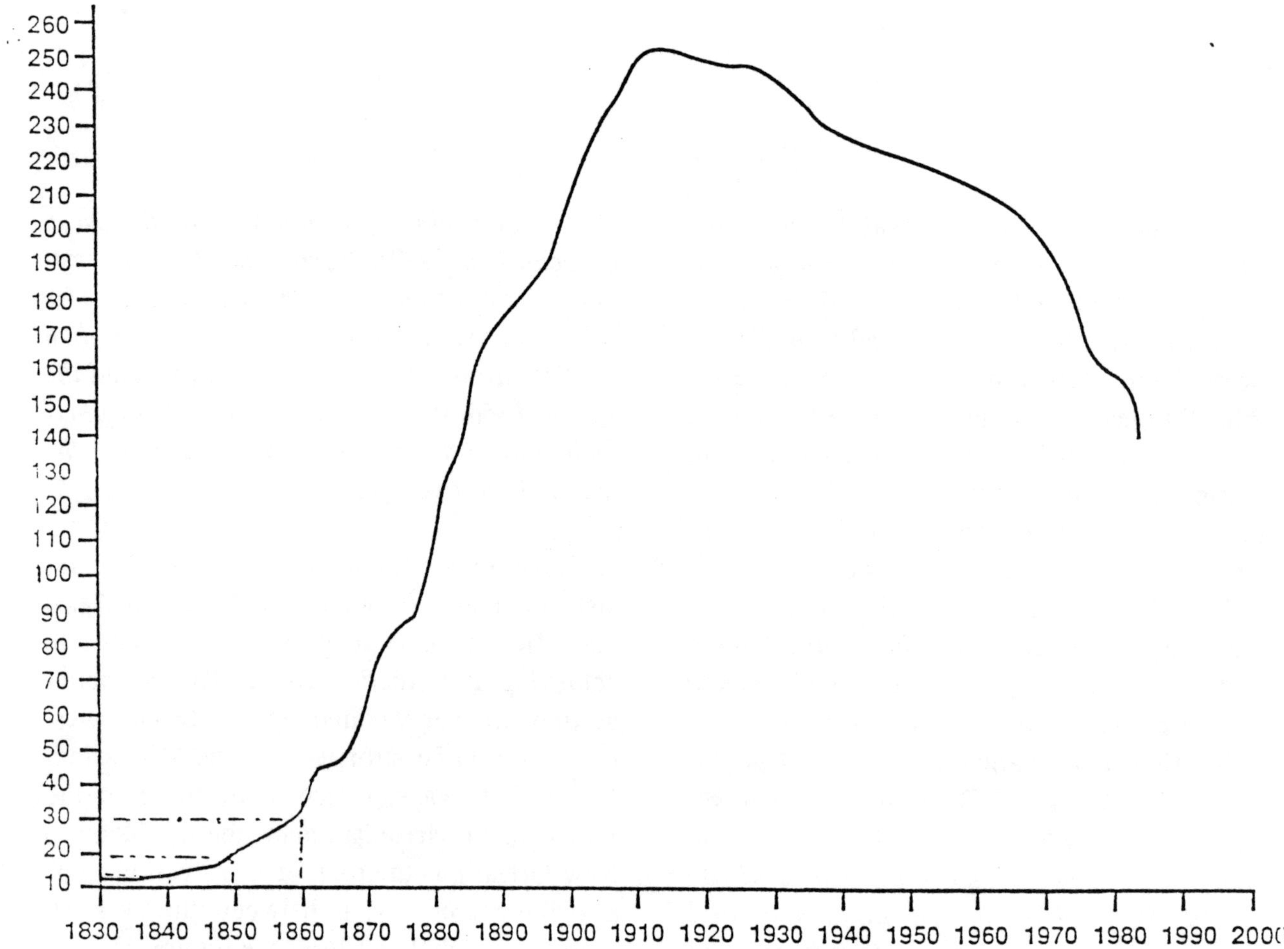

260
250
240
230
220
210
200
190
180
170
160
150
140
130
120
110
100
90
80
70
60
50
40
30
20
10
1830 1840 1850 1860 1870 1880 1890 1900 1910 1920 1930 1940 1950 1960 1970 1980 1990 2000

V, 2

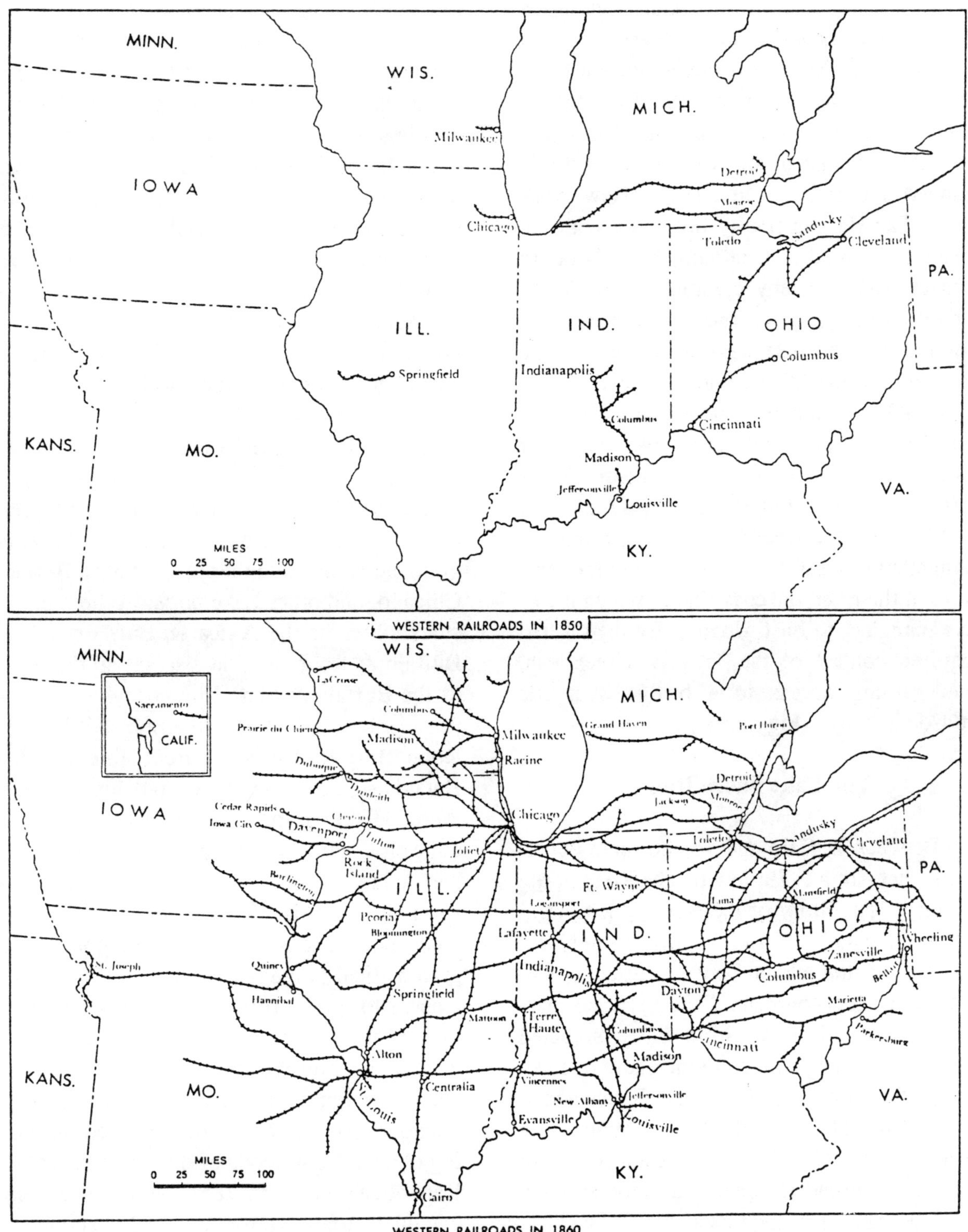

WESTERN RAILROADS IN 1850

WESTERN RAILROADS IN 1860

charter had been amended in 1840 to allow it to build north to Albany. Progress was slow, but by 1844 White Plains had been reached. In 1842 the president of the road had sounded out the president of the Erie about building a branch to the Hudson opposite Piermont. In a decision which Mott calls incredible, startling, stupid, and even criminal, the Erie turned down this offer which would have given it entry into Manhattan and would have forever changed the railroad history of New York State. The Harlem finally linked up with the Western Railroad at Chatham, New York, in January, 1852, thereby creating a New York-Albany all-rail route, though ferries were required to transport passengers across the Hudson between Albany and Rensselaer. (See Figure #3, which should be consulted for the rest of this chapter, and Figure #4.) The year before, a better route, the Hudson River Railroad, organized by Poughkeepsie interests in 1847, was opened from a terminal on Manhattan's West Side, thence up the east shore of the river, the coastline of which it forever mangled, to East Albany. By then it had acquired control of the Troy & Greenbush, thus gaining access to a bridge over the Hudson at Troy. (Figure #5.)

The Lake Shore Route

Between Buffalo and Toledo there developed what Alvin F. Harlow in The Road of the Century: The Story of the New York Central called "a gaggle of little roads strongly remindful of the chain between Albany and Buffalo but less coherent." The first to be chartered was the Erie & North East, projected from Erie, Pennsylvania, up the shore of Lake Erie to the New York State line. It was hoped that this would induce the Erie to build a line to meet it from Dunkirk. One state could not charter a railroad to operate in another state. Fiscally exhausted upon its arrival at Dunkirk, however, the Erie had perforce to curtail plans for further expansion, so a separate company, the Dunkirk & State Line, was organized to close the gap but found difficulty obtaining funds.

Meanwhile, another road was promoted by the village of Fredonia three miles south of Dunkirk. Stock was sold to residents of Chautauqua and Erie counties, and on June 6, 1849, the Buffalo & State Line (State Line was a village located appropriately enough on the boundary of Pennsylvania and New York) was organized at Fredonia. Presiding at its creation were Dean Richmond of Buffalo and James S. Wadsworth of Geneseo. Like many early Buffalonians, Richmond had been born in Vermont. His parents moved west to Syracuse where they operated a salt mine. Orphaned as a teenager, Richmond came to Buffalo in 1842 and entered the grain forwarding business, sharing in the prosperity brought to the port by the completion of the Albany-Buffalo chain of railroads in 1843. He operated a fleet of steam and sailing vessels on the Lakes and owned grain elevators and other properties in Buffalo, Chicago, and other Lake ports. A director and stockholder of the Attica & Buffalo and the Buffalo & Rochester, he also sat on the board of the Buffalo & State Line, of which he was president at his death in 1866. When the Rochester & Buffalo direct line reached Batavia in 1852, he transferred his residence there. His biographer writes that "he had little education and no cultural opportunities. He had a large frame and uncommon muscular strength. All his life he swore to excess; he could not make a speech or even converse in grammatical language." Hence he was never elected to public office, but was State Chairman of the Democratic Party from 1850 until his death. Wadsworth grew up as heir apparent to his family's extensive landed estate in Genesee County, which he managed on coming of age. He was one of the organizers of the Republican Party in 1856, and unsuccessful candidate for governor in 1862. Though he had no previous military experience, he fought at First Bull Run, Fredericksburg, Chancellors-

V, 3

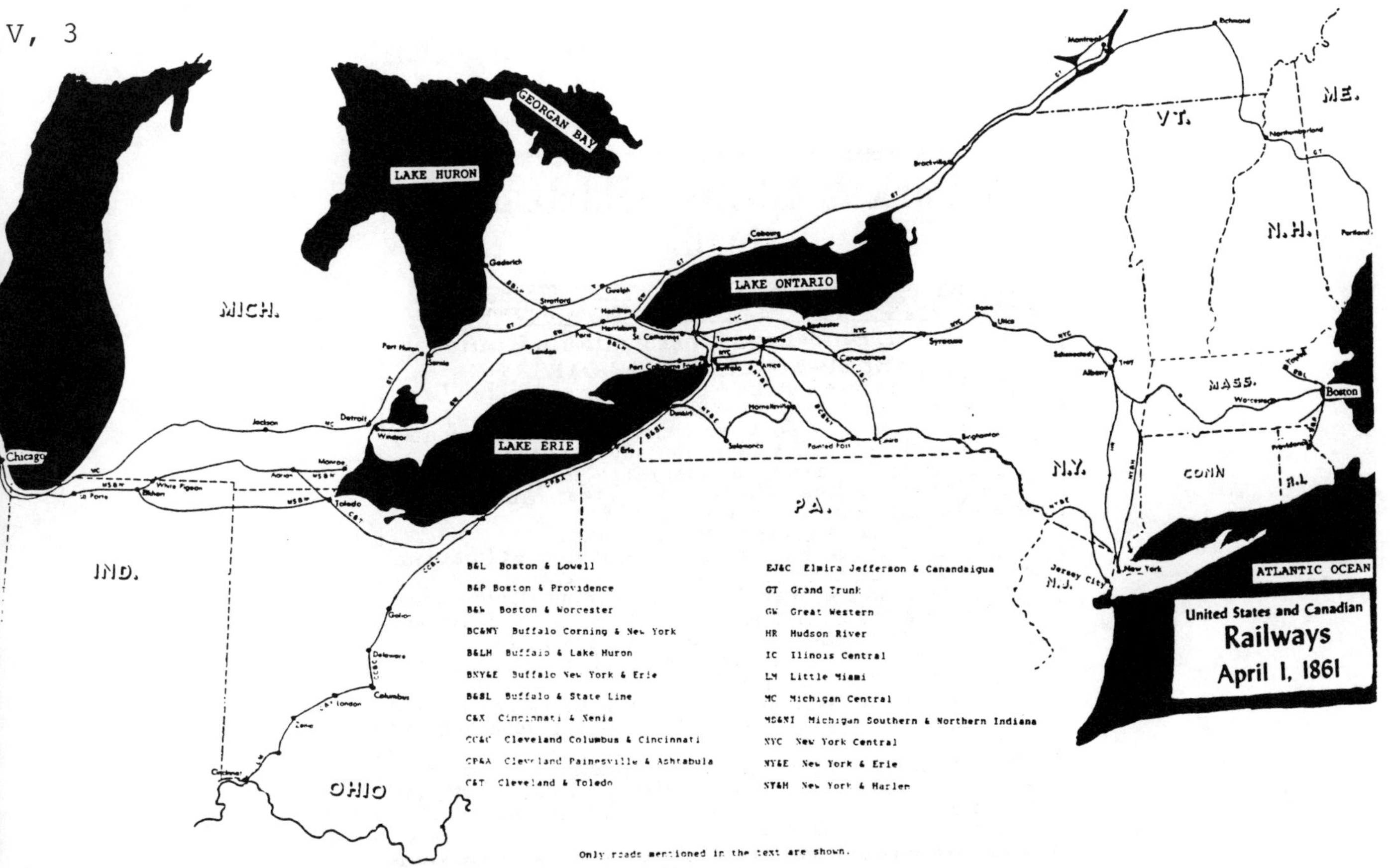

ville, and Gettysburg, while rising to the rank of brigadier general. He was shot at the Battle of the Wilderness, May 6, 1864, and died two days later.

Among the stockholders of the Buffalo & State Line was the Albany-Buffalo chain of railroads since it would extend their reach toward lines being projected in the Midwest. The Syracuse & Utica had signed up for $63,200, the Rochester & Syracuse for $105,000, and Richmond's Buffalo & Rochester for $94,000. The Erie was built to a six foot gauge, and both the Erie & North East and the Dunkirk & State Line were planned to be of the same width. The Buffalo & State Line began to assemble contiguous parcels of property in Buffalo and along the lake shore south and west of the city to the Pennsylvania border during 1850 and 1851, along which trains were soon running sixty-nine miles to State Line. Oddly enough, Fredonia was left off the main line and had to be satisfied with a branch. Testifying to the dominance of Richmond and the Albany-Buffalo railroads was the fact that the Buffalo & State Line's gauge was not six feet but the standard gauge of the central New York roads, four feet eight and a half inches.

With the consent of New York, Massachusetts, and Connecticut, Congress had in 1792 sold to Pennsylvania a forty mile lake front neck to provide it with a corridor to Lake Erie. On the western side of that neck in Ohio the four feet ten inch gauge had been established by state law in 1848 to discourage out-of-state traffic. The legislature at Harrisburg reacted to this exercise in mercantilism by banning the Ohio gauge within the borders of Pennsylvania, thus denying to Ohio continuous rail connections with the Atlantic coast. Moreover, a charter which would have created a thirty-mile long railroad from Erie to the Ohio line was rescinded at the behest of Philadelphians, who were building the Pennsylvania Central toward Pittsburgh and had their eyes on Erie as a terminal on the

V, 4

New York & Albany—Harlem Rail Road.

Cheapest, Safest and Most Reliable Route.

FARE $1—NO CHANGE OF CARS.

TICKETS procured at the office, corner of Maiden Lane and Dean streets, Albany, or at the Depot, East Albany.

Passengers for New York, who wish to go by this route, should buy tickets at the Rochester office for Albany.

On and after Wednesday, January 26th, 1853, the Trains of the Harlem Railroad will run as follows, (Sundays excepted,) at the remarkably low sum of $1:

LEAVE ALBANY FOR NEW YORK.

1st Train—7.30 A M, Express Train, stopping at Chatham and Croton Falls, arriving in New York at 12.30 M.

2d Train—10.45 A M, Way Mail Train, making all stoppages.

3d Train—3.30 P M, Express Train, stopping at Chatham and Croton Falls, and arriving in New York at 9 P M.

LEAVE NEW YORK FOR ALBANY—From City Hall Station.

1st Train—7.30 A M, Way Mail Train.

2d Train—9 A M, Express Train, Arriving in Albany at 2 P M

3d Train—3.45 P M, Express Train, arriving in Albany at 9 P M.

☞ Baggage checked through at Rochester, and transferred from the Buffalo to the Harlem Railroad Depot, free of charge. M. SLOAT, Superintendent.

Albany, January 25, 1853. fe14

V, 5

Hudson River Railroad.

WINTER ARRANGEMENT.—FARE REDUCED.

On and after Monday, December 5, 1853, the trains will leave Albany from the foot of Maiden Lane, as follows:

4.30 A. M. Express Passenger Train for N. York, stopping at Hudson, Poughkeepsie, Fishkill and Peekskill.

6.15 A. M. Way Mail and Passenger Train for New York, stopping at all Mail Stations.

8.45 A. M. Express Train for New York, stopping only at Hudson, Rhinebeck, Poughkeepsie, Fiskill and Peekskill.

11 A. M. Way Train, stopping at Castleton, Stuyvesant, Coxsackie, Hudson, Oakhill, Tivoli, Barrytown, Rhinebeck, Staatsburgh, Hyde Park, Poughkeepsie, New Hamburgh, Fishkill, Cold Spring, Garrison's and Peekskill.

1.15 P. M. Way Freight and Passenger Train for Poughkeepsie, stopping at all stations.

4.45 P. M. Express Train for New York, stopping at Hudson, Poughkeepsie and Peekskill.

4.55 P. M. Milk, Freight and Passenger Train, stopping at all stations on signal.

Sunday Mail Train for New York at 3 o'clock P. M.

☞ Passengers can have their Baggage checked and procure Tickets at the office, No. 13 Maiden Lane, corner of Dean street.

EDMUND FRENCH, Superintendent.

Albany, December 5, 1853. de18

Great Lakes. For three years Pennsylvania excluded foreign roads that would channel traffic out of state until the building of the Great Western across the Ontario Peninsula from Niagara Falls to Detroit made Quaker Staters realize that they were preventing their state from becoming a vital link in the course of interstate commerce between the Atlantic and the interior.

Thereupon the Pennsylvania legislature came up with a law which required that all railroads from Erie to the New York border must be of either six feet or four feet eight and a half inch gauge, while all from Erie to the Ohio line must be four feet ten inches. This would compel a change of trains by all passengers at Erie, possibly a layover of a few hours, and the expenditure there of some money by travelers. Freight would also have to be transshipped, to the benefit of Erie stevedores.

Since it was situated on Lake Erie and joined to the Ohio river at Portsmouth by the aptly named Ohio & Erie Canal, which had been completed in 1832, Cleveland held aloof from railroad building during the 1840s. However, road transportation eastward along the lake shore to Buffalo had become increasingly important. In 1849 the Cleveland Painesville & Ashtabula was chartered to build from Cleveland (population 15,000) along this route to the Pennsylvania line. By 1852 the railroad had reached Conneaut on that line, sixty-eight miles east of Cleveland. To penetrate the adjoining strip, the CP&A acquired control of the Franklin Canal, a Pennsylvania company, which had the foresight to obtain a change in its charter enabling the company to build a railroad with a four foot ten inch gauge from Erie to the Ohio line, over which the first train ran from Cleveland to Erie in November, 1852. At the same time the nineteen mile six foot gauge Erie & North East was completed to a junction with the standard gauge Buffalo & State Line. Since in April, 1853, the legislators at Harrisburg were induced by fair means and foul to repeal the law requiring a change of gauge at Erie, the Erie & North East and the Buffalo & State Line agreed to change their gauge to the four foot ten inch Ohio gauge. For four weeks violent mobs of irate residents of Erie, aided by local lawmen, attempted to halt the introduction into their city of this foreign gauge by ripping up track whenever it was laid, but eventually cooler heads and federal intervention prevailed. Thus was made possible continuous service between Buffalo and Cleveland, where further connections could be made for either Chicago or Cincinnati. In Figure #6, a Buffalo & State Line advertisement of October 1, 1853, this route is already being referred to as the Lake Shore Railroad.

Lake Erie ships handled most of the traffic between Toledo and Cleveland during the 1840s. (For the genesis of the Cleveland & Toledo and its eastern and western connections see Figure #7.) However, intermediate lake towns were not happy with this arrangement. Therefore in 1846 Sandusky interests planned the Junction Railroad to link Toledo with Cleveland via Fremont, Sandusky, and Elyria. The swing inland to Fremont was made to avoid the need to bridge Sandusky Bay. There matters stood until Norwalk took the initiative and in September, 1850, organized the Toledo Norwalk & Cleveland. This was to be an 87.5 mile southeasterly arc from Toledo through Fremont and Norwalk to Grafton on the Cleveland Columbus & Cincinnati, twenty-five miles from Cleveland. The gauge of the projected road was standard in order to connect with the standard gauge Northern Indiana at Toledo.

This development jolted the promoters of the Junction into action, and they began construction on their line between Sandusky and Cleveland. They now decided to bypass Toledo and link up with the Northern Indiana at Swanton, eighteen miles west of Toledo. (Note the dotted line in Figure #7.) This involved a long and difficult grade and an expensive bridge across the Maumee River.

V, 6

Lake Shore Railroad.

From Buffalo to Cleveland, Pittsburgh, Columbus, Cincinnati, Toledo and Chicago, connecting at Cleveland with the Steamboats for Detroit.

Buffalo and State Line Railroad—Fall Arrangement—4 Daily Trains, (Sundays excepted.)

LEAVING THE DEPOT OF THE BUFFALO AND ALBANY RAILROAD, EXCHANGE STREET.

First Train, 7.30 A. M., Cleveland Express, th[illegible]h in 6½ hours—connecting with Trains for Pittsburg, [illegible]ving at 9 P. M., also with Trains for Wellesville and W[illegible]ling.

Second, 10.45 A. M., Express Mail, leaves Cleveland at 8 P. M.

For Cincinnati and Chicago—Leaves Toledo at 2 A. M., and arrives at Chicago at 12 o'clock, noon.

Third Train, 2.30 P. M., Accommodation and Freight to State Line.

Fourth Train, 9.30 P. M., Express.—Leaves Cleveland at 7 A. M. for Cincinnati and Chicago—Leaves Toledo at 12.30 P. M. and arrive at Chicago at 10.30 P. M.

First class fare to	Cleveland		$4 00
" " "	Detroit		6 00
" " "	Toledo		6 00
" " "	Chicago		12.25
" " "	Cincinnati		9 50
" " "	Louisville		11 50
" " "	St. Louis		18 50
Second " "	Cleveland		2 00
" " "	Detroit		3 00
" " "	Toledo		3 05
" " "	Chicago		5 50
" " "	Cincinnati		4 75

Tickets should be procured at the Office of the New York Central R. R. at the Depot.

☞ Passengers who design going by this Road, are cautioned against purchasing Tickets before they arrive at Buffalo.

☞ Passengers going to Detroit, by taking either of the morning trains, arrive at Cleveland in time for the evening line of boats to Detroit, arriving at Detroit next morning.

To THE PUBLIC—We show you no distorted map of the lakes and western country to make Air Lines, but give you the ACTUAL starting, running, and arriving hour of trains as agreed upon in convention of Superintendents of the principal western railroads, which will be worked to, unavoidable accidents only excepted.

C. C. DENNIS, Sup't B. & S. L. R. R.

Buffalo, 1853. oc1

V. 7

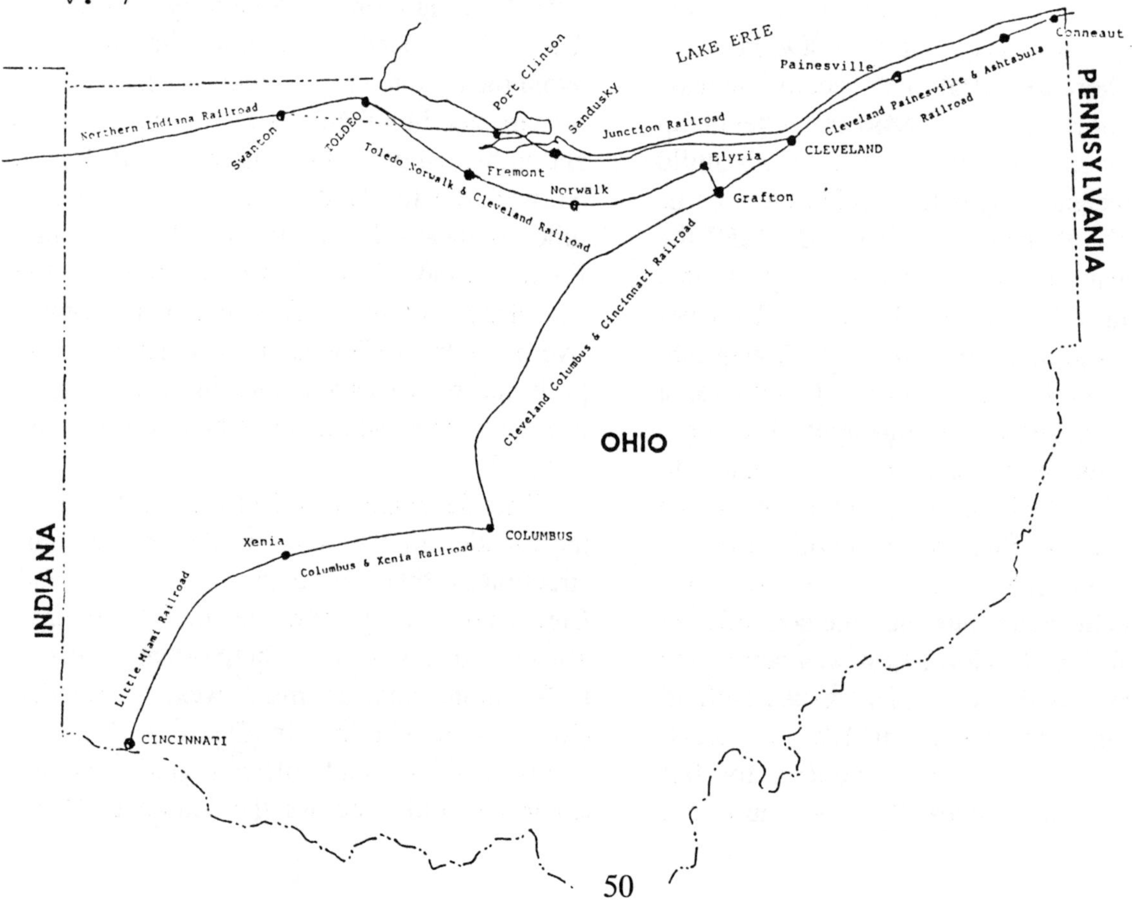

Neither the steep grade nor the expensive bridge were ever used since the Junction interests again changed their plans and decided to bypass Fremont and build west from Sandusky across Sandusky Bay and through Port Clinton. The hapless Junction also ran into trouble at its eastern end when Cleveland declined to grant permission to enter the city across the Cuyahoga River.

On January 24, 1853, the Toledo Norwalk & Cleveland ran its first train from Toledo to Cleveland via Grafton. The Junction people gave up the fight, and both railroads merged in September into the Cleveland & Toledo which finally bridged Sandusky Bay. The C&T consisted of a Northern Division (Cleveland to Toledo via Sandusky) and a Southern Division (Cleveland to Toledo via Fremont.) The latter division, though longer, bore the lion's share of the through traffic because the former route involved a ferry across the Cuyahoga. Hard times followed the Panic of 1857, and the Northern Division dismantled its line west of Sandusky, including the bridge, in 1858. Fourteen years later, however, like "the stone which was rejected by the builders" but "became the head of the corner," the Northern Division's more direct route was reactivated and became the mainline of the lake shore route. The resulting anomaly was that the main line of the Michigan Southern did not run through Michigan at all but through Ohio and Indiana.

Next west on the Lake Shore's future route to Chicago was the Michigan Southern, which originated as part of a daring plan for a railroad network adopted by the Michigan legislature in 1836, months before the territory became a state. It was to run from Monroe on the western end of Lake Erie between Detroit and Toledo and New Buffalo on Lake Michigan in the southwesternmost corner of Michigan across from Chicago. It was conceived of as a portage route across the state eliminating the 700 mile detour up Lake Michigan and down Lake Huron on lake ships. However, the state had difficulty finishing even the first sixty-eight miles west of Monroe by 1843 when construction was halted. In 1846 the state sold the road to private investors who received permission to run it through northern Indiana to Chicago. La Porte, Indiana, was reached in 1851, and on February 20, 1852, the Michigan Southern became the first railroad to reach Chicago from the east, beating the Michigan Central by three months. The line through Indiana had been constructed by the Northern Indiana Railroad which was soon combined with the Michigan Southern to produce the Michigan Southern & Northern Indiana. In addition to the 243 mile line from Chicago, which dead-ended at Monroe, a shorter route from Toledo west to Elkhart, Indiana, was built which soon became the mainline.

From Cleveland to the Ohio River railroad connection was provided by the Cleveland Columbus & Cincinnati, the Columbus & Xenia, and the Little Miami, all of which had been completed by 1851. After the Civil War the CC&C was merged with other midwestern roads to become the Cleveland Cincinnati Chicago & Saint Louis, *alias* the Big Four. (Figure XI, #7.)

Chicago via Canada

Buffalo was to enjoy alternate routes to Chicago (Figure #3) which, as a result of railroad construction in the Midwest and Canada during the 1850s and the building of transcontinentals after the Civil War, was destined to play the key role in America's railroad system, hailed by Carl Sandburg as "Hog Butcher for the world, Tool Maker, Stacker of Wheat, Player with Railroads and the Nation's Freight Handler; stormy, husky, brawling City of the Broad Shoulders." The first and shorter (525.1 miles) route was via the south shore of Lake Erie through Ohio and Indiana. Of this the Buffalo & State Line was, as noted, the easternmost link, and the Northern Indiana the westernmost. The second and slightly longer

(537.7 miles) route crossed the Ontario Peninsula and southern Michigan. The eastern link in the second route was Canadaís Great Western Railroad, incorporated in 1845 as a shortcut across Canada for American traffic to and from the burgeoning Midwest. It was a 233 mile road with a five foot six inch gauge (mandatory from 1851 to 1871 for all Canadian railroads receiving government assistance) from Niagara Falls to Windsor across the Detroit river from Detroit by way of Hamilton, Paris, and London, Upper Canada, later called Canada West and still later Ontario. At the same time the Michigan Central was in the process of linking Detroit with Chicago. The author and finisher of the Great Western was Sir Alan MacNab, a Scottish immigrant who had been knighted for his role in putting down the rebellion of 1837, a minor armed uprising of some disaffected residents of Upper Canada, who resented the ruling clique in the province known as the Family Compact. "Though he lived to be premier of Canada," writes the historian of the Canadian National Railways concerning MacNab, "he may have regarded January 17, 1854, as the crest of his career. On that day the first train of the Great Western railroad ran from Niagara Falls to Windsor."

Since it was difficult to raise the money needed for the Great Western in Canada and since the Imperial government and City bankers turned Sir Alan down when he traveled to London for financial assistance, he approached the Canadian government. (In Canada as in America, only more so, politics and railroads went hand in hand.) He argued that the Great Western would provide a western link for the Grand Trunk, a Canadian road projected to run along the Saint Lawrence River from Montreal to Kingston and along the north shore of Lake Ontario to Toronto. He was successful to the extent that in 1849 the Canadian government guaranteed the interest on money borrowed for railroad construction. MacNab also interested Americans in his scheme. At the end of 1851, after the legislators in Albany had abolished canal tolls that had to be paid by the railroads, the Albany & Schenectady, the Utica & Schenectady, the Syracuse & Utica, the Rochester & Syracuse, and the Rochester Lockport & Niagara Falls subscribed to almost $500,000 in Great Western stock. The Buffalo & Rochester begged off because it had already invested in the Buffalo & State Line. Also it was the Lockport, not the Buffalo line, that would profit from the Great Western.

The role of the Irish in building the Erie Canal has been exaggerated, but not in railroad construction a generation later. On the building of the Great Western, a contemporary wrote:

First through Lincoln came the surveyors, followed during the winter of 1851-52 by obstreperous construction gangs. Comprising the largest part of the construction forces were the Irish immigrants who had fled the famine in their homeland. They were a rootless, irresponsible lot, suffering under the brutal and dishonest behaviour of sub-contractors and straw bosses, and they returned their treatment in like measure. Farmers along the route constantly lost chickens and other livestock to the workers, and payday brawls occurred regularly. [2]

The Great Western's Chicago connection was the Michigan Central, whose origins went back to the Detroit & Saint Joseph, which had been chartered along with the Michigan Southern in 1836. It was to run from Detroit to Saint Joseph on the southeast shore of Lake Michigan. Like the Michigan Southern it was intended as a portage route between Lakes Michigan and Huron. By the time the road reached Kalamazoo, 144 miles west of Detroit and about four-fifths of the way to Saint Joseph, money had run out. A group of Boston capitalists bought it from the state, reorganized it as the Michigan Central, redirected it toward New Buffalo, acquired an Illinois road (the

New Albany & Salem), and arranged with the Illinois Central for running rights into Chicago. The first Michigan Central train pulled into Chicago on May 20, 1852.

Meanwhile, back east, the connection between the Great Western at Niagara Falls and the western terminal of the Rochester Lockport & Niagara Falls was furnished by the ferry steamer *Maid of the Mist.* This was highly inconvenient because it required descending the escarpment on one side Of the Niagara Gorge and ascending it on the other. The solution to the problem was a suspension bridge. John N. Jackson and John Burtniak write in Railways on the Niagara Peninsula:

The Niagara Gorge was an ideal location for a bridge. Although the water was exceptionally turbulent in its confined chasm, the land was high and even on both banks of the river and it was the narrowest point along the entire length of the River. The rock formations on both banks were firm and more than adequate to support the weight and stress of a railway bridge. The gap of 800 feet could be crossed, but only if a suitable single span structure could be designed. [3]

The first suspension bridge across the gorge had been built by a private contractor in 1848, but it was not strong enough to support trains. In connection with this bridge the story is told that the contractor offered a prize of five dollars to the first boy who could land a kite on the other side of the bridge, after which stouter wires and then cables were pulled across. Another contractor was engaged, John A. Roebling, who was to plan and whose son Washington was to complete the Brooklyn Bridge:

The construction of this stronger bridge [over the Niagara River] *began in 1851 and occupied the next four years. The design was novel, breath-taking in appearance, and in absolute conflict with the accepted engineering tenets of the period. It was nothing less than a melding of the principles of a suspension bridge, then regarded as undulating and frail, with the demands of rigidity and strength needed for the passage of heavy locomotives and loaded freight trains. Roebling's solution was to provide stiffening by trusses, braces, and stays from above, below, and within the structure in order to resist any wind or swaying motion that might occur. The bridge was completed in 1855 when the first train, with twenty loaded freight cars weighing 326 tons passed safely over the structure. Agreement had been reached in 1853 that the Bridge Company would lease the upper deck in perpetuity to the Great Western which became its principal user.* [4]

Suspension Bridge, the proper name given to the new bridge, was tracked to handle three gauges, five foot six inches for the Great Western, four feet eight and a half inches for the Rochester Lockport and Niagara Falls, and six feet for the Canandaigua & Niagara Falls which connected at Canandaigua with the Canandaigua & Elmira. The Canandaigua road had been chartered in 1851 and was doing business by October, 1853. (Figure #9.) Like the Lockport line, it was aimed at tapping Great Western traffic, and like the Hornellsville and Corning roads it was conceived of as a feeder of the Erie at Elmira.

The Great Western threw out a branch from Hamilton to Toronto the year the bridge was opened in order to link up with the Grand Trunk which, as noted, was putting together a line paralleling Lake Ontario and the Saint Lawrence River. With a line from Montreal to warm water at Portland, Maine, the Grand Trunk provided Canada with year-round access to the Atlantic, since the Saint Lawrence is frozen for several months during winter. Unfortunately, the two companies could not agree on terms so the Grand Trunk built its own line paralleling the Great Western on the north via Gulf and Stratford to Sarnia, across the Saint Claire River from Port Huron, Michigan. When completed in 1856 the Grand

V, 8

V, 9

Canandaigua & N. Falls Railroad.

OPEN TO THE FALLS.

New Broad Guage Route between New York and Niagara Falls.

The Express Train leaves Niagara Falls at 2 45 P. M. Mail Train at 8 A. M.

The Express trains leave Canandaigua at 8 A. M. The Mail train leaves Canandaigua at 4 P. M.—each connecting with the Night Express Trains on the New York & Erie and Canandaigua and Elmira Railroads; and with trains on the New York Central Railroad at Batavia and Canandaigua.

The Mail Train also connects with the Mail Train on the Canandaigua & Elmira Railroad.

Through Tickets to be had at the offices of the Company at the Falls and Canandaigua, and at the offices of the New York and Erie Railroad Company, at foot of Duane street, and corner of Dey street and Broadway, New York.

N. B.—Baggage checked through. No charge for handling.

SAM. BROWN, Sup't.

Sup't office, C. & N. F. R. R., Canandaigua, Oct. 14, 1853.

oc17tf

Trunk possessed the longest railway system in the world - a continuous stretch of 1,100 miles over sparsely settled territory. A later Canadian prime minister was to remark that while other nations had too much history, Canada had too much geography.

The following account of the last Canadian rail link with Buffalo before the Civil War is from G. R. Steven's history of the Canadian National:

The citizens of Brantford, Ontario, spat blood when the Great Western failed to build through their flourishing community, despite its traffic potential of 15 million feet of lumber, and 400,000 bushels of grain annually. They particularly wanted a link with Buffalo, and as early as 1851 had incorporated the Buffalo & Brantford. James Wadsworth [who was to be killed at the Wilderness], *mayor of the American city* [in 1851], *had become the leading figure in this promotion and visited England on several occasions to obtain support for it. The route ran from Fort Erie (a Canadian suburb of Buffalo) through Brantford to Goderich on Lake Huron, 162 miles away.* [5]

Like the Michigan Central and the Michigan Southern, this road was originally conceived of as a portage route, enabling passengers and freight to bypass Lake Erie. A contemporary, however, emphasized even more than Stevens Buffalo's role in the project, asserting in 1864 that "this road originated in a desire on the part of the populous city of Buffalo to render tributary to herself the rich peninsula of Canada West; and also to divert the stream of eastern and western travel and freight away from the Suspension Bridge route to her own hotels and stations."

Construction began in 1852, and the line to Caledonia, fifty-seven miles from Fort Erie, was opened in late 1853 (Figure #10); to Brantford on January 6, 1854, and later that year to Paris with a junction with the Great Western, which enabled it to share in the considerable traffic between Detroit and Buffalo. However, money ran out in the attempt to push on to Goderich. Laborers were not being paid regularly, the result being riots at Ridgeway in 1855 in which one man was killed and several wounded. The company was reorganized in 1856. The sequel is narrated by Stevens:

On June 28, 1858 the first train crawled into Goderich on temporary trestles. Only then did the promoters learn that the harbor was too shallow for ships of even moderate burden to come alongside and that all transfers of cargo must be effected in the fairway by means of lighters. From then on the Brantford & Goderich line was a dying duck. [6]

To eliminate its nuisance value as a potential competitor, it was taken over in 1864 by the Grand Trunk.

Passengers on the Buffalo Brantford & Goderich took the ferry across the Niagara River at Fort Erie to the foot of Porter Avenue on the American Side and the Buffalo & Niagara Falls to its terminal on Erie Street. (Figure #11.) The first ferry, the *International,* did not carry railroad cars and took twenty five minutes to cross over between Fort Erie and Black Rock. It burned in 1854 and by 1857 had been replaced by a second *International* which had been built in Buffalo. As described by a contemporary:

The new ferry boat was a wooden sidewheeler, 226 feet long, 40 feet 8 inches wide, 13 feet depth of hold, 1, 121 gross tons register. Two sets of tracks, capable of holding eight passenger cars were laid on the main-deck. The machinery consisted of two engines placed athwartship. Each engine was connected to the side-wheel on its side. This permitted the greatest flexibility when maneuvering the vessel. [7]

V, 10

Buffalo, Brantford and Goderich Railway.

Open from Buffalo to Caledonia--60 Miles.

On and after Tuesday, 20th December, 1853, one train will run daily, Sundays excepted, leaving Buffalo at 9 o'clock A. M., and Caledonia at 1 o'clock P. M.

Passengers are requested to procure tickets at the office, No. 13 Exchange street, nearly opposite the Mansion House, Buffalo, and at the Ticket Office, Caledonia.

de12tf WILLIAM WALLACE, Sup't.

☞ The following papers in Canada are requested to publish the above as a regular yearly advertisement, until forbid, and send bill to the office of the company in Brantford:

'Welland Reporter,' Drummondville; 'Niagara Chronicle,' do; 'Journal,' St. Catherines; 'Leader,' 'Globe,' 'Colonist,' 'Message,' Toronto; 'Spectator,' 'Canadian,' Hamilton; 'Reformer,' 'Reporter,' Galt; 'Backwoodsman,' Elora; 'Warder,' Dundas; 'Telegraph,' Berlin; 'German Canadian,' do; 'American,' Woodstock; 'Messenger,' Simcoe; 'Reformer,' do; 'News,' Perth; 'Signal,' Huron; 'Times.' Free Press,' 'Prototype,' London; 'Despatch,' St. Thomas; 'Chronicle,' Ingersoll; 'Herald,' 'Pilot,' Montreal; 'Chronicle,' Quebec; 'Sachem,' Vienna; 'Planet,' Chatham; 'Advertiser,' do.

de24

Buffalo, Brantford and Goderich Railway.

NEW ARRANGEMENT.

Buffalo, Brantford & Gooderich Railway, connecting with the Rochester, Lockport & Buffalo Railway at Black Rock.

On and after Tuesday, the 3d January, 1854, one train will run daily, (Sundays excepted,) leaving the new Depot, at the foot of Erie street, at 8 o'clock A. M., and Caledonia at 10 P. M.

Freight for this line will be received at the Freight Depot of the Buffalo & Niagara Falls Railway, on Sixth street, by JOHN BANNERMAN, Freight Agent.

Buffalo, 2d January, 1854. ja2tf

V, 11

6
The Civil War

Before the American Civil War, railroads had not played a decisive role in military actions. In the Crimean War (1854-1856) and the Italian War of Liberation (1859), they were used to bring up supplies and evacuate the wounded rather than for mass troop movements. But, whereas Europe had well-developed road systems, the United States for the most part had decaying turnpikes and trails. By 1860, however, it had, at least in the Northeast and Midwest, an extensive and integrated railroad network.

Lincoln Travels from Springfield to Washington

Abraham Lincoln's journey from Springfield, Illinois, to Washington in February, 1861, to assume the presidency recapitulated the previous thirty years of American railroad development. (Figure #1.) His election had triggered the secession of the Deep South and the creation of the Confederate States of America. On the 11th he left Springfield with his party by special train. Eight states, fourteen days, twenty railroads, and 1,979 miles later, he arrived in Washington. Along the route he conferred with local leaders, addressed the state legislatures, and attempted to reassure the people, over a million of whom saw and heard him.

On Saturday the 16th Lincoln arrived at Buffalo on the Buffalo & Erie at Exchange Street, where he was welcomed by ex-President Millard Fillmore, who rode with him behind a military escort through crowded streets to the American Hotel on Main Street. Lincoln made a brief speech from the balcony of the hotel, followed by a reception for him and Mrs. Lincoln. On Sunday, the Lincolns accompanied Fillmore to services at the Unitarian Church at Eagle and Franklin, and had dinner with him, after which the president-elect spent the day resting his throat. On Monday the party, accompanied by Governor Edwin D. Morgan, left for Albany on the New York Central.

Railroad Military Strategy [1]

After the firing on Fort Sumter on April 12, 1861, Lincoln declared that a State of Insurrection existed and called for 75,000 three-month volunteers. This prompted the secession of Virginia, North Carolina, Tennessee, and Arkansas. Washington was

VI, 1

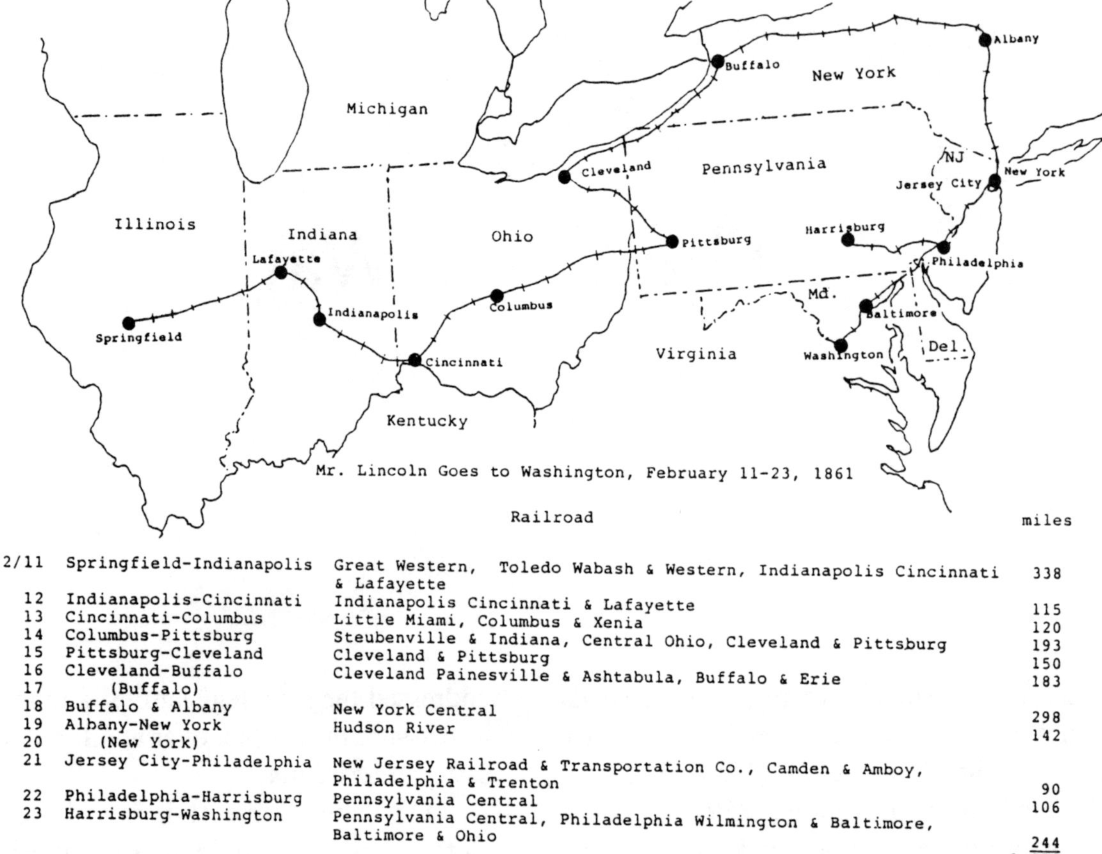

Mr. Lincoln Goes to Washington, February 11-23, 1861

		Railroad	miles
2/11	Springfield-Indianapolis	Great Western, Toledo Wabash & Western, Indianapolis Cincinnati & Lafayette	338
12	Indianapolis-Cincinnati	Indianapolis Cincinnati & Lafayette	115
13	Cincinnati-Columbus	Little Miami, Columbus & Xenia	120
14	Columbus-Pittsburg	Steubenville & Indiana, Central Ohio, Cleveland & Pittsburg	193
15	Pittsburg-Cleveland	Cleveland & Pittsburg	150
16	Cleveland-Buffalo	Cleveland Painesville & Ashtabula, Buffalo & Erie	183
17	(Buffalo)		
18	Buffalo & Albany	New York Central	298
19	Albany-New York	Hudson River	142
20	(New York)		
21	Jersey City-Philadelphia	New Jersey Railroad & Transportation Co., Camden & Amboy, Philadelphia & Trenton	90
22	Philadelphia-Harrisburg	Pennsylvania Central	106
23	Harrisburg-Washington	Pennsylvania Central, Philadelphia Wilmington & Baltimore, Baltimore & Ohio	244
			1,979

VI, 2

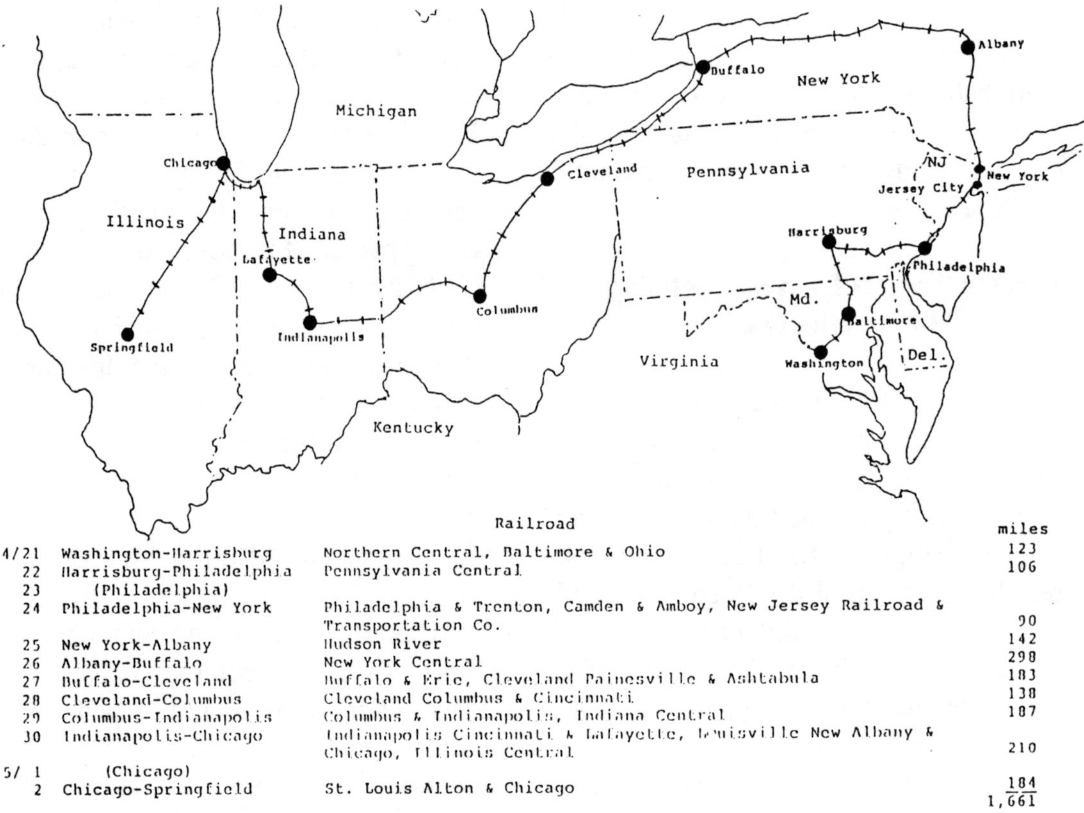

		Railroad	miles
4/21	Washington-Harrisburg	Northern Central, Baltimore & Ohio	123
22	Harrisburg-Philadelphia	Pennsylvania Central	106
23	(Philadelphia)		
24	Philadelphia-New York	Philadelphia & Trenton, Camden & Amboy, New Jersey Railroad & Transportation Co.	90
25	New York-Albany	Hudson River	142
26	Albany-Buffalo	New York Central	298
27	Buffalo-Cleveland	Buffalo & Erie, Cleveland Painesville & Ashtabula	183
28	Cleveland-Columbus	Cleveland Columbus & Cincinnati	138
29	Columbus-Indianapolis	Columbus & Indianapolis, Indiana Central	187
30	Indianapolis-Chicago	Indianapolis Cincinnati & Lafayette, Louisville New Albany & Chicago, Illinois Central	210
5/ 1	(Chicago)		
2	Chicago-Springfield	St. Louis Alton & Chicago	184
			1,661

Route of Lincoln's Funeral Train, April 21-May 2, 1865

now in a vulnerable position, across the Potomac from Virginia and surrounded by Confederate sympathizers in Maryland. Yet within a few weeks the city was secured by thousands of troops brought in by the Philadelphia Wilmington & Baltimore, the Northern Central, and the Baltimore & Ohio. The B&O would suffer from frequent Confederate sorties in the years to come.

The first battle won by railroads was First Bull Run, July 21, 1861. Screaming "On to Richmond!" the Federals advanced from Washington against the outnumbered Confederates drawn up across Bull Run under command of General Pierre G. T. Beau-regard. But just in time, General Joseph Johnson brought his troops in from the Shenandoah Valley on the Manassas Gap Rail-road, shored up Beauregard's right, and drove the Yankees back to Washington. Eleven months later, Generals Robert E. Lee and Stonewall Jackson turned back General George B. McClellan's Peninsular Campaign against Richmond by a similar strategy. With the Shenandoah Valley cleared of Yankees, Jackson transferred his 10,000 man command on ten trains from eastern Virginia on the Virginia Central, joined Lee, and repulsed McClellan. (Figure #3.)

In the West the Confederates had been less successful. February saw the surrender to General Ulysses S. Grant of Forts Henry and Donelson in Tennessee and the abandonment of Nashville. Falling back to northern Mississippi, General Albert Sidney Johnson used the railroads converging on Corinth to assemble 40,000 men from Humboldt, Jackson, New Orleans, Mobile, and Pensacola to stop Grant. But Johnson did not move fast enough. His army was defeated and he was slain at the Battle of Shiloh, April 6-7, 1862. (Figure #4.)

Failing to follow up on this victory, the Union army under General Don Carlos Buell moved eastward toward Chattanooga, Tennessee, a railroad center. Buell's supply line was the railroads from Louisville on the Ohio to Nashville and on to Stevenson and Bridgeport, Alabama, thirty miles from Chattanooga. Confederate cavalry cut the line in July and slowed down Buell, which gave Confederate General Braxton Bragg, commander of the Army of the Tennessee, opportunity to relieve Chattanooga by sending his command by train on a circuitous route via Tupelo, Mobile, Montgomery, and Atlanta, to Chattanooga in August, 1862. George E. Turner opines in Victory Rode the Rails that "by a comfortable margin he had won their race with Buell for Chattanooga and the consequences can be measured in the loss of an untold number of lives and the indefinite prolongation of the war." (Figure #4.)

A year later, in August, 1863, a month after the twin disasters of Gettysburg and Vicksburg, the Confederates went on the offensive at Chattanooga, where the armies of Bragg and Union General William S. Rosecrans, Commander of the Army of the Cumberland, who was laying siege to the city, were about equal. Confederate General James Longstreet's veterans were to be shipped via rail from Virginia through Lynchburg, Bristol, and Knoxville, about 500 miles, to Chattanooga, a four days journey. Then "Fighting Joe" Hooker charged in from Kentucky and cut this route, forcing the Confederates to go the long way round via Petersburg, Wilmington, and Augusta to Atlanta, almost 1,000 miles on ten different railroads. Turner calls it "the outstanding operational feat of Confederate railroads during the war;" but by the time Longstreet neared Chattanooga, Bragg had abandoned the city and retreated to Dalton, Georgia, on the Western & Atlantic. (Figure #4.)

Reinforced, Bragg took the offensive, and won the Battle of Chickamauga, as a result of which Rosecrans was trapped in Chattanooga, the relief of which was to be the most dramatic railroad operation of the war. (Figure #3.) Two army corps, totaling nearly 60,000 men with their battle gear, were carried from

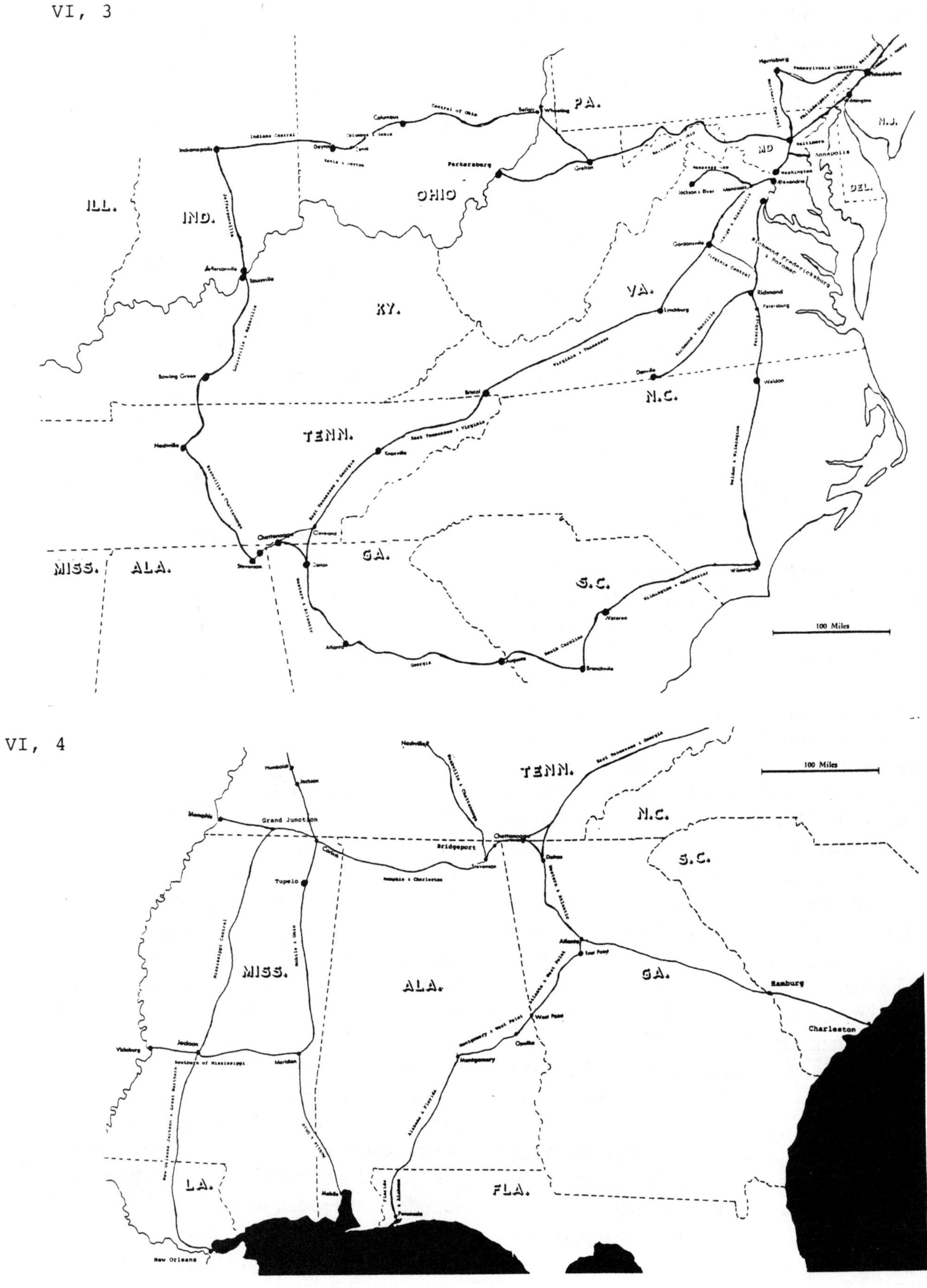
VI, 3
PA.
OHIO
ILL.
IND.
KY.
VA.
MD
N.J.
DEL.
N.C.
TENN.
MISS.
ALA.
GA.
S.C.
100 Miles
VI, 4
TENN.
N.C.
S.C.
MISS.
ALA.
GA.
LA.
FLA.
100 Miles
Grand Junction
Bridgeport
Tupelo
Hamburg
Charleston
New Orleans

Northern Virginia 12,000 miles in eleven and a half days via twelve railroads. (Figure #3.) Grant was given charge of the western armies and replaced Rosecrans with General George H. Thomas who with the reinforcements broke out of Chattanooga on November 23-25, 1863. During the winter General William T. Sherman determined to destroy the Army of the Tennessee and push on through the heart of the South via Atlanta to the sea. His army of over 100,000 men and 35,000 horses was supplied with provisions from his base at Knoxville, 477 miles from Atlanta, a feat that would have been impossible with horses and wagons. Atlanta fell on September 2, 1864, and the way was open for Sherman's brutal march through Georgia. In Virginia, the fall of Petersburg on April 2, 1865, deprived Lee of his supply line to North Carolina. His surrender at Appomattox on April 9 was forced by Grant's severing the railroad Lee had hoped to use in his retreat to Danville, which broke the Confederate line of supply. Starvation mandated surrender. Appomattox Station was on the Richmond & Danville Railroad, only nineteen miles from Richmond.

Buffalo's Railroads and the War

While soldiers raged and politicians devised vain things, Buffalo grew rich rapidly. It was a prosperity stimulated almost entirely by the sudden increase of commerce on the Great Lakes. The city had never carried on much business with the South, so the closing of the Mississippi did not adversely effect Buffalo's economy. The boom in lake-borne traffic was phenomenal. Buffalo historian John T. Horton notes that despite labor unrest on the docks, caused by the refusal of employers to raise wages and their use of black labor to break the strike which followed, during the forty-eight hours of May 10th and 11th, 1863:

...there arrived in port one steamer, thirteen brigs, fourteen propellers, thirty barks and a hundred thirty-six schooners bearing a total cargo valued at $3,500,000. The cargo consisted of 1,454,315 feet of lumber; 543,500 pounds of bacon, 1,800,000 pounds of lard; and 2,478,997 bushels of grain, mostly wheat and maize. The total receipts that year in wheat alone amounted to more than 21,000,000 bushels; but brisk as the business was, it registered a decline from the previous year when the receipts of wheat had reached an all time high of over 30,000,000 bushels, and had prompted the Express to break forth in lyrical language, "Every wind from the West has wafted to our wharves argosies of golden grain." [2]

The Civil War turned the fortunes of the Erie Railway around. Since it now reached every town of importance in the southern and western parts of the Empire State, when the regiments came marching out of Rochester and Buffalo, and the companies out of towns and villages, it was the Erie that carried many of them toward their destination. There was a large army camp, and later a notorious prisoner of war camp at Elmira, and another large camp at Hancock on the upper Delaware.

Wartime freight also rose to record heights, and for the first time coal began to play an important role in generating revenue for the Erie. At 2:00 P. M. July 15, 1864, an Erie train carrying 800 Confederate prisoners from Jersey City to Elmira crashed head-on into a westbound coal train at Shohola. Trackside graves received the bodies of the victims of the wreck, fifty-one Confederates and nineteen Union guards. The fireman of the eastbound and the engineer of the westbound were also killed. The injured numbered 123, some of whom died later. A drunken dispatcher had cleared the freight coming in on the Hawley branch for the mainline. Of the 12,123 prisoners confined at Elmira 1864-1865, 2,963 died because of foul sanitation, poor diet, and the cold.

Out of an 1860 population of 81,129, Erie County contributed 15,249 men to the Union

Army during the Civil War. In addition, there were about 7,000 local men in state militia regiments for state service, and in Federal service in miscellaneous branches. Casualties in killed, wounded, dead of disease, and captured were 4,740. The first company (a company was roughly between 70 to 100 men) of Erie County volunteers was organized at Buffalo on May 1, 1861. By May 3 three more companies had been formed. All four set out from Buffalo for Elmira, which had been designated as the rendezvous point for the volunteers of Western New York. Elmira was the junction point of the Erie and the Williamsport & Elmira, which ran due south through north central Pennsylvania. At Williamsport the W&E joined the Philadelphia and Erie, which in turn joined the Northern Central at Sunbury, whence a direct route led through Harrisburg to Baltimore and Washington. (Figure VII, #1.) Lincoln's Secretary of War, Simon Cameron, held a large interest in the Northern Central, to which he gave military traffic. This arrangement greatly enhanced the road's and the Secretary's own profits. Concerning the first departure of Buffalo troops for the front, Horton writes:

An immense number of people witnessed their departure. They were escorted to the Erie railroad depot by the 'Union Continentals,' a body of elderly citizens, who had donned the old "Continental" Uniform and organized themselves into a company, with ex-President Fillmore as Captain, to encourage warlike spirit among the more youthful part of the community. At Niagara Square a short halt was made, and a handsome flag was presented to the volunteers by the young ladies of the Central school. On arriving at Elmira the four companies went into camp and awaited the arrival of the other six. These were rapidly formed, several companies of the 74th [Regiment Buffalo] *Militia being used as nuclei of the new organizations. On the 11th of May the remaining six companies proceeded to Elmira where the whole ten (758 men] were organized into a regiment which took the name of the 21st New York Volunteer Infantry,* [Colonel William F. Rogers commanding.] [3]

Known popularly as the 1st Buffalo Regiment, the 21st fought at Second Bull Run, South Mountain, and Antietam. Two officers and fifty-one men were killed at Bull Run, and eighteen enlisted men at Antietam. Kept in reserve at Fredericksburg, it was detailed to provost duty around Washington before being ordered home at the end of April, 1863, since the two years the men had signed on for were over. They returned by train to Buffalo to a grand reception on May 18, 1863, by which time the regiment was down to 495 officers and men. The unit was disbanded but many reenlisted in other regiments.

Shortly after the attack on Fort Sumter, a company was raised in Buffalo named the Richmond Guards, after Dean Richmond. It proceeded to Elmira under Colonel Theodore B. Hamilton, and in May, 1861, became Company G of the 33rd Regiment New York, which saw action at Marye's Heights south of Fredericksburg in May, 1863. The 33rd was brigaded with the 49th New York Volunteer Infantry, the 2nd Buffalo Regiment, Colonel Daniel D. Bidwell commanding, which had been mustered into federal service in September, 1861. Four companies of the 33rd were raised in Buffalo, four in Chautauqua County, one in Niagara County, and one from Westchester. Before organization was complete, the 49th was ordered to New York on September 16, and later that month left for the front. It participated in McClellan's Peninsular Campaign in May and June, 1862, and at Antietam and Fredericksburg. In the spring of 1864 the 49th fought in Grant's Wilderness Campaign, where it suffered casualties of sixty-eight dead and twenty-two wounded. Transferred to the Shenandoah, it saw active duty under General Philip Sheridan, especially at Cedar Creek, where Bidwell, its former colonel, by then a brigadier general, was killed. Of the 1,350 men the regiment had received into its ranks in the course of the war, 316 died of all causes. The three year men were returned to Buffalo where they were discharged on October 18, 1864.

The 3rd Buffalo Regiment was the 100th New York Volunteer Infantry, commanded by Colonel James M. Brown of Chautauqua County. Authorities did not wish to subject the troops to a raucous send off so it was announced that the regiment was to entrain on the NYC for New York in the regularly scheduled 6:45 P. M. train. Instead, as reported in the *Courier* for March 8, 1862, the regiment "made a sudden, unexpected, and unobstructed flight from the city on a special N. Y. Central train yesterday morning about 10 o'clock." The whole regiment was not involved in this stratagem, since at least one company, with its colonel, had left a few weeks before. The 100th went to the front in March, 1862, and fought in the Peninsular Campaign. By the end of July it could muster only fifteen officers and 436 men. To prevent it from being merged with another unit, the Buffalo Board of Trade undertook refitting it and promoted recruiting in Buffalo and the rest of Erie County. During 1863 the 100th again sustained heavy casualties campaigning along the South Carolina coast and in the attack on Fort Wagner at Charleston Harbor. Toward the end of the war the regiment saw service against Petersburg and Richmond. Colonel Brown was killed during the Peninsular Campaign, and 373 other officers and enlisted men died as a result of wounds, disease, or in enemy prisons. The unit was mustered out at Albany on August 28, 1865.

The failure of the Peninsular Campaign brought a call from Lincoln in July, 1862, for 300,000 volunteers, and Governor Morgan directed that a regiment be recruited in each of the thirty-two senatorial districts of the state. Major Edward P. Chapin was named colonel of the 116th New York Volunteers, the new regiment which rapidly filled up in Erie County and was at full strength when ordered to Baltimore on September 5, 1862. Thousands of roaring flag wavers turned out to witness the line of march from Fort Porter to the Erie Depot where a special train waited for its coming. "Twenty-one cars were soon filled with their contents; but the scene at the depot we shall not attempt to describe," wrote a reporter in the September 6th *Daily Courier.* "An immense concourse of people succeeded in gaining admission inside the fence, and were soon crowded on the platform, mounted on an opposite train of cars, or wedged in compactly between the out-going and the stationary lines of cars." The regiment first saw action in the advance on Port Hudson on the Mississippi in May, 1863, when Chapin was killed at the head of his brigade. From March to June, 1864 the 116th took part in the Red River Campaign, and in July was ordered north to join Sheridan's forces in the Shenandoah Valley. On June 13, 1865, the regiment returned to Buffalo to a warm reception. Dead from all causes were 220 officers and men.

Erie County, moreover, contributed twenty eight companies to nine cavalry regiments. In addition, an artillery company of Buffalo Germans, organized on the eve of the war by Captain Michael Wiedrich, Battery 1 of the 1st New York Artillery, left Buffalo on September 5, 1861, for Albany on the NYC. It participated in Cross Keys, Second Bull Run, Chancellorsville, Gettysburg, Lookout Mountain, Missionary Ridge, and Sherman's March to the sea, returning to Buffalo to a gala reception on June 23, 1865. In August 1862, Colonel John E. McMahon was authorized to recruit a regiment with headquarters at Buffalo for the Irish Legion, also known as Corcoran's Brigade. McMahon's unit, which left Buffalo October 2, 1862, was consolidated with other units to form the 164th regiment. Companies B, C, and D of this regiment were composed of men from Buffalo, Lockport, Newfane, and Ridgeway. The regiment served in Virginia and was mustered out near Washington on July 15, 1865. Colonel McMahon died in Buffalo of an illness contracted while in service. Another Buffalo Irish unit was Company K of the famous 69th New York Infantry.

A minor early troop transportation contretemps is described in the Western New York Railway Historical Society's *Railway Flyer* for the summer of 1991. (Figure III, #1.) A Colonel Paine of the 4th Wisconsin Regiment had entered an agreement with several railroads for passage from Chicago to Harrisburg, with the option of going either by way of Dunkirk or Buffalo. He chose the Dunkirk route since it was more direct. The Erie went to the expense of setting out nine cars at Dunkirk to take the troops to Elmira. When Paine reached Dunkirk, he discovered that he needed six more cars which were available at Buffalo. So he took his men instead over the Buffalo & State Line to Buffalo, where he arrived on July 17, 1861. From there he proceeded to Corning over the Buffalo Corning & New York. This infuriated the Erie's superintendent, Charles Minot, who refused the Wisconsin regiment passage from Corning to Elmira over the Erie. After fruitless negotiations, Paine declared martial law and commandeered the eastbound *Night Express.* A locomotive and cars were added, a crew was found among the men in the regiment, and the train pulled out for Elmira. Later it was determined that the Buffalo Corning & New York had to reimburse the Erie full passenger fare for several hundred men between Corning and Elmira.

War was not all bands and flag waving. Casualties, dead and wounded and diseased, began to pile up. The return of the bodies of dead soldiers was a frequent event in Buffalo. During the Peninsula Campaign, the May 14, 1862 *Buffalo Morning Express* contained this sad news:

The bodies of Adjutant William Bullymore and Capt. Henry W. Trowbridge arrived from Yorktown together on the 8:00 P. M. train, New York Central Railroad, last evening. The Buffalo Tigers, the Citizen's Light Guard, and Co. D of the 74th with officers of other military organizations were in waiting at the Depot to receive the remains. A great throng of people was also in attendance.

It was also during the Peninsula Campaign that the *Express* noted that the Boston & Albany had recently converted two passenger cars into hospital cars. About half the seats in each car were removed and replaced with berths, six on a side, furnished with mattresses, pillows, blankets, and covers. The cars, which also carried ice water, could accommodate thirty soldiers each. Earlier, forty-eight Confederates captured at Fort Donelson in February arrived in Buffalo. There they entrained on the Central for Fort Warren in Boston Harbor, which had been converted into a prison of war camp. Paroled Union ex-prisoners also passed through the city on their way to report to the Adjutant General in Albany. The *Express* predicted that the vast increase in freight and passenger traffic as a result of the war would break all records and that 1862 would be a very prosperous year for Buffalo's railroads.

There were at the beginning of the war two Buffalo New York National Guard infantry regiments, the 65th, which had been organized in 1848, and the 74th, which had been organized in 1854. The 65th was not called out in 1861, but the 74th was. However, the order was countermanded, and many of the regiment's disappointed officers and men joined the 21st. But when Lee's Army of Northern Virginia invaded Maryland and Pennsylvania in June, 1863, these two regiments were needed to help repel the invaders. On June 16, the call went out to men of both units to assemble at the state arsenal on Batavia Street (later Broadway), between Milnor and Potter, at 6:00 A. M. on Friday the 19th. There about 900 fell in line at 9:20 A. M. for the march down Main Street to Exchange Street and the Erie Depot. Tearful and almost impenetrable crowds lined the way from Michigan to Chicago Streets.

The previous afternoon a cavalry company had taken the afternoon train from the same station. At Elmira the troops were transferred to the Northern Central and the war zone. After the 3rd of July at Gettysburg, where the ability of Lee's army to mount a serious offensive had been destroyed, both regiments were sent to New York City to repress draft riots that had broken out on July 13 and continued for four days. By the end of the month, the two regiments had returned to Buffalo, and the men were mustered out of service. Accompanying this brief expedition was Private Nelson H. Baker of Company A, later Father Baker of Lackawanna, who had signed up on June 18, 1863.

Lincoln's Funeral Train Passes Through Buffalo

Abraham Lincoln was shot on April 14, 1865, and died the next morning. From Philadelphia to Cleveland his funeral train followed the same route as the president-elect had followed from Springfield to Washington four years before. (Figures #1 and #2.) The funeral train left Washington on April 21st and arrived at Springfield on May 2 after a 1,700 mile journey which took thirteen days. Aboard the train were military and political dignitaries. Local delegations rode the train for several miles into their city. Hundreds of thousands waited at trackside to watch the train pass by. New York City especially outdid itself in a vast outpouring of grief on April 24 and 25. Thereafter, as Carl Sandburg wrote:

Up the Hudson River east bank on the night of April 25 chugged the locomotive named Union, *with its train of seven cars. On every mile of the route to Albany those on the train could see bonfires and torches, could hear bells and cannon and guns, could see forms of people and white sorry faces. . . . At Garrison's Landing, opposite West Point, were assembled the academy staff and professors - and a thousand precise and caped cadets. At each station farther en route to Albany were crowds, at Strasburg an ingenious circle of light, at Rhinebeck and Barrytown torch formations, at Tivoli lighted lamps, at Catskill huge bonfires with flags at half-mast, at Hudson minute guns and two hotels with all windows illuminated and black-draped.* [4]

As reported in the *Buffalo Morning Express* for April 28, 1865, a dozen prominent Buffalonians, headed by ex-President Fillmore, left Buffalo by special car at 6 P. M. Wednesday and spent the night at Batavia in order to board the funeral train there. The Batavia depot had been draped in mourning and many of the prominent buildings and homes in the village were similarly shrouded. Upon the arrival of the train at the packed station, a choir of young men and women sang two dirges during a ten minute stop, after which the train departed for Buffalo. No further stops were made along the way but "almost continuously along the route the train passed between long lines of people who had come to catch but a fleeting glimpse of their beloved president."

Scheduled time of arrival at Exchange Street was 7:00 A. M. on April 26th, "but long ere that hour the streets near the depot were filled with the eager and expectant multitude. At ten minutes before 7:00 o'clock the pilot engine [which tested the safety of track and roadbed] arrived to announce the approach of the funeral train." The train was right on time and "came in slowly and silently. The crowds received it with uncovered heads and every mark of respect." The station had been "elaborately decorated as also the Wadsworth House, Bloomer's Dining Saloon, and other buildings in the vicinity." The Express's account of the decorations on the train was most detailed:

The train which bore the remains and the funeral party was a grand affair and attracted much attention. The engine, the Dean Richmond, *Leonard Ham, engineer, was very tastefully and richly draped. It had a full-*

length portrait of the president underneath the headlights in front, which was surrounded by the graceful folds of two national flags thrown over the upper part of the engine, each trimmed in black and white crepe. Two exquisite bouquets took the place of the engine flags and another surmounted the sandbox. The hand rails were neatly adorned with festoons of black and white tasteful rosettes. The cab was draped with the national colors. The cars which made up the train were also draped with exquisite taste.

But the chief attraction of all was the funeral car which has borne the remains thus far from Washington and is designed to bear them to the hero's western home. It was built by Mr. B. P. Jamison [actually Lamason] *of Alexandria for the United States Military Railroad and was intended for the use of the president and other dignitaries while traveling over the military road. It contains a parlor, sitting room, and sleeping apartment, all of which are fitted up in the most approved modern style. Around the top of the stateroom small panels are fixed upon which are painted the coats of arms of each state. The car has sixteen wheels, eight on each side. Black curtains have been fixed at all the windows. Inside and out the car is robed in black, the mourning out side being festooned in two rows above and below the windows, while between each window is a slip of mourning connecting the upper with the lower row. A deep silver fringe also hangs from the edge of the roof and festoons of crepe are looped over each window with a silver star and a large silver tassel.*

At 8:00 A. M. the coffin was carried from the car to a hearse parked in front of the depot and taken to Saint James Hall at Main and Eagle Streets. All places of business along the route were closed and "every window and housetop was filled with a mass of human beings." At the hall the coffin was placed on a dais after which members of the Saint Cecil Society sang the solemn dirge, "Rest Spirit Rest." Then the lid was removed revealing the body of the deceased. During the rest of the day and part of the next from eighty to a hundred thousand people passed through the hall to view the remains.

The Express noted that the "place was oppressively silent save for the constant tramp of the passing multitude." Across the river at Fort Erie a minute gun brought in on the Grand Trunk Railway thundered during the day at half hour intervals. The next day, the cortege left for the west on the Buffalo & Erie.

7
Gilded Age Railroading

Though marked by intervals of business downturns - 1873-1878, 1882-1885, and 1893-1897 - the period from Appomattox to the assassination of President William McKinley in 1901 was one of extraordinary growth in the United States, especially in the North and West. The closing of the Mississippi at the beginning of the war had meant that more western farm produce had to reach market by rail, a shift which had benefited Buffalo immensely. The insatiable demands of armies for supplies and of farms for machinery had led to expanded production capacity. The high war tariff, the new national banking system enacted by former Whigs now in the guise of Republicans, and the massive issues of fiat money and government bonds had helped create liquid capital that gravitated to the large money marts in New York and Philadelphia. The war had produced dozens of millionaires. Others were eager to add to their fortunes by exploiting the great resources and markets of the nation. The movement from country to city accelerated. By 1880 there were fewer farm than non-farm workers, and by 1900 the pre-Civil War imbalance had been reversed. Ten years later industry had replaced agriculture as the chief source of national wealth.

Markets for goods which had been chiefly local before the war were becoming national, a development promoted by railroads as they reached across the continent. In the six years from 1867 until the Panic of 1873, 33,000 miles of track were laid, more than the total trackage in 1860! By 1880 railroads totaled 93,000 miles. (Figure V, #1.) Much of this new construction was concentrated in the South and in the trans-Mississippi West since the basic network of Northeastern and Midwestern roads was in place by 1860. Probably more than half of the funds for this unprecedented expansion came from abroad, and more than $1 billion from public funds. By 1900 $10 billion had been invested in railroads, and railroad securities represented the bulk of the New York Stock Exchange listings.

Interest in industrial stocks developed as expanding industries, fueled by railroad demands, required more capital to be raised through stock issues. Between 1860 and 1900 there was a tenfold increase to $10 billion of funds invested in manufacturing. The value of American manufactures, which was less than that of Germany, France, or Great Britain in 1860, equaled the total for all three by the early 1890s.

Buffalo New York & Philadelphia

Though water transportation was long to remain vital to Buffalo as a transportation center, the city's lake and canal shipping went into a relative decline after the Civil War. Many attributed this to the Welland Canal, the third edition of which enabled larger lake boats to bypass Buffalo, but the radical cause was the post-bellum growth of the railroads. The optimistically named Buffalo & Washington, incorporated on February 4, 1865, projected from Buffalo to Olean, and backed by leading citizens of that Allegheny Valley town on the Erie Railroad, reached East Aurora, seventeen miles from Buffalo on December 22, 1867, where construction was halted for three years. Bronson Case Rumsey, a member of Buffalo's elite, was the first president. The Rumseys had made their money in tanning and then began acquiring real estate, especially in North Buffalo, where the rapid growth of the city generated healthy profits. Vice president was Henry A. Richmond, Dean Richmond's son, a prosperous grain merchant and lithographer who later became president of the road. In 1870 B&W trains left Buffalo for East Aurora at 5:00 P. M. and at 10:00 A. M. Buffalo-bound trains left East Aurora at 6:10 P. M. and 11:00 A. M. Intermediate stops were made at Junction [with the Erie and the Buffalo Creek], Indian Church Road, Ebenezer, Springbrook, Woodward [Elma], Jamison Road, and Aurora. The timetable for May of that year announced that "Stages are run from Aurora to South Wales, Holland, Protection, Sardinia, Yorkshire, Arcade, Wales, Strykersville, Java Village, and Currier Corners." Renamed the Buffalo New York & Philadelphia, it was extended five miles further to South Wales, another temporary terminal, until the latter part of 1870. It was then pushed with more vigor so that it reached Olean on July, 18, 1872, and Emporium on the Philadelphia & Erie on January 1, 1873. (Figure #1.) In Buffalo the BNY&P's depot occupied the block bounded by Carroll, Exchange, Michigan, and Chicago Streets. (Figure #2.)

The following account of the backers of the Buffalo & Washington is from Horton's History of Northwestern New York:

That road stretching southward through East Aurora toward Olean and Emporium was little likely to compete with the Erie Canal; but a more positive advantage made it a favorite project in Buffalo where the Common Council itself had subscribed half a million dollars toward its completion. The Council had done this contingently on the raising of a like sum by private capitalists; and in 1870 the capitalists were fulfilling the condition. By the end of June only $69,000 remained to be subscribed as the merchants James Adam and Philip Becker, the old lawyer Stephen Austin, the meat-packer Jacob Dold, the manufacturers Josiah Letchworth and George W. Tifft, together with Elbridge Gerry Spaulding, added at that time to the sum already raised by other leading citizens. Early in the month a dozen men, as widely representative of the city' s business, had subscribed $25,000 each. Among them had been Myron P. Bush and Bronson Case Rumsey of the leather interest, James Braley, the manufacturer of farm implements; Sherman S. Jewett and Pascal Paoli Pratt of the iron interest; ex-Mayor William G. Fargo of express fame; Walter Cary, Henry A. Richmond, Jonathan Scoville, and finally, the great connoisseur of horses, Cicero J. Hamlin, whose wealth originally acquired in mercantile pursuits and real estate was about to be greatly augmented through the manufacture of glucose. Of the Buffalo-Washington Road Hamlin like Jewett was one of the foremost patrons and promoters. The fact put him in the front rank of local capitalists who were discerning enough to understand that if the city was to have a future as an industrial center it must establish direct access to the coal mines. Thence and thence only was to be had the cheap fuel [soft coal] *indispensable to large scale manufacturing. Cheap fuel, as the local*

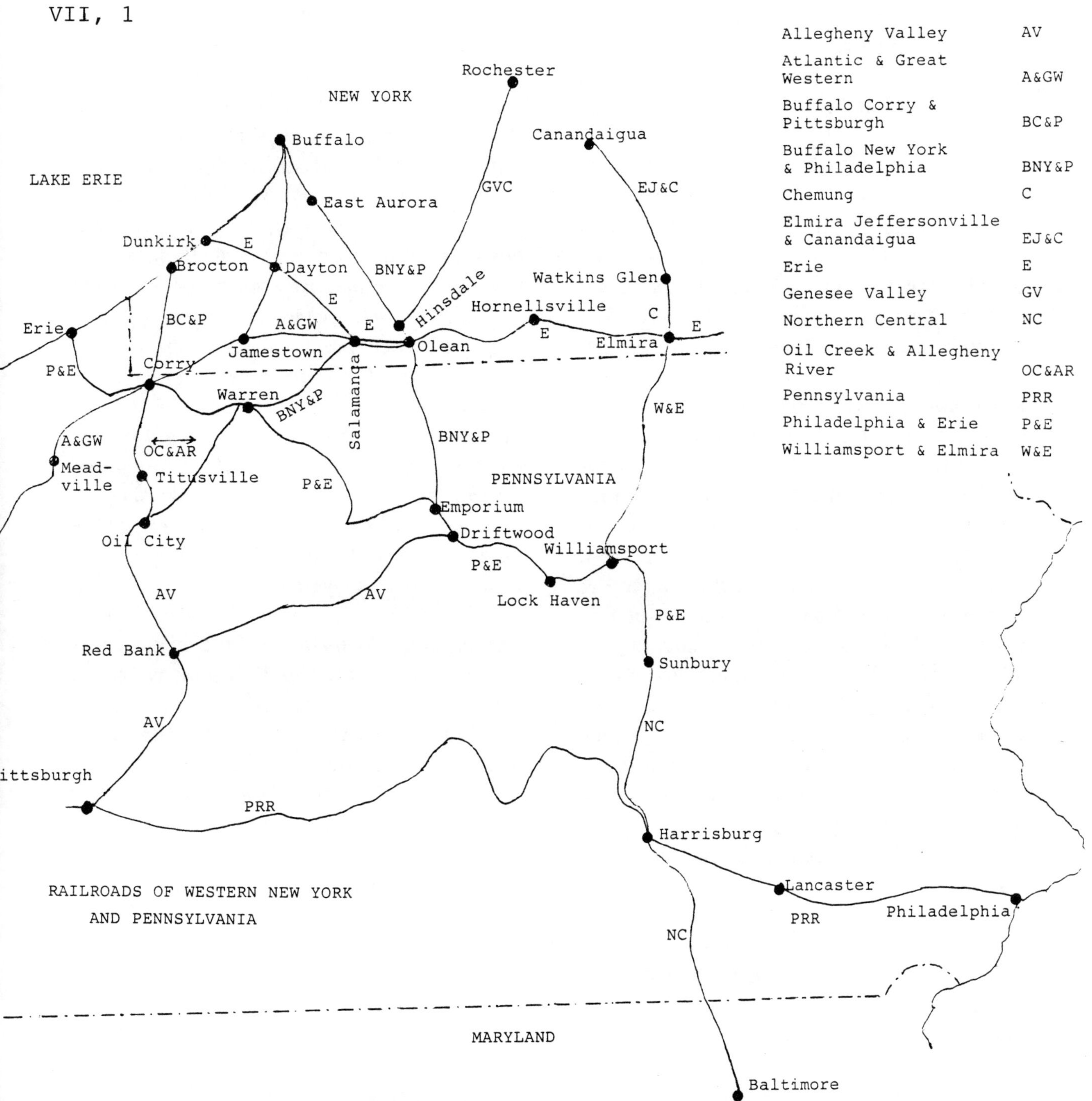

RAILROADS OF WESTERN NEW YORK AND PENNSYLVANIA

press asserted again and again, was the motive of Buffalo's interest in a railroad into Pennsylvania. That interest so motivated had been keen even before the Civil War. With the completion of the Buffalo-Washington Railway to Emporium by January, 1873, a long-felt need began to be satisfied. [1]

Northern Central

The Philadelphia & Erie had been incorporated as far back as 1837 as the Sunbury & Erie to link Erie, Pennsylvania's sole port on the Great Lakes, with Sunbury on the Susquehanna Division of Pennsylvania's canal system. Near Sunbury this division branched east to connect with the New York State canal system and west to reach Williamsport. At Harrisburg it joined the Philadelphia-Pittsburgh Mainline Canal, Pennsylvania's answer to the Erie Canal. The Mainline (with a gravity railroad across the Alleghenies and a railroad from Columbia on the Susquehanna to Philadelphia) had been completed in 1834. (Figure #3.) Construction of the Sunbury & Erie was delayed until 1854, at the end of which the first link was open from Milton to Williamsport. It reached Sunbury and a connection with the Northern Central in 1856, Emporium in 1863, and Erie in 1864, by which time its name had been changed to Philadelphia & Erie, and the road had been leased to the Pennsylvania.

The Northern Central began life as the Baltimore & Susquehanna in 1829, a year later than the better known Baltimore & Ohio. (Figure #1.) As its name indicated, the B&S was intended to tap Pennsylvania's fertile Susquehanna Valley. Opposition from Philadelphia slowed progress, and the line to York, Pennsylvania, was not completed until 1838. Bridgeport, across the Susquehanna from Harrisburg, was reached in 1854, when the road's name was changed to Northern Central. A connection with the Sunbury & Erie was achieved in 1858. As Robert L. Gunnarsson writes:

Reaching Sunbury also gave the Northern Central access to the Great Lakes - after a fashion. From Sunbury to Williamsport, Pennsylvania, business moved over the Sunbury & Erie. At Williamsport, a transfer was made to the Williamsport & Elmira Railroad, which ran north to Elmira where it connected with the broad-gauge Erie Railroad; the Erie completed the route to Buffalo. By 1859 the Erie signed a formal agreement allowing the Northern Central to forward business over its line on a pro-rata basis. In 1858 the opening of the Buffalo route was considered a substantial accomplishment in Baltimore. The event was given ample coverage in the newspapers; the Northern Central advertised itself as forming 'the shortest route between Baltimore and the Great Lakes,' and exalted the 'increased benefits.' But in reality, the route was slow, disjointed, and required several transfers. A passenger trip between Baltimore and Buffalo took the better part of three days. The Williamsport & Elmira [which would be leased by the Northern Central in 1863] *had been built on a shoestring budget, and, although completed in 1854, already was dilapidated. Rail and ballast were poor, and weather and floods had taken their toll of the roadbed. In fact, several documents of the time referred to the railroad as one laid on 'quick sand.' It would be some years before it would become a true main line route.* [2]

Its strategic position as a link between upstate New York, the Susquehanna Valley, and Baltimore produced a dramatic rise in the Northern Central's income during the Civil War. By 1865 total revenue had swelled a spectacular 186 percent above the 1861 level. Gunnarsson writes that "war-time traffic had rescued the railroad from another financial collapse and had helped start it on the way to becoming a first-class facility."

By 1867 the Northern Central was in contact with Buffalo via the Chemung Railroad

VII, 2

VII, 3

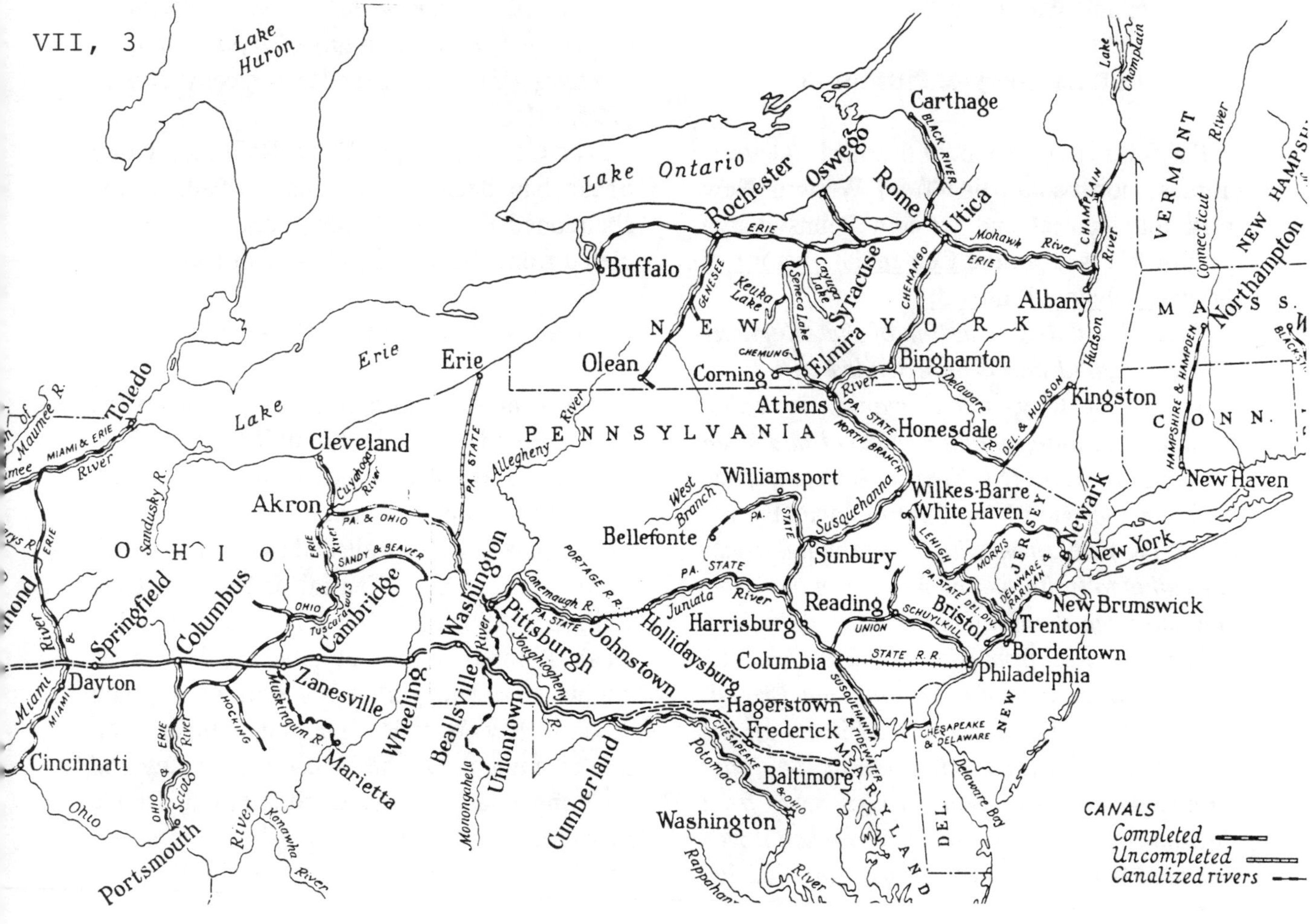

Lake Huron
Lake Ontario
Lake Erie
Carthage
Oswego
Rochester
Rome
Utica
Buffalo
Syracuse
Albany
Elmira
Binghamton
Erie
Olean
Corning
Athens
Honesdale
Kingston
Toledo
Cleveland
Akron
Williamsport
Wilkes-Barre
White Haven
Newark
New York
Bellefonte
Sunbury
Reading
Bristol
Trenton
New Brunswick
Bordentown
Philadelphia
Harrisburg
Hollidaysburg
Johnstown
Pittsburgh
Washington
Columbia
Hagerstown
Frederick
Baltimore
Washington
Cumberland
Uniontown
Beallsville
Wheeling
Zanesville
Marietta
Cambridge
Columbus
Springfield
Dayton
Cincinnati
Portsmouth
Northampton
New Haven
N E W Y O R K
P E N N S Y L V A N I A
O H I O
VERMONT
NEW HAMPSHIRE
M A S S.
C O N N.
N E W J E R S E Y
M A R Y L A N D
DEL.
Lake Champlain
Connecticut River
Hudson River
Mohawk River
Delaware
Susquehanna
Juniata River
Allegheny River
Monongahela
Potomac
Ohio River
Miami River
Muskingum R.
Scioto
Cuyahoga River
Sandusky R.
Maumee R.
Genesee
Keuka Lake
Seneca Lake
Cayuga Lake
Chenango
Chemung
Black River
Erie
Champlain
Miami & Erie
Ohio & Erie
Pa. & Ohio
Sandy & Beaver
Pa. State
Portage R.R.
Union
Schuylkill
Lehigh
Morris
Delaware & Raritan
Del. & Hudson
Chesapeake & Ohio
Chesapeake & Delaware
Susquehanna & Tidewater
Hampshire & Hampden
Hocking
Delaware Bay
Rappahannock
Kanawha River

CANALS
Completed
Uncompleted
Canalized rivers

and the Elmira Jefferson & Canandaigua which had been leased from the Erie the previous year. These were six foot lines since the Chemung had been built as a feeder to the Erie at Elmira and the EJ&C as a continuation of the Canandaigua & Niagara Falls (which had a six foot gauge until taken over by the Central in 1855.) The lease led to problems with the Erie's prickly management, so by 1872 the Northern Central had obtained a majority of the stock of both companies and thereafter operated them as part of their own line. Their gauge was changed to standard, and at Canandaigua a harmonious interline relationship was developed with the New York Central via its Canandaigua & Niagara Falls line. The Northern Central advertised in Buffalo papers, but its trains did not enter the city. It was necessary for passengers to take the Peanut to Canandaigua on the Northern Central or the Erie to Elmira to access its trains to and from Baltimore and Washington.

Buffalo Corry & Pittsburgh

The following account of the third and westernmost north-south line from Western New York into central and western Pennsylvania (Figure #1) is from the Centennial History of the Pennsylvania Railroad:

From Pittsburgh, the line of the Allegheny Valley Railroad had been extended to a point opposite Oil City, Pennsylvania, in 1868. Prior to this date, another railroad had been constructed from Oil City to Brocton, New York, on the New York Central [actually the Buffalo & Erie], *from which point it had trackage rights to Buffalo. The nucleus of the latter line had been the Oil Creek Railroad, built in 1862 to carry oil from the wells near Titusville to the Philadelphia & Erie and the Erie at Corry. As the Buffalo Corry & Pittsburgh the line was continued on to Brocton in 1867, and formed part of a natural through route from Pittsburgh to Buffalo, particularly when it was extended from Brocton to Buffalo in 1882* [as the Buffalo Pittsburgh & Western in cooperation with the Nickel Plate]. *A line from Hinsdale, New York, on the Emporium-Buffalo line, to Rochester, New York, was completed in 1882, and a line from Warren, Pennsylvania, to Olean, New York, in 1883. By means of this latter line and the Oil Creek & Allegheny Valley, plus a short piece of trackage on the Philadelphia & Erie, a route was opened between Pittsburgh, Oil City, and Rochester, and an alternative route* [to that by way of Corry] *between Oil City and Buffalo via Emporium. All of these lines, except the one to Rochester, were consolidated into the Buffalo New York & Philadelphia Railroad Company in 1883 and this company became the lessee of the Genesee Valley Canal Railroad, which was the line from Hinsdale to Rochester. By this time the prosperity of the oil regions was on the wane. The BNY&P went into receivership in 1885. It was reorganized in 1887 as the Western New York & Pennsylvania Railroad Company, but this company also failed to earn its charges and was forced into receivership in 1893.* [3]

The Genesee Valley Canal Railroad, whose tracks had been laid on the towpath of the abandoned Genesee Valley Canal, was completed from Olean to Rochester in 1882.

New York Central & Hudson River

The most important development on the local railroad scene shortly after the Civil War was the 1867 take-over of the New York Central by Cornelius Vanderbilt who joined it to his Hudson River Railroad two years later to form the New York Central & Hudson River Railroad. Socially, Vanderbilt was another Dean Richmond, but at business he was a genius. He had gotten his start in shipping around New York Harbor and branched out into steamboats on the Hudson to Albany and on Long Island Sound to Stonington, Rhode Island, and a system of steamships and stagecoaches from New York to California via

Nicaragua. The self-styled Commodore did not turn to railroads until his late sixties when in 1862 he began buying up a controlling interest in the New York & Harlem, which had reached a connection at Chatham with Albany in 1852. Next, he interested himself in the Harlem's rival, the Hudson River Railroad, which had reached East Albany in 1851, and by 1864 he had become its majority stockholder. He obtained control of the Central by tactics in which nineteenth century business tycoons gloried. With the two Albany-New York lines in his pocket, he began buying Central stock in 1865. Within a year he had accumulated $2.5 million worth of shares, and was able to put two of his creatures on the board. Unhappy because his Hudson River line transferred most of its westbound freight to the NYC at Albany but got little of the latter's eastbound freight in return (except in winter when the river was frozen), Vanderbilt worked out an agreement whereby the NYC gave his line a prorated share of its long-distance freight charges and a bonus of $100,000 annually.

When a new group headed by William G. Fargo and two Wall Street operators, Henry Keep and Legrand Lockwood, who had taken over the Central's board, learned of this agreement, they were furious. At the December 1866 stockholders' meeting Keep and Lockwood arranged to throw Vanderbilt's men off the board and elect a new president who canceled the bonus. On January 14, 1867, when boats could not sail on the frozen Hudson, Vanderbilt's Hudson River Railroad informed the NYC it would no longer accept its freight. The Hudson's passenger trains began stopping short of the bridge that had been opened across the Hudson to Albany the previous year, forcing the Central's passengers to cross over on foot in the bitter cold to make the connection. Unable to transport its freight to New York City, the NYC saw its stock drop from $130 to $95, at which price Vanderbilt began buying and soon had $6,000,000 of the road's $20,000,000 capitalization. The board gave in and invited him to accept the presidency. In 1869 he merged the Central and the Hudson River to form the New York Central & Hudson River Railroad, which in 1872 leased the Harlem. Vanderbilt's strategy, writes Maury Klein, "was as elemental as it was effective: buy a road, put in honest management, improve its operation, consolidate it with other roads when they can be run together economically, water the stock, and still make it pay dividends." His victory, however, was not a one-man show. Leading stockholders of the NYC realized that, with growing rivalry and rate-wars with the Erie and Pennsylvania, their road could no longer compete with these longer lines based on Atlantic coast seaports. The NYC had to throw in with a line leading directly into New York City.

At the same time as this takeover and merger a memorable event occurred in the annals of the Gilded Age, which Harlow narrates with unwonted conciseness:

After the Commodore became head of the New York Central, he sought to end the rate-cutting hostilities between Central, Erie and Pennsylvania. The last-named was agreeable, but the Erie was recalcitrant, wanting too large a share of the profits, and Vanderbilt, much annoyed, decided to get rid of the nuisance by taking it over. In this he reckoned without the genius of two newcomers to Wall Street, Jay Gould and James Fisk, Jr., who in alliance with none other than Daniel Drew, now dominated the Erie. When Vanderbilt tried to corner Erie, these worthies simply printed and threw on the market millions of counterfeit stock, and when New York became too hot for them as a result, all fled to New Jersey. Vanderbilt was unused to that sort of strategy, and the courts were too corrupt to depend on for relief.

Presently the conspirators' agents were in Albany, asking the Legislature for a law that would legalize their acts. Gould himself ventured up there with a trunk said to be full of

$1,000 bills, and though under technical arrest, negotiated actively with the lawmakers. The New York Herald remarked that 'the Drew party were willing to spend $2,000,000 to secure the success of the measure,' which was 'a godsend to the hungry legislators and lobbymen, who have had up to this time such a beggarly session that their board bills and whiskey bills are all in arrears.' Vanderbilt sent a flock of agents to Albany, including [son-in-law Horace] *Clark and a young lawyer named Chauncey M. Depew, who now for the first time comes into the Central picture; but they found themselves so outclassed that the old man decided to withdraw his opposition to the bill. When, says* [Charles Francis] *Adams* [in *Chapters of Erie*], *news of this, 'as of some great public disaster, spread panic and terror through hotel and corridor,' it is asserted that the asking price of votes dropped in a few minutes from $5,000 to $100. The bill passed, and Vanderbilt, after losing somewhere between one and two millions, gave up for all time the notion of controlling Erie.* [4]

Mott writes of this chapter of Erie:

Judging from the results that followed his subsequent ownership and control of the Harlem, Hudson River, and New York Central Railroads, it more than likely has been many times since a matter of great regret to the holders of Erie securities that he did not follow to success the promptings of his early ambition and his later efforts toward the control of Erie. [5]

Atlantic & Great Western

The desire of civic leaders in three towns in three adjoining states, Franklin, Ohio, Meadville, Pennsylvania, and Jamestown, New York, for broad gauge railroad service to the Atlantic seaboard led to the creation of the Atlantic & Great Western which was destined to become the Erieís connection with Chicago and Saint Louis. As early as 1850 visionaries in northwestern Ohio projected a six foot line that would connect their region with the Atlantic on the east via a connection with the New York & Erie at some point in southwestern New York, and with the Mississippi Valley via the six foot 340 mile Ohio & Mississippi Railroad between Cincinnati and East Saint Louis, the final segment of which would be completed in 1857. Marvin Kent of Franklin, Ohio, obtained a charter in 1851 for the Franklin & Warren Railroad to run west to Akron, and east through Warren to the Pennsylvania line. (Figure #4.) Thereupon a contract was let to grade the road all the way through Ohio down to Dayton where it would connect with the Cincinnati Hamilton & Dayton. Early in 1853 the name Franklin & Warren was changed to Atlantic & Great Western of Ohio, and in July grading commenced. About half the work was completed, when a shortage of funds compounded by severe drought intervened, and no further work was done for several years.

Getting through Pennsylvania also proved a stumbling block for the A&GW of Ohioís vision, as Mott reported:

The ultimate object of the projection of this work [the Atlantic & Great Western of Ohio] *was communication with New York and eastern markets by connection with some through line in that State. The Erie was open between Dunkirk and New York, and the New York Central had come into existence on the consolidation of the five local railroads between Albany and Buffalo. But to form any connection with either of those trunk lines it was necessary that the Oho interests should have a railroad through Pennsylvania, and that was not an easy thing for a foreign corporation to secure in those days. The Pennsylvania Railroad was completed from Philadelphia to Pittsburg* [sic], *and work was in progress from Pittsburg to Cleveland. The Sunbury and Erie Railroad was projected from Sunbury to Erie Harbor, and the Pittsburg and Erie Railroad from Pittsburg to Erie. Neither of these lines*

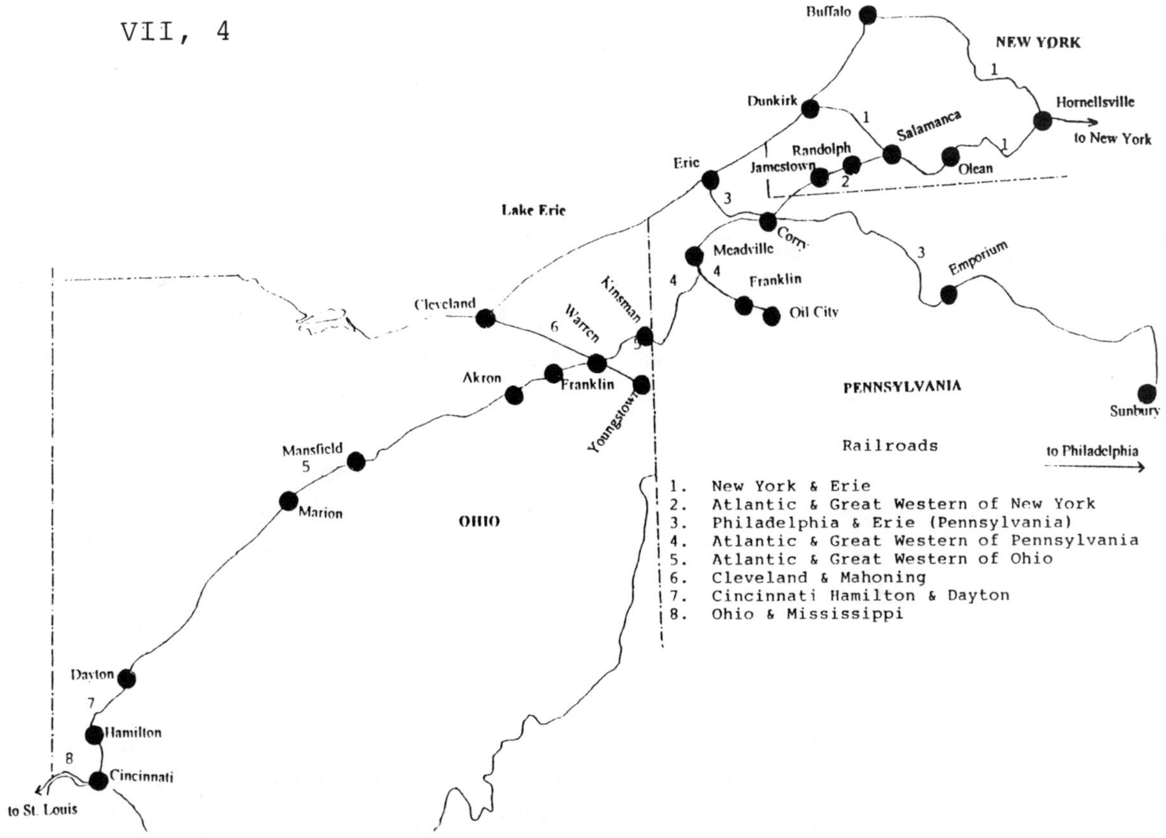

was yet built. [The Sunbury & Erie, renamed the Philadelphia & Erie in 1861, would not reach Erie until 1864.] *There was no railroad across the State of Pennsylvania between Ohio and New York, and such transit was jealously guarded against by the selfish interests of Philadelphia, Pittsburgh, and Erie.* [Pennsylvaniaís forty mile wide neck fronting on Lake Erie was finally bridged by continuous rail at the conclusion of the 'Battle of the Gauges' in Erie, Pennsylvania, in 1853. See Chapter V. 'Lake Shore Route.'] *Railroad charters in Pennsylvania could only be granted by legislative enactment, and all legislation was controlled by the united interests of these cities. Many attempts had been made to pass the barrier by open and covert attempts in the legislature without avail. The decision had gone out that all land commerce to and from the East, through Pennsylvania, must pass by way of Pittsburgh and Philadelphia.*

This was the embarrassing dilemma the projectors of the Atlantic and Great Western undertaking were in, when it was found that under the liberal privileges of the Pittsburgh and Erie Railroad Company's charter as to the construction of branches to the main line, a branch could be constructed from the Ohio line, near Kinsman, across Pennsylvania to a point in Warren County at the New York State line. To further the interests of its own railroad project, the Pittsburgh and Erie company was willing to permit the building of such a branch by Meadville interests under its charter. [6]

The Meadville Branch would ostensibly serve as a feeder to the projected Pittsburgh & Erie. As Huntington writes

Thus the stage was seemingly neatly set. The Branch would be built to Meadville, then cautiously, on east of there until finally the New York State line would be reached, while at the same time connection would be made with the Franklin and Warren Road. It was a pretty plan and adroit and it seemed almost certain to go through. But it did not then nor for a long time thereafter. [7]

Ground for the Meadville Branch of the Pittsburgh & Erie was broken on August 19, 1853, but was abandoned after a few miles had been graded. The six foot Erie had held out some hope of financial aid to this six foot gauge enterprise, but its own fiscal straits prevented this from happening. Four years later, on April 3, 1857, the Meadville Railroad was chartered by the Pennsylvania legislature to build a railroad from Meadville to Erie and was vested with the right to receive from the P&E a transfer of its branching privileges. The Meadville Railroad was organized on July 13, 1857, with William Reynolds as president. Ten days later the P&E sold its branching privileges to the Meadville Railroad. Now a branch could be constructed from the Ohio-Pennsylvania line near Kinsman across Pennsylvania to a point in Warren County on the Pennsylvania New York boundary. A construction contract was made with the Erie & New York City, but the Panic of 1857 intervened, and the contract was canceled. A year later the name of the road was changed to the Atlantic & Great Western Railroad of Pennsylvania.

In western New York support for a connection with the projected Pennsylvania and Ohio roads came principally from citizens of Jamestown, unhappy that their town had been left off the Erie. The result was the organizing of the Erie & New York City at Jamestown on June 30, 1851, to build a railroad from Great Valley (later Salamanca) on the New York & Erie through Randolph and Jamestown to the Pennsylvania line. Work was not begun until May 19, 1853, and was abandoned on January 5, 1855, for lack of funds. Realizing the importance of cooperation and of securing a link through New York, representatives of the Ohio and Pennsylvania roads went to England and induced James McHenry, a wealthy businessman, to provide financing. They also organized the Atlantic & Great Western Railroad of New York on May 7, 1859, with William Reynolds of the Meadville road as president. This company purchased the assets of the Erie & New York City. Construction was recommenced on May, 1860, and the road was opened to Jamestown, September 11, 1860, and to Corry, Pennsylvania, on what was now the Philadelphia & Erie on May 7, 1861. On March 12, 1862, control of the three A&GW companies was placed under a central board of two directors from each. The first train from Salamanca rolled into Meadville on November 11, 1862. (Salamanca had been named after the Duke of Salamanca, a banker and financial adviser to Queen Isabella of Spain. He had earned his fortune building railroads in Spain, France, and Italy, and had been interested by McHenry in the A&GW.) Two years later the Atlantic & Great Western built a branch to Franklin, Pennsylvania, which in June, 1864, was extended to Oil City, being the first railroad into the Oil Regions.

In July, 1863, the Cleveland & Mahoning Railroad was leased for ninety-nine years by the Atlantic & Great Western of Ohio, and a third rail was laid on it to give the Atlantic broad gauge access to Cleveland. Completing the gaps across Ohio and Pennsylvania was hindered by the high cost of labor and materials during the Civil War, but the work was completed with money raised in Europe by McHenry; and the Atlantic & Great Western connected up with the Cincinnati Hamilton & Dayton on June 20, 1863. New York now enjoyed a continuous six-foot gauge connection with Cleveland on the Lakes (Erie, A&GW, C&MV) and with Saint Louis (Erie, A&GW, CH&D, Ohio & Mississippi) in the Mississippi Valley

Shortly after its completion, the A&GW contracted to deliver its business to the Erie at Salamanca. This was a major factor in fattening the latter's earnings in 1864-1865. In addition, the A&GW's strategic location brought the business of many other connections to the Erie. In return the Erie was to supply the

A&GW with $5,000,000 of rolling stock. This happy arrangement did not last. As already noted, the Pennsylvania Central (soon to be called simply the Pennsylvania) had been completed from Harrisburg to Pittsburgh in 1852 and had established a connection with Philadelphia over its own tracks by 1861. By the summer of 1866, the Pennsylvania tapped the oil regions by controlling three lines, the Philadelphia & Erie, the Allegheny Valley, and the Oil Creek, which ran through Titusville. (Figure #1.) The Oil Creek had been built with a six-foot gauge to connect at Corry with the A&GW-Erie, an arrangement which had made sense since the Philadelphia & Erie was not completed in 1864. When that happened and when the P&E, the Allegheny Valley, and the Oil Creek had been taken over by the Pennsylvania, the A&GW's profits tumbled. As a result of cutthroat competition for the oil business, a post-war business recession in 1866, and bad management, the A&GW went into receivership, April 1, 1867.

An 1874 lease of the A&GW to the Erie did not last long. The lessor went into bankruptcy in 1875, and in 1880, having been converted to standard gauge, was sold at foreclosure. It was again leased by the Erie in 1883, went bankrupt again, and was purchased at foreclosure by the Erie in 1896. At that point, Mott remarks, "It began, with the Erie, an unharassed career at last."

The Atlantic & Great Western was an exception to the rule that during the Civil War little railroad building took place. Prices of materials were high and the labor supply diminished by enlistment in the army and concentration on military production. In addition to the oil traffic, the A&GW'S strategic location brought the business of many other connections to the Erie. To obtain the money to buy the rolling stock for the A&GW the Erie had to sell its soul to Daniel Drew, the "Speculative Investor," whose influence on its history was wholly malign. The financial situation of the Erie itself had also worsened because of a general post-war business decline and the interest charges on the equipment bought for the A&GW for which there was now little use.

An example of the indifference that Daniel Drew and his henchmen on the board of the Erie had toward its interests is related by John S. Gorden in *The Scarlet Woman of Wall Street* about the Buffalo Bradford & Pittsburgh. This was an ambitiously named twenty-five mile line from Carrollton near Salamanca on the Erie's mainline through Bradford to Gilesville, Pennsylvania.

The Erie bought this small, derelict, and nearly worthless enterprise from a group of its own directors. The road cost the purchasers as financiers, some $250,000; as proprietors, they then issued in its name bonds for $2,000,000, payable to one of themselves, who now served as trustee. This person then, shifting his character, drew up as counsel for both parties, a contract leasing this road to the Erie Railway for four hundred and ninety-nine years, the Erie agreeing to assume the bonds; reappearing in their original character of Erie directors, these gentlemen then ratified the lease, and thereafter it only remained for them to relapse into the role of financiers and divide the proceeds. All this was happily accomplished, and the Erie Railway lost and someone gained $140,000 a year by the bargain [the annual 6% interest on the bonds]. *It would subsequently cost the Erie $1,000,000 more to put the road into usable shape.*[8]

Vanderbilt, Gould, and the Lake Shore

It was at this juncture that Jay Gould, in October, 1868, became president of the Erie. Sensation mongering journalists loved to hate Gould, and for almost a century historians, with the exception of Mott, exhibited a similar loathing. A revision of this assessment was begun by Julius Grodinsky in 1957, and carried further by Maury Klein's already cited biography of Gould. Be that as it may, Gould's four years (1868-1872) as president of the Erie were not the high point of his career. His part in the clearly illegal but successful scheme to deny Vanderbilt control of the Erie and in the even more nefarious plot hatched by Jim Fisk to corner the gold market in September of 1869 placed Gould's reputation under a cloud from which it never emerged.

On taking over, Gould determined to seize western connections for the Erie, which at that time dead-ended at Buffalo (and Dunkirk.) Four routes (Figure #5) dominated the business between New York, Philadelphia, and the West: (1) the lake shore route; (2) the A&GW with its connections to Dayton and thence to Saint Louis; (3) the Pittsburgh Fort Wayne & Chicago; and (4) the Panhandle Road, a recent amalgamation, sponsored by the Pennsylvania Railroad, of lines between Pittsburgh and Columbus, which reached Chicago via the Columbus Chicago & Indiana Central.

To that end, in December, 1868, Gould disposed of the A&GW's receivership and leased the road to the Erie for twelve years. A month later he leased the Indiana Central and through the purchase of stock and proxies obtained enough votes to control the Cleveland & Pittsburgh's annual meeting. There he revamped the company's by-laws to secure his control of this road which provided the Fort Wayne with access to the oil refineries of Cleveland. These rapid moves galvanized the Pennsylvania into action. Before the Indiana Central's stockholders met to approve the Erie lease, they accepted a higher bid from the Pennsylvania. In Ohio, the Pennsylvania enjoined Gould's highhanded actions at the Cleveland's annual meeting and forced a compromise giving him influence but not control of the road. Klein takes up the story at this point:

As for the Fort Wayne, Jay controlled the stock but the Pennsylvania dominated the state legislature. The Fort Wayne's and the Pennsylvania's managers did not want the road's traffic diverted to New York via the Erie, and neither did the state's businessmen.They rushed to Harrisburg and in only thirty-four minutes obtained a classification act staggering the election of Fort Wayne directors over a four-year period, a sure-fire method of preventing sudden hostile take-overs. Later the Pennsylvania locked up the road with a perpetual lease. [9]

Gould's attempt to secure the lakeshore route as a western outlet for the Erie was also foiled. In 1868 he planned a line from his Atlantic & Great Western at Akron to Toledo and suggested to the president of the Michigan Southern & Northern Indiana that his road lay a third rail from Toledo to Chicago so Erie trains could run through to the Windy City. The two Cleveland to Buffalo roads, the Cleveland Painesville & Ashtabula and the Buffalo & Erie, protested this threat to their through traffic; and Vanderbilt, dreading the effect of the proposed alliance upon his New York Central, began buying heavily into Michigan Southern & Northern Indiana stock early in 1869. By May of that year the string of railroads from Buffalo to Chicago had been merged into the Lake Shore & Michigan Southern, the controlling interest in which was held by Legrand Lockwood, head of a New York brokerage and an ally of Gould.

The denouement is briefly described by Grodinsky:

It was the gold panic of September [1869] which defeated this combination. The gold speculation, which has generally been interpreted as a Gould success, was in fact a calamity to Gould. One of its immediate effects was a stock-market shake-out which forced Lockwood, one of the leading Lake Shore stockholders, to sell his stock. It was Vanderbilt, the businessman with funds, and not Gould, the speculator without funds, who bought the distressed stock. Through this speculative windfall, Vanderbilt acquired control of the Lake Shore.[10]

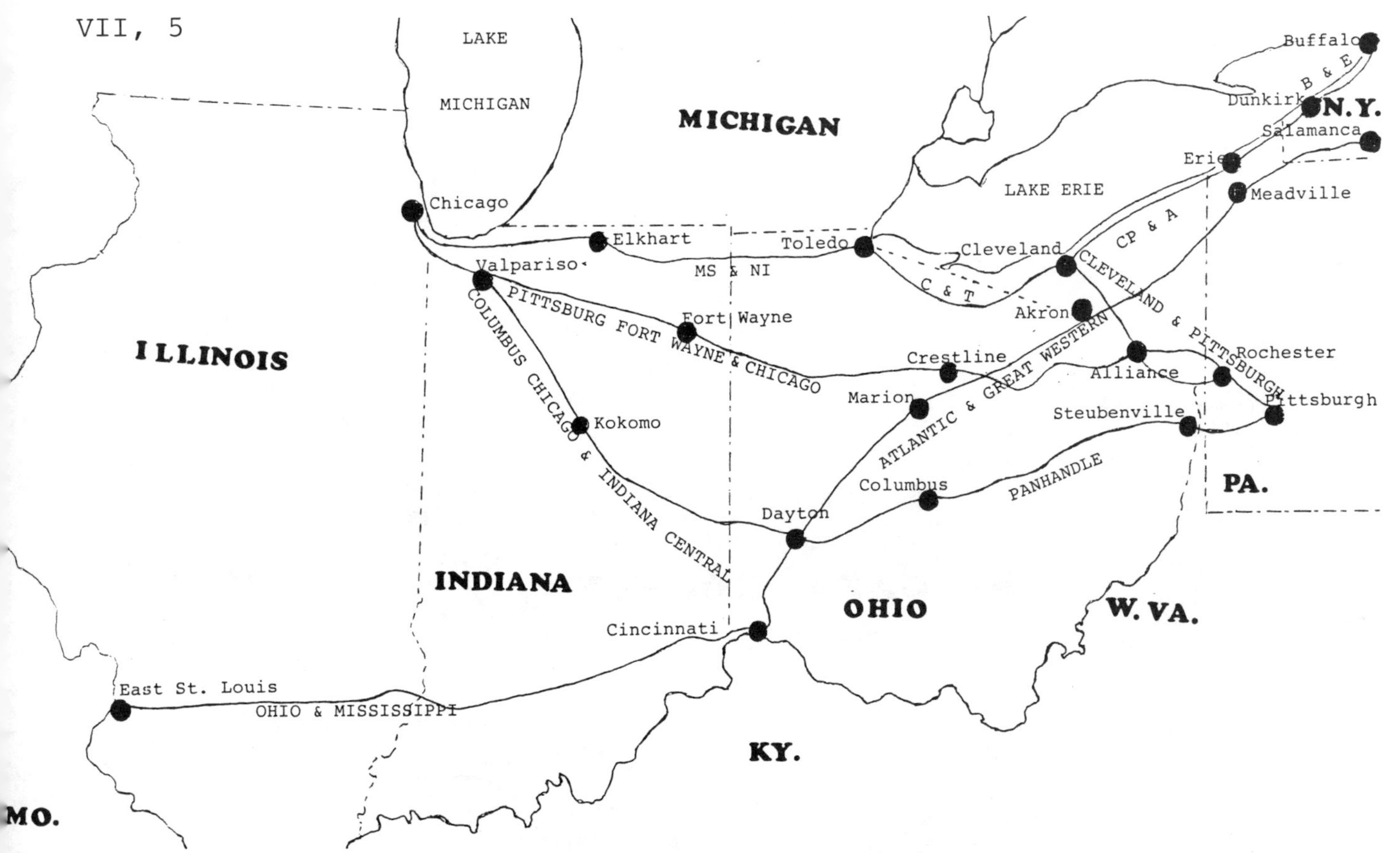

Suspension Bridge & Erie Junction

The situation at Buffalo created by Vanderbilt's capture of the Lake Shore confronted the Erie with a serious problem since the Commodore followed it up by closing that route to the Erie. To open an alternate route, Gould revived plans for a parallel road to the Central's Niagara Falls line to be called the Suspension Bridge & Erie Junction Railroad. Early in 1867, prior to Gould's becoming president, the Erie management had determined to build this connection with Canada's Great Western, which ran from Suspension Bridge to Windsor, across the Saint Clair River from Detroit, whence it reached Chicago over the tracks of the Michigan Central. (Figure V. #3.) Gould's extension was built, according to Niagara County historian William Pool, during the fall and winter of 1870-1871 and was opened for business on May 15, 1871. It left the mainline at William Street in Buffalo just southwest of the intersection of William and Bailey (then called the Williamsville Road) and headed northwest to Niagara Falls, crossing Main Street just north of Hertel. (Figure #6.) By 1893 stations of this branch within the city of Buffalo were located at Clinton Street, East Buffalo, Walden Avenue, Delavan, Kensington, Main Street, and International Junction. Beyond the city passenger trains stopped at Ellwood Park, Gratwick, La Salle, Niagara Falls, Suspension Bridge, and Clifton in Canada, where connections could be made with the Grand Trunk and the Canada Southern. Not all Erie local stations were agency stations.

Erie International

Gould had lost control of the Erie by the time the next extension of the Erie on the Niagara Frontier, the Erie International, was incorporated on December, 16, 1872.

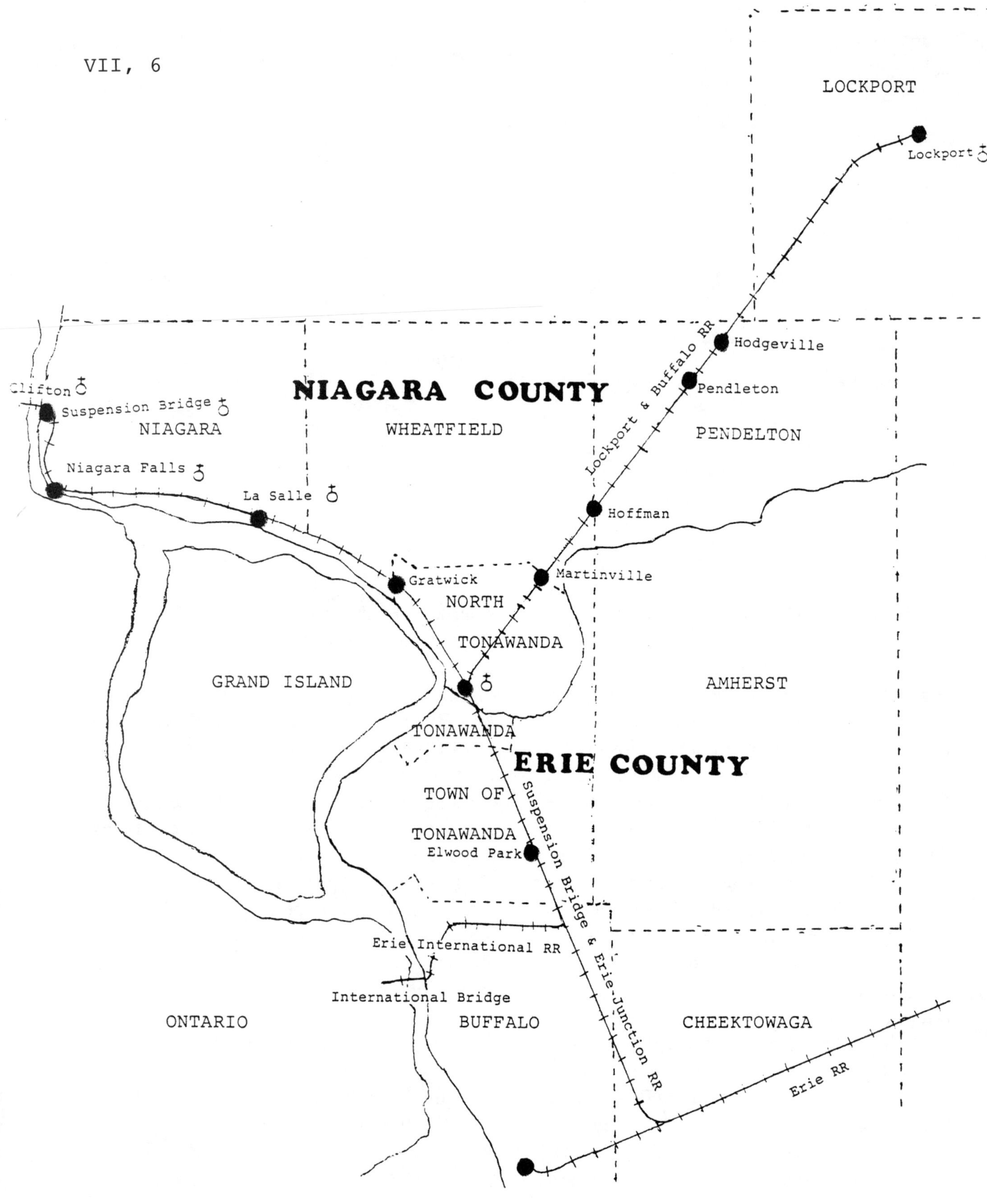
VII, 6
LOCKPORT
Lockport
NIAGARA COUNTY
Clifton
Suspension Bridge
NIAGARA
WHEATFIELD
Lockport & Buffalo RR
Hodgeville
Pendleton
PENDELTON
Niagara Falls
La Salle
Hoffman
Gratwick
Martinville
NORTH
TONAWANDA
GRAND ISLAND
AMHERST
TONAWANDA
ERIE COUNTY
TOWN OF
TONAWANDA
Elwood Park
Suspension Bridge & Erie Junction RR
Erie International RR
International Bridge
ONTARIO
BUFFALO
CHEEKTOWAGA
Erie RR

According to its deed the EI was to "begin at a point near the crossing of the Ellicott Turnpike (Main Street) and the Suspension Bridge and Erie Junction Company's railroad" and run due west across North Buffalo "to a point in the Eastern Abutment of the International Bridge on the Niagara River." The Erie now had its own Buffalo Belt Line. The International Bridge was the second railroad bridge across the Niagara River, the first being the Suspension Bridge below the Falls. Construction of this bridge which would eliminate the ferry at Fort Erie was done by the Grand Trunk Railway, which had taken over the Buffalo & Lake Huron in 1864. (Figure V, #3.) Sir Casimir Gzowski, who had built the Grand Trunk's mainline from Toronto to Sarnia, was the chief engineer of the International Bridge. As Jackson and Burtniak write:

He had now to cope with the difficult task of placing the supporting piers in the deep, fast-flowing river and of counteracting the destructive force of the winter ice. At the time of its construction this was the only bridge across the Niagara River with piers in its turbulent waters - all other bridges spanned the river from bank to bank. The site selected for the crossing was located 3.5 miles north of Buffalo harbour, where advantage could be taken of Squaw Island, situated close to the American side, to cross both the River and the Erie Canal. The piers had to be constructed in the swift current and several coffer dams were swept away before they were anchored by heavy stone. The crossing, which consisted of a bridge across the main river channel, an embankment across Squaw Island, and a swing span across the Erie Canal, was opened for single track traffic in November, 1873, and its success was immediate. (Figure #7.) [11]

The International Bridge was the Grand Trunk's answer to the Great Western's Suspension Bridge. Grand Trunk trains used the New York Central's station at Erie Street (Figure II, #18), formerly that of the Buffalo & Niagara Falls, since the eastern end of the

VII, 7

bridge connected with the Niagara Falls line at Lower Black Rock.

Junction Railroad

In order to achieve a similar direct connection with the Grand Trunk's International Bridge, the New York Central had begun as early as 1870 to acquire property for the Junction Railroad, better known as the Belt Line, which was in place by 1872. It left the mainline in East Buffalo, ran north across Broadway, Genesee, Ferry, Delavan, and Leroy before swinging west through North Buffalo parallel to Amherst Street until it reached the Central's Niagara Falls line near International Bridge. (Figure #8.) In its early years the Junction Railroad was for freight only, and Grand Trunk passenger trains continued to operate out of the dead-ended Erie Street Station. To handle its burgeoning freight business, the Central developed a huge complex of freight and stock yards, car repair shops, a roundhouse, and an ice house to the north of William Street between Fillmore and Bailey. (Figure #9.)

Lockport & Buffalo

The Lockport & Buffalo was organized in 1876 to liberate this old canal town from the monopoly enjoyed by the Central. (Figure #6.) As early as 1868 a public meeting at Lockport had appointed a committee to plan a railroad to connect Lockport with the Erie, but nothing came of the idea at the time because of the difficulty of locating a route. The first president of the L&B, which was finally chartered in 1871, was Thomas Thorn Flagler of Lockport, who had made his money in the hardware business and then founded the Holly Manufacturing Company at Lockport. The City of Lockport agreed to purchase $100,000 of the road's bonds; the Erie Railroad seems to have been the majority stockholder. By early 1877 grading and bridge building was finished between North Tonawanda and Lockport, and ties were laid along the line; but for three years the Central refused to permit its rival to cross NYC tracks in North Tonawanda. As narrated by Mott, Colonel Lewis S. Pain, a wealthy lumber merchant of that city who had fought at Seven Pines, White Oak Swamp, and Malvern Hill, was "a leading spirit" in the projected railroad, "with a force of several hundred men forced a crossing at midday, and held it, accomplishing in a short time the desired object." The first passenger train from Buffalo to Lockport arrived on August 29, 1879 and the first excursion train ran to Niagara Falls via Tonawanda on June 5, 1880. William R. Gordon, author of *90 Years of Buffalo Railways,* writes:

The opening of the Lockport & Buffalo branch of the New York & Erie R. R., with new rates on September 15,1879, was of great economic importance to Lockport. Freight rates that had been 28 cents per hundred-weight between Buffalo and Lockport dropped to 6 cents, and of course, Lockport absorbed the benefit. [12]

Buffalo & Jamestown

A line to Jamestown was destined to be the last branch acquired by the Erie in Western New York. The A&GW had ambitioned its own line into Buffalo. In a biographical sketch of residents of Jamestown, Mott writes:

In 1867 the Atlantic & Great Western Railroad had surveyed and was grading a route for a railroad from Randolph [on the A&GW halfway between Salamanca and Jamestown] *through Cattaraugus County, by way of the Zoar route. Daniel Griswold believed that by this route the road would be of little value to Chautauqua County. After making several trips through that region, at his own expense, he discovered what appeared to him to be a more feasible and practical route for the railroad, and one that would be an everlasting benefit to the people of*

VII, 8

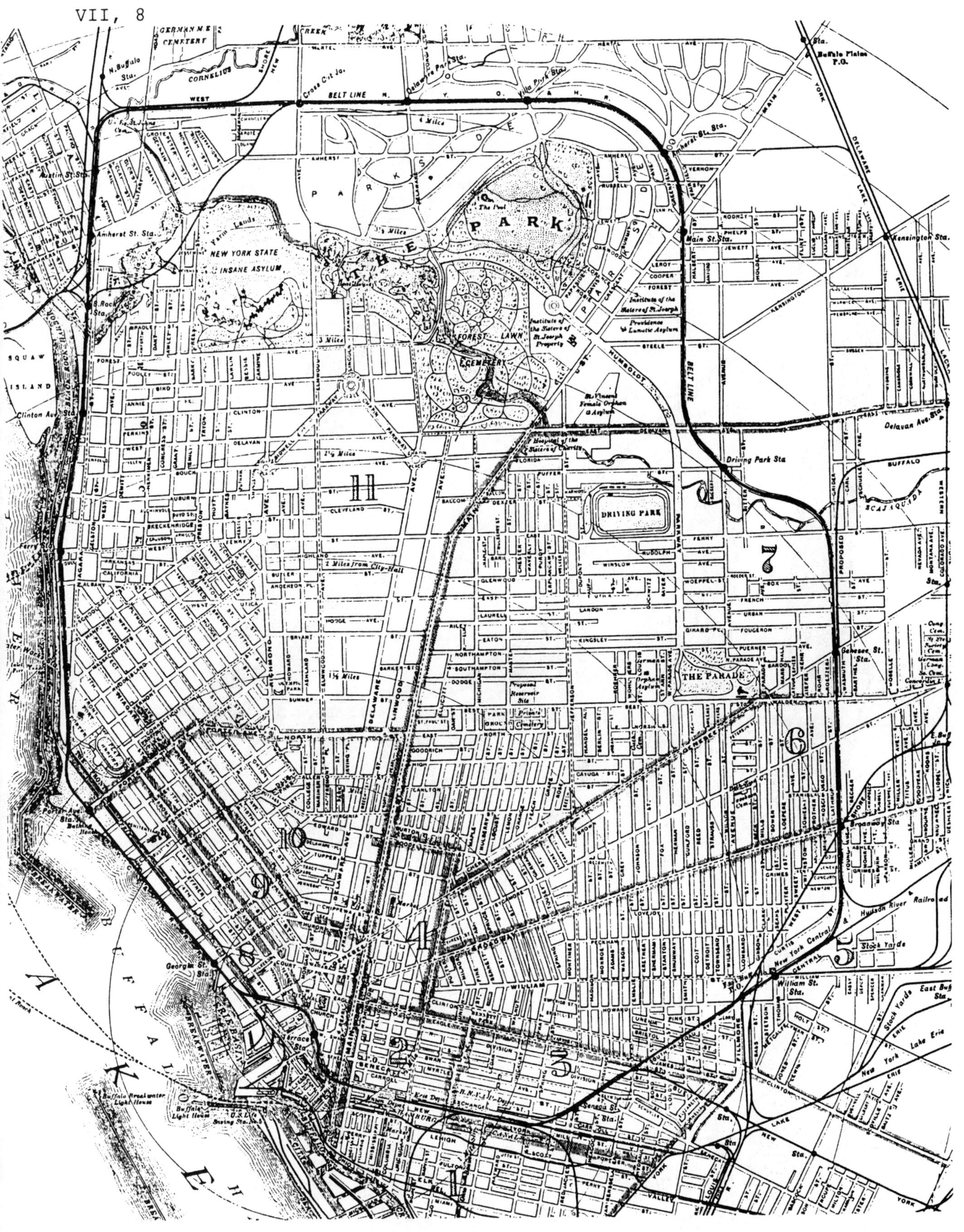

GERMAN M.E. CEMETERY
N. Buffalo Sta.
Cross C.t. Jc.
BELT LINE
Delaware Park Sta.
Villa Park Sta.
Buffalo Plains P.O.
Amherst St. Sta.
Austin St. Sta.
Amherst St. Sta.
NEW YORK STATE INSANE ASYLUM
THE PARK
The Pool
FOREST LAWN CEMETERY
Institute of the Sisters of St. Joseph
Providence Lunatic Asylum
Main St. Sta.
Kensington Sta.
Delavan Ave. Sta.
SQUAW ISLAND
Clinton Ave. Sta.
St. Vincent Female Orphan Asylum
Hospital of the Sisters of Charity
Driving Park Sta
DRIVING PARK
SCAJAQUADA
2 Miles from City Hall
3 Miles
1½ Miles
Proposed Reservoir Site
THE PARADE
Genesee St. Sta.
Broadway Sta
Porter Ave. Sta.
Georgia St. Sta.
Terrace Sta.
Seneca St. Sta.
William St. Sta.
New York Central & Hudson River Railroad
Stock Yards
East Buffalo Sta.
Lake Erie
Buffalo Breakwater Light House
Buffalo Light House
BREAKWATER
B U F F A L O
L A K E
1
2
3
4
5
6
7
8
9
10
11

VII, 9

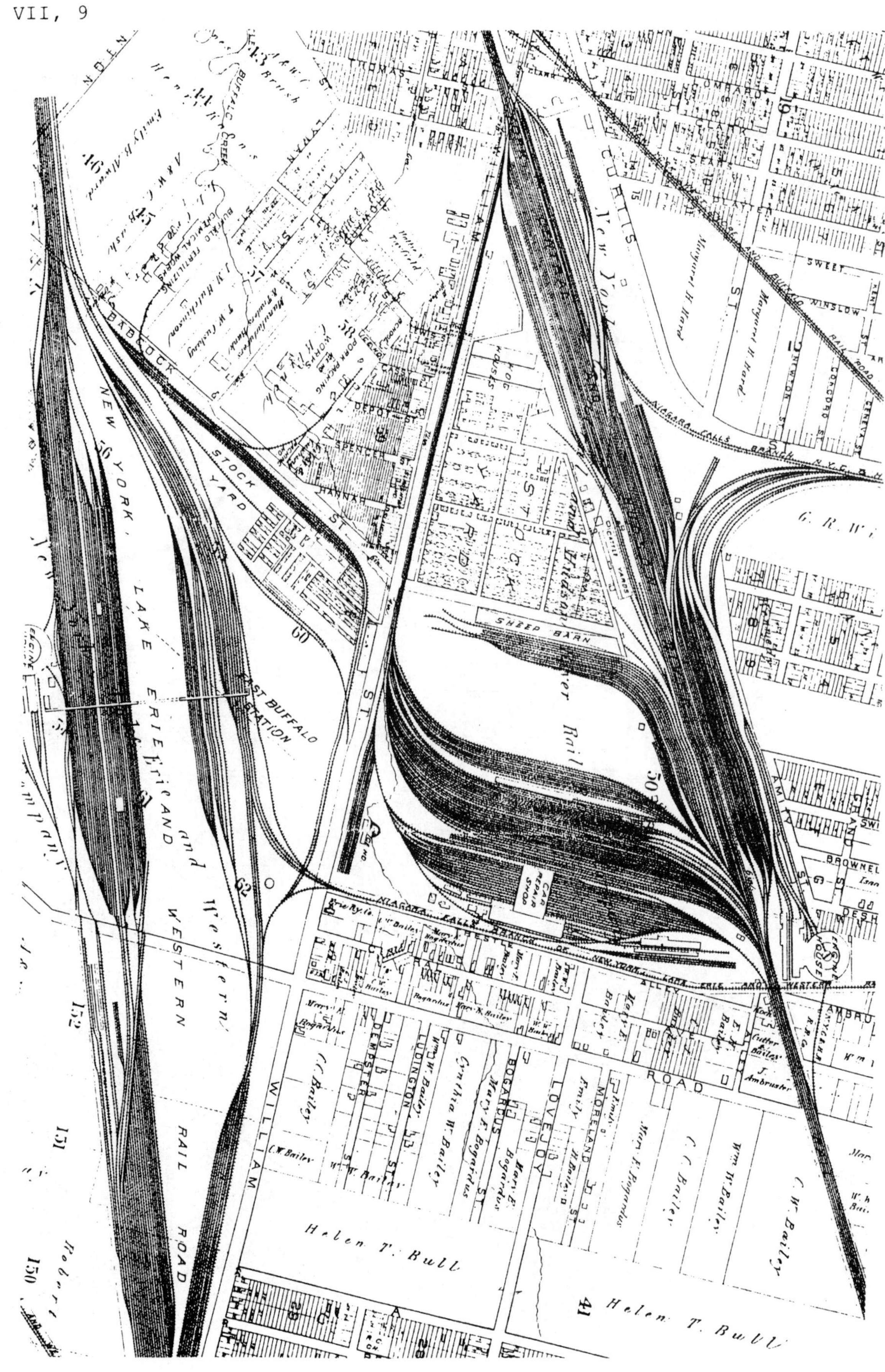
NEW YORK, LAKE ERIE AND WESTERN RAIL ROAD
New York Lake Erie and Western
EAST BUFFALO STATION
STOCK YARD
BABCOCK
DEPOT ST
SPENCER
HANNAH ST
WILLIAM ST
SHEEP BARN
CAR REPAIR SHOP
NIAGARA FALLS BRANCH OF NEW YORK LAKE ERIE AND WESTERN
SWEET
WINSLOW
BROWNELL
ROAD
DEMPSTER
LUDINGTON
BOGARDUS
LOVEJOY
MORELAND
WILLIAM
Helen T. Bull
C. W. Bailey

Chautauqua County. He called on Mr. Shyrock and Mr. Reynolds, of the Atlantic and Great Western Railroad Company, at Meadville, Pa., and explained to them the feasibility of the new route. They sent their engineer, Thomas Bridgen, with him to examine it. The engineer was so impressed with the route, which lay between Jamestown and Buffalo, passing through Cherry Creek, Dayton [where it crossed the Erie's old mainline to Dunkirk] *that the old Zoar route was immediately abandoned and the new route was adopted. Later, Buffalo capitalists, with the aid of the bonded towns, built the railroad over that route.* [13]

The road in question was the Buffalo & Jamestown which was organized on March 25, 1872. (Figure #10.) Rail laying began on October 21, 1872, and by the end of the next month an excursion was made over the first five miles. Gowanda was reached to the accompaniment of the usual celebration on October 24, 1874. This sixty-four mile road joined the mainline of the former A&GW, which had emerged from receivership as the New York Pennsylvania & Ohio, at Falconer, 3.5 miles east of Jamestown. Entrance to downtown Buffalo was over the tracks of the Buffalo Creek and the Buffalo New York & Philadelphia whose station it shared. During the long depression following the Panic of 1873 the road went bankrupt and was sold by a referee for $1,000,000. Renamed the Buffalo & Southwestern, it was sold to the Erie on August, 1, 1881, which thereafter operated it as the Buffalo & Southwestern Division. Stations within Erie County were located at Buffalo Creek Junction, West Seneca, Blasdell, Big Tree, Abbott Road, Hamburg, Water Valley, Eden Valley, Eden Center, North Collins, Lawton's, and Collins.

By means of a hoist which lifted car bodies while trucks were changed, the Erie had exchanged traffic at Suspension Bridge with the now standard gauge Great Western since the early seventies. By 1874, however, the principal point of interchange between the Erie and its western connections was East Buffalo. Here its classification yards contained fifteen miles of track, and large transfer sheds on an immense tract of land stretching south of William Street and the NYC's yards from Babcock Street almost to the city limits. (Figure #9.)

Canada Southern

The Niagara Frontier had not felt the last of Commodore Vanderbilt's influence. During the 1860s besides his lake shore route to Chicago, his New York Central & Hudson River Railroad also employed the Great Western of Canada-Michigan Central as an alternate route west from Buffalo. (Figure V, #3.) The Canadian road employed a five and a half foot gauge, but in 1866 a third rail was installed, and thereafter trains with sleepers ran over the two roads between Chicago and Buffalo, and at times even to Albany and New York. Cutthroat competition in the early 1870s, however, by trunk lines between the Atlantic coast and Chicago, undermined the Michigan road's fiscal stability. As Harlow puts it:

With the collapse of 1873, the proud Michigan Central, whose stock had sold as high as 130, now had to pass dividends, and saw its shares fall below par in the market. But a new force was gathering strength behind it. It was Commodore Vanderbilt who, on behalf of the New York Central, began buying its stock in 1869 when it seemed doubtful whether he or the Erie would gain possession of the Lake Shore. His son William urged his purchases in both roads. The aging Commodore had settled into provincialism in his thinking, and at first saw no reason for owning lines west of Buffalo. "If we take hold of roads running all the way to Chicago," he retorted to William, "we might as well go on to San Francisco or even to China." But William recognized the growing importance of Chicago as a national solar plexus, and the necessity of

VII, 10

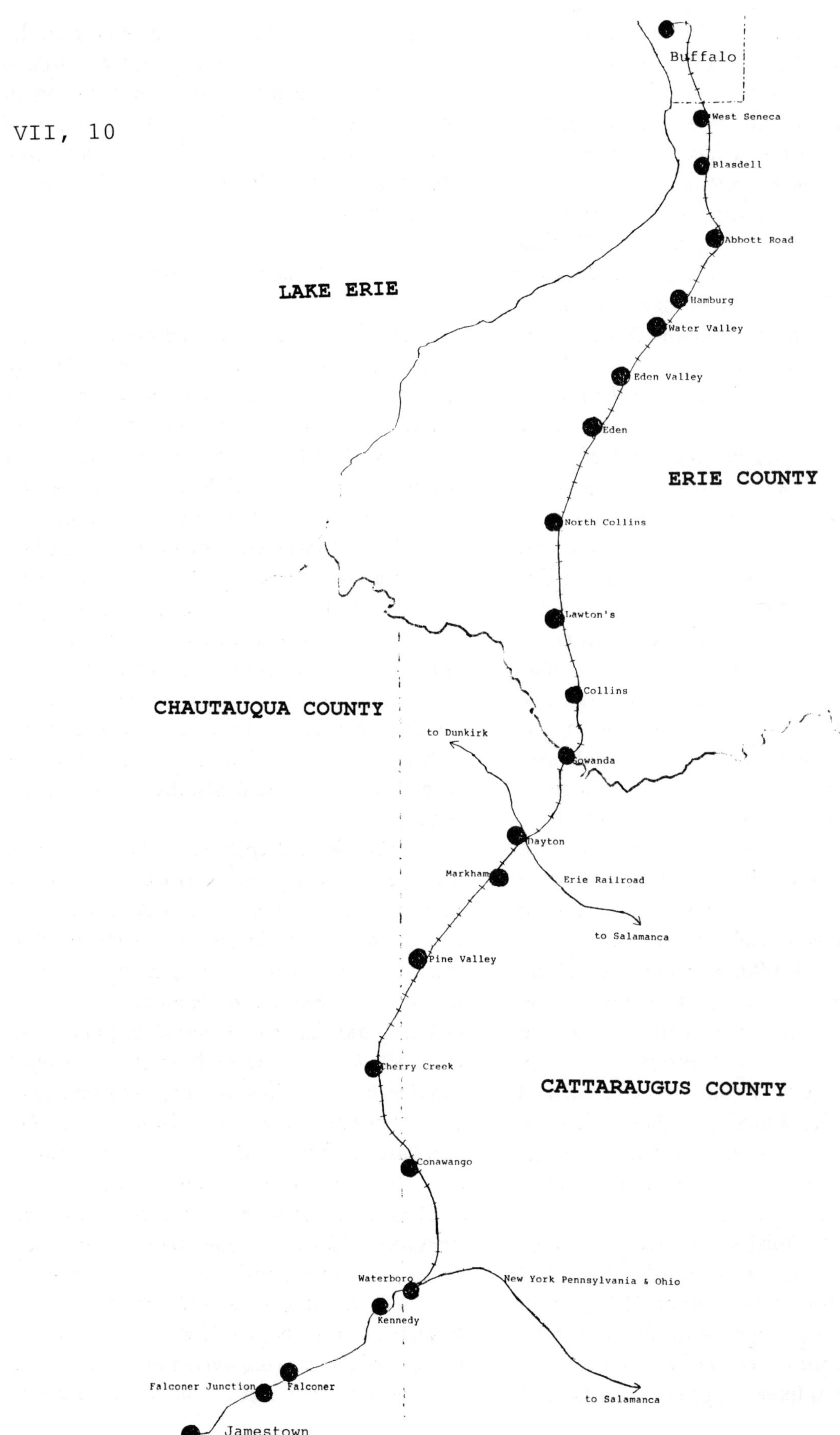
Buffalo
West Seneca
Blasdell
Abbott Road
LAKE ERIE
Hamburg
Water Valley
Eden Valley
Eden
ERIE COUNTY
North Collins
Lawton's
Collins
CHAUTAUQUA COUNTY
to Dunkirk
Gowanda
Dayton
Markham
Erie Railroad
to Salamanca
Pine Valley
Cherry Creek
CATTARAUGUS COUNTY
Conawango
Waterboro
New York Pennsylvania & Ohio
Kennedy
Falconer Junction
Falconer
to Salamanca
Jamestown

not merely fragile traffic agreements with carriers west of Buffalo, but actual control of them; and Cornelius was wise enough not only to yield to his counsels, but to enter into the plan with enthusiasm. [14]

By 1875 it was clear that the New York Central held a controlling interest in the Michigan Central. New York management supplanted the previous Boston management early in 1877.

It remained only to fill in the gap between Buffalo and Detroit. British directors of the Great Western refused to sell out, so Vanderbilt proceeded to move in on its rival, the Canada Southern. This was a road with low grades and easy curves across the Ontario Peninsula from Fort Erie to Amherstburg on the Detroit River south of Windsor which was completed in 1873. (Figure #11.) At Fort Erie it used the ferry until the completion of the International Bridge in November of that year. The Canadian terminus of the structure was thereafter known as Bridgeburg. The Canada Southern had been completed across the Ontario Peninsula from Detroit to International Bridge in 1873 and had acquired the Erie & Niagara, which ran north-south along the Niagara River on the Canadian side. The Canada Southern went bankrupt in 1876 and was snapped up by Cornelius Vanderbilt in what Harlow calls "his last earthly triumph," for a mere guarantee of five percent interest on its bonds. In 1882 the Canada Southern was formally leased by the Michigan Central for twenty years. For decades, MC trains stopped at Falls View or Inspiration Point in Niagara Falls, Canada, to give passengers a look at the Falls. With the breakup of relations between the Great Western and the Michigan Central, the Grand Trunk, which had taken over the Great Western in 1882, sought to retaliate by threatening to stop the MC's use of the Grand Trunk's Suspension Bridge at Niagara Falls. The Canada Southern had also built a branch from its mainline at Welland northeast to Niagara Falls, Canada. William Vanderbilt's answer was to build the Michigan Central's own bridge, a great 500 foot long double-tracked cantilever, immediately south of Suspension Bridge. Increased weight and speed of trains had rendered Roebling's Suspension Bridge obsolete. It was replaced in 1896 by a steel arch bridge. However, the area on the American side of the bridge, and even the bridge itself, continued to be called Suspension Bridge for decades thereafter.

The Great Western did not take the threat of competition from the Canada Southern lying down, but rather built a line into Fort Erie to parallel the Canada Southern and to introduce the Great Western into the southern part of the Niagara Peninsula. (Figure #12.) The first train passed over this line in 1873. The route departed from the Great Western's mainline at Glencoe, twenty-two miles west of Saint Thomas, and ran east to Welland, where one branch ran to the International Bridge at Fort Erie. Another branch, employing trackage rights over the north-south Welland Railway as far north as Allanburg, ran to Niagara Falls. It was called the Canada Air Line because it did not climb the Niagara Escarpment (unlike the Great Western's line from the Falls to Hamilton, which involved a double crossing of the Escarpment) and because it enjoyed the shortest distance between Glencoe and the Niagara River. It was also called the Loop Line, since the line from Simcoe through Allanburg rejoined the old mainline at Niagara Falls.

The original idea had been to run the Air Line east from Canfield Junction on the Buffalo & Lake Huron, but since that had been leased to the Great Western's competitor, the Grand Trunk, that plan was abandoned. The merger of the Great Western and the Grand Trunk in 1882 made this construction superfluous, a frequent development in the history of Canadian railroads. For the major railroads of the Ontario Peninsula, which was a stepping stone between Western New York and the American Middle West, see Figure #13.

VII, 11

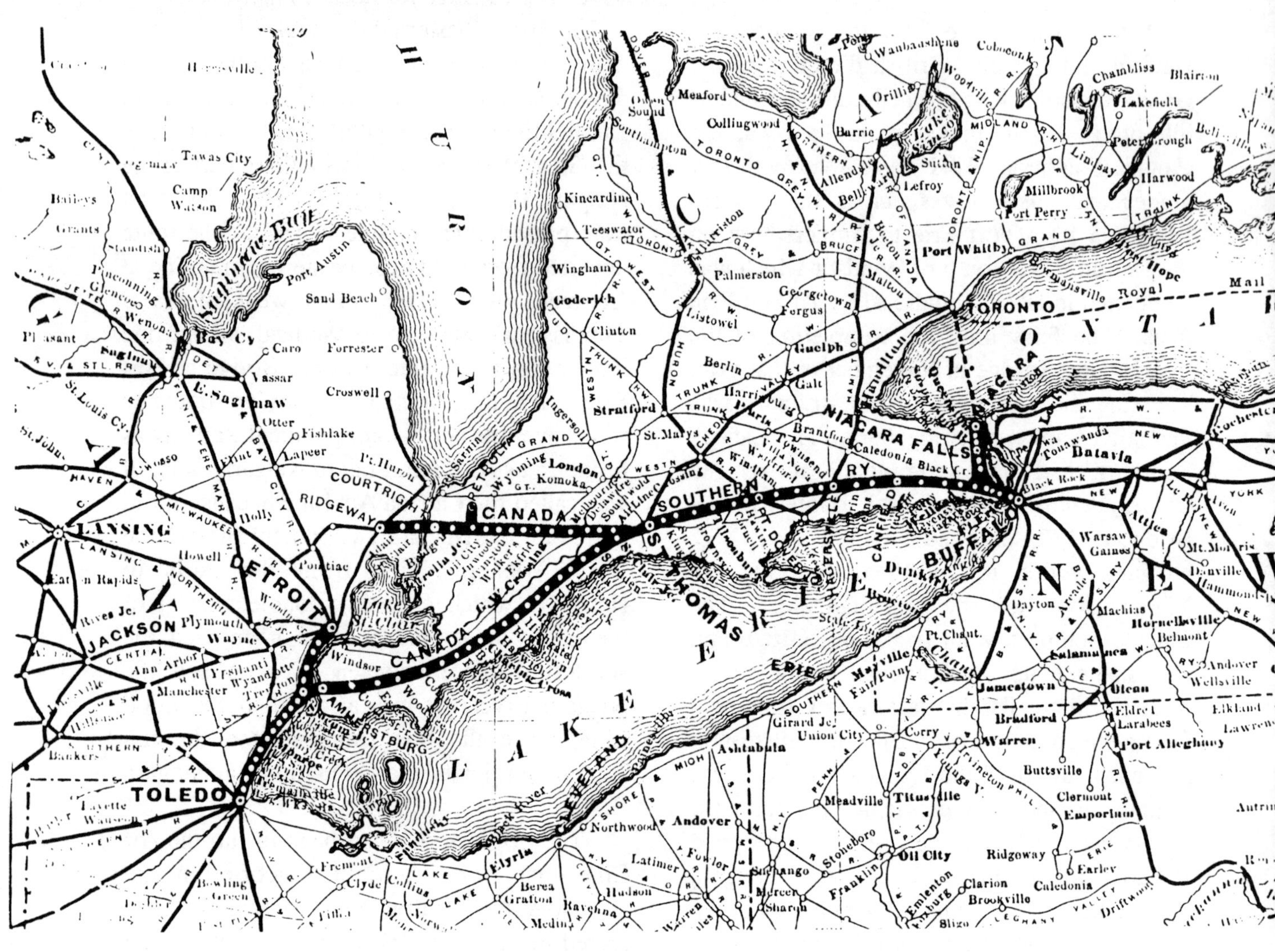
TORONTO
NIAGARA FALLS
BUFFALO
DETROIT
TOLEDO
LANSING
JACKSON
AMHERSTBURG
CANADA SOUTHERN RY.
ST. THOMAS
LAKE ERIE
CLEVELAND
Windsor
London
Batavia
Hamilton
Guelph
Stratford
Goderich
Port Whitby
Barrie
Orillia
Collingwood
Meaford
Kincardine
Wingham
Palmerston
Listowel
Galt
Brantford
Caledonia
St. Marys
Ingersoll
Komoka
Courtright
Ridgeway
Pt. Huron
Croswell
Forrester
Sand Beach
Port Austin
Caro
Vassar
E. Saginaw
Bay Cy
Tawas City
Fishlake
Lapeer
Holly
Pontiac
Howell
Plymouth
Wayne
Ann Arbor
Ypsilanti
Manchester
Dunkirk
Jamestown
Olean
Bradford
Warren
Corry
Union City
Titusville
Meadville
Oil City
Franklin
Ashtabula
Andover
Elyria
Berea
Hudson
Ravenna
Fremont
Clyde
Salamanca
Hornellsville
Belmont
Wellsville
Andover
Attica
Warsaw
Dayton
Machias
Eldred
Port Allegheny
Emporium
Ridgway
Clarion
Brookville
Stoneboro
Port Hope
Peterborough
Lindsay
Millbrook
Lakefield
Harwood
Lefroy
Sutton
Allendale
Milton
Georgetown
Fergus
Berlin
Clinton
Teeswater
Owen Sound
Southampton
Meadville
Girard Jc.
Erie
Black Rock
Tonawanda
Mail
Royal
Northwood
Latimer
Grafton
Bowling Green
Fayette
Wauseon
Bankers
Hillsdale
Eaton Rapids
Reves Jc.
Pt. Chaut.
Mayville
Fair Point
Buttsville
Clermont
Earley
Caledonia
Driftwood
Sligo
Emlenton
Sharon
Mercer
Shenango

VII, 12

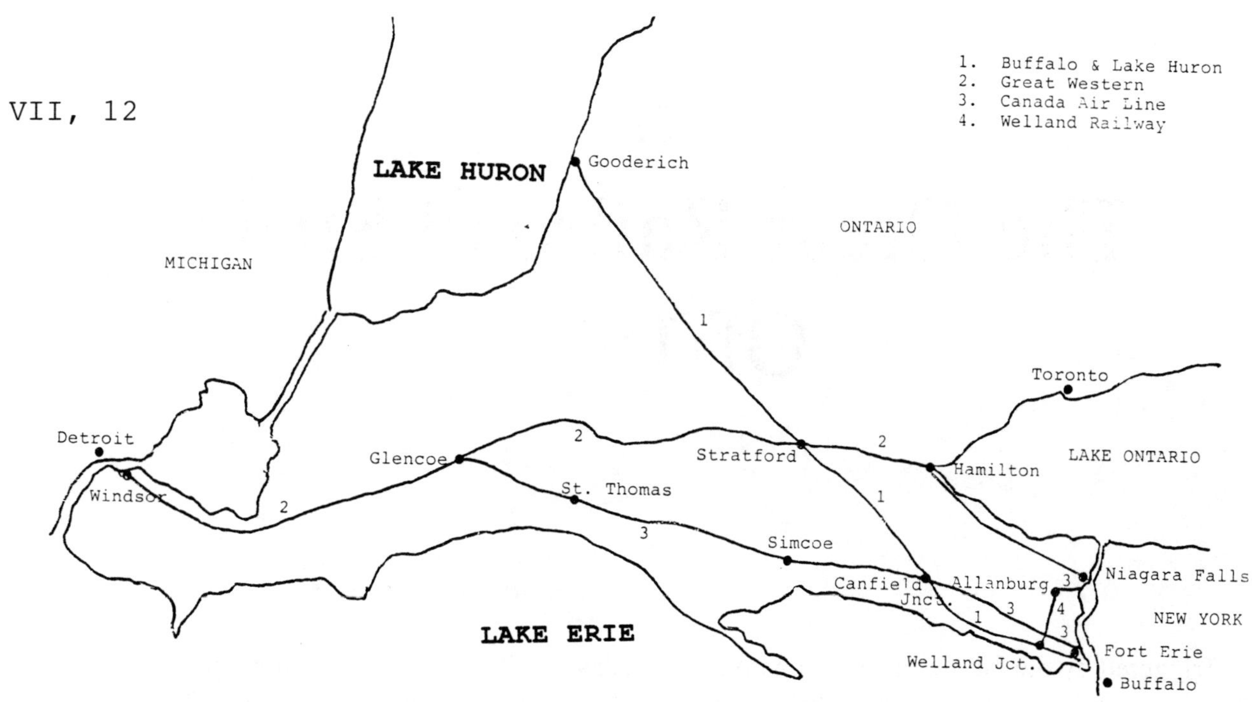

VII, 13

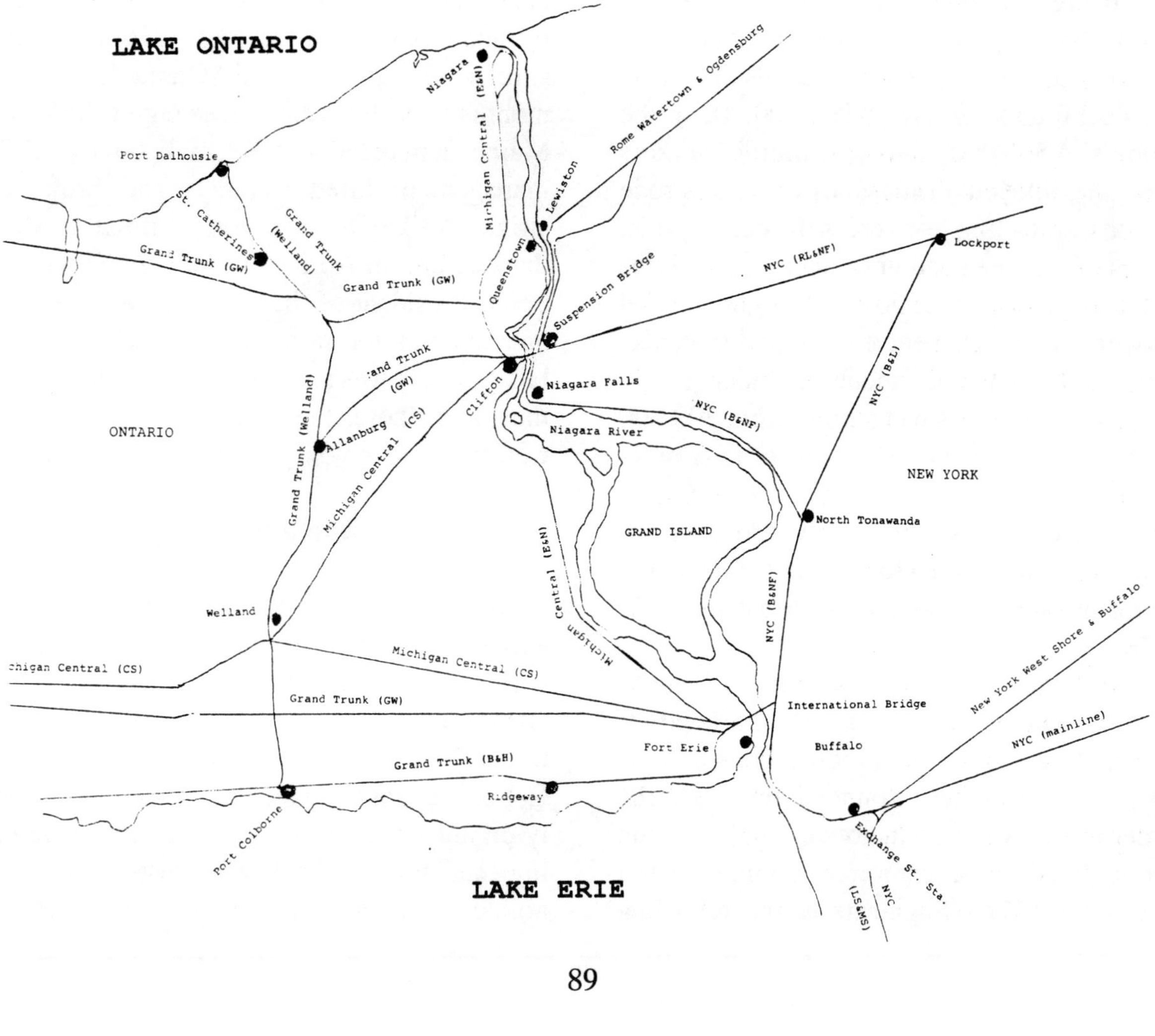

LAKE ONTARIO
Niagara
Rome Watertown & Ogdensburg
Port Dalhousie
St. Catherines
Grand Trunk (Welland)
Grand Trunk (GW)
Michigan Central (E&N)
Lewiston
Queenstown
Suspension Bridge
NYC (RL&NF)
Lockport
Grand Trunk (GW)
Clifton
Niagara Falls
NYC (B&NF)
NYC (B&L)
ONTARIO
Allanburg
Michigan Central (CS)
Niagara River
NEW YORK
Grand Trunk (Welland)
North Tonawanda
GRAND ISLAND
Michigan Central (E&N)
NYC (B&NF)
Welland
Michigan Central (CS)
Grand Trunk (GW)
International Bridge
New York West Shore & Buffalo
Fort Erie
Buffalo
NYC (mainline)
Grand Trunk (B&H)
Ridgeway
Port Colborne
Exchange St. Sta.
NYC
(LS&MS)
LAKE ERIE

8
The Great Railroad Strike Of 1877

Triggered by the failure of several banking houses which had invested unwisely in overbuilt railroads, the Panic of 1873 was followed by a depression which lasted until 1879 and saw the bankruptcy of a majority of America's railroads and the idling of two-thirds of its iron and steel foundries. By 1875 1,000,000 of the nation's 4,500,000 non-agricultural workers were unemployed. Thousands of tramps rode the rods, spreading fear across the countryside. Gangs of teenage hoodlums, denizens of slums that had grown up almost overnight, ranged through city streets bent on loot and violence. Stunned by unemployment, membership in national craft unions had shrunk from 300,000 in 1870 to 50,000 in 1875. Since most managers regarded labor as merely a commodity whose price was set by supply and demand, wage reductions in factories, coal mines, and railroads swept across the northeast in 1875-1878.

Railroad shopmen, brakemen, and trackworkers had no union. The Brotherhood of Locomotive Engineers, the aristocrats of railroad labor, had been founded in 1863, the Order of Railway Conductors in 1868, and the Brotherhood of Locomotive Engineers and Firemen in 1873. (Engineers averaged $3.35 a day 1875-1879, conductors $3.06, firemen $1.82, and brakemen $1.80.) [1] Though they concentrated at first on temperance and insurance, the engineers forced the Jersey Central to rescind a pay cut in October, 1876, and won a similar victory over the Grand Trunk two months later; but when those on the Boston & Maine demanded a raise in February, 1877, management hired standbys and broke the strike. A like fate overtook a similar strike on the Reading in April. On May 24 Thomas A. Scott, President of the Pennsylvania Railroad, announced a ten percent cut effective June 1. His example was soon followed by the Lehigh, the Lake Shore, the Erie, and the New York Central, to name only roads serving Buffalo.

Martinsburg [2]

Seeing that the roads which had made cuts experienced no serious trouble, John W. Garrett, President of the financially troubled Baltimore & Ohio, ordered a wage cut effective July 16, 1877. On that day trainmen in Baltimore, who had signed up with the recently organized Trainmen's Union, began deserting their trains. They were dispersed by the police, fired, and quickly replaced. But at

Martinsburg, West Virginia, 100 miles west of Baltimore, strikers warned that no trains would move until the cut was rescinded. Though ordered by the Governor to preserve the peace and prevent interference with men willing to work, the local militia, after a brief scuffle the next day, proved unwilling and/or unable to restore train service. The Governor sent troops from Wheeling on the 18th, but being warned that intervention by the militia would precipitate bloodshed, wired President Rutherford B. Hayes for federal troops. The next day, 330 regulars arrived at Martinsburg, and some freight trains began moving under military protection. Trouble, however, moved west to Cumberland, Maryland, where on the 20th striking canalboat owners, the unemployed, tramps, and teenage boys had stopped all freights sent west from Martinsburg. Since the local authorities were unable to stem the violence, Governor Charles L. Carroll called out Baltimore's 5th and 6th Maryland National Guard Regiments.

Baltimore

Baltimore, where a third of the working population was unemployed, had the reputation of "the most mobbish city in America." Answering Carroll's call, units of the militia marched to the Camden Street Station to entrain for Cumberland, but were mobbed and shot at on the way. Some soldiers fired back, but many deserted. (Figure #1.) Ten residents were killed and scores seriously wounded. No trains left Baltimore that night as rioters ringed the station, torched passenger cars, and drove the firemen off. Carroll called upon President Hayes for assistance. The next day rioting continued, but by nightfall of the 22nd 500 federal troops had arrived, and the strike was soon over.

Pittsburgh

The day the B&O wage cut went into effect, the superintendent of the Pennsylvania Railroad's Pittsburgh Division decreed that, as of the 19th, freights on the eastbound grade from Pittsburgh would be pulled by two engines, a labor saving arrangement which halved the number of conductors and brakemen needed. On the 19th, trainmen refused to work and by intimidating strikebreakers brought train service to a standstill. (Figure #2.) The freight yard was soon thronged by a

VIII, 1

VIII, 2

mob in which railroad men were outnumbered by tramps and street punks.

Pittsburgh was a blue collar city, a showcase of the rapid industrialization of the last third of the nineteenth century and home to dozens of factories, mills, mines, and oil refineries. Its workers were a testy lot and had won some recent strikes. Moreover, most Pittsburghers hated the Pennsylvania Railroad, which they believed had bribed the legislature into discriminating against their industries. By the morning of the 19th, incoming freights with hundreds of cars of perishables were clogging the yards and scores of oil cars were blocking the mainline. Crowds with railroad men in the minority were roaming the streets crying, "Bread or Blood!" It seemed as if war had begun between capital and labor.

When a committee of strikers presented their demands to Alexander Cassatt, Vice President of the PRR, he refused to negotiate and asked the sheriff to make a pro forma call on the mob to disperse, so that when it was ignored, Governor John F. Hartranft's office could be asked to call out the militia. Since the Governor was out of state, the request was directed to the Adjutant General in Philadelphia. Pittsburgh militiamen were slow to answer the call, so the Adjutant General activated the Philadelphia-based 1st Division, 600 members of which were on their way by the afternoon of Saturday, the 21st. Their train was pelted with rocks as it approached Pittsburgh. The troops were dispatched to a crossing thronged by a crowd of about 6,000, composed of toughs, drunks, men getting out of work, and the curious. With bayonets drawn, the soldiers drove the crowd back to permit making up trains. The crowd answered with a barrage of coal and rocks, and some pistol shots were heard. The soldiers fired back, and it was all over in five minutes. The toll was ten Pittsburgers dead and about thirty wounded. No soldiers were killed, but fifteen were injured. Though the track was now clear, railroad officials were unable to raise crews to run the trains.

Pittsburghers were now furious and up in arms. Mobs emptied gun stores and the militia's armory. Pistol fire was directed at the roundhouse to which the Philadelphia militia had retreated. Burning boxcars were rolled downhill to flush the soldiers out. Rioters aimed a cannon captured from the armory at the roundhouse, but rifle fire held them off. On Saturday night, the entire city stayed up as looting began in earnest. At daybreak Sunday the Philadelphians marched out of their burning roundhouse to the U.S. Arsenal where a timid commander denied them sanctuary. Along the way, bystanders opened up with rifle fire, killing several soldiers. The militia retaliated with a gatling gun, after which the unit, covered by a skirmish line, marched to safety in the countryside. Many Pittsburgh militiamen changed into civilian clothes and melted into the mob. The sheriff cowered in his office, the popular mayor was thrown off the platform at Union Station when he tried to address the mob, and the Catholic bishop was roughly handled when he did the same. The Adjutant General, who had come out from Philadelphia, wandered the streets aimlessly. Exaggerated newspaper accounts of events in Baltimore on Saturday were broadcasted and believed. Drunks torched empty freight cars. The Union Station (Figure #3), the Adams Express Company building, the Pan Handle freight depot, and a huge grain elevator were burning furiously. Firemen were prevented from wetting down railroad property, but when flames spread to private houses many returned to their homes to save them. By nightfall things had quieted down. The mob was exhausted and hung over. Next morning, twenty regulars arrived to protect the Arsenal. Smoke and fog hung over smoldering ruins for two miles along the mainline. Destroyed were 104 locomotives, 2,152 freight and passenger cars, and 79 buildings from grain elevators to shanties. Twenty-four persons perished in the weekend violence, three of them railroaders. The Pittsburgh militia reassembled and marched through the streets without incident. A Committee of Public Safety was formed and armed from the Arsenal. But the strikers, joined by hundreds of mill workers, continued their work stoppage.

Chain Reaction

From Sunday to Friday, July 22-27, 1877, violence broke out in cities from the Middle Atlantic States to the Mississippi Valley. Across the river from Pittsburgh, strikers patrolled the yards and pushed freight cars onto the mainline to keep them from rioters. In Altoona on Sunday, 500 Philadelphia militia stopping over for breakfast enroute to Pittsburgh were turned back, and rioters disarmed the battered Philadelphia militia returning from Pittsburgh. Militia garrisoned the state

VIII, 3

arsenal, and the mayor and sheriff organized a posse which discouraged looting. Reading, where bitter memories lingered from the failed engineers' strike in April, did not get off so easily. A meeting of the engineers on Saturday probably planned mayhem for the next day in solidarity with the rioters in Baltimore. On Sunday afternoon a mob tore up the tracks around the station and set fire to the railroad bridge across the Schuylkill. It burned all night and finally collapsed, isolating the city. Militia from Easton and railroad police tried to clear rioters out of a cut beyond the station to free a blocked passenger train. From the sides of the cut and from a bridge across it, rocks, bottles, and small arms fire greeted the advancing militia and the train moving up behind it. Shots rang out from the militia, at random at first, then in a volley. Eleven died that night, and a score were wounded. The next day, six companies of the United States Artillery arrived, and by Wednesday train service had been restored. Philadelphia was the headquarters of the PRR, which was therefore not regarded as an absentee landlord. Moreover, civic officials there took a firm stand from the beginning. At the first sign of trouble the police headed off a mob, and the mayor wired for federal troops. On Thursday the 27th, 300 police scattered a mob and then formed a hollow square to protect firemen extinguishing a blaze on a torched train. Early that afternoon, 125 marines arrived, followed next day by 500 men of the 1st United States Artillery, who joined 400 armed police, 400 armed firemen, 2,000 special police, and 1,500 members of the Grand Army of the Republic, the Civil War veterans' organization, to keep the peace.

Hornellsville [3]

On July 1, 1877, the brakemen, yardmen, and trackmen's wages were cut ten percent on the Erie Railroad. Of the fifty members of a grievance committee sent to New York City headquarters of the bankrupt road to protest the cut, a dozen were fired by Hugh J. Jewett, who had been appointed receiver two months before. At a meeting of employees at Hornellsville at midnight, July 19-20, an immediate strike was voted. From Friday the 20th until Wednesday the 25th, Erie train movements in central and western New York were suspended. On Friday at 9:30 P. M., Superintendent E.S. Bowen reached Hornellsville by special train to find the yards and shops in possession of 400 strikers. Under the leadership of Barney J. Donohue, a red-headed little Irishman, they allowed no one to work and sidetracked all arriving trains, passenger as well as freight.

The sheriff, unable to put the Erie in possession of its property, notified Governor Lucius D. Robinson, a director of the railroad, who ordered the 54th Regiment of Rochester to the scene. It arrived 400 strong Saturday evening to the jeers of the strikers. The 110th Battalion and Battery A of the 20th Brigade also arrived from Elmira. The militia cleared and guarded the yards and placed them under martial law. However, most of the soldiers sympathized with the strikers. Conductors and engineers, who were not affected by the cut, were willing to take trains out; but Donohue told them they did so at their own peril. The same day the Governor ordered the 74th Regiment to Hornellsville from Buffalo.

The *Pacific Express* carrying United States Mail, but no passengers, arrived at 9:00 on Sunday morning the 22nd. Superintendent Bowen was determined to send it on under military escort. The train with two passenger coaches, a baggage car, and a mail car was started up at 10:00 with forty men of Company D, 110th Battalion, aboard. A sergeant and four men were placed on the locomotive and two guards were stationed on the platform of each car. The rest of the detachment was scattered through the cars. The soldiers had orders to fire if attacked. Scores of detained passengers were informed that a train was departing, but only fourteen ventured aboard.

A steep grade began half a mile west of the Hornellsville depot. Starting at that point the strikers' wives had covered the rails with soft soap. The train pulled out and was moving fast when the engine struck the soaped rails. The wheels began slipping and the train labored up the grade very slowly. The 500 trackside strikers and their women and children yelled and screamed. They poured onto the track in front of the train, and large torpedoes were placed on the rails to lift the locomotive and still further check it. The engineer spurted sand and pounded ahead.

The strikers swarmed onto the locomotive, climbed the steps of the cars, and clung to the railing in spite of the guards, many of whom were pale with fright. Beyond a feeble attempt at presenting bayonets, the soldiers did not resist the strikers who with wild shouts pushed the troopers aside and soon had possession of the train. Setting the brakes on the passenger cars, they uncoupled them from the baggage car; and the engine, mail car, and baggage car went on. The engineer stopped and backed up to recover the rest of his train, but the strikers surrounded him and told him to proceed or he would never leave Hornellsville alive again. Seeing resistance was useless, he resumed his trip without the passenger cars. The strikers drove the guards from the cars, ordered the passengers out, smashed the brake wheels with axes, and sent the cars careening down the hill into the village. An engineer in the yard threw a switch just in time to turn the flying cars off the main, thus preventing a disastrous collision at the depot. The strikers captured the soldiers, marched them back to the yard, and handed them over them to their comrades with hoots and jeers. An effort to send a train out on the Buffalo Division via Attica under guard of the 54th Regiment also failed. The emboldened strikers seized a locomotive that was being readied to take a train east with a posse of sheriff's deputies aboard and ran it out of town, where they drew its fire and let the water out of the boiler. Donohue warned the yardmaster and all conductors and engineers that, unless they ceased aiding in the making up of trains, their lives would be forfeit.

Late that afternoon, 300 militiamen of the 74th Regiment of Buffalo arrived at Hornellsville after their train had been held up by the strikers for several hours. The 23rd Regiment from Brooklyn was also ordered to the scene. William W. MacFarland, counsel for the Erie, had taken one look at the upstate troops on hand and wired Governor Robinson for a New York or a Brooklyn regiment. The Governor consented and also proclaimed the strike a riot, warning all to desist, and calling upon all good citizens and authorities, civil and military, to aid in suppressing it. Local authorities issued a proclamation banning the sale of intoxicants and warning all to stay away from the disturbances. The 23rd left New York at 11:00 A. M. Sunday. No trouble was met until the train reached Susquehanna, but from there on the regiment had to fight its way. Toward evening the Brooklynites marched into Hornellsville, having left the cars at the bridge east of town. Their bearing at once impressed the strikers. There was no hooting. In fact, a strange silence prevailed. The 23rd was placed on guard in the yard that night. Strikers attempted to pass through the line as they had been doing. The first to try was challenged. He paid no attention but kept on going. Instantly, a bullet from the sentinel's gun whistled over his head, and he quickly retreated. From that moment, a change came over the spirit of the strikers.

The next day, a strike committee headed by Donohue requested an interview with Superintendent Bowen which was held in his private car. Donohue delivered his ultimatum, which was the original demands of the strikers. MacFarland reminded the committee that, since the property of the company was in receivership, they were in contempt of federal court. He advised the men to return to work and trust the magnanimity of the officials of the company, as no concessions would be made. Since he "spoke as with the voice of Receiver Jewett himself," as the Erie's historian put it, the strikers' hopes for a favorable settlement were dashed. That night, while Donohue was at supper at strike headquarters, he was arrested for contempt of court and jailed in default of $2,500 bail.

The next day, July 24 at 7:30 A. M., a train with two locomotives and four soldiers from the 23rd on each, the rest of the unit in escort, and the 110th Battalion in the coaches, started for the east. The military accompanied the train for the first four miles and returned on foot. At Corning the strikers had thrown freight cars across the tracks and spiked the switches. The train arrived there at 12:30 P. M. where it met a train from New York which had fought its way through with 128 more men from the 23rd. The soldiers removed the obstructions, and both trains proceeded after a two hour struggle with the strikers. The westbound had to fight its way to Hornellsville and got there only after skirmishers, with orders to fire if resisted, were sent ahead to disperse strikers who were tearing up track. When confronted by the militia drawn up in a line, the strikers scattered into the woods.

The strike was settled the next day, Wednesday, July 25th, on the basis of an agreement worked out by local lawyers that the men should acquiesce in the ten percent cut. Members of the grievance committee were to be reinstated at the option of their superintendents. No employee would be fired or proceeded against unless he had destroyed property. Donohue's case would be left to the courts. On Thursday morning all military surveillance was removed. There was great rejoicing in Hornellsville, which had been cut off from the outside world since July 19th. Business had been practically suspended during the strike, which cost the Erie $1.3 million. It was a week before regular operations resumed. Donohue pleaded guilty to conspiracy and drew three months in the Steuben County jail.

Buffalo [4]

To understand the events to be narrated, R. V. Bruce's observation in his *Year of Violence* that ìthe Canal Street section of Buffalo was as lawless and depraved as any in the countryî should be kept in mind. [5] Canal Street ran southeasterly below the Erie Canal from Erie Street to Main and was about 300 yards from the Erie and New York Central terminals where much of the action took place. For locations mentioned below, see Figure #4.

Saturday, July 21

At about 1:00 A. M. Saturday, striking Erie switchmen, following the example of their brethren in Hornellsville, boarded a switch engine in the Erie passenger yard just east of the Erie's Buffalo depot at Exchange and Michigan streets and asked the engineer to take them to the East Buffalo Station, which adjoined the road's freight yards southeast of Babcock and William Streets. He agreed, supposing the head switchman was on the locomotive. When he had gone two blocks and discovered otherwise, he stopped, refusing to take his passengers any farther. They got off quietly, intending to walk to East Buffalo. The fireman, without whose services a locomotive could not long be conveniently operated, accompanied them, an indication that Buffalo's firemen were supporting the switchmen, something that was made explicit at a meeting of the firemen the next morning. Two hours later Charles Calligan, assistant superintendent of the Erie, wired Police Superintendent John Byrne for help. Byrne was a native of County Wicklow, Ireland, who came to America in 1844. He enrolled as captain in the 155th New York Volunteers in 1862, had his eye shot out at Spottsylvania in 1864, was captured, did time in Richmond's infamous Libby's Prison, and was paroled early in 1865. Mustered out as lieutenant colonel, he joined the recently organized Niagara Police Force in 1866 and became the first superintendent of the Buffalo Police Force. Mayor Philip Becker visited

VIII, 4

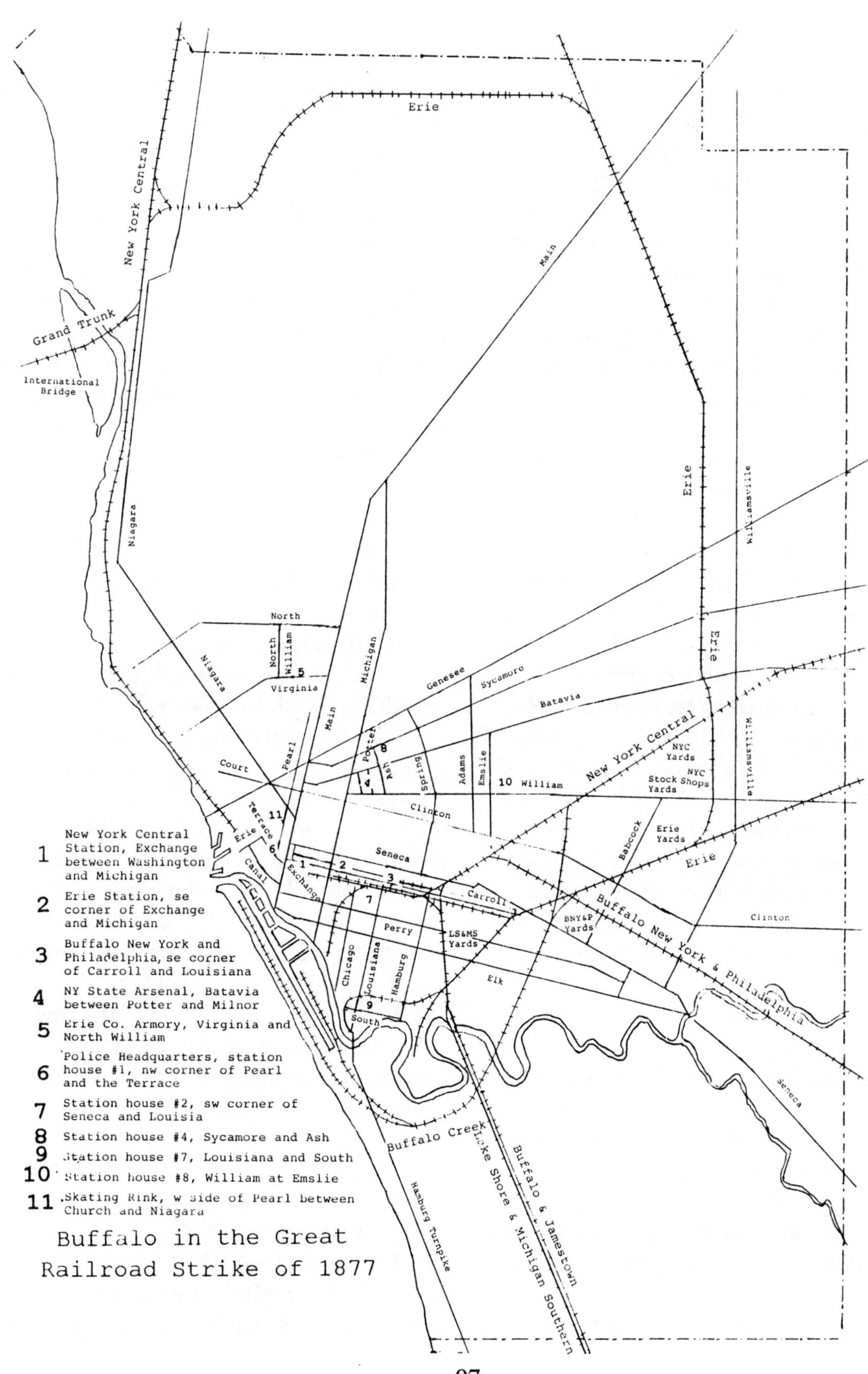

Buffalo in the Great Railroad Strike of 1877

Richard G. Taylor, superintendent of the Buffalo Division of the Erie, and told him that the 74th Regiment had already assembled and was ready to offer whatever aid was needed.

The *Erie Express* , due in Buffalo at 12:20 A. M., arrived thirty minutes late, having made the trip by way of Corning, Avon, and Attica instead of Hornellsville. (Figure III, #1.) Though the conductor reported no opposition from the strikers, after his train cleared Corning they blockaded the yard to prevent further train movement. Strikers boarded the engine at Buffalo and warned the crew to quit work immediately. They pointed out that if any engines were run out in the morning, the engineers would have to act as their own firemen.

Walter Licht, a historian of nineteenth century railroad labor, writes:

Through a conscious process of selection and rejection, engineers, conductors, brakemen, and firemen formed social ties within their own grades which were based on shared work and career experiences. This process reinforced the craft distinctions created, maintained, and encouraged by railroad managers. Engine drivers established their own social world, complete with singular customs and traditions and a developed argot. Firemen were allowed entry into this private universe, but only as junior members. Cabmen accordingly spent a good portion of their leisure hours in each other's company. They worked together as a team and the master-apprentice relationship strengthened the link. Relations, however, were not always frictionless. In hard times especially relations easily soured. When companies announced cutbacks during periods of retrenchment, it became a serious matter whether enginemen were to be laid off or demoted, thereby replacing the now endangered firemen. This festering issue, among others was responsible for the creation of separate craft unions among locomotive engineers and firemen. [5]

Interviews with prominent members of the local engineers' and conductors' brotherhoods revealed that neither had any intention of participating in the strike, and that they intended to adhere to their agreement to accept the July 1st reduction.

Saturday was the first full day of the strike of the Erie's brakemen and firemen at Buffalo. Policemen were stationed throughout the company's yards; but no demonstrations were made, and the day passed quietly. Some locals were run on the Buffalo Division from Attica to Hornellsville. At 6:00 P. M. the accommodation from Buffalo to Hornellsville steamed out of the Erie terminal. On arriving at East Buffalo, the fireman deserted his post at the orders of his striking brethren. Learning of this and fearing mischief, Calligan obtained a switch engine and, with police and a new fireman, headed east behind the accommodation. About a mile from East Buffalo the accommodation was flagged by one William Lahy, who with others boarded the engine and ordered the fireman off. Before he could do so the switch engine arrived, and Lahy was arrested, taken to police headquarters at Pearl and the Terrace, and charged with conspiracy.

When the train reached Attica it was met by strikers who had gone to Batavia on the Central and thence to Attica. They forced the fireman off and saw to it that the train was abandoned. Notice of this was telegraphed to the officials at Buffalo who applied to the military for aid. Immediately parts of Companies K and F of the 74th Regiment were ordered to entrain for Attica. Sixty soldiers were aboard the train when it left at 11:40 P. M. There was a large crowd at the depot to see them off, but no violence, though many feared for the safety of the train and its passengers. It arrived without incident at Attica about 1:30 A. M.

Buffalo's two National Guard regiments, the 65th and the 74th, consisted in theory of 780 officers and men each. Lewis M. Evans was Colonel of the 74th and Richard Flach of the 65th. The 65th's armory was the State Arsenal on Batavia Street, later Broadway,

VIII, 5

between Potter and Milnor. (Figure #5.) That of the 74th was on Virginia and North William, which latter street afterwards became part of an extended Elmwood Avenue. These regiments made up Buffalo's 31st Brigade under Brigadier General William F. Rogers, who had commanded the 21st Infantry Regiment during the Civil War. Major General Rufus L. Howard was commander of the 8th Division, which embraced all western New York.

Sunday, July 22

Late Saturday night, Erie strikers invaded the roundhouse and machine shop of the Lake Shore & Michigan Southern on the block bounded by Red Jacket, Scott, and Heacock Streets. From early Sunday morning the yards near the roundhouse were thronged by strikers and sympathizers. All trains were stopped and firemen forced off. Passenger trains arrived and departed on time until afternoon, but freight trains were embargoed. Other strikers stationed themselves at the Buffalo Creek bridge, halted a livestock train, and removed the fireman. The obstructionists, five firemen and four brakemen, were arrested and taken to #2 Station House on the southeast corner of Seneca and Louisiana Streets. They accompanied the officers quietly to the station house, where no attempt was made to rescue them. The train got through to East Buffalo but it was the last freight to do so for some time.

Toward noon, the crowd near the Lake Shore & Michigan Southern roundhouse steadily increased, the strikers receiving large accessions from uptown. About 2:00 o'clock, an attempt was made to take a train of loaded freight cars to East Buffalo, preparatory to sending it out on the road. Then the fun began. Engine #251 was attached to the cars, but all efforts to take the train out of the yard were unavailing. The strikers stationed themselves along the cars, pulled the pins, and threw them away. Captains John M. Flanagan of the 7th Precinct on Louisiana near South Street and Michael Donovan from headquarters, with about twenty other policemen, were on the scene giving what assistance they could. The officers were deployed along the cars to guard the couplings, but the crowd only laughed at them.

With the officers' attention distracted, some nimble fellow would pull a pin and run away to the cheers of his friends. The yardmaster wanted to get the train moving, since then the coupling pins could not be removed. For two hours he kept trying but was constantly thwarted. Finally, he got the train started, but it had gone only a short distance when a switch was thrown, and the train had to stop. Again a crowd gathered and, despite the efforts of the police, the train was cut in four or five places. The temper of the crowd was good-natured but determined. The vain efforts of the police to guard the couplings were jeered, but they themselves were not harmed. The yardmaster finally gave up and sent a message to the city for help.

Meanwhile, as ordered by Governor Robinson the previous day and despite trouble brewing in Buffalo, early Sunday afternoon the 74th Regiment (except the two companies sent to Attica the previous evening) left for Hornellsville. It numbered about 300 men under Lieutenant Colonel L. P. Reichert, Colonel Evans being out of the city. The train consisted of five passenger and two baggage cars, the latter filled with commissary stores and camp equipment. Reichert spent all Saturday and Sunday morning securing rations for the troops. Ample supplies of cooked hams, sausage, pressed beef, and bread were purchased from local merchants. Before leaving the armory, the troops were inspected by General Howard, who cautioned them to act with discretion but to do their duty as soldiers in case of emergency. At the depot there was a large crowd. Some were strikers, but the great majority were drawn by curiosity. A large force of police was in attendance, and after the soldiers were drawn up inside, the entrances were guarded and no spectators were allowed to enter without a pass. The train pulled out of the depot to the accompaniment of a few feeble shouts and reached Hornellsville shortly after 7:00 P. M., although for a long distance west of town the rails had been soaped. At 6:00 P. M. another train left for Hornellsville carrying General Howard and his staff.

Meanwhile, to keep the peace at home, shortly before the departure of the 74th the 65th was ordered under arms by Colonel Flach around noontime, and by 3:00 P. M. over 225 men had reported to the arsenal ready for duty. From there they were sent to the Erie depot. In very few cases was it necessary to dispatch a guard for the men, as almost all responded as soon as they knew their services were required. At 7:00 P. M. supper was served to the men at the station, no easy task since the 74th had exhausted the surplus provisions in town.

Back at the troubled LS&MS yards on Perry Street east of Van Rensselaer, after the first attempt to start a train was given up, members of the crowd circulated among themselves swapping rumors. One was that three or four companies of soldiers had been annihilated at Hornellsville, news that was greeted with cheers. There was an impression abroad that the strike had only just begun and that it would soon be general among all the employees on all the roads.

About 4:30 P. M. the railroad authorities made another effort to move a freight train but encountered the same opposition as before. Two policemen were stationed at each coupling, and finally part of the train was started up. Company A of the 65th Regiment then arrived with General Rogers. After about twenty-five soldiers were drawn up across the tracks, the crowd quickly gathered around and began hooting. The soldiers did not react until the crowd closed in and tried to take a musket from a private at the end of the line. He resisted and a scuffle ensued. General Rogers rushed over and was roughed up, but quickly drew his large revolver. The company was then placed in a car and taken back to the depot, since Rogers realized that the soldiers were too few for the job.

Shortly after 7:00 P. M. when the soldiers

returned to the city, the police arrested a man named Francis for creating a disturbance. He was escorted to #2 Station House followed by a howling mob which made desperate attempts to rescue him. Stones were thrown at the officers until they drew their revolvers. Sergeant John H. Conley was struck in the back of the head by a heavy stone and badly cut. Patrolman Dennis Maloney was also hit in the head and stunned. Patrolman Patrick Gilroy took a large stone full in his back, and Patrolman Michael Roach was struck in the arm. Francis was clubbed over the head two or three times, cut severely, and lodged in the station house overnight. The police were reinforced after this melee, but as darkness gathered the crowd began to grow more demonstrative, and stones were thrown with more abandon. Several bystanders were hit, none seriously. Even the Central's *Saint Louis Express* which left for New York at 8:40 P. M. was stoned as it passed through East Buffalo.

From headquarters all day Sunday policemen were dispatched to wherever the most violent demonstrations took place or trouble was anticipated. At the Erie depot there were thirty-five under Captain H. Schwartz of the 4th Precinct at Sycamore and Ash. At the LS&MS roundhouse there were about twenty-five under Sergeant Conely until he was injured. On guard along the tracks to East Buffalo and elsewhere were about twenty more. During the evening the arrangement was changed so that a larger detail was sent to East Buffalo, and at the other places the forces were cut down. They maintained excellent order, considering the crowds, and without their assistance the affair at the roundhouse would have been more serious.

Monday, July 23

Monday the excitement continued unabated. Wild rumors were flying about; and law-abiding residents and property owners were uneasy. No one could be sure of the temper of the mob, and, with the example of Pittsburgh in mind, it was natural for people to fear the worst. Rumors of threats from the strikers to burn railroad property at night were bruited about, and uptown everyone seemed to feel that a serious crisis was impending. On the East Side and around the railroad shops and depots the strikers were in control.

Nonetheless the soldiers guarding the shops were not bothered, and the police discharged their duties without interference. Three LS&MS cattle trains which had been stopped beyond the Buffalo Creek bridge on Sunday got through to the NYC's stockyards at William Street west of the Williamsville Road about 4:00 A.M. Monday. Later, however, a large crowd of strikers assembled at the East Buffalo yards. A stock train was made up about 9:00 A. M., but an attempt to start it failed. The crowd took over, forced the fireman and the brakemen off the train, and pulled the coupling pins. The livestock had to be unloaded and returned to the stock pens.

About 9:30 A. M. a large crowd of strikers descended upon the LS&MS roundhouse armed with clubs and stones and forced the employees to stop working. After the invaders left, Companies E, D, and G of the 65th Regiment were stationed at the roundhouse and guarded it throughout the day. The crowd moved on to the Erie machine shop at Louisiana and Exchange Streets which was guarded by Company A, 65th Regiment. The strikers pushed past the soldiers into the shop. All were told to quit working at once. The master mechanic wisely closed up shop immediately. No property was damaged.

The strikers believed that the military would not fire on them even if ordered. The conduct of the soldiers at the Erie machine shop seemed to prove this. A prominent strike leader explained the matter to an *Express* reporter:

We were determined to get into that shop and would have gone in there no matter what. When we approached the shop the soldiers told us to halt, and we stopped. One of the officers asked us where we were going, I said, "We are going in." He said, "If you do, we'll fire." Says I, "Captain, if you fire, you can kill only a few of us, and after that your life won't be worth one cent. You can only fire one volley before these men behind me will have your muskets. So you'd better let us pass." He said, "Well, all right, go ahead, but don't damage any property." Then they let us pass.

The mob that had stopped the stock train at East Buffalo next descended upon the Buffalo New York & Philadelphia shop at Seneca and Babcock Streets. All employees were driven out, and some firemen were taken off their engines. At noon all work there was abandoned. Early in the afternoon some 400 or 500 strikers and their sympathizers gathered at the Hamburg Street crossing of the Erie, the BNY&P, the LS&MS, and the NYC. Most were armed with heavy sticks and all appeared firm in their devotion to their cause. The strikers had agreed that there should be no resort to violence and that mail trains should be allowed to pass. This last resolution, it was said, was telegraphed to the government in Washington. During the whole afternoon the large and still growing crowd was quiet except when cheering the strikers' successes in stopping trains. However, most sympathizers made no attempt to join the strikers. Still there were many non-railroad workers who cursed loudly and made violent threats.

About 1:00 P. M. a train of the Buffalo & Jamestown, which entered Buffalo on Erie tracks, was halted at Hamburg Street, a favorite spot for the forced stopping of trains. Several strikers quietly boarded it and took the fireman and two brakemen off. The train then moved on. Shortly afterwards, the crowd hurried over to the NYC and tried to halt the express due at 2:50. The police, however, were too numerous and the strikers' efforts futile. After this, every engine that came along was stopped and the firemen removed. Several engines pulling cabooses on the BNY&P were brought to a standstill, and the firemen and the brakemen forced off. At 3:00 the crowd gathered at the Erie crossing on hearing that the Buffalo & Jamestown was going to send out another train. When it appeared, it was immediately boarded by the strikers. The crew offered no resistance. On learning that the B&J men's pay had not been reduced and that they had no desire to strike, the strike leaders allowed the train to proceed. The engine started up, but a troublemaker pulled the pin, causing the locomotive to go ahead alone. At the same time, the coach became separated from the baggage car. The strikers surrounded the baggage car and threatened to thrash anyone who tried to pull a pin. The coach was then coupled on by the strikers, and many of them walked along each side of the train and got on the platform until the train passed safely through the crowd. Two of the strikers then went through the car informing the passengers that they owed their safe passage to the strikers of the Erie and LS&MS.

At 4:00 P. M. Company C, 65th Regiment, was sent from the Erie depot to the former NYC shop at the junction of Seneca Street and Peacock Street which had been abandoned for a new shop at East Buffalo. A large crowd congregated around the building after the troops arrived, and urchins began to pelt the soldiers with stones. The strikers immediately checked this outburst and told the police captain that they deplored these acts and should not be held responsible for them. It was feared that an attempt would be made to burn the empty building but an 11:00 P. M. check uncovered no criminal activity. On the crossing outside, however, were numerous spectators, many of them women and girls. On a coal car a long pole was set up with a lantern on the top, illuminating a banner with the device, "We Will Let the Mail Go." Many similar placards had been printed for posting on railroads and buildings. All the strikers agreed that the mail must go through.

At quitting time a large delegation of strikers visited the NYC's machine shop near the stock yards. There was no violence, but the employees were ordered not to show up for work the next day. Nearly all assured the strikers that their order would be obeyed. In the evening Company K of the 74th returned from Attica where it had been stationed since Sunday and was detailed to duty at the NYC depot on Exchange Street. On the same train came the 4th Separate Company of Warsaw and the 5th Separate Company of Batavia. Both units were dispatched to the NYC's East Buffalo yards.

Meanwhile, at the Hamburg Street crossing, the crowd swayed backward and forward, charging about as rumors were spread; but nothing happened until a NYC passenger train came out from the city. It consisted of three coaches and a mail car and had left the depot at 6:00 P. M. Police were placed on the engine and on the platforms of the cars except between the baggage car and the first passenger coach. The train came along at some speed and for a while it looked as though it would get through unscathed. But then several men jumped onto the unguarded platform and set the brakes, stopping the train. The engine was surrounded, the fireman taken off, and the coaches were uncoupled from the mail car and pushed back to the depot. The engineer was then ordered to proceed with the mail car alone.

The crowd dwindled with the coming of darkness. So far no one here had been seriously injured. During the lull a group of strikers met and resolved that if anyone of them became intoxicated, he should be placed in protective custody so that no personal or property damage could be blamed on the strikers. At a meeting of the Brotherhood of Locomotive Engineers it was decided that Erie and LS&MS engineers would not work until the troubles were over.

Mayor Becker issued a statement that life and property in Buffalo were in great danger, that the military had been called out by the governor, and that the police force was doing its best, "and yet it is feared that these will not be sufficient and that the citizens themselves should take immediate action." His Honor invited law-abiding citizens to a public meeting at 7:30 P. M. "at the Skating Rink (on the west side of Pearl Street between Church and Niagara Streets) to consider what precautions, if any, should be adopted and what action should be taken . . . for the protection of the city." This document was printed in the evening papers, and 5,000 copies were distributed around the city in the shape of small handbills. At the same time the Common Council authorized the Mayor and the Board of Police to appoint as many special policemen as necessary "to preserve the public peace." Railroad workers present at the meeting agreed to act as special patrolmen, if needed, and to abstain from intoxicating liquors during the strike. A committee appointed by the meeting resolved that "the Mayor be requested to enroll two thousand citizens who will volunteer for general duty, who shall, when a signal is given, be ready to move at a moment's warning, for the protection of the lives and property of the city." The mayor was instructed to be at the office of the Police Commissioner at 9:00 next morning to swear in the special policemen.

First blood was shed on Monday. At 9:30 P. M. a LS&MS train with Westfield's militia company aboard was stopped at the bridge over Buffalo Creek. As later described by its captain, J. H. Towle, the unit left Westfield with fifty-seven men. On arrival at the NYC depot ten were missing and seven wounded. The survivors were covered with mud and their coats were torn. When the train was halted and surrounded at the bridge, Towle addressed the rioters, and his words seemed to have a quieting effect. However the obstructionists demanded that the soldiers give up their arms, after which they would be allowed to continue on to the city. This the captain refused to order his men to do. The demands of the rioters were supported by drawn revolvers. Since none of the Westfield men had ever seen active service, some of them thought their last hour had arrived. The rioters wrested some rifles from the militia, whereupon Towle gave orders to clear the car, and the main body of his men set about doing it. Then firing commenced. The mob fired through the windows and doors, and the soldiers from inside the cars. The company got out on the tracks and fired another volley which put to flight the rioters, a dozen of whom were badly wounded, including a carpenter whose left arm had to be amputated. The captain led his men, two of whom were so badly injured that they had to be carried, along a road leading to the Hamburg Turnpike. They were put up at the residence of Dr. Dennis B. Wiggins which stood on a twenty acre tract near Lake Erie in the part of West Seneca that later became Lackawanna. A druggist whose store adjoined the Western Savings Bank at Main and Court Streets, Wiggins attended to the wounded and served the whole company breakfast next morning. None of the injured militiamen died. Of the rioters eighteen year old Michael Lyons who was not a railroader was killed, and seven others were wounded, including John Cleary, Patrick Brahan, James Hickey, and Michael Murphy. To rescue the badly demoralized Westfield company, Captain Henry W. Linderman's company of artillery was sent from Buffalo and spent the night guarding the bridge.

One of the cars that carried the militia from Westfield was set afire near the LS&MSís roundhouse at Heacock and Porter Streets. This was the first instance of destruction of property at Buffalo. The crowd, 500 strong, surrounded the burning car and refused to let anyone approach. An alarm was sent to Chemical Engine #2 at Chicago and Folsom, but on its arrival the mob threatened the firemen if they tried to put out the fire. An alarm was sounded later from box #127 on Perry Street by the LS&MS shops, and more firemen responded. On arriving they were received with shouts of derision and taunts of "Go home and put out the fire in your stoves!" Seeing there was no danger of the flames spreading to nearby buildings, Fire Department Superintendent Thomas B. French ordered his men back. The crowd was made up chiefly of frenzied young men who seemed capable of anything. Several times during the burning of the car they proposed to push it down to the roundhouse and burn it up. But cooler heads prevailed, and the proposal was not carried out. The crowd was in an ugly mood, and warnings were issued that if soldiers interfered any further they would be killed. Threats were also made that this was only the beginning, and that worse was to follow.

Tuesday, July 24

Tuesday was the fourth day of intense anxiety for Buffalonians. The bloody riot of the previous night raised the specter of anarchy and mob rule. All over the city throughout the day clusters of people discussed the situation and exchanged sensational reports. Many called for the most summary measures in dealing with the troublemakers. Others thought that the melee with the militia had taught the mob a lesson. Still others believed that the success of the rioters at the Buffalo Creek bridge - it was not clear which side, if either, had won - would only incite them to further acts of lawlessness. Not much censure or indignation was expressed against the railroad men, but the role played by roughs and tramps in the disturbances was redounding to the discredit of the strikers.

Tuesday was a repetition of Monday as far as crowds were concerned. After an exciting night, mobs were up early to prevent the arrival or departure of any trains. At the shops and on the railroads they gathered in force, but as most trains had been canceled, the crowds were at a loss what to do. Knots of people wandered about uneasily, and whenever the incident at the bridge was mentioned, the Westfield militia was bitterly denounced.

Threats were aired to capture and hang Captain Towle, and the more violent declared that not one man of the company would ever go back to Westfield alive.

In the morning a delegation of the strikers waited on Postmaster Isaac M. Schermerhorn to assure him they would not interfere with the movement of the mail. They even volunteered men to take the mail trains through in safety. The postmaster declined the offer, saying that postal clerks would not take the responsibility of going except on the regularly scheduled passenger trains, most of which carried mail cars.

At 9:30 A. M. about 150 turbulent men and boys confronted the employees of the Niagara Grain Elevator and demanded that they quit work immediately. They replied that they were satisfied with their wages and declined to join the riot. On the arrival of a squad of policemen, the agitators left but headed for the City Elevator, the principal grain elevator of the NYC railroad, where they made a similar demand. Once again the police were on hand and once again the workers declined to join in the work stoppage. Both elevators continued unloading lake vessels and loading canal boats. No railroad cars, however, were loaded at City Elevator.

Another mob, composed largely of tramps, boys, and women, stormed Boler & Rechtenwalt's planing mill (a woodworking establishment) at Chicago and Carroll Streets and Quipp & Duke's lumber yard on the north side of Seneca west of Michigan where the employees were compelled to stop work. Early in the afternoon the heavers employed by George Dakin, agent for the Anthracite Coal Company, in its coal yard by the docks at the foot of Genesee Street, struck for higher wages. Some of these strikers went to a nearby stone yard to incite the men there to strike. The police were notified, and strike leader Fred Maison was arrested by Patrolman Hugh Kennedy and taken to police headquarters. The strikers were, according to the Express, ignorant Mecklenburgers, victims of "strike fever, who didn't know what they wanted." Another crowd broke into John T. Noyes's lumber yard on Washington Street to persuade the men to quit work. The police were informed and quickly scattered the troublemakers. Other ineffectual attempts to promote a general strike were made at Jewett & Root's stove works at Perry and Mississippi and at the nearby steam engine factories of Farrar & Treft on Perry Street, George W. Tifft on lower Washington Street, and Dempster & Comstock across the way at 19 Main Street. The police dispersed the mob, whose thirsty members then headed off for their favorite saloons.

On the East Side scare tactics were more successful. About 200 men and boys proceeded up Exchange Street shortly before noon. They visited the Buffalo Scale Works on 332 and Drullard & Hayes's Foundry at 344 Exchange Street. In both places they made an unopposed entrance and ordered all the men to put on their coats and leave. They obeyed and the firm closed for the day. The car wheel works of J. C & N. Scoville at Louisiana Street and the Main and Hamburg Canal were also targeted by the mob and the employees forced to go home. Yet another gang operated on Clinton Street, invading the tannery of Laub & Zeller near the NYC crossing, the planing mill and bellows factory of Joseph Churchill at Clinton and Adams, the tin works of Sidney Shepherd across the street, and the Buffalo Bolt & Nut Works of Plumb Burdict & Barnard near the corner of Clinton and Watson.

A fourth band of strikers marched out William Street on a similar mission. They compelled the carpenters to suspend work on the new hog yards. Then they turned back to the Farthing Distillery at William and Spring Streets. They were boisterous and turbulent and, as they passed #8 Station House on the north side of William near Emslie, a squad of officers swooped out and arrested a ringleader. After driving off the workmen the intruders did not damage any shops or factories. Their object seemed to be, as one sturdy fellow put it, "to keep up the excitement."

As requested by Mayor Becker, a strikers' committee met in his office in the afternoon. Lauren C. Woodruff said that he belonged to a citizens committee appointed to confer with Receiver Jewett of the Erie to devise some means for stopping the strike. Referring to the excitement in the city, he stated that the people were observing the strikers closely and would blame them for any violence. Michael Callahan, speaking for the Erie's engineers, said they had no grievances, but had joined in the stoppage for the sake of the firemen and brakemen who were out of work and wanted their jobs back. He agreed with Woodruff on the need to keep order and claimed that none of the railroaders meant to harm the city. Tenth Ward Alderman P. J. Ferris supported Callahan but observed that that there were those in the guise of strikers who were harming the strikers' cause. He told the strikers present, "I believe you have rights and that they have been trampled on."

Bowing to the demand made upon him by the general superintendent of the NYC, James Tillinghast, Sheriff Joseph L. Haberstro summoned special deputy sheriffs to aid in protecting property and suppressing demonstrations. About 300 men responded, a large number from the Ninth and Tenth Wards (the West Side) being notified shortly after 6:00 P. M. At 7:30 the deputies, who had assembled in the grand jury room of the courthouse, were distributed among the different station houses where they were issued batons and badges. The regular sheriff's deputies were sent out into the country to enlist additional forces. Proprietors of shops and factories were instructed to tell the sheriff how many men they needed to guard their properties. About 500 special policemen were sworn in and assigned to station houses. During the afternoon a threat was received at #2 Station House that unless the prisoners confined there, who had been arrested for inciting to riot, were released by 4:00 P. M. the station would be stormed, the police overpowered, and the prisoners set free. Precautions were taken to prevent any such attempt.

By Tuesday these militia companies were quartered at the Exchange Street Station: 74th Regiment, Company K, 60 men; 65th Regiment, Company F, 35 men; Company D, 50 men; Company G, 43 men; Company H, 8 men; Battery A, 60 men; Cavalry Troop, 60 men; 6th Separate Company, Niagara Light Guards from Lockport, 64 men; 4th Separate Company, Warsaw, 64 men; 5th Separate Company, Batavia; 2nd Separate Company Westfield, 34 men. Old soldiers were also heard from. Members of the G. A. R. assembled at the office of the Firemen's Benevolent Association in the Young Men's Association Building at Clinton and Washington at 7:30 P. M. to discuss volunteering as patrolmen or deputy sheriffs. A committee waited on the mayor, and seventy-three Civil War veterans reported to City Hall for duty. Their first assignment was to guard the arsenal. The mayor announced that a large number of "good men and true" had responded to the call for special patrolmen. "I do hereby admonish and advise every citizen," he added, "to keep himself and those under his charge within his own domicile between the hours of 10:00 P. M. and 5:00 A. M." He also ordered all places of business to be closed during the same hours.

In the evening a party of strikers rode out on handcars to Dr. Wiggins's home in West Seneca where some of the wounded Westfield soldiers were being treated. The strikers denied any intention of harming the wounded; but to forestall mischief some of them were removed to safety further south and two were brought to City Hospital on High Street in carriages. Some suspected that the strikers were looking for Captain Towle. Later, thugs called at the home of Mrs. Erastus Clar[?] on Franklin near Allen demanding money, saying if she refused they would ransack her house. Frightened and alone, the woman complied, and the unwelcome guests departed. At 10:40 P. M. an alarm was sounded after a fire was discovered in some freight cars at the NYC's East Buffalo yards. Another car near Jacob Dold's slaughterhouse on West Market Street between Scott and Perry was torched. Both fires were put out before much damage was done. The alarm caused great excitement, and within minutes the streets were alive with spectators.

Wednesday, July 25th

Shortly after midnight a huge throng of men and boys drawn by curiosity gathered near the depots on Exchange Street. By morning there was such a crush of people on the adjoining tracks that Company K, 74th Regiment, and Companies of the 65th tried to drive them off. The police charged the mob and drove it back to Michigan Street, clearing the tracks. Shortly afterwards the crowd dispersed.

Overall the feeling throughout the city Wednesday was one of somewhat diminished anxiety. The prompt measures of citizens and authorities, the reinforcement of the troops by special police and deputy sheriffs, and the arrival of a regiment from Auburn had a reassuring effect. Law-abiding people relaxed, judging that although the disaffected might be disposed to violence, the force which had been mobilized against them was more than adequate. But authorities did not relax their vigilance. Special policemen continued to be sworn and were sent out as needed. Among the special police were Rev. George W. Cutler, Pastor of the Unitarian Church, Rev. Darius H. Muller, Pastor of Grace Methodist Episcopal Church, and Rev. Dr. L. Van Bokkelen of Trinity Church. Buses were stationed at police headquarters to carry police promptly to trouble spots. Military surveillance of the depots was continued, and the streets, so far as possible, kept clear. The strikers indulged in bitter threats but were overawed by the large force of military and police. The spirit of violence was ebbing, and all signs indicated a speedy return to peace. Still, all the strikers questioned by reporters were determined not to return to work until the railroads yielded to their demands.

The 49th Regiment of Auburn, which was ordered to the city by Adjutant General Townsend following a request from Mayor Becker, arrived at 7:00 A. M. The unit had left Auburn at midnight and came through over the NYC without incident. On reaching the city the regiment marched to the Skating Rink where it was quartered during the morning. It numbered 325 men, strapping specimens, many of whom, unlike the hapless Westfield troopers, had seen hard service in the late war. They were led by General Clinton D. MacDougall, United States Marshall for the Northern District of New York, an ex-congressman who had served with distinction in the Civil War and commanded a brigade of the state militia. The men of the regiment, known as Shield's Guard, were uniformed in gray and presented a soldierly appearance. At 10:00 A. M. they marched to the NYC depot to relieve the soldiers on duty who retired to the Arsenal and the North William Street Armory. The Batavians who had been guarding the depot were treated to dinner at the Terrapin Restaurant by Samuel Seymour, passenger agent for the Northern Central Railroad.

Crowds were astir since early in the morning. About the depots on Exchange Street, at the LS&MS switching yard near Elk Street, in East Buffalo, and at other points knots of people mustered, most armed with sticks and ready for action but without leaders. The special policemen were hooted at but most kept their mouths shut to avoid further confrontation.

At about 9:00 A. M., a large crowd of men and boys went to Haines & Company's lumber yard at the foot of Erie Street to scare off the workers. Help was summoned. Sergeant Conley and a squad of police responded quickly, and the crowd fled. Hugh O'Melia and

Michael Dorlan were arrested and taken to headquarters where they were jailed. Two hours later the mob returned bent on more mischief. Help was again summoned, and Sergeant Edward G. Burns answered the call with twenty bluecoats who charged the crowd in dashing style, laying about them with their batons and scattering the crowd. Fourteen were arrested and jailed at headquarters. The lumber yard was quiet for the rest of the day.

Shortly after 1:00 P. M., a large mob gathered at Dakin's coal yard near the corner of Louisiana and Ohio Streets. About seventy-five employees joined the crowd. Disorderly demonstrations broke out, and eighteen patrolmen were sent from #1 under command of Sergeants Conley and Burns to aid Captain Flanagan in dispersing the mob. Officers Gorman, Collins, and Sweeney were injured, but not seriously. The mob resisted fiercely but could not stand up before expertly wielded batons.

About thirty men resumed work at the yard after the disturbers of the peace had left. They returned at 3:00 P. M., however, breathing vengeance against the men in the yard and threatening to lynch them if they did not stop working. Help was again requested from headquarters, and Sergeants Burns and Conley arrived with twenty men. Together with Captain Flanagan's detachment they divided into three sections and with a dash charged the disorderly from different directions. Batons fell with telling impact right and left. The mob wavered for a moment, then turned and fled. Stones were thrown, and Officer Thomas Dowd was hit and slightly injured. About thirty employees guarded by two lines of police were safely escorted back to work, though hooted at along the way. Their tormentors dared not attack them. Two of the ringleaders of the demonstration were arrested and jailed.

An incident of man-to-man encounter was related by an eye witness. Phillip McDonell, a muscular stevedore who was unloading the *Annie L. Craig* at the foot of Lloyd Street at about 2:00 P. M., was accosted by a burly ruffian named Carroll who ordered him to stop work and join the strikers. McDonell refused, saying he had a family to support and could not afford to leave his job. Carroll, without parley, struck McDonell a terrific blow in the mouth. McDonell turned on his assailant and forced the fighting until Carroll took to his heels. He fled into Vosburgh & Baker's, ship chandlers on NYC Wharf, with McDonell in pursuit. When Carroll got inside, McDonell tripped him up and pummeled him until he roared for mercy. After disposing of his tormentor, McDonell, whose dander was now fully aroused, strode into the street and asked if any other striker wanted to tackle him. He had no takers. Carroll was arrested and taken to headquarters where he was attended to by Police Surgeon Byron H. Daggett, who set his fractured jaw.

Other violent episodes occurred on Wednesday. A drunk, Frederick Danebrook, entered Louis Sandman's bakery on Ellicott Street and Barton Alley about 2:00 P. M. with a gun and ordered the men there to stop working. His description was given to two specials who quickly collared him. He was committed to jail by Superintendent Byrne himself. Around 4:00 P. M. a large crowd gathered on Chicago Street between Seneca Street and the railroad where a disturbance quickly developed. Special Policeman Persall arrested one of the crowd but was set upon and his prisoner released. Persall sent for assistance and twenty regular policemen were soon on hand, followed by thirteen mounted men. Superintendent Byrne, who was passing by, jumped out of his carriage and led the police. The crowd broke up into small clusters, but took no hostile action, except for hurling an occasional insult. While driving the crowd off the street corner, Officer Thomas Driscoll of #2 Precinct arrested John Howard, an Erie switchman, and Detective John Riley took into custody Valentine Gallestone, a railroad fireman. The crowd thereupon dispersed.

On the NYC no trains arrived or departed except the one carrying the Auburn militia. On the LS&MS a like inaction prevailed. Superintendent William P. Taylor tried to send out the 12:40 P. M., but the strikers warned him that they would not allow it through, so he gave up the idea. Only one mail train on the Erie got through, and the 6:00 P. M. from Hornellsville did not arrive until after 11:00. On the BNY&P all trains were canceled, though a mail train was scheduled for the next day. In the afternoon a train arrived from Jamestown on the B&J. The passengers were unloaded at Tifft Street and taken to the city in omnibuses. A train was started for Jamestown from the same location. The passengers arrived there in hacks and buses from the company's office on Main Street.

Trains on the Great Western were running regularly to and from Fort Erie. Passengers from Buffalo were sent down to Black Rock on Niagara Street horsecars and taken across the International Bridge on a dummy engine. No trouble was anticipated for passenger runs on the Great Western, although all freight trains were canceled. On the Canada Southern a train due in Buffalo Tuesday night did not arrive until 2:00 P. M. Wednesday, having been delayed by strikers at Hagersville and Bismarck. The morning train from Niagara arrived safely. The regular afternoon train to Niagara, however, was stopped at Victoria at the western end of the International Bridge by the strikers who pulled a coupling pin and extinguished the fire in the engine. Suddenly, all train operations on the Canada Southern were halted. At Saint Thomas, the strikers occupied the depot but made arrangements to protect railroad property. They notified Tillinghast, who doubled as president of the Canada Southern, that they would allow mail trains to pass, but he declined, he said, to "operate mail trains by courtesy of the mob."

Alternate means of transportation were being devised. From the pier at the foot of Main Street a tug, the *O. H. Nolton*, took on passengers for Dunkirk. A traveler from Rochester took the NYC's Falls Road to Niagara, Ontario, and thence via the last train to run on the Canada Southern to Fort Erie. A traveler from Syracuse reached Buffalo on the NYC's Falls Road to Lockport and from there by carriage. Without Buffalo's extensive yards, the Falls Road was less crippled by the strike than Buffalo's railroads.

Thursday, July 26th

At 12:30 A. M. it was announced that a committee of Erie switchmen, brakemen, and firemen at Hornellsville had accepted the terms offered by the railroad and ended their strike. They agreed to the wage cut as described above. The ranking official of the road at Buffalo ordered yardmasters and other employees to get trains running again at once. However, a misunderstanding arose between the strikers on the Erie at Buffalo and those at Hornellsville. The Buffalonians had struck for a recission of the July 1st wage cut, while in Hornellsville the main object was the reinstatement of the discharged committee members. Many of the Buffalo strikers were not happy with the settlement made by their Hornellsville brethren.

Nevertheless, Erie officials at Buffalo decided to run all their regularly scheduled trains during the day. Shortly after 8:00 A. M., the Elmira mail train left with a squad of police under charge of Sergeant Conley. Before it could be started, die-hard strikers drove the fireman off the engine, but another was obtained, and the train pulled out for Attica, which it reached without further incident. At the outskirts of the city police boarded westbound #7 which arrived at Buffalo at 1:00 P. M. bringing back many residents stranded for several days in eastern cities. The Erie's Niagara Falls train left at noon with only four policemen aboard. On its arrival at the Hamburg Street crossing, four blocks from the station, it was stopped by a mob which uncoupled the cars, pushed the coaches back to the depot, and permitted the mail car to proceed. A squad of police from #2 Precinct led by Superintendent Byrne was soon on the scene. The crowd was quickly dispersed after the club had been freely used. Daniel O'Leary, C. O'Leary, and Louis Primo were arrested on a charge of riot, and thirty-eight others were taken into custody for blocking the sidewalk. The train was afterwards reassembled and dispatched to the Falls. During the afternoon the Erie's regular trains left as scheduled and went through without any trouble. Most were filled with passengers. Regular freights were scheduled for Friday, and no further interruption was expected from the strikers.

Although no formal agreement was made between the LS&MS and the strikers, it was decided to send trains out anyway. At 12:40 P. M. the first passenger train on the road since the beginning of the strike headed west. It was filled with passengers and proceeded without molestation. No police were on board since Superintendent Taylor had been assured that it would not be stopped. The 5:00 P. M. accommodation departed safely, but after that no trains were dispatched. The passenger train from the west due at Buffalo at 1:30 P. M. arrived shortly before 3:00 without any interference by strikers. It had waited for an hour at Hamburg for orders. Its consist was two mail cars, a baggage car, and seven passenger cars. Freight trains were yet to run since some of the freight engineers refused to go out on the road with inexperienced firemen.

NYC officials, believing that the back of the strike had been broken, planned to resume passenger service. The regular 2:40 P. M. eastbound was made up, but its departure was delayed to connect with the LS&MS's delayed eastbound. Conversation aboard the ten car NYC train was animated, as passengers who had been detained in Buffalo or points west expressed their pleasure in many ways. Freights were also dispatched and encountered no obstacles.

Superintendent Peter Doyle of the B&J sent out the regular accommodation from the Erie depot in the afternoon. The ubiquitous Sergeant Conley and a police detachment were stationed in the baggage car, but there was no need for their services. The train stopped at Hamburg where the police got out and boarded the northbound, which they guarded on its approach to Buffalo where it arrived at 6:00 P. M. While at Hamburg, Doyle treated the police to lunch at Drummers' Hotel. The BNY&P and the Grand Trunk resumed regular passenger service with freight trains scheduled for Friday. No trains as yet moved on the Canada Southern, but a regular schedule was announced for Friday. The general superintendent of the Northern Central advertised that "our passenger trains are all running through and about on time. Sleepers to Philadelphia and Washington have been running as usual." There was no trouble on the Great Western, since none of its employees had gone on strike.

The 74th Regiment under command of Colonel Reichert returned from Hornellsville at 6:15 P. M., having left there at 6:15 A. M. Wednesday. (Twelve hours to cover ninety one miles! Regularly scheduled expresses did it in five.) The strikers at Hornellsville and their sympathizers quickly learned that the 74th meant business. While there, the soldiers did guard duty or piloted trains. On arrival in Buffalo, the regiment garrisoned the NYC depot until the next day.

After the tumult of the early part of the week Buffalo was fast resuming its normal tranquillity. There were no crowds or demonstrations on the streets. In East Buffalo, along the main lines, and on Elk Street, where mobs rallied on previous days, scarcely anybody was to be seen. The strikers were less defiant and confined themselves to denouncing railroad management for oppressing the working man. They were beginning to fear the loss of their jobs. Many even declared that they had never sympathized with the strike. Little incentive remained for obstructing trains. Two muskets lost by the Westfield Company in the fracas Monday night were recovered by Patrolman Quinn of #7 in a house on Folsom Street. The Police Commissioner stopped swearing in specials. Nine hundred had taken the oath.

Friday, July 27th

On the Erie few signs remained of the violence the road had just experienced. Passenger trains ran regularly along with several freights. On the LS&MS passenger trains arrived and departed on time, though the freight engineers held out. Superintendent Taylor warned that they had until Monday to report for work, after which no-shows would be discharged. On the NYC all trains were running regularly. One hundred and forty-four stock cars left East Buffalo together with other categories of freight cars. All employees had returned to work except for a few the superintendent refused to take back. The strike continued on the Canada Southern where President Tillinghast reiterated his determination to make no concessions to the strikers until they went back to work.

All the out-of-town military organizations left the city, the Batavia and Warsaw companies on special morning trains. The embattled Westfield company left on the LS&MS at 12:55 P. M., escorted to the depot by Battery A. At about 3:00 P. M. the more popular 49th Regiment left for Auburn on another special train, a departure attended by General Rogers and his staff. The Light Guards from Lockport returned home in the afternoon. Buffalo's own 74th Regiment assembled at the armory at 6:00 P. M. and was dismissed with thanks. Each of the city's charitable organizations was invited to send a representative to the Skating Rink next morning between nine and ten when the unused commissary stores would be equally divided.

Patrolmen Dugan and William F. Stage of #2 traced John Clary (*alias* "Reddie Jack") to a house on Perry Street, reputedly the home of his girlfriend who had concealed him the past few days. He was taken to headquarters and from there to jail. Clary, a switchman, was reportedly one of the most prominent organizers of the work stoppage and the leader in all the brawls in which the strikers engaged. He was also believed to have led the assault on the Westfield company at the Buffalo Creek bridge. Other alleged strike leaders, William Quirk, William Burtiss (*alias* "Dirty Dick"), Frederick Frelberger, Joseph Scott, and Christopher Capperson, were also apprehended and imprisoned.

By Friday, most Buffalonians were in a congratulatory mood. Many boasted that they would have taken a hard line and crushed the outbreak of violence the very first day if they had been in charge. These critics notwithstanding, most citizens approved the restraint of the authorities. The affair ended with little loss of life, unlike what happened at Pittsburgh and Chicago. General Rogers and his officers deserved credit for their discretion in not firing into turbulent crowds, a tactic which would probably have killed more innocent spectators than guilty toughs. There was no blunder in the use of the troops. Except for the melee on Monday night at Buffalo Creek, which could scarcely have been provided against, bloodshed was prevented and law maintained by the simple power of civil authority backed by the presence of the military.

The *Express* concluded its coverage of the strike week in Buffalo with an editorial on Saturday, July 28th:

It seems certain that one of the results of the recent riots will be the increase by the next congress of our standing army. The fact that a few companies of readily available troops might have prevented the strike by promptly suppressing the demonstration at Martinsburg is an effective answer to those who have argued that the country needs no army beyond its militia. It is evident that the army will have to be larger than it now is to form sufficient protection against outbreaks like the one we have just passed through. While there is every reason for sustaining and encouraging the state militia, it is clear that it is not well calculated for occasions like riotous outbreaks. While the men lack nothing in personal courage and in case of invasion or military service of any legitimate kind would be of great service, there are reasons why they are not so valuable in suppressing riots. The chief is that the principal use of the military is to overawe the mob by its presence. The work of dispersing crowds can best be done by police, who, however, need the support of the military; but it has often been proved that the presence of the United States soldiers has much more influence than the presence of militia. The reason why police have proved much more effective than militia is because suppressing riots is really their function. They may go ahead, fearless of consequences, striking right and left with their clubs, while the militiaman must stand back, the target for insults and brickbats, and must not use his weapon - the musket - till matters have gone to extremes. It is to be hoped that a way will be found for removing the cause and so preventing in the best way strikes and violent demonstrations. But it is not safe nor profitable to be without means for meeting and suppressing formidable mobs in every city in the Union.

Bruce thus concludes his brief account of the strike at Buffalo:

It was Buffalo's regular police force that took the honors [for breaking the strike]. *Throughout Tuesday's disturbances, squads of police had effectively broken up roving bodies of rioters. The showdown came at the NYC 's East Buffalo depot at dusk. An unruly mob of boys and tramps (but no railroad men) pelted the depot with stones and threatened to burn it. They did burn a freight car and dismantle a flagman's shanty. When they stoned and blackguarded the police detachment, Captain Philip Wurtz of #8 Precinct summoned a wagon load of reinforcements. A feint by a few policemen distracted the mob while Wurtz formed a line of seventy-five police across the wide street at the rioters backs. 'Now boys, slash 'em!' shouted Captain Wurtz and the charge began. In the appreciative words of the* Weekly Courier: *'Like lightening the clubs descended and descended. Every stroke hit a new head whose owner went solid to the ground or bowled in continued somersaults. The officers seemed to put their whole souls into this commendable work . . . Those who did not get hit fled as fast as their legs could carry them, and . . . a howling chorus of pain could be heard at the high trestle more than a mile away. The rout was complete and final.' Next day rioters made sporadic attempts to invade mills and shops but were frightened off easily by the newly respected constabulary.* [6]

The house historian of the NYC lightly dismissed the strike as it affected his subject:

The LS&MS men decided to go out on the 21st. Bee Line [Cleveland Columbus Cincinnati & Indianapolis, another Vanderbilt line] *trainmen and shopmen in Cleveland reported for duty on the morning of the 23rd, but there was such a crowd of the disaffected there to interfere with and threaten them that management thought it best to declare a holiday. Cattle, hogs, and chickens died by thousands from starvation, thirst, and suffocation on stalled trains at Cleveland. There was greater loyalty on the NYC. Shopmen at West Albany and Syracuse went out, and some others at Buffalo, where they were influenced by the LS&MS and Erie strikers. There was little or no disorder anywhere on the NYC. Freight movement was halted for about three days, but passenger service was affected hardly at all.* [Sic.] *The LS&MS strike gradually faded on the 28th and 29th, with no concessions by management, which was true practically everywhere. On October 3, half of the wage cut* [on the NYC] *was restored, and in February, 1880, full salaries were back in force. After that they began rising.* [7]

The Strike Moves West [8]

By Monday, July 23, the strike had spread though Ohio, Indiana, and Illinois and into Kentucky, Missouri, and Iowa. In Ohio the LS&MS and the Ohio & Mississippi suspended operations, the Bee Line and the Cincinnati Hamilton & Dayton canceled the pay cut, the Atlantic & Great Western had never initiated one. Some leadership was provided by locals of the Brotherhoods and the Trainmen's Union, but the national officers of the brotherhoods adopted a hands off policy. Increasingly, the strike, its impact heightened by sensational reporting, sparked violence by marginal groups.

An element of ideology appeared as the strike moved west. Communist ideas had been introduced to America by English and German socialists. The property conscious saw the violence which accompanied the strike as a reenactment of the horrors of the Paris Commune of 1871, and employers branded all union activity as communistic and un-American. In Cincinnati, the German Section of the Workingman's Party of the United States (WPUS) sponsored a parade followed by speeches which portrayed communists as friends of the workers. However, party leaders opposed violence and advocated measures like the eight hour day and nationalization of the railroads.

Misery was rampant among the lower classes of Chicago, the hub of the nation's railroad system, where the large foreign-born population was susceptible to communist propaganda. With an organization, a program, and a string of practiced speakers, the WPUS made a bid for strike leadership. On Monday the 23rd the party sponsored a rally where thousands were inflamed by speeches calling for support of the strike, nationalization of the railroads, and class warfare if the minions of capitalism fired on working men. The next day switchmen struck the Michigan Central and marched through its shops and freight houses closing them down. Strident teenagers soon shut down all freight traffic.

The mayor ordered Chicago armories under guard. At his request the Secretary of War directed six companies of regulars traveling east from Dakota to stop over at Chicago. The mayor also closed the saloons and ordered firebells, reminiscent of Baltimore, to be rung summoning militiamen to their armories. Few showed up. Civil War veterans assembled, and six more companies of regular army infantry were transferred from Omaha to Rock Island, a trouble spot on the Chicago Rock Island & Pacific. Hundreds of special policemen were sworn in, as the local WPUS called for a nationwide general strike for the eight hour day and an across the board twenty percent wage hike.

On Wednesday gangs shut factories and businesses. The Chicago & Alton and the Burlington halted passenger service. A teenage mob tried to close down the MC yards, but the police let the young rowdies have it with billies. It was all over in five minutes. That evening a few police were repulsed when they tried the same at the Burlington yards where a motley lot of strikers, workers, and punks were enforcing compliance with the strike. When bullets would not stop the advancing mob, now numbering in the thousands, the police retreated to the yards. There, picking up reinforcements, they went on the offensive. The fleeing mob left behind nine wounded, three fatally. That evening two companies of hardened veterans of war against the Sioux and the Cheyenne arrived in Chicago.

Wednesday's rioting moved the mayor to ask President Hayes to order the regular army to play a more active role in Chicago. The President did so. A hundred Illinois Central and Chicago & Northwestern employees were deputized to guard the property of their employers. The G. A. R. mobilized, and in most of the wards of the city citizens patrols were organized. But it was the police who took the lead in Thursday's showdown, which began at the Halsted Street viaduct where a large and nasty mob gathered. Rioters cut telegraph lines, stoned and stopped streetcars, and terrorized anyone who was well dressed. In midmorning a police squad charged the mob which fled across the viaduct and down the opposite slope where they were met by 5,000 enraged rioters. Stones of the mob were answered by pistol fire from the police. Then some rioters commenced firing. Police bullets dropped man after man in the crowd, which pressed on relentlessly. Running out of ammunition, the police fled, with the mob in hot pursuit. A block from the viaduct, the retreating police were met by more of their own and a company of mounted militia. (Figure #6.) The augmented forces of law and order rallied and scattered the rioters into side streets, at which point a company of regulars showed up.

All afternoon Halsted Street swarmed with thousands, mostly in groups of 100 or more. Police and mounted militia constantly harassed them. Brief scuffles kept breaking out, adding to the dead and wounded. A crowd would scatter at the approach of the cavalry and reassemble after the troopers cantered past. The 1st National Guard Regiment, several hundred regulars, and special police set up a base near 12th and Halsted from which detachments were sent out as needed.

In mid-afternoon police and mounted militia broke up a mob on Canal Street. During the fighting, mobs continued to terrorize the city's factories. At stockyards and the gasworks, employers were made to sign promises to raise wages. They did so gladly since the promises were unenforceable. Lake vessels swung at anchor for lack of dockworkers. The tanneries, rolling mills, and every factory from

VIII, 6

Chicago Avenue to North Avenue stood idle. Sporadic violence lingered into Thursday night, but the worst was over as more federal troops arrived. The strike was broken. Chicago got through it without another fire. Eighteen men and boys were known dead and dozens were wounded.

Saint Louis was a gateway of trade with many transients and foreign born. Though steamboats lined its levees, their great days were over, and railroads and factories employed a growing proportion of the city's 300,000 people. The Panic of 1873 hit the area hard, its impact sharpened by a string of bank failures in mid-July, 1877. Most of the city's railroads had instituted a ten percent pay cut. The WPUS was strong here with German, English, Bohemian, and French sections.

On Sunday the 22nd, as telegraphers reported the defeat of the militia at Pittsburgh, railroad workers attended a mass meeting in East Saint Louis dominated by WPUS speakers predicting that workers would soon be ruling the country. Delegates of employees of six railroads called for a strike at midnight. The Missouri Pacific rescinded the cut, but for the sake of worker solidarity, the strike committee refused to let the men return to work. Another mass meeting Monday night established the WPUS as the directing force of the strike. The next day the Saint Louis Kansas City & Northern followed the MoPac in rescinding its pay cut, but the strike committee once again refused to acknowledge the gesture. Other railroads discontinued passenger service to inconvenience the public and turn popular sentiment against the strikers. On Tuesday the 24th the mayor, since the militia was weak and the police inert, organized a citizens guard.

That evening, answering a request from the receiver of the Saint Louis & Southwestern, six companies of regulars arrived with Springfield breechloading repeaters and two Gatling guns. They marched to the arsenal, their commander insisting that they came not to break the strike or to run trains but to protect government property. But that could include the StL&SW since James H. Wilson, its receiver, argued, like the Erie's counsel at Hornellsville, that a road operated by a receiver appointed by a federal court was entitled to federal protection. Federal Judge Thomas Drummond of the Eastern District of Illinois agreed with Wilson. A third mass meeting was convoked by the WPUS that eclipsed Monday's in size and enthusiasm and endorsed a general strike for the eight hour day and the abolition of child labor.

Employees of all railroads serving Indianapolis, including the bankrupt SL&SW, somewhat belatedly went on strike on Monday, July 23. Walter Q. Gresham, United States District Judge for Indiana, swung into action, and at his request 200 regulars arrived in the city on Friday. This ended the strike on the bankrupt road and soon on all the others. The strike reached Kansas City on Tuesday when men of the four wage cutting roads walked off their jobs and closed down all streetcars, packing houses, grain elevators, and even the shops of the Kansas Pacific, which never made a cut.

There was no vandalism since citizens, including strikers, organized patrols to keep the peace. Denver got by without a strike. Trouble on the Union Pacific was averted when its officials, frightened by news reports from the East, rescinded their cut. In San Francisco the discontent of tramps and the unemployed, incited by a mass meeting of the WPUS, was turned against the hated Chinese, but within a day citizens patrols restored order.

Though by now Baltimore, Pittsburgh, Buffalo, and Reading had passed their crises, and Chicago's was yet to come, overall the Great Strike reached its climax on Wednesday, July 25, 1877. Only two regions were exempt: New England, where memories of the unsuccessful strike on the B&M in February were fresh, and the South where race divided railroad workers, most of whom were black except for engineers and conductors.

Collapse

On July 25, 1877, two-thirds of the nation's 75,000 miles of railroad lines were struck. Most freight and some passenger trains stopped running. Saint Louis was about to experience the first formal general strike of the industrial era. Karl Marx was writing to Friedrich Engels, "What do you think of the workers of the United States?" The nation's 24,000 man regular army was spread very thinly over a growing number of disturbed areas. Tom Scott was urging President Hayes to call for 75,000 volunteers as Lincoln did in 1861, but William T. Sherman, Commanding General of the Army, thought that would start a revolution. However, what the nation was undergoing was not yet a disaster. Only nine days had elapsed since rioting began in Baltimore. Cities had food for a week or more on hand and wagons began conveying supplies from the countryside, which had hardly been affected.

Then suddenly the movement began to flounder. The leaders of the WPUS in Saint Louis lost their self-confidence. The police, supported by the army and militia, stormed party headquarters and arrested seventy. It was on the 25th that NYC strikers at Syracuse and Erie strikers at Hornellsville elected to resume work. Governor Hartranft, with several hundred militia, set out from Philadelphia on Thursday aboard two special trains followed by more than 500 regulars. Arriving at Pittsburgh they found that the local Committee of Safety had matters well in hand. On Sunday morning, July 29, a double-header freight pulled out for the east with thirty-four cattle cars and two filled with troops. More freights departed and others arrived. Pennsylvania Railroad officials set Tuesday morning as the deadline for reporting for work. By Monday night the roll book was full. In the case of the Erie and the Saint Louis & Southwestern the legal principle was being established that obstruction of a railroad in receivership was in contempt of a federal court. MC strikers had given in on July 27. LS&MS employees at Cleveland held out until August 3.

The PRR suspended dividends for two quarters, and Tom Scott, unpopular because of the role the PRR played in the strike, failed to get an expected federal subsidy for his Texas & Pacific Railroad. At Baltimore thirteen rioters drew jail terms of from three to eight months. Hundreds were arrested in Pittsburgh, but many were discharged at preliminary hearings, and the rest were given short terms in the workhouse. In Chicago, Saint Louis, and Philadelphia those imprisoned during the riot were released after two or three days in a sort of general amnesty. For several years, railroad management avoided wage cuts, which the return of prosperity in 1879 made unnecessary. The near universality of the strike prevented reprisals against more than a small fraction of strikers. The rest lost only one or two week's wages, of which most made up at least part in the subsequent rush of business. At the end of July the MC began equalizing wages which meant increases of from four to twelve percent. The Jersey Central paid off half the back wages due its men, and the Illinois Central gave all its employees full pay for July. William H. Vanderbilt ordered a bonus of $100,000 to be distributed among the NYC employees who did not go on strike. Of the eleven thousand employees of the road at this time, 8,904 shared in the bonus. Loyal engineers received $30 each, passenger conductors $20, switchmen and brakemen $9, and laborers $7. The Knights of Labor began eight years of phenomenal growth with their first national assembly. The Brotherhood of Railroad Trainmen, however, did not come into being until 1883. The United States Army was not increased, but stricter training programs, less gaudy uniforms, and improved armories were in store for state militias.

9
Railroading In The '80's And Early '90's

The most productive decade yet in terms of American railroad construction was the 1880s. In 1880 there were 93,272 miles of railway lines (first track) in the United States. By 1890 the figure had risen to 166,703, a seventy-eight percent gain of 73,441 miles, which was roughly equal to the total mileage as late as 1875. The 1890s, blighted by a depression from 1893 to 1897, saw a gain of only 26,643 miles, producing a grand total of 193,346 miles by the end of the century. (Figure V, #1.) During the 1880s, five railroads, the New York Chicago & Saint Louis, the Delaware Lackawanna & Western, the Buffalo Rochester & Pittsburgh, the New York West Shore & Buffalo, and the Rome Watertown & Ogdensburg reached Western New York, and a sixth, the Lehigh Valley, made the scene in 1892.

The Lehigh Valley

Anthracite coal, the sole American source of which is located in northeastern Pennsylvania, principally Lucerne and Lackawanna Counties, was the premier fuel for home heating in the United States throughout much of the nineteenth century. It was almost pure carbon and burned without giving off smoke. In 1791 anthracite was discovered in Mauch Chunk, Pennsylvania, where a canal was dug to float coal barges down the Lehigh Valley to the Delaware River at Easton. By the 1820s, the Lehigh Coal & Navigation Company had a near monopoly on mining and transporting hard coal. To break this monopoly, the Delaware Lehigh Schuylkill & Susquehanna Railroad was incorporated in 1846 to build a line from Mauch Chunk to Easton. Renamed the Lehigh Valley in 1853, the road was completed in 1855. In 1867 it was extended to Wilkes-Barre in the Wyoming Valley. From there, a junction was made with the Erie Railroad at Waverly, New York, via the Pennsylvania & New York, which was completed under LV auspices in 1869. The roadbed of this line was the towpath of the defunct North Branch Division of the Pennsylvania canal system. (Figure VII, #3.) The P&NY gave the Lehigh a western outlet for its hard coal. To avoid the inconvenience of transferring cargoes and passengers to the Erie's broad gauge cars at Waverly, the LV furnished men and money for a third rail providing standard gauge service all the way to Buffalo, which commenced in May, 1876.

To the east the LV had two outlets. At Easton, it connected with the Jersey Central and the New York Bay area. Also at Easton, the LV interchanged with the Belvidere Delaware Railroad, which ran along the east shore of the Delaware to Philadelphia. When the Lehigh's rival anthracite carrier, the Lackawanna, acquired the cross-Jersey Morris & Essex in 1868, and the Jersey Central invaded the hard coal fields by leasing the Lehigh & Susquehanna (Easton to Wilkes-Barre) in 1871, the LV built its own line to Perth Amboy, New Jersey, on Raritan Bay in 1875. A year later, the LV took control of the Geneva Ithaca & Sayre, which connected with the NYC at Geneva.

With its trains running to Buffalo over the Erie, the LV set about securing land and developing facilities for its terminal operations there. The Buffalo Creek had been organized in 1869 by Buffalo businessmen, but next year the LV became its majority stockholder. The BC originally extended 3.5 miles from its junction with the mainline of the NYC near the intersection of Howard Street and Fillmore Avenue with the head of the City Ship Canal. Along its route, the BC intersected the Erie, the Buffalo New York & Philadelphia, the Buffalo & Jamestown, and the Lake Shore. During the 1870s, the BC was gradually extended along Ganson Street up the narrow strip of land between Buffalo Creek and the City Ship Canal (known as the Island) to a point 700 yards north of Michigan Avenue. (Figures #1 and XV, #6.) Its completed mainline was 4.08 miles long. (Correspondingly, the BNY&P had a spur running up the equally narrow strip of land between the Ship Canal and Lake Erie, the eastern shore of which between the U.S. slip and the foot of Michigan on the sea wall was called the Beach. The area bounded by the BC on the east, the LS&MS on the west and the NYC became known as the Iron Triangle.) In 1879 the Erie became interested in the BC and succeeded in placing three Erie officials on its board of directors. On January 1, 1890, the Erie and the LV leased the BC and operated it thereafter as joint lessees.

In 1882 the LV bought the Tifft Farm, located on the waterfront between Tifft Street and Buffalo Creek, and built an East Canal and a West Canal joined by a Cross Cut Canal as extensions of the City Ship Canal. These serviced lake ships carrying inbound grain, lumber, and iron ore and outbound coal. (Figure #2.) The previous year the LV had established its own shipping line, the Lehigh Valley Transportation Company, operating lake vessels between Buffalo and Chicago, Duluth, and other cities on the Great Lakes. By 1885 the LV's fleet boasted five ships. Five years later the shipping line's flag, a red banner emblazoned with a black diamond symbolizing anthracite, was adopted by the road as its logo. (Figure #3.)

Before it could establish its own passenger and freight terminals in downtown Buffalo, the LV determined to reach the city on its own tracks. Accordingly in March, 1882, a charter was issued for the Lehigh Valley Railway Company, a ten mile spur diverging from the Erie at Lancaster and ending at the LV's downtown station site between the Hamburg Canal and Scott Street. The new line was opened to freight traffic in 1884. Construction of a passenger terminal at Washington and Scott Streets began in 1883. The three story brick depot housed passenger waiting rooms and ticket offices on the first floor and company offices on the floors above. (Figure #4.) Double tracks approached the station at street level, branching out to six stub tracks terminating beneath a train shed to the rear of the station. When completed, the terminal was shared by the Grand Trunk, an arrangement that proved so amicable that by 1888 the LV began running through Pullman service between Philadelphia and Chicago in conjunction with the GT, eventually expanding this service to New York City.

Construction of its own line west from Geneva to Buffalo across the rolling hills and

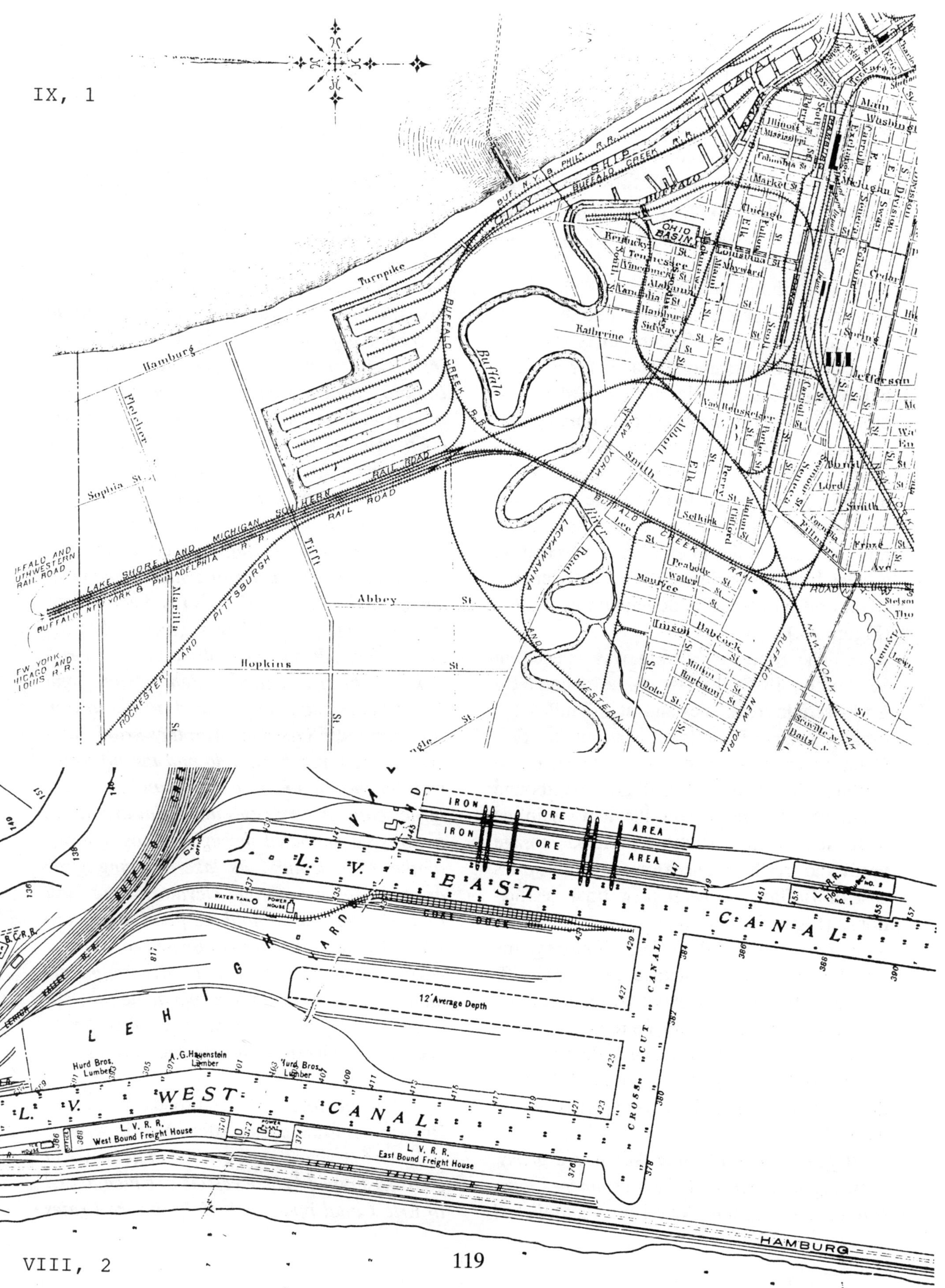

IX, 1
SHIP CANAL
BUFFALO CREEK R.R.
BUF. N.Y. & PHIL. R.R.
BUFFALO RIVER
OHIO BASIN
Turnpike
Hamburg
BUFFALO CREEK R.R.
Buffalo
LAKE SHORE AND MICHIGAN SOUTHERN RAIL ROAD
BUFFALO NEW YORK & PHILADELPHIA R.R.
ROCHESTER AND PITTSBURGH
NEW YORK
LACKAWANNA AND WESTERN
BUFFALO CREEK RAIL ROAD
BUFFALO NEW YORK
Sophia St.
Abbey St.
Hopkins St.
Katherine
Smith
Selkirk
Peabody St.
Maurice
Babcock
Illinois
Mississippi
Columbia St.
Market St.
Chicago
Louisiana
Hayward
Kentucky
Tennessee
Main
Washington
Michigan
Jefferson
Van Rensselaer
Fillmore
IRON ORE AREA
IRON ORE AREA
L. V. EAST CANAL
COAL DOCK
WATER TANK
POWER HOUSE
LEHIGH VALLEY R.R.
BUFFALO CREEK
B.C.R.R.
ENGINE HOUSE
LEHIGH
12' Average Depth
CROSS CUT CANAL
Hurd Bros. Lumber
A. G. Hauenstein Lumber
Hurd Bros. Lumber
L. V. WEST CANAL
L. V. R. R. West Bound Freight House
POWER HOUSE
L. V. R. R. East Bound Freight House
LEHIGH VALLEY R.R.
HAMBURG
VIII, 2

flatlands of Western New York was next on the LV agenda. This relatively easy project was undertaken by the Buffalo & Geneva Railway Company organized in 1889. Next year the B&G was consolidated with a bypass route in central New York and with the existing Lancaster to Buffalo line to form the Lehigh Valley Rail Way Company, mortgaged at $15 million to defray construction costs. Since the rental agreement with the Erie for trackage rights to Buffalo would expire in 1892, the LV pushed to complete its own line by then. Beyond Manchester, fifteen miles west of Geneva, the new mainline headed for Buffalo, bypassing Rochester, the state's third largest city. Eager for another rail connection, Rochester offered to build the necessary railroad bridges over waterways. Leaving the mainline at Rochester Junction, the Rochester & Honeoye Valley, another Lehigh subsidiary, ran north 12.9 miles to a terminus perched on a steel framework directly over the Genesee River on Court Street in downtown Rochester. (Figure #5.)

The route to Buffalo was opened in September, 1892, the last of the major New York-Buffalo trunk lines and, at 447 miles, the longest. The LV's local stations in Erie County were at Lancaster, Cheektowaga, and William Street in East Buffalo Westbound anthracite shipments over the new mainline were sent to the newly completed storage yards and trestle at Cheektowaga, eight miles east of Buffalo, to await their final destinations. (Figure X, #4) Operated in conjunction with the Lehigh Valley Coal Company, the Cheektowaga facility helped keep the Tifft Terminal free of congestion from incoming coal trains from the anthracite region.

The LV's western terminal is described by Robert Archer, from whose history of the road the account of the LV in this chapter is chiefly derived:

Buffalo of the '80s and '90s was a grimy, brawling lake port and the preeminent industrial center of upstate New York. Established as the western terminus of the Erie Canal in 1825, it soon became a major commercial center and shipping transfer point, its harbor and warehouses handling the heavy east-west tonnage transported by canal barge and lake ship. Farm products coming off the Great Lakes for the eastern seaboard were stored at Buffalo for transshipment by canal, as were manufactured goods heading west. Streams of settlers and adventurers bound for the frontier aboard canal packets awaited their connections west at Buffalo, and scores of hotels sprang up to accommodate the tide of human traffic. To insure its future commercial livelihood, Buffalo concentrated on developing a solid industrial base during the boom years of pre-Civil War expansion. The railroads were drawn not only by its new and growing manufacturing industries, but also by the proximity of convenient waterborne shipping connections. Predictably, Buffalo rapidly evolved into a major American rail center in the post-war period. As the railroads reached the city, its industrial potential was given a healthy boost. The LV and Erie offered a direct rail link with the coal regions of Pennsylvania, and Great Lakes shipping provided access to iron ore from Lake Superior. With these raw materials in easy reach, Buffalo had the prerequisites for the manufacture of iron and steel on a large scale. As the city's industrial expansion progressed unabated through the last quarter of the 19th century, its lake shipping grew apace. Massive storage elevators were built on the waterfront to hold the flood of western grain destined after transshipment to railroad cars for eastern markets. Extensive freight terminals were built to accommodate eastern manufactured goods arriving for transfer to lake ships or western rail connections. [1]

On the role of the railroads in making Buffalo a milling center, Albro Martin writes:

For a few years, most grain and flour would be transshipped to lake vessels at Chicago and to Erie Canal boats at Buffalo, but rail rates

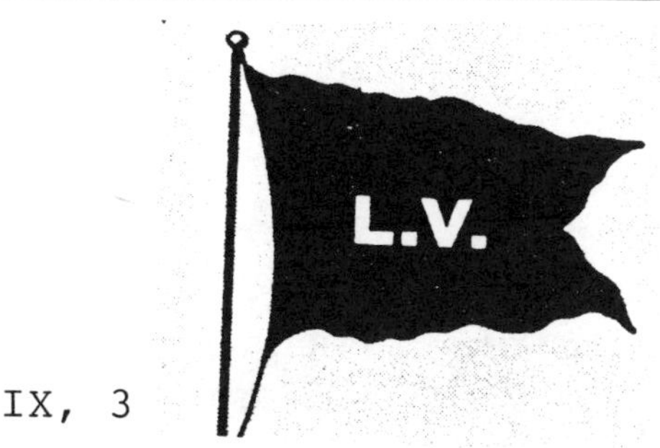
L.V.

IX, 3

LEHIGH
VALLEY

IX, 4

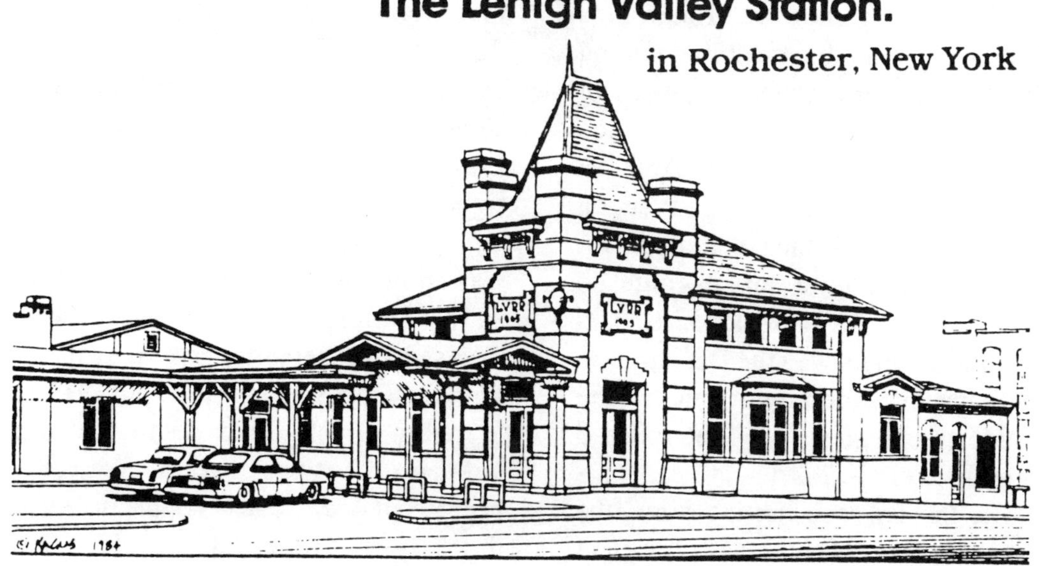
The Lehigh Valley Station.
in Rochester, New York

IX, 5

declined steeply after 1873, and long before the century was over the railroads had claimed most of the grain movement east. . . . Flour deserted the water for the rails sooner than grain, because of its greater value per pound. In fact, the railroads made long distance shipment of flour feasible, and thus flour milling declined east of the Appalachians, although it has never entirely disappeared. Buffalo became the logical point at which to terminate wheat's progress as wheat and to turn it into flour, as reflected in freight rates for wheat inbound by lake to Buffalo that fell from twenty cents per bushel in 1854 to six cents in 1858, quoting end-of-season rates. Of course, once the short, hot summer of the Midwest ended and the lakes and canals froze over, the railroads got it all. By end-of-the century standards, Buffalo's facilities for producing flour were truly eye-popping. The tall, wooden grain elevators that lined the lakefront gave the city a skyline even before the age of the skyscraper arrived, and on one occasion awed the citizenry with one of the most spectacular conflagrations in memory. [2]

The LV had regularly interchanged its Canadian traffic to and from Suspension Bridge with the NYC at Batavia on the Peanut. To speed up shipping schedules and to lower costs by a more direct route, the Lehigh in 1895 organized the Depew & Tonawanda Railroad. This was a double track line linking the mainline line at Depew, nine miles east of Buffalo, with the Peanut at Tonawanda Junction, just west of the Tonawanda-Amherst Line. This 10.5 mile road was opened on November 15, 1896, furnishing a short cut for international traffic and a direct route to Niagara Falls for the LV's brisk tourist and honeymoon trade. On its way the D&T passed through Williamsville, thus giving one of Erie County's oldest settlements its first railroad station. (Figure XVI, #2.)

Fiscally, the LV was hurting since the Buffalo extension had left little cash for plant improvements and the regular five percent stockholders' dividend. An offer the latter could not resist was made by Archibald A. McLeod, President of the Reading, who with the backing, at least initially, of J. Pierpont Morgan, aimed at dominating the anthracite industry. The Reading leased the Lehigh for 999 years on February, 1892, an arrangement which was terminated after only eighteen months amid mutual recriminations. Earnings continued to drop following a decreased demand for anthracite, increased competition from other coal carrying roads, the Panic of 1893, and a disastrous year-end strike.

The Delaware Lackawanna & Western

Similar to the Lehigh in origin, development, geography, and traffic was the Delaware Lackawanna & Western Railroad. (For a map of this railroad at its fullest extent see Figure #6.) The DL&W began its corporate existence in 1849 as the Liggett's Gap Railroad. When it was completed in 1851, the Ligettís Gap was renamed the Lackawanna & Western, since it linked Scranton in the heart of the Lackawanna Valley coal fields with Great Bend, Pennsylvania, on the mainline of the Erie, eleven miles east of Binghamton. In 1853 the L&W acquired the charter of the Delaware & Cobb's Gap Railroad, which had also been incorporated in 1849 to build a railroad through the Pocono Mountains from the Delaware Water Gap on the Delaware River to Cobb's Gap, six miles southeast of Scranton. Little work was done on the D&CG until its rights were acquired by the Lackawanna & Western in 1853, after which the enlarged road was aptly renamed the Delaware Lackawanna & Western. The Scranton-Delaware Water Gap section, thereafter known as the Southern Division, was completed in 1857. The Scranton-Great Bend section became the Northern Division. The Delaware River was bridged in 1858, and a connection made with the Central Railroad of New Jersey at

IX, 6

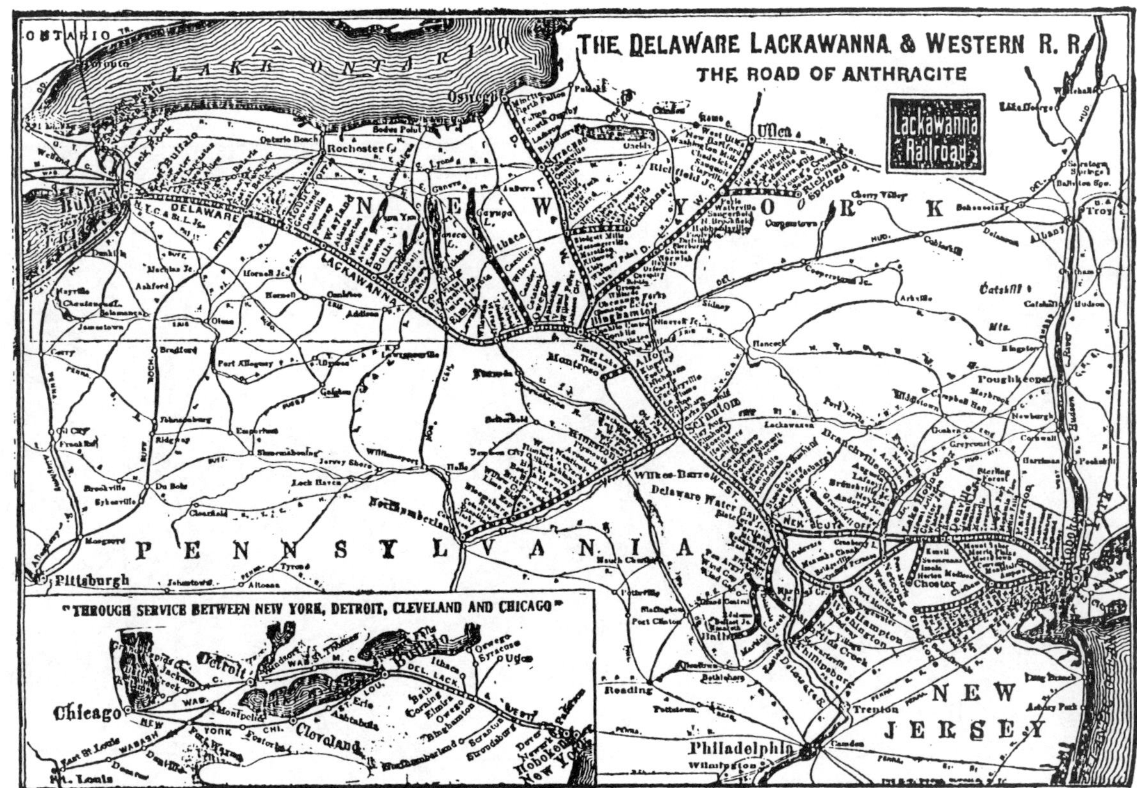

Hampton, New Jersey, via the Warren Railroad which the DL&W was to lease in perpetuity in 1877 for a guaranteed seven percent annually on the Warren's stock.

In 1861 the DL&W sent George Dakin to Buffalo to establish a yard at the foot of Erie Street between the mouth of Buffalo Creek and the Coit Slip on the Erie Basin from which coal could be carried further up the Lakes by colliers. Until 1876 the DL&W's gauge was six feet because of the ex-Liggett's Gap connection with the Erie. In order to avoid sharing revenue with the Jersey Central, the DL&W in 1868 leased the Morris & Essex Railroad which had been chartered in 1835 to build a line from Morristown to Newark. By 1869 the M&E was running from Phillipsburg, New Jersey on the Delaware to Hoboken on the Hudson across from New York City. It was also in 1869 that the DL&W secured control, but not absolute ownership, of the six foot Syracuse Binghamton & New York which had been chartered in 1849. A lease by the DL&W that same year of the Oswego & Syracuse brought the parent company to the shores of Lake Ontario. Construction by the DL&W of the Valley Railroad, chartered that busy year of 1869, closed the gap between Great Bend and Binghamton and ended dependence by the DL&W on the Erie for the route to Lake Ontario.

The scene was set for the DL&W's western extension from Binghamton to Buffalo. By 1881 Jay Gould's southern and western empire included the Union Pacific, the Kansas Pacific, the Denver & Rio Grande Western, the Missouri Pacific, the Texas & Pacific, the International & Great Northern and the Saint Louis Iron Mountain & Southern. Extending this network further east was the Wabash, which may be conceived of as a giant letter X, one arm of which linked Kansas City with Toledo (later extended to Detroit) and the other Chicago with Saint Louis, intersecting at Decatur, Illinois. Moreover, the Wabash enjoyed running rights over Canada's Great Western across the Ontario Peninsula from Detroit to Buffalo. (Figure #7.) Grodinsky takes up the story at this point:

While building the Wabash system in the

IX, 7

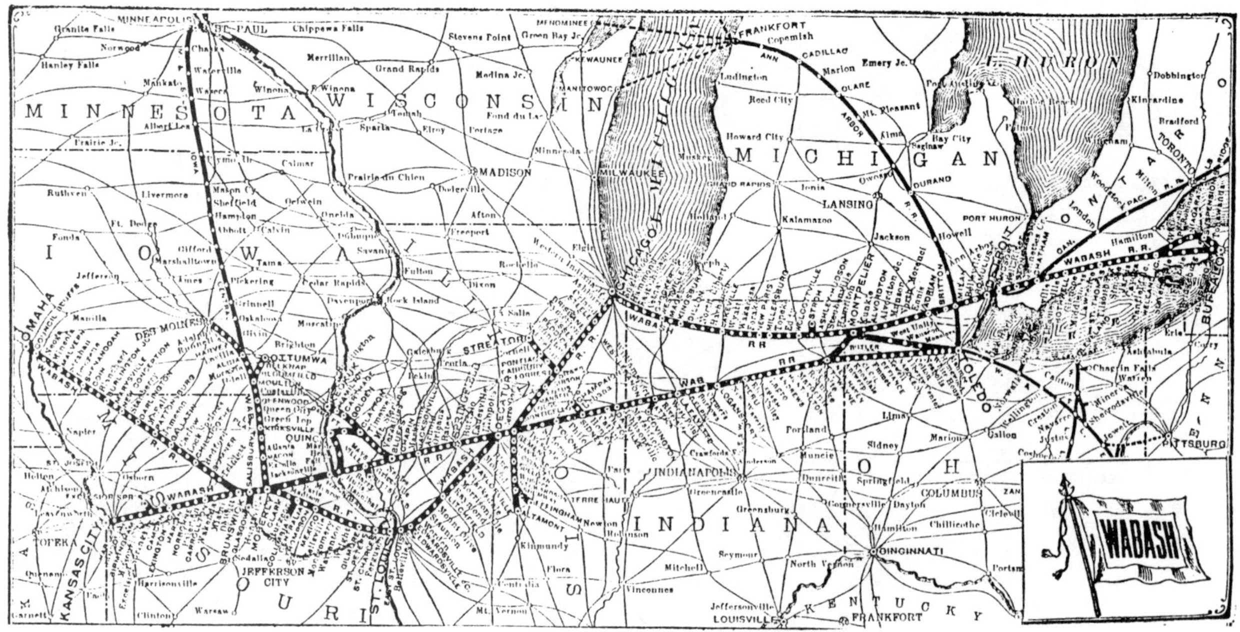

West, Gould was developing a new strategy in the East. In that region he entered upon a program of buying the stock of the DL&W, one of the anthracite carriers serving the northeastern Pennsylvania mines. Its lines extended west to Binghamton, New York, and east to the seaboard at Hoboken, New Jersey. The road was a competitor of the Pennsylvania and worked closely with the NYC on traffic to Buffalo and the West [via Syracuse]. If it were extended to Buffalo, Vanderbilt's NYC would be hard hit, although the Wabash would not necessarily be helped.

In the summer of 1880 Gould's hand in this new railroad strategy was revealed. On heavy trading volume the price of DL&W stock rose rapidly, and in August came the announcement of the incorporation of a wholly owned subsidiary for the purpose of building a Buffalo extension [the New York Lackawanna & Western]. The incorporators of the new railroad included Gould, his two major associates on the Union Pacific, Sidney Dillon and Frederick L. Ames; his associate on the Wabash, Humphreys; General Thomas Eckert, president of American Union Telegraph; and Samuel Sloan [eponym of Sloan, New York], the aggressive president of the DL&W. The Buffalo extension was a surprise to both railroad and financial groups, but Gould's interest in the venture was an even greater one. With the completion of the Detroit extension [from Toledo] early in 1881, the Wabash had a connection with the Great Western and could now send its traffic over that road to Buffalo. In anticipation of this lucrative business, the Great Western refused to merge with the Grand Trunk, since such action might lead the wily Gould to change his mind and transfer the Wabash business to another line, perhaps to Vanderbilt. A few weeks after the organization of the new company for the Buffalo extension, the Wabash, the Lackawanna, and the Great Western entered into a traffic alliance for a through route to the seaboard.

The Wabash accordingly was about to

become a competitive line in eastern trunk-line territory, and its financial out look appeared to be favorable. A leading eastern railroad journal reported Chicago opinion as believing that the various combinations in which the Wabash was then engaged would make it "one of the most important and formidable of any in the West." Despite his brilliant success in the handling of the Wabash, Gould's policy was unsound. His projects involved largely a diversion of traffic from existing lines. It is probable that had Gould made a cooperative arrangement with the existing Chicago roads, the traffic could have been equitably divided with profit to all. [3]

Thomas Taber, the DL&W's historian, writes:

Unlike the start of the railroads constructed thirty or more years previous, this new railroad would have ample financial backing money was no problem. Some of the directors of the DL&W and their friends created the Central Construction Company, which was given the contract for constructing the railroad. With the backing of the DL&W they advanced the required cash. It has been said that the actual cost of construction was $12 million, but that the completed line was turned over to the DL&W for a book value of $22 million. Stockholders of the construction company received a handsome profit on their investment! [4]

Save for some stiff eastbound grades from Groveland to Wayland, the line of the NYL&W was relatively level with few sharp curves. The Buffalo Division, as it was soon known, was well built and became the "racetrack" of the DL&W, widely celebrated for speed records made between Elmira and Buffalo. Work began near Binghamton on October 6, 1880, and by April, 1882, four trains were running daily to and from Elmira. From Binghamton to Elmira the new road paralleled the Erie while from Elmira to Buffalo the two roads were never more than a few

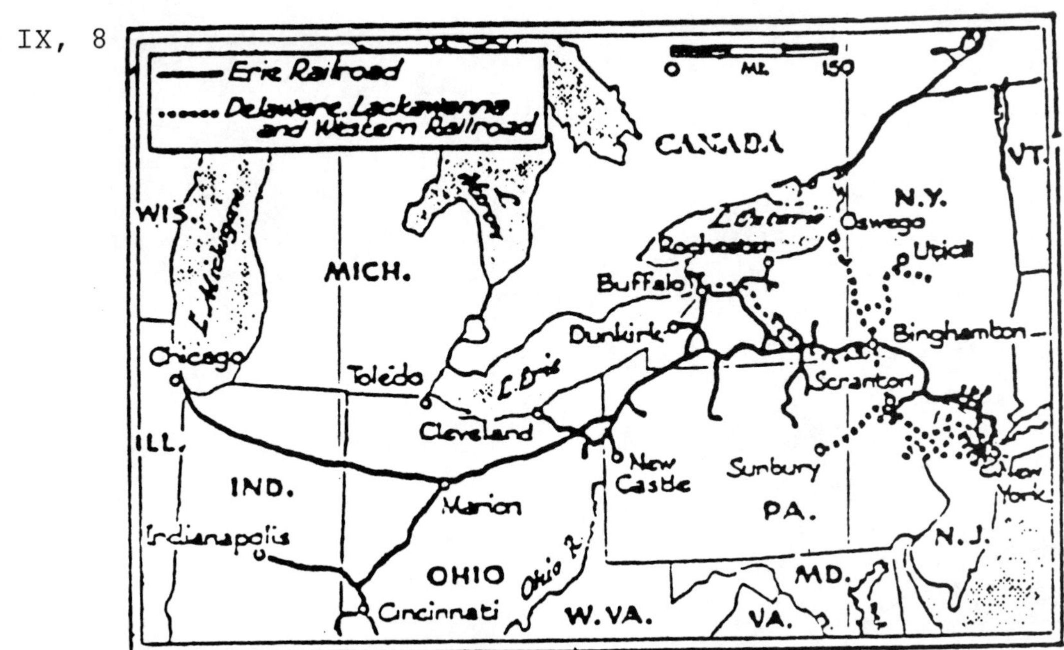

miles apart. (Figure #8.) The road had some trouble in the winter of 1881-1882 getting permission from the City of Buffalo to lay track on Ohio Street to reach the docks and the huge coal trestle which had been constructed at the foot of Erie Street in 1879. These facilities antedated the arrival in Buffalo of the DL&W by three years. Eventually the differences were adjusted. Paralleling the Erie's Suspension Bridge & Erie Junction-Erie International route to International Bridge was the DL&W's branch which left the mainline near the Buffalo-Cheektowaga border, ran up the East Side, and across North Buffalo to the bridge. The DL&W's principal western connection was the Grand Trunk owner of International Bridge. The Lackawanna's branch to this bridge was another needless reduplication of railroad trackage. (Figure #9.) Nevertheless, the reduplication lasted for almost a hundred years.

The first passenger train for New York left Buffalo from the Aetna Building on Prime Street at 8:00 A. M. on May 14, 1882. The original station was a makeshift affair intended for temporary use until a permanent station could be built at a more convenient location. A correspondent with a limited vocabulary reported in the Express on June 28, 1885:

Tomorrow the DL&W will occupy its new

IX, 9

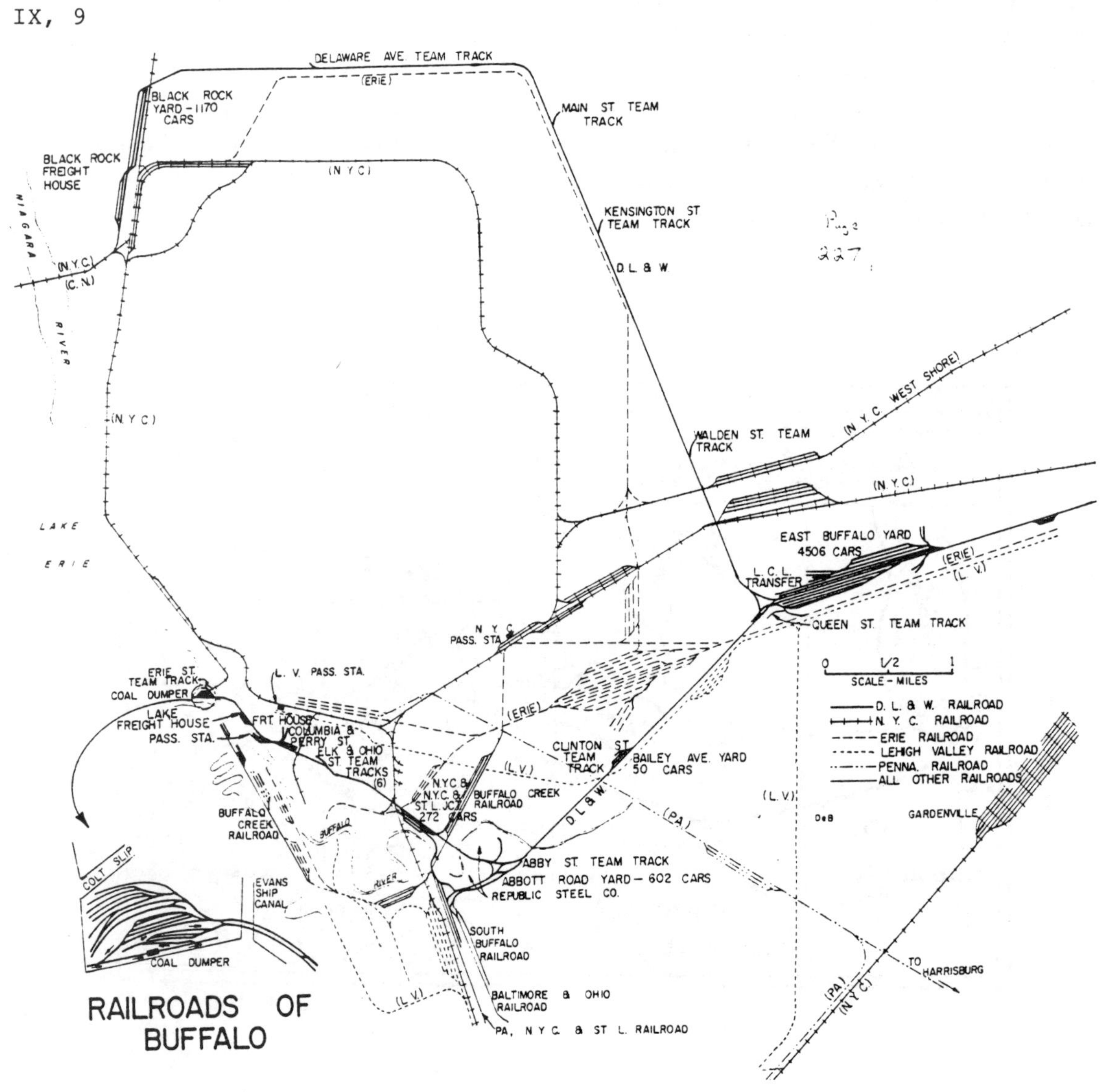

station at the foot of Main Street. The building though small is a pretty one and will prove a pleasing substitute for the old Aetna building. The large waiting room, which extends from Main Street through to the tracks is well lighted and the effect of the light wood, with which it is finished, is pleasing. The local ticket agent, Mr. Seth E. Wells, has a handsome office on the Main Street side of this room, fitted up with handsome desks and ticket cases. This ofice, though small is very convenient, The baggage room is located at the southern end of the building and is roomy and pleasant. An express platform is being built at the Dayton Street end. Although not making any pretensions as to size, the company now has one of the brightest and pleasantest stations in the city. (Figure #10.)

By 1890 the Lackawanna was scheduling thirteen daily (or daily except Sunday) trains westbound into Buffalo. (Figure #11.) Two were coal trains, three fast freights, three mixed trains, one mail train, and four passenger trains. Eastbound a total of fifteen trains left Buffalo daily: four passenger trains, one cattle train, two fast freights, four second class freights, three coal trains (returning empties or carrying soft coal), and one mixed train. Passenger trains covered the Buffalo Division at an average speed of up to thirty-eight miles an hour; first class freights averaged up to seventeen miles an hour. On the subject of speed Taber writes:

The DL&W never showed a timetable schedule between Hoboken and Buffalo even in the twentieth century, when the road had reached its highest development and had reduced the mileage from Hoboken to 396 miles [from 409 by constructing a cut-off across western New Jersey and northeastern Pennsylvania] *of less than eight hours! It may be surmised that the Vanderbilt-NYC interest represented on the Board of Managers opposed faster schedules which would equal those of the NYC, and might result in taking business away from the*

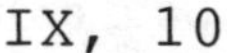
IX, 10

IX, 11

DELAWARE, LACKAWANNA & WESTERN R. R.—BUFFALO DIVISION.

TIME TABLE, No. 39.

FOR GOVERNMENT AND INFORMATION OF EMPLOYEES ONLY. TAKES EFFECT MONDAY, OCT. 6, 1890.

WEST. EAST.

STATIONS.

F. A. SEABERT, Asst. Superintendent. W. F. HALLSTEAD, General Manager

NYC. [5]

In the heart of Cheektowaga near Forks the DL&W constructed for local distributors a huge coal trestle with a capacity of 150,000 tons, the equivalent of about 200 train loads. (Figure #12; see also Figure X, #4.) Since most of the large tracts of land in Buffalo suitable for railroad yards had been preempted, the DL&W, as befitted a latecomer, erected its roundhouse and yards in the westernmost part of Cheektowaga. The tract was bounded by William Street on the south, Harlem Road on the east, Broadway on the north, and the Buffalo city limits on the west. To accommodate the railroad this area was incorporated in 1896 as the Village of Sloan. (Figure X, #4.)

The New York Chicago & Saint Louis

As John H. Rehor wrote at the start of his history of the Nickel Plate:

Throughout the lower Great Lakes basin and especially along the south shore of Lake Erie, the early 1880s were years of dynamic growth. Here proximity to much of the nation's mineral wealth, its markets, and principal trade routes had led to the establishment and rapid expansion of the iron and steel industry and related manufacturing activity. The region was served by a single east-west railroad, the owners of which were concerned only with the continued accumulation of great wealth and the preservation of their monopoly. Local facilities for handling the growing volume of travelers and goods were inadequate, service was poor, and rates were based on what the traffic would bear. Discrimination against shippers and commodities, connecting railroads, and even against entire communities was not uncommon. [6]

Rehor is referring to the LS&MS, which Cornelius Vanderbilt had acquired in 1869, and on his death in 1877 had passed on along with the NYC and other railroads to his son

IX, 12

lrawing shows the original trestle, built in 1883, and the superstructure where the coal was dumped.

William H. The Commodore's heir was to spend the rest of his life trying to preserve this Buffalo-Chicago monopoly primarily, but not solely, against his arch rival, Jay Gould.

During 1879-1880 a syndicate headed by George I. Seney, a New York banker, put together several short railroads in Ohio and Indiana to form the Lake Erie & Western, a 353 mile road from Bloomington, Illinois, to a junction with the LS&MS at Fremont, Ohio. Although the LE&W offered Vanderbilt an excellent opportunity to retaliate against Gould, Vanderbilt's previous agreement to turn over the bulk of his NYC's westbound traffic to the Wabash prevented him from concluding amicable exchange of traffic with the LE&W. Therefore, Seney and his associates decided to build their own Buffalo-Chicago line. Accordingly, on February 3, 1881, they organized the New York Chicago & Saint Louis Railway Company. A Norwalk, Ohio, newspaper referred to it as the "great double-track nickel-plated railroad," and the name stuck. By the beginning of June, 10,000 men and 5,000 teams of horses were in the field at forty points between Buffalo and Chicago. East of Cleveland, the Nickel Plate was built on the narrow level shelf of land between Lake Erie and the Appalachian foothills. For this entire distance the road was located south of and adjacent to the LS&MS. Here the NKP crossed the deep gorges of many streams, and so most of the permanent bridges on the line were on this Cleveland-Buffalo section. The construction boss was Jack Casement, who had held a similar position during the building of the Union Pacific in the mid-1860s. By March, 1882, Casement's track layers had reached Brocton, New York, forty-eight miles from Buffalo. There they met construction crews of the Buffalo Pittsburgh & Western (formerly the Buffalo Corry & Pittsburgh and soon to be absorbed by the Buffalo New York & Philadelphia). It was arranged that the NKP and the BP&W would lay track simultaneously, the NKP's track to the north of the BP&W's. The PB&W's track would be operated as the eastbound main for both lines and the NKP's the westbound.

The last 15.6 miles from Derby to a junction at Seneca Street with the Erie in Buffalo, 1.6 miles from its downtown terminal, were finished during early August, 1882. (Figure #13.) Full operation commenced on October 23, 1882. There were no through passenger trains. The sole varnish runs were daily except Sunday accommodations between Buffalo and Bellevue and between Cleveland and Chicago. Trains #3 and #4 were scheduled to cover the 340 mile Cleveland-Chicago run in fourteen

IX, 13

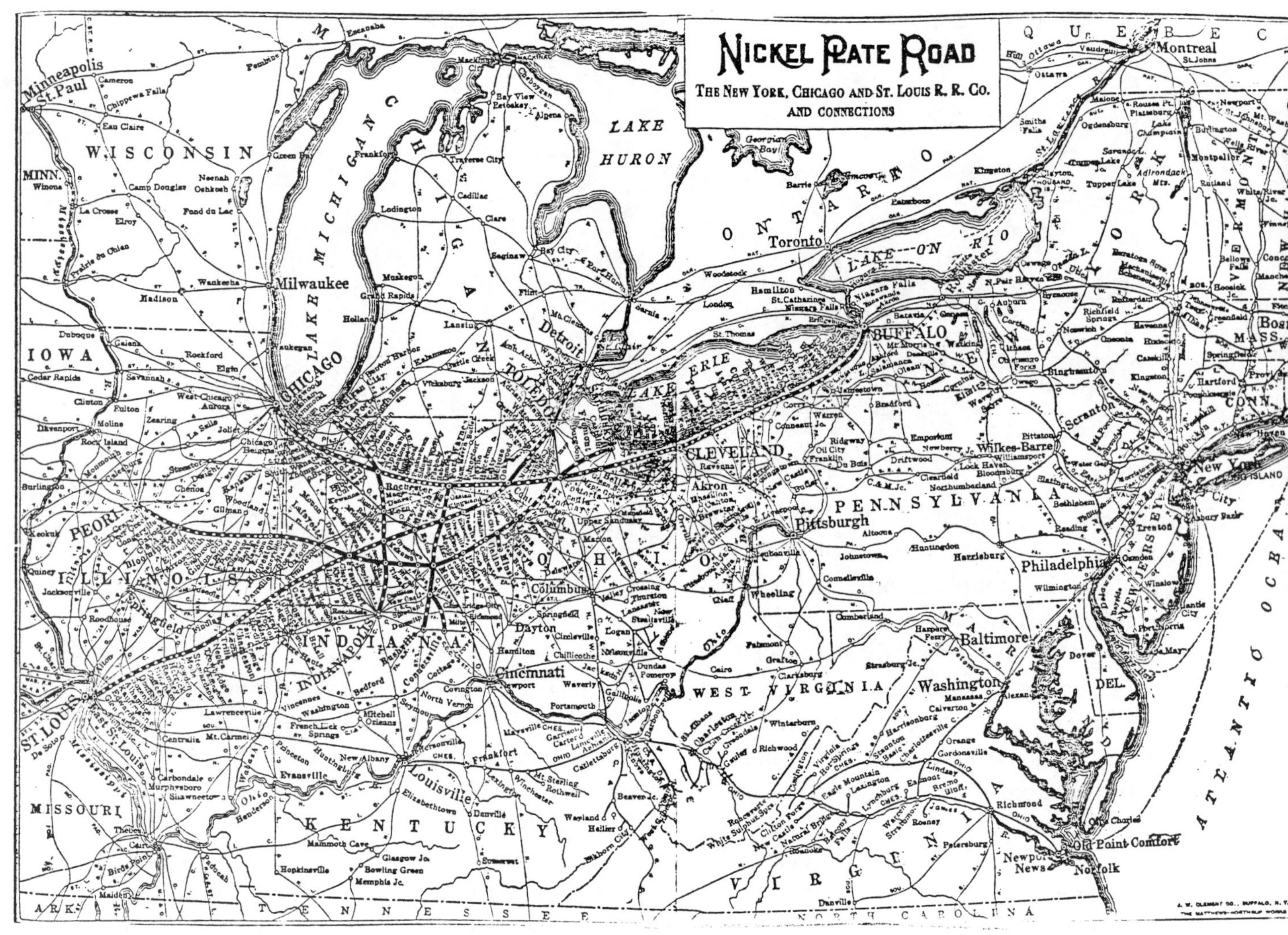

hours; Bellevue-Buffalo trains #1 and #2 required ten hours and twenty-five minutes to get over the road. Local freight trains, one in each direction over each of the three districts, carried passengers in the caboose. Clearly NKP officialdom was not competing with the LS&MS for passengers. Western New York stations were located at Ripley, Westfield, Brocton, Dunkirk, Silver Creek, Irving, Angola, Lake View, and Buffalo (i.e., Erie Railroad) Junction.

On October 25, 1882, two days after the road had opened for business, William Vanderbilt offered to buy it. Jay Gould would have dearly loved to have been the successful suitor but he simply lacked the funds. The NKP would have provided a more dependable link between his Wabash and the DL&W at Buffalo than the Great Western. Vanderbilt paid the Seney Syndicate $7,205,000, about ten percent more than had been paid into the entire capital stock of the NKP. Rehor analyzes the transaction:

The purchase was a stunning victory for Vanderbilt and the turning point in his long war with Jay Gould. As for Gould, he had stood at the zenith of his career, ready to administer the coup de grace to the one man who stood between him and his dreams of a transcontinental dynasty. After October 1882 it was all downhill for Gould.

Wall Street concluded that the NKP had been built as a bold speculation by shrewd men who intended all the while to sell it to the highest bidder. While this may have been the case, the fall of 1882 found most of the syndicate members treading on the brink of financial chaos. For several weeks prior to the sale, the prices of Nickel Plate stocks had been dropping due to widespread fear that the road's opening would set off a rate war. Most of the promoters had so overextended themselves financially that they could afford no further risk. Certainly the syndicate could not hope to match Vanderbilt's losses in a rate war.

[Syndicate member Calvin] *Brice estimated the profit realized by the syndicate members at 75%. In this day and age such a return seems spectacular, but in a time when fortunes were made and lost overnight it was really quite modest considering the risks undertaken. Whatever their motives, the Seney group had built and opened the Nickel Plate and, ironically, by selling out to Vanderbilt had assured its survival.* [7]

The NKP underwent bankruptcy two years later, though in the reorganization which followed Vanderbilt retained control. However, his handpicked president, Darius Caldwell, a holdover, was given a reasonably free hand in running the road. No longer would he be encumbered with restrictions imposed by Vanderbilt that had bankrupted the NKP. The road's new status was due in part to the Interstate Commerce Act of 1887, which prohibited pooling freight traffic between common points on competing roads and outlawed rate discrimination against persons, commodities, and localities. The Sherman Anti-Trust Act three years later strictly forbade the restraint or destruction of competition through ownership or control of competing roads. Taking advantage of the autonomy granted him, Caldwell quickly put the NKP on a paying basis. In 1893 he worked out an operating alliance with the New York West Shore & Buffalo, acquired by Vanderbilt at foreclosure in 1885. These two roads formed a through New York-Chicago route 952 miles long.

The Buffalo Rochester & Pittsburgh [8]

What anthracite was for home heating, bituminous or soft coal was for smelting and generating steam for locomotives and stationary engines. The success of the first industrial enterprises in Buffalo was due largely to its accessibility by water to the coalfields of Ohio and Pennsylvania. By 1850 the city had many foundries, but it was not until coal reached Buffalo by rail that manufacturing became prominent. By the time of the Civil War the city was growing so fast that a serious fuel shortage developed. This led to the construction of what became the Buffalo New York & Philadelphia and the Buffalo Corry & Pittsburgh Railroads which connected Buffalo with the soft coal fields of western Pennsylvania.

Rochester also stood in need of a direct rail link to these coalfields. By the late 1840s the city enjoyed good east-west lines of transportation: the Erie Canal and the Tonawanda and the Attica & Buffalo Railroads to the west, and the Auburn & Rochester to the east. But this arrangement delivered the industrialists of what was still being called the Flour City to the tender mercies of Buffalo and Syracuse coal dealers. The opening of the Buffalo & Cohocton Valley from Corning northeast through Avon to Buffalo offered a way out since Avon was only eighteen miles south of Rochester on the Genesee River. The connecting Rochester & Genesee Valley was opened in 1853. It was a six foot gauge road since the Corning line and the Erie to which it was a feeder were of that gauge. However, the Tonwanda, the Attica & Buffalo, and the Auburn & Rochester were amalgamated to form the NYC in the "Great Consolidation" of

1853, and the Erie soon controlled the Cohocton Valley and the Genesee Valley. Now Rochester business interests were dependent on two mighty railroad corporations. The Genesee Valley Canal was of little help. Begun in 1834 and finally completed between Rochester and Olean in 1857, it was 107 miles of leaky waterway which never lived up to the expectations of its promoters. (Figure I, #1.)

Rochester was ready for the Rochester & State Line Railroad, which was organized by prominent men from Genesee Valley towns on April 8, 1869. While it was common knowledge to the industrialists of Rochester and founders of the railroad that its purpose was to tap the coalfields of Pennsylvania, the public, especially farmers and townsfolk along the line, were led to believe that it was to aid them in shipping farm produce to market. Communities along the proposed route subscribed to $500,000 worth of stock, and Rochester raised $600,000 for the project through the sale of city bonds. By May, 1874, the first section was completed from Rochester through Scottsville to Le Roy, where construction stopped because of the spreading effects of the Panic of 1873. Work began anew, and rails reached Salamanca on the Atlantic & Great Western on January 28, 1878, though the line was not open for through freight and passenger service until May 16. Before tracks reached Salamanca, traffic was chiefly farm produce and lumber. After that the big moneymaker was crude oil, solid trains of which ran to Rochester over a supposed coal road. Since Vanderbilt interests, which had once considered the State Line as a source of coal, lost interest in purchasing it, and since even its oil business began to fall off, the company found itself losing money and went into receivership in February, 1880. The major reason for this was the road's failure to tap the coalfields which was why it had been organized in the first place.

The Rochester & State Line was sold early in 1881 to a New York syndicate for $600,000 and was reorganized as the Rochester & Pittsburgh Railroad. The new company purchased the Pitkim Building on West Main and Oak Streets in downtown Rochester and built a two story Gothic addition in the fall of 1881. Though asymmetrical, this edifice long remained an impressive Rochester landmark. (Figure #14.) Construction south from Salamanca toward the coal fields began early in 1882. The major problem encountered was the monumental one of building across a plateau called the Big Level which was split by Kinzua Creek Gorge. The Erie was also building in this area. The upshot was that the R&P ac-

IX, 14

quired trackage rights over the Erie for thirty-eight miles between Howard Junction and Clarion Junction. It took ninety-four working days to build the Kinzua Viaduct over the gorge. This viaduct was the highest railroad bridge in the world at the time, 301 feet above the gorge and 2,053 feet long. This single track bridge shared with the Erie proved a bottleneck which later led BR&P management to construct its own line which skirted the valley around the bridge from Mount Jewett to Howard Junction. This forty mile detour was opened for traffic in 1893. At Falls Creek trackage rights into Pittsburgh were secured from the PRR. Passenger service between Rochester and Pittsburgh began in June, 1883. Beyond Falls Creek, southern extensions tapped coalfields around Punxsutawney and Wilson which furnished the bulk of the railroad's coal traffic, the original promoters' primary goal objective.

At the same time as track was being laid south into Pennsylvania, a subsidiary, the Buffalo Rochester & Pittsburgh, was organized on August 18, 1881, to build from Machias on the mainline to Buffalo. However, since this would merely parallel the Buffalo New York & Philadelphia, a route through virgin territory was adopted departing from the mainline at a point in the Town of Ashford soon known as Ashford Junction. Two obstacles to construction were Cattaraugus Creek near Springville and quicksand just to the south. Springville was so anxious for a standard gauge railroad that it donated most of the needed right-of-way through the town to the railroad.

Next town north on the projected route was Orchard Park which had yet to enjoy the ministrations of a railroad. According to John N. Printy's brief sketch of the village published in 1969, an old lady, then in her nineties, recalled that:

. . . much of the roadbed was accomplished by Irish immigrant labor. She was told by her parents to be prepared for a severe whipping if they heard of her so much as looking at one of those 'rough, crude individuals!'

In Buffalo, the BR&P purchased thirty acres along the Buffalo Ship Canal on the Island south of the intersection of Michigan and Ganson Streets where yards were built for handling coal trains and interchanging coal cars with other railroads. In addition, a slip was dug to accommodate canal boats. (Figure XV, #6.) At first the DL&W's terminal facilities were used for local freight and passenger service. These proved so inadequate, however, that within a few months the arrangement was abandoned, and a similar one was entered into with the NYC for use of its Exchange Street Station, the junction point being at William Street. The Buffalo Creek Railroad provided the connection from Buffalo Creek to the NYC's mainline. (Figure #1.) In addition to coal and iron ore, the Buffalo line produced some on-line traffic. Besides lumber, feed, and general merchandise business generated by the small towns along the line, brick yards were located at Orchard Park, Loveland, and Jewettville.

The first passenger train left Buffalo for Pittsburgh on June 5, 1883. Pullman cars were added in December. An 1884 timetable claimed that "our equipment consisting of elegant coaches with air brakes and all the latest improved appliances, with smooth track, fast time, and polite conductors combine to make the Rochester & Pittsburgh Railroad one of the most desirable routes for travel." Two trains left Buffalo daily, the *Buffalo Express* at 8:30 A. M, and the *Pittsburgh Express* at 6:00 P. M. Local stations on the forty-eight mile Buffalo line, almost all of which doubled as telegraph stations, were at West Valley, Riceville, Springville, East Concord, Glenwood, Colden, West Falls, Orchard Park, West Seneca, Buffalo Creek, and East Buffalo.

As later with the LV, expansion had been too rapid, and the R&P went bankrupt in May, 1885. It reemerged in October as the Buffalo

IX, 15

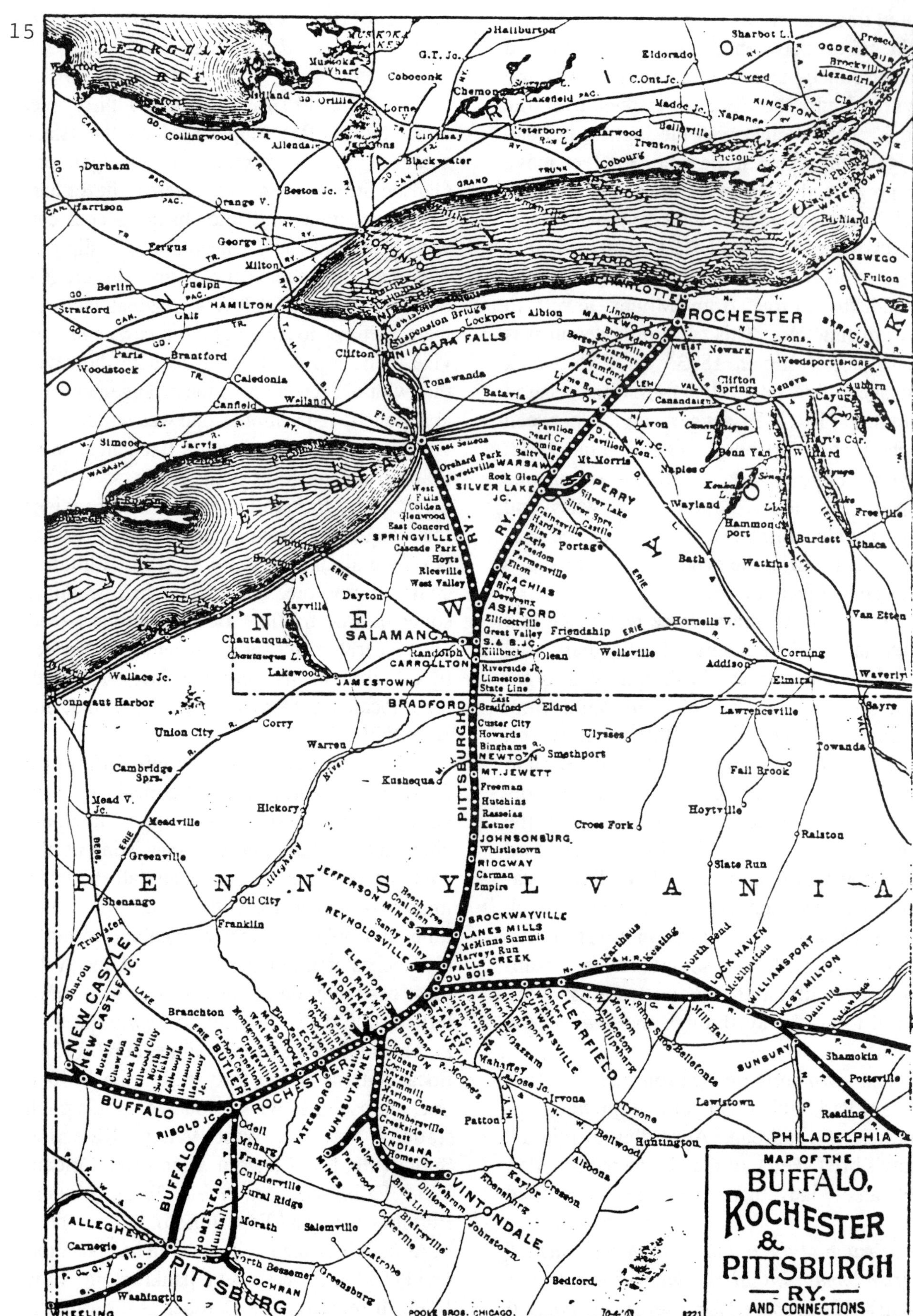
MAP OF THE
BUFFALO,
ROCHESTER
&
PITTSBURGH
RY.
AND CONNECTIONS
POOLE BROS. CHICAGO.
ROCHESTER
BUFFALO
NIAGARA FALLS
Lockport
Albion
Batavia
Lewiston
Suspension Bridge
Tonawanda
Clifton
West Seneca
Orchard Park
WARSAW
SILVER LAKE JC.
PERRY
Silver Lake
Portage
Mt. Morris
Avon
Pavilion
Charlotte
SPRINGVILLE
West Valley
MACHIAS
ASHFORD
Great Valley
SALAMANCA
Olean
Friendship
Wellsville
Hornells V.
Bath
Corning
Elmira
Addison
Waverly
Sayre
Ithaca
Watkins
Geneva
Auburn
Newark
Lyons
Canandaigua
Naples
Wayland
JAMESTOWN
Lakewood
Chautauqua
Mayville
Dayton
Randolph
CARROLLTON
Killbuck
Riverside Jc.
Limestone
State Line
BRADFORD
East Bradford
Eldred
Custer City
Howards
Binghams
NEWTON
Smethport
MT. JEWETT
Kushequa
Freeman
Hutchins
Ketner
JOHNSONBURG
Whistletown
RIDGWAY
Carman
Empire
BROCKWAYVILLE
LANES MILLS
McMinns Summit
Harveys Run
FALLS CREEK
DU BOIS
Sandy Valley
REYNOLDSVILLE
JEFFERSON MINES
CLEARFIELD
CURWENSVILLE
PUNXSUTAWNEY
INDIANA
Homer Cy.
VINTONDALE
Ebensburg
Johnstown
Cresson
Altoona
Bellwood
Tyrone
Huntingdon
Bedford
Latrobe
Greensburg
Salemville
Blairsville
Black Lick
YATESBORO
Dillwyn
Kaylor
Odell
Frazier
Cummerville
Rural Ridge
Morath
BUTLER
RISOLD JC.
HOMESTEAD
North Bessemer
COCHRAN
PITTSBURG
ALLEGHENY
Carnegie
Washington
WHEELING
NEW CASTLE
NEW CASTLE JC.
Sharon
Branchton
Greenville
Shenango
Meadville
Mead V. Jc.
Franklin
Oil City
Hickory
Warren
Corry
Union City
Cambridge Sprs.
Conneaut Harbor
Wallace Jc.
Ulysses
Cross Fork
Lawrenceville
Towanda
Fall Brook
Hoytville
Ralston
Slate Run
LOCK HAVEN
WILLIAMSPORT
WEST MILTON
SUNBURY
Danville
Shamokin
Pottsville
Reading
PHILADELPHIA
Bellefonte
Lewistown
Irvona
Patton
Mahaffey
N. Y. C. & H. R.
Karthaus
Keating
North Bend
Philipsburg
Mill Hall
NEW
PENNSYLVANIA
HAMILTON
Galt
Stratford
Berlin
Guelph
Fergus
Milton
Paris
Brantford
Woodstock
Caledonia
Welland
Canfield
Jarvis
Simcoe
TORONTO
Orange V.
Durham
Collingwood
Allendale
Beeton Jc.
Blackwater
Lindsay
Coboconk
Haliburton
Cobourg
Trenton
Belleville
Napanee
KINGSTON
Picton
Tweed
Eldorado
Sharbot L.
Brockville
Prescott
OGDENSBURG
WATERTOWN
Richland
OSWEGO
Fulton
SYRACUSE
ONTARIO
ERIE
GRAND TRUNK
PITTSBURGH
RY.

Rochester & Pittsburgh, a title more in keeping with its "Y" shaped route. (Figure #15.) A major figure in the reorganization was Arthur Yates, who served as president of the road from 1890 to 1910. He was a Rochester coal merchant with interests in several coal mines around Du Bois, Pennsylvania. He was also the largest coal shipper on the BR&P. His son Harry came to Buffalo in 1892 as President of the Rochester & Pittsburgh Coal & Iron Company. Later he branched out into steel making and the hotel business. He moved to Orchard Park where he began with a horse farm and eventually owned 3,599 acres, becoming the town's largest taxpayer. He donated land for a Protestant church, a Catholic church and cemetery, a public park, and a garbage disposal plant. Yates also arranged the elimination of several grade crossings and the construction of a station grander than Orchard Park's population at the time warranted.

Concerning the towns along the line of the BR&P, Horton writes:

They had good reason for their gratitude; since they were among the last in the county to obtain a road. Nigh desperate at being bypassed, Springville in the early '70s through Hugh Leland, C. J. Shuttleworth and Bertrand Chaffee attempted to persuade Buffalo capitalists to join in the project of a narrow gauge railway to connect the village with the county seat. Nothing came of this project, but a similar one was carried out. From 1878 well into the '80s the narrow gauge Springville & Sardinia Railroad operated between Springville and a junction with the Buffalo & Washington at Chaffee. The place was named in honor of Bertrand Chaffee. Of portentous weight and girth, this tutelary god of the narrow gauge experiment was the kind of being of whom men invented legends. After heavy rains had unsettled the bed of the Springville & Sardinia, he was wont to tread the track ahead of the engine to make the passage of the train steady and safe. [9] (For an S&S engine, see Figure #16.)

IX, 16

The three-foot 11.57 mile long S&S had cost $61,813 to build and was laid with very light twenty-five pounds to the yard rail. With the coming of the BR&P through Springville in 1883 the short line became superfluous and was abandoned in 1886. "Its last great surge of business," Pietrak writes, "was 3000 tons of stonework, huge quantities of rail, timber and iron materials for the Cascade Bridge [over the Cattaraugus Creek Gorge] - a bridge that would carry the very railroad which would put the little S&S out of business."

Narrow gauge construction in America flourished during the twenty years after the Civil War. At its peak there were 750 narrow gauge roads (anything less than standard) in the United States. Colorado once had twenty-five narrow gauge railroads including the multibranched 1,641.87 mile Denver & Rio Grande and the 265.24 mile Denver South Park & Pacific. New York had nineteen narrow gauge railroads totaling 389.31 miles, the longest of which was the 58.89 mile Allegany Central. As Paul Darrell wrote in his introduction to Narrow Gauge Railways in America:

Powerful arguments in their favor were economy of construction, even in difficult country, and light locomotives and rolling stock. The distinct disadvantages of transshipment of goods from narrow gauge to standard gauge cars, and vice versa, plus the active enmity of the older established standard gauge lines, soon undermined the advocacy of the narrow gauges. As our railroad system expanded, the undesirable break of gauge made operations more difficult for any line that was not of standard gauge. The principle of interchangeability of equipment is the backbone of the great American network. Anything that interfered with this precept was bound to be bypassed as the railroad system expanded. [10]

The New York West Shore & Buffalo [11]

The mid-eighties mark a critical period in the growth of American railroads and the development of the management policies on which their golden age of prosperity was based. Nowhere was the stability of the railroad industry more seriously threatened than in the northeast, the economic heart of the nation, where the outcome depended of the creation of a balance of power between the NYC and the PRR, giants that were not in harmony in the early 1880s. Nor did the public really benefit from the lower rates, supposedly the result of cutthroat competition, since the inequities of discriminatory short haul rates, by which lines sought to make up in some localities what they were losing elsewhere, would become a principal grievance of the Progressive Era. The critical stage of the period of rugged individualism came in 1885 when the NYC and the PRR came face to face in two railroad building projects undertaken to duplicate their mainlines. This West Shore-South Pennsylvania episode marked J. P. Morgan's first major effort to bring harmony, as he called it, to the uncontrolled and often destructive individualism of late nineteenth century American capitalism.

By the mid-1870s there was a growing feeling that a railroad paralleling the NYC from New York to Buffalo, where it could connect with existing roads to Chicago, would be a money-maker. The more cynical believed that such a road could be sold to the NYC on a blackmail basis. William H. Vanderbilt showed his horror of competition in 1882 when he hurriedly bought control of the NKP which threatened his highly profitable LS&MS between Buffalo and Chicago. But there was a real need for another rail artery up the west shore of the Hudson, at least to Albany, to service river communities lacking major railroad service like Newburgh, Kingston, and Catskill. Especially attractive was the prospect of avoiding the New York City bottleneck to through travel from Washington, Baltimore, and Philadelphia to the increasingly popular resorts in the Catskills and Adirondacks. Through service from the

South to Boston would also become possible via the west shore of the Hudson to Albany, and from there to Boston via the projected Boston Hoosac Tunnel & Western. The Hoosac's president had moved in this direction by acquiring a bankrupt New Jersey railroad which had begun a west shore line, the New York West Shore & Chicago, incorporated in 1870, but he died before he could pursue his plans further. The NYWS&C's promoters had a survey done which envisioned a line with slight grades twenty-four miles shorter from New York to Buffalo than the NYC. Another victim of the Panic of 1873, it was ordered sold in 1879, having constructed only two miles of track. The only real progress in the area had been made by the Jersey City & Albany which opened its first twenty-four mile section from the PRR's Jersey City terminal to Tappantown just across the New York line in August, 1873, before going bankrupt.

With the return of prosperity in the early eighties, Edward F. Winslow, a former Union cavalry general, had managed the construction of the New York Ontario & Western. This was an anemic line which meandered diagonally across New York from Oswego to Middletown, aiming for Cornwall on the Hudson. Winslow then consolidated the Jersey City & Albany with his own North River Railroad, a paper corporation, in May, 1881, and a month later merged those two properties together with the unbuilt New York West Shore & Chicago into a new corporation, the New York West Shore & Buffalo. Support for the new line began to appear. George Pullman, the nation's leading builder and operator of sleeping and parlor cars, had not forgiven the NYC for substituting Wagner Palace Cars for Pullmans. Pullman's New York representative, General Horace Porter, became president of the West Shore, and construction progressed rapidly.

By the end of 1882, $7 million of the authorized $10 million capital had reportedly been paid in. The NYWS&B was a well engineered railroad. If it had obtained enough working capital to carry it through its first few years and had solved the problem of a convenient entry to Manhattan (a very big "if"), it might have become a serious competitor of the NYC. But the West Shore faced initial construction tasks which quickly absorbed most of the capital raised during the first rush of enthusiasm. Just outside its terminal at Weehawken, New Jersey, across the river from 42nd Street, a 4,225 foot tunnel had to be bored through Bergen Hill before trains could go anywhere. Eight more tunnels were required on the way to Albany. Eventually $50 million in first mortgage bonds were issued by the NYWS&B, but to whom and at what price cannot be determined. While as much as $35 million may have actually been raised, much less was available for actual construction. The company, therefore, found itself in trouble before it reached the point where it could even meet operating expenses.

The first passenger train ran from Jersey City to Newburgh in June, 1883. By October the line was open to Syracuse, and service to Buffalo began in January, 1884. A through route to Chicago was secured by an arrangement with the Grand Trunk west of Buffalo, but the NYWS&B's bid for this lucrative business was not successful. Unable to match the speed and convenience of the NYC, the road was forced to cut fares to attract more than local passengers, of whom there were not many. The month the road reached Buffalo it went bankrupt, which induced more rate cuts, forcing the NYC to do the same with disastrous results on Wall Street. Harlow records the ultimate indignity:

Then one day the Buffalo New York & Philadelphia, with whom the NYWS&B was sharing a makeshift depot at Buffalo (Figure VII, #2) ordered the NYWS&B out because of non-payment of rent and tore up some rods of its track. The receivers made hurried promises by wire, scraped up some money, the tracks were replaced overnight, and the road had a place to hang its hat though precariously. [12]

While the NYWS&B's promoters were still permitted to dream, they envisioned a splendid terminal in Buffalo of steel and pressed brick. After the flamboyant fashion of the eighties it was to have a clock tower, a port cochere, and a train shed 600 feet long arching over eight platform tracks. The BNY&P was to share in this magnificence, and four platform tracks were assigned to it. The hope was that the NKP, the Erie, or the recently completed DL&W might eventually come in, but these roads were already provided for and evidenced no intention of moving. Instead of the initially calculated $200,000, it was discovered that this terminal would cost twice that sum. Therefore the WNY&P, a poor relation at best, backed off the new terminal project which was quickly abandoned.

While the NYWS&B failed to take over much NYC business, it did succeed in upsetting the NYC's owner. Ordinarily, William Vanderbilt was a coolheaded man, but the assault of the NYWS&B, following so closely what he considered the Nickel Plate blackmail, upset his balance, and, as in that case, he moved too quickly and in the wrong direction. He believed, moreover, that his rival was receiving substantial assistance from the PRR beyond the use of its Jersey City terminal. Determined not to submit to extortion this time, he decided to fight back by invading the territory of his supposed tormentor. No evidence exists to support the widely held belief that Vanderbilt's suspicions were correct.

Means for retaliation were at hand. Beginning in 1881, Vanderbilt's son-in-law, Hamilton McK. Twombley, had bankrolled a survey for a railroad from Harrisburg to Pittsburgh, the South Pennsylvania, a route that had been proposed even before the Pennsylvania had been built in the 1840s. Vanderbilt's decision to undertake what had become his son-in-law's project was due in part to the willingness of Robert B. Sayre of the LV to assume responsibility for building and operating the South Pennsylvania. Another powerful ally was Andrew Carnegie, who had chafed for years at the lack of an viable alternate to the PRR as an outlet for his mills in Pittsburgh. He assumed, moreover, that the NYC and the PRR would continue as rivals for the foreseeable future. When he was shown the plans for the new undertaking while visiting Vanderbilt in New York, Carnegie expressed his delight and offered to raise $5 million for the enterprise. Equally delighted, Vanderbilt decided to put up another $5 million. Vanderbilt, Carnegie, and twenty eight other investors formed the "South Pennsylvania Syndicate." They agreed to raise the $15 million estimated cost of a railroad from Harrisburg to a connection with the Vanderbilt-controlled Pittsburgh & Lake Erie southeast of Pittsburgh. Only about five miles of actual railroad were ever built. From the beginning of the project in November, 1883, emphasis was placed on its main features, nine tunnels totaling about seven miles, and a bridge over the Susquehanna at Harrisburg. When the final halt was called in 1885, $5.7 million of the Syndicate's money, thirty-eight percent of the $15 million subscribed, had been spent. It was estimated that $4 million more would have finished the job.

As Vanderbilt contemplated the unstable railroad situation aggravated by his launching of the South Pennsylvania and as he watched NYC common stock sink below par for the first time since the Commodore had taken control, he must have shuddered at what his father would have thought. Where was the South Pennsylvania's traffic to come from? His experience with the NKP had shown that most of the new line's traffic would have to be donated by the NYC, and in this case it would have to be shared with the Reading east of Harrisburg. Vanderbilt had invested heavily in the Reading and was an ally of its mercurial president, Francis B. Gown, a member of the South Pennsylvania Syndicate who loathed the

PRR. When Vanderbilt decided to abandon ship, most of the other Syndicate members went along. But a way would have to be found to recover some of the Syndicate's money and Vanderbilt's pride. When overtures were made to the PRR, however, its officials warned that the South Pennsylvania problem was not going to be solved in isolation from the problems of rates, service, and invasion of the territory of one road by another.

Enter J. P. Morgan, on whose recommendation many European investors had poured hundreds of millions into American railroads. The NYC had just caused a sensation on Wall Street by cutting its annual dividend from $8 to $6, and its stock price dropped ominously. Lower earnings, stemming from the rate war with the NYWS&B, were part of the reason. Morgan saw that the NYC would have to take over the NYWS&B, and in view of its sad financial condition, he was sure it could be gotten at a bargain price. George Roberts, President of the PRR, would have let the members of the Syndicate swing in the breeze, but Morgan explained that the PRR's gain would more than justify the price. Aboard the *Corsair*, Morgan's yacht, as it steamed up the East River to Long Island Sound and back on July 7, 1885, were Morgan, Roberts and his heir, Frank Thomson, and Chauncey Depew, President of the NYC. It was agreed that the PRR would buy the South Pennsylvania at a price acceptable to most of the Syndicate. The PRR would also be permitted to buy the Beech Creek Railroad, a coal carrying road which Vanderbilt interests had built into PRR territory. The NYC was to take over the NYWS&B, thus removing it as a disruptive force in the eastern trunk line picture. Passenger and freight rates in competitive territory would be reestablished and maintained at their former profitable levels.

The agreement was not implemented. The PRR was enjoined by the Pennsylvania Supreme Court from purchasing either the South Pennsylvania or the Beech Creek since they were both competitors of the PRR, so the Syndicate did not recover any of its investment at this time. Vanderbilt died on December 8, and his heirs bought out the other Syndicate members for sixty cents on the dollar. The PRR honored what its management called its "moral obligation" to the Vanderbilts at the rate of thirty-two cents on each dollar William H. had sunk in the South Pennsylvania. On December 4, the NYWS&B was sold under foreclosure to three representatives of the Vanderbilt interest who had organized a new West Shore Railroad Company with capital of only $10 million, all of which was provided by the NYC. The new corporation was then leased to the NYC for 474 years. The West Shore Railroad Company, now with solid backing, issued $50 million in four percent bonds of which half went to the holders of the $50 million old bonds. They thus recouped fifty cents on each dollar they had invested in the NYWS&B. The other $25 million would be used to pay off the debts of the road and to finish and equip it. The Central had thus acquired cheaply - only $2 million in interest a year - an alternate low-grade line to Buffalo which was to become a valuable property. (Figure #17.)

On its way through Erie County the NYWS&B passed through Clarence (population 1875, 3,349). From land surveys that were being made, residents learned in November, 1881, that a railroad was projected through the southeast corner of Clarence, and that some of the village's finest buildings and oldest landmarks were on the right of way and would have to be moved or torn down. Two indignation meetings were held, one at Harris Hill where the farmers announced their refusal to sell their land at the price offered by the railroad.

These problems were ironed out, and early next summer the surveyors finished their work. Some homeowners supplemented their income by boarding laborers, and one resident of Harris Hill began turning out ties. Trees were cut down and grading across Main Street

IX, 17

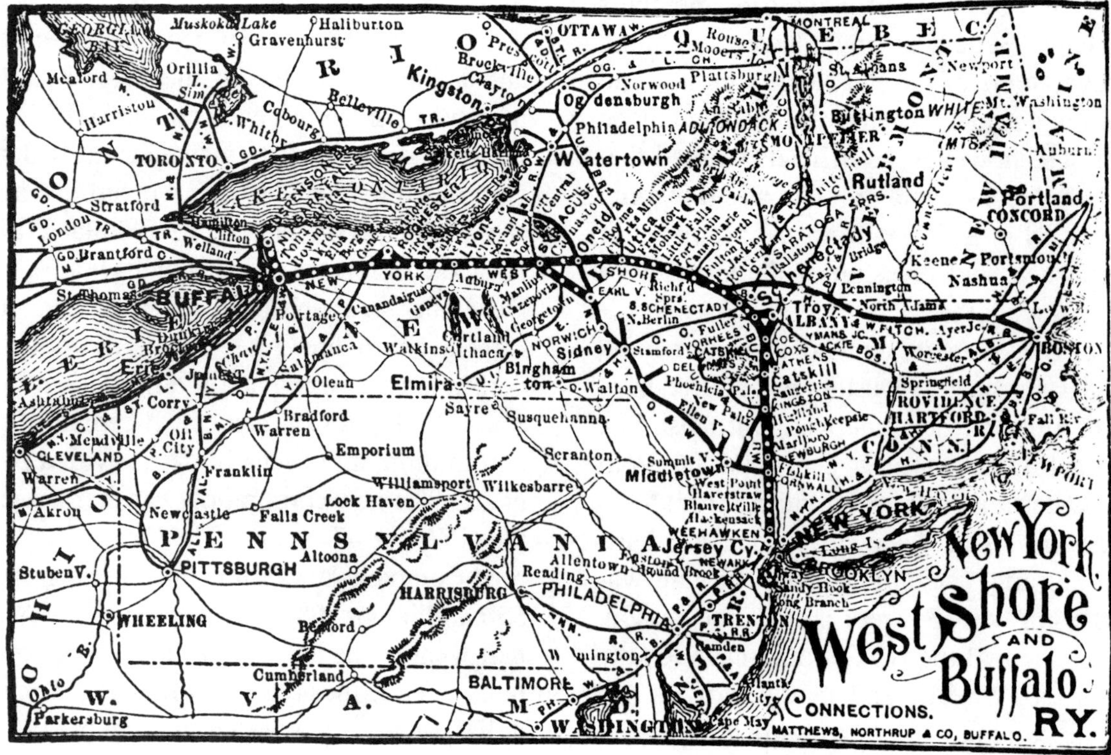

began. One senior citizen remarked, "Our sleepy hollow village looks like the day after the Resurrection." Men and horses did most of the construction work. However, some steam engines were used, including a steam drill and a steam shovel that was kept going day and night at the gravel pit excavating ballast. Local farmers earned extra money with their teams, while other teamsters came from as far away as Rochester. Stone cutters were imported for the stone facing on the abutments of the bridge over Ransom Road. In the late summer of 1883, architect's plans for the depot were put on display in a local store window awaiting bids. In November, 1883, the first freight rumbled over the line from Syracuse to Buffalo, and on New Year's Day, 1884, the first passenger train passed through Clarence, as reported by the local paper:

Many of the citizens gathered at the depot yesterday to welcome the first train from the east due at 11:11 A. M. It was some two hours late but they stood the cold northeast wind which came sweeping down the track, heroically, and at 1:10 P. M. the whistle was heard and upon approach loud cheers were sent forth with the tossing of hats and the waving of handkerchiefs. [13]

Telegraphy preceded regular train operations. With Christmas at hand, inhabitants began to think about distant friends and relatives to whom they sent messages from a temporary telegraph station set up in a shanty pending the completion of the depot in December, 1883. A crossing shanty was placed on Main Street for a flagman. Despite his warning, however, numerous accidents occurred here until the residents got used to the trains.

In the spring of 1884 the depot was completed. Figure #18 shows the nearby Bowmansville station. Its gingerbread design and balcony were characteristic of West Shore structures. Students of the country railroad station write:

IX, 18

The West Shore accepted the idea of standardized depots, understandable since it built them in the early heyday of carbon copy architecture. The parent New York Central seemed sufficiently impressed to adopt the West Shore's plans. [14]

The local paper remarked that "the employees at the depot have their new suits with brass buttons and caps to match. They now present quite a nobby appearance." There arose good-natured rivalry between Clarence and Clarence Center (three miles north on the Peanut) over the merits of their respective trains. Clarence Centerites boasted that a train was old stuff to them, while Clarentians boasted that their train at least arrived on time. Stations on the West Shore between Rochester and Buffalo were located at Churchville Junction, Churchville, Bergen, Byron Center, Elba, Oakfield, Alabama, Akron, Clarence, Bowmansville, and East Buffalo Junction.

Eastward the West Shore provided through passenger service to Boston as well as New York. Its partner in this arrangement was the Fitchburg Railroad, which had put together an east-west route across Massachusetts through the Hoosac Tunnel, paralleling to the north the Boston & Albany. This 4.6 mile long tunnel had been completed in 1875 at a cost of 195 lives. The Fitchburg, which was taken over by the Boston & Maine in 1900, linked up with the NYWS&B at Rotterdam Junction, eighteen miles west of Albany.

The Rome Watertown & Ogdensburg

Watertown was a thriving lumber mill town on the lower Black River in the North Country near Lake Ontario. Though the Watertown & Rome had been chartered back in 1832 to link Watertown with the projected Utica & Syracuse, construction under the auspices of the Watertown & Rome Railroad did not begin until 1849. In September, 1851, this seventy-two mile line was opened between its titular terminals and was extended next spring twenty-five miles farther to Cape Vincent where Lake Ontario flows into the Saint Lawrence River, a ferry ride across from Kingston, Ontario.

At the beginning of the Civil War, the Watertown & Rome took over the financially troubled Potsdam & Watertown, a seventy-six mile line from Watertown northeast to a junction with the Northern Railroad. The Northern (after 1864 the Ogdensburg & Lake Champlain) ran from Ogdensburg, a busy Saint Lawrence port above rapids of the Saint Lawrence, to Rouses Point on the northern tip of Lake Champlain. There a connection was made with New England's railroad system via the Vermont & Canada and the Vermont Central, both of which later became part of the Rutland. Thus came into being a route from Boston to the Great Lakes via Northern New England and Northern New York.

The result of the merger of the Watertown & Rome and the Potsdam & Watertown was christened the Rome Watertown & Ogdensburg, since a branch, which soon became the mainline, was built to Ogdensburg from De Kalb Junction. From Richland, about halfway between Rome and Watertown, another branch extended twenty-eight miles westward to the historic Lake Ontario port of Oswego, thirty-six miles north of Syracuse. The RW&O reached Syracuse in 1868 by leasing the Syracuse & Northern. The result of this topsy-like growth by absorption was a regional network with three southern terminals, Rome, Syracuse, and Oswego. (Figure #19.)

The road's directors should have quit while they were ahead. Their next move, the acquisition of the Lake Ontario Shore Railroad, led to bankruptcy. Niagara County historian Edward T. William's tells the story:

In the Spring of 1870 the Lake Ontario Shore Railroad Company was organized at Oswego. The road which the company was formed to build was intended to be part of a future trunk line from Boston to the west. The

IX, 19

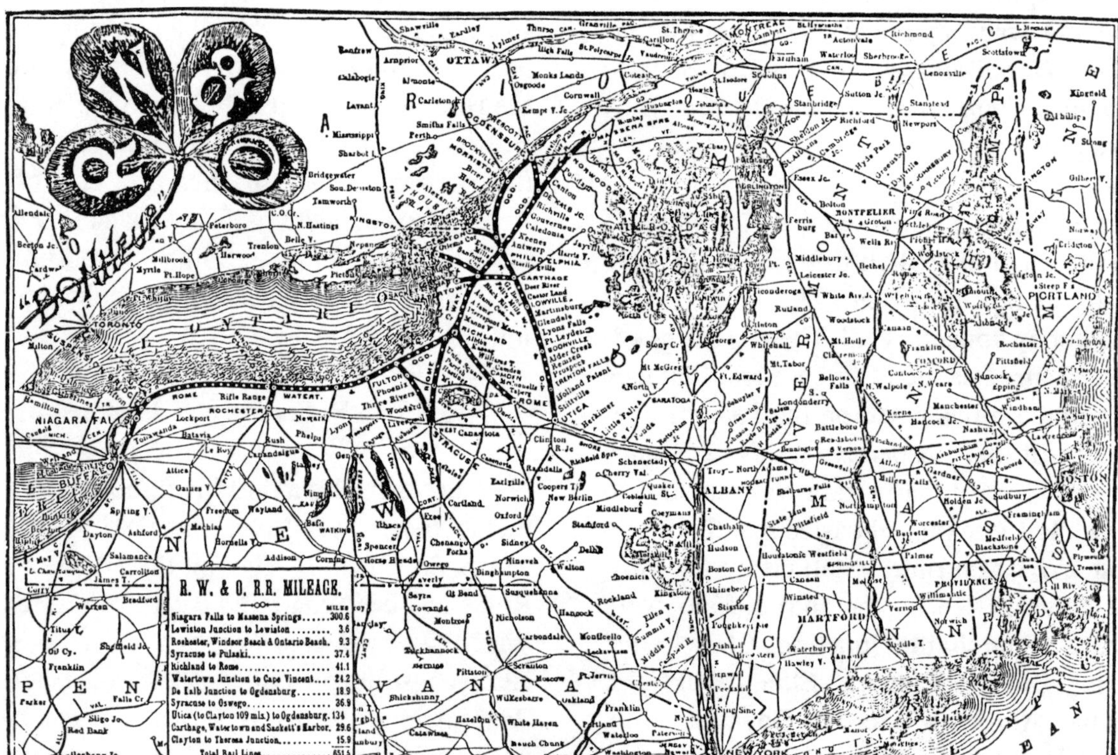

R. W. & O. R.R. MILEAGE.

	MILES
Niagara Falls to Massena Springs	300.6
Lewiston Junction to Lewiston	3.6
Rochester, Windsor Beach & Ontario Beach.	9.3
Syracuse to Pulaski	37.4
Richland to Rome	41.1
Watertown Junction to Cape Vincent	24.2
De Kalb Junction to Ogdensburg	18.9
Syracuse to Oswego	36.9
Utica (to Clayton 109 mls.) to Ogdensburg.	134
Carthage, Watertown and Sackett's Harbor.	29.6
Clayton to Theresa Junction	15.9
Total Rail Lines	651.5
St'mb't & Ferry Lines controlled by this Co.	84
Total	[illegible]

town of Kendall, Orleans County, gave its bonds for $60,000 worth of the stock; Yates, $100,000; Somerset, Niagara County, $90,000; Newfane, $88,000; Wilson, $117,000; Lewiston $152,000. The work of construction proceeded slowly. Litigation over the town bonds checked their sale and crippled the company so that it could not complete the road. In May, 1874, the Rome, Watertown & Ogdensburg Railroad Company assumed the undertaking. The road was then principally graded, but it was more than a year before the bridges on the western end of the line were finished. In the latter part of July, 1875, track was laid twenty miles west of the Genesee River, and was carried through Orleans County during the autumn, and to Lewiston in the following spring. Afterward the road was built into the then village of Suspension Bridge. In its early days the road had a heavy passenger traffic by reason of the fact that immigrant trains from New York bearing immigrants bound for the west through Canada over the New York Ontario & Western were run to Niagara Falls over the Rome Watertown & Ogdensburg. As the railroad runs through the great fruit belt of Niagara County the freight business is heavy, especially in the fall. [15]

The mainline of the LOS, which was bought at auction at seventy-three cents on the dollar of its bonded indebtedness by interests representing the RW&O, missed most major cities including Rochester. It quickly became a drain on the finances of its owner, which entered bankruptcy in 1878 and fell into the hands of the DL&W. Samuel Sloan, President of the DL&W, became President of the RW&O, and deliberately sabotaged the little railroad in favor of his first love.

A savior of the road appeared four years later in the person of Charles Parsons who picked up enough of the road's cheap stock to oust Sloan. Parsons rehabilitated the road and acquired the Black River & Utica which connected Utica on the south with Sackett's Harbor, Clayton, and Ogdensburg on the north via three separate branches. Thus was expanded the dream of linking Boston with the Great Lakes which had been the original purpose of purchasing the LOS. Parsons also built a spur into Rochester from Charlotte, and extended the mainline past Potsdam Junction to Massena, near the Canadian border, from which a branch of the Grand Trunk provided access to Montreal. Threatened, the NYC moved to head off competition by stock purchases, an expensive proposition since in early March, 1891, RW&O stock, which had sold for $10 a decade before, was quoted at $123. On March 14th it was announced that the 643 mile system had been leased to the NYC.

At the western end of the RW&O, access to Buffalo was via the NYC from Suspension Bridge. Niagara County stations were at Lewiston, Ransomville, Wilson, Newfane, Hess Road, and Somerset. Between Lewiston and Suspension Bridge a right of way had been run up the Niagara Escarpment and straight through the campus of the College and Seminary of Our Lady of Angels (later Niagara University). (Figure #20.) An article in Niagara's November, 1990, faculty and staff newsletter discusses this phenomenon:

Long a part of its history, the railroad tracks that once severed the Niagara University campus have themselves become history. The 1,4000 foot section of tracks was removed after the right-of-way was deeded to the university by Consolidated Rail Corp. (Conrail), the last owner. A small section of track behind Clet Hall has been preserved as a memento of this significant part of the university's lore.

A curiosity to more recent students who have never seen them in use, the tracks had been a part of university life for more than 100 yers. To more seasoned Alumni, the rail line was once a source of cheap transportation to and from campus. For some former students, it was an obstacle to on-time attendance at classes in St. Vincent's Hall.

IX, 20

A reading of the university's early history indicates that no tracks existed on the present campus when the university was founded. [Our Lady of Angels was founded in 1851 and moved to Mounteagle Ridge in 1857.] *A previous right-of-way had been abandoned, the tracks removed, and the roadbed returned to a highway. There was a* [trolley] *line, however, which ran along the gorge* [from 1895 to 1935].

The late Jack Weber, an alumnus of the class of '47 with a keen interest in railroads, found local newspaper accounts which reported that tracks were laid through the NU campus in September, 1880. Almost a year later, in August, 1881, the first freight train traveled to Lewiston on the Rome Watertown & Ogdensburg Railroad.

The tracks were viewed back then as a distinct advantage for the university because of their ability to bring "special Pullman carloads of Alumni from the east and the west right to the very door." In a report on the silver jubilee of the seminary, an occasion celebrated Nov. 23, 1881, the Niagara Index reported that on that day "the giant smoking steed on the RW&O Railroad puffed into the precincts of the seminary grounds at 10 a.m. The two palace coaches annexed bore over 130 persons - the patrons, friends, and former students of Old Niagara."

Referring to efforts to establish a post office on campus, something accomplished in 1887, the diamond jubilee history noted: "The railroad at the side of the athletic field, instead of being a nuisance, would be a distinct help; a help not only for the periodic events of bringing alumni to meetings and crowds to commencement and to games, but a daily help, several times daily, by the receiving and sending of mail."

In her book on local history, Under the Mountain, Margaret D. Robson recounts another interesting story on how the tracks became know as the Hojack line. She writes:

"Whoa Jack!" was applied to the line because one of its first engineers, "Big Jack Welch," being more of a farmer than an engi-

IX, 21

ROME, WATERTOWN AND OGDENSBURG RAILROAD.

New York Central and Hudson River Railroad Co., Lessee.

H. WALTER WEBB, 3d Vice-President, N. Y. C. & H. R. R.R. Co., Grand Cent. Depot, New York.
E. V. W. ROSSITER, Treasurer, "
E. VAN ETTEN, Gen. Superintendent, "
THEO. BUTTERFIELD, Gen. Pass'ger Agt., Syracuse, N.Y.
S. GOODMAN, Gen. Freight Agent, New York.
F. L. WILSON, Asst. Gen. Fht. Agt., Watertown, N. Y.

W. L. KINGMAN, Gen. Coal Agent.
JOHN CARSTENSEN, Comptroller, New York.
ALLAN BOURN, Purchasing Agent, "
F. C. ROOT, Aud. of Disbursements, "
J. F. FAIRLAMB, Aud. of Pas. Accounts, "
W. B. POLLOCK, Aud. of Fht. Accounts, "
C. H. EWINGS, Car Accountant, "

E. G. RUSSELL, Superintendent, Watertown, N.Y.
WM. BUCHANAN, Supt. Motive Power and Rolling Stock, New York.
O. E. JENKINS, Gen. Western Passenger Agent, 95 Clark St., Chicago, Ill.
F. J. WOLFE, Gen. Baggage Agent, Albany, N.Y.
C. HARTIGAN, Traveling Agent, Syracuse, N.Y.

NIAGARA FALLS LINE.

115	117	No. 185	127	M.	*May* 23, 1893.	No. 104	114	124	182	102
N'HT	NO'N		A.M.		LEAVE] [ARRIVE		A.M.	A.M.	A.M.	
*12 20	†12 00	†3 50 P.M.	†6 45		.....**Buffalo**.....	3 05 P.M.	7 25	4 30	11 50	
3 20	*12 52	5 05 P.M.	7 40		..**Niagara Falls**..	1 46 P.M.	5 10	11 00	10 55	
3 30	1 00	5 15 "	7 50	0	**Suspension Bridge**	1 35 "	5 00	10 50	10 45	
....	1 03	5 25 "	7 59	5	+..**Lewiston**..δ	1 25 "	4 45	10 40	10 33	
3 53	1 23	5 42 "	8 15	13	+...Ransomville..δ	1 07 P.M.	4 19	10 13	10 12	
c..	1 37	5 53 "	8 27	19	+.....Wilson......	12 57 NO'N	4 07	10 07	10 01	
c..	1 50	6 04 "	8 40	25	+...New Fane.....	12 46 "	3 54	9 54	9 48	
c..	c..	6 10 "	8 46	28	... Hess Road....	....	3 47	9 48	9 42	
c..	2 08	6 20 "	8 57	33	+...Somerset...δ	12 31 "	3 36	9 37	9 32	
c..	2 19	6 28 "	9 06	37	...County Line...	12 24 "	3 27	9 29	9 23	
4 52	2 27	6 37 "	9 15	41	+..Lyndonville....	12 17 NO'N	3 18	9 20	9 15	
c..	c..	6 45 "	9 24	45	......Carlyon......	....	3 09	9 12	9 06	
5 05	2 44	6 50 "	9 30	49	+...Waterport....	...	d..	9 05	9 00	
5 12	2 51	6 55 "	9 37	51	+....Carlton....δ	11 58 A.M.	d..	8 59	8 53	
5 17	c.	7 02 "	9 43	54	...East Carlton...	....	d..	8 53	8 47	
5 27	3 03	7 11 "	9 54	59	+....Kendall....δ	11 43 "	2 40	8 43	8 37	
5 31	c..	7 16 "	9 59	61	+..East Kendall...	....	d..	8 33	8 3[illegible]	
5 38	c..	7 23 "	10 09	66	+....Hamlin......	11 30 "	d..	8 29	8 22	
5 45	c..	7 29 "	10 16	69	+..East Hamlin...	....	d..	8 23	8 16	
5 52	3 37	7 36 "	10 24	72	+.....Parma......	11 17 "	2 12	8 16	8 08	
5 58	c..	7 43 "	10 31	75	......Greece......	11 12 "	d..	8 09	8 01	
6 12	3 55	7 55 P.M.	10 45	82	arr..Charlotte δ lve.	11 01 A.M.	1 55	8 00	7 48	
6 35	4 23	8 20 P.M.	11 21	89	arr..Rochester..lve.	*10 15 A.M.		†7 15	†7 15	
*5 45	*3 30	†7 15 P.M.	†10 15	89	lve..Rochester..arr.	11 21 A.M.	6 35	8 20	8 05	
6 15	4 00	8 00 P.M.	10 50	83	lv.Windsor Bch.ar.	10 58 A.M.	1 50	7 55	7 45	
....	e..	8 10 "	10 58	87	...Forest Lawn...	g..	....	7 42	7 36	
6 34	4 20	8 18 "	11 08	92	+....Webster....	10 40 "	1 29	7 31	7 25	
6 40	4 25	8 24 "	11 13	95	+...Union Hill....	g..	1 23	7 24	7 20	
6 50	4 34	8 35 "	11 23	99	+....Ontario....δ	g..	1 13	7 13	7 10	
7 00	4 43	8 45 "	11 33	104	+..Williamson....	10 16 "	1 03	7 02	7 00	
7 12	4 54	9 00 "	11 45	110	+....Sodus.......	10 04 "	12 50	6 48	6 47	
7 18	5 00	9 05 "	11 52	113	+.**Wallington** δ	9 58 "	12 43	6 42	6 42	
7 31	5 12	9 21 "	12 06	120	+.....Rose.......	g..	12 27	6 24	6 28	
7 39	5 21	9 31 "	12 15	125	+....Wolcott....δ	9 36 "	12 13	6 13	6 20	
7 50	5 33	9 45 "	12 27	131	+...Red Creek....	9 25 "	12 05	6 03	6 09	
7 59	5 41	9 55 "	12 37	136	+...**Sterling**..δ	9 15 "	11 55	5 53	6 01	
8 10	5 52	10 08 "	12 49	141	+...Hannibal.....	....	11 42	5 39	5 50	
....	e..	10 12 "	12 54	144	.... Wheeler's	....	....	5 32	5 45	
8 30	6 10	10 30 P.M.	‖1 10	151	.....**Oswego**...δ	*8 45 A.M.	*11 20	†5 15	†5 30	
A.M.	P.M.		P.M.		ARRIVE] [LEAVE		P.M.	P.M.	A.M.	102
A.M.	P.M.		P.M.		LEAVE] [ARRIVE		P.M.	P.M.		NO'N
†9 35	†6 30	†6 20 A.M.	1 30	151	+...**Oswego**.....	8 20 A.M.	9 15	5 16		12 15
9 48	6 46	6 35 "	1 49	159	.......Scriba......	8 04 "	8 56	4 58		11 57
9 57	6 53	6 42 "	1 57	162	...New Haven....	7 57 "	8 47	4 50		11 47
10 08	7 05	6 52 "	2 08	167	+....Mexico....δ	7 47 "	8 36	4 39		11 36
....	7 15	7 03 "	2 15	172	.....Sand Hill.....	7 35 "	8 24	4 27		11 23
10 30	7 25	7 10 "	2 28	176	+....Pulaski....δ	7 28 "	8 15	4 13		11 15
10 40	‖7 35	7 20 "	2 38	180	arr.+**Richland** δ lve.	7 20 "	8 05	4 10		11 05
A.M.	7 50	7 30 "	2 58	180	lve. **Richland**...arr.	‖7 10 "	‖7 40	4 05		11 00
	8 02	7 40 "	3 08	186	+..Sandy Creek..δ	7 00 "	7 23	3 53		10 47
	8 12	7 50 "	3 17	190	.... Mannsville..δ	6 50 "	7 19	3 45		10 39
	8 17	7 54 "	3 21	192	Pierrepont Manor δ	6 46 "	7 15	3 42		10 35
	8 30	8 04 "	3 32	198	+ ....Adams....δ	6 35 "	7 05	3 32		10 25
	8 38	8 12 "	3 40	202	..Adams Centre.δ	6 26 "	6 55	3 20		10 16
	9 15	8 45 "	4 10	212	....**Watertown**...δ	†6 05 A.M.	6 30	2 57		9 55
	9 25	8 55 "	4 20	216	Sanford's Corners δ		6 09	2 37		9 42
	9 35	9 07 "	4 30	221	+..Evans Mills..δ		5 58	2 28		9 32
	9 53	9 35 "	5 00	228	+..**Philadelphia**..δ		5 45	2 15		9 20
	10 05	9 48 "	5 20	234	+....Antwerp...δ		5 20	2 00		8 46
	10 14	9 58 "	5 30	240	..... Keene's...δ		5 08	1 49		8 36
	10 30	10 13 "	5 45	246	+..Gouverneur .δ		4 55	1 36		8 23
	10 43	10 26 "	5 58	254	.....Richville...δ		4 39	1 19		8 08
	11 00	10 50 "	6 15	262	+.**De Kalb Jn.** δ		4 25	‖1 05		7 55
	11 17	11 08 "	6 33	270	+.....Canton....δ		4 05	12 27		7 37
	11 40	11 35 "	6 53	280	+....Potsdam...δ		3 43	12 04		7 15
	11 55	11 50 A.M.	7 05	286	+...**Norwood**..δ		3 30	11 50		†7 00
	P.M.	12 20 NO'N	7 30	299	.**Massena Springs**.		†3 00	†11 20		A.M.
			P.M.		ARRIVE] [LEAVE		P.M.	A.M.		
					.....**Malone**.....			9 10		
					.**Rouse's Point**.			†7 00		
					.....**Fabyans** ...			A.M.		
					....**Portland**....					
					ARRIVE] [LEAVE					

CARTHAGE, WATERTOWN & SACKETT'S HARBOR LINE.

Pas.	Pas.	Pas.	Pas.	Mls.	*May* 28, 1893.	Pas.	Pas.	Pas.	Pas.
P.M.	P.M.	A.M.			LEAVE] [ARRIVE	A.M.	P.M.		P.M.
†5 50	†1 20	*5 50		0	........**Utica**........	9 50	1 00		10 05
7 13	2 37	7 13		35	......Boonville.......	8 30	11 38		8 42
8 03	3 23	8 15		58	.......Lowville.......	7 30	10 41		7 40
P.M.	P.M.	A.M.			LEAVE] [ARRIVE	A.M.	A.M.	P.M.	P.M.
†8 35	†4 05	*8 55		74	+....**Carthage**....δ	6 47	9 38	1 02	6 52
8 48	4 18	9 08		81	+....Great Bend....δ	6 37	9 28	12 52	6 42
8 53	4 23	9 13		83	+....Felt's Mills....δ	6 32	9 23	12 47	6 37
8 58	4 28	9 18		85	+....Black River....δ	6 25	9 18	12 42	6 32
9 10	4 40	9 30	A.M.	92	ar.+ **Watertown** δ lv.	†6 10	†9 05	†12 30	*6 20
P.M.	4 40	A.M.	†7 00	92	lve..**Watertown**..arr.	A.M.	9 05	NO'N	6 00
	5 05		7 40	104	+..**Sackett's Harbor**....		†8 10		†6 30
	P.M.		A.M.		ARRIVE] [LEAVE		A.M.		P.M.

CAPE VINCENT LINE.

Pas.	Pas.	Pas.	M	*May* 28, 1893.	Pas.	Pas.	Pas.
	A.M.	P.M.		LEAVE] [ARRIVE		P.M.	A.M.
	7 40	5 05		...**Niagara Falls**...		11 30	5 10
	A.M.	P.M.		LEAVE] [ARRIVE		P.M.	A.M.
	7 50	5 15		..**Suspension Bridge**..		10 50	5 00
	A.M.	P.M.		LEAVE] [ARRIVE		P.M.	A.M.
	10 15	7 15		......**Rochester**....		3 20	6 35
	P.M.	A.M.		LEAVE] [ARRIVE	NO'N	P.M.	P.M.
	1 30	6 20		......**Oswego**......	12 15	5 15	9 15
	P.M.	A.M.		LEAVE] [ARRIVE	NO'N	P.M.	P.M.
	1 10	5 40		......**Syracuse**.....	12 30	5 45	9 45
	P.M.	A.M.		LEAVE] [ARRIVE	NO'N		P.M.
	1 40	5 50		........**Rome**........	12 08		9 25
31	29	27			28	30	32
P.M.	P.M.	A.M.		LEAVE] [ARRIVE	A.M.	NO'N	P.M.
†6 35	†4 05	†8 55	0	+...**Watertown**..δ	8 27	12 12	6 12
6 50	4 20	9 10	5	+....Brownville....δ	8 12	11 57	5 57
6 57	4 27	9 17	9	......Limerick.....δ	8 03	11 48	5 50
7 07	4 37	9 27	14	+....Chaumont......	7 55	11 38	5 41
7 14	4 44	9 34	17	+..Three-mile Bay.δ	7 46	11 31	5 34
7 30	5 00	9 50	25	+.**Cape Vincent**.δ	†7 30	†11 15	†5 20
P.M.	P.M.	A.M.		ARRIVE] [LEAVE	A.M.	A.M.	P.M.
				(*Via Steamer*)			
	7 00	12 00		.....**Kingston**......	†5 00		†2 30
	P.M.	NO'N		ARRIVE] [LEAVE	A.M.		P.M.
				..**Alexandria Bay**..			
				ARRIVE] [LEAVE			

OSWEGO AND ROME LINE.

Pas.	Pas.	Pas.	Ml.	*May* 28, 1893.	Pas.	Pas.	Pas.
P.M.	P.M.	A.M.		LEAVE] [ARRIVE	A.M.	NO'N	P.M.
†5 50	†1 15	†5 25		........**Utica**........	9 13	12 30	9 45
†6 15	†1 40	†5 50	0	+.......**Rome**......δ	8 45	12 08	9 25
6 28	....	....	7	......Humaston	8 28	....	....
6 34	1 53	6 10	11	........Taberg......δ	8 23	11 51	9 00
6 38	2 03	6 15	13	...McConnellsville..δ	8 18	11 46	8 55
6 48	2 13	6 25	18	+......Camden......δ	8 10	11 38	8 45
6 58	2 22	6 35	23	.....West Camden...δ	7 59	11 29	8 34
7 06	2 31	6 45	28	.....Williamstown...δ	7 51	11 21	8 25
7 12	2 37	6 51	31	........Kasoag......δ	7 46	11 16	8 13
7 21	2 46	7 01	36	+......Sand Bank....δ	7 38	11 08	8 10
‖7 30	2 53	7 10	41	arr+.**Richland**...lve.	7 30	11 00	8 00
8 05	4 10	7 20	41	lve...**Richland**.δ arr.	7 20	10 40	‖7 35
8 15	4 18	7 28	45	+......Pulaski......δ	7 10	10 30	7 25
8 24	4 27	7 35	49	.......Sand Hill......	7 00	....	7 15
8 36	4 39	7 47	54	+......Mexico......δ	6 52	10 08	7 05
8 47	4 50	7 57	59	......New Haven......	6 42	9 57	6 53
8 56	4 58	8 04	62	.........Scriba........	6 35	9 48	6 46
9 15	5 15	8 20	70	+.....**Oswego**.....δ	†6 20	†9 35	†6 30
P.M.	P.M.	A.M.		ARRIVE] [LEAVE	A.M.	A.M.	P.M.

Trains marked * run daily; † daily, except Sunday; § Sunday only; ‡ stops on Sunday. + Coupon stations; δ Telegraph stations. ‖ Meals. *c* Stops Sunday to leave passengers from Niagara Falls; *d* stops Sunday to take passengers for Niagara Falls; *e* stops Sunday to leave passengers from Windsor Beach; *g* stops Sunday to take passengers for Windsor Beach.

STANDARD—*Eastern time.*

ROCHESTER & ONTARIO BEACH LINE, AND ROCHESTER, CHARLOTTE & ONTARIO BEACH TRAINS.

Trains leave Rochester for Charlotte †7 15, *10 15 a.m., †7 15 p.m.; for Forest Lawn †10 15 a.m., †7 15 p.m.; for Windsor Beach *5 45, *7 15, *10 15 a.m., †3 30, †7 15 p.m. Returning, leave Charlotte *6 12, †10'45 a.m., *3 55, †7 55 p.m.; leave Forest Lawn †7 36 a.m., †7 42 p.m.; leave Windsor Beach *6 15, †7 45, *11 00 a.m., *4 00, *8 00 p.m.

neer, would yell "Whoa!" as he pulled the train up to a stop at a station. Even today [1958] *this name is used for the line, though many spell it "Ho Jacki" and do not realize the origin of the name."* [16]

In a remarkable instance of metonymy, the entire road came to be known locally as the Hojack. (For an 1893 RW&O timetable see Figure #21.)

Update on the Central

To meet the challenge of new and old boys on the block the NYC had to do more than simply buy out the competition. It had to provide better service. The first step in this direction was four-tracking the 297 miles from Albany to Buffalo, a program which the Commodore himself had announced in January, 1873. This involved a track on each side of the existing double tracks. (Figure #22.) The new tracks were for freight only, the interior tracks being reserved for the growing number of passenger trains which were being delayed by slow moving freights. The program was funded by the issuance of $10 million in sterling bonds which were easily disposed of in London. Work went on steadily during the summers of 1873 and 1874 but was halted temporarily at Rochester whose citizens objected to having four mainline tracks crossing the center of their town at grade. Yet when management suggested that the two freight tracks be placed on a timber trestle above the two passenger tracks there was a public outburst against this projected eye sore.

The historian of the nineteenth century NYC relates the sequel:

Eighteen hundred and eighty saw the New York Central & Hudson River in stronger shape than it had ever been before. Traffic was running freely once again, the senseless rate wars between the trunk lines, if not exactly under control, were being better regulated than four or five years before; the Central had already proved the wisdom of the men who had

IX, 22

four-tracked it, first from Albany to Rochester, and then, under the second Vanderbilt, from Rochester to Buffalo. When this last step had been taken at the beginning of the 'eighties, and when the much mooted and much needed direct connection between the Erie Street and Exchange Street stations in Buffalo had been built, the Central removed practically all the through passenger trains for the Michigan Central from the single-track Niagara Falls branch out of Rochester. This ended the glory of Rochester as one of the chief junction points on the system. Much of the railroad activity which previously centered there was now transferred to Buffalo.

Rochester did not take very kindly to this. There had been friction for a long time between the town and the Central, and Mr. Vanderbilt was quite aware of it. But he gave a fine sop to the town in the shape of the first important grade crossing removal program in the United States (with the exception of the Central's newly completed job through Park Avenue, New York city) and a brand new passenger station. . . .

Buffalo, to which for years the Vanderbilts had promised a station, did not propose to be outdone by Rochester at the very beginning of the prosperous 'eighties. A fortuitous, although tragic, circumstance helped the town to a new passenger terminal. There were in 1880 not less than three principal passenger stations of the NYC there - the station at east Buffalo, almost on the present site of the really magnificent Central Terminal (opened in the summer of 1929) which was used chiefly by through trains of the Central and the Lake Shore [which diverged from the Central 600 yards east of the Exchange Street Station (Figure XV, #1)]; *the second Exchange Street Station, built in 1855-56 and by 1880 an extremely sad and decrepit affair* [(Figure #23)], *and the Erie Street Station* [(Figure II, #18)] *on the west of Main Street, close to the harbor, which was used by trains running between Buffalo and Niagara Falls and Lockport.*

After much effort and litigation, the Central succeeded (in 1879) in getting a [600 yard long] *track connection down between the Niagara Falls line and the Exchange Street Station and in the following summer the Erie Street Station was abandoned for passenger purposes, and the station now known as the Terrace was opened to replace it for local travel.* [(Figure #24.)]

This all was in accordance with a plan thought out in cooperation with the town. For a long time the Central had been much hampered by the lack of a direct connection between its two downtown stations in that city. On the other hand, the citizens of Buffalo did not like having the principal station of the road out at East Buffalo, then relatively much farther out than today. Here was a trading point. The trade was made. Buffalo sacrificed, to a degree, its historic and once beautiful Terrace which was already going to seed, and the Central was permitted to put tracks through from Erie to Exchange Street. In return, it promised these new tracks to passenger trains [(at street level freights would have tied up Main Street traffic interminably)] *and promised always to maintain a passenger station west of Michigan Street. . . . The railroad did more. With the new connection track finished, it agreed to utilize it in the installation and operation of belt line passenger service all the way around the town* [using the Junction Railroad which was built to reach the International Bridge in the early 1870s. (Figure VII, #7)] *which in that day was a needed facility. This belt line service, after many delays, began operating in July, 1883, with twelve small trains a day in each direction. It carried only 2,100 passengers in its first week, but thereafter its patronage increased, slowly, but steadily for a long time.* [The railroad] *did even more; it enlarged and greatly extended Exchange Street Station, both trainshed and headhouse. The East Buffalo passen-ger station was then practically abandoned.* [17]

IX, 23

IX, 24 "

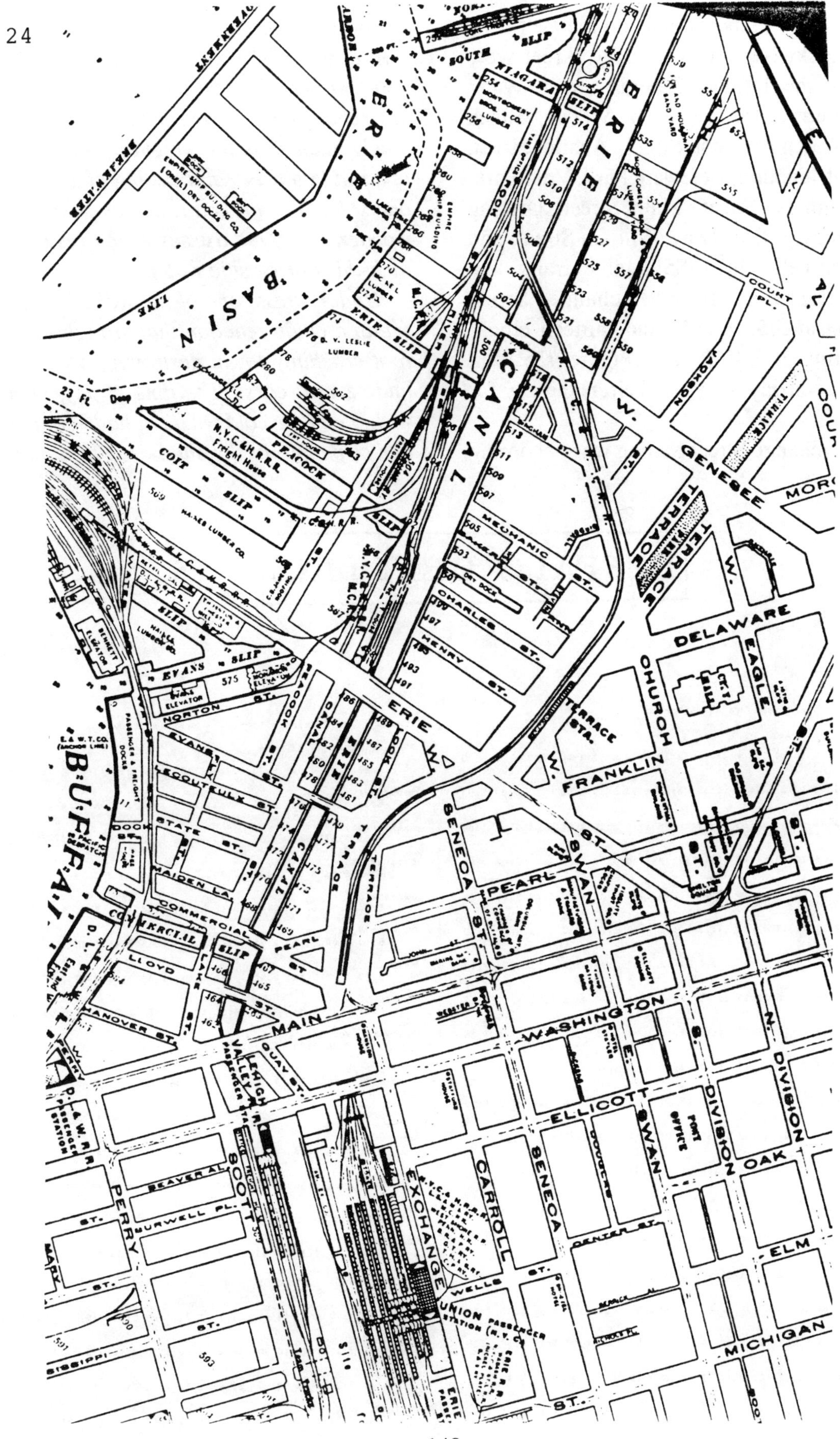
ERIE BASIN
ERIE CANAL
BUFFALO
DELAWARE
GENESEE
FRANKLIN
CHURCH
EAGLE
PEARL
SWAN
SENECA
WASHINGTON
MAIN
ELLICOTT
DIVISION
OAK
ELM
MICHIGAN
EXCHANGE
CARROLL
SCOTT
PERRY
TERRACE
COMMERCIAL
LLOYD
HANOVER ST.
EVANS
NORTON
LECOUTEULX ST.
STATE ST.
MAIDEN LA.
MECHANIC ST.
CHARLES ST.
HENRY ST.
POST OFFICE
UNION PASSENGER STATION (N.Y.C.)
N.Y.C.&H.R.R.R. Freight House
PEACOCK
COIT SLIP
HAINES LUMBER CO.
BURWELL PL.
BEAVER AL.
WELLS ST.
CENTER ST.
COURT PL.
JACKSON
LEHIGH VALLEY R.R.
D.L.&W.R.R.
SOUTH SLIP
NIAGARA SLIP
ERIE SLIP
23 Ft. Deep
DOCK ST.
QUAY ST.
WATER ST.
MORGAN

In its early years, stations on the Belt Line counterclockwise from Exchange Street were located at the Terrace, Georgia Street, Water Works, Ferry Street, Clifton Avenue, Black Rock, (West) Amherst Street, Austin Street, Cross Cut Junction, Delaware Park, Villa Park, (East) Amherst Street, Main Street, Driving Park, Genesee, Broadway, William Street, and Seneca Street. In 1885 twelve trains ran counter-clockwise from Exchange Street beginning at 5:55 A. M., and thirteen clockwise ending at 7:45 P. M. (Figure #25.) In those halcyon days one could circle the city for a nickel.

The Exchange Street Station was becoming a disaster area. As Cousins writes::

At about 9:00 a. m. on February 8, 1881, the 120-feet-wide by-450-feet long trainshed roof at Exchange Street collapsed, an accident variously blamed on the weight of snow, breaking of a rod in a truss, and cutting of a doorway in one side. The arched roof was constructed of wooden bow type trusses which rested on 13-inch-thick brick side walls.

Under stress, one of the walls buckled and set up a chain reaction that brought the whole roof crashing down, destroying a yard engine and several cars. The time of day, combined with the bitter cold weather, had kept the number of people in the shed area to a minimum.

IX, 25

BUFFALO BELT LINE

1885

Trains leave Exchange Street via Black Rock:

			AM					PM					
	6:30	7:15	9:00	10:00	11:00	11:30	12:30	1:30	3:15	4:00	5:00	6:00	7:00
Terrace	6:33	7:18	9:03	10:03	11:03	11:33	12:33	1:33	3:18	4:03	5:03	6:03	7:03
Georgia St.	6:35	7:20	9:05	10:05	11:05	11:35	12:35	1:35	3:20	4:05	5:05	6:05	7:05
Porter Ave.	6:38	7:23	9:08	10:08	11:08	11:38	12:38	1:38	3:23	4:08	5:08	6:08	7:08
Waterworks	6:40	7:25	9:10	10:10	11:10	11:40	12:40	1:40	3:25	4:10	5:10	6:10	7:10
Ferry St.	6:42	7:27	9:12	10:12	11:12	11:42	12:42	1:42	3:27	4:12	5:12	6:12	7:12
Clinton Ave.	6:43	7:28	9:13	10:13	11:13	11:43	12:43	1:43	3:28	4:13	5:13	6:13	7:13
Black Rock	6:45	7:30	9:15	10:15	11:15	11:45	12:45	1:45	3:30	4:15	5:15	6:15	7:15
Amherst St.	6:46	7:31	9:16	10:16	11:16	11:46	12:46	1:46	3:31	4:16	5:16	6:16	7:16
Austin St.	6:47	7:32	9:17	10:17	11:17	11:47	12:47	1:47	3:32	4:17	5:17	6:17	7:17
Crosscut Jnct.	6:50	7:35	9:20	10:20	11:20	11:50	12:50	1:50	3:35	4:20	5:20	6:20	7:20
Delaware Ave.	6:52	7:37	9:22	10:22	11:22	11:52	12:52	1:52	3:37	4:22	5:22	6:22	7:22
Colvin St.	6:54	7:39	9:24	10:24	11:24	11:54	12:54	1:54	3:39	4:24	5:24	6:24	7:24
Main St.	6:57	7:42	9:27	10:27	11:27	11:57	12:57	1:57	3:42	4:27	5:27	6:27	7:27
Driving Park	7:00	7:45	9:30	10:30	11:30	12:00	1:00	2:00	3:45	4:30	5:30	6:30	7:30
Genesee St.	7:04	7:49	9:34	10:34	11:34	12:04	1:04	2:04	3:49	4:34	5:34	6:34	7:34
Batavia St.	7:06	7:51	9:36	10:36	11:36	12:06	1:06	2:06	3:51	4:36	5:36	6:36	7:36
William St.	7:09	7:54	9:39	10:39	11:39	12:09	1:09	2:09	3:54	4:39	5:39	6:39	7:39
Seneca St.	7:12	7:57	9:42	10:42	11:42	12:12	1:12	2:12	3:57	4:42	5:42	6:42	7:42
Exchange St.	7:15	8:00	9:45	10:45	11:45	12:15	1:15	2:15	4:00	4:45	5:45	5:45	7:45

Trains leave Exchange Street via William Street

Running time: 45 minutes

	5:55	6:45	8:00	9:30	10:30	12:30	1:30	2:30	3:30	4:40	5:30	6:30
Seneca St.	5:58	6:48	8:03	9:33	10:33	12:33	1:33	2:33	3:33	4:43	5:33	6:33
William St.	6:01	6:51	8:06	9:36	10:36	12:36	1:36	2:36	3:36	4:46	5:36	6:36
Batavia St.	6:04	6:54	8:09	9:39	10:39	12:39	1:39	2:39	3:39	4:49	5:39	6:39
Genesee St.	6:06	6:56	8:11	9:41	10:41	12:41	1:41	2:41	3:41	4:51	5:41	6:41
Driving Park	6:10	7:00	8:15	9:45	10:45	12:45	1:45	2:45	3:45	4:55	5:45	6:45
Main St.	6:13	7:03	8:18	9:48	10:48	12:48	1:48	2:48	3:48	4:58	5:48	6:48
Colvin St.	6:16	7:06	8:21	9:51	10:51	12:51	1:51	2:51	3:51	5:01	5:51	6:51
Delaware Ave.	6:18	7:08	8:23	9:53	10:53	12:53	1:53	2:53	3:53	5:03	5:53	6:53
Crosscut Jnct.	6:20	7:10	8:25	9:55	10:55	12:55	1:55	2:55	3:55	5:05	5:55	6:55
Austin St.	6:23	7:13	8:28	9:58	10:58	12:58	1:58	2:58	3:58	5:08	5:58	6:58
Amherst St.	6:24	7:14	8:29	9:59	10:59	12:59	1:59	2:59	3:59	5:09	5:59	6:59
Black Rock	6:25	7:15	8:30	10:00	11:00	1:00	2:00	3:00	4:00	5:10	6:00	7:00
Clinton Ave.	6:27	7:17	8:32	10:02	11:02	1:02	2:02	3:02	4:02	5:12	6:02	7:02
Ferry St.	6:28	7:18	8:33	10:03	11:03	1:03	2:03	3:03	4:03	5:13	6:03	7:03
Waterworks	6:30	7:20	8:35	10:05	11:05	1:05	2:05	3:05	4:05	5:15	6:05	7:05
Porter Ave.	6:32	7:22	8:37	10:07	11:07	1:07	2:07	3:07	4:07	5:17	6:07	7:07
Georgia St.	6:35	7:25	8:40	10:10	11:10	1:10	2:10	3:10	4:10	5:20	6:10	7:10
Terrace	6:37	7:27	8:42	10:12	11:12	1:12	2:12	3:12	4:12	5:22	6:12	7:12
Exchange St.	6:40	7:30	8:45	10:15	11:15	1:15	2:15	3:15	4:15	5:25	6:15	7:15

Nevertheless four persons were killed, three of them railroad employees. The tragedy spurred agitation for a new station. After investigating the wreckage, however, Central officials decided to repair the damage and concentrate on improving, rather than replacing the structure. [18]

The question of a union station for Buffalo was becoming entwined with that of grade crossing elimination which had a long history. The first attempt to abolish grade crossings had been made in 1856 by Peter Emslie, City Engineer, who proposed a bridge over the four tracks of the NYC at Michigan Avenue. Nothing came of it. In 1874, Alderman Joseph Churchyard called on Commodore Vanderbilt and submitted plans for a similar bridge. The Commodore replied that "until the city of Buffalo expresses a more emphatic desire for that improvement, and until they, the company, are obliged to do the work, they would decline to consider the matter." Railroads regarded their long established grade crossings as a matter of vested rights of which they could not easily be deprived. Moreover, grade crossing elimination was very expensive.

A bill providing for the creation of a Grade Crossing Commission with the power of forcing the railroads to comply and letting contracts and apportioning costs between the city and the railroads was signed by Governor David B. Hill on May 22, 1888. The first chairman was Robert B. Adam, who was particularly upset about the situation on three streets where a traffic tally had been made for a single day, April 7, 1887, between six in the morning and six in the evening:

Street	Vehicles	Pedestrians	Trains
Washington	1,603	5,724	132
Michigan	2,682	12,995	412
Louisiana	2,158	6,405	428

Shortly after the creation of the commission, the following article appeared in the *Express:*

The efforts to solve the grade-crossing problem in this city have resulted in a grand scheme which has been authorized by legislative enactment, and will be brought to speedy fulfillment. The plan was prepared by Mr. C. W. Buckholz of the Erie Railroad from whose drawings the accompanying illustrations are made. [(Figure #26.)] *The total cost of the projected improvement is estimated at between $2,000,000 and $3,000,000.*

In accordance with the plan the roads entering the city will approach their terminus by a common route, the tracks of which will cross the streets east of Louisiana above grade, but run under Louisiana, Chicago, and Michigan streets. These thoroughfares will cross the railroads by wide overhead bridges, extending from Seneca street across the Hamburg Canal. The tracks are to run into the Grand Union Depot which will front on Washington street at the corner of Exchange. West of the depot the tracks of the NYC will cross Washington and Main streets below grade, coming to grade on the Terrace about opposite the foot of Franklin street.

It is proposed to begin the depression of the tracks at Van Rensselaer street and continue the descent until a level is struck two feet below the present grade at Louisiana street. This level will be continued to Michigan street and thence carried into the Train-house at such a grade that the platforms of the cars will be on a level with the landings. Chicago street can be bridged or closed in accordance with the value placed upon that thoroughfare by those who have occasion to use it. The estimated cost of the bridges and approaches is $100,000 each. The plans call for the widening of Carroll street so as to make it a thoroughfare convenient for the loading and unloading of freight; the doubling of the present width of Michigan Street from Exchange to Seneca street to facilitate heavy traffic; the abandonment of the horse-car tracks on Exchange street east of Michigan, and the con-

fiscation of the Continental Hotel property and the other buildings on Exchange street opposite the Washington Block and on the east side of Washington street between Exchange street and the Hamburg Canal.

The Passenger Station provided in Mr. Buckholz's plan merits description in detail. It will be the finest Passenger Station in the United States, with a Train-house more capacious than any other in this country if not in the world. The Washington street elevation represents an ornate brick and cut-stone building, with a frontage of 300 feet, seven stories high, covered by a mansard roof with numerous dormer windows, and over-topped by a massive clock-tower over 200 feet high. A paved plaza 100 feet wide separates the building from the street proper. Over the main entrances is a broad port cochere, and to the right of this, about 75 feet further south, is a massive arch from which emerge the double tracks of the New York Central Belt Line and the Niagara Falls branch. The Exchange street elevation drops to three stories after passing the tower and continues for 300 feet. Beyond this stretches away the mammoth Train-house for 500 feet more. A heavy archway securely gated on this side furnishes an exit for all passengers leaving the depot. Some of the express and baggage-rooms are in the corresponding building on the canal side of the station, which is separated from the canal by a driveway of ample proportions. The ground plan of the passenger station shows a general waiting-room, 76 by 132; a smoking-room, 37 by 81; a spacious ladies' room; wide hallways extending up to the roof to afford light and ventilation; a grand stair-case leading to the regions above from the hall on the right of the general waiting-room; four elevators; a spacious ticket-office; and a platform 50 by 280 between the waiting-room and the Train-house.

On the second floor is a restaurant, while all the floors above are given up to offices of the railroad companies making use of the terminal facilities. The south wing contains baggage rooms, express-rooms, a storeroom, and a kitchen, with offices on the two floors above. The north wing, on the Exchange street side, contains baggage and express-rooms only on the ground floor, with offices above.

The plans for the Train-house call for a grand arched structure, 108 feet high in the center and 280 feet wide, with 14 tracks and eight broad platforms between them. To appreciate the size of this building, it is only necessary to state that the Train-house of the Grand Central Depot in New York is but 140 feet, while the present NYC Train-house in this city measures less than 100 feet from wall to wall.

The estimated cost of the new Passenger Station complete is $700,000. The accompanying plans show the Washington street elevation, a portion of the Exchange street side, the arrangement of tracks in the great Train-house, and the system of approaches, freight-houses, etc., according to the new scheme. The land bounded by Michigan, Carroll, Alabama, and Exchange streets it is proposed to devote to Union Freight-houses, to which ample track approaches will be made as shown in the map.
Accompanying the article but not mentioned in it was a sketch of the proposed Terrace Station, reminiscent of Stanford White's Union Station in Lockport. (Figure #27.)

In the end, nothing came of this union station plan. The Erie was unwilling or unable to spend any money, Chauncey Depew, President of the Central, disliked the idea from the beginning, and various parties haggled endlessly over details, e.g. viaducts or tunnels. Moreover, the railroads could not agree on the financing of the Terminal Improvement Company which was to build the station.

However, the issue of grade crossing elimination remained. The railroads found legal grounds for refusing to enter into contracts with the Grade Crossing Commission for this purpose. One argument was that when the union station plan fell through the commis-

IX, 26

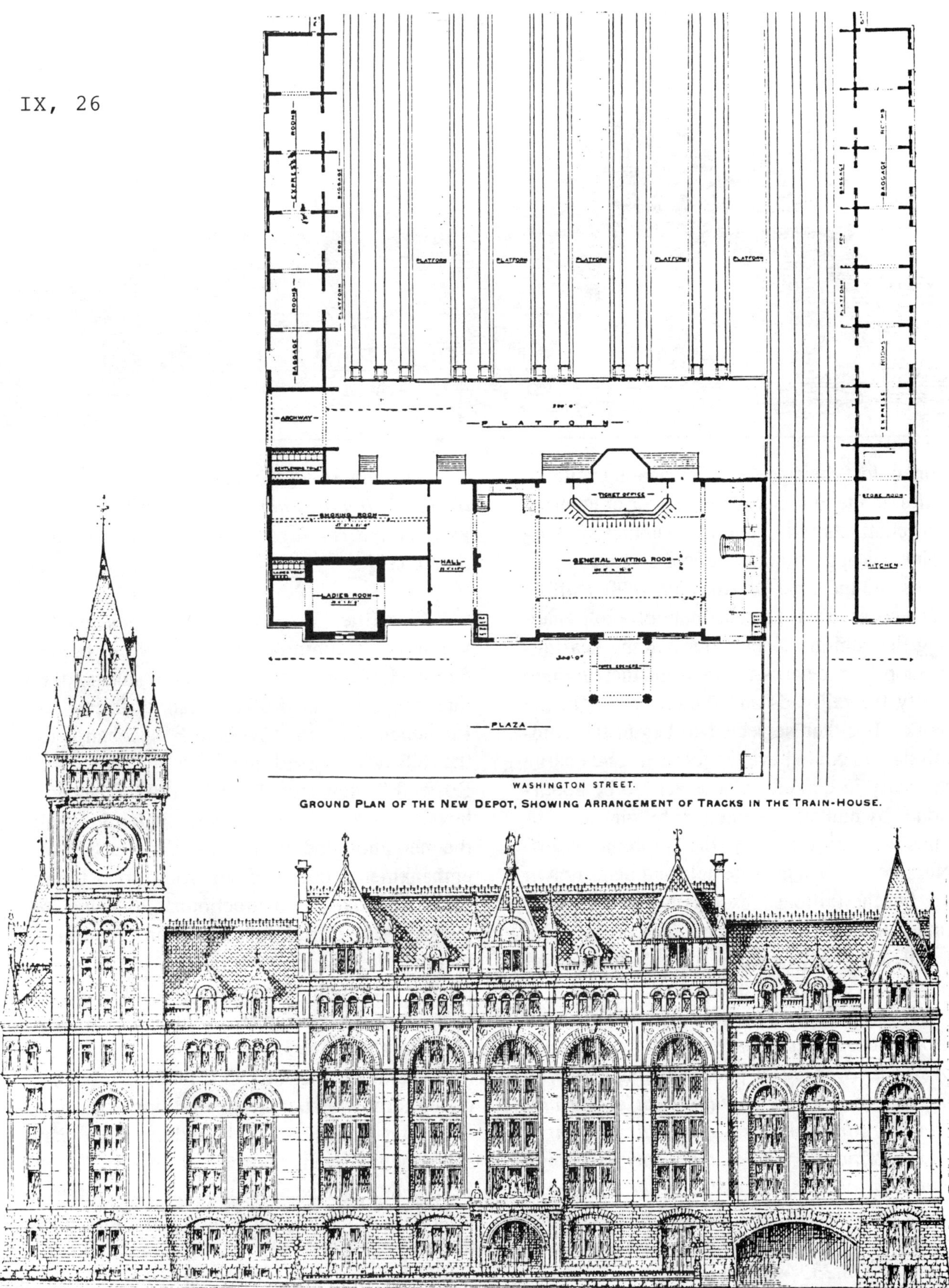

GROUND PLAN OF THE NEW DEPOT, SHOWING ARRANGEMENT OF TRACKS IN THE TRAIN-HOUSE.

ELEVATION ON WASHINGTON STREET

IX, 27

sioners lost their power of mandating railroad action in the grade crossing area or of entering into contracts with anyone. Another sticking point was apportionment of costs between railroads and the city. On April 30, 1890, Buffalo interests secured the enactment of a bill enabling the commissioners after holding hearings to adopt a grade crossing plan and thereupon to notify the railroads and the city to begin the work. If either neglected to begin, the commissioners could have the job done and charge the party in default. Costs were to be apportioned by mutual agreement or by special commission appointed by the supreme court. Numerous hearings were held and plans drawn up, but the railroads, especially the Erie, continued to throw up obstacles. The preamble to a bill that would enlarge the commissioners' power of compulsion declared:

This grade crossing evil has reached such proportions as to be unbearable - the number of accidents, the killing and maiming of people increasing with the rapid growth of the city and its railroad traffic - a record of a single day's traffic of two of the many crossings shows the pressing necessity for the abatement of the evil and the great danger of the existing conditions. At Michigan Street Saturday, Feb. 20, 1892, 3,230 wagons and carriages, and 13,402 [foot] *passengers crossed the tracks. At Louisiana Street the record was: passenger trains 87, freight trains 43; light engines 110; wagons and carriages 1,387, foot passengers 5,716.* [19]

The Erie's lawyers and lobbyists fought valiantly, claiming that they were being deprived of their property without substantive due process; but Buffalo had a friend in Lieutenant Governor William F. Sheehan, and the bill was signed into law by Governor Roswell P. Flower on April 20, 1892. The end, however, was not yet in sight. Individuals in the neighborhood of proposed viaducts and embankments provided vigorous opposition. Some accused the obstructionists of being in the pay of the Erie. A bill was proposed disbanding the commission since it had accomplished nothing in five years. The bill failed of passage in the legislature. Actual work would not begin until 1895.

Outside the city the NYC pursued a policy of vigorous expansion, building on the Lancaster-Cheektowaga boundary huge car shops which were opened in April, 1893. Before the year was out other large ancillary industries, including the Union Car Company, the National Car Wheel Works, and the Gould Coupler Company erected facilities nearby which spurred the rapid growth of a village more urban than rural. It was incorporated in 1893 as the Village of Depew after Chancy M. Depew, President of the NYC 1885-1899 and United States Senator from New York 1899-1911. While senator, he was also Chairman of the Board of the NYC, ensuring that railroads had at least one friend in Washington during a disastrous time politically for the railroad industry.

In the Valley of the Tonawanda

The Tonawanda Railroad had been chartered in 1832 to run southwest from Rochester to Batavia on the Tonawanda River and from there up the Tonawanda River to Attica. The line to Batavia was completed in 1837; but the extension to Attica was not opened until 1842 and then only to link up with the Attica & Buffalo, which was sold to the Erie after the construction of the shorter and more direct Buffalo & Rochester in 1853. From Attica the Erie proceeded southeast via the old Attica & Hornellsville to the mainline to New York. In 1836, the same year as the chartering of the Attica & Buffalo, the Attica & Sheldon (Sheldon is the town in which Java is located) was incorporated to build south up the Tonawanda to Java in order to tap the lumber and agricultural resources of the region. This project was doomed by the Panic of 1837.

It was not until 1852 that the idea of building south from Attica resurfaced, this time with a grander role envisioned. That year the Attica & Allegany Valley was organized to build a three-foot gauge railway seventy-four miles south from Attica to the Pennsylvania line where it would connect with a companion company chartered to push on to Pittsburgh. The similarity between this project and that of the 1869 Rochester & State Line is striking. Work began on the Northern Division (Attica to Arcade) of the A&AV immediately. By September, 1853, the grading, masonry, fencing, and placement of ties on most of this section had been completed at the high cost of over $350,000. Then disaster struck, due to the dishonesty of the project's promoters, who were more interested in marketing securities than in building a railroad. On February 2, 1856, the property was sold under foreclosure and the project abandoned. Not until ten years later would investors be found to sink money in the Tonawanda Valley.

In 1866 a group of bondholders of the defunct A&AV led by Henry A. Richmond filed articles of association for the Batavia Attica & Salamanca. Richmond had been involved in the Buffalo & Allegany Valley which had been incorporated in 1854 to build southeast from Buffalo to a junction with the A&AV. Acquisition of the A&AV's property and improvements would put his B&AV well on the way to Salamanca. In line with this project, the legislature in 1868 authorized the towns of Arcade, Java, and Sheldon to purchase the right-of-way of the defunct A&AV. The next year Charles Benedict, a prominent resident of Attica, organized the Attica & Arcade Railroad in an attempt to snatch the almost completed line of the A&AV away from Richmond. The resulting conflict plus some sleight of hand financing by Benedict delayed the building of the Attica & Arcade for many years. Finally, on April 5, 1880, the Tonawanda Valley Railroad was incorporated to build a three foot road from Attica to a point on the Buffalo New York & Philadelphia in the Town of Sardinia. Erie Railroad officials had agreed to finance the road, provided localities along the route would support the project. Shortly before this the legislature had passed a law permitting narrow gauge lines to charge higher rates than standard gauge ones. The first train on the line was a September 11, 1880, excursion from Attica to Curriers on a branch of Cattaraugus Creek, a temporary terminal until a route further south could be determined. Completion of the road was rapid because the roadbeds of the former A&AV and A&A were followed for most of the distance. The TV owned no passenger cars so flat cars,

IX, 28

The Tonawanda Valley Railroad.

TIME TABLE No. I.

Distance.	TRAINS NORTH.	A. M.	P. M.	Distance.	TRAINS SOUTH.	A. M.	P. M.
	Lv. CURRIERS......	7.00	2.00		Lv. ATTICA	10.30	7.00
2^{38}	JAVA CENTRE..	7.10	2.13	3^{24}	- *SIERKS.........	10.45	7.13
5^{31}	- NORTH JAVA...	7.24	2.20	5^{46}	- *EARL'S.........	10.58	7.23
6^{51}	- *PERRYS.........	7.28	2.34	7^{48}	- VARYSBURG....	11.08	7.31
9^{53}	- JOHNSONBURG.	7.40	2.50	9^{58}	- JOHNSONBURG.	11.20	7.40
11^{46}	- VARYSBURG....	7.50	3.02	12 [illegible]	- *PERRYS.........	11.36	7.52
13^{46}	- *EARL'S.........	7.58	3.12	13 [illegible]	- NORTH JAVA...	11.40	7.56
15^{37}	- *SIERKS.........	8.07	3.24	16 [illegible]	- JAVA CENTRE..	11.58	8.10
19^{18}	Ar. ATTICA	8.20	3.40	19^{18}	Ar. CURRIERS......	12.10	8.20

At Stations marked thus * Trains will stop only on signal.

☞ Trains on this Road run by New York Time.

J. V. D. LOOMIS,
Superintendent.

ATTICA, Sept. 27th, 1880.

one of which was fitted up with a canopy and board seats for the ladies, were used for the trip. (Figure #28.)

To obtain the funds needed to complete the line, the Tonawanda Valley Extension Railroad was incorporated on November 3, 1880. Though it was supposed to be built to Sardinia, the contractors instead utilized the grade of the long bankrupt A&AV to Arcade. Regular service on the twenty-six miles between Attica and Arcade began on May 16, 1881. Shortly thereafter, on July 14, 1881, the Tonawanda Valley & Cuba Railroad was incorporated to build from Arcade to Cuba on the mainline of the Erie Railroad. (Figure #29.) A month later all three short lines were consolidated into a new Tonawanda Valley & Cuba Railroad which went into operation along its entire 59.1 mile length on September 4, 1882. At Cuba the TV&C connected with the mainline of the Erie and with the Bradford Eldred & Cuba, another narrow gauge line controlled by the Erie. Edward A. Lewis, historian of the A&A, upon whose work this entire account depends, remarks concerning the recently completed TV&C:

Service consisted of one first class passenger train and two mixed passenger and freight second class trains in each direction daily except Sunday. The first class train required

IX, 29

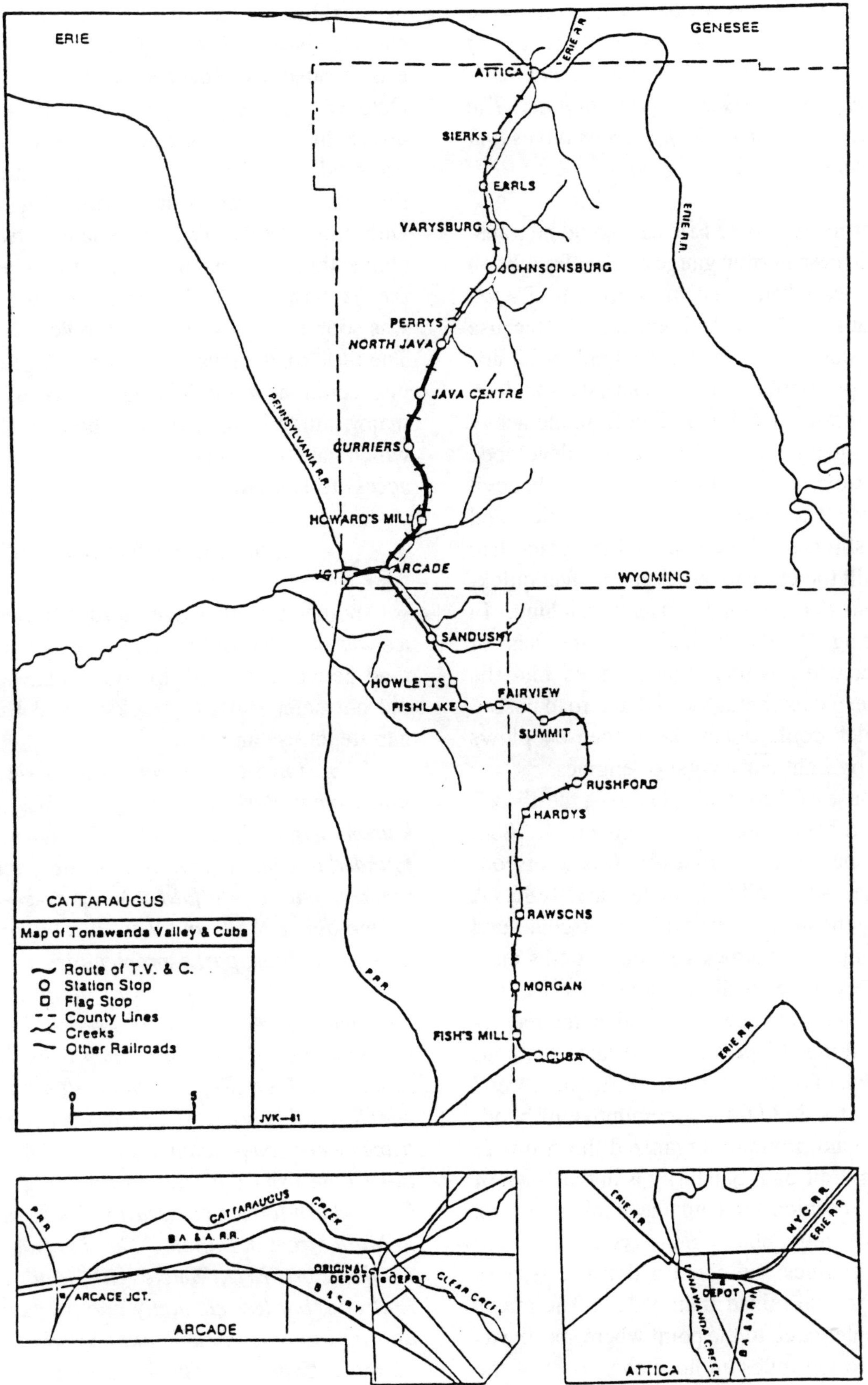
ERIE
GENESEE
ERIE R.R.
ATTICA
SIERKS
EARLS
VARYSBURG
JOHNSONSBURG
PERRYS
NORTH JAVA
JAVA CENTRE
PENNSYLVANIA R.R.
CURRIERS
HOWARD'S MILL
JCT.
ARCADE
WYOMING
SANDUSKY
HOWLETTS
FISHLAKE
FAIRVIEW
SUMMIT
RUSHFORD
HARDYS
RAWSONS
MORGAN
FISH'S MILL
CUBA
P.R.R.
CATTARAUGUS
Map of Tonawanda Valley & Cuba
Route of T.V. & C.
Station Stop
Flag Stop
County Lines
Creeks
Other Railroads
0
5
JVK—81
CATTARAUGUS CREEK
B.A. & A. R.R.
ORIGINAL DEPOT
DEPOT
CLEAR CREEK
ARCADE JCT.
ARCADE
NYC R.R.
DEPOT
TONAWANDA CREEK
ATTICA

three and a half hours to cover the 59 mile route while the mixed trains took a scheduled six and a half hours on the Attica-Cuba run. Speed did not seem important, and because of the light rail and equally light trackwork, trains seldom exceeded 17 miles an hour. The rolling stock . . . included five locomotives and twenty cars. [20]

Unfortunately, only Erie cars could be transferred to these narrow gauge tracks. Freight on all other cars had to be transferred to TV&C cars, causing delay and expense. Because through traffic could be handled only with difficulty, profitable freight business was lost. The light rails took a pounding from the heavy standard gauge cars. The roadbed developed several trouble spots that continued to bedevil the line. The heavy clay at the Attica end caused slippage of the ties, and the grade had been built too close to the river and over quicksand beds that required constant watching. In the spring floods washed out stretches of roadbed, while winter snows drifted into the many deep cuts through which the road passed and which could not be kept open by plows pushed by light narrow gauge engines.

Because of these multiple flaws, the TV&C went into bankruptcy on November 24, 1884. One of the receiver's first acts was to discontinue the daily mail train in January, 1885. A few months later all service was discontinued when employees struck for four months back pay. They were finally paid, and service was resumed until October, 1886, when the receiver discontinued operation of trains south of Sandusky. On January 19, 1891, the TV&C was sold for $33,000 to a committee of bondholders who promptly organized the Attica & Freedom Railroad (Sandusky is in the Town of Freedom) which took up the tracks between Sandusky and Cuba. Train service, provided by two engines and about a dozen cars, was limited to one mixed train a day. The tracks had disintegrated to the point where speed was limited to ten miles an hour over most of the line. Ties were rotten and hidden by weeds. In the wake of falling revenues and rising deficits, the road again went bankrupt. It was sold in March, 1894, to New York City interests headed by Spencer S. Bullis, who in October secured reorganization of the road under the name Buffalo Attica & Arcade Railroad. The entire line between Attica and Freedom was relaid to standard gauge by December, 1895. Two years later a two mile connection was installed between Arcade and the Western New York & Pennsylvania, which was soon to be absorbed by the Pennsylvania. The little road, elevated to standard gauge status, could now interchange easily with two major railroads, the Erie and the PRR, both of which gave residents of the Tonawanda Valley access to Buffalo.

The Sandfly Express

Another narrow gauge railroad of the eighties was also part of the Niagara Frontier's railroad network, though, like the Tonawanda, it did not enter Buffalo. Jackson and Burtniak narrate its rise and fall:

A . . . tourist route served the Erie Beach Amusement Park at Fort Erie. This resort, known originally as Snake Hill Grove, was founded in 1885 to provide a picnic ground for the residents of Buffalo. A merry-go-round, casino-dance hall, outdoor swimming pool, athletic stadium, parks, promenades, and a zoo were added, attracting crowds of up to 20,000 on summer weekends. It was served by a narrow gauge steam railway which began operation in 1885, until a pier was built about 1910 which enabled boats to land at the beach. The tracks were constructed along the shoreline of Lake Erie from the old ferry landing in Fort Erie, where ferries crossed the Niagara River to Main Street in Buffalo. The line was known as the Fort Erie, Snake Hill, and Pacific Railroad, but less elegantly and perhaps more appropriately as the "Peanut Special" or the "Sandfly Express." The fare was $2.00 return

IX, 30

which included both the ferry crossing and the train ride. [21]

A September 7, 1931, article in the *Buffalo Times,* on the occasion of the abandonment, contains some historical data on the line:

Rolling stock consists of eight coaches and two locomotives built in 1878. They are older even than the most ancient of Buffalo's street cars. They were purchased second hand in 1900 from the New York City elevated lines, when the "L" changed over from steam to electricity. [(Figure #30.)] *No one wants eight wooden coaches 52 years old. They are equipped with a vacuum braking system that was abandoned for air brakes about the time the cars came to Fort Erie, so they can't be hooked onto a regular train. In 1880 William B. Pierce of Buffalo and Ben Baxter of Fort Erie, who built the line, bought some land on the lake front and started "The Snake Hill Grove." In those days resorts were called groves or gardens. There were not so many kinds of concessions, almost no mechanical thrillers such as the "Wild Cat." Pleasure seekers came to the groves and sat around green tables under the trees. They played dominoes, bean bag, and cards, and drank brown October ale.*

Another Buffalo man, Fred J. Weber, bought the grove in time to reap a rich harvest during the Pan-American Exposition. He changed the name to Erie Beach Grove. The pier was not built until 1910, so everyone who came to the beach had to ferry across the river and take the train. Some made the trip in spring buggies, but most Buffalo folk who went to the beach on Sundays left the gig and horse tied up at the foot of Ferry Street. Almost every one rode [the train]. *It was part of the fun of going to the beach.*

Frank Baron bought the beach property, the ferry, and the railroad from Weber after the Exposition and kept it until 1914. Baron sold the resort to its present owner, J. H. Pardee in 1925. From Decoration Day until Labor Day the train made a trip every 20 minutes from the ferry to the beach. It started at 6:30 a. m. and stopped a little after midnight.

Epilogue

As Walter S. Dunn has written in his <u>History of Erie Count y:</u>

The [Buffalo] Express's *illustrated supplement for 1888 noted eleven railroads terminated in the city, the shortest of them 346 miles long. Within the city were four transfer or switching railroads. By 1897 another such publication reported that Buffalo's eleven trunk lines aggregated 13,000 miles of track, while within the city proper there were 660 miles of tracks used for storage, switching service, and the making-up of trains. A note added that while the supplement was being printed two more roads had reached the city.*

10
The Buffalo Switchmen's Strike Of 1892

The Knights of Labor in August, 1890, waged a brief, unsuccessful strike against the NYC. In 1891 and1892 coal miners in eastern Tennessee, trying to halt the use of convict labor, were crushed by the state militia. In the silver and lead mines of the Coeur d'Alene district of Idaho in July, 1892, a dispute over unionization led to violence that had to be put down by federal troops. The same month in the Carnegie steel works at Homestead, Pennsylvania, one of the great labor battles of the late nineteenth century was fought between the steel workers' union and management. In the course of this strike, strikers fired upon two barges towed up the Monongahela with 300 Pinkerton detectives engaged by the company's general manager, Henry Clay Frick, resulting in seven deaths. The strike was broken as state militia took over on July 12th. The rapid industrialization of the northeastern United States had produced in many areas a sharp conflict between workers on one side and capitalists and their servants on the other.

On Friday night, August 12, 1892, according to the next day's *Express,* at a meeting at Gammel's Hall at Seneca and Emslie Streets in the Hydraulics of the John M. Hannon Lodge #39 of the Switchmen's Mutual Aid Association of North America, with Frank Sweeney of Chicago, Grand Master of the union, in attendance, a strike to begin at midnight was voted for by switchmen of the Lehigh Valley, the Erie, and both roads' jointly leased Buffalo Creek Railroad. (From February, 1892, until August, 1893, the LV was itself leased by the Philadelphia & Reading and operated as the Buffalo & Seneca Division of the lessee.) The strike arose from a dispute between the switchmen and management about wages and hours. Hitherto, day yard brakemen had been paid $60 for a twelve hour a day twenty-six day month (19 cents an hour), and day yard conductors had received $65 (21 cents an hour.) For the same work at night, brakemen had been paid $65 (21 cents an hour) and conductors $70 (22.5 cents an hour.) They now demanded the same pay, but for only ten hours, and extra pay by the hour for any time in excess of half an hour beyond that. They claimed that they sometimes worked as much as fifteen hours with little or no time off to eat and no adequate extra pay. The context of their demands was New York's Ten Hour law signed by Governor Roswell P. Flower on May 20th, which enacted that ten hours' labor:

. . . performed within twelve consecutive hours shall constitute a day's labor in the operation of all steam surface and elevated railroads owned and operated within this state. . . [and] *for every hour in excess of said ten hoursí labor that any conductor, engineer, fireman, or any trainman of any railroad company or corporation, owned or operated within this state, who works under the direction of a superior, or at the request of such company or corporation, shall be required or permitted to work, he shall receive comparative compensation for said extra service in addition to his daily compensation.* [1]

The switchmen wanted to make sure that the law would not lower their daily wages, while the railroads wished to assure that it would, by maintaining the same hourly pay as before. In February, 1889, the Central Labor Union accused the Buffalo East Side Railway Company (a horsecar line) of violating the Ten Hour Day Law. The case went to the courts, where State Supreme Court Justice Loren L. Lewis of the Eighth Judicial District dismissed it on the ground that the worker involved had not proved that the company had coerced him into working beyond the limit. If he had done so, the judge ruled, he had acted as a volunteer and so had no cause of action. George E. Matthews, editor of the *Express* and no champion of unions, remarked that employers could easily coerce employees into volunteering. This decision blunted the applicability of the law locally.

Gerald Eggert has argued in Railroad Labor Disputes: *The Beginnings of Federal Strike Policy* that in the two decades after the Great Railroad Strike of 1877 Congress regularly declined to meet the problems created by strikes on the nation's railroad system, which seriously disrupted interstate trade. This placed the burden on the executive and especially the judicial branch of the federal government. Many members of the judiciary had been railroad lawyers and tended to adopt management's viewpoint. Some even saw such railroad strikes as conspiracies in restraint of trade, which indeed they were, and therefore subject to action by federal courts. The Sherman Anti-Trust Act (1890) could be and was used by federal judges to interdict combinations of labor as well as of capital. What was lacking in 1892 was a congressionally sponsored machinery for resolving railroad labor disputes, which were growing in intensity and violence, impartially and definitively

John McMahon and two other members of the switchmen's grievance committee at the Erie's East Buffalo yard had approached Superintendent Charles A. Brunn of the Erie with their demands on June 1st. Brunn asked them to come back, which they did four times. "The only reply they could get," McMahon said, "was a repetition of the old story about the poverty of the Erie." (Next year, the Erie went bankrupt for a third time.) In desperation, the members of the committee traveled to New York to confront General Manager Walter at his office at 21 Cortlandt Street on July 22. He was absent so they returned two days later when Walter told them, "I can do nothing for you." Joseph Boss, a member of the grievance committee from the LV's yards, experienced the same stonewalling from Reading officials as had McMahon's delegation. General Manager Schweigart of the Reading, whom Boss and his committee called upon July 20 in Philadelphia, refused to see them. Superintendent Stevenson gave them the same answer when they called on him at Sayre on their way home.

It was a settled principle among most railroad managers of the time not to deal with their employees through a representative chosen by them. (Eggert writes that "sometimes companies negotiated wages and work rules with unions for the sake of convenience, or out of necessity, but never as a matter of right.") On returning to Buffalo, McMahon reported the results of his interviews at an August 12th meeting of the Erie switchmen, who voted eighty to fifteen for a strike to begin at midnight. Grand Master Sweeney approved the strike call, which included Waverly (Erie and LV) and Elmira and Binghamton (Erie). The strikers expected that switchmen on non-striking roads would refuse to handle cars of the three strike-bound roads at interchange points. Sweeney claimed not to like strikes, and said, according to the *Express:*

The whole thing was precipitated by a remark by Assistant Yardmaster Anthony Barrett of the Erie Friday when he said to members of the committee of switchmen, "You sons of bitches dare not strike." Possibly the men would have struck anyway, but such expressions went a long way toward hurrying the strike along.

Saturday, August 13

Saturday was quiet, as reported in the *Express* for August 14th, with management and strikers giving very different descriptions of the strike's impact. Superintendent T.H. Fennell of the LV asserted that "the trains are being moved almost the same as usual, and we have employed a number of competent yard men to take the place of the strikers." Brunn of the Erie pointed out that the twelve hour shift was necessary because "all railroad men know that a railroad day is 24 hours;î and he added that "the men are allowed an hour's nooning, so that they actually work 11 hours." He disputed Sweeney's claim that there were 1,000 men on strike saying, "There are 65 men out on our road in Buffalo, six in Black Rock, and six at Suspension Bridge. There may possibly be 65 Lehigh Valley men out and I understand Mr. [Edward F.] Knibloe [General Agent of the Buffalo Creek] says 25 of his men have quit. You know these figures don't foot up to 1,000." He was whistling in the dark. An Erie engineer said that westbound freight was being stored "on the sidings at Hornellsville, Burns, Canaseraga, Hunts, Warsaw, and all other stations along the line where there were sidings;" and a policeman at the Erie crossing on Seneca Street said he had seen "only three strings of cars pass the crossing during the day of 10 or 15 cars each, instead of seven or eight strings of 30 or 35 cars each" as was usual. Two or three dozen switchmen hanging around Barney Ward's, a saloon-hotel on Swan Street between Michigan and Seneca, were laughing because two Poles had been employed in the Erie yard. The strikers sneered saying that "it would take two men to watch each Pole." A gang of youths went to one of the Poles and threatened to kill him.

Trouble was brewing in the 7th Precinct stationhouse on Louisiana near Elk Street (the boundary between the First and Second Wards) where reserves were called to cover the line of the Erie from Exchange to Smith Street. The first arrest of a striker took place there. John Gibson was charged with assaulting an Erie yardmaster riding on top of a boxcar on a train going from the Ohio Street freight house to the yards in East Buffalo. Captain Emil Zacher of Station #8 between Watson and Emslie dispatched his reserves further east to the Bailey Avenue crossings of the Erie and Lackawanna where strikers were holding up an Erie train, but there was no violence. Fearing the worst, officials of the WNY&P yielded to the switchmen's demands and conceded a ten hour day with twelve hours pay.

Sunday, August 14

On Sunday all hell broke loose, readers of the next day's *Express* learned. At 2:00 A. M. the brakes were released on a string of coal cars on the fueling trestle of the LV's machine shops at Dingens and New South Ogden Streets. The cars came hurtling down the incline to the bottom where they crashed into a string of standing cars. Fifteen cars were destroyed as well as the standpipe from which engines took on water. Twelve empty boxcars and a flagman's shanty were torched. Firemen responding to the alarm found that it was a long way from the fire to the nearest hydrant. "Take your time boys," they were advised by bystanders who then disappeared into the night. Shortly afterwards someone stuck a link from a coupler into the gears of Engine #56, which broke when it was started up. Superintendent Fennell estimated the damage at $4,000. Returning from that conflagration, the firemen came across a boxcar that had been derailed and set on fire near the intersection of the LV and the WNY&P near Clinton and Bailey. Captain Valentine Wurtz of Precinct #11 (Broadway and Bailey) sent a detachment into the Lehigh's yards, but the police made no arrests. Much of the vandalism perpetrated both now and later against the railroads seems to have been done by men who knew their way around a railroad yard, but they might not all have been striking switchmen.

It was also early Sunday morning that Conductor Martin Neville was aboard an Erie freight train out of the Ohio Street yards which ran into two deliberately opened switches at the intersection of the Erie and the WNY&P just south of Clinton and Bailey. The train was derailed and broken in two places. Neville was knocked senseless, taken to Precinct #9 at Seneca and Babcock Street, and then home. For whatever reason, he gave no account of the attack.

Erie #3, the *Pacific Express* from Jersey City, was scheduled to arrive at Buffalo at 11:10 A. M. Just inside the city line the LV and the Erie crossed William Street at grade along-side each other. The train was flagged (an engineer cannot run a flag) and boarded by a gang of strikers, who emptied a car and a half of strikebreakers hired by the railroad in New Jersey. One Henry Schraeder panicked, ran through the car, jumped onto the platform, and was set upon by three or four strikers, who punched and kicked him. He escaped and was taken by a special policeman on a William Street trolley car to the Fitch Accident Hospital on Swan and Michigan where his wounds were dressed, and he was let go. The strikers' confederates down the line had obviously gotten the word through that strikebreakers were on the way.

Early Sunday evening, strikers pulled the pins on two loaded Erie freights just east of William Street causing a blockade of the westbound track. Accordingly, #17, the local from Hornellsville which was due at Exchange Street at 7:45 P. M., was sent in on the eastbound tracks from Lancaster. After it passed the obstructions, it was backed onto the westbound track just west of William Street for the rest of the way into the city. A striker threw the switch after the engine passed over it, tipping the train onto the adjoining tracks. There were four coaches on the accommodation, and all were crowded with passengers, many standing on the platforms preparing to detrain. The engine stayed on the track, but the baggage car was thrown diagonally across the space between the main track and the sidetrack onto which the switch opened. There were empty freight cars on the siding, and the side of the baggage car crashed into the end of one of them. No one was injured, but it was clear that tampering with moving passenger trains was a potentially lethal activity. The last three coaches did not leave the track and, after a delay of about half an hour, they were backed onto the westbound track and brought into the city, arriving at 9:30 P. M. Now both tracks were blocked. LV #3 from Easton, Pennsylvania, which was due in at 7:50 P. M. was also derailed on reaching William Street.

Some time later, an Erie train came out from the city to the William Street Station to pick up passengers from the blocked trains that continued to pile up. Aboard one of these was the corpse of a late resident of Middletown, New York, destined for burial in Michigan. It was accompanied by the deceased's wife and daughter. Many of those marooned at William Street had planned to connect at Buffalo for points west. As each train arrived at William Street, it was boarded by strikers who searched the cars to make sure no strikebreakers were aboard. When indignant passengers asked how long they were going to be detained, they were told that when the strikers got through with them they might proceed but not before. For this the strikers were roundly cursed out by their victims.

About 9:00 P. M. the skies were suddenly lit up by the flames of burning freight cars in the LV yards at Dingens Street and North Ogden. On the ground surrounding the burning cars and atop others, strikers and their sympathizers cheered the destruction of property and jeered the efforts of railroaders, including a few officials, to drag some cars to safety by hand. It was not until after 10:00 P. M. that Acting Battalion Chief Jacob Petzing, with twenty of his men, was able to begin playing water on the flames. Though companies from East Buffalo and Best Street came to his assistance, the blaze continued. By 3:15 A. M. 150 freight cars were burning, according to Superintendent Brunn, and new fires were breaking out every few minutes. (Figure #1.) For the second time he called upon Sheriff August Beck for protection from the train wreckers and incendiaries.

Meanwhile, Grand Master Sweeney kept to his room at the Genesee Hotel at Main and Genesee. He defended his inaction by asking, "What would have been the use of my marching about among the members today? The conduct of the strike is in the hands of the local lodge, and it is not my business to interfere with them." He reiterated his opposition to strikes except as a last resort. When queried about the burning of the LV cars last night, the running of the string of cars down the trestle, and the attacks on the non-union switchmen and the strikebreakers, he answered, according to the August 15th *Express*:

It is unfortunate that when strikes occur there are many who have no connection with the men who are out but who believe they are doing the strikers a favor in resorting to violence. I do not say that our men are entirely innocent, nor do I care to say that they are

X, 1

THE GREAT SWITCHMEN'S STRIKE AT BUFFALO: FREIGHT-CAR FIRES AT THE LEHIGH YARDS. — SKETCH BY C.W. BRADLEY
The Buffalo Express, August 21, 1892

guilty. In any large body you will find men whose zeal runs away with their reason and they may do something which will bring odium on the entire body, while probably 99 out of 100 would most strenuously oppose such forcible action.

Monday, August 15

Tuesday's *Express* reported on the results of the previous day's incendiarism:

With the ditched passenger trains back on the track and out of the way, the scene yesterday in the vicinity of the wrecked freight cars was not an inspiring one. The fire, which must have been started by oil, had done its work thoroughly, nearly all the cars fired being burned to the trucks. The freight cars were lined up for miles at the Cheektowaga yards on Sunday, and one of the principal fires occurred half a mile or so above the Lackawanna's brick hotel on a private roadway. Here at least 20 cars were destroyed, and the clearing away of this wreck was one of the principal duties of the Erie's wrecking crews which got to work early. [Since the Erie had no yards in Cheektowaga, the reference must be to cars stalled on the Erie's main.] *The spot is comparatively in the country, and this has not prevented a crowd gathering. Still there were a few interested spectators and many striking switchmen and others viewing the wreck. These cars had all been loaded, some with carpets and other merchandise. So thoroughly had the fire done its work that by daylight there was little remaining of the cars except the iron work.*

The wrecking crew, which worked without molestation, at once waded into the job, and before long, the smoldering woodwork together with wheels, trucks, etc., were tossed over into the ditch beside the track. The coal had become so thoroughly heated that when piled alongside the track the space was hot as a furnace. The rolls of charred carpet were sorted out and those worth saving were stored in the empty freight cars, while the rest was abandoned to a flock of Polack women, who struggled for possession of the best pieces with which to carpet their East Buffalo parlors. It did not take long to eat up the stuff by this means, although the unpleasant odor lingered long in the vicinity. After the smoldering remnants were heaped alongside the track, the crew turned its attention to restoring the westbound track, which was badly warped by the heat. About 5:00 o'clock in the afternoon trains could have been run over it carefully, but there were no trains to run. It was declared by the officials present that it would be in apple-pie order today.

Strikers were confident and claimed that the strike would spread and quickly too if they could not force the LV and the Erie to yield. On the other hand, railroad officials declared Monday night that they would have matters straightened out in a few days if given proper protection by the authorities. In a special dispatch to the *Express* from Reading, Pennsylvania, it was reported that Archibald A. McLeod, president of the Reading Railroad, had said that "no concessions will be made to the strikers. The company views the trouble in a serious aspect, but expects to win." In speaking of the sending from Philadelphia of fifty non-union switchmen to Buffalo last night and today, he said: "There are 1,000 men who are ready and willing to take the places of the strikers. All that is needed is the assurance of the authorities that they will be protected." The DL&W was less confrontational. Anxious to avoid trouble, its officials declared that they would not handle freight from the LV or the Erie. These roads had asked to ship their freight from Buffalo to Waverly over the DL&W and there take it up again, but the DL&W refused to cooperate.

At 9:30 A. M. Monday, the LV's through train from Jersey City arrived at Buffalo with seventy-two men aboard who had been picked up along the Reading System in accordance with McLeod's directive. They were taken to the United States Hotel on Pearl Street and the Terrace where rooms had been engaged for them. During the day, they were visited by a committee of the strikers and asked not to go to work for the LV. They agreed to return home if the local union of switchmen would pay their way home. This was referred to a union meeting that evening, where it was urged, "If we pay the fares of these men to go home, they may drop off, come back, and sell their tickets to brokers, as was done by some of them during the NYC strike. If they are sent out of town by us, we will know were they have gone." The imported strikebreakers had dinner at the hotel and quietly slipped away.

The same issue of the *Express* described the reaction of local law enforcement authorities on Monday to the disturbances created by the strike:

At Police Headquarters [on the corner of Franklin and Seneca Streets] *a bustling scene of activity was presented. The corridors were crowded in the morning with would-be policemen. In the morning seventy special patrolmen were sworn in and the number kept increasing during the day. Superintendent Daniel Morgenstern was asked how many would eventually be added to the force. He replied that at least 150 specials would be sworn in. Asked what preparations were being made, the Superintendent said the city would be thoroughly protected. The regular policemen will be stationed near the scene of disorder while the specials will take their places around the city. He said he could at once throw 200 men into any disorder without leaving the city at all unprotected. Captain* [Patrick] *Kilroy will be in command at East Buffalo. He spoke of the unfortunate circumstance of the* [Chicago World's] *Fair coming just as it does. "The people who come here for that must be protected just the same," he said, "and they will be."*

"Outside the city limits the Sheriff will have to quell any disturbance that may arise," he continued, "but inside the city police will see that quiet is kept. It is strange that the strikers should take the steps they are, for they are not hurting the railroads at all. The City and the County will have to pay for all damage done, and in this way the strikers will have to pay their share." No disturbance occurred along the LV or Erie tracks between Seneca Street and the city line up to midnight Monday. Captain Kilroy had a force of about 60 patrolmen guarding these tracks all evening. The men were placed at intervals along this extent of track and patrolled a line over six miles long.

Further east in the LV yards more cars, empty ones this time, were still smoldering with the remains of Sunday night's fire. They were not so badly in the way here, but they also received the attention of the wrecking crew. The steady progress of the fires despite the efforts of the Fire Department was explained when daylight discovered many slits cut in the hose under cover of darkness. It was in this manner that steamers' streams were made ineffectual.

The office of the Sheriff in the City Hall [on Franklin between Eagle and Church] *has not been the scene of so much activity as it was all day yesterday in many years. The Sheriff's call and the substantial inducement in the hope of $3 per day drew a large crowd of men to the office early in the morning. Beck went out in the morning with the first posse of 48 men, but all deserted at the solicitation of the strikers who were ranged along the fence at Lackawanna Avenue* [three blocks into Cheektowaga from the Buffalo line.] *The sheriff soon had 48 clubs to carry back into the city.* [(Figure #2.)] *Another batch of almost 30 special deputies with blue badges and white batons went out on the 2:35 Erie accommodation, which succeeded in making three or four miles in two hours. Arrived at Lackawanna Avenue and William Street, the deputies alighted and marched down towards the stalled freights. Near the wrecked passenger*

X, 2

train, they met a handful of strikers who counseled the deputies to be "white men." The deputies at once tendered Sheriff Beck their clubs and when he refused to accept them tossed them over the fence, blue badges and all, while the strikers applauded. Once started the desertions quickly spread along the line, and before the Sheriff could leave, his buggy was filled with the clubs and badges he had furnished. "I'm going to town now and make a requisition for the militia," he said, "as I find that I cannot keep the men I have sworn in. It is time to do something besides getting a lot of friends of the strikers to act as officers. Why the engineers, firemen, and train hands seem to be in league with the men, and will not move the trains."

A deputy who did not cave in so quickly reported that "the strikers came up and mixed in with us and took our clubs away." An ex-policeman who had been sworn in as a deputy gave his explanation of the fiasco to a reporter from the *Express*:

When we got there, instead of a line being regularly formed and the men placed in twos or threes at regular intervals along he track, they were all huddled together on the track just outside the city limits. A good many were mere lads, and the strikers intimidated them. That's all there was to it. There was no competent officering, and half the men were scared blue.

John McMahon, the chairman of the committee which had ordered the strike, said that the Grand Master had offered a reward of $100 for the identification of the man who derailed the Hornellsville local Sunday night. McMahon said he was using every influence he had to prevent a repetition of the lawless acts of Sunday night and to preserve the strike from any violence. "The strikers have pickets out to prevent the introduction of non-union men," he insisted, "but that is all."

It was on his return from East Buffalo that Sheriff Beck called on General Peter C. Doyle for the aid of the militia. Concerning the general, Horton writes:

Peter C. Doyle, the powerful Democratic politician who had served the city well in effecting the nomination of Grover Cleveland as mayor, now stood prepared to serve it in another capacity. President of the Merchants' Exchange in 1890 and passenger and freight agent of the LV, Doyle was a versatile man who had accumulated military as well as civic distinctions. He was a member of Buffalo's 21st Infantry Regiment in the Civil War from which he emerged a major; and thereafter he kept up his military interest unabated. [2]

In 1892 Doyle was a general in the National Guard and the commanding officer of the 4th Brigade. The state militia consisted of four brigades. The 4th was made up of the 65th and 74th regiments of Buffalo, separate infantry companies from Rochester, Jamestown, Canadaigua, Elmira, Oswego, Geneva, Syracuse, Geneva, Olean, Tonawanda, and Niagara Falls, and an artillery company from Syracuse.

The property authorities were particularly concerned with protecting was the great LV coal trestle in a section of Cheektowaga called Bellevue, which with its contents was valued at about half a million dollars. A small train of empty cars nearby had been set on fire early Monday morning. Telegraph wires were also cut, those strung along the Erie connecting the LV trestle with company offices on Scott Street and those connecting the nearby DL&W trestle with the DL&W terminal at the foot of Main Street. It was largely to guard the LV trestle that the sheriff had earlier sworn in deputies and sent them out to Cheektowaga.

The switchmen's union held a long meeting Monday night at which no reporters were present nor were any resolutions promulgated. However, rumors circulated that the strike would soon spread to other roads, even those that had already given in to the strikers' demands. Accordingly, Attorney Daniel H. McMillan and several officials of the NYC called on Sheriff Beck shortly after midnight and demanded protection for their road's property. Although the NYC's switchmen had not yet gone on strike, the company had received intimations that they might do so and had decided to warn the sheriff.

Tuesday, August 16

Sheriff Beck made his call upon General Doyle at Brigade headquarters at 6:00 P. M. on Monday. Doyle, struck by the novelty of giving orders of a warlike character by telephone, called out Buffalo's two regiments which assembled promptly. A little after midnight on Tuesday morning, the First Battalion of the 65th, about 150 men under command of Colonel Samuel M. Welch, a lawyer, left their armory at the State Arsenal on Broadway and, preceded by drummers, marched to the Erie depot, where Welch, according to the August 16th *Express*, declared ominously:

The National Guard is never ordered out at midnight to put down a riot armed with blank cartridges. Every man that leaves this arsenal tonight carries 38 rounds of ball cartridge, prepared to shoot. The regiment has a fine record at rifle practice and was never in better condition for duty than tonight.

From Exchange Street the troops were taken to a point east of the Erie's William Street Station, just inside Cheektowaga. (Figure #3.) Arriving there about 1:00 A. M. Tuesday, they were given the task of protecting both the LV's and the DL&W's coal trestles. (Figure #4.) The 74th under Colonel George C. Fox left its armory on Virginia Street at 1:30 A. M. Tuesday for the Erie depot. On the way out to East Buffalo, soldiers were stationed on the train and the engines, prepared to pick off anyone interfering with switches. Asked when was the last time his regiment had been called out to repress lawlessness, Fox replied, "Not since 1877, the time of the railroad riots, when the 74th went to Hornellsville." The troops,

X, 3

X, 4

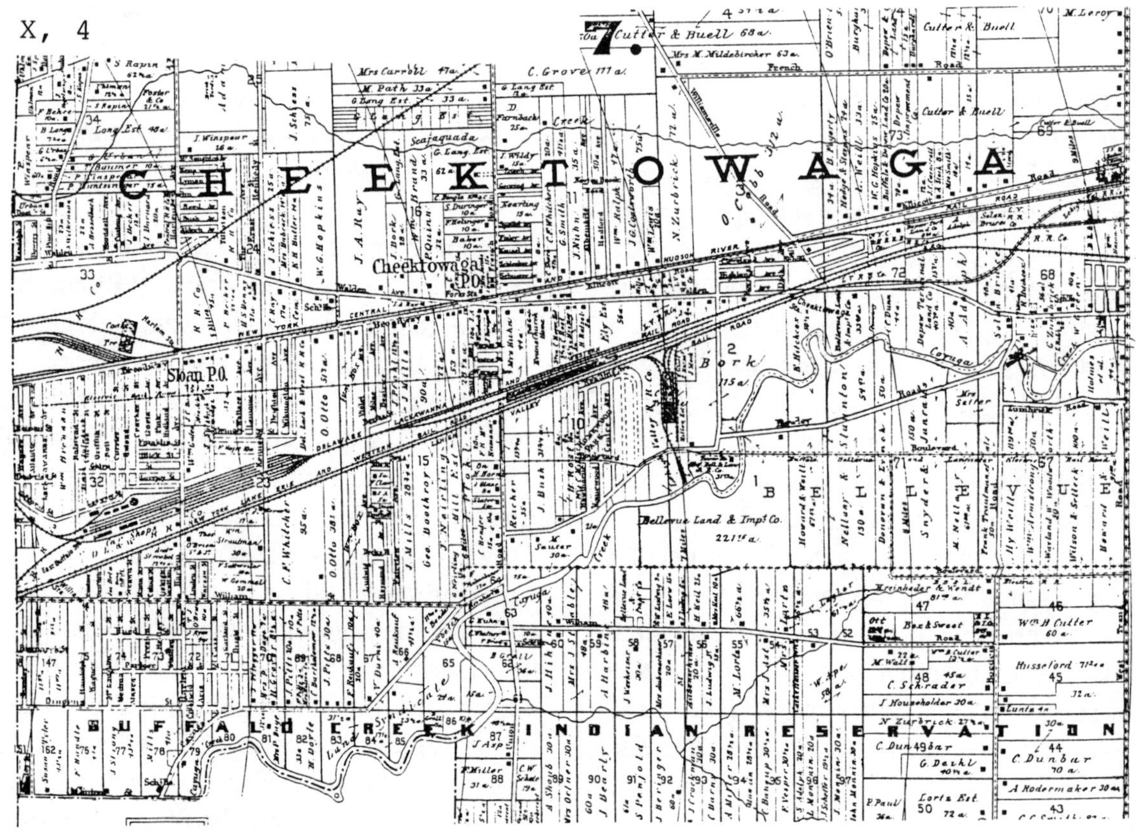
CHEEKTOWAGA
Cheektowaga P.O.
Sloan P.O.
Bellevue Land & Impt Co.
BUFFALO CREEK INDIAN RESERVATION
BELLEVUE
Cutler & Buell
Cayuga Creek

over 200 in all, reached William Street at 2:35 and took up a position next to the 65th. Camp fires were lit, and the scene was that of a picturesque bivouac. Colonel Welch announced that his men were there not for patrol duty but to repress disturbances, a distinction, as it turned out, without a difference. To secure the LV's threatened trestle, Colonel Welch, leaving a squad to guard the William Street Station, marched the rest of his regiment along the DL&W's tracks four miles out to the trestle. The sleepless soldiers said it was the hardest march they had ever made. They reached their objective at 6:00 A. M. and waited there until 9:00 whence they returned to William Street at about 10:30. Captain Babcock with seventy-five men from Companies F and D was left to guard the trestle.

A reporter from the *Express* tried to interview Frank Sweeney in the lobby of the Genesee Tuesday afternoon, but he professed to know nothing about anything connected with the strike. "I've been around the hotel nearly all day, and have seen but few who knew of anything," he added. The same afternoon, the Buffalo Rochester & Pittsburgh yielded to the demands of Sweeney's union. The matter was settled at a meeting held at the office of Trainmaster E.D. Wells at Buffalo Creek Junction, at which General Superintendent J. H. Barrett and the grievance committee of the trainmen were present. The agreement had not been signed, however, and so the yards were tied up at 4:00, the men refusing to work without a formal pact. Barrett agreed to sign it next morning, and, with that understanding, work recommenced at 6:00 P. M.

Throughout Tuesday, passenger trains continued to run. Interference with passenger trains would have quickly antagonized the public and, since most through trains and some locals were regularly assigned mail cars, the federal government. The Erie sent out five day freights on the Buffalo Division and five on the Buffalo & Southwestern Division, but the LV did nothing. From the headquarters of the Reading at Philadelphia came assurance "that President McLeod was ready to send in all the men needed as soon as he was assured of proper protection." Fennell of the LV declared:

We will be in good shape to handle all our business, as we have 60 men who are not afraid to work, and will not leave us. We do not wish to hold any one who does not care to work, as they are not the class of men we want. At East Buffalo we have fitted up fine quarters, and with the best of cooks we will look after the interests of the men.

These men were brought in shortly before noon on the LV on two cars and housed in temporary quarters in the car shops on New South Ogden Street. None of them went to work, however, since the strike at Sayre had tied up the line. What these men needed most of all was protection, and General Doyle intended to cooperate with his employer. On Tuesday night the general ordered all the separate companies of his 4th Brigade to report for duty in Buffalo on Wednesday. This involved fourteen infantry companies, two from Rochester, two from Elmira, one each from Auburn, Jamestown, Tonawanda, Geneva, Syracuse, Niagara Falls, Olean, Geneva, Oswego, and Cortland, and a battery (sans artillery but with pistols and sabers) from Syracuse. With the 65th and 74th Regiments already on the ground, this addition of approximately 1,140 would bring the total militia in and around Buffalo to about 2,000. This new call to the colors was made pursuant to an order from Federal Judge Manly C. Green, before whom representatives of Buffalo's railroads had appeared and requested more protection.

Tuesday was marked by sporadic violence. In the afternoon, an Erie crew set out fifteen cars of ice for L. B. Banks & Company on its siding on Hamburg Street. Returning with empties the train was stopped at Heacock Street, and a mob began pulling pins from the train. In a few minutes, a squad of police from Station #2 (Seneca Street east of Louisiana) arrived and dispersed the pin pullers. The train proceeded to East Buffalo without further incident. Shortly before 5:00 P. M. about a dozen strikers gathered at the Dingens Street crossing of the LV and threatened several non-union men working in the yards there. Suddenly, one of the strikers drew a revolver as if to shoot at a strikebreaker. Patrolman John Paten and Detective Cruse dove at the man, who boldly grabbed the patrolman's club. Two other strikers came to their confrere's assistance. Paten drew his revolver, which was in turn clutched at by the striker, who released his hold on the club, one blow from which laid him in the dust. When he came to, he was arrested. Meanwhile, one of his abettors was captured and arrested by Cruse. The pair, Philip Saltier and James Hanlon, were charged with riot and locked up at #7 Station House on Louisiana near Elk. A Buffalo & Southwestern Division Erie passenger train was derailed by a tampered switch at the Seneca Street crossing at about 11:00 P. M. Fortunately, the passengers were not shaken up and were taken into the city on trolley cars. Half an hour later, Captain F. E. Wood of Company H, 74th Regiment, which had also been detailed to guard the DL&W bridge at William and North Ogden Streets over the Erie and the LV (Figure #5), fired on a man on a moving freight car who had thrown a stone at him.

About 9:00 P. M., a gang of about twenty hard-bitten characters sauntered up to a three-man detail from Company C, 65th Regiment, at the same bridge. With an air of braggadocio, the troublemakers attempted to force their way through, but with bayonets fixed, the detail forced the leaders back. The strikers then changed their tactics and claimed they were boarders at the DL&W's brick hotel and wished merely to go up Queen Street to get there. Corporal W. F. Caddie agreed to let them through, if they would fall in line and follow him. They refused, withdrew, and returned within a few minutes with about thirty reinforcements, who stood across the street

DOING PICKET DUTY ON WILLIAM STREET NEAR CITY LINE

jeering at the pickets. When some of the mob began throwing stones, Lieutenant Lambrecht of Company C came up with a relief of fourteen men on the double who with pointed bayonets again charged the crowd which again dispersed but soon returned. By now the crowd had swelled to about 200, many of them women. At this point, the police took over. Captain Kilroy called up his reserves who came running, brandishing clubs. Some men in the crowd would not budge and had to be clubbed. Most fled, however, and the police gave chase for several blocks.

Philip Day was standing allegedly in the doorway of his coal, wood, and feed store on the corner of Schiller and Queen Streets. He was no part of the mob and so refused to run. As a result, he was clubbed by several zealous policemen and knocked unconscious. After the excitement had died down, he was carried into his office and the Fitch ambulance summoned. Before it arrived, Dr. Adelbert G. Gummer, whose office was located nearby on Bailey Avenue, came along and sewed up an inch and a half cut in Day's head. (Police Superintendent Morgenstern would later claim that Day was on the sidewalk, not in his doorway, and was clubbed because he refused to comply with a reasonable request from a police officer to move.) As Jack Dennison, a DL&W engineer, was coming back from the grocery with five pounds of sugar, he was clubbed on the shoulder by a policemen. In the confusion, the sugar was lost. After the police returned from the chase, they cleared out five saloons on Queen Street and closed them down for the night. The ambulance from Fitch remained on the scene ready for emergencies.

On Tuesday afternoon the switchmen's strike committee met with Theodore Voorhees, General Superintendent of the NYC, who arrived in Buffalo aboard the private car *Marquis* along with Third Vice President H. Walter Webb, in charge of operations and Vice President of the Wagner Palace Car Company. Voorhees refused to yield to the union's demands. In a night session at Lodge #39's regular meeting place, Kaiser's Hall on Seneca Street, a call for a strike to begin at midnight was sent out to lodge members in Buffalo, Black Rock, Niagara Falls, and Suspension Bridge. The NYC had in service about twenty-five day and about a dozen night switch engines, each having a switching crew of three men besides the enginemen, which brought the total to 125, nearly as many as were already striking on the Erie, the LS&MS, and the Buffalo Creek. The previous week a vote had been taken in the yards in which three fourths of the switchmen agreed to strike for a ten hour day if necessary. Tuesday night's action, following Voorhees's refusal, was taken in accordance with this earlier vote. The switchmen also demanded that the roads which had already granted the ten hour day order their trainmen to refuse to handle any NYC cars, lest they also be struck. Given the size of the NYC's interchange business, this would seriously cripple railroad operations in Buffalo. Puffing on a cigar while standing in a secluded platform of the Exchange Street Station early Tuesday evening, Webb told a reporter that "there is no danger to be apprehended on our lines here as the men will work if given protection, and I believe they will get that all right," referring, no doubt, to Judge Green's order.

After the NYC switchmen went out, another reporter interviewed Voorhees, since Webb had retired, in the *Marquis* at 1:00 A. M. Wednesday. The superintendent said that the day men would not go out because they did not belong to the union. He also claimed that the men employed by the NYC in Buffalo "have been receiving more pay than any other men performing like service on this road in the State of New York." In answer to the question "What do the strikers demand - fewer hours or increased wages?" Voorhees replied:

That's just what I'd like you to make clear to the public through the press. It is purely a strike for increased pay. The pretension of the men that they want fewer hours is all humbug. They have worked in the past 11 hours a day actual work and they expect to continue to work that way, but they want their hourly compensation increased by an amount which is practically 10 percent. It is, as I said before, a strike for increased pay. The men have never before made the slightest objection to the number of hours they work."

With the strike spreading to the NYC, navigation on Lake Erie was brought to a near standstill. In fact, before the strike most coal shipments had stopped. Grain forwarders up the Great Lakes were complaining that their elevators were bursting with wheat. A cattle boat was unable to leave the Port of Boston because no cattle cars had gotten through from Buffalo. The lumber trade was less affected because the Erie Canal offered an alternate means of transport. Westbound package freight was increasingly being sent over the canal. Tuesday night State Arbitrator Florence F. Donovan met with Sweeney and the strike committee at the Broezel Hotel on the southeast corner of Seneca and Wells and listened to their side of the dispute.

Wednesday, August 17

At daybreak, the switchmen on the NYWS&B, following the example of their brethren on the NYC, went out on strike. The first death stemming from the walkout occurred at the LV trestle in Cheektowaga on Wednesday morning. Quarter Master Sergeant F. W. Elsaesser of Company F of the 74th, in civilian life a shipping clerk, was accidentally shot in the head by a private who was tinkering with a rifle he did not realize was loaded. The sergeant was taken by ambulance to Emergency Hospital on the corner of South Division and Michigan, where he died in the early afternoon. He had enlisted in the 74th in 1881 at the age of twenty.

Throughout the day rumors abounded of other railroad workers going out on strike. The national heads of both the Brotherhood of Locomotive Engineers and the Brotherhood of Locomotive Firemen were reportedly in the city, and S. E. Wilkinson, Grand Master of the Brotherhood of Railway Trainmen, came in from Galesburg, Illinois, for a meeting of his organization at Grimm's Hall at Seneca and Michigan Streets. He declined to be interviewed. Police Superintendent Morgenstern, having spent a sleepless night at headquarters, swore in fifty-eight more special policemen.

The major development of the day, however, was the long conference at the Buffalo Club between city and county officials on the one hand and railroad officials on the other. The upshot was the dispatch of a telegram to Governor Flower dated August 17th, though it was actually dispatched at 12:45 A. M. Thursday: "We have become satisfied that the situation here in Buffalo under the pending strike has become so serious that we ask that the National Guard of the State be called out to protect the lives and property of citizens of this city and county." It was signed by Sheriff Beck and Mayor Charles F. Bishop.

The August 18th *Express* reported that those present at the conference and representing the civil authorities were, besides the sheriff and the mayor, Superintendent Morgenstern and General Doyle. Speaking for the railroads were Webb and Attorney McMillan for the NYC, Wilson S. Bissell, a former law partner of Grover Cleveland and soon to become Postmaster General, for the Reading, and E. Carlton Sprague for the Erie and the Buffalo Creek. Webb had earlier asked the Governor to call out the entire National Guard but was told that this could be done only at the request of the proper civic authorities. Sheriff Beck was extremely reluctant to appeal to Albany. He had made a tour of inspection of the yards and found everything comparatively quiet. He also deplored the expense to the state and county that summoning the guard would entail. The argument of the railroad men was that although no very serious outbreaks had occurred yesterday, this was simply because the roads had not tried to move freight. (This conflicted with their earlier claims that the strike was not seriously disrupting their business.) Not only were freight trains torched, they continued, but passenger trains were derailed and stoned in the very heart of the city. The lives of people traveling over the roads were not safe and property was liable to destruction at any moment. If this was the case when the roads were practically idle, they argued, nothing short of bloodshed and mob rule would result from an attempt to operate the lines at full capacity.

After two hours of discussion, Beck gave in and signed the request. Adjutant General Josiah Porter, the chief of staff of the National Guard, had been notified that a request for troops might be expected during the night and was waiting in his office in Albany for the call. Webb said that the 12th and 22nd Regiments from New York City, the 10th Battalion of Albany, and six separate companies had been waiting under arms in their respective armories and would start early Thursday morning on trains provided by the NYC. He asserted that "the strike is practically over with the calling out of the Guard. All the roads have men enough to work these trains with if they have protection." Oddly enough, earlier Wednesday evening, in answer to the question whether he had ordered any troops to get ready, Porter had stated:

I have not. No companies or regiments outside of the 4th Brigade have been notified to be in readiness. If New York regiments are assembling, they are doing it, the same as the 10th Battalion here, of their own volition and because they have heard it rumored that they will be called out.

While the Buffalo Club conference was going on, over on the East Side Sergeant Herman G. Burkhardt and Patrolmen William McNamara and Matthew Slavin apprehended two men whom they took to be striking switchmen, John Ball and Martin Beyer, in the act of tampering with a switch on the NYC's mainline near Fillmore Avenue. The miscreants had opened the switch and were adjusting the light so that it would indicate clear. The officers readjusted the switch and the light, and not long afterwards the westbound *Fast Mail* due in Buffalo at 8:00 P. M, the second fastest train on the road, roared past at its usual rate. The murderous duo were arraigned in Police Court and jailed.

Thursday, August 18

The New York National Guard listed 13,290 men on its roster, but Porter planned to send only about 7,000 to Buffalo, the remainder being kept in reserve. The 12th and 23rd Regiments from New York City and the 13th from Brooklyn left for Buffalo shortly before noon on Thursday, the first two on the NYC from Grand Central, the latter by ferry to Weehawken and from there on the NYWS&B. The two city regiments had about a thousand men each, and the one from Brooklyn half that number. Station platforms were crowded with wives and sweethearts. Troops began arriving at Buffalo at 7:30 Thursday evening. First on the scene was the 10th Battalion, 490 strong, from the Albany area. It was assigned to the NYC's Seneca Street shops where the offices were turned into headquarters, temporary bunks with mattresses from Wagner cars were set aside for officers and the injured, and the main building was given over to the enlisted men. Two or three Albanians were jailed for refusing to answer the call to arms. Also heading for Buffalo on the 18th were the 4th Separate Company from Yonkers, the 6th from Troy, the 46th from Amsterdam, the 44th from Utica, and the 48th from Oswego (a member of which was run over and killed his first day of duty at the NYC yards.)

Shortly before 1:00 A. M. Thursday, the NYC offered to the LS&MS's westbound yard at East Buffalo the cars of two freight trains. The two switching crews working the yard refused to handle them when ordered to do so by the yardmaster. Since all Buffalo's railroads terminated there, interchange between them was the major part of their business. The yardmaster fired the recusants, and the yard was struck. When word of the firings reached the Lake Shore's Buffalo yard at Elk Street and Abbott Road, the switchmen there also walked off the job. The LS&MS was controlled by the NYC. The Commodore's grandson, Cornelius Vanderbilt II, was chairman of the board of the NYC and his brother, William K., was chairman of the board of the LS&MS. Though its headquarters were at Grand Central Station in New York City, the LS&MS retained its own corporate identity and management and operating structure. Its labor policy, however, was different from that of the Central.

Confident now of protection for strikebreakers, the Erie and the LV advertised in New York papers for a hundred "able bodied men to leave the city for work." About 150 men, most of them young and unkempt, met an agent of the roads at a saloon on Hester Street on Manhattan's Lower East Side. They were told that they would received from $2 to $2.50 a day, depending on their skills, that they would be fed by the company, and that they could sleep in yard buildings. About eighty signed on. The others, when they learned where they were going, said they did not want to have their heads cracked or to be sent back from Buffalo in a pine box. Meanwhile in Buffalo, about 150 strikebreakers were hired at the United States Hotel.

Frank Sweeney, who grew more loquacious as the strike continued, claimed that the railroads "are getting in carloads of men, but they are not practical switchmen. I'll bet 500 men have been shipped into the city since the trouble began, but they are the worst class of men in the country." He based this assertion on information provided by scouts who reported to him that "the roads are picking up tramps and bums and bringing them here." When asked what conduct by strikers he considered "within the law," he replied, "Moral suasion and that only. I do not include pulling pins, turning switches, or threatening men who are at work." His critics pointed out that Sweeney failed to go out and preach this gospel to the members of his union.

Upon the arrival of National Guard units from the east, General Doyle repositioned his brigade. He transferred headquarters from the Erie station at Queen and William to 476 Main Street between Court and West Mohawk, maintaining contact with his men in the field by telephone. The 65th was based on the Lehigh roundhouse on New Ogden Street. The 74th was given the responsibility of patrolling everything along the Erie and the LV from William Street east into Cheektowaga. The main camp, an agglomeration of tents and railroad cars with headquarters at the Erie's William Street Station, was known as Camp Lehigh, though the men called it Camp Bush after Captain Bush, the oldest man in the 74th. The sub-encampment of three companies guarding the Lehigh trestle was known as Camp Cheektowaga. Near Camp Lehigh on 963 William Street was the Milsom Rendering & Fertilizing Company from which emerged an awful stench. During the day a merciless sun beat down on the men. Nights were cool and damp. However the camp saw many visitors, particularly females, who came bearing delicacies. The fare for dinner on Wednesday, according to an *Express* reporter, was boiled ham, canned Boston beans, and coffee. S.& H. Davis, fish dealers, promised half a ton of their goods, while Vice President Webb sent smoking and chewing tobacco to all the soldiers guarding the Vanderbilt roads and cigars to their officers. A less roseate picture was painted for the *Express* by a young man in the regiment from Delaware Avenue:

The men had to sleep five in a tent, with loose straw for bedding. That's nothing, though, when you get used to it. What came hardest at first was the grub. They brought us a big basket full of hunks of meat and each man had to grab for himself with his fingers. If a man got more than three pieces of meat, two rolls, and two cups of awful muddy coffee for his breakfast, he was voted a hog. These rations come from what the guardsmen irreverently term "the grub cars" switched out on a side track just below camp. Here Lieut. Buck presided with an easy grace born of long experience in the hotel business, and what is known as wet goods, sent down by the Lehigh officials. [(Figure #6.)]

"We privates don't get very near those wet goods," remarked a trooper, "but a bottle from outside finds its way into the tents now and then." Erie and Lehigh officials claimed that there was more switching and dispatching of trains on Thursday than previously.

The legislature had decreed in 1887 that:

Whenever a strike or lockout shall occur, or is seriously threatened in any part of the state, it shall be its [the New York State Arbitration Board's] *duty to proceed to the locality of such strike or lockout and put themselves in communication with the parties to the controversy, and endeavor by mediation to effect an amicable settlement of such controversy; and, if in their judgment, it is deemed best to inquire into the cause or causes of controversy; and to that end the board is hereby authorized to subpoena witnesses, compel their attendance, and send for persons and papers.* [3]

William Purcell, chairman of the Arbitration Board, an Irish-Catholic Democrat and editor of the *Rochester Union and Advertiser*, had on Tuesday met with Sweeney, who agreed to submit his union's dispute with the railroads to

X, 6

COMMISSARY BUCK'S KITCHEN AT CAMP BUSH.

arbitration. However, at a meeting Wednesday with the railroad officials, Purcell got no satisfaction whatsoever. Accordingly, he sent identical letters to the ranking official of each struck railroad in Buffalo urging submission of the issue to arbitration.

All railroad officials contacted absolutely refused to submit the dispute to arbitration. Webb replied that most of the switchmen on the NYC struck because they had been intimidated by a minority. Freight service was continuing, he insisted, and any interference therewith "has simply been owing to the fact that the properly constituted authorities of the city and county have been unable to furnish protection to those who were in the company's service and who sought to continue in the performance of their duties." McLeod instructed his man in Buffalo, M. F. Bonzano, General Superintendent of the LV, to tell Purcell that the Reading would have no dealings with outlaws who abandoned the service of the company, destroyed its property, and threatened to murder its employees. The superintendent of the Eastern Division of the LS&MS wrote sharply to Purcell saying that he referred the request for arbitration to the general superintendent, William. H. Canniff, in Cleveland. Nineteenth century railroad executives had no intention of letting outsiders determine the wages paid to railroad workers.

Either the situation had improved for the railroads or their representatives at the Buffalo Club conference had deceived the mayor and the sheriff. On Thursday the NYC's Assistant Superintendent Rossiter told an *Express* reporter:

We are running our passenger trains with but little trouble and find little difficulty beyond the delay necessary in running carefully over the switches. We are looking carefully after the safety of our passengers and a few minutes of delay will not seriously inconvenience them. In our freight department we are getting along splendidly. We are not refusing any freight and our East Buffalo agent reports that the freight is being handled better than ever. At Ohio Street we are working our full force and have sent out today about 150 cars of grain and lake freight.

In an attempt at humor which spoke volumes about the economic state of his road, General Superintendent Bradley of the NYWS&B said with a laugh, "We do not do enough business to let such a little thing as a strike bother us. We are moving everything we have to move and are not worrying after our men."

Things were not so serene elsewhere. A string of cars from the LV was handed over to the Nickel Plate for interchange at its yards between Seneca Street and Abbott Road before noon on Wednesday. Shortly after 2:00 P. M., a crew of switchmen were ordered to handle these cars. They refused and were discharged, whereupon every other crew in the yard walked off the job, leaving it to Yardmaster Curry and one or two of his assistants to cope as best they could. As of Thursday night, switchmen had struck the Erie, the LV, the Buffalo Creek, the NYC, the LS&MS, the NYWS&B, and the Nickel Plate.

Thursday night a striker brought to the office of the *Express* an affidavit signed by eleven men who had been engaged in New York City to work as foremen and time-keepers for a gang of men at Buffalo. They were to be brought near no place where a strike was in progress and were not to take the place of any strikers. Passage was engaged for them over the NYC, and they were given orders valid for their return passage, signed by C. A. Brunn of the Erie. They arrived in Buffalo on Tuesday and were taken directly to the Erie yards, where they were given their breakfast in the presence of soldiers with drawn bayonets. They refused to act as strikebreakers and went looking for Brunn, but were told that he was out and that the man in charge could do nothing for them. The prospective strikebreakers had no money and approached Adam Rehm,

Superintendent of the Poor, who told them to go back to the road that had engaged them.

Friday, August 19

On Friday Sweeney made another attempt to have the strike arbitrated. He wrote to the heads of all the struck railroads proposing that:

. . . the disputed points in question, viz: the hours of their labor per day, the schedule of wages, and the right of appeal of a discharged or suspended switchman to a higher authority on your road, be submitted to a committee of three citizens of the City of Buffalo, one to be named by the officials of your company, and one to be named by the switchmen, and the third to be named by the two thus appointed. This committee to investigate all matters in dispute and hear all evidence presented by either side, and after such investigation and hearing the final conclusion of the committee to be binding upon the officials and the switchmen.

Pending a settlement, Sweeney ordered that all the switchmen employed as of August 12, 1892, the day the strike was called, who were since discharged for refusing to work, should resume their former employment.

Webb declared that "the NYC does not employ union men, and there is no reason why we should treat with him." Canniff, of the LS&MS, said the same thing. He pointed out that the LS&MS switchmen had walked out Thursday morning when ordered to handle freight cars of the struck NYC. They were told that "as a common carrier the LS&MS was compelled by law to receive and forward all freight offered our company, and that it was impossible to receive freight from one road and not another." Caniff was on solid ground since secondary boycotts, a relatively new weapon in railway-labor disputes, had been declared illegal by two federal judges in connection with the strike against the Chicago Burlington & Quincy in 1888, and not long afterward Circuit Court Judge William Howard Taft, the future President of the United States, ruled that the Interstate Commerce Act (1887) obliged all interstate carriers to exchange freight with all other carriers without discrimination. Railroad officials interpreted Sweeney's offer as a sign that support for the strike was weakening. After all, his strikers had not been paid for almost a week. A reporter for the *Express* had a long interview with Grand Master F.P. Sergeant of the Brotherhood of Locomotive Firemen, who saw no reason why its members should be drawn into the strike since they had no grievances of which he was aware. William Buchanan, Superintendent of Motive Power for the NYC, had been in Buffalo for several days and so far had heard no complaints from either engineers or firemen. He had no fear that any of them would go out on strike. In the morning, Sweeney held a conference at Kaiser's Hall with representatives of lodges of the Switchmen's Association in Pennsylvania, and in the afternoon he attended a meeting of the switchmen and the local lodge of the trainmen at O'Grady's Hall on Broadway near Bailey.

A committee of four striking switchmen called on Mayor Bishop and Sheriff Becker at 10:30 Friday morning and requested that the militia be withdrawn. They declared that the switchmen "had more right to protection from burdensome taxation [to support the troops] than the railroads had to have State troops act as guards to keep non-union men at work." Many of the new men, they asserted, wanted to quit, but were prevented from so doing by rigid military surveillance. The committee insisted that none of the lawlessness and violence had been the work of the strikers (this was more than Sweeney had claimed), and promised that if the troops were taken away there would be no further trouble. The only danger of trouble resulted from the presence of the military. Both mayor and sheriff assured the committee that as soon as they were convinced that the presence of the state troops was no longer necessary to protect life and property, and the railroads were allowed to transact business without interference, they would ask the governor to withdraw the militia. Superintendent Morgenstern had notices posted at police headquarters that no more special patrolmen were needed. He already had 250 which he considered enough. "The strike is over, I guess," he concluded, quite inaccurately.

Violence was not over. Yardmaster Barrett of the Erie was riding in from East Buffalo on a string of freight cars in the afternoon when stones were thrown at him as the train crossed Seneca Street. He recognized his tormentors as former switchmen and took down the names of a several for prosecution. At about the same time Albert Bowen of Westfield, a brakeman who had begun work on the LS&MS Thursday, was attacked by a striker who had sneaked through the military pickets into the yards near the roundhouse at Perry Street and climbed up on to Bowen's train. Bowen gave as good as he got and eventually threw his attacker off the train. The striker ran away, and the Fitch ambulance was called for Bowen. As the badly injured man was being led to the ambulance beyond the picket line, cries of "Scab!" erupted from a score of throats. The victim had just gotten into the ambulance when one member of an advancing mob reached the ambulance and succeeded in striking Bowen three times. The mob was driven back by the militia at bayonet point, but did not disperse. A policeman telephoned Precinct #2 for reserves, and Sergeant Ryan and four patrolmen rushed to the scene where, wielding their clubs, they restored order. Henry Duggan, one of Bowen's attackers, was arrested and taken to the stationhouse, where he was locked up for disorderly conduct. Meanwhile at Fitch, two of Bowen's wounds were pronounced serious. The doctors believed he had been hit in the head with brass knuckles.

In the evening on NYC's Ohio Basin branch, three switch engine crews were at work when a shower of stones, chunks of coal, and coupling pins descended on them. Since General Doyle informed Vice President Webb that there were not enough soldiers to protect this particular operation, the workers had to be sent home for the night. Thomas Mills was given three months for beating Patrick Welch, a LV switchman, into insensibility with a large stone. Martin Hanlon, a striker, was arraigned in Police Court for having with other strikers surrounded a non-union workman in the NYC yards in East Buffalo and "threatening to kill him if he did not quit work."

Strikebreakers had other problems than those created by strikers. Michael Costello, a penniless resident of Lowell, Massachusetts, who had been working as a switchman on the Erie for only four days, had his right arm caught between the bumpers of two freight cars. It was crushed so badly that it had to be amputated when he was taken to Emergency Hospital. Several men who had been brought to Buffalo by the Erie and the NYC went to the switchmen's meeting place on Seneca Street and were given money to return home on the DL&W. They claimed that they had been hired in New York City to work as laborers on Western railways.

A second and more distinguished delegation called on the sheriff at 4:00 P. M. on Friday. The *Express* tried to put its members down by observing that they were "all of the South Side" - i.e., the First Ward. The chief spokesman was Michael Martin, an engineer for the LS&MS. Accompanying him were another LS&MS engineer, George Mackintosh, Doctor Thomas M. Crowe, and the Lieutenant Governor of New York, William F. ("Blue Eyed Billy") Sheehan, who had been elected six times to the assembly, where he opposed Prohibition and supported big corporations against the predecessors of the progressives. In 1891 he had served as speaker. Upon him had fallen the mantle of his elder brother, John C. Sheehan, as boss of the First Ward. Martin pointed out that there were thirty soldiers in town for every striker and that the county was incurring unnecessary expense by the presence of the militia. Someone muttered something about Beck having been "actuated by 'boodle' in calling for the militia," which was unfair since he had been the last local official to hold out against calling for troops.

Trains were moving on most railroads, but not as many as before the strike. The LS&MS accommodation due in Buffalo at 9:40 A. M. was delayed near Buffalo Creek by an open switch. The trainmen were afraid to touch it, but several of the passengers got off and appealed to a crowd of bystanders to let the switch be thrown. They did, and the train was allowed to proceed. Police and militiamen guarded rights of way, stations, and railroad company offices. Under the banner, "Where To Find Friends," the *Express* listed the locations of the camps, the units (regiments and separate companies) assigned there, telephone numbers, and commanding officers:

#1, Seneca Street crossing of Erie RR, 12th Regt., 15th, 19th, and 47th Separate Companies, tel. 319D, Col. Herman Dow

#2, Tifft Farm Hotel, part of the 22nd Regt., 4th, 16th, 23rd Separate Companies, tel. 1319, Col. John T. Camp

#3, D & H Canal Co. docks, lower Louisiana and Ohio Sts., part of 22nd Regt., tel. 770 and 1050A

#4, Market Grounds, Elk and Michigan Sts., part of 13th Regt., tel. 355, Col. David E. Austin

#5, Erie crossing, Elk St. and Abbott Rd., 9th Regt. and 5th 10th, 16th, and 31st Separate Companies, tel. 319, Col. William T. Seward, Jr. (son of the late governor, senator, and Lincoln's Secretary of State)

#6, Ganson St. south of Michigan, part of 13th Regt., tel. 515 and 184D, Capt. Cochrane

#7, Erie's East Buffalo Station, William east of Bailey, 71st Regt., 8th and 28th Separate Companies, tel. 1363, Col. Frederick Kopper

#8, Lehigh Valley shops, Dingens St., East Buffalo, 65th Regt., 13th, 25th, 42nd, 43rd Separate Companies, tel. 861, Col. Samuel M. Welch

#9, NYC shops, William St. east of Bailey, 1st Provisional Regt. (2nd, 29th, 34th, 41st, 45th, 48th Separate Companies), Gallup's Signal Corps, tel. 721, Capt. W. Maurice Kirby

#10, Black Rock, Tonawanda St., 2nd Provisional Regt. (7th, 32nd, and 39th Separate Companies), tel. 923, Capt. A. Austin Yates

#11, NYC freight house, Erie St., 2nd Provisional Regt. (36th and 37th Separate Companies).

#12, NYC car shops, Seneca St. near Jefferson, 10th Battalion, 6th, 21st, 42nd, 44th Separate Companies, tel. 721D, Col. William E. Fitch

#13, Wagner Palace Car Co., Broadway and Bailey, 23rd Regt., 18th Separate Company, tel. 721D, Col. John N. Partridge

#14, Lehigh Valley, William Street crossing, 74th Regt., 1st and 20th Separate Companies, 5th Battery, tel. 1380, Col. George C. Fox

Company "A," Cavalry. Alternated between stockyards on William St. and Camp #10.

Where They Came From

Regiments

9th	New York City	23rd	Brooklyn
12th	New York City	65th	Buffalo
13th	Brooklyn	71st	New York City
22nd	New York City	74th	Buffalo

Separate Companies

1st	Rochester	26th	Elmira
2nd	Auburn	28th	Utica
4th	Yonker	30th	Elmira
5th	Newburgh	32nd	Hoosac Falls
7th	Cohoes	34th	Geneva
6th	Rochester	36th	Schenectady
(10th Battalion	Albany)	37th	Schenectady
10th	Newburgh	39th	Watertown
13th	Jamestown	41st	Syracuse
15th	Poughkeepsie	42nd	Niagara Falls
16th	Catskill	43rd	Olean
18th	Glens Falls	44th	Utica
21st	Troy	45th	Cortland
23rd	Hudson	46th	Amsterdam

25th Tonawanda 47th Hornellsville
48th Oswego
Troop "A" New York City
Signal Corps New York City

Saturday, August 20

Despite the presence of fifteen camps at trouble spots in the city (Figure #7) and the fact that many trains were escorted by soldiers (Figure #8), violence continued on Saturday. Guards stationed at intervals along the DL&W coal trestle at Erie Basin, in what the police considered the worst section in the city ("Below the Terrace"), were stoned by a mob which they chased with bayonets affixed, nicking some of the troublemakers. Another crowd of brickbat throwers soon gathered at the corner of Ohio and Michigan Streets. There ensued a lively chase by the militia down back alleys, and the bayonet-wielders soon cleared out the district. Colonel Welch detailed an eighty-man guard to escort a sixty-car LV freight train at Tifft Terminal. Every car had a soldier atop it. John E. Niven, a drunken striker, was noticed bending over a switch that the train was bearing down on. The soldiers nabbed him in time, placed him aboard the train, and handed him over to the police. Another striker was apprehended trying to wreck a train in broad daylight near the LV yards on Dingens Street. He was seized and placed temporarily in the guardhouse of the 65th at Camp Lehigh. The Erie's *Day Express* from Jersey City due in Buffalo at 10:15 P. M. was derailed six miles east of Attica by an iron fish-plate spiked to the inside of a rail. Damage was minimal, since the train had been proceeding slowly because of orders to lookout for open switches. At 10:00 P. M. an Erie freight was stopped east of Babcock Street, and its pins were pulled.

The switchmen's union held another closed meeting Saturday afternoon at O'Grady's. "We are as firm as ever," one of the participants said. "There is not the slightest indication of a backdown on our part, and we feel confident of winning our point." He asserted that the railroads had brought about 2,500 strikebreakers into the city to take the place of 500 switchmen, and the job was still not getting done. "The railroad officials can make their statements about the excellent condition their roads are in, but we don't see much freight moving and we do see any number of idle engines." Delegations of strikers and their sympathizers continued calling on the mayor and the sheriff asking that they petition the Governor to recall the troops, and several supervisors concurred; but the sheriff's reply to all comers was that while stone throwing, turning switches, and interfering with the railroad companies' property continued, the troops were by no means superfluous. Police Superintendent Morgenstern issued a general order to police captains to arrest all bums, tramps, and vagrants found within the city limits. Captain Reagan of the notorious First Precinct and his men arrested about seventy-five persons within those categories, most of whom were given ten or fifteen days in the penitentiary. Morgenstern wanted to get these good-for-nothings off the streets during the strike, since they were apt to hang around with the strikers, incite them, and even engage in mischief themselves. He also requested all law-abiding citizens not to congregate near railroad crossings or yards, since when a charge against a mob is made by police or militia, it is impossible to tell troublemakers from bystanders.

Superintendent Fennell of the LV said that, since the yards at Sayre were now open, he was able to send out seven eastbound freights on Saturday. The LV was again interchanging westbound freight with the Nickel Plate. Rossiter of the NYC stated, "We have our full number of [yard] engines at work and now have 16 road engines here waiting to take trains east." His road handled 471 freight cars Saturday, but he admitted that he received nothing from the struck LS&MS. The most

X, 7

BUFFALO, N. Y., SUNDAY, AUGUST 28, 1892.

MAP OF BUFFALO SHOWING LOCATION OF CAMPS N. G. S. N. Y. DURING STRIKE AUG 1892

R. C. DOYLE BRIG. GEN. 4th BRIGADE

Scale 1 in. = 3000 ft.

Camps	Number of Troops				
	Aug 20	Aug 21	Aug 22	Aug 23	Aug 24
1	615	648	712	711	707
2	756	753	765	774	662
3					
4	623	666	675	674	777
6					
5	547	629	617	613	612
7	498	619	622	623	624
8	629	707	711	726	714
9	411	409	427	424	425
10	208	203	219	221	216
11	170	169	171	171	171
12	575	578	591	597	591
13	530	660	678	684	691
14	617	547	545	551	558
Troop A	85	93	93	85	85
1st Batty	56	56	56	57	57
Total	6340	6737	6882	6911	6890

MOVING LEHIGH VALLEY FREIGHT IN A DANGEROUS DISTRICT

sanguine was Brunn of the Erie, who announced:

We have sent out nine freights so far, and three are ordered to go out this evening. We have sent these out on the main line and three on the Falls Branch. We are working 10 yard engines today, and have every protection except between Michigan and Fillmore Avenues. We are in splendid shape.

Whether the Erie was in splendid shape or not, the price of perishables like meat, poultry and eggs was on the rise in New York City. Wholesalers claimed that their supplies of these commodities, which came chiefly from the west, had steadily dwindled during the past week because of the inability of the railroads to get their trains through. Retail butchers claimed that their wholesalers had ten days supply on hand and that the strike would be settled before then, but the wholesalers were taking advantage of the strike to raise prices anyway. Poultry dealers went further and claimed that their suppliers had six months supply on hand, and were simply gouging their customers. Thus far, those who suffered most because of the strike were grain merchants who complained that they were losing thousands of dollars every day. For some local merchants, however, the strike proved a boon. On Saturday night, employees at a Michigan Avenue bakery worked overtime turning out 5,000 loaves of bread, 3,000 French rolls, 5,000 fried cakes, and 700 pies for the soldiers.

Sunday, August 21

Railroads hitherto tied up stepped up operations over the weekend with protection from the militia and the police and began running freights slowly but surely. The August 22nd *Courier* reported:

The reappearance of coal trains indicated that the yards were being cleared out, since coal was the last commodity that would suffer by delay. On Sunday the companies were doing their normal stepped-down Sunday business. Sporadic acts of violence continued, but to a much lesser extent than before.

Much of the operating personnel of Buffalo's railroads was made up of Irish-Catholics, who in the 1890s were zealous Sunday mass goers.

At 9:30 A. M. Sheriff Beck drove out to the troubled areas with the county clerk and three supervisors to find out whether the troops should be withdrawn. As an elected official, he feared retaliation at the polls by railroad workers and their many sympathizers, who resented the presence of militia in the city. The party first drove out in carriages to the Tifft Terminal, where all was quiet. From there they proceeded up Louisiana to Elk, east on Elk to Smith, north on Smith and Fillmore to Clinton, east on Clinton to Bailey, and north on Bailey to the infamous William Street crossing of the Erie and the LV. "Everything was in good condition there," the sheriff told a reporter for the *Courier*, "no rows occurred while we were there, and we saw well guarded trains moving without any outside interference. Every train was guarded with soldiers, but of course they were not acting as train hands - merely protecting property." From there the sheriff went out to the LV trestle in Cheektowaga where the 65th Regiment was stationed and where he learned from Colonel Welch that the soldiers had been hustled out of bed three times during the night by of the presence of suspicious characters. One trespasser had been discovered trying to get under the trestle, and shots were fired, but by whom the colonel did not know. Asked whether any of the troops could be withdrawn, he replied, "If you want to keep that trestle where it is, the troops had better remain where they are."

Continuing his interview with the reporter, Beck said:

While we were there, a switch engine coming down the trestle was by some interference with a switch suddenly thrown onto a track with a very steep grade and dashed along through a narrow space, destroying some of the trestle beams as well as the cab and steam pipe of the engine. The engineer stuck to his engine, calling on the others to jump. The fireman was slightly bruised from his leap for life.

After this experience, the sheriff drove back to Camp #13 at Broadway and Bailey, site of the Wagner Car shops and the NYC yards, where Police Captain Kilroy asked the sheriff that no troops be withdrawn. From there the sheriff drove south on Bailey to Dingens Street, where the 74th Regiment was based. As he got there, he saw a striker hit a strikebreaker on the back with a coupling pin, knocking him down. This assault was committed in the presence of 200 soldiers at the post. Returning downtown by way of Ohio Street, Beck noticed that the NYC had been moving its freight trains out of the yards all evening. Beyond gathering in small knots and talking, the striking switchmen made no demonstration. The recently turbulent lower wards of the city were quieter than usual.

Back from his thirty-mile round trip, the sheriff met General Porter at the Iroquois Hotel at Main and Eagle and told him that it was not time yet for any troops to be withdrawn. But then Beck made a proposal to the local railroad officials which indicated that, despite what he had learned, he was still anxious to get the troops out of Buffalo. The proposal, which its author believed would end the strike "within twenty-four hours and enable the ordering home of the troops at once," was that the railroad officials should permit "the soldiers to go to their homes, and I, as Sheriff, will swear in all your non-union switchmen as deputy sheriffs, give them badges and clubs, and let them protect your property." Given the sheriff's experience with defecting deputies, this was a ridiculous proposal.

The response of General Freight Agent Pomeroy to Beck's suggestion showed that railroad officials had not been truthful when they described the imported strikebreakers as competent. Pomeroy, as reported in the

August 22 *Courier*, stated:

I have heard this proposition and while I appreciate the dignity which would be conferred upon the Erie the swearing in of its employees as deputy sheriffs, I have serious doubts about the wisdom or efficiency of the proposition. These men that we have employed, whom he proposes to swear in, we have picked up in all sorts of places. They are strangers to us, men idling here and there, and of whose antecedents and character we know absolutely nothing. We have no knowledge that they are responsible men. Some of them we know are not. We have hired them and set them at work, learning a business of which most of them know nothing. We are watching them closely and culling out the best of them, whenever we find any who show a fitness for regular service. It would be the height of absurdity for us, even if they were all honest, sober, responsible men, to expect that they could adequately guard our property armed with clubs and badges, when now they are so terrorized that they have to be guarded by soldiers when they sleep in the sheds at night and with troops in the trains which they are moving by day. When the Erie road is unable to do more than work by day, under the protection of hundreds of troops, without attempting to work at night, it is nonsense to think that 125 green men can learn switching and protect themselves and our property at the same time.

Adjutant-General Porter had come to Buffalo to observe, not to command. Shortly after noon, as narrated in the same issue of the *Courier,* Porter, accompanied by General Doyle and other high ranking officers, including Captain George H. Bush of Ulster County, Speaker of the Assembly, inspected the camps along the Erie and the LV that had been set up during the past few days. By then, over half the National Guard of the state was in Buffalo. Unlike Sheriff Beck, the military went by train from the Erie depot, accompanied by W. J. Nivens, freight agent for the Erie. As the train moved out to East Buffalo, what the officers noticed first was the large number of militiamen strung along each side of the tracks. First stop was at Camp #1, where the Erie crossed Seneca Street. Colonel Dowd of the 12th Regiment conducted the officers through the camp and told the Adjutant-General that "all he had to ask was that the rations should be rushed forward." His men were hungry, and their camp "not located in a desirable spot." Saturday afternoon, the officers learned, the pins had been pulled on a nearby freight train. The soldiers helped to get it into the yards. After dark, a striker had broken through the lines and assaulted a working switchman. A guard nicked the intruder with his bayonet, but not enough to stop him. In all, ten shots were fired in this sector during the night. While Porter and his staff were at the camp, "one long freight train went eastward and two went into the yards. Every second car was mounted and guarded by a soldier with a loaded rifle." From Camp #1 the train carried its prestigious passengers to the Babcock Street Station, where part of the 71st Regiment along with the Rochester and Utica Companies was located. Soldiers' quarters were found to be comfortable, and no complaints about food were heard. Camp Lehigh at the William Street Station of the Erie, which was actually in Cheektowaga, was the next stop. This station was the headquarters of Buffalo's 74th Regiment "where overpowering stenches from the garbage crematory and the Buffalo fat rendering establishment made life . . . almost unbearable." In the commissary's car of the 74th General Porter found a bill of fare for Sunday, which he thought satisfactory:

Breakfast - Yarmouth bloaters [cured herring], *hot cross buns, rolls, and coffee. Dinner - Roast beef, boiled potatoes, bread and butter, pie, coffee, and cheese. Supper - Cold roast mutton, bread and butter, ginger snaps, and tea.*

The party turned southwest to the headquarters of Buffalo's other regiment, the 65th, at Dingens Street. Here, the *Courier* continued, "was seen the most lively spectacle presented at any of the camps. The tents and surrounding area were crowded with women, young and old, who had come to have a Sunday visit with their soldier friends. The boys thoroughly enjoyed this part of military life, while the music of the regimental band added zest to their enjoyment." Preparation of food here at Camp #8 was much improved, according to Colonel Welch, by erecting a cooking shed and acquiring two huge boilers for coffee and soup.

The last stop was the Erie's East Buffalo Station on William Street between Bailey and Babcock Streets. Here at Camp #7, Colonel Greene escorted Porter's party to the William Street Bridge over the Erie's Niagara Falls branch to witness a dress parade of the regiment. The 71st Regiment had an extensive area to cover, and the colonel said that he could use more troops. The men of this regiment were quartered in freight cars, a much better arrangement than many other commands enjoyed. The officers' quarters were on the second floor of the freight house. Back at Iroquois, reporters badgered Porter about whether more troops were needed when the troops now in Buffalo were withdrawn. The general artfully fielded the question without saying anything definite.

Monday, August 22

On Sunday a crew on the WNY&P was asked to switch some LV freight cars. They refused, and at a union meeting in the evening voted to join the strike. At 3:00 P. M. on Monday they walked off the job, but were orderly and simply went home. The WNY&P switchmen had no grievance against their employer other than the order to handle a struck road's cars. In fact their wages and hours were exactly what the men on the other roads were striking for. Now only two of Buffalo's railroads with mainlines in the city remained unaffected, the DL&W and the BR&P. Though nearly all the other lines were running some freight trains, they were operating well below capacity.

The steamer, *John Pridgeon Jr.*, unloaded about twenty-five carloads of LV freight at the DL&W freight house near the mouth of Buffalo Creek where some of the goods were loaded onto freight cars. When the switchmen learned that LV freight was involved, they refused to handle the cars. The freight was reloaded onto the steamer, which sailed to the LV freight house at Tifft Farm to dispose of it. About thirty LV car handlers working on the coal trestles and who sympathized with the switchmen went on strike at 4:00 P. M. Even though they were receiving $1.25 a day with extra pay for overtime, they had been persuaded by Erie strikers. Rank and file firemen, especially those on the LV, were anxious to strike, but their Grand Master dissuaded them.

At least during daytime, freight train movements were picking up on Monday. Superintendent Voorhees claimed that "the Central had 'slipped back into its old groove.' Nearly 200 cars were sent out, and trains were moving on nearly schedule time." The same was allegedly true of the Erie, with eleven switching crews at work. Five eastbound freights departed for Hornellsville, and seven westbounds had arrived. The LV received "a good many cars from other roads" and was constructing a boarding house for its strikebreakers at the Tifft Farm, where its tracks crossed the Hamburg Turnpike. Trains at Black Rock seemed to be running as regularly as ever during the day, but at night "one might stand on the tracks for an hour without being disturbed except for the sentinel on duty."

Varying fates befell the soldiers in the camps around the city. The men of the 22nd at Camp #3 on lower Louisiana Street sat around the fire at night singing. The got so used to sleeping out of doors that they continued to do so after tents arrived. Neighbors along the line of the Erie branch to the Ohio Basin were very kind, some even bringing the soldiers dinner when they were on picket duty. Troops from the same regiment at Camp #2, at Tifft Terminal, experienced no clashes with locals. But the captain of the guard reported "that several squads were patrolling the streets on the double quick in addition to the regular pickets, and all bore an appearance of forced peace." The Crandall House at William and Newell across from the NYC yards put on an elegant dinner for boys of the 71st from Camp #4. It was the first square meal these New Yorkers had enjoyed in some time. Colonel Dowd of the 12th issued a general order to his command that stone throwing at men on cars or at switchmen was to be answered under penalty of expulsion with a shot; while on the other hand Colonel Austen of the 13th ordered his men not to even load their pieces unless by order of a commissioned officer. Most fortunate were the soldiers of the 1st Provisional Regiment at Camp #9, 450 men quartered in the NYC's paint shop in East Buffalo. Through the kind offices of Vice President Webb, their dinner on Monday consisted of soup, roast beef, roast pork, a variety of vegetables, bread and butter, rice pudding, and coffee. This repast was prepared and dispensed by a large corps of cooks and waiters aboard three dining and two baggage cars under the supervision of J. C. Yager of the Wagner Palace Car Company. A special engine and car were made several trips a day between East Buffalo and Exchange Street transporting provisions.

Tuesday, August 23

On Tuesday afternoon the switchmen on the last two railroads with trackage in Buffalo that had not been struck, the BR&P and the DL&W, walked off the job, not because of a grievance over wages and hours but in sympathy with their striking brethren. The BR&P soft coal yards were located on the west shore of the Island along the City Ship Canal, just south of Michigan Avenue, and were worked by fifteen switchmen on four engines. The men went on strike when they were ordered to handle cars of struck railroads. They quit and went home. The DL&W employed about 125 switchmen in its Erie Street, Black Rock, and Cheektowaga yards. At the latter facility, a striker explained that they had gone on strike "because the DL&W handled 'scab' freight." This news was announced to a union meeting at Kaiser's Hall to the accompaniment of loud applause. Shortly afterwards, a delegation from the union waited on Superintendent Frank A. Seabert and volunteered to be sworn in as special policemen to patrol the DL&W yards. Seabert thanked the men but said that the company did not need guards, military or otherwise.

As a result of this development, the *Courier* came out on August 24th with the banner headline, "All Out Now." (The Michigan Central and the Grand Trunk remained unstruck, but they owned no trackage in Western New York.) However, officials of the Erie, the WNY&P, the NYC and the Nickel Plate reported increased activity. The LV was digging in for a long struggle. General Agent Knibloe was quoted by the paper as saying:

We have been building a sort of hotel for our men and fully equipping it with beds, cooking utensils, and all the necessary paraphernalia for taking care of our new men. We expect to put 25 new men at work in the morning. That is about our usual number. Unless the unexpected happens we will be working everything all right then.

The building was located near the southern tip of the City Canal, where the railroad crossed the Hamburg Turnpike. A different picture was painted by a striker who observed that ordinarily a train or engine would pass the Amherst Street crossing on the Erie's line to Niagara Falls about every three minutes (clearly an exaggeration), whereas now "you can sometimes watch for an hour before you'll see any go by."

At about 5:00 P. M. John McGlukin of Philadelphia and Charles Gable of Titusville, two imported LV switchmen working the LV yards on Ganson Street on the Island, were attacked by five strikers. Gable was hit in the face with a stone and his associate McGlukin was kicked so viciously that he had to be taken to Emergency Hospital. Aboard the engine on the train on which the strikebreakers were working was a detail of five privates and Sergeant William S. Conrow under command of Lieutenant Charles E. Austen of the 2nd Battalion, 22nd Regiment, part of which was stationed at Camp #2 on lower Louisiana Street. Austen ordered the strikers to leave the yard, which they refused to do. Thereupon, the lieutenant ordered his men to fire. They did so and apparently hit only the right elbow of the foremost of the assailants, Thomas Monaher. The *Express* (whose account differed from the *Courier's*) described the sequel:

After this volley was fired the strikers and others attracted all crowded to the spot where Monaher lay. The militia charged the strikers and drove them back. A host of them crowded into O'Brien's saloon on Ganson Street and locked the door. The soldiers forced in the door, drove them out, and finally dispersed them.

Monaher's wounds were attended to by the surgeon of the 22nd, after which the patrol wagon was called, and the injured man and his four companions, Thomas O'Laughlin, Bernard Dunn, Patrick Madigan, and William Cotter, were taken to the #7 Precinct station house on Louisiana Street. There Monaher's four partners in crime were locked up on a charge of riot, since Police Justice Thomas S. King refused to accept bail for them. Monahar was taken to Emergency Hospital, where he was found to have been hit by three bullets, one of which pierced his body and lodged just above his kidneys. It was removed by Dr. W. H. Heath, after which the patient improved rapidly. From his sickbed he exclaimed, "I'm a dammed fool. I've been a switchman only eight weeks, and here I am out on strike and leading a lot of strikers and getting shot." He had a criminal record and was long unemployed until he went to work for the Buffalo Creek.

Lieutenant Austen and Sergeant Conrow went to the station house with a detail of policemen. Word went out among the soldiers that they had been arrested. Major Franklin Bartlett, commander of the 2nd Battalion, communicated this information to General Doyle, who ordered him to send a company to the station house and liberate the soldiers. He sent Captain Hart with a squad who, according to one account, met their two comrades returning from #7, who told them that the police had merely wanted to take their statements. But according to Colonel Camp of the 22nd, Austen and Conrow "were not returned, however, and it was not until there had been a demonstration in force made, which convinced the police that the military arm was not to be trifled with, that they were released from custody."

Adjutant-General Porter inspected several of the National Guard camps Tuesday afternoon "and found everything quiet." There were at the time 6,911 troops in the city. "Some of the men leave each day," Porter said, "but enough more come in to more than make up for the loss." Commissary-General Thomas H. McGrath also inspected the camps and claimed that he had received no complaints about food. However, an Associated Press dispatch from Poughkeepsie dated August 23rd reported: "The members of the 15th and 19th Separate Companies at Buffalo have been sending messages home telling of their sufferings from the lack of proper food and clothing. The friends and relatives of the soldier boys thus appealed to have furnished a carload of provisions and clothing which will be forwarded to Buffalo." Closer to home, hungry militiamen from the 8th Company of Rochester and the 28th of Utica confiscated a load of provisions intended for the Erie's non-union switchmen, who as a consequence went to work hungry.

General Porter insisted that "the troops will remain here until the law is obeyed and respected and there is no further danger of violence to persons or property. If more troops are needed, they will be brought here and will be kept under the same terms." Sheriff Beck, who earlier favored withdrawing the militia, supported Porter and declared, according to the *Express:*

We are now in the most serious part of the business. More roads have gone out today, and it stands to reason that more ground will have to be covered. People think this is the same as in 1877, when there was only Exchange Street and a few roads to guard. They don't comprehend the enormous increase of railroad facilities. Look at only one of these big trestles. Their destruction would make the County liable for considerably more than the cost of the soldiers will amount to.

Grand Master Sweeney had a long conference with James Fullerton, attorney for the switchmen, at the Genesee Hotel but neither would speak to reporters. Nevertheless, the rumor spread through the switchmen's union that Sweeney was about to order all members between Buffalo and New York out "in order to bring the railroads to time," a report that Vice President Webb quickly discounted.

From his home in Terre Haute, Indiana, Eugene V. Debs, Secretary of the Grand Lodge of the Brotherhood of Locomotive Firemen, who was to become nationally famous during the Pullman Strike in Chicago two years later, said that "a sympathy strike is out of the question under our present laws, which state that only a grievance of a member can be considered, and if a strike is participated in under any other circumstance the member so offending shall be expelled." He described the strike in Buffalo as the old story of a fight between corporations and labor. "It does not require the prophetic vision of a seer to foretell the result," he added. "Justice to labor will never come until labor federates and wields its united power for the good of all." From Chicago, S.E. Wilkinson of the Brotherhood of Railway Trainmen, said in regard to the Buffalo strike, "Unless our men have grievances to settle, we will not care to express any sympathy in that way." It was his belief that, "but for the acts of violence resorted to, the strike would have been amicably settled." An unnamed engineer on the Erie felt sure his union would not join the strike. He did not believe in making the switchmen work more than ten hours a day, but asserted that, "when the rioting and burning of cars was begun, they went too far." Peter M. Arthur of Cleveland, since 1874 Chief Engineer of the Brotherhood of Locomotive Engineers and through shrewd investments a millionaire, declined Sweeney's invitation to come to Buffalo. The Chief Engineer, as reported in the August 24th *Express,* gave it as his opinion that "the brotherhood would not interfere in the strike, as it had definite contracts with all the railroad companies to run their locomotives on certain conditions, which have not yet been violated." For all his conservatism, it should be remembered that Arthur had authorized a strike against the Burlington in 1888 and in 1893 would authorize another against the Toledo Ann Arbor & North Michigan.

Later in the day, the level of violence picked up. Three strikebreakers were riding atop a slow moving, unguarded southbound freight on the Buffalo & Southwestern which was boarded at 8:00 P. M. by seven strikers who brutally assaulted the workers, beating them on the head with coupling pins and trying to throw them off the train and kill them. The attacked fought back, and the strikers fled before an alarm could be given and so avoided arrest. One of the victims was taken to the hospital. The 1st Provisional Regiment at the

NYC shops in East Buffalo, the same which had earlier benefited from Vice President Webb's largess, was raked by friendly fire by outposts of Camp #13 on Seneca Street near Jefferson. A detachment from Camp #6 on Ganson Street encountered a hailstorm of stones in attempting to close Dennis Collins's Saloon at 114 South Michigan Avenue. The patrons of the establishment were driven off at bayonet point, but soon returned. Only poorly aimed, perhaps deliberately so, rifle fire restored order. Colonel Austen of the 13th had ordered all saloons in the vicinity of Camp #6 closed between 7:00 P. M. and 7:00 A. M. Camp #14, at the LV crossing at William Street, was stoned constantly throughout the night. The soldiers fired back every time, but succeeded only in killing a dog. A former prizefighter and all-round sportsman, Danny Moran, tried to run the lines of the 22nd Regiment at Camp #2 at Tifft Farm and was halted by the butt end of a picket's gun. Badly bruised about the head and face, he was locked up on a charge of disorderly conduct at #7 Station House. Almost all the other camps were subject to stone and brickbat barrages during the night.

Tuesday's violence was not confined to Buffalo. Shortly before 10:00 P. M., a NYWS&B freight bound for Buffalo was derailed by a turned switch as the cars passed over it on Lewiston Avenue in Niagara Falls. The crossing was wrapped in total darkness, since the electric street light there had been extinguished. Trying to stop a string of runaway cars which had become uncoupled from the wrecked train, a gatekeeper was critically injured. A suspect, "Butch" Mahaney, was jailed on a charge of disorderly conduct.

The August 24th Courier appended to its account of Tuesday's strike activities statistics, indicating that "The Railroads Own One Fourth of Buffalo." Of the 24,000 acres within the city, the railroads owned 6,400. The total assessed valuation of the city's twenty-five wards was $170,583,385. Of this the roads bore an assessment of $19,000,000. The assessed value of railroad property in the First, Second, Fourth, and Tenth Wards, through which the NYC, the Erie, the DL&W, and the LV passed on their way into their respective Buffalo yards and passenger terminals and along which most of the strike-connected disturbances had occurred, was $9,133,995, almost half the worth of their holdings in the city. Total value of private property in the same four wards was $15,722,440.

Wednesday, August 24

As reported in the August 25th *Courier,* the New York State Board of Mediation and Arbitration, created by the legislature in 1887, met at 10:00 A. M. Wednesday in the New Era Hall at Main and West Swan Streets. The board was authorized to "compel the production of all books, papers, and documents, subpoena witnesses, issue warrants, and to commit for contempt of court in default of compliance therewith." It could arbitrate a dispute only when requested to do so by both sides. Charles J. Madden, secretary of the board, had sent an official circular on Tuesday to concerned railroads and labor organizations inviting them to appear "by officer or other representative and take part in the investigation." No subpoenas were issued. The commission consisted of Chairman Purcell, Utica lawyer Gilbert Robertson, Jr., and F. F. Donovan of Brooklyn. The railroads were not formally represented, although railroad attorneys ex-Senator McMillan for the NYC, ex-Judge Frank Brundage for the Reading, and Carlton Sprague for the Erie, "dropped in and out," and Superintendent Brunn of the Erie "was in the hall for a few minutes before the opening of the afternoon session." At first, there were only about a dozen switchmen in attendance, but by noon their number had increased to about fifty.

Attorney for the switchmen, John J. Hynes, opened proceedings by placing on record a copy of the recently passed Ten Hour Law. His first witness was Erie switchman John McMahon, who testified that he regularly worked from 7:00 A. M. to 7:00 P. M. with half an hour off for dinner, but often worked as late as 7:30 and even 8:00 without compensation. When the chair noticed that there was no reference in the statement of grievances to the Ten Hour Law, McMahon replied, "No, but it was referred to in the talk we had [with Brunn and Walter]." But when further asked, "Was it ever called to your attention that a violation of the [Ten Hour] law by the road was punishable, or did your lodge take any action to enforce it or to proceed against the Erie?" McMahon was unable to answer.

Joseph Boss from the LV testified that the switchmen's dinner hour was sometimes at ten o'clock in the morning and sometimes at five in the afternoon. Matthew Colgan from the LV's Cheektowaga yards testified that his hours were from six in the morning until seven at night. During the last two months, he never got a dinner hour and worked thirteen hours a day. "Did you get no time to eat?" Purcell asked, to which Colgan replied: "We went right along with the engine and took a bite out of our pails when she was taking water or something of that kind. I have worked 36 hours at a stretch without going home to eat or sleep." He added that "the appeal [of disciplinary decisions] asked for was to remedy the grievance of the men in regard to whimsical discharge by the yardmaster, who had a great deal of authority and frequently abused it."

About 500 switchmen crowded the hall for the afternoon session, where the examination of witnesses was resumed by Attorney Hynes in the presence of the railroad lawyers. George Dalton, formerly in the employ of the Buffalo Creek, had the same experience with General Agent Knibloe as had earlier witnesses with their employers. Dalton had once worked thirty-six hours at a stretch and rather often nineteen hours three times a week. He failed to protest because he was afraid of losing his job. John Scanell was a non-union switchman who had worked for the Erie since 1873 but he went out with the union men anyway. He testified that he had worked five and six hours a day extra and had gotten nothing for it because it did not amount to a full day's work. The hours he worked after seven at night were credited to him until it amounted to a day, which was reckoned as twelve hours. But when he and a companion had gone to collect for what they calculated as fifty-one hours they were paid for only forty-three. F. H. Learman, formerly a yard conductor for the LV who had put in sixteen to seventeen hours at stretch, complained that when men like himself approached Yardmaster McGowan to collect their overtime he tampered with the figures on the pay card. Learman claimed that he was cheated out of as much as thirty-four hours pay in a month. Refusing to put up with this, he protested to Train Dispatcher Broadhead and was told, "If you don't like it, you can quit." A few days later he was discharged, with no reason given.

John Gorman was a member of a grievance committee of non-union switchmen in the NYC's East Buffalo yards, who immediately after the passage of the Ten Hour Law on May 24 waited on officials of the road with a petition signed by seventy-six men, mostly non-union, objecting to working a twelve hour day. Acting Superintendent Rossiter gave them no satisfaction. "Didn't you ask him about the Ten Hour Law?" Gorman was asked, to which he replied, "We couldn't touch him on that subject. He wouldn't hear of it." General Yardmaster Bernard Mulvaney suspended all three of the committee because they went to Superintendent Rossiter about the new law. After five days' suspension, they were discharged. Witnesses from the NYWS&B corroborated the charge that twelve hours was still being treated as a day's work and that switchmen were not being paid according to the old scale for overtime. But A. W. Shaw, a switchman for the LS&MS until he had gone out on strike on August 18, testified that there "the men had what was known as standard pay, and ten hours was deemed a day's pay. Over thirty minutes counted as an hour, and extra pay was allowed for Sundays. Men were given an hour for the noon meal, and were thus in better shape than those on some other roads." When Purcell asked, "What did you quit work for?" Shaw replied, "We had no grievance of our own, but, being in sympathy with the men on strike, we refused to handle scab freight." Committeeman Robertson showed himself unsympathetic to this line of reasoning, since railroads were required by the Interstate Commerce Act to handle all freight offered to them.

Sweeney did not attend the afternoon session of the Mediation and Arbitration Committee. At his request, Clark of the Order of Railway Conductors, Wilkinson of the Trainmen, and Frank P. Sargent of the Firemen had come to Buffalo and were closeted with Sweeney at the Broezel Hotel from three until six in the afternoon. Arthur of the Engineers was conspicuous by his absence. Sweeney's visitors extended their sympathy to him, assured him that the switchmen had a just grievance, but told him that the constitution and by-laws of their organizations forbade sympathy strikes. The answer, they added, to the railway labor problem was a federation of existing unions. They left Buffalo that night.

After a gloomy gathering of the strike committee of the switchmen in his room at the Genesee Hotel Wednesday night, Sweeney issued this statement to reporters which was reprinted in the August 25th *Courier*:

A conclusion has been reached by the duly authorized representatives of the switchmen and it is that this trouble is ended at midnight tonight. That is all I have got to say. Four hundred and fifteen switchmen can't fight 8,000 troops and four or five railroad companies.

The third killing and the first non-accidental one in connection with the strike occurred about 11:00 Wednesday morning. William Broderick, age seventeen, who with his parents had emigrated from Ireland five months previously, was standing a block from his home with other boys near the corner of South and Louisiana Streets. They were throwing stones at a passing Erie freight train and at soldiers of the 22nd Regiment from nearby Camp #3 who were guarding the train. (It was a soldier from this regiment that had shot Monaher.) The soldiers charged with fixed bayonets at the boys who ran along Louisiana Street. Ordered to halt, all did so except Broderick, who ran between two houses and climbed a fence. At that point, a soldier fired, and the boy tumbled over into the next yard. He picked himself up and ran for a few steps and fell again. A policeman was notified, and Broderick was conveyed to Fitch Hospital, where it was found that he had been hit by three bullets. The doctors operated but the boy's case was hopeless, and he died at 6:10 P.M. Neighbors engaged in tirades against the soldiers for their brutality, and a Mrs. Lee, who lived in one of the houses between which Broderick had run, asserted that the soldier who shot the boy ran to the fence, drew a revolver, and shot him again while he lay bleeding on the ground. She also claimed that "a small army of soldiers then rushed back to the fence, invaded her house, turned things upside down, took her ax, broke down the small section of fence that belonged to her, and chopped the legs of one of her chairs to make a headrest for the wounded boy." Questioned by a reporter for the *Express*, Major Bartlett at first justified the killing saying that "the young man was stoning a train and refused to stop when ordered to." But he added, "I have instructed my men from the start not to shoot unless their lives are in danger or in case of an attack on the men under their protection" - neither of which conditions were verified in Broderick's case. The soldiers had been ordered not to have their pieces loaded, and no order to fire had been given.

Bartlett discounted Mrs. Lee's statement about a soldier shooting the boy with a revolver, noting that privates did not carry revolvers. Higher-ups gave vague answers when asked about a military investigation of the killing. Three of Broderick's companions were arrested and locked up at #7 Precinct House on Louisiana Street. Their names were Michael Clifford, James Murphy, and John Kelly. The next day they were released uncharged.

Relations between the troopers and the people among whom they were quartered were deteriorating. Broderick's neighbors complained bitterly that females were regularly insulted by soldiers of the 13th Regiment as if they believed there were no honest women in Buffalo. The men of the 13th, in turn, complained that the location of their camp on Louisiana Street was the worst of all since "the population is denser and almost to a soul sympathizes with the strikers and their friends." (The First Ward, where Camp #3 was situated, was bounded by Exchange Street, lower Main Street, Lake Erie, and on the east by Louisiana Street as projected southward across Buffalo Creek and the Ship Canal to the Lake. It included the Beach and the Island. In 1880 its teeming population numbered 14,951, chiefly Irish-Catholics.) William Dray and Patrick Burns, residents of the Beach above Michigan Street, complained to Captain Reagan of the 1st Precinct that at midnight on Wednesday their lives were endangered by shots fired by soldiers. Both claimed that bullets had entered their shanties and narrowly missed some of the inmates. Reagan investigated and found that this was indeed the case.

Not all Buffalonians were antagonistic to the soldiers, as is indicated in this excerpt from the August 25th *Express*:

The work of the police in gathering in tramps, vagrants and bums has been going steadily on. The first female vagrant arrested in connection with the strike was taken into custody by the police of the 9th Precinct [Seneca & Babcock Streets] *Wednesday. She is Gertrude Haigh, a pretty and well formed young woman of 18 years. She was found about dawn in a flag-shanty in the railroad yards near Smith Street close to a military camp* [probably Camp #1.] *A number of queer reports were in circulation as to what brought her there. From what she told she police, it seems that she has for some time been staying away from the fold of virtue, and she blames her mother for her fall, dating her waywardness from a couple of years ago when, so she alleges, she was unjustly arrested at her mother's instance. This was the second time the police had found her hanging around the camp during the past few days, so when she came before the morning justice she was sentenced to a two months term in the Penitentiary.*

Thursday, August 25

The Arbitration Board resumed its investigation on Thursday morning with questioning of Sweeney by Attorney Hynes. The union leader described his coming twice o Buffalo at the request of members of the local lodge, his unsuccessful meetings with railroad officials, and the strike vote which he claimed wrongly was unanimous. He concluded with the assertion made in the face of evidence to the contrary that "the depredations were not committed by any member of the association." In the afternoon session, Superintendent Brunn of the Erie and Fennell of the LV gave their testimony. Telescoping events, Brunn said that "the [strike] committee had called on officials of the road and presented their requests, but the company did not feel it could accede to the demands, and the next he learned was that a general strike was on, and that cars were being burned." What the switchmen asked for was the adoption of the ten-hour day for the pay they had been receiving for twelve hours, which amounted to a ten percent raise. (This would be true only if they worked two hours overtime.) Brunn explained further that a railway day was twenty-four hours and that the roads which adopted the ten hour day all worked their men twelve hours, allowing two hours for meals.

Rank and file of the switchmen's union met in Kaiser's Hall Thursday afternoon. After an open and rancorous debate, they voted by an overwhelming majority to continue the strike which, they claimed, Sweeney and his committee had no right to call off. Michael J. Moriarty, head of Lodge #39, was proposed for Sweeney's post. As the discredited leader left the New Era Hall where he had spent the morning testifying, he was assaulted by a member of Lodge #39, Arthur Quinn, a Nickel Plate switchman, who punched Sweeney in the eye, knocked him down, and kicked him until bystanders intervened. Sweeney got up and walked to a nearby drug store where three doctors attended to his injuries. A threatening crowd gathered outside, and a call was put through to police headquarters. Sergeant John M. Lynch was dispatched with a patrol wagon and several patrolmen to escort the Grand Master to the Genesee in safety.

Late Thursday afternoon, soldiers from the 22nd Regiment were transporting a keg of beer from the city to their camp at the Tifft Farm Hotel on a handcar. Somewhere between Abbott Road and the DL&W tracks two passenger trains approached, one going north the other south. Frightened, the soldiers took the handcar off the rails and placed it between the tracks, where it was struck by one of the trains and thrown under one of the cars. The handcar and presumably the keg of beer were completely destroyed, and the damaged passenger car had to be uncoupled in order to permit the train to proceed.

Freight operations, which had never completely closed down, began to approach normal, and newspapers were filled with advertisements for regular passenger service. The old hands failed to return on the Buffalo Creek, but they were expected back on Friday, and General Agent Knibloe announced that all would get their jobs back. The Nickel Plate refused to take back strikers. The LS&MS, the NYC, and the DL&W would take them back only as vacancies occurred. Announced policy was not to discharge strikebreakers. However, Vice President Webb of the NYC came up with the extremely flexible principle that "good men who had been forced out could make application and would be taken on when there was room." The Erie had not decided what to do with ex-strikers, but for the present was getting along with the switchmen on hand. Forty men, hired under false pretenses arrived via the WNY&P; but, since the strike was over, they were paid off and sent back home.

Led by Troop "A" with its "sleek steeds," the militia started for home. The cavalry left from the NYC's stockyards on William Street at 2:00 P. M. followed a half hour later by the Albany, Troy, Utica, and Amsterdam Companies, which shipped out on the NYC from the Seneca Street crossing at 2:30 P. M. Someone was going to pay for the militia, and the sooner the soldiers left, the less the bill would be. (It was estimated that the county's bill for the militia and the damage done to railroad property was about $400,000.) At 9:00 P. M. the Catskill Company departed from Exchange Street, and shortly after 10:00 the 23rd left the Wagner Palace Car shops followed by Brooklyn's other regiment in Buffalo, the 13th, which left from Exchange Street. Because of their destination, the Catskill and Brooklyn units traveled east on the NYWS&B. The 41st Company from Syracuse took over at the Wagner shops. The five companies from New York which had been grouped together to form the 1st Provisional Regiment were scheduled to depart from Exchange Street on the NYC over the Auburn Road, but at the last moment were ordered to replace the 13th at Elk Street. Some railroad officials, especially those of the Erie, feared that the troops were being withdrawn too quickly. Accordingly, General Doyle announced that his 4th Brigade would be kept on for another day or so. General Porter judged the troubles to be "practically over." He added that "of all the cases of lawlessness that had come to my personal knowledge, only one had been the act of one who was not a striker." On this point Horton, a laboristic historian, wrote:

Whether the rioters . . . were all strikers is more than doubtful, though the Express tried hard to create this impression. On the other hand the Enquirer, the Catholic Union and Times, and to a less extent the Courier combated it. In an interview with the Evening News, Sweeney maintained that the strikers were staying at home, pointed out by way of proof that none of them had been arrested, and hinted darkly that incendiaries and other lawless acts were the work of toughs whom the railroads had planted for the purpose. Sweeney in the nature of the case was no impartial witness. . . As touching the incendiaries and rioting that disturbed the city before the guard had brought the situation under control, the Governor preferred to ascribe them not to the strikers themselves, but to 'the hangers on who find pleasure and profit in stirring up strife and causing wreck and ruin.' [4]

"Laboristic society" was a term coined by Harvard economist Sumner Schlichter and, according to Albro Martin in Railroads Triumphant, "was one in which the interests of organized labor are identified closely with those of the 'general public,' and the knottier the issues in a labor dispute the more likely the government is to resolve them in the direction of some net gain, at least, to the union." Of thirty arrested during the strike as reported in the *Express*, six were clearly switchmen. The most numerous category was "laborer." Two were teamsters, one was sailor, another a watchman, a fifth a saloon keeper.

Friday, August 26

Most of the remaining troops, except Buffalo's two regiments, left town for points east beginning at 9:00 A. M. Friday on special trains. Five thousand people turned out at the Erie Station in Jamestown to greet the returning members of the 13th Separate Company. The cheering lasted several minutes, and the mayor congratulated the company on its faithful service. The soldiers, sobered by their Buffalo experience, gave three cheers for "Jamestown, the best place on earth." Bands and crowds thronged the platform of the Tonawanda station, eight miles from downtown Buffalo, to welcome home the men of the 25th Company, for whom a banquet was planned for Monday at Post Office Hall. The 43rd Company of Olean arrived home at 7:00 P. M. Friday to a royal welcome. It was escorted to its armory by the local post of the G. A. R. and by about half the population of the city to a sumptuous banquet at the Capitol Hotel.

All day Friday, dejected switchmen hung around Kaiser's Hall debating warmly what should be done. "Some of us will go back to work Sunday morning," one of them said. "The strike has been declared off, and we might as well be doing something as sitting around. Of course, there are some among us who will not be allowed to resume work, but I think that the roads will be glad to get most of us back again." Another spoke up, "Why, only this morning the NYWS&B, LS&MS, Erie, LV, and some of the other roads sent word to the men to go back to work. That is a certain indication that they are anxious to have us back." Sweeney was roundly criticized. "He had no backbone," one disgruntled striker said. "As long as the law gave us 10 hours a day, why did not the Grand Master allow us to fight it out." Another spokesman for the diehards said:

Why we had the strike practically won. All we wanted was time. We only had the roads tied up in Buffalo and vicinity. We could have extended the strike from the Atlantic to the Pacific. Yes, our meeting this afternoon was a big one. I think over 300 were present; and we decided there was no use to fight any longer after the strike had taken the turn it had.

Entries in a police blotter give the impression of a mopping-up operation "William Sullivan was discharged in Police Court yesterday on a charge of intimidating switchmen." "Sergt. [Florence] Driscoll and his men mistook several non-union switchmen for strikers at the LS&MS roundhouse last evening and some severe clubbing was done before the error was discovered. The reserve was called out but all ended peacefully." "Detective Kilroy, who has been in charge of the police in the strike district will remove his quarters from the 11th Precinct [Broadway and Bailey] to the 7th [Louisiana and Elk] today, as that is expected to be the most promising field for trouble between the strikers and non-union men." "Two more rioters were arrested in the 7th Precinct last evening. They are Daniel J. Delaney, an ex-patrolman, and Owen Kief, an ex-NYC switchman. They are charged with stoning a train on the NYC between Perry and Fulton Streets." "John Carey, John Lang, and John Dugan were given 15 days each yesterday. They are three of the tramps captured by the militia on the Tifft Farm last Wednesday. Hogan and O'Niel, the other two, were let go, as no case could be made out against them." "John Hess, a 'scab' switchman living at 733 Michigan, fell under a car early Friday while at work in the NYC yards at Michigan. He was taken to the Fitch.."

Saturday, August 27

Superintendent Voorhees of the NYC had arranged for trains carrying the New York and Brooklyn regiments to travel by way of Niagara Falls, where a forty-five minute layover gave most of the men their first view of the famed Cataract. The four New York regiments arrived in the city Saturday morning, where the men were given a hearty breakfast at Grand Central and then marched to their respective armories and, after listening to a few speeches, disbanded. Colonel Camp of the 22nd, whose headquarters had been at the Tifft Farm, told a *New York Times* reporter, "There can be no question about the sympathy of the Buffalo police with the striking switchmen." The *Times* for August 28th informed its readers:

In the 9th and 12th Regiments the expression of commanding and subaltern officers and of the better class of enlisted men who had personal experience in the matter was unanimous in regard to the action of the police in not only having extended sympathy but aid and countenance to the strikers. Instances of the release of rioters who had been turned over to the police were also given by the officers and men of the 13th and 23rd and 71st Regiments, all of which were susceptible of proof. The members of the 12th Regiment [at Camp #1] *were especially delighted over the arrest of a policeman by Lieut. Tilton at the Seneca Street crossing. All the trouble the regiment had in its stay in camp was at this crossing, where strikers openly gathered and hurled jeers, gibes, and insults at the troops. A six-foot policeman made himself particularly objectionable on Friday morning* [August 26] *by asserting that his sympathy was with the strikers, that he wouldn't arrest one of them, and that he would break the head of the first soldier whom he found in Buffalo.* [An odd threat since the out-of-town soldiers had been in Buffalo for over a week.] *Lieut. Tilton, the mildest officer in the regiment, heard the remark. He called a squad of men and ordered them to load their pieces. Then turning to the policeman, he said, "Drop that club!" The guardian of Buffalo's peace with an oath refused. Tilton advanced toward him with drawn revolver. "Drop that club or I will blow the top of your head off," said the Lieutenant. The policeman looked at Tilton's weapon, then at the guard whose pieces were ready to be turned on him and obeyed the order. "Hand over your revolver!" was the next order. The policeman complied. "Now, men,' said Tilton, "march him off to the guardhouse." The burly bully was forced to proceed with his captors. He cursed the troops and declared that in a fair fight ten strikers could defeat a hundred of them. As one of the 12th Regiment officers said, "The arrest was the last official act the regiment performed in camp, and it was the neatest piece of work you ever saw."*

Meanwhile back in Buffalo, Police Superintendent Morgenstern was calling the 22nd "a pack of curs." The *Express* summed it all up by stating that "one thing was established, i. e., there was a great deal of friction between the military and the police." The editor might have added, "and between the military and the local population." Discipline in some regiments seems to have been better than in others.

Switchmen met outside Kaiser's Hall Saturday morning and discussed the strike situation. About two-thirds had been in favor of continuing the strike, but the other third took the opportunity of Sweeney's calling it off to return to work. When this was known, it was decided that all should apply for their old places. Buffalo's two regiments, the 65th and the 74th, the last militia units to remain under arms, marched, with colors flying up, Main Street in the morning to their respective armories. Sheriff Beck, in response to requests from Erie and LV officials, said that he had sent fifteen deputies from the Harlem Avenue crossing of the DL&W, Erie, and LV to the LV's Cheektowaga trestle. Major Harding of the 74th had been guarding the structure with three companies for the past week, and their safety had been feared for throughout the strike.

The strike was all over, except for the shouting. As usually happened during the nineteenth century, management won. But the cost was great to the railroads in lost business, to the strikers in lost wages, to the state, county, and city in money owed for soldiers and extra deputies and patrolmen, and to the public which had suffered serious and prolonged inconvenience. Apparently the strikers, at least those who had not engaged in violence or destroyed company property, got their jobs back. Many of those arrested during the troubles were later released for lack of evidence.

The year after the Buffalo Switchmen's Strike, the Philadelphia & Reading Railroad failed, triggering the Panic of 1893, which lasted until 1897. Eighteen ninety-four was the year of the Great Pullman Strike, which started in May as a walkout by employees resident in George Pullman's company town outside Chicago. Pullman had cut wages twenty-five percent, but not rents. This soon turned into a general strike where members of Eugene V. Debs's recently organized American Railway Union refused to handle trains with Pullman cars. This was the kind of secondary boycott the courts had already condemned. Nevertheless, the local strike soon developed into a general railroad tie-up throughout the West by June 28, 1894. A federal judge issued a blanket injunction prohibiting all interference with trains, which was defied by the strikers, who also resorted to violence. Almont Lindsey, laboristic author of the standard but dated history of the Pullman Strike, wrote:

Debs had hoped that all railroad workers would support the strike and sustain the boycott; but, to his chagrin, the brotherhoods, without exception, rejected his appeal for cooperation. This policy was not due to a lack of sympathy for the Pullman employees. It was primarily because of a mounting fear that in case of victory the American Railway Union would continue its unprecedented growth and ultimately absorb all railroad unions into one mighty industrial organization. [5]

Lindsey fails to mention that that the problems of one group of railroad employees were not necessarily those of another and that, a year into the worst industrial depression America had ever known, rank and file members of the brotherhoods were probably glad to have any jobs at all. Moreover, "One Big Union" would be a combination as threatening to the Republic as the industrial giants of which progressives professed to be so frightened. One reason why Debs's strike did not spread eastward was that several lines in the East had contracts with the Wagner Palace Car Company (this was the case with the NYC) or the Monarch Sleeping Car Company.

A refreshing and perceptive observation from Albro Martin, is germane here and will go far to explain the downward slide of American railroads:

As for Debs, he has been virtually canonized as a saint of the labor movement, but still it must be admitted that he drank too much, was something of a muddle-headed, self-taught socialist, and had a penchant for getting into fights he could not possibly win. The U. S. government, for example, reacted vigorously against the violent boycotts resorted to by the strikers at George Pullman's car-building plant in Chicago in 1894, and President Cleveland firmly backed up with force the refusal of the railroad executives to let the men take out their trains without their normal complement of Pullman sleeping cars. The nation was far from ready to support the men's challenge to the unfettered exploitation of private property, but the event was not without its embarrassment to the nation's leaders. Mark Hanna, a leader of the Republican party who was grooming his man, William McKinley, to return the party triumphantly to the White House in the campaign of 1896, declared about George Pullman that "any man who won't negotiate with his men is a damm fool!" The Pullman strike, however, was the low-water mark of America's traditional favoritism towards the underdog. Theodore Roosevelt's brand of Republican Progressivism burst upon the nation in 1901, notably in the trust-busting movement and his Olympian settlement of the strike in the anthracite coal industry in 1902. And Teddy was one-upped by Wilson in the eight-hour day threats by the railroad brotherhoods in 1916, after which railroad executives must have felt "naked to mine enemies" in future disputes. They have seldom had much more than a fig leaf since. [6]

Debs dispatched countless emissaries and telegrams trying to solicit national support for a strike that he had reluctantly supported. On July 8, 1894, he wired the president of the Central Labor Union of Buffalo:

We ask your cooperation . . . we are making a great fight for labor, and deserve the support of all railroad employees. Capital has combined to enslave labor. We must all stand together or go down in hopeless defeat. It is impossible for the companies to fill vacancies. We can solve this problem only by quitting in a body and standing together, one for all and all for one, upon each and every road throughout the land. [7]

His summons to arms elicited no warm response in Buffalo. For a few days, business and civic leaders, reading the headlines about violence and carnage in Chicago - thirteen dead, fifty-six injured, $3,500,000 in railroad losses alone - held their collective breath, as rumors went through the city of railroad men joining their midwestern and western brethren. The brotherhoods, where a two-thirds vote was required for a strike, held firm. The American Railway Union was weak here. Its president, James Mallican, refused Debs's order to call upon members to strike. Fear was expressed with regard to the switchmen who had tied up the city two years before, but experience had made them cautious. They too stayed out.

In the aftermath of the strike of 1892, as had been the case in 1877, when many had feared the reenactment here of the horrors of the Paris Commune of 1871, armories were constructed in many American cities. In Buffalo, two vast medieval piles were built, one for the 65th Regiment, the other for the 74th. The 74th's, begun in 1897, occupied the West Side block bounded by Prospect Avenue and Connecticut, Niagara and Vermont Streets. (Figure #9.) The 65th's, begun in 1902, stood on the south side of Best Street opposite the reservoir which had been built in 1894 on the site of the later Civic Stadium. (Figure #10.)

X, 9

204. 74 th Reg. Armory, Buffalo, N. Y.

X, 10

65th REGT. ENTERING THEIR ARMORY FOR THE FIRST TIME, BUFFALO, N. Y.

11

Buffalo's Passenger Service In The Nineteenth Century

1868

The Travelers' Official Guide of the Railways and Steamship Lines of the United States & Canada first appeared in 1869. It contained passenger timetables of all railroads in the two countries. Later editions included also timetables of Cuba, Puerto Rico, Mexico, and Central America. During 1869 Commodore Vanderbilt merged the NYC, control of which he had acquired two years before, with the Hudson River Railroad, which he had taken over in 1863, to form the New York Central & Hudson River Railroad. However, since the Official Guide went to press before the merger, it is only the NYC that is listed as terminating at the dead-end Exchange Street Station in Buffalo. Moreover, most of the data in this, the first edition of the Official Guide, is from May, 1868.

West of Buffalo, the American route to Chicago ran along the south shore of Lake Erie. Under the name Lake Shore & Michigan Southern, it was taken over by Vanderbilt in 1869. He acted to thwart Jay Gould's ambitions for a western outlet for his Erie. A second dead-end terminal was that of the Erie Railway in the shadow of the NYC's on Exchange Street. A third stub station was that of the former Buffalo & Niagara Falls on Erie Street next to the Erie Canal. (Figure II, #18.) The gap between the Exchange Street and the Erie Street stations was not closed until 1879. (Figure IX, #24.)

In 1868, according to the Official Guide, four trains were scheduled to arrive on weekdays at the NYC's Exchange Street Station from New York/Boston, the junction point being Albany. In addition, a westbound emigrant train arrived daily from Albany. The first leg of that journey was by cheaper Hudson River steamboats. A sixth westbound was an accommodation from Syracuse. The express which left New York at 8:00 A. M. and was due in Buffalo sixteen hours later at midnight was the fastest westbound (twenty-seven miles per hour). The emigrant train, with a consist of boxcars with a few windows and wooden benches added, was the slowest (thirteen miles per hour). The express which arrived at Buffalo from New York at 6:20 A. M. carried sleeping cars, though this was not indicated in the Official Guide. John H. White, author of the definitive study of American passenger cars, notes in The American Railroad Passenger Car that the Central Transportation Company, a predecessor of Pullman, had 119 cars in service on sixteen major railroads in the East in 1869. The 11:30 A. M. arrival from New York/Boston was also a mail train. There were likewise four eastbound New York/Boston expresses (one of which was a mail train), a fifth express which did not have a Boston section, and a Rochester accommodation. It would have come as no surprise to Horace Greeley that there was no eastbound emigrant train. The Boston & Albany had been formed in 1867 out of the Boston & Worcester (1835) and the Western Railroad (Worcester to Albany, 1841). It was not until 1900 that the NYC succeeded in leasing the B&A, but relations between the two roads had always been friendly, since their routes were complementary rather than competitive. One of the New York/Boston trains, the *Steamboat Express*, originated in Buffalo/Niagara Falls and made no connections with any runs from the West.

There were four westbound expresses from Buffalo on the lake shore route in 1868, three to Chicago and one to Toledo. At Cleveland they made connections to Cincinnati on the Cleveland Columbus & Cincinnati. For years, one eastbound Chicago-New York express was called the *New York Express*, while its westbound opposite was the *Chicago Express*. Another pair of through trains was the *Atlantic Express* and the *Pacific Express*. There was also in 1868 a mail train to Erie, Pennsylvania, but no westbound emigrant train, since emigrants found it cheaper to proceed further west by lake steamer. Express train arrivals were scheduled to make connections with departures, and through cars saved passengers the annoyance of changing cars. Thus the midnight express from New York left for Chicago at 12:05 A. M., the 6:20 A. M. arrival from New York left for Chicago at 6:30 A. M., and the 11:30 morning train from New York left for the west at 11:40 A. M. Eastbound, the same arrangement held for three arrivals on the lake shore route. Travel time between New York and Chicago was between thirty-six and forty-two hours. All westbound departures were from Exchange Street on the former Buffalo & Erie, reaching Chicago via the Michigan Southern & Northern Indiana, or the Pittsburgh Fort Wayne & Chicago. A shortcut to accommodate both the standard gauge NYC and the four-foot ten-inch Buffalo & Erie was known as the Compromise Track. (Figure #1.) The name remained, even after the LS&MS had adopted standard gauge.

On the eve of the adoption of time zones by the United States and Canada in 1884, there were seventy-five systems of time in use by the railroads of the two countries. The Boston & Albany ran by Springfield time, the NYC by Albany time, the LS&MS in Ohio by Columbus time and further west by Chicago time, while the Great Western followed Hamilton time. It is, therefore, often difficult to plot the time of New York-Chicago passenger schedules, since a Boston-Chicago train operated through four time systems, Boston being one hour and seven minutes ahead of Chicago. Western New Yorkers were given this warning in the 1868 timetable: "STANDARD OF TIME; The Clock in the Depot at Albany which is twenty-one minutes faster than Buffalo."

There was also a Canada-Michigan route to Chicago made up of the Great Western (Suspension Bridge to Windsor, Ontario) and the Michigan Central (Detroit, across the Detroit River from Windsor, to Chicago.) (Figure V, #3.) The four westbound NYC trains from New York were split up at Rochester, some cars going on to Buffalo on the former Buffalo & Rochester, the rest to Suspension Bridge on the former Rochester Lockport & Niagara Falls for connections with the Great Western. A car ferry operated between Detroit and Windsor. Three eastbound express arrivals from the west at Buffalo on the lake shore route were paralleled by corresponding arrivals at Suspension Bridge on the Great Western, all of them destined for consolidation at Rochester.

XI, 1

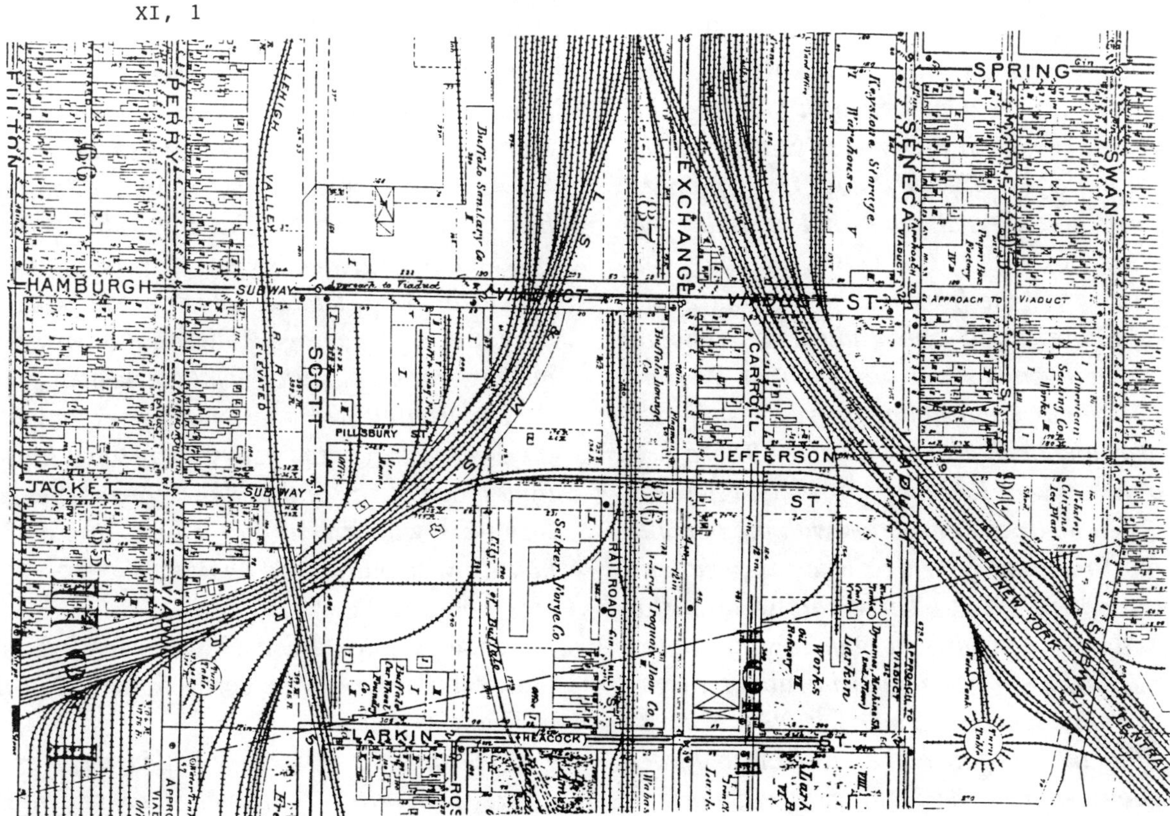

Until the construction of a tunnel under the Detroit River and an electrified line between Windsor and Detroit in 1910, freight and passenger trains crossed the river on time-consuming car ferries. As Stauffer and May write in their study of NYC motive power:

Old timetables show the elapsed time between the two cities being upwards of 30 minutes but during severe winter weather conditions numerous delays and backups occurred that tied the railroad up for days on end. During the worst of these circumstances, traffic was diverted to rival Vanderbilt line Lake Shore & Michigan Southern via Toledo. The Detroit River Tunnel Co., 2.72 miles in length, work on which began October 1906, brought these operating miseries to an end and cut the time to fifteen minutes. [1]

The name Pullman was once synonymous with the sleeping car, and it was widely believed that George Pullman invented this mode of transportation. However, he did not enter the field until 1858. The first sleeping car had appeared twenty years before on the Cumberland Valley Railroad (Harrisburg to Chambersburg, Pennsylvania), providing a break for travelers between Philadelphia and Pittsburgh. Early railroads were short, but as they lengthened and trips took up to a day or more, a demand arose for sleeping cars. White notes that sleepers were operated on at least eight railroads before 1850, but adds that it was "during the 1850s that long-distance travel became a dramatic reality and precipitated demand for more luxurious accommodations," as "the Eastern lines were being rapidly extended into the heart of the continent." Unfortunately, early editions of the Official Guide frequently do not indicate whether a given train carried through sleepers or even sleepers.

On the subject of luxurious accommodations on the NYC at this time, Hungerford writes:

In these early days, none of Pullman's own

cars ran regularly upon the Central. The road had its own sleeping car genius in Webster Wagner, a resident of Palatine Bridge, who organized the New York Central Sleeping Car Company, which a number of years later he merged into the Wagner Palace Car Company and which continued under that name for two decades or more. The Gates Sleeping Car Company had the franchise on the contiguous Lake Shore Road and Pullman's company operated over the combined Great Western and Michigan Central line between Rochester, Suspension Bridge and Chicago. There was also the showy "Red Line" to which reference has been made in connection with the opening of the first Albany bridge when it went into operation [in 1866]. *These cars were parlor cars. Each car consisted of three state rooms, and a large center room with about twenty comfortable chairs. They left New York at 10:30 in the morning and arrived at Rochester at about 9:40 in the evening, where through passengers were transferred to the sleeping cars for Chicago, going either by way of Suspension Bridge and the Michigan Central or by way of Buffalo and the Lake Shore.*

It took thirty-six hours to go from New York to Chicago in the mid-'seventies and the majority of through travelers preferred the schedule that gave them two nights and one day on the train rather than two days and one night. So the Pacific Express, leaving New York at 8:00 in the evening and arriving at Chicago at 7:25 on the second morning, became the heaviest train on the road. On it the sleeping cars ran through to Chicago without change and one had only to get off the train at mealtimes - breakfast at Rochester, lunch at Erie and supper at Toledo on the one line and lunch at Niagara Falls and supper at Detroit on the other. Dining cars were still in the distance, although on the Michigan Central Pullman was already experimenting with what he called his "hotel-cars." For this route he built three of them at the end of the 'sixties - the Viceroy, the President, and the New World. These were remarkable productions. Each was seventy-five feet long and was mounted upon eight-wheel trucks. They contained in addition to the berths, a small kitchen and each carried a chef, waiters, and a porter. Meals were served in the sections after they had been made up for the day. This was as good an arrangement as was feasible, until the advent of the vestibule, which made possible easy and safe passage between the cars of a moving train, no matter what the weather was.

The trouble with these hotel-cars was that they were entirely too heavy (sixty tons) for the light locomotives of that day. For that reason they were withdrawn after a time, and eating houses were patronized again. [2]

A hotel car contained a kitchen and fed only those who occupied the berths in the car itself, as White explains:

The hotel car, though hailed as a great advance in railway travel, had its faults. Travelers who suffered from motion sickness found it disagreeable to be cooped up in a car where the smell of food lingered. The price of the meals was high: an entree with potatoes cost 50 to 60 cents, coffee and tea 25 cents apiece. The crew was too large for the number of patrons. The investment required for a kitchen, linens, and the other accessories added to the economic risk of the hotel car. [3]

Wagner was killed in a rear-end collision on one of his own cars at Spuyten Duyvil on the northern tip of Manhattan Island in 1882. His company continued until 1899, when it was sold to Pullman, who thus posthumously achieved his dream of a national sleeping car network. Wagner's factory was located in Buffalo on the northeast corner of Broadway and Bailey, later the site of a Pullman plant. (Figure #2.) The fortunes of the Pullman company during its century long rise and fall can be seen in Figure #3.

On February 6, 1871, disaster struck the train cited by Hungerford as the heaviest on

XI, 2

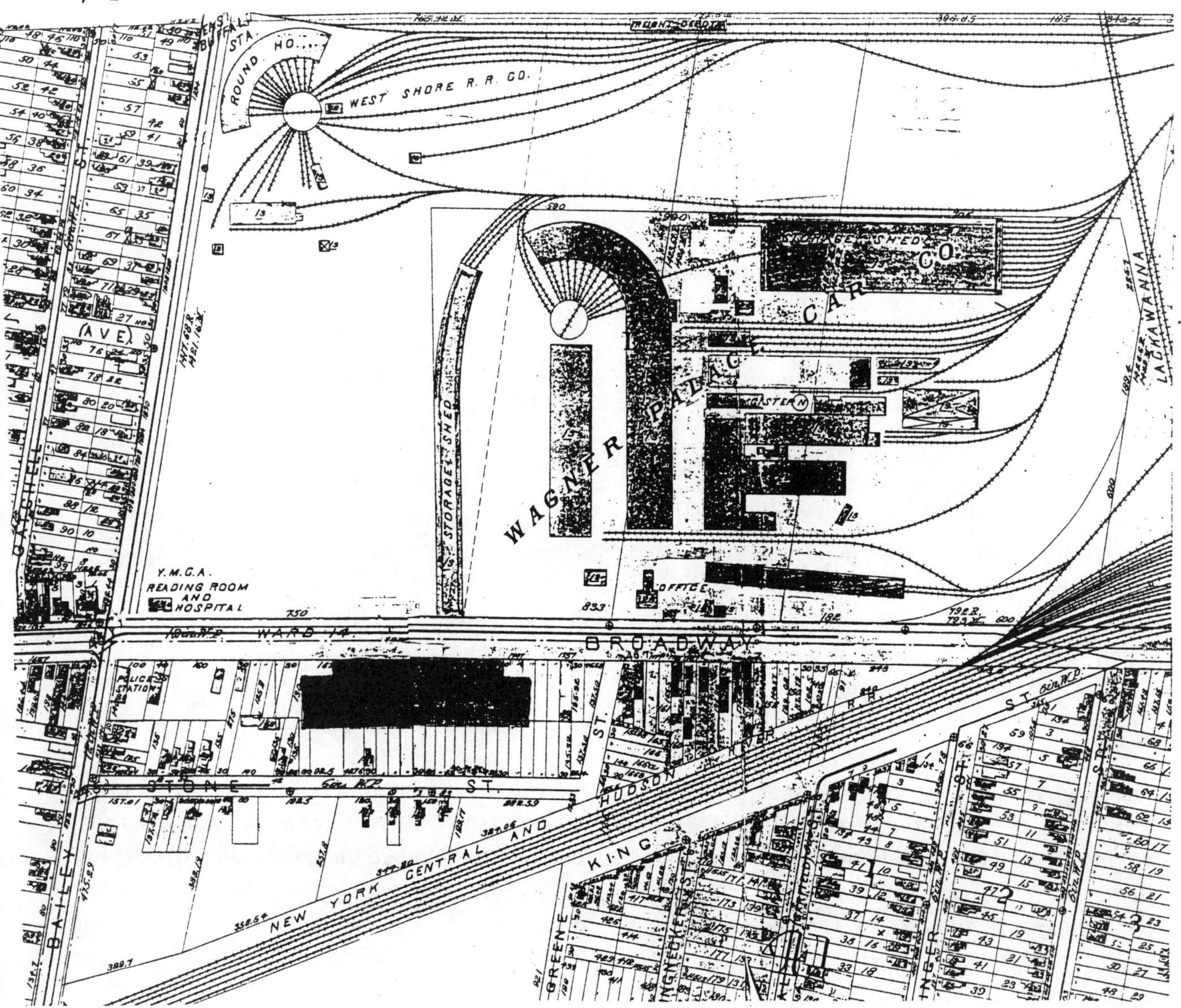

the line:

> *The* Pacific Express . . . *had left Thirtieth Street at eight o'clock in the evening. The train had a locomotive and tender, baggage car and express car, five sleeping cars and a day coach. They were all moderately filled. The train approached the New Hamburgh station* [south of Poughkeepsie] *at a little after ten o'clock in the evening. As it entered the drawbridge crossing over Wappinger's Creek the engineer, David Simmons, saw that a freight train which was passing south over the bridge on the opposite track was derailing and piling itself up within the structure. The fireman noticed the same thing. He called to Simmons to jump and himself jumped, saving his life. The engineer refused to leave. He stuck by his throttle and so lost his life.*
>
> *The southbound freight which consisted of twenty-five cars, the most of them tank cars filled with oil, had that very moment been derailed by the breaking of an axle on one of the forward cars. Couplings parted and the train massed itself within the walls of the bridge trusses. When the locomotive of the northbound train struck the oil-soaked wreckage its fires quickly ignited the debris. . . .*
>
> *The engine plunged from the tracks into the water and the engineer was instantly killed.*

XI, 3

Table 3.3 The Pullman Company, 1868–1968

YEAR	NO. CARS	ROUTE MILES	ASSETS	GROSS	PROFIT, LOSS	PASSENGERS
1868	50*		$ 1,470,800	$ 258,000	$ 169,700	
1870	300*		3,312,800	746,500	331,800	
1875	600*	30,000*	11,257,000	2,568,600	1,260,800	
1880	700*	60,000*	13,280,000	2,635,000	1,416,400	2,000,000*
1885	1,195	71,400	28,466,000	5,613,600	2,793,400	
1890	2,135	120,680	43,013,000	8,860,900	4,563,700	5,023,000
1895	2,556	126,660	62,792,000	8,547,600	4,290,300	4,788,000
1900	3,258	158,500	78,895,900	15,022,800	6,623,400	7,752,000
1905	4,138	184,100	96,151,900	26,922,000	13,038,000	14,969,000
1910	5,285	124,100	135,989,600	38,880,800	18,050,300	20,203,000
1915	7,287	215,800		41,512,800	20,580,100	24,252,000
1920	7,752	119,700	143,678,000	14,519,700	12,913,500	39,255,000
1925	8,776	130,300	329,148,900	81,490,300	16,779,000	35,526,000
1930	9,801	133,800	352,276,400	19,061,600	7,404,000	29,360,000
1935	8,007	115,400	276,275,300	50,063,400	*Loss* – 502,000	15,479,000
1940	6,910	109,500	304,469,800	60,095,500	2,411,800	14,765,000
1945	8,590	95,700	327,446,500	147,855,700	26,150,924	31,484,000
1950	6,226	102,700	83,131,400	103,756,600	1,325,200	15,606,000
1955	4,776	89,100	44,129,000	94,506,500	282,317	11,438,000
1960	2,650	67,400	28,000,000	55,876,900	286,046	4,484,000
1965	1,494	51,000	24,162,000	35,805,900	*Loss* – 21,513,000	2,507,000
1968	765	33,400	20,126,500	17,778,100	*Loss* – 22,000,800	1,073,000

* Estimates

The baggage and the express cars fell on it. Next came the Buffalo sleeper from which no person escaped alive. It was enshrouded in flames which spread to the next two sleeping cars, but not before their passengers escaped. In ten minutes the wooden bridge and the Buffalo sleeping car also dropped into the river, the three final sleeping cars and the day coach were saved. It is a commentary on the light rolling stock of that day when it is related that their passengers alighted and with their hands uncoupled them and pushed them out of the way of danger [4]

Twenty-two persons were killed and many more were injured.

The lake shore route was the scene of two of America's most notorious wrecks, one at Angola, New York, the other at Ashtabula, Ohio. On December 18, 1867, a Buffalo bound express, running fast to make up time, was derailed on the bridge over Three Sisters Creek near Angola. Before the train crossed the bridge, a wheel on a defective axle on the rear car struck a crossover rail known as a frog. The rear car jumped the track and, still coupled to the train, bumped along the ties. The jolting of this car derailed the car ahead. A moment before reaching the bridge, the last car became uncoupled and fell against the bridge abutment. The car's coal stove broke apart, scattering red hot coals on the wooden car and its passengers, forty-two of whom were burned alive. The other derailed car was dragged along the track for 300 feet. Then it too broke loose and fell down the embankment. Remarkably, only one passenger in this car was killed. (Figure #4.) A mass funeral for the victims of what became known as "The Angola Horror" was held in the Exchange Street Station in Buffalo three days before Christmas.

Almost exactly nine years later, on December 29, 1876, just east of Ashtabula, the LS&MS's *Pacific Express* plunged through a high but defective bridge. Eighty passengers

XI, 4

met fiery deaths. Nineteen of the victims were so badly burned they were never identified. The cause may have been the use of compromise cars on the four-foot ten-inch Ohio gauge of the lake shore route. These cars were standard gauge with treads extended to reach the wider gauge. A severe lateral motion could cause them to derail, since the tread did not cover all of the rail.

Nineteenth century railroads were killers. The national census report on transportation listed 8,216 railroad accidents for 1876. After the creation of the Interstate Commerce Commission in 1887, national railroad statistics become more meaningful. In 1891, 293 passengers were killed and 2,972 were injured. In absolute terms, the numbers did not improve for decades. The worst year was 1907, when 710 passengers were killed and 13,041 were injured. That year also saw an all-time high of railroad workers killed, 4,534. As the author of a book on train wrecks puts it:

After the Civil war there began a slow improvement of some railroad equipment to reduce the terrific toll. At the same time, however, traffic became swollen; the burgeoning train traffic and increased speeds of the 1870's and 1880's took place without corresponding improvement either in the cars themselves or the roadbeds they ran over. The telegraph re-

placed the old signal posts, but the telegraph was not universally adopted by railroads until late in the century. Rails, too, were gradually improved after the Civil War, but many lines failed to replace old strap- or wrought-iron rail with steel after disastrous derailments. As safety devices were developed, the speeds at which passenger trains traveled accelerated. As Lucius Beebe said, "The grim reaper has never been altogether outdistanced by progress." [5]

The lake shore route connected at Brocton (birthplace of George Pullman) with the Buffalo Corry & Pittsburgh, which ran three trains each way daily between Brocton and Corry on the Atlantic & Great Western. At Corry the BC&P also connected with the Oil Creek Railway, which, via the Allegheny Valley Railroad, led to Pittsburgh. However, no effort was made to synchronize Corry trains with those of the Buffalo & Erie. The BC&P's timetable advised patrons that it "connects at Mayville with Steamboats on Chautauqua Lake for Jamestown and Randolph . . . Trains stopping at Fish & Barnes connect with Line of Stages for Westfield."

Close by the NYC's station on Exchange Street was that of the Erie Railway, billed as the "Broad Gauge [true] Double Track [false] Route between the Atlantic and the South, Southwest, West and Northwest." In 1868 the Erie featured "Four Express Trains Daily, 460 Miles, without change of Coaches between New York and Salamanca, Dunkirk, Buffalo, and Rochester." At this early date, the Erie's Buffalo-New York service matched the NYC's. The westbound expresses were the *Express Mail* which arrived at 6:12 A. M., the *First Night Express* at 11:40 A. M., the *Fast Night Express* at 1:25 P. M., and the *Day Express*, which was scheduled to pull into Buffalo at the first stroke of midnight. (Names were assigned from the point of view of the station of origin.)

The four eastbound expresses and their scheduled time of departure were: *New York Day Express*, 5:45 A. M., *Lightning Express*, 2:20 P. M., *New York Night Express*, 6:10 P. M., and the *Cincinnati Express*, 10:45 P. M. The Erie assured prospective patrons that "the best and MOST LUXURIOUS SLEEPING COACHES in the world accompany each night train." Meal stops were at Turner's near Monroe, Susquehanna, and Hornellsville. There were two daytime westbound locals, one from Corning on the former Buffalo Corning & New York and the other from Hornellsville on the former Buffalo & New York City. Eastbound, there were two locals to Corning. (Figure III, #1.) The Erie's expresses took from sixteen to nineteen hours between Jersey City and Buffalo. In addition, the timetable contained the notation that "a daily Emigrant Train leaves New York 8:00 p. m. Jersey City 8:15 for Rochester, Salamanca, Buffalo, Dunkirk, and the West."

Regarding railroad station restaurants, White observes:

They could be wonderful or terrible. The depot hotels at Altoona, Springfield, and Poughkeepsie had a national reputation for excellent fare, and the Harvey Houses along the Santa Fe were recognized as model establishments from their beginning in 1876. But most depot eating houses seemed to fall below any conceivable standard of decency and were vigorously denounced in the nineteenth century press. One account insisted that they were the most infamous of all the "pernicious institutions" in America. . . .

Because of the time factor, meals at even the best depot restaurant were not always a pleasant experience. The train could afford to stop for no more than half a hour; fifteen or twenty minutes waiting to be fed at the same time created an atmosphere that was not conducive to civilized dining. If the train were running late, the scheduled thirty-minute stop might be cut back by the conductor. The fear of being left behind ruined many a stomach.

The contrast between the depot restaurant

and the dining car was remarkable. To the good food, good service, and pleasant surroundings of the diner was added the enchantment of the pleasing landscape. Few other places can induce the same feeling of serenity and well-being than a seat on a railway dining car. It was in many travelers' experience one of the most civilized pleasures created by Western society. [6]

West of Main Street stood the NYC's Erie Street Station, from which trains ran to both Lockport and Suspension Bridge, the fork being at North Tonawanda. There was no rail link between the Exchange and Erie Street depots. In 1868 there were four trains from Buffalo to Suspension Bridge, one of which went on to Lewiston, where it connected with a steamboat to Toronto, weather permitting. Two of the four trains from Buffalo went to Lockport. Eastbound, this service was reversed. At Suspension Bridge connections were made with through NYC trains to and from Rochester via the Falls Road and through Canada on the Great Western. At Tonawanda connections were made with the one train a day each way on the former Canandaigua & Niagara Falls, the Peanut, to Batavia. This was a rural line with stations at Getzville, Transit, Clarence Center, Clarence, Akron, Falkirk, and Pembroke. A tenant at the Erie Street Station was the Grand Trunk Railway, which scheduled two daily departures to Goderich, 160 miles away, one to Stratford, 115 miles, and one to Brantford, 75 miles on the former Buffalo & Lake Huron. Eastbound, the process was reversed. Fort Erie was reached by car ferry from the foot of Porter Avenue. (Figure V, #10.)

If Buffalo and Suspension Bridge be considered a single railroad center, there were in 1868 thirty-six arrivals and thirty-five departures for a total of seventy-one passenger train movements on any given weekday. Of this total, the NYC was responsible for thirty-two (45%), the Erie thirteen (18.3%), and the lake shore route ten (14%). Of the Canadian roads, the Grand Trunk operated eight (11.25%), and the Great Western eight (11.25%). This does not take into account special excursion trains and the fact that when traffic was heavy a train would be run in two or more sections five or ten minutes apart, which could be an invitation to disaster.

Trains were labeled express, accommodation, or mail. Express trains took between thirty-five and forty-two hours to cover the 980 miles of track (air distance 713 miles) between New York and Chicago on the NYC and its western connections. For the night portion of their run, express trains usually carried sleepers. In theory, express trains were fast since they made fewer stops (hence the name "limited"). Some expresses did omit many station-stops, but others were actually long-distance accommodations.

During fiscal year 1871-1872 the Buffalo-Chicago line carried daily 50,000 to 60,000 letters each way and three to ten tons of newspapers, magazines, and parcels. For one year, 1875-1876, the NYC ran a solid mail train New York-Chicago with specially designed white cars, in which mail was processed en route. On its maiden trip on September 16, 1875, the train raced from New York to Buffalo at the astonishing speed of 40.9 miles an hour, including stops. On the Lake Shore portion of the run, the average speed dipped to 33 miles an hour, an indication of the comparative merits of the track on the two lines. Nevertheless, the train overall completed its run in twenty-seven hours and fifteen minutes, shaving ten hours off the time of the fastest express up to that time. But a vindictive Congress reduced the rate of compensation to railroads for carrying the mail by ten percent in July, 1876. A furious Commodore Vanderbilt canceled the *Fast Mail*.

Most mail trains carried passengers. In fact, many mail cars were combination baggage, mail, and passenger cars. This was the case especially on runs through less populated

XI, 5

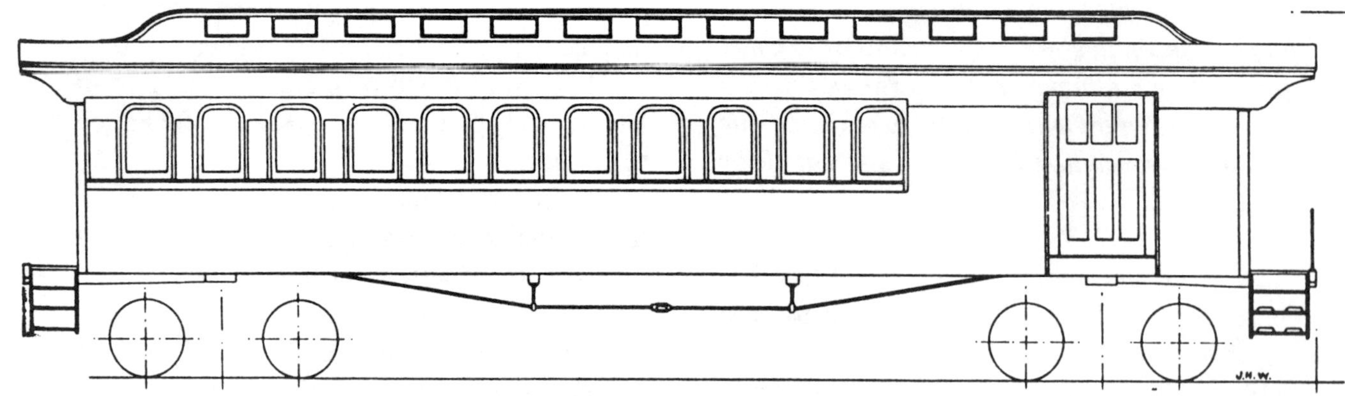

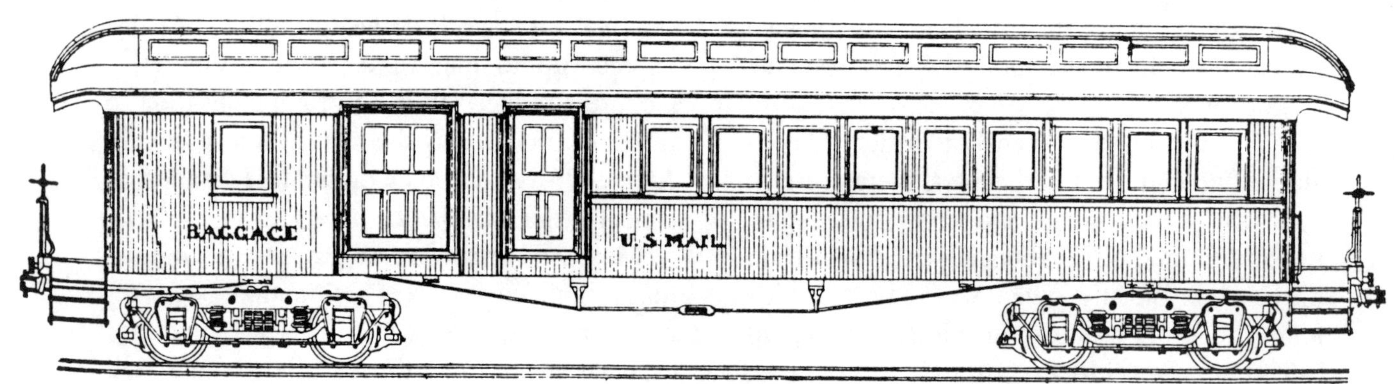

areas. (Figure #5.) In contrast with later years, the number of locals when compared with long-distance trains was very small. Most long-distance trains made frequent stops. As greater speed became possible, the number of limited-stop trains increased, as did also that of accommodations to service the bypassed local stations.

The following list demonstrates weekday train movements at Buffalo-Suspension Bridge in 1868:

Road	Expresses	Locals	Total
NYC	(9)	(3)	(12)
LS&MS	(8)	(2)	(10)
RL&NF	(8)	-	(8)
B&NF	-	(8)	(8)
B&L	-	(4)	(4)
Future NYC System	25	17	42
B&NYC	(3)	(3)	(6)
BC&NY	(5)	(2)	(7)
Erie Railroad	8	5	13
Great Western	8	-	8
Grand Trunk	6	2	8
Grand Total	47	24	71

Given the growing importance of bulky items like oil, coal, grain and lumber in Buffalo's booming economy and the fact that the light American (4-4-0) type locomotive dominated in both freight and passenger operations during the second half of the nineteenth century, the number of Buffalo freight trains must have been considerably greater than seventy-one passenger trains in and out of Buffalo in 1868. An ordinary freight train consisted of about ten cars. Very few Western New Yorkers at this date lived beyond the sound of a locomotive whistle or the smell of soft coal smoke.

1878

By the late 1870s passenger operations on the Niagara Frontier had undergone a stupendous transformation as a result of a period of explosive railroad construction. International Bridge to Fort Erie had been opened in 1873. The NYC had completed the Junction Railroad, better known as the Belt Line, from the mainline in East Buffalo to the bridge at lower Black Rock the previous year. Commodore Vanderbilt took over the Lake Shore in 1869, and the Michigan Central in 1875. In 1877 he assumed control of the Canada Southern (CaSo), which had been completed from Windsor to International Bridge in 1873. The NYC's longtime but ill matched rival, the Erie, had completed the Suspension Bridge & Erie Junction Railroad to connect with the Great Western at Suspension Bridge in 1871. At the same time, the Erie built the Erie International across North Buffalo from Main Street to the Grand Trunk at International Bridge. (Figure VII, #6.) The Great Western had completed its Airline from Glencoe to Bridgeburg (with a branch from Welland to Suspension Bridge) in 1873. (Figure VII, #12.) That same year the Buffalo New York & Philadelphia established a connection at Emporium by way of East Aurora and Olean with the Pennsylvania's Philadelphia & Erie. (Figure VII, #1.) In the summer of America's Centennial Year, the Rome Watertown & Ogdensburg reached Lewiston. The Buffalo & Jamestown, moreover, was now operating passenger trains between its titular cities. (Figure VII, #10.)

In 1878 four westbound express trains arrived daily at Buffalo from New York on the NYC. Three of them carried cars from Boston. All four trains had split at Rochester with cars going on the Falls Road to the Great Western at Suspension Bridge. A fifth through train arrived at Suspension Bridge without having been split at Rochester. With the completion of International Bridge, NYC cars could now be sent to Chicago directly, either via the LS&MS, as before, or via the Junction Railroad, the bridge, and the CaSo. Three of the four expresses from New York made connections with both the Great Western, the LS&MS, and the CaSo. The Erie Street Station was no longer used to reach the Great Western at Suspension Bridge. The Belt Line, in a routing necessitated by the break in trackage between Exchange and Erie Streets, was used for that purpose. Trains to Suspension Bridge ran out the mainline to East Buffalo, where they took the Belt Line to Lower Black Rock and the Niagara River route to the Falls. Four trains a day went this way to, and four arrived from Suspension Bridge and the Great Western, so that the latter road advertised them in Buffalo papers as Great Western trains to Toronto, Hamilton, Saint Thomas, London, Detroit, and Chicago. In addition, there were three NYC mainline westbound locals arriving at Buffalo daily, one from Amsterdam, one from Rochester, and one from Albany. They stopped at every station along the way and carried mail and express packages. Three emigrant trains arrived at East Buffalo on the NYC daily, the early morning *Boston Emigrant and Accommodation*, and in the evening the [Lake] *Shore Emigrant* and the *Canada Southern Emigrant.*

Westbound from the NYC's Exchange Street Station in 1878 were four expresses to Chicago, Cincinnati, and Saint Louis on the LS&MS, and three on the CaSo-International Bridge-MC route, and four heading for Suspension Bridge and the Great Western via the former Buffalo & Niagara Falls. The excess of westbound departures on these western routes over westbound arrivals on the NYC may be explained by the very existence of these three Buffalo-Chicago routes and by competition from the Erie on the New York-Buffalo run. The Erie's western connections were less numerous than those of the NYC. There was also a late afternoon daily local to Erie, Pennsylvania, on the LS&MS.

Eastbound arrivals at the NYC's Exchange Street Station were four express trains on the LS&MS and three on the CaSo. Three through trains from the west arrived daily on the Great Western at Suspension Bridge. Included in these arrivals were two GW connections with Toronto. Suspension Bridge also welcomed a westbound arrival from the Rome Watertown & Ogdensburg, which had been completed to Lewiston two years before, and which used the former Buffalo & Niagara Falls to reach the bridge. There was a single inbound local on the LS&MS from Erie. Besides Chicago, major western points in the United States that boasted connections either by through cars or otherwise with Buffalo were Cleveland, Detroit, Toledo, Cincinnati, and Saint Louis. (For a Wagner sleeping car, see Figure #6.)

Departures from Buffalo eastward on the NYC consisted of four expresses. One of these was scheduled for a meet with a Falls Road eastbound at Rochester; two carried Boston cars, and were similarly scheduled. There was also a single local to Rochester. The fastest trains on the NYC between New York and Buffalo were the westbound *Chicago Special*, which left Grand Central at 10:30 A. M. and arrived in Buffalo at 12:50 A. M., and its eastbound companion, the *New York Special*, which left Buffalo at 4:35 A. M. and arrived in New York at 7:00 P. M., thus covering 440 miles in roughly fourteen hours and twenty minutes. The slowest train on the line was the *Boston Emigrant and Accommodation*, which averaged sixteen miles an hour between Albany and Buffalo. A tenant of the NYC at Exchange Street was the Allegheny Valley Railroad, whose trains left for Brocton on the LS&MS, and thence on the former Buffalo Corry & Pittsburgh and the Oil City Railroad through the oil regions to Pittsburgh at 7:10 A. M. and 12:15 P. M., returning at 1:00 P. M. and 8:20 P. M. (Figure VII, #1.)

At the adjacent Erie Station, there were in late 1878 three express trains from Jersey City, one less than on the NYC. The *Day Express* arrived here at 12:05 A. M., the *Night Express* at 8:00 A. M., and the *Second Night Express* at 11:50 A. M. Four express trains, however,

XI, 6

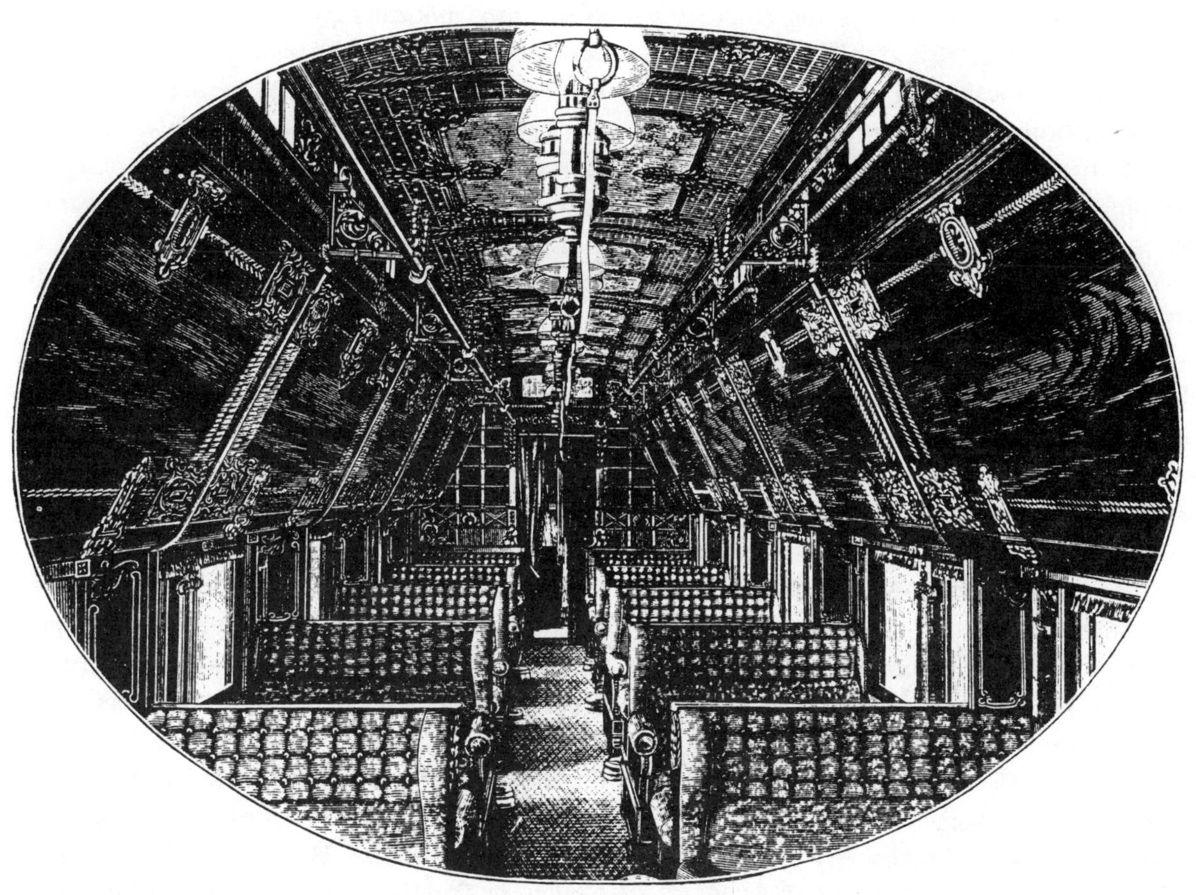

departed for Jersey City: the *Special New York Express* at 8:00 A. M., the *Atlantic Express* at 2:50 P. M., the *Night Express* at 5:50 P. M., and the *New York Night Express* at 9:20 P. M. The Erie proclaimed itself "the only Line running Pullman Palace Hotel and Sleeping Coaches through without change between Chicago, Cincinnati, Cleveland, Niagara Falls, Rochester, Buffalo, and New York." (The NYC used Wagner Palace Car Company sleepers.) The Erie's through trains matched the NYC's in speed, averaging between twenty-five to thirty miles an hour. Prospective patrons were assured that "the best ventilated and most LUXURIOUS SLEEPING COACHES in the world accompany each night train." But there was always the inconvenience of the ferry crossing to Manhattan.

The Erie also operated two locals daily from Corning to Buffalo and one to Corning, all three on the former Buffalo Corning & New York, that is, via Avon. (Figure III, #1.) There was a westbound local from Hornell and one from Castile, both on the former Buffalo & New York City. At Attica the train from Castile picked up Buffalo bound cars from Avon on the former BC&NY. In addition, there were five locals each way on the Suspension Bridge & Erie Junction line between Buffalo and Suspension Bridge, which connected with the Great Western. The GW advertised these trains as its own, as it had done with NYC connecting trains to Suspension Bridge. Erie Station was also the terminus of the Buffalo & Jamestown, recently renamed the Buffalo & Southwestern, which scheduled two trains each way daily, one of which was named the *Pittsburgh Express*, and the other the *Night Express*. This branch provided connections with Bradford and with the Atlantic & Great Western, which had been leased by the Erie in 1874, thus extending the lessee's reach to Cleveland, Cincinnati, and Chicago. (Figure VII, #4.)

Grodinsky provides a comparison of the Erie and the NYC during the 1870s:

At end of three and half years of Gould power, the Erie "was an incomplete concern, its track disconnected at different points, largely single track, no terminal improvements, defective machinery, iron rails, largely wooden bridges, in a condition that it could not be worked with economy." Such was the language of Hugh Jewett, president and receiver of the road who took over the executive responsibilities after the departure of Gould [March 11, 1872] *and the McHenry satellites who followed him. Jewett's conclusions were confirmed by another railroad man who in the interests of his English clients made an elaborate survey of the property. The Erie, he wrote, needed iron to replace its wooden bridges. It lacked steel rails and durable sleepers* [ties], *and it badly needed an improvement in its grades. Its terminal arrangements were inadequate. The road, furthermore, had only a single track, while the NYC had four and the PRR two tracks and in many places a third. The NYC with its additional tracks between New York and Buffalo was able to reduce the running time of trains and the cost of freight transportation. The absence of double tracks on the Erie, on the other hand, led to delays, expense, and operating risks.* [7]

The NYC's Erie Street Station no longer handled trains to Suspension Bridge, but was still the terminus of the Grand Trunk, the Great Western's Loop Line, CaSo locals to Niagara-on-the-Lake, and the NYC's Lockport branch. Trains on the GT used International Bridge which, as has been noted, had been built as the GT's answer to the GW's Suspension Bridge. In 1878 the GT operated three trains each way from the Erie Street Station. Two (one each way) ran daily between Buffalo and Stratford on the former Buffalo & Lake Huron. At Stratford, connections could be made to Goderich on Lake Huron or Detroit and Chicago. The Great Western's Loop Line sent two locals daily west to Saint Thomas and received one from there. The CaSo operated two round trip locals daily between Buffalo and Niagara-on-the-Lake on the former Niagara & Erie. There were two round trip NYC locals between Buffalo and Lockport daily. At Tonawanda, one Lockport train split, with a section going on the C&NF to Batavia. This train set something of a negative speed record - nine miles an hour. When the Erie Street Station (Figure II, #18), which had been built in 1852-1853, was demolished in November, 1903, it was discovered that its walls were four feet thick, and its foundation twenty feet deep. The wreckers judged that it would have lasted for another century or more.

The Buffalo New York & Philadelphia's ramshackle station at Exchange and Louisiana Streets sponsored one train daily each way between Buffalo and Emporium (121 miles), where connections could be made for Harrisburg, Philadelphia, and other points on the PRR. In addition, another train was scheduled each way between Buffalo and Port Allegheny, Pennsylvania (ninety-six miles).

If Suspension Bridge and Buffalo be viewed once again as a single hub, there were at that expanded rail center in 1878 fifty-eight arrivals and fifty-five departures, a total of 113 daily passenger train movements, up by forty-two (59%) since ten years before. This is all the more remarkable when it is remembered that the depression which followed the Panic of 1873 did not lift until 1879. The speed of the New York-Chicago express trains had not improved over the past decade, however, most still averaging thirty-six hours on the trip. The primacy of the Vanderbilt lines in the Western New York railroad picture can be seen in the fact that fifty-nine (52%) of the total passenger train movements there took place on the NYC or its subsidiaries. The Erie was a distant second with thirty trains (26%) of the total.

The following is a list of train movements in 1878. Since the gap between the NYC's Exchange and Erie Street stations had not yet been closed, and through trains on the NYC continued to be divided (or consolidated) at Rochester, Niagara Falls and Buffalo are taken as a single transportation center for express trains.

Railroad	Expresses	Locals	Total
NYC	(8)	(7)	(15)
LS&MS	(8)	(1)	(9)
CaSo	(6)	(2)	(8)
RL&NF	(7)	(3)	(10)
B&NF	(7)	(3)	(10)
B&L	-	(4)	(4)
C&NF	-	(1)	(1)
JRR	-	(2)	(2)
Future NYC System	36	23	59
B&N	(7)	(2)	(9)
BC&NY	-	(3)	(3)
SB&EJ	-	(10)	(10)
B&J	-	(4)	(4)
EI	-	(4)	(4)
Erie Railroad	7	23	30
BNY&P	2	-	4
AV	4	-	4
GT	5	1	6
GW	7	3	10
Grand Total	61	52	113

1888

As noted in Chapter IX, the 1880s were the most productive decade ever in railroad building in America. On the local scene, four railroad companies extended their trackage into Buffalo, the NKP and the DL&W in 1882, and the BR&P and the NYWS&B next year. With the closing of the gap between the NYC's Exchange and Erie Street stations in 1879 (Figure IX, #24) and the completion of the four-tracking of the mainline from New York to Buffalo in the early 1880s, NYC trains could now conveniently reach Chicago across Canada by way of Buffalo. As a result, all through NYC trains between New York and Chicago across the Ontario Peninsula were taken off the single-track Falls Road and routed through the Rochester-Buffalo mainline and the former Buffalo & Niagara Falls to either International or Suspension Bridge. The Grand Trunk absorbed the Great Western in 1882. That same year, the Michigan Central leased the Canada Southern and integrated operations with it. (For American-Canadian connections on the Niagara Frontier, see Figure VII, #13.) The Pittsburgh & Lake Erie had been completed from Pittsburgh to Youngstown, Ohio, in 1879. Commodore Vanderbilt had acquired fifteen percent of its stock, seeing in the road an entering wedge into Pittsburgh and competition with the PRR. His LS&MS already had a branch from Ashtabula on Lake Erie to Youngstown. The P&LE supplied a third route between Buffalo and the Steel City, in addition to those of the Buffalo Rochester & Pittsburgh and the Western New York & Pennsylvania. In 1889 the NYC acquired complete control of the P&LE and thereafter operated this extremely profitable industrial carrier as a part of its own system.

It was also during the 1880s that the new Big Four (Cleveland Cincinnati Chicago & Saint Louis) was formed under Vanderbilt auspices by consolidation of the old Big Four (Cleveland Indianapolis Saint Louis & Chicago) with the Bee Line (Cleveland Columbus Cincinnati & Indianapolis.) Behind this development lay forty years of bewildering railroad construction and amalgamation in the southern tier of the Midwest. (Figure #7.) During the 1880s, the Commodore's grandson, Cornelius Vanderbilt II, chairman of the NYC and master of *The Breakers* at Newport, had become a power in the midwestern railroad scene. By 1882 he had secured control of the Bee Line, which ran east and north from Cincinnati and Indianapolis toward Sandusky and Cleveland. Even before the construction of railroads along the south shore of Lake Erie, the Cleveland Columbus & Cincinnati, a forerunner of the Bee Line, had been the preferred route between Buffalo and Cincinnati because of regularly scheduled connections by lake steamers between Cleveland and Buffalo.

By 1880 Melville Ingalls of Cincinnati, a Massachusetts born graduate of Harvard Law School, had put together another string of midwestern railroads from Cincinnati to Indianapolis, Saint Louis, and Chicago, known as the (first) Big Four. The author of the account of Ingalls's life in the Dictionary of American Biography wrote:

His skill as a railroad reorganizer had attracted the attention of the Vanderbilts, who controlled the Cleveland, Columbus, Cincinnati, and Indianapolis Railway, popularly known as the Bee Line. In 1889 the Ingalls and Vanderbilt interests were consolidated, and the Cleveland, Cincinnati, Chicago, and Saint Louis was organized. Of the new system, known as the [second] *Big Four, Ingalls was elected president. He held this position until the New York Central in 1905 assumed of the various properties under his direction; he then became chairman of the board of directors, an office he retained until his resignation, Nov. 14, 1912. He was also president of the Kentucky Central Railroad from 1881 to 1883 and president of the Chesapeake and Ohio from 1888 to 1900.* [8]

The new Big Four provided the NYC at Buffalo with access to Saint Louis, Indianapolis, Cincinnati, and Columbus. Vanderbilt lines now reached from the Atlantic to the Great Lakes and to the Ohio and Mississippi Rivers. This extensive growth and complexification of connections between railroads entering Buffalo made for an increasingly complicated shuffling of through cars, especially at the NYC's Exchange Street Station. For freight trains it also called for greatly expanded classification yards.

In addition, a new amenity had been added to long-distance railroad passenger travel, the

XI, 7

C&C	Cleveland Columbus & Cincinnati		
I&B	Indianapolis & Bellfontaine	Cleveland Columbus Cincin-	
B&I	Bellfontaine & Indianapolis	nati & Indianapolis (Bee	
S&C	Springfield & Columbus	Line) 1868	
C&S	Cincinnati & Springfield		
I&C	Indianapolis & Cincinnati		
I&StL	Indianapolis & St. Louis	Cincinnati Indianapolis	
TH&A	Terre Haute & Alton	St. Louis & Chicago (1st	Cleveland Cincinnati
L&I	Lafayette & Indianapolis	Big 4) 1880	Chicago & St. Louis
CL&C	Cincinnati Lafayette & Chicago		2nd Big 4) 1890
MR&LE	Mad River & Lake Erie		
(SD&C	Sandusky Dayton & Cincinnati)		
O&ISL	Ohio and Indiana State Line		
I&OSL	Indianapolis & Ohio State Line	Peoria & Eastern 1880	
IC&D	Indianapolis Crawfordsville & Danville		
DUB&P	Danville Urbana Blomington		

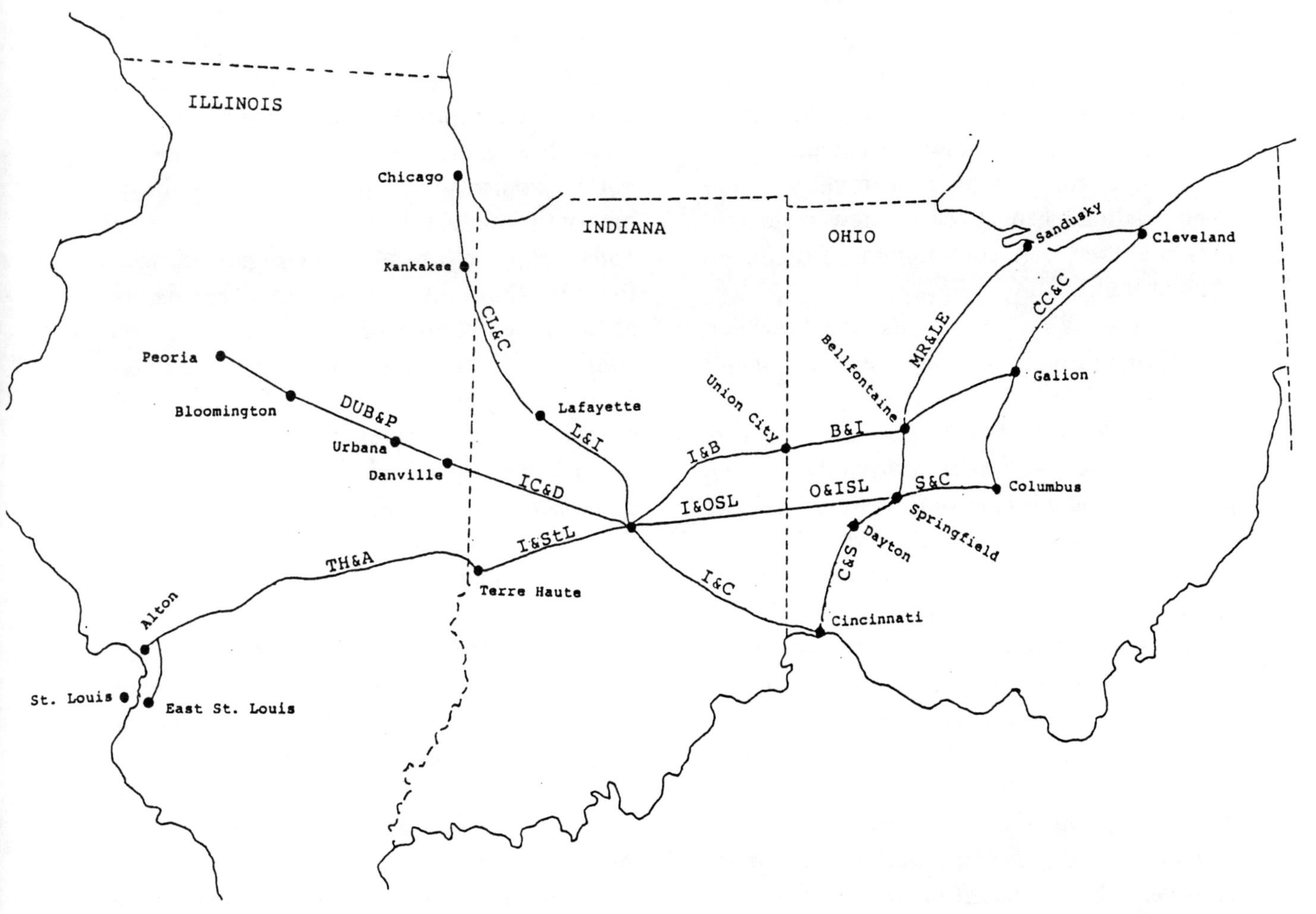

dining car. George Pullman resolved to overcome the problems associated with hotel cars by constructing a car that did nothing but prepare and serve meals for everyone aboard a train. In 1868 he built a magnificent restaurant car, the *Delmonico*, named after the most posh eating and drinking establishment in America, located at Fifth Avenue and Twenty-Sixth Street in New York. The car boasted a kitchen, ice chest, and hot-water heating system, and was manned by two cooks and four waiters, capable of serving 250 meals daily. By the mid-1870s, dining cars had been widely adopted by Midwestern railroads. For competitive purposes, all railroads serving Chicago with long-distance trains now carried dining cars, despite the losses they inevitably generated. Eastern railroads were initially less enthusiastic about the new departure. Led by its more daring western subsidiaries, the MC and the CaSo, the NYC reluctantly added dining cars to its through trains beginning in 1883. "By the mid-eighties," writes White, "the dining car was no longer an unwanted stepchild but the pride of the passenger car family. Every major railroad had at least a few restaurant cars, and they were common on all first-class express trains."

Throughout their history, however, American railroads found serving food a major problem, as White explains:

Even well patronized trains could not seem to make money on their restaurant cars. High fixed costs and a limited market were the basic reasons for their fiscal difficulties. A sizable crew, generally ten men, was necessary to serve thirty to forty patrons efficiently. Even in the days of cheap labor, and even though the same crew served several seatings, this was a disproportionate ratio. The crew had to be fed and housed throughout the trip, and at least some of them had to be carried back to their homes as deadheaded passengers. Unlike a restaurant, the railroad could not use part-time help. . . . Unused or spoiled food was another large expense. Cars were usually overstocked so that no customer would be disappointed, and what was not used could not always be salvaged. The old-fashioned icebox was not entirely effective in storing perishables. Moreover, the clientele was limited to those aboard the train. No matter how good or cheap the meal, the dining car could not draw upon the population at large. And many travelers brought their own food; others, being country folk intimidated by the posh diner and its crew, skipped their meals. Only the first-class passengers could be depended on to patronize the diner. [9]

By 1888 the *Official Guide* had achieved a sophistication it would retain for the rest of its existence. Its pages were enlarged to seven by ten inches, and in thickness it began to approach a modern city telephone directory. Detailed maps were provided, the names and condensed schedules of through trains were included, and their consist was described in detail. Unfortunately, Buffalo's Belt Line schedule was omitted, and hence its trains are not considered in this study, since few timetables of this circular line have survived. (For an 1884 Belt Line timetable, see Figure IX, #25.) In 1884 the United States and Canada had agreed to adopt a series of time zones to overcome the difficulties caused by conflicting local time systems. Henceforth, there would be only two time zones, Eastern and Central, east of the Great Plains. (Hereafter in this book, times given will be in terms of Eastern Standard Time, which is one hour ahead of Central Standard Time.)

Locally, six westbound daily expresses arrived at Buffalo on the NYC's mainline from New York. Three of them, the *Chicago Express*, the *Fast Western Express*, and the *Pacific Express*, were split at Buffalo, with one section continuing west on the LS&MS, the other on the MC via Suspension Bridge. The three other arrivals continued west only on the LS&MS: one, the *Vestibule Limited*, ran to Chicago; the second, the *Fast Mail*, only to

Cleveland; and the third, the *Night Express*, carried through cars for Cincinnati on the Bee Line. All three LS&MS only trains also carried cars for Saint Louis on the Cincinnati Indianapolis Saint Louis & Chicago, *alias* the first Big Four. (The Bee Line and the CCC&I would be merged within a year to form the Cleveland Cincinnati Chicago & Saint Louis, *alias* the second Big Four.) Four of the six westbound departures from Buffalo carried through cars from Boston. All MC express trains ran via Suspension Bridge, which is why that road billed itself as "The Niagara Falls Route."

Since the NYC had leased the NYWS&B in 1883, the lessor used the NYC's Exchange Street Station for the three westbound express trains it operated daily between Weehawken, across the Hudson River from Manhattan's Forty-second Street, and Buffalo. All these trains carried through cars from Boston via the Fitchburg Railroad, the junction point being Rotterdam Junction. All three carried through cars for Chicago, and two carried cars for Saint Louis. In the case of the *Chicago & Saint Louis Express*, Chicago was reached via the Grand Trunk to Detroit and the Wabash from there to Chicago and Saint Louis. Connections were made with the GT at Suspension Bridge over the NYC's ex-B&NF line. The second NYWS&B train, the *Pacific Express*, carried cars for Chicago, which was reached over both the Grand Trunk and the Grand Trunk Western (GT's Michigan subsidiary) and the GT-Wabash routes. This train also carried cars for the Wabash to Saint Louis. The NYWS&B's last arrival at Buffalo, *Chicago Express,* went all the way to Chicago on the GT and its Michigan subsidiary, the GT Western. All three NYWS&B trains carried through cars for Toronto by arrangement with the GT. The different Buffalo/Boston-Chicago routes seem to have been adopted to attract patrons at intermediate points.

Note the complex routing of the *Pacific Express* from Boston: (1) Fitchburg - Boston to Rotterdam Junction (2) NYWS&B - Rotterdam Junction to Buffalo (3) B&NF - Buffalo to Suspension Bridge (4) GT - Suspension Bridge to Detroit and Toronto (5) Wabash or GT Western - Detroit to Chicago. Coupling and recoupling sleepers was not conducive to uninterrupted sleep. The Interstate Commerce Act had been passed the previous year, and the NYC management may have been creating the impression that the NYC and the NYWS&B were actually competing for the New York/ Boston-Buffalo/Chicago passenger trade.

Seven trains left Buffalo daily on the NYC heading for salt water: the *New York Express* (New York only); the *New York Limited* (New York only); the *Fast Eastern Express* (Boston only); the *South Shore Limited* (New York only); the *Atlantic Express-South West Limited*; the *Saint Louis Express*; and the *Cincinnati Express*. The last three trains carried both Boston and New York cars. Four of the Central's seven eastbound express trains from Buffalo were the result of consolidating LS&MS and MC trains at Buffalo. Three arrivals from the west came into Buffalo only on the LS&MS, which traversed a far more populous territory than the MC. The NYWS&B participated in running a series of trains eastbound, in concert with the Wabash, the GT, and the Fitchburg. These trains corresponded to its westbound offerings, that is, three expresses from Chicago and Saint Louis.

Express trains on the Vanderbilt lines were faster during the late 1880s than previously due to improved equipment and track, the use of dining cars, and the elimination of some station stops. On the New York-Chicago run, time elapsed ranged from thirty-three hours on the *Pacific Express* to twenty-five hours on the *Vestibule Express* and the phenomenal twenty-two hours and forty-five minutes on the eastbound *South Shore Limited*, which averaged forty-one miles an hour on the Buffalo to New York section of the trip. The *Fast Mail* justified its name on that part of its run on the

LS&MS from Cleveland to Buffalo, averaging forty miles an hour. However, these were all scheduled times. What percentage of trains were on time is unknown.

There were in 1888 two westbound main-line NYC arrivals at Buffalo of intermediate distance, without parlor, dining, sleeping cars. One came in from Lyons, the other from Rochester. Correspondingly, there were two eastbound departures, one to Syracuse and the other to Albany. Two MC locals ran each way between Buffalo and Detroit, and two each way between Buffalo and Welland via International Bridge and the MC. On the LS&MS the only passenger run that was not a through train was the Toledo local. However, it should be realized that many of the slower express trains made numerous local stops. The NYWS&B operated two round trip locals between Buffalo and Lyons, one set of which originated and terminated in East Buffalo. Obviously, this was not primarily a passenger operation. Another NYWS&B round trip between Buffalo and Weehawken is classified here as a local (although its eastbound edition was called *West Shore Express*) because it carried no diners, parlor cars, or sleepers and stopped at most stations on its sixteen hour run.

The former Buffalo & Niagara Falls operated a dozen weekday trains westbound, but three of these, making no intermediate stops between Buffalo and the Falls, were actually the MC's three expresses to the west. Three others carried NYWS&B through cars for interchange with the GT, which had an arrangement with the Wabash, at Suspension Bridge. These, however, made many of the intermediate stops on the way (Terrace, Black Rock, North Buffalo, Tonawanda, and La Salle). Of the remaining six, three went all the way to Lewiston, two terminated at Suspension Bridge, and one went only as far as Tonawanda, where it turned onto the Peanut. Similar but reverse arrangements prevailed on the B&NF eastbound, which resulted in twenty-four daily trains on this line, twelve expresses and twelve locals. Running time for the twenty-four miles to Suspension Bridge was an hour. Thus, anyone traveling between Buffalo and Niagara Falls had the choice of twelve trains each way daily. North Tonawanda was the junction point for the Lockport line, which saw many more trains (five each way) than ten years before. At this time, there was only one stop, at Sawyer's Creek, on the sixteen miles between Tonawanda and Lockport. Patrons of these locals were undoubtedly shoppers, theater-goers, students, and commuters who worked in Buffalo and wished to enjoy rural living. Since Buffalo and Lockport were both county seats, the Lockport line must have seen its share of lawyers, petitioners, defendants, and witnesses. The Lewiston train connected with lake steamers to Toronto and with the Rome Watertown & Ogdensburg, which operated one train a day to and from communities on the south shore of Lake Ontario and in the North Country.

Figure VII, #13 illustrates the NYC's presence on the Niagara Frontier and the Vanderbilt roads' connections with the west via the Niagara Peninsula. The B&NF played a key role in passenger service in this area. Its Erie Street passenger station was located just across the street from the notorious Canal Street and between the Erie and the Evans Ship Canals. Although the station had lost its importance with the closing of the gap between Exchange and Erie Streets by tracks which bypassed the station to the east, the GT continued to use it for two trains a day each way between Buffalo and Saint Thomas. The GT also maintained two freight houses in this crowded commercial and industrial district. (Figure #8.)

The Erie, having converted from six feet to standard gauge by June 2, 1880, scheduled twenty-five daily arrivals and an equal number of departures. The road ran three express trains each way daily between Jersey City and

XI, 8

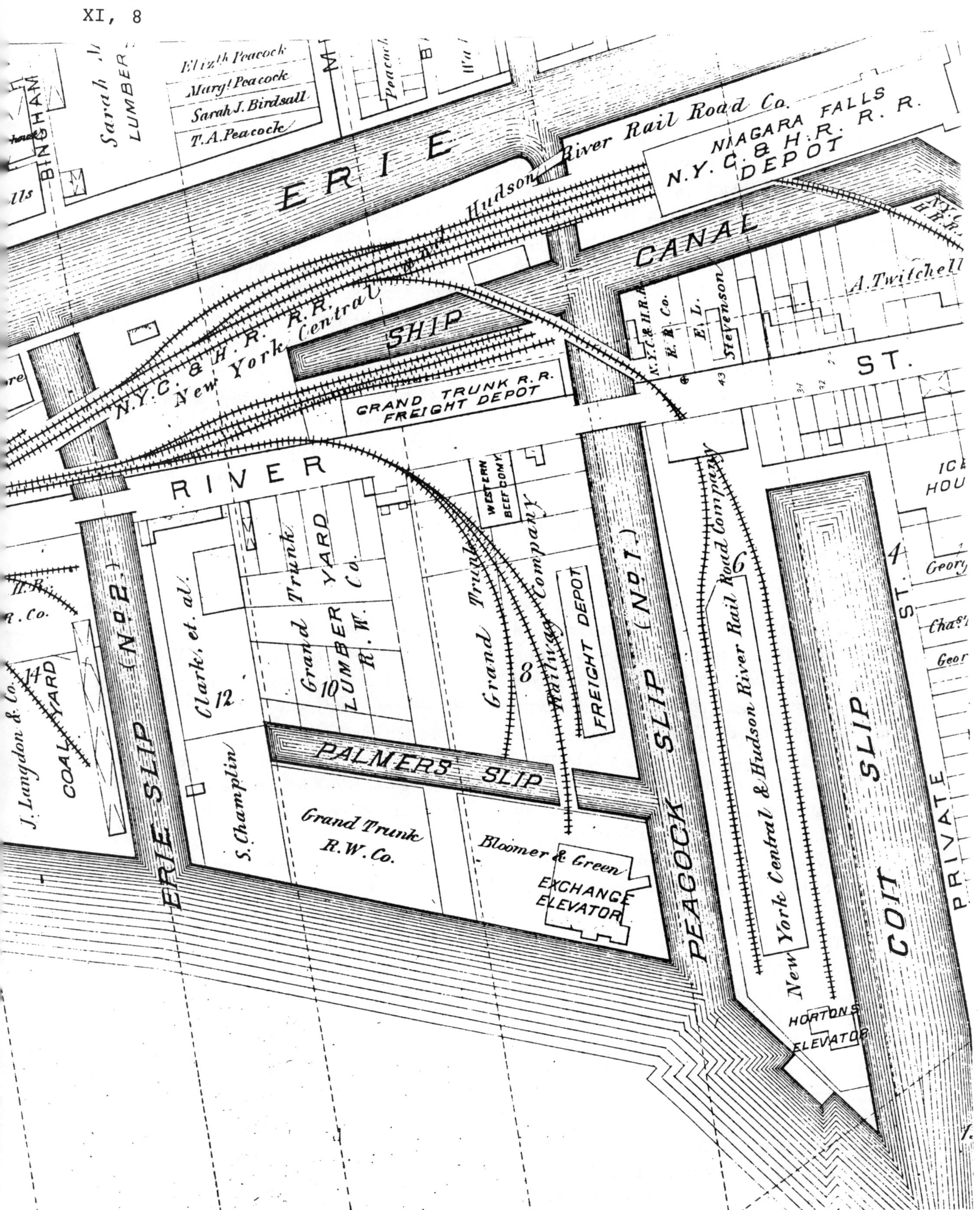
Eliz'th Peacock
Mary! Peacock
Sarah J. Birdsall
T.A. Peacock
BINGHAM
LUMBER
ERIE
CANAL
Hudson River Rail Road Co.
NIAGARA FALLS
N.Y.C. & H.R. R.R.
N.Y.C. & H.R. R.R. DEPOT
New York Central
N.Y.C. & H.R. R.R.
SHIP
GRAND TRUNK R.R. FREIGHT DEPOT
A. Twitchell
Stevenson
ST.
RIVER
WESTERN BEEF COM'Y
Grand Trunk YARD
Grand Trunk
Grand Trunk LUMBER R.W. Co.
Railway Company
FREIGHT DEPOT
Clark, et. al.
12
10
8
6
4
14
COAL YARD
J. Langdon & Co.
ERIE SLIP (No 2)
PEACOCK SLIP (No 1)
PALMERS SLIP
S. Champlin
Grand Trunk R.W. Co.
Bloomer & Green
EXCHANGE ELEVATOR
New York Central & Hudson River Rail Road Company
HORTONS ELEVATOR
COIT SLIP
PRIVATE
ICE HOU
ST.

Buffalo. A decade previously, it had run three westbound and four eastbound. During Hugh Jewett's presidency, the Erie completed double-tracking its line from Jersey City through Hornellsville to Buffalo. This enabled the fastest Erie trains to cover the distance between the Buffalo and Jersey City in twelve hours and forty-two minutes at an average speed of thirty-two miles an hour. The Lehigh Valley had yet to reach Buffalo, but through LV cars were attached to two eastbound Erie trains from Buffalo to Waverly, where the LV took over and brought them to the PRR's Exchange Place Station in Jersey City and to the Philadelphia & Reading Station in Philadelphia. Travelers - but not through cars - from further west came in on any of three Wabash trains to Clifton, on the Canadian side of Suspension Bridge. There they entrained on the Erie's Niagara Falls branch to Buffalo. The Wabash trains linked Clifton with Chicago and Saint Louis. These were the same three Wabash trains which exchanged through cars with the NYWS&B. The reverse process held for westbound Erie trains. (Figure VII, #6.) The Erie's Niagara Falls branch trains carried coach passengers only. Pullman passengers on the Erie between New York and Chicago took mainline trains that left the Erie at Salamanca and bypassed Buffalo by way of the New York Pennsylvania & Ohio (NYPANO), successor to the bankrupt Atlantic & Great Western. (Figure VII, #4.) The Erie had leased the NYPANO in 1883 and was to acquire all its stock in 1896. Three other Clifton-Buffalo locals ran each way daily. The Lockport branch featured four trains daily each way, so that between the Erie and the NYC, Lockport was linked to Buffalo by eighteen trains a day. There were three daily round trips to Jamestown on the Erie's Buffalo & Southwestern Division. The late morning departure on this line carried a through Pullman parlor car to Cleveland on the NYPANO. On the former Buffalo & New York City, three eastbounds ran to Hornellsville, and two only as far as Attica. Westbounds contributed two arrivals from Attica and two from Hornellsville. Corning accounted for two trains each way daily. (On the Erie's routes in Central and Western New York, see Figure III, #1.)

The NKP, which was a tenant at the Erie's station, had begun passenger service to Buffalo in October, 1882. By 1888 it was dispatching and receiving one passenger train a day to and from Fostoria, Ohio, 286 miles away, on the Indiana Bloomington & Western, later part of the Big Four. The NKP's westbound also made a connection of sorts at Fostoria with a B&O train to Chicago. At this time, NKP management did not envision its road as a major passenger hauler.

The BNY&P had been reorganized as the Western New York & Pennsylvania in 1887, by which time it had acquired a chain of smaller railroads from Buffalo to Pittsburgh via Brocton and Oil City known as the Pittsburgh Division. (Figure XI, #3.) This division was billed as "The only line running night trains with sleeping cars between Buffalo and Pittsburgh *[sic]* and parlor cars on day trains." Prospective patrons were given this assurance in the Official Guide:

> *All* [trains are] *equipped with the Westinghouse Air Brake and Miller Platform. In the case of air brakes, a reciprocating steam pump on the locomotive supplied compressed air to a tank located under the cab floor. When a valve was opened in the cab, air was sent back to the cars through a pipe with flexible hoses between the platforms. The pipe directed the air into cylinders attached to the brake rigging.*

Westinghouse successfully tested his invention in 1868, and orders immediately began to flow into his Pittsburgh plant. As White points out:

> [By 1870] *eight railroads were now using the apparatus on 355 cars. Of these, 200 were on the Pennsylvania. In less than two years 85*

railroads and 4,000 cars were equipped with the Westinghouse brake. By 1874 the number of cars so fitted had nearly doubled. At the time of the Centennial [1876], *nearly three-quarters of the passenger equipment in this country had air brakes. So rapid a conversion is almost without precedent an industry famous for its wait-and-see attitude.* [10]

So the WNY&P's boast was somewhat hollow. Colonel Ezra Miller's platform, again the source is White:

. . . was a combination trussed end platform, draft gear, and coupler that diminished the likelihood of telescopes and eliminated the link and pin coupler. It was widely adopted in the United States for passenger cars between 1875 and 1900. For most of that period it was the national standard. [11]

Because of the expense, the railroad industry was much slower to adopt air brakes for freight cars. The pace picked up only after the passage of the Safety Appliance Act in 1893, which also provided for automatic couplers. The WNY&P operated one night train and one day train each way between Buffalo and Pittsburgh, all four of which, stopping at every station, averaged only twenty-four miles an hour. The Pittsburgh Division, which advertised itself as "THE ONLY ALL-RAIL ROUTE TO CHAUTAUQUA ASSEMBLY GROUNDS," reached the grounds of the Institute by means of a junction near Mayville with the Chautauqua Lake Railway, which continued on to Jamestown. The Pittsburgh Division also ran a daily local to and from Oil City. The Buffalo Division featured two trains to and from Emporium, where connections could be made on the PRR's Philadelphia & Erie to Philadelphia, Baltimore, and Washington. No sleepers, diners, or parlor cars were carried on this division. In addition, it operated a local each way to Franklinville. Two further accommodations, the 8:35 A. M. arrival from and the 5:50 P. M. departure to Olean, were commuter runs servicing Ebenezer, Elma, Jamison Road, and East Aurora. As demonstrated by this line and also by the Attica, Lockport, Jamestown, and Niagara Falls lines, and by some mainline locals and slower express trains, there was incipient suburban life before streetcars.

At the foot of Main Street, Lackawanna Station welcomed three westbound arrivals from Hoboken and dispatched four eastward to Hoboken. Two trains each way were night trains carrying sleepers and two were daylight trains with parlor and dining cars. There were also two mixed trains daily in opposite directions between Elmira and East Buffalo. Their average speed was less than fifteen miles an hour. Finally, there was a local from Elmira arriving at 8:00 P. M., but none in the opposite direction.

At the time of its arrival at Buffalo in 1883, the BR&P did not reach further south than Punxatawney, 105 miles from Buffalo, so arrangements were made with the PRR to connect with its Allegheny Valley Division at Falls Church, in order to reach Pittsburgh. In 1888, however, the morning and evening round trips of the BR&P, originating at and terminating in the NYC's Exchange Street Station, ran only as far as Bradford, just over the Pennsylvania line.

By 1888 there were, exclusive of Belt Line trains, eighty-four arrivals at Buffalo and eighty-six departures for a total of 170 weekday train movements, up fifty-seven (50%) from ten years before. Noteworthy during the '80s was the diminished importance of the Falls Road from Rochester to Suspension Bridge because of the closing of the gap between Exchange and Erie Streets. Eighty-two of the total 170 train movements took place at the NYC's Exchange Street Station. Of the total train movements, sixty-four were express trains and 106 were locals or trains of intermediate distance which lacked what White calls "first class cars," that is diners, parlor cars, or sleepers, which were becoming more common on long distance trains. Grouped on this basis, the distribution of Buffalo's passenger trains in 1888 was:

Railroad	Expresses	Locals	Total
NYC	(13)	(5)	(18)
LS&MS	(12)	(1)	(13)
MC	(8)	(11)	(19)
NYWS&B	(8)	(4)	(12)
B&NF	(5)	(10)	(15)
B&L	-	(10)	(10)
Future NYC System	46	41	87
B&NYC	(6)	(13)	(19)
BC&NY	-	(4)	(4)
SB&EJ	-	(12)	(12)
L&B	-	(8)	(8)
Erie Railroad	7	42	49
BNY&P	-	(8)	(8)
BC&P	(4)	(2)	(6)
WNY&P	4	10	14
BR&P	-	4	4
DL&W	7	3	10
NKP	-	2	2
GT	-	4	4
Grand Total	64	106	170

1893

The so-called "Gay Nineties" were good times only from 1890 until May, 1893, and again from 1897 to the end of the century. The Panic of 1893 had come about because capital investment in the 1880s, especially in railroads, had exceeded the possibilities of immediately profitable use, and the trend of prices continued downward. On the panic and its aftermath, Harold U. Faulkner writes in Politics, Reform and Expansion, 1890-1900:

[On February 22, 1893] *the Philadelphia & Reading Railroad, with no warning, suddenly went bankrupt. The volume of sales on the day of its collapse was the greatest in the history of the New York Stock Exchange. The air was filled with anxiety. Then on May 5 the National Cordage Company failed in spectacular fashion shortly after having paid its regular dividend. The market collapsed abruptly. Banks called in their loans; the stream of credit dried to a trickle. Businesses failed daily. The Erie went down in July* [for the third time in its history], *the Northern Pacific in August, the Union Pacific in October, the Atchison in December. . . . The panic broadened into a major depression. In the following year railroad traffic for the second time in history suffered an absolute decline. Railroad construction fell off drastically, reaching its lowest point since 1851. By 1895, new mileage shrank to 1,800 as compared to 4,700 in 1892. By the end of June, 1894, more than 40,818 miles and one-fourth of the capitalization of American railroads were in the hands of receivers. Three-fifths of railroad stock paid no dividends.* [12]

Buffalo's passenger service in 1893 was as follows:

Railroad	Expresses	Locals	Total
NYC	(34)	(8)	(42)
LS&MS	(25)	(3)	(28)
MC	(14)	(8)	(22)
NYWS&B	(10)	(4)	(14)
C&NF	-	(4)	(4)
B&NF	(6)	(24)	(30)
B&L	-	(11)	(11)
Future NYC System	89	62	151
B&NYC	(6)	(10)	(16)
BC&NY	-	(4)	(4)
SB&EJ	-	(14)	(14)
B&J	-	(10)	(10)
L&B	-	(8)	(8)

Erie Railroad	6	46	52
BNY&P	-	(8)	(8)
BC&P	(4)	(6)	(10)
WNY&P	4	14	18
BR&P	-	6	6
DL&W	8	3	11
NKP	5	1	6
GT	-	4	4
LV	8	4	12
Grand Total	120	140	260

These 260 weekday passenger train movements at Buffalo's five railroad terminals in 1893 (Figure #9) were up a whopping ninety (52%) in only six years. In 1893 the nation's railroads, despite the onset of depression, carried a record 593,561,000 passengers, after which a sharp decline set in which lasted until 1901. (Figure #10.) It was in 1893 that Chicago hosted the immensely successful Colombian Exposition, the greatest international fair of its time, which drew an average daily attendance of 172,712 and a total attendance of over twenty-seven million. The NYC put on an *Exposition Flyer* and a *World's Fair Special*, and the NYWS&B a *World's Fair Special.* A major argument in securing the fair for Chicago was its position as the hub of

XI, 9

The following timetable illustrates the immense size Buffalo's passenger train service had attained by the last decade of the nineteenth century. Since several of the roads serving Buffalo had multiple lines into the city, these are identified by an earlier incarnation. New York Central: B&NF (Buffalo & Niagara Falls), NYC (mainline from Rochester), LS (Lake Shore & Michigan Southern), MC (Michigan Central), WS (New York West Shore & Buffalo), B&L (Buffalo & Lockport), RW&O (Rome Watertown & Ogdensburg), C&NF (Canandaigua & Niagara Falls), P&LE Pittsburgh & Lake Erie.) New York Lake Erie & Western: (SB&EJ) Suspension Bridge and Erie Junction, B&NY (Buffalo & New York City - Hornellsville to Buffalo), BC&NY (Buffalo Corning & New York, L&B (Lockport & Buffalo), B&J (Buffalo & Jamestown). Western New York & Philadelphia: BC&P (Buffalo Corry & Pittsburgh), BNY&P (Buffalo New York & Philadelphia). Grand Trunk: GW (Great Western), B&LH (Buffalo & Lake Huron.) Single line roads in 1893 were DL&W (Delaware Lackawanna & Western), BR&P (Buffalo Rochester & Pittsburgh), NKP (Nickel Plate), LV (Lehigh Valley.) CLR (Chatauqua Lake Railway.) NFSL (Niagara Falls Short Line) stands not for a railroad but a route, Grand Trunk from Suspension Bridge through Hamilton and London to Detroit and Wabash through Adrian to Chicago. C> is the Chicago & Grand Trunk which ran on the Grand Trunk from Suspension Bridge to Detroit and thence on the Chicago & Grand Trunk to Chicago. Lines connecting arrivals and departures indicate continuity through Buffalo. * means that this train does not stop at Buffalo.

1893

New York Central Station. Exchange & Washington Sts.

Westbound

AM	Arrivals: road # from	Departures: road # to	mon
12:10	NYC (15) Boston (B&A 15) 10:30a "Boston & Chicago Special"		36
12:15	WS (1) Weekauken 10:25a "Day Exp." Fitchburg 1 Boston 9:00a "Day Exp."		30 31
12:15*	NYC (41) NY 3:00p "Exposition Flyer"		48
		LS (41) Chicago 11:00a "Exposition Flyer"	48
12:20		LS (15) Chicago 3:30p "Buffalo & Chicago Special"	31
		B&NF (1) Susp. Bridge 1:10a [connects with RW&O 115 to Richland 10:40:a NFSL 51 to Chicago 7:15p C> #1 to Chicago 5:50p]	36
12:30		LS (3) Chicago 7:45p "Chicago Accommodation"	28
3:15	NYC (19) NY 4:30p B&A 19 Boston 2:00p xf "North Shore Ltd."		40 37
3:20	WS 15 Weehauken 3:55p "World's Fair Special"		37
		MC (19) Chicago 5:30p via Ft. Erie xf North Shore Ltd."	38
3:40		MC 17 Welland 4:35a	25
6:00		MC 11 Chicago 7:50a via Ft. Erie	39
6:05	WS (3) Weehauken 5:30p s "Niagara Falls Chicago & St. Louis Ltd." Fitchburg 3 Boston 3.00p "Fast Exp."		34 31
6:15	NYC (5) NY 6:00p "Fast St. Louis & Chicago Exp."		35
6:20		B&NF (3) Susp. Bridge 7:10a [connects with NFSL 53 to Chicago 11:15p C> 7 to Chicago 10:30p Wabash 7 to St. Louis 8:35a]	28
6:30	NYC (25) Boston (B&A 7) 4:20p "Chicago & Western Exp."		35
6:35		B&L 241 Lockport 7:30a	24
6:40		LS (5) Chicago 10:00p "Pacific Exp."	35
6:45		MC (5) Chicago 10:10p via Niagara Falls St. Louis (Wabash 53) 8:35a "Fast St. Louis & Chicago Exp."	36
		B&NF 5 Lewiston 7:55 [connects with RW&O 127 to Massena Springs 7:30p]	24
[6:50		NKP (5) Chicago 10:50p "Western Exp." from Erie Sta.]	32
6:55		LS 21 Cleveland 1:50p	26
7:00		MC 50 Niagara-on-the-Lake 8:30a b	22

Eastbound

AM	Arrivals: road # from	Departures: road # to	
1:40	LS (6) Chicago 11:30a Pittsburgh (P&LE) "Chicago & Boston Special"		41
1:50		NYC (16) NY 2:10p B&A 16 Boston 3:40p "Boston & Chicago Special"	42 42
2:15*	LS (10) Chicago 3:00p "Exposition Flyer"		48
		NYC (40) NY 11:15a "Exposition Flyer"	48
2:50	MC (20) Chicago noon via Ft. Erie "North Shore Ltd."		36
3:00		NYC (20) NY 2:40p B&A Boston 4:45p "North Shore Ltd."	37 36
4:05	LS (2) Chicago 8:10a		27
4:20	LS (3) Chicago 1:30p "World's Fair Special"		36
4:30	B&NF (20) Susp. Bridge 3:30a [connects with RW&O 124 from Massena Springs 11:20a and with NFSL 58 from Chicago 10:00a]		24
4:40		NYC (22) NY 3:45p World's Fair Special"	39
		NYC (2) NY 7:00p B&A 18 Boston 8:30p "Day Exp."	30 31
4:45		WS (10) Weehauken s 7:30p	29
6:00		NYC 102 NY 8:50p	29
[6:40		WS 86 Lyons 4:15p at East Buffalo Jnct.]	11
6:55	LS (18) St. Louis (CCC&StL 18) 9:05a Cincinnati 7:00p "Southwestern Ltd."		33 37
7:00		NYC (18) NY 6:00p B&A 18 Boston 8:30p "Southwestern Ltd."	39 36
7:20	LS (12) Chicago 4:10p Pittsburgh (P&LE) "Atlantic Exp."		35
7:25	MC (6) Chicago 4:10p via Niagara Falls "NY & Eastern Exp." [connects with RW&O 114 from Massena Springs 3:00p		36
[7:30	NKP (6) Chicago 3:30p at Erie Sta.]		30
7:45		NYC (6) NY 8:50p Boston 11:45p	33 30
8:10		BC&P Brocton 10:08a	25
8:20	B&NF (2) Susp. Bridge 7:15a [connects with NFSL 54 from Chicago 3:30p C> 4 from Chicago 4:00p]		28
	LS Westfield 5:20a		19
		WS (2) Weehauken s 8:33p Fitchburg 2 Boston 10:30p "Day Exp."	35 33
		BNY&P 102 Emporium 1:05p	25
8:25	B&NF 202 Lewiston 7:15a		24
	BR&P Springville 7:00a		22

Time	Train	Connection	No.
7:15	BC&P 3 Pittsburgh (AVR 3) 9:10p a		2
7:30	NYC 43 NY 7:30p "Buffalo & Niagara Falls Special"		43
7:45	NYC 7 NY 8:00p "St. Louis Exp."		37
		B&L 243 Lockport 8:45a	26
7:50		B&NF 201 Lewiston 10:10a	12
7:55	BNY&P 113 East Aurora 7:13a		24
		LS 7 St. Louis (CCC&StL 7) 8:45a Cincinnati (CCC&StL 7) 8:30p "St. Louis Exp."	30 35
8:35	BNY&P 105 Olean 5:55a		18
8:40		BR&P 9 Walston 6:10p "Pittsburgh Mail & Exp."	19
8:45	NYC 101 Rochester 6:15a		27
9:00		B&NF 203 Lewiston 10.20a b	21
9:25	BC&P Jamestown (CLR) 6:15a		27
9:35	NYC 11 NY 9:00p "Ltd. Fast Mail"		34
		LS 11 Cleveland 2:25a Pittsburgh (P&LE)	37
10:00		MC 31 Kalamazoo 10:50p via Ft. Erie	28
10:10	WS 92 Lyons 6:50a		31
10:15	NYC 103 Batavia 9:05a		31
10:25		B&NF 205 Susp. Bridge 11:20a	26
10:50	NYC 105 Lyons 7:10a		28
10:55		B&L 245 Lockport 11:55a	26
11:40		MC 52 Niagara-on-the-Lake 1:15p b	21
PM			
12:00		B&NF 207 Lewiston 1:00p [connects with RW&O 117 to Massena Springs noon]	29
12:15	NYC 9 NY 9:15p B&A 9 Boston 7:15p "Chicago Exp."		29 29
12:30	WS 5 Weehawken 8:40p		27
	Fitchburg 5 Boston 7:00p "Pacific Exp."		27
	BC&P Oil City 7:05a Jamestown (CLR) 9:00a		25 25
12:40		B&NF 5 Susp. Bridge 1:40p [connects with NFSL 55 to Chicago 8:15a C> 9 to Chicago 8:32a]	24
12:50		LS 9 Chicago 8:35a Wabash 9 to St. Louis 9:00p "Chicago Exp."	27
[1:05		NKP 1 Chicago 9:10a "Chicago Exp." from Erie Sta.]	26
	BNY&P 101 Emporium 8:35a		21
1:10		MC 9 Chicago 8:55a via Niagara Falls "Pacific Exp."	28
1:30		B&L 247 Lockport 2:30	26
2:20		B&NF 209 Lewiston 3:45p	23
3:00		BR&P Springville 4:22p	23
3:50		B&NF 211 Lewiston 5:15p [connects with RW&O 185 to Oswego 11:00p]	20

Time	Train	Connection	No.
8:40	LS 20 Chicago 6:30a "Buffalo Special"		39
	MC 4 Chicago 6:30p via Niagara Falls "NY & Chicago Ltd."		39
		BC&P 2 Pittsburgh (AVR) 6:35p Jamestown 11:45a	26 28
8:45	B&L 242 Lockport 7:50a		24
8:50		NYC 4 NY 7:30p "NY & Chicago Ltd."	41
9:00		NYC 104 NY 10:30p	33
9:40	B&L 26 Lewiston 7:55a		16
9:45		NYC 26 Boston (B&A 6) 11:[illegible] "Chicago & Western Exp."	34
9:50	B&L 161 Lockport 8:50a		26
10:25	BR&P Bradford 7:20a		30
10:50	B&NF 206 Lewiston 8:55a [connects with RW&O 182 from Oswego 5:30a]		15
11:00	MC 51 Niagara-on-the-Lake 9:20 b		20
11:50	B&FL 208 Lewiston 10:30a b		21
PM			
12:05		NYC 30 Albany midnight	21
12:25	B&NF Susp. Bridge 11:35a		36
12:45	LS 34 Erie 9:50a		30
12:50	MC 18 Chicago 9:40p via Niagara Falls "Niagara Falls & Buffalo Exp."		37
12:55	LS 26 Chicago 10:00p "Buffalo Exp."		36
1:15		NYC 50 NY 10:30p "Empire State Exp."	47
1:35	B&L 224 Lockport 12:35p		26
2:05	B&NF 212 Susp. Bridge 1:10		26
2:50		BC&P Oil City 8:40p	23
3:00	MC 53 Niagara-on-the-Lake 1:25p b		21
		NYC 110 Batavia 4:10p	31
3:05	B&NF 214 Lewiston 1:25p [connects with RW&O 104 from Watertown 6:05a]		17
3:15		WS 94 Lyons 6:40p	20
3:20	MC 8 Chicago 8:30p via Niagara Falls "Atlantic Exp."		29
3:30	LS 14 Chicago 8:[illegible]0p "NY & Boston Exp."		25
		BNY&P 104 Emporium 8:15p	25
3:50		NYC 8 NY 6:30a B&A 10 Boston 10:50a "Atlantic Exp."	29 26
4:25	B&NF 216 Lewiston 2:45p		19
5:00		NYC 112 Lyons 8:20p	30
5:23		BC&P Jamestown 8:35p	27
5:30	B&L 246 Lockport 4:30		26
		BNY&P 106 Olean 8:15	18
5:35	B&NF 6 Susp. Bridge 4:35p [connects with NFSL 55 from Chicago 11:30p C> 8 from Chicago 9:15a]		24
5:45	LS 26 Chicago 7:00p		23
	B&NF 215 Lewiston 3:55p		13

Time	Eastbound Arrival	Westbound Departure	
4:15	NYC (21) Albany 5:15a "Day Exp."		
4:25		B&NF (21) Lewiston 5:35p	24
4:30		MC 54 Niagara-on- the-Lake 6:00p	13
4:35		B&L 164 Lockport 5:35	26
[4:40	WS 85 Lyons 7:05a at E. Buffalo Jnct.]		11
5:00	NYC 109 Syracuse 10:30a		23
5:15		B&NF 51 Lewiston 6:35p	21
		BR&P Bradford 3:30p	28
5:30		LS 19 Chicago 9:30a "South Shore Exp."	33
5:40		B&L 249 Lockport 6:40p	26
6:00	BC&P 1 Pittsburgh 8:40a Jamestown (LCR) 3:00p		28 29
6:10	NYC 51 NY 8:30a "Empire State Exp."		45
6:30		B&NF 213 Lewiston 7:45p	23
6:35	BC&P Brocton 4:37p		25
6:50	BNY&P 103 Emporium 1:50p		24
7:00	WS (9) Weehawken 3:40a		27
7:05		B&NF (9) Susp. Bridge 8:05p	24
7:45p	NYC 111 Syracuse 2:30p		28
8:00	NYC (13) NY 9:10a B&A 13 Boston 5:00a "Fast Mail"		40 33
8:10		LS (13) Chicago 10:10a "Fast Mail"	38
8:38	NYC (1) NY 10:00a "NY & Chicago Ltd."		41
8:45		LS (1) Chicago 10:45a "Chicago Special" Pittsburgh (P&LE)	38
8:50		MC (1) Chicago 10:45a via Niagara Falls "NY & Chicago Ltd."	40
9:05		MC 17 Chicago 11:40a via Niagara Falls "Chicago Special"	38
9:10		B&NF 215 Susp. Bridge 10:05p	26
11:00	NYC (23) NY noon "World's Fair Special"		39
11:10		LS (23) Chicago 2:00p "World's Fair Special"	34
11:20	NYC (3) NY 10:30a B&A 3 Boston 8:30a "Day Exp."		34 33
11:30	NYC (17) NY 1:00p "Southwestern Ltd."		41
11:45		MC (3) Chicago 5:10p via Niagara Falls "Chicago Day Exp."	32
11:50		LS (17) St. Louis (CCC&StL 17) 8:30p Cincinnati (CCC&StL 17) 11:45a "Southwestern Ltd."	35 37
5:50	BP&P 6 Walston 5:30a "Buffalo Rochester Mail & Exp."		20
6:00	MC (10) Chicago 11:10a St. Louis (Wabash) 5:00p via Niagara Falls "NY & Boston Exp."		29 33
	[NKP (2) Chicago 10:30p at Erie Sta.		26]
6:15		WS (6) Weehawken 7:25a & Fitchburg 6 Boston 10:00a "Atlantic Exp."	35 27
6:20		NYC (10) NY 7:00a B&A 10 Boston 10:50a "St. Louis & Chicago Exp."	34 30
6:35		BNY&P 112 East Aurora 7:17p	24
6:45	LS 24 Chicago 9:00p		24
7:00		WS 16 Weehawken 7:30 "World's Fair Special"	22
7:10	B&NF 220 Lewiston 5:50p		21
7:30	MC 16 Chicago 8:05a via Ft. Erie		23
		NYC 46 NY 7:30a "Buffalo Special"	36
7:55	B&NF 222 Lewiston 6:35p		21
8:20	LS (16) Chicago 12:30a Cincinnati (CCC&StL 12) 8:30a St. Louis (CCC&StL 12) 8:45 "NY Exp."		27 36 30
8:30		NYC (12) NY 7:55a "Southwestern & Chicago Exp."	38
8:35	MC 55 Niagara-on- the Lake 6:00p b		13
8:45	B&L 248 Lockport 7:45p		26
9:00	B&NF (4) Susp. Bridge 8:00p [connects with C> 2 from Chicago 12:30a]		22
9:05	LS 2nd 20 Cleveland 4:00p		37
9:10	B&NF 224 Lewiston 7:55p		23
9:15		WS (4) Weehawken 9:55a Fitchburg 14 Boston 12:40p	33 31
		BC&P 4 Pittsburgh (AVR 4) 7:30a s	26
9:30		NYC 48 NY 10:20a	34
11:30	LS (4) Chicago 9:00a "NY Mail"		40
11:40		NYC (14) NY 10:35a "Fast Mail Ltd."	40

New York Central Station. Erie St. & the Erie Canal

	Eastbound Arrival	Westbound Departure	
AM			
7:30		GT 71 Stratford 11:55a St. Thomas 1:20a	30 20
PM			
1:20	GT 70 Stratford 8:55a St. Thomas 7:20a		15
4:30		GT 75 Stratford 9:20p St. Thomas 10:35a	24 20
8:40	GT 74 Stratford 4:15a St. Thomas 3:15p		25 22

XI, 10

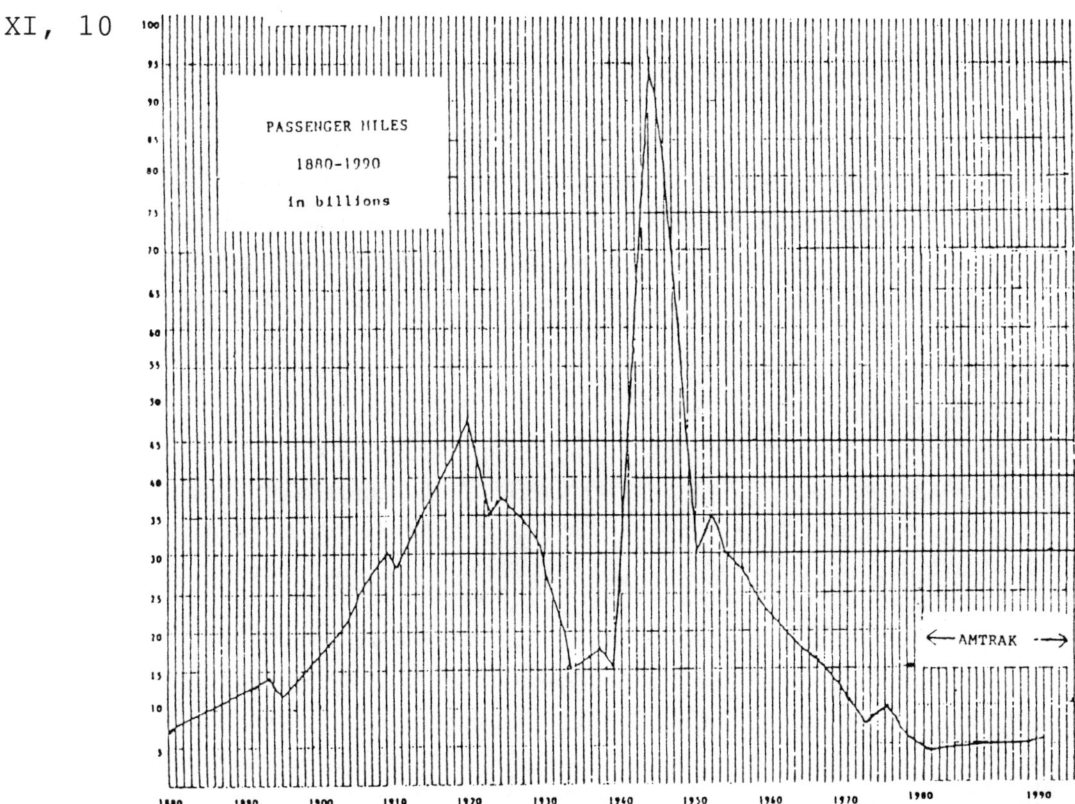

America's railroad system. On the local scene, the NKP and the NYWS&B, in anticipation of increased patronage, instituted joint New York-Chicago passenger trains on May 28, 1893. Since the NKP used the Erie Station, and the NYWS&B that of the NYC which was nearby, transfer of through cars was effected by building about 500 feet of track between the two stations.

One hundred and five of Buffalo's 260 train movements took place at the NYC's Exchange Street Station (or the road's East Buffalo Station). Four westbound through trains (through Buffalo, that is) were split at Buffalo with one section going to Chicago through Canada on the MC, and the other along the lake shore route. The same process was reversed for the two eastbounds between the same terminals.

Buffalo's local service provided by short and intermediate distance runs of the NYC consisted of four arrivals on the mainline: one from Syracuse (making forty stops on the 150 mile five hour and fifteen minute trip), one from Lyons (twenty-nine stops), one from Rochester, and one from Batavia. Eastbound locals consisted of a departure to Batavia and another to Lyons. The MC ran three trains each way over International Bridge to Niagara-on-the-Lake and a westbound to Welland. The LS&MS dispatched one train to Westfield and another to Erie. The NYWS&B ran two locals each way to Lyons; and that was it as far as trains of this category were concerned on almost all the main routes of the Vanderbilt lines. However, several of the slower expresses on these same routes made many stops at rural points in Erie County such as Forks, Looneyville (later Dellwood), Wende, Athol Springs, Lake View, Angola, Farnham, Bowmansville, Clarence, and Akron. The only exception was the B&NF, which functioned both as a local line between Buffalo and Niagara Falls and as the MC's extension from Suspension Bridge into Buffalo. In 1893 there were fifteen departures from Exchange Street daily to the Falls, and fifteen arrivals from there. Most of these trains made local stops at the Terrace, Black Rock, Tonawanda and La Salle. The exceptions were through trains on the MC and the NYWS&B, which all stopped at Niagara Falls. The result was frequent train service between the two metropolises of Western New York.

The 9:00 A. M. B&NF train to Lewiston connected there with a lake steamer which docked at Toronto at 1:30 P. M. Correspondingly, the 7:00 A. M. boat from Toronto was met by the 10:30 train from Lewiston, which arrived at Buffalo shortly before noon. (Figure #11.) Lockport, was no longer on a trunk line, but was serviced by five accommodations to and six from Buffalo daily on the NYC alone.

It is obvious, however, that through trains with a full consist of parlor, dining, and sleeping cars provided the lion's share of the NYC's Buffalo passenger business. There were six trains westbound from the Atlantic Coast to the Midwest via the LS&MS alone: #5, the *Boston & Chicago Special*; #41, the *Exposition Flyer*; #7, the *Saint Louis Express*; #13, the *Fast Mail*, #23; the *World's Fair Special*; and #17, the *Southwestern Limited.* To save time, the crack *Exposition Flyer* and its eastbound opposite did not come into the Exchange Street Station and did not take on or discharge passengers at Buffalo, using the Compromise Track to bypass downtown. They did, however, stop to change crews and take on a fresh locomotive. LS&MS trains carried through cars for Pittsburgh, Cincinnati, and Saint Louis. One train operated New York/Boston to Chicago only on the MC, #19, the *North Shore Limited.* Four trains divided at Buffalo into MC and LS&MS sections: #1, the *New York & Chicago Limited*; #3, the *Day Express*; #5, the *Fast Saint Louis & Chicago Express*; and #9, the *Chicago Express.* Terminating at Buffalo were #11, the *Limited Fast Mail*, and #51, the *Empire State Express.* Originating at Buffalo were MC #17, the *Chicago Special*, and LS&MS #19, the South

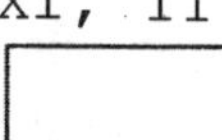
XI, 11

This photo from July 1925 captures the steamer Cayuga of the Canada Steamship Lines, which traveled between Lewiston and Toronto.

Shore Express.

Eastbound from the interior and traveling only on the LS&MS to New York/Boston were seven trains: #2, the *Boston Day Express*, #4, the *New York Mail*, #6, the *Chicago & Boston Special*, #8, the *World's Fair Special*, #12, the *Southwestern & Chicago Express*, #18, the *Southwestern Limited*, and #40, the *Exposition Flyer*. In the same direction but on the MC alone were #10, *New York & Boston Express*, and #20, *North Shore Limited.* Trains from both western roads combining at Buffalo for the run to the sea were #6, *New York & Eastern Express*, and #8, *Atlantic Express.* LS&MS trains terminating at Buffalo were: #20, the *Buffalo Special*, #26, the *Buffalo Express*, and #24 and 2nd #20 from Cleveland. MC trains of this type were #18, *Niagara Falls and Buffalo Express*, and #16. New York bound trains originating at Buffalo were #46, *Buffalo Special*, #50, *Empire State Express*, #102, and #104. Residents of Lockport were provided with a sleeping car to and from New York on the Falls Road.

Also operating out of the NYC's Exchange Street Station was the NYWS&B, with four daily arrivals from Weehawken, three of which continued on the B&NF to Suspension Bridge, where through cars were handed over to the GT and/or Wabash for Chicago and Saint Louis deliveries. These arrangements were reversed for eastbound trains. The arrangement with the Fitchburg for through trains to and from Boston by way of Rotterdam Junction was continued. A fourth New York-Buffalo trainset, oddly enough called the *World's Fair Special,* originated and terminated in Buffalo. Two of the NYWS&B's trains were handed over to the NKP at Buffalo to be taken to Chicago. It had taken the NKP ten years from its completion to initiate a Buffalo-Chicago passenger service of three westbound and two eastbound trains. After the Fair was over, the NKP reduced its passenger train offerings to two round trips between Buffalo and Chicago daily. A third eastbound operated between Cleveland and Buffalo. Wagner sleepers were assigned to the three westbounds, but only one carried a diner; the other two stopped for meals at company dining rooms at Conneaut, Cleveland, Bellevue, and Fort Wayne.

Three non-Vanderbilt lines were tenants of the NYC at Buffalo: the BR&P and the WNY&P at Exchange Street, and the GT at Erie Street. A southbound BR&P *Pittsburgh Day Express* ran from Buffalo to Walston, a hundred miles northeast of Pittsburgh. Its northbound companion was the *Buffalo & Rochester Mail and Express.* These day trains carried neither diners nor sleepers. Another brace of locals ran between Buffalo and Bradford. In addition, Springville was served by an early morning departure for and a mid-afternoon arrival from Buffalo.

Service on the WNY&P's two divisions consisted of eighteen trains every weekday. On the Pittsburgh Division there was a day train (with parlor-buffet cars) and a night train (with sleepers) each way between Buffalo and Pittsburgh, a train to and from Oil City, and a local to and from Brocton. Three of the trains that ran each way past Mayville picked up or deposited passengers from or to Jamestown on the Chautauqua Lake Railway at Mayville Junction. On the Buffalo Division, the former BNY&P, there were two round trips daily between Emporium and Buffalo. At Emporium sleepers could be boarded on the PRR for Philadelphia, Baltimore, and Washington, but there were no through sleepers from Buffalo. In addition, there was an early morning accommodation from and a late afternoon train to Olean, and a matched pair of East Aurora commuter trains. The BR&P and the WNY&P served the same overall area, but the passenger service of the latter was at this point more ample, since it consisted of older, more established routes.

Passenger train activity at the once busy Erie Street Station of the NYC was down to two trains each way over International Bridge on the GT's Loop Line. At Welland westbound trains divided, with one section going to Saint Thomas and the other to Stratford on the former Buffalo & Lake Huron. Eastbound trains merged at Welland.

The number of trains using Buffalo's Erie Railroad station in 1893 was up slightly from fifty in 1888 to fifty-eight. Management stuck with its traditional three daily expresses each way between Buffalo and Jersey City. As noted above, two of the NKP Chicago-Buffalo trains used the Erie Station, though their through cars between Buffalo and Weehawken had to be shuffled over to the NYC's station for connections with the NYWS&B. The DL&W ran four through trains each way between Buffalo and Hoboken, an indication that the Erie had not been sufficiently aggressive in exploiting passenger potential in their common area. The Erie's day trains and two of its night trains were called *Vestibuled Expresses.* Employing a slight variation, the DL&W christened a pair of its day trains *Vestibule Day Express.* Vestibules were enclosed platforms at both ends of a passenger car and were first successfully employed by American railroads in 1887. Together with "accordion-like appendages called diaphragms, at each end of the vestibules," White explains:

[They] *united the individual cars of the train into a single unit, just as the couplers and drawbars hold it together physically. Passengers and crewmen alike can pass from one end of the train to the other, safeguarded against falling under the wheels and fully protected from the elements and the train's own smoky trail... For a time the name "vestibule" was used to indicate an extra-deluxe train.* [13]

A new kid on the Buffalo railroad block in 1892 was the Lehigh Valley, which completed its line into the city in September, 1892. As part of a plan to establish control over the anthracite industry and to stabilize prices, Archibald A. McLeod, President of the Philadelphia & Reading, had leased the LV for 999 years on February 2, 1892. He then planned to expand his empire through control of the Boston & Maine. At this point, his backers, Anthony Drexel Biddle and J. Pierpont Morgan, regarding him as a megalomaniac, withdrew their support, and then the Panic of 1893 struck. In August, 1893, the LV repudiated the lease, alleging that the P&R had not lived up to the terms of the agreement. Nevertheless, for a few months in 1892-1893 the LV was operated as part of the Reading System. In May, 1893, it was announced that the Reading, in concert with the BR&P, would operate, with "Superb Train Equipment and Double Daily Service," two trains each way on a "New Route" between Buffalo and Rochester. The hookup was at "Reading Junction" near Mumford. The new departure did not long survive the lease. During the summer of '93, the LV, in addition to the daily double service to Rochester, operated four eastbound expresses to Jersey City-Philadelphia and four westbounds from there, with appropriate dining, parlor, and sleeping cars. In addition, there was one train each way between Buffalo and Sayre, where the LV had shops and extensive yards.

The LV attempted to make up in luxury what it lacked in speed. Despite its economic troubles during the hard times that followed its entry into Buffalo and the depression following the Panic of 1893, management introduced a glamorous new train in a bid for a share of the New York-Buffalo through passenger business. As Archer records:

The Black Diamond Express made its inaugural run on May 18, 1896, shamelessly touted as 'The Handsomest Train in the World.' It did its best to live up to management's extravagant laudation, its Pullman-manufactured consist a car-builder's gem. At the head end was a combination baggage and cafe car outfitted with a library and smoking room for gentlemen. This was an era in which discreet female travelers did not yet brave smoking in public. Kitchen and dining facilities were to the rear of the car, presided over by chefs whose "culinary artistry in preparing and serving substantials and delicacies in most appetizing fashion" was glowingly extolled by a zealous passenger department. The second and third cars were day coaches equipped with smoking rooms and finished with interiors of polished Mexican mahogany, accentuated by inlaid beveled French plate mirrors. The observation-parlor car was given a similar interior treatment. Bringing up the rear end of the early Black Diamond were observation parlors Lehigh, and Ganoga, and Seneca, complete with open observation platforms and suffocating velvet interior decor so favored in the late Victorian period. Motive power for the Black Diamond's glamorous consist was furnished by Baldwin in the form of five graceful Atlantics [4-4-2s], *capable of maintaining the train's tight schedule in spite of stiff mountain grades on the Wyoming Division. So reliable were the high-drivered camelbacks in their first year of service that the Black Diamond in 1897 was able to complete its run within five minutes of the advertised schedule 92% of the time - an impressive routine performance, considering the LV's jagged operating profile. . . . Operating on a daily except Sunday schedule, the Black Diamond made its daylight run between Jersey City and Buffalo in just under ten hours.* [(Figure #12.)]

New York City passengers made connections with the train at the Pennsylvania Railroad's Jersey City Terminal, necessitating a Hudson River ferry crossing from Manhattan boat slips at the foot of Cortlandt, Desbrosses, or West 23rd St. Philadelphia-Buffalo passengers were accommodated by a through coach connection via the Reading between Philadelphia's Reading Terminal and Bethlehem. From its inception the Diamond was so popular with Niagara Falls-bound newlyweds that it was nicknamed the Honeymoon Express. Although its running time was slightly longer than the NYC's Empire State Express, the Black Diamond offered the traveler al-ternate first class accommodations between New York and Buffalo, with an armchair view of the mountainous terrain of eastern Pennsylvania and the Finger Lakes. [14]

Besides numerical growth, increased speed at least on the NYC's through trains, was a characteristic of Buffalo's passenger train scene in the 1890s. The *Exposition Flyer* negotiated the 940 miles between New York and Chicago in twenty hours, an average of forty-eight miles an hour. The metropolitan areas of New York and Chicago were the largest population centers in the United States, and the railroads serving them, especially the NYC and the PRR with their superb roadbeds and trackage, vied for a share in that lucrative business. George H. Drury remarks in his Guide to North American Steam Locomotives that the NYC "carried perhaps two-thirds the number of passengers as the PRR but NYC's average passenger traveled one-third again as far as Pennsy's." It was during 1893 that the *Empire State Express*, the premier daylight train of the NYC, allegedly set a record of 112.5 miles an hour over a section of track between Batavia and Buffalo as a publicity stunt conceived by general passenger agent George H. Daniels. The engine at the point was #999, a 4-4-0 designed by William Buchanan, superintendent of motive power. (Figure #13.) James E. Kranefeld tells the story:

Daniels saw to it that nothing was spared in the execution of the engine's cosmetic appearance. The tall drivers gave her that leggy showgirl look. Her svelte boiler, including the smokebox, was sheathed in gray Russia iron. The cab was of maple and mahogany, but perhaps the most elegant flair was the name Empire State Express in silver-leaf script across the tender flanks. The engine exuded elan. . . .

The plan was to see how she behaved in ser-

XI, 12

"BLACK DIAMOND EXPRESS"

HANDSOMEST TRAIN IN THE WORLD

DAILY EXCEPT SUNDAY

BETWEEN

NEW YORK CITY AND BUFFALO

ON LIMITED TIME,

CONNECTING AT BETHLEHEM WITH TRAINS TO AND FROM

PHILADELPHIA

AS PER FOLLOWING SCHEDULE:

☞ Everything Strictly First-Class.
☞ Sumptuous Dining-Car Service, *á la carte.*
☞ Baggage Checked to and from residences and hotels.

No. 9 Westward		STATIONS.		No. 10 Eastward
		NEW YORK.		
11.55 am	Lv	Foot of West 23d Street	Ar.	10.15 pm
12.00 n'n	Lv	Foot of Cortlandt Street	Ar.	10.08 pm
12.00 n'n	Lv	Foot of Desbrosses Street	Ar.	10.08 pm
11.45 am	Lv	Brooklyn Annex (Fulton Street)	Ar.	10.20 pm
12.14 pm	Lv	Jersey City	Ar.	9.56 pm
e 12.28 pm	Lv	Newark (Market Street)	Ar.	9.43 pm
12.51 pm	Lv	South Plainfield	Ar.	9.20 pm
1.50 pm	Lv	Easton	Ar.	8.18 pm
2.06 pm	Ar	Bethlehem and South Bethlehem	Lv.	8.01 pm
12.30 pm	Lv	PHILADELPHIA, Reading Terminal	Ar.	9.26 pm
2.11 pm	Lv	Bethlehem and South Bethlehem	Ar.	7.56 pm
2.19 pm	Lv	Allentown	Ar.	7.48 pm
3.03 pm	Lv	Mauch Chunk	Ar.	7.09 pm
....	Lv	Glen Summit	Ar.	....
4.32 pm	Lv	Wilkes-Barre	Lv.	5.37 pm
5.11 pm	Lv	Tunkhannock	Lv.	4.49 pm
6.05 pm	Lv	Towanda	Lv.	3.58 pm
6.29 pm	Lv	Sayre	Lv.	3.38 pm
7.45 pm	Lv	Geneva	Lv.	2.09 pm
....	Ar	Clifton Springs	Lv.	1.54 pm
8.30 pm	Ar	Rochester Junction	Lv.	1.24 pm
9.00 pm.	Ar	Rochester	Lv.	12.35 pm
7.50 pm	Lv	Rochester	Ar.	1.47 pm
9.55 pm	Ar	BUFFALO	Lv.	12.10 pm

e Will stop only to take on passengers.

SPECIAL NOTICE.

Second-class or immigrant tickets. Theatrical or party tickets, Advertising mileage tickets, Sixty-trip monthly and forty-six-trip school tickets, Clerical tickets, Employes' tickets, Special tickets of all classes, Charity tickets, Tickets for corpse are not good on the "**Black Diamond Express.**"

BAGGAGE RESTRICTIONS.

The accommodations on these trains, for baggage, being limited, no baggage will be carried except that belonging to passengers on same train.

Station Baggage Masters will, so far as possible, send baggage either by train preceding or train following the Black Diamond Express.

No Bicycles, Theatrical or Commercial baggage will be carried except when accompanied by the passenger and provided the space in the car is sufficient to warrant acceptance.

No baggage will be carried on train No. 9 destined to Wilkes-Barre or points east.

XI, 13

vice and then when the time was right, top 100 mph and tell the world. The nearly level Western Division from Syracuse to Buffalo was chosen as the logical section of the road for 999 to stretch her legs. Central Vice President H. W. Webb, informed by Buchanan that the locomotive was ready, now called upon the ranking engineer on the division, Charles Hogan, offering him the chance to break the world's speed record. Hogan, one of the nation's most respected engine drivers, eagerly accepted as did his regular fireman, Al Elliott. All players were now cast in their respective roles with 999 taking center stage. Her date with history, fame - and controversy - was at hand.

In May of 1893, 999 was finally assigned to work the train for which she was built, the Empire State Express under the careful hand of Charlie Hogan, between Syracuse and Buffalo. On the 9th it was reported that Hogan had coaxed her up to 102.8 mph. Daniels now instructed all concerned that it was time to make their move. On the following day, May 10, Charlie Hogan would, as has oft been written, "take the bridle off" and ride his charge into history. The story of that day's memorable run, as related in many sources, is legendary - perhaps deliberately so. It has Hogan and Elliott waiting at Syracuse with 999 to make the engine change, the needle of her pressure gauge trembling at the 190 pound mark. The Empire State Express arrives conveniently a few minutes late. This means, of course, that 999 will have to make up time over the 150 mile stretch to Buffalo in order to bring the Empire in on the advertised. After coupling up to the train and testing the air, Hogan whistles off and the dash to Buffalo is on!

Hogan keeps the running routine past Rochester and to a few miles west of Batavia where the grade evens out and then descends for the final 30-some miles to Buffalo. On this stretch he coaxes his steed past the 100 mph mark and then bests the previous day's top of 102.5. With the throttle wide open and Elliott shoveling to beat the devil, 999 rolls the Empire at a faster and faster clip. Back aboard the train the mileposts are called out and the readings of several stop watches are recorded. [Locomotives did not have speedometers.] *When the data is compared and evaluated, everyone realizes that one of the miles west of Batavia was covered at the rate of 112.5 mph. Unfortunately, this scenario has always been looked upon as dubious for various reasons not the least of which was the fact that the engine was built and the run was conducted for publicity. Some students of motive power design have doubted whether the 999's cylinders could have taken and exhausted enough steam to top the 112 mph mark.* [15]

Staufer describes the sequel:

The star locomotive was rushed back to West Albany for cleaning, polishing, and general trimming-up. The woodwork on her cab (alternating maple and mahogany strips) shone like a mirror. She was then hurried to Chicago where she became the undisputed hit of the fair. This was her shining hour, brief but glorious. The locomotive and the railroad were household words for months thereafter. Toy makers jumped on the bandwagon and miniature 999s rolled over the floors of thousands of homes. Never before in the history of railroading had an event captured the public imagination as this had done. [Experience was to prove that she could run but she couldn't pull the heavier consists coming into vogue.] [16]

In 1888 the fastest train on the NYC from New York to Chicago had been #1, the westbound *Vestibule Limited,* which covered the distance in twenty-five hours and twenty minutes, thirty-eight miles an hour. Several other 1893 NYC trains hovered around the forty mile an hour average which had not been the case five years before. However, the Erie's fastest train between Buffalo and Jersey City, *Vestibuled Day Express*, averaged only thirty-five miles an hour and its slowest, *Pacific Express*, twenty-eight miles an hour. The best the DL&W could do was thirty-five miles an hour and the LV thirty-seven. The problem with these roads were stiff grades in Pennsylvania, absence of four tracks on their mainlines, and stops for on-line passengers, whereas the NYC boasted about its "Water Level Route. You can sleep." Moreover, its main was four-tracked from New York to Buffalo, and slower through trains could pick up on-line patrons. The Erie's mainline to Chicago was not completely double-tracked until the twentieth century. It also had a talent for avoiding major cities. Its New York-Chicago route was forty miles longer than the NYC's and ninety miles longer than the PRR's. However, it had no major grades except in Pennsylvania and, as a result, developed into a fast freight line. From the late '60s on, it never ran more than three passenger trains each way between New York and Chicago, and they took four to eight hours longer than those of the NYC and PRR.

The consist of a typical passenger train of the 1890s was four or five cars. (Figure #14.) If traffic was unusually heavy, trains were run in sections with two green flags on the engines of all but the last section, indicating that more was to follow. Specially scheduled trains showed white flags. Cars were still wooden with telltale underslung rods stabilizing the sides. Also, typically, the train was pulled by a 4-4-0, an *American.* The *American* was a general purpose locomotive. The only difference between *American* passenger and freight engines was that the drive wheels on the former were larger. The two engines involved in Andrew's Raid during the Civil War, the engines that brought Lincoln to Washington in 1861, the ones that brought his body back to Springfield in 1865, and those that met at Promontory for the driving of the golden spike on the first transcontinental in May, 1869, were all *Americans,* as was NYC #999 in 1893. For most of the second half of the nine-

XI, 14

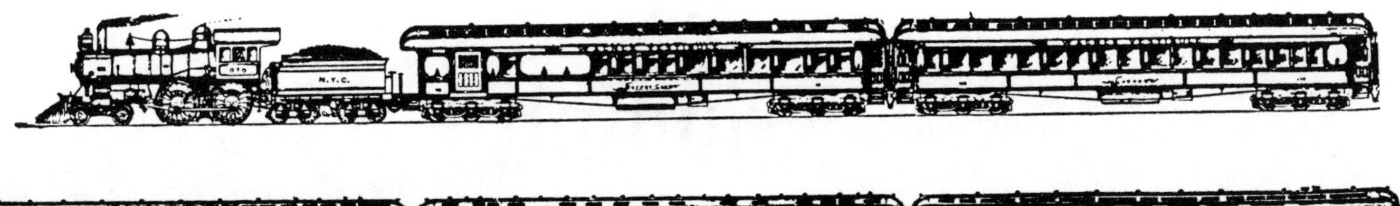

teenth century, the *American* dominated railroad operations in the United States, hence its name. Staufer writes:

However, the twilight of the eight-wheeler era was fast approaching, particularly at the heads of the limiteds. Clearly, heavier power was the order of the day and Buchanan's last contributions was a set of ten 4-6-0's designed for heavy passenger service. The turn of the century was to usher in a new breed of iron-horses. An era was at an end, and its seems almost right that William Buchanan [he retired in 1899] *and his Americans should fade fron the scene together.* [17]

The turn of the century was also "an ending and a beginning," for another Buffalo railroad, as its historian, Thomas Taber, put it:

The Delaware, Lackawanna & Western Railroad did not end when the nineteenth century closed, but a very imporant era had. Happily, it was succeeded by an even greater period of success. The corporate lifespan of the Delaware, Lackawanna & Western Railroad was from 1853 to 1960. Almost half was in the nineteenth and the balance in the twntieth century. It was during the nineteenth century that the railroad reached practically its full growth, insofar as extension of trackage was concerned. The regime of Samuel Sloan as President was one of conservative policies, aided by a phenomenal increase in the use of anthacite coal, which established the DL&W as a sound, financially sucessful railroad. When, in March 1899, at the grand old age of eighty-two, Samuel Sloan stepped down after thirty-two years as president, that action marked the end of a way of life on the DL&W Railroad. [18]

12
Triumph

La Belle Époque of American Railroading

The two decades before the First World War were the glory days of American railroads. Before the depression of the 1890s they had been overbuilt, underfinanced, and starved by rate wars which drove many poorer roads to bankruptcy. The depression, however, which began in 1893, changed all that, providing a shake out which brought strength out of weakness through financial reorganization and consolidation. Instrumental in this development was the formation after 1890 of communities of interest which introduced a stability the earlier pools had failed to achieve. The community of interest which particularly affected the railroad scene in Buffalo was that of the eastern trunk lines under the leadership of the PRR's President Alexander Cassatt (1899-1906) and the NYC. Managements of these lines reduced rate competition with each other to a minimum and, through stock acquisition, obtained control of the policies of the Baltimore & Ohio, the Erie, the Chesapeake & Ohio, the Norfolk & Western, and several anthracite roads including the DL&W. The result was fiscal stability, which made possible an extensive program of physical improvements which enabled the railroads to handle upcoming unprecedented demands for their services. Among these improvements were the construction of Penn Station and Grand Central in New York (and the concomitant tunneling of the Hudson and East Rivers and the electrification of the lines of both the PRR and the NYC into the city), the doubling and even quadrupling of hundreds of miles of mainline throughout the country, and the acquisition of all-steel passenger cars, bigger boxcars, and more powerful locomotives. It was in 1916 that the route mileage of American railroads reached its high point of 254,251 miles. (Figure V, #1.)

Spanish-American War: Going and Returning

In 1898 the United States fought a brief and immensely popular war with Spain, ostensibly to free Cuba. The explosion of the battleship Maine as she rode at anchor in Havana harbor on February 15, 1898, exacerbated already strained relations between the American and Spanish governments, especially when on March 28th a Naval Court of Inquiry determined (most likely erroneously) that the ship had been sunk by a submerged mine. On April 24th Congress declared that a state of war had begun between the United States and Spain on April 22nd.

There were three military units in Buffalo in 1898: the 65th and 74th Regiments, New York National Guard, and five companies of the 13th Regiment, United States Army. Headquarters of the 65th were still at the Arsenal on Broadway and those of the 74th at Elmwood Avenue and Virginia Street, site of the later Elmwood Music Hall. The 13th had come east from Indian Territory in 1894, and since 1897 its headquarters, regimental band, and five companies were located on the Front at Fort Porter. The band was an excellent one, and its open air recitals during the summer made the regiment highly popular in Buffalo. On April 19th, three days before the war began, the 13th entrained for Tampa Bay, Florida, which was to be the port of embarkation for the invasion of Cuba. About 10,000 well-wishers gathered in the rain at the Porter Avenue Station of the Belt Line to see the troops off on the first leg of their journey. All but thirteen of the 524 men at Fort Porter left for the war.

Unlike World War II when almost anyone could volunteer, during the Spanish-American war only the active militia or National Guard could sign up for service. President William McKinley's administration did not envision a big war. The War Department determined that the 65th should be mustered into federal service while the 74th was to remain in Buffalo as part of the Home Guard. At 4:15 P. M., May 1, 1898, the day Admiral George Dewey's Asiatic Squadron annihilated the Spanish fleet in Manila Bay, the 65th, over 700 strong, marched from the Arsenal down Broadway to Main to the Erie depot on Exchange Street where two trains were waiting to take the men to Jersey City. From there they would travel to Camp Black at Hempstead Plains, Long Island. An estimated 125,000 well-wishers packed the sidewalks along the line of march. American flags could be seen everywhere. The first train left at 5:15 and the second at 5:30 P. M. They were preceded by a special train carrying separate companies from Niagara Falls and North Tonawanda. On the way, these trains overtook other trains carrying companies from eleven other cities and towns in Western New York. Nine days later, three companies of the 65th which had been left behind followed their comrades to Camp Black. On May 20th, the 65th was moved from Camp Black to Camp Alger at Dunn-Lording, Fairfax County, Virginia, near Washington. This is as close to Cuba as the regiment ever got. There were 60,000 men at Alger by early June when an epidemic of typhoid fever broke out. The water was foul and sanitary facilities inadequate. By the beginning of August the hospitals were filled, and the ranks were depleted.

The 13th succeeded in getting to Cuba, where it participated in the Battle of San Juan Hill on July 1, 1898, the bloodiest battle of the war, in which the regiment had two officers and fourteen men killed and six officers and eighty men wounded. Subsequently there was much sickness in the 13th due to the heat and malaria. About eighty-four out of 334 were down with the fever. Some died in Cuba but most dribbled back during August to Fort Porter hoping for a cure from the cooling breezes that blow across Lake Erie in the summer. The main body of the regiment was sent aboard transports to Montauk Point at the eastern end of Long Island, where the men were quarantined in a hospital camp for several days.

For many men of the 65th their return to Buffalo was not as their departure had been. News of the lethal conditions at Camp Alger trickled into Buffalo from soldiers' letters. Members of the Woman's Volunteer Aid Society met in late August and wired Governor Frank Black, Secretary of War Russell Alger, and Buffalo Congressman De Alva Stanwood Alexander, asking that the

65th be sent home. The governor assured the ladies that the regiment would soon be back in Buffalo. They began preparations for outfitting a hospital train to go to Alger and collect the sick of the 65th. The ladies raised money and enlisted Doctor Roswell Park in equipping the train and assembling a staff of five doctors and five nurses. As Frank Mogavero writes in his account of military activity in Buffalo during the war:

On August 30, 1898, over one hundred sick men of the 65th returned to Buffalo from Camp Alger on a special hospital train. The train was met by physicians and nurses. Dr. Herman Mynter was in charge. The train consisted of six ordinary cars and one baggage car. Sixty or more ambulances and carriages were waiting at the depot. Dr. William Bissell, Major of the 74th Regiment, was in charge of removing the sick men from the train. The ambulance officers and corps from the 74th Regiment were on hand. Within fifty minutes every soldier was moved out of the train. Twenty nine of them were sent to the General Hospital, twelve to Sisters Hospital, six to Homeopathic Hospital, and the rest to other hospitals or to their homes. The sick men were pale and weak and the more serious cases were very worn and thin. [1] (Figure #1.)

On the train the sick were divided according to their illness. There were forty-seven cases of typhoid, fourteen were suspected of typhoid, eleven had malarial fever, two had simple fever, and one had measles. Of these men three died within three days, and fourteen others within two months. In contrast to the navy which was relatively speaking ready for action, the army was ill-prepared for the Spanish-American War. Its high command, training, and equipment were inadequate, and it lacked proper supply and medical services for waging a tropical campaign. Of the more than 274,000 officers and men who served in the army during the war, 5,462 died in the various theaters of operation and camps in the United States. Only 379 of these deaths were battle casualties, the remaining being attributed to disease and other causes.

"Home. Sixty-Fifth Gets a Deserved Welcome - City Aglow - One Ceaseless Roar - Soldiers Marched to the Arsenal Between Two Walls of Glad People - 1,102 Men in the Ranks - Every Street Along the Route Jammed with the Regiment's Grateful Admirers" was the way the *Express* headlined its account of the 75th Regiment's homecoming on Monday, September 5, 1898. The article which followed described the scene:

The crush was heaviest about the station. Entrance to the station shed was refused to all. Supt. Bradfield had cleared four tracks outside the shed on the south and had an engine waiting for the prompt transfer of the hospital cars. All buildings looking down on the scene of debarkation were crowded at the windows and on the roofs. Michigan Street bridge even to the ironwork overhead swarmed with people. It was noised that the hospital-train would be the first to arrive. Doctors and nurses bustled to and fro. Suddenly out beyond Michigan Street sounded a short sharp toot. A switch signal red as a bullock's blood dropped, and as if it were a race-horse a big iron steed sprang forward. In its wake swung eleven cars. They rocked and swayed as they crossed the switches and at every plunkety-plunk the crowd cheered.

It was the hospital-train. In the first car was Company B, one of the healthiest in the regiment. In the last cars were 33 sick men. Capt. Henry Mead was in charge of the train and almost before he alighted the rear cars were cut off, hauled back and sent into the shed where the sick were unloaded carefully, one by one, and carried out in the ambulances or carriages. It was a small repetition of last Tuesday's scene, wan, shriveled fellows, hollowed by disease and within easy haling distance of death. While they were being taken out, Company B disembarked outside, south of the train shed, and the middle cars with the offi-

XII, 1

cers horses were unloaded on a platform.

It was 9:45 [A.M.] *when the first section arrived. Eight minutes later came the second section racing in, the window of every one of the twelve coaches choked with one or two blue-shirted fellows wearing their old campaign hats and cheering lustily. As the train stopped, every head popped out of sight, then finding they could not tumble out of the cars pell-mell, every head popped out again like hundreds of Jacks-in-the box. Companies G, I, and F were aboard the train under Major Babcock with Company B. They made the first battalion. When the order came they scrambled out shouldering their knapsacks as they went. Col. Welch and Adjt. Nursey were in the last car of the train with the band under John Powell in the car ahead. Before the last of the men were out of the cars, the third section appeared. It was 10:00 A. M., but it waited four minutes out by Michigan Street for a clear track. It had the second battalion, Companies H, C, A, and D under Major Smith. Fifteen minutes later the last section arrived with Companies E, K, L, and M aboard under Lieut-Col. Chapin and Major Howland. . . . As the regiment moved up Main Street it was as if they were marching in the Cave of the Winds, with the roar of the Falls surging about, unable to do aught but beat against the walls.*

The 13th Regiment returned to by way of New York City and Niagara Falls, where one company was left off. The rest arrived on September 15, 1898, on a single train of two horse cars, two baggage cars, five coaches, and a sleeper. It was the only Buffalo regiment that had seen action, and most of its members were not Buffalonians. Of the 334 who had marched off to war in April only 177 returned for a victory parade in Buffalo. The train had left the West Shore's Weehawken station on 7:00 P. M. Wednesday but did not reach Buffalo until 2:55 Friday afternoon. As befitted a regiment of regulars, "there was no tumbling pell-mell upon the platform, no wild rush to get off, no frantic waving of arms. In single file they marched out of the cars on to the platform, falling in quickly and forming company front." Each coach bore a car length streamer. One read "Home Sweet Home," another "Long Live Buffalo," and a third "Put Me Off At Buffalo." Reminiscent of earlier arrivals, "three sick men, stooped, yellow as if jaundiced, with bulging eyes and hollow cheeks and gulping throats were assisted out to the ambulances." The line of march led west on Exchange Street from the station, up Main Street to North and west on North to Porter and the fort. A delirious crowd estimated at 300,000 roared, cheered, waved flags, wept, and tossed bouquets at the marching survivors. The next year the regiment left to engage in putting down what Americans called "the Philippine Insurrection."

Toronto Hamilton & Buffalo

The two decades before World War I witnessed the last big push in railroad construction. On the Niagara Frontier this produced the Toronto Hamilton & Buffalo (1895), the South Buffalo Railroad (1902), and the Buffalo & Susquehanna (1906). In addition, two detours to the southwest, the NYC's Buffalo Terminal Railway (1896) and the LV's Lehigh & Lake Erie (1907), were built. Meanwhile the two major railroads in the northeast, the PRR and the NYC strengthened their position, the former by acquiring entrances into Buffalo and Rochester, the latter by streamlining somewhat its corporate structure.

Ontario's Niagara Peninsula was destined for one more railroad before the close of the nineteenth century. The joint promoters of the Toronto Hamilton & Buffalo Railway were the Michigan Southern, the Canada Southern, the NYC, and the Canadian Pacific. The CP was making its first entrance into the peninsula. The Vanderbilt roads owned 72.9 percent of the TH&B's stock and the Canadian Pacific 27.1 percent. The original plan had been to build from a junction with the MC at Welland through Hamilton and on to Toronto, but when the Grand Trunk conceded running rights on the 38.7 miles between Hamilton and Toronto, the extension between these cities was shelved. A double-tracked thirty-eight mile line ascending the Escarpment at Stony Creek seven miles east of Hamilton was opened in 1895, and through Toronto-Buffalo service established the next year. (Figure #2.) At first, the Grand Trunk, the TH&B, and the MC provided their own locomotives on their own tracks, with engine changes at Welland and Hamilton, but this cumbersome method of interchanging was finally abandoned in 1912. Jackson and Burtniak write:

Through passenger service was heavy, with the bulk of the passengers riding from Toronto and Hamilton to New York, Boston, Cleveland, Pittsburgh, and Cincinnati during the summer. Within the peninsula the importance of the TH&B lay in the fact that it provided the shortest route on land from either Toronto or Hamilton to Buffalo. It introduced a new transverse route from northwest to southeast and provided railway access to an extensive area not previously served. [2]

A line from Smithville to Dunnville was completed in 1916 connecting Hamilton by rail with Lake Erie, and ferry service was established to Ashtabula, Ohio, to bring coal to Hamilton's steel mills.

The Pennsy Comes to Buffalo

A railroad from Philadelphia to Erie had been considered second in importance only to the mainline to Pittsburgh by the founding fathers of the PRR. The Philadelphia & Erie from Sunbury to Erie was subsequently constructed to achieve this purpose, with an assist from the Northern Central from Sunbury to Harrisburg; but it became clear that Erie, like Dunkirk, would never supersede Buffalo as the Great Lakes port. The Buffalo New York & Philadelphia succeeded in reaching Buffalo

XII, 2

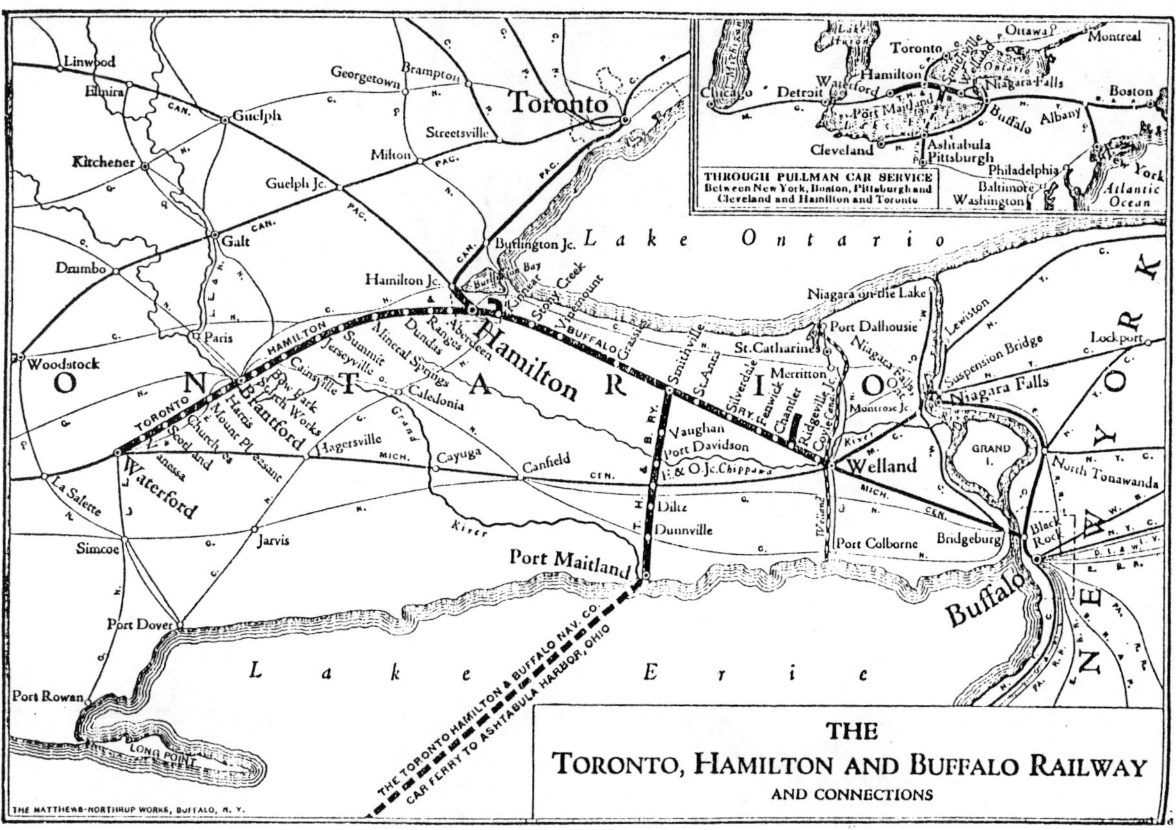

from Emporium on the Philadelphia and Erie in 1872. (Figure VII, #1.) The BNY&P, which was reorganized as the Western New York & Pennsylvania in 1887, had by then acquired a line from Buffalo to Pittsburgh via Brocton made up of the ex-Buffalo Corry & Pittsburgh [later the Buffalo Pittsburgh & Western], the Oil City & Allegheny River, and the Allegheny Valley. A line to Rochester, the ex-Genesee Valley Railroad, which had been built in 1882 along the towpath of the abandoned Genesee Valley Canal, joined the Buffalo line at Hinsdale, just north of Olean, which had been the southern terminus of the Genesee Canal. In 1883 a line from Warren, Pennsylvania, on the Philadelphia & Erie, near Oil City, was completed to the terminus of the Genesee Valley Railroad at Olean. The Rochester line and that from Warren to Olean were also acquired by the WNY&P. By means of the latter two lines and the Oil Creek & Allegheny River, plus a short stretch on the P&E, a route was opened between Pittsburgh, Oil City, and Rochester, with an alternative route between Oil City and Buffalo via Emporium. (Figure #3.)

It was during Cassatt's presidency that the PRR expanded its presence in the eastern Great Lakes by purchasing the WNY&P, which since its reorganization in 1895 up to 1899 had earned barely enough to pay interest on its fixed interest bonds, much less its income bonds or dividends. The prosperity of the oil regions which the lines were built to service had long passed. Some of the security holders of the WNY&P must have balked at the take-over since in February, 1900, the PRR made plans to build its own line from Kane, Pennsylvania, on the Philadelphia & Erie to Buffalo. This brought the reluctant around, and on August 1, 1900, as Burgess and Kennedy write:

The two companies entered into an agreement whereby the PRR was to operate the Western Company at cost (operating expenses, equipment, rents, and taxes); any surplus to be

available for bond interest and dividends. Under this arrangement the WNY&P failed to earn its fixed interest charges in every year prior to 1926, despite the additional millions which were supplied to improve its lines and facilities. On the other hand, the results of its acquisition were quickly apparent in the improved earnings of the Allegheny Valley and the Philadelphia & Erie, which had previously struggled to make ends meet, so that the results were not all negative by any means. The main trouble was that there were so many miles in the total that were not susceptible of any material improvement in traffic. A part of the deficits in the earlier years was the result of a major rehabilitation program made necessary by the run-down condition of the property and the demands of the heavier traffic which resulted from PRR operation. . . Major expenditures incurred shortly after acquisition were for new docks and supporting facilities at Buffalo [the 33 acre Burrows Lot on the Hamburg Turnpike and along Buffalo Creek]*; and a new classification yard at Olean. These together cost about $2.1 million.* [3]

A comparison of the NYC and PRR systems indicates that they were natural candidates for membership in a community of interest. (Figure #4.) While in the Midwest their lines paralleled each other extensively, the NYC's mainline through New York State and the PRR's through Pennsylvania were separated by well over a hundred miles. As far as local passenger service was concerned, they did not compete at all. The NYC's presence in Pennsylvania was on a par with the PRR's in upstate New York. As writers on the subject would later assert:

In operating style, in marketing philosophy, in personnel, they differed sharply. The PRR, stolid, steady, and traditional, carried ore over mountains. It was "volume oriented," and its operations were highly decentralized. . . The NYC carried manufactured goods along its "water level route." It was profit oriented and centralized. [4]

Acquisition of the WNY&P did not threaten any major New York Central interest there.

The South Buffalo Railway

At Slocum Hollow in the anthracite fields of northeastern Pennsylvania, where Roaring Brook flows into the Lackawanna River, the Scranton brothers, George and Selden, began an iron mill which by 1847 was turning out durable rails for the New York & Erie, then being built through New York's Southern Tier. With the profits from this venture, the firm was reorganized as the Lackawanna Iron & Coal Company. The Lackawanna River rises in northeastern Pennsylvania and flows southwesterly for fifty miles to join the Susquehanna near Pittston. It traverses the chief anthracite regions of the state, passing through the cities of Scranton, Dunmore, Dickson City and Carbondale. Lackawanna is an Indian name meaning "fork in the river."

Slocum Hollow became first Scrantiona and then simply Scranton. The location was a natural for smelting because it was during the 1840s that anthracite supplanted wood in iron making. In 1875 the company installed a Bessemer furnace to produce steel rails with which railroads were rapidly replacing their iron tracks. However in the seventies and eighties coke made from soft coal was being used in place of anthracite for smelting, and in the nineties huge deposits of iron ore, including the fabulous Mesabi Range, were being exploited to the west of Lake Superior.

The stage was set for the move to Buffalo. Horton suggests that the transmission of electric power from the Falls to Buffalo which was first effected in 1896 made the city more attractive than ever to manufacturers, especially iron and steel makers; but Dunn in his history of Erie County concludes:

Ultimately the steel industry benefited as electric furnaces were introduced, but there is not necessarily any immediate and pressing

XII, 4

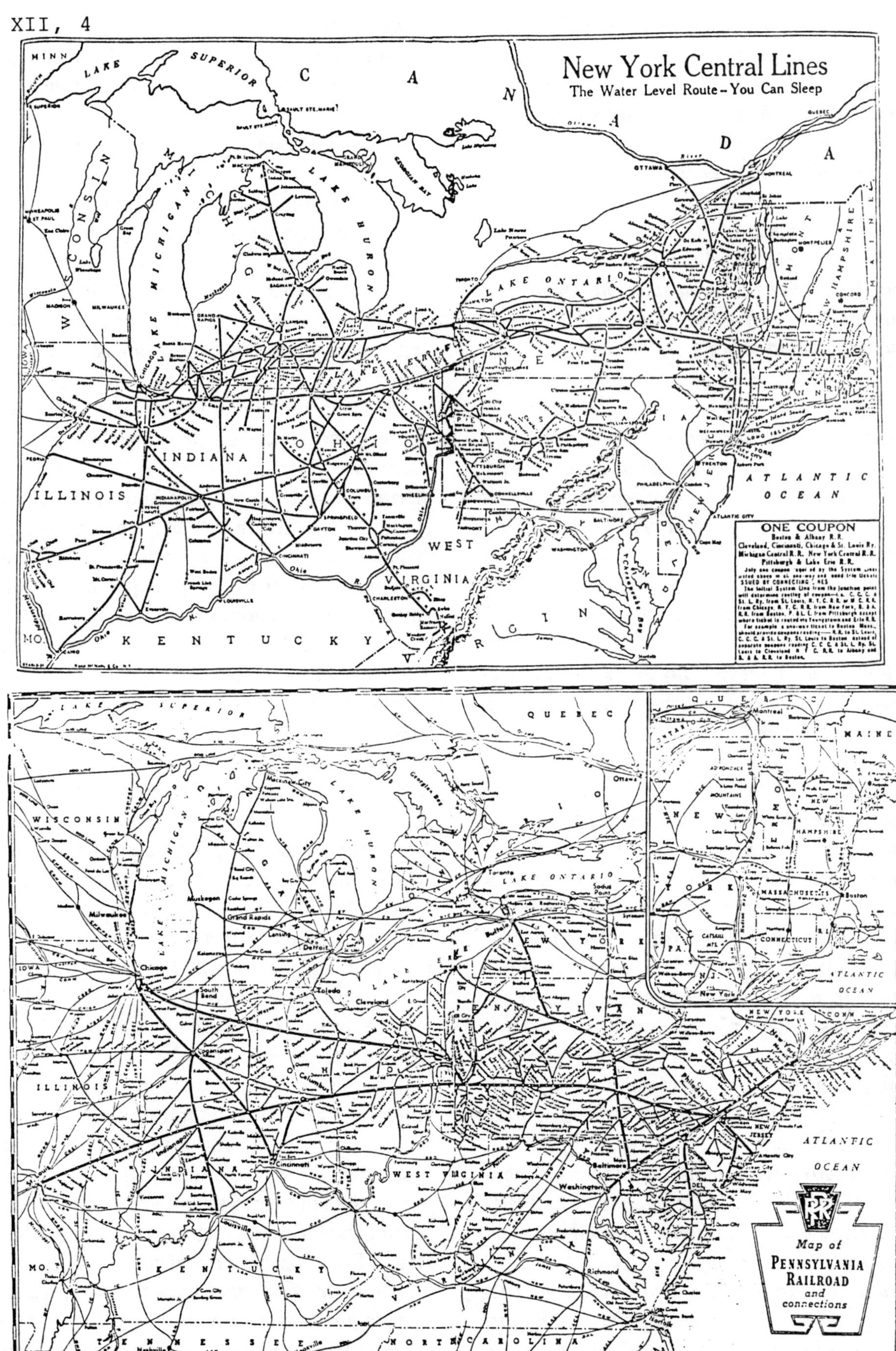
New York Central Lines
The Water Level Route - You Can Sleep
ONE COUPON
ATLANTIC OCEAN
INDIANA
ILLINOIS
OHIO
KENTUCKY
WEST VIRGINIA
WISCONSIN
LAKE MICHIGAN
LAKE HURON
LAKE ONTARIO
LAKE SUPERIOR
CANADA
Map of
PENNSYLVANIA
RAILROAD
and
connections

connection with the new steel plant that put Buffalo into the big leagues. This was the DL&W Steel Company developed by a number of Buffalo men. Among them were Franklin D. Locke, John G. Milburn, J.J. Albright, Edmund Hayes, and Sullivan A. Rogers. They had persuaded Walter Scranton that his family's already ancient (1840) DL&W Iron & Coal Company (since 1891 DL&W Iron & Steel Company) should be placed more advantageously. Since the Scranton family were already looking for such a spot, they were amenable. The decision to move was made in 1899 and in 1903 steel was being poured in buildings on the new site, a thousand acres along three miles of lakefront just south of Buffalo. (Figure #5.) [5]

Historians of the Lackawanna steel plant write:

In the spring of 1899, a group of prominent Western New York businessmen met at the exclusive Buffalo Club on Delaware Avenue. The purpose of the meeting was to complete plans for enticing DL&W Iron & Steel Company to the shores of Lake Erie by meeting the Scranton, Pennsylvania, company's request for capital, land, and dockage facilities. Local capital raised in that historic meeting was substantial - $2.5 million out of $15 million total - involving subscriptions from several prominent area capitalists led by John J. Albright. Albright had already acquired rights to 1,500 acres south of the city under the nominal ownership of the newly incorporated Stony Point Land Company; by December, 1899, he would buy still more from the city of Buffalo, then resell it to the land company at a profit of $644,154 to himself. Stony Point Land was a designated agent for DL&W Iron & Steel. [6]

The argument these local businessmen had used on the Scrantons was that it made more sense to ship ore on steamers from the Upper Lakes to the shores of Lake Erie where it would meet the soft coal being brought up from western Pennsylvania on the railroads, especially the BR&P, than to ship ore to a lake port and then send it by train to northeastern Pennsylvania, which was not a soft coal area anyway. These investors held a considerable block of company stock in the early years, with 16.7 percent or $5 million out of $30 million worth of shares and two out of twenty three directorships. "But after 1910," as Leary and Sholes tell the story, "when the directors expanded the number of shares that sold below par to generate new capita, Buffalo investors - among the first in the company - were left with overpriced low-income stock. Consequently, local investment fell sharply, as faith in the company declined."

The area occupied by the steel plant was situated in District #3 of the Township of West Seneca which was known as Limestone Hill. Resentment by inhabitants of the district, whose population had swelled to 15,000, over inequities in taxation and spending, led to the incorporation of the district into a city on May 29, 1909. The presence of the plant had attracted hordes of immigrants whose lot is patronizingly described by Horton:

In Lackawanna Serbs, Croats, Slovenes and Hungarians dwelt in long dismal rows of squat tenements owned by the Company. The streets between them were dirty. The air was dirty that came in at their windows. The belching chimneys of the steel plant gave to the whole place a look of dinginess and grime that was relieved in but two places. One was the interior of the plant itself, where clangor and flame and lightning created a magnificent Inferno. The other was the church nave with an altar gleaming at the far end and inspiring hopes of rest, peace, and Heaven at the last. [7]

Horton fails to mention the saloon which along with the church constituted the two focal points of the ethnic neighborhood. Actually, company housing could accommodate only a third of the plant work force. Those who could

XII, 5

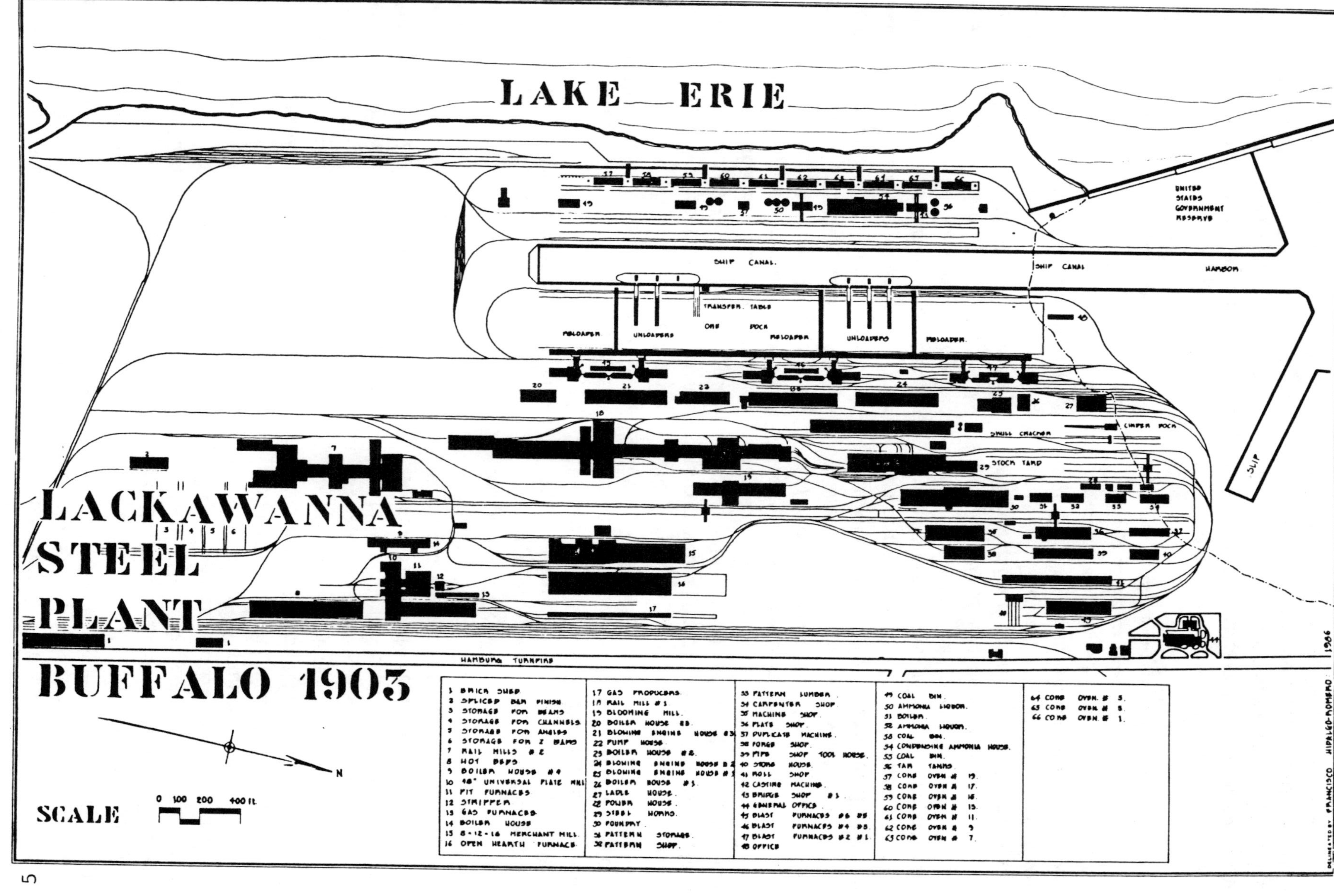
LAKE ERIE
UNITED STATES GOVERNMENT RESERVE
SHIP CANAL
HARBOR
TRANSFER TABLE
ORE DOCK
RELOADER
UNLOADERS
SKULL CRACKER
CINDER DOCK
STOCK YARD
SLIP
HAMBURG TURNPIKE
LACKAWANNA
STEEL
PLANT
BUFFALO 1903
N
SCALE
0 100 200 400 ft.
1 BRICK SHOP
2 SPLICE BAR FINISH
3 STORAGE FOR BEAMS
4 STORAGE FOR CHANNELS
5 STORAGE FOR ANGLES
6 STORAGE FOR Z BARS
7 RAIL MILLS # 2
8 HOT BEDS
9 BOILER HOUSE # 4
10 48" UNIVERSAL PLATE MILL
11 PIT FURNACES
12 STRIPPER
13 GAS FURNACES
14 BOILER HOUSE
15 8-12-16 MERCHANT MILL
16 OPEN HEARTH FURNACE
17 GAS PRODUCERS
18 RAIL MILL # 1
19 BLOOMING MILL
20 BOILER HOUSE # 3
21 BLOWING ENGINE HOUSE # 3
22 PUMP HOUSE
23 BOILER HOUSE # 2
24 BLOWING ENGINE HOUSE # 2
25 BLOWING ENGINE HOUSE # 1
26 BOILER HOUSE # 1
27 LADLE HOUSE
28 POWER HOUSE
29 STEEL WORKS
30 FOUNDRY
31 PATTERN STORAGE
32 PATTERN SHOP
33 PATTERN LUMBER
34 CARPENTER SHOP
35 MACHINE SHOP
36 PLATE SHOP
37 DUPLICATE MACHINE
38 FORGE SHOP
39 PIPE SHOP TOOL HOUSE
40 STORE HOUSE
41 ROLL SHOP
42 CASTING MACHINE
43 BRIDGE SHOP # 1
44 GENERAL OFFICE
45 BLAST FURNACES # 6 # 5
46 BLAST FURNACES # 4 # 3
47 BLAST FURNACES # 2 # 1
48 OFFICE
49 COAL BIN
50 AMMONIA LIQUOR
51 BOILER
52 AMMONIA HOUSE
53 COAL BIN
54 CONDENSING AMMONIA HOUSE
55 COAL BIN
56 TAR TANKS
57 COKE OVEN # 19
58 COKE OVEN # 17
59 COKE OVEN # 16
60 COKE OVEN # 13
61 COKE OVEN # 11
62 COKE OVEN # 9
63 COKE OVEN # 7
64 COKE OVEN # 5
65 COKE OVEN # 3
66 COKE OVEN # 1
DELINEATED BY FRANCISCO HIDALGO-ROMERO 1986

afford to do so lived in Buffalo and traveled to work on streetcars. But even for them, life was harsh. As Leary and Sholes note:

Most plants, including Lackawanna at the outset, operated their open hearths round the clock with only two turns. Continuous operation meant 10-14 hours of work seven days a week; a man changing shifts had to work 24 hours straight every two weeks - the infamous "long turn." [8]

From its beginnings, Lackawanna Steel aimed at backward and forward vertical integration, i.e., expanding control over raw materials like fuel and ores and over shipping and sales. Into these categories falls the South Buffalo Railway which, as Leary and Sholes put it, "transported materials into, around, and from the mills, tying the steel plant in Buffalo to other rail lines which could ship goods to the markets of the east and midwest." (Figure #6.) The road, incorporated in 1899 and completed in 1902, extended from the plant north to Buffalo Creek intersecting the New York Central, the Buffalo & Susquehanna, the PRR, NKP, and the BR&P as they swept north alongside each other on their way to Buffalo from the southwest, the south and the south east. (Figure #7.) At Buffalo Creek, moreover, the SB connected with the Buffalo Creek Railroad and the DL&W. The SB was also an industrial line like the BC and serviced other manufacturers along its route. Until 1915 it even conducted commuter service from the DL&W Station in Buffalo to the steel plant. (For a picture of the SB's Blasdell roundhouse in 1911, see Figure #8.)

The Buffalo & Susquehanna [9]

The virgin hemlock forests of north central Pennsylvania in McKean and Potter Counties had been visited by lumber men earlier, but it was not until the 1880s that large scale lumbering began there. Adequate transportation to markets was lacking, and the forests that lay beyond streams were virtually unreachable. Onto the scene in 1885 burst Frank H. Goodyear, who during the next quarter century built an empire of sawmills, coal mines, coalfields and timber stands in Pennsylvania, a steel plant in Buffalo, lake steamers to supply the plant with ore, and the short-lived Buffalo & Susquehanna Railroad. The empire did not survive Goodyear's death in 1907.

Goodyear was born in Groton, Tomkpkins County, New York, in 1849. He came to Buffalo in 1872, where, with the backing of Elbridge G. Spaulding, he purchased timber lands and erected sawmills around Port Allegany on the Buffalo New York & Philadelphia about twenty-five miles north of Emporium. In 1800 he purchased 1,900 acres of virgin timberlands near Keating Summit, also on the BNY&P, to the south of his existing holdings. By 1884 his operations moved into high gear as he purchased vast tracts of hemlock along Freeman Run and Sinnemahoning Creek east of Keating Summit. (Figure #9.) To get logs from forests along these streams to a sawmill at Keating Summit, Goodyear built his first railroad, the Sinnemahoning Valley.

The SV ran east from Keating Summit to a switchback (a zigzag set of tracks used to get trains up and down steep grades) and from there south down the north branch of Freeman Run to Austin. It was completed and opened as a common carrier on December 14, 1885. Logs were brought to Keating Summit for processing until sawmills were built at Austin. The next year the railroad was extended south to a hamlet called Costello, where a tannery was already in operation, a new customer for Goodyear since hemlock bark is necessary for curing leather. In 1887 Frank Goodyear was joined in the lumber business by his brother, Charles W., a former law partner of Grover Cleveland. Temporary railroads known as trams were extended from the mainline of the SV up nearly every creek and valley. As fast as the wood supply was exhausted in one sec-

XII, 6

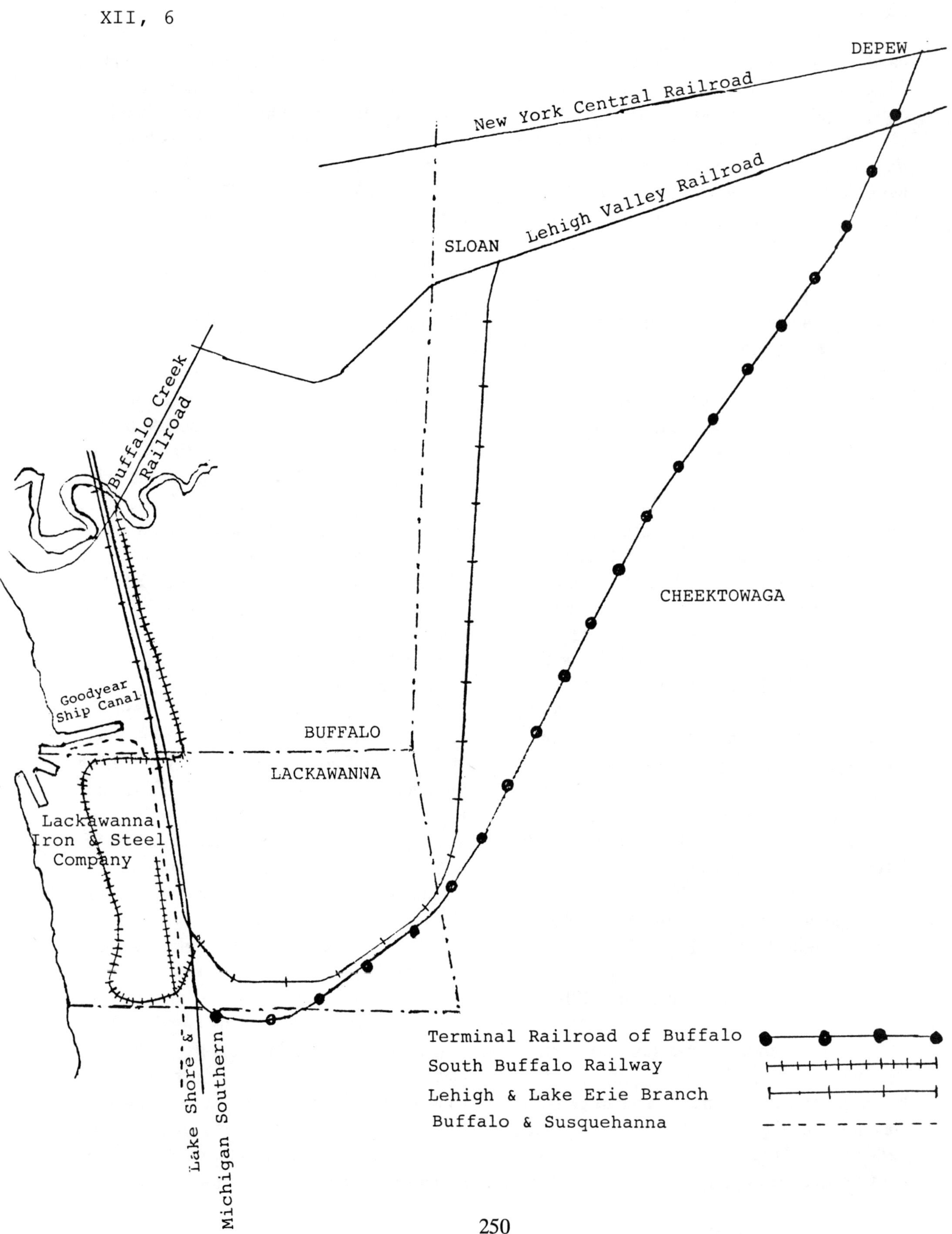
DEPEW
New York Central Railroad
Lehigh Valley Railroad
SLOAN
Buffalo Creek Railroad
CHEEKTOWAGA
Goodyear Ship Canal
BUFFALO
LACKAWANNA
Lackawanna Iron & Steel Company
Lake Shore & Michigan Southern
Terminal Railroad of Buffalo
South Buffalo Railway
Lehigh & Lake Erie Branch
Buffalo & Susquehanna

XII, 7

Joseph Bros. Co.
Buffalo Brake & Beam Co.
Round House
WARD
B ST.
PENNSYLVANIA
LEHIGH VALLEY
HUDSON RIVER R.R.
NEW YORK CENTRAL & HUDSON RIVER R.R.
PENNSYLVANIA R.R.
BUFFALO & SUSQUEHANNA R.R.
SOUTH BUFFALO
Shenandoah Steel Wire Co.
Stony Point Land Co
12.63a.
Rail Road Co.
9.26a.
C. V. Franks
15a.
Franks
ERIE
NEW YORK CHICAGO & ST. LOUIS
12in

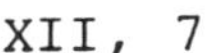

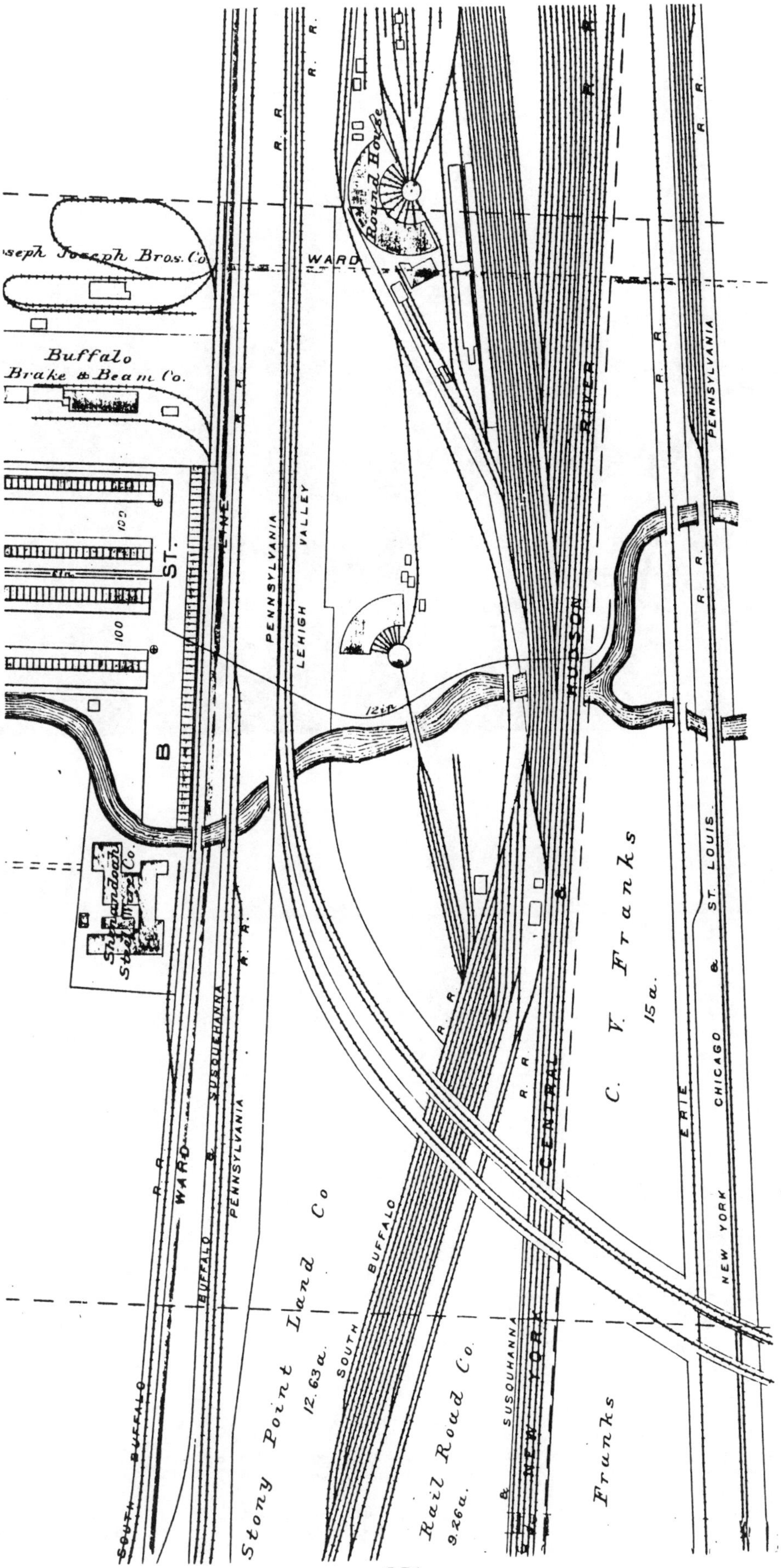

XII, 8

XII, 9

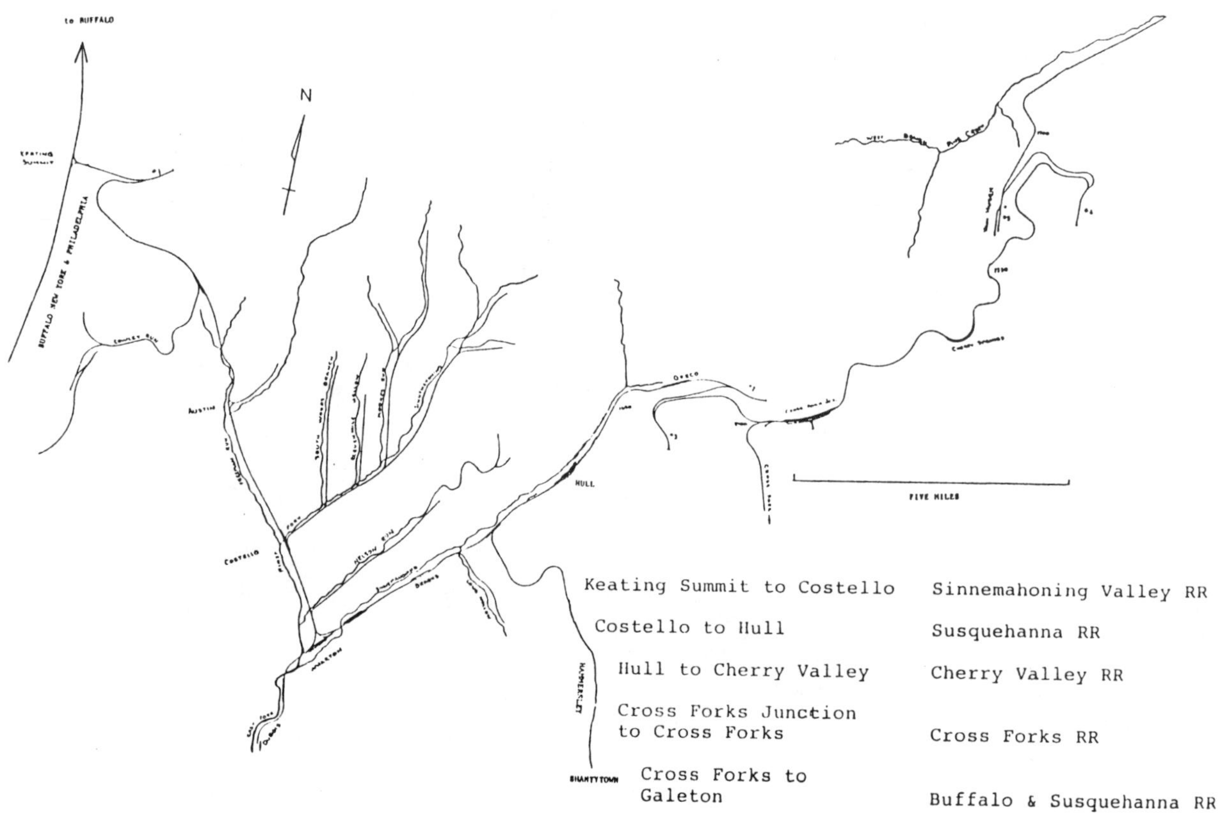
N
Keating Summit to Costello
Sinnemahoning Valley RR
Costello to Hull
Susquehanna RR
Hull to Cherry Valley
Cherry Valley RR
Cross Forks Junction to Cross Forks
Cross Forks RR
Cross Forks to Galeton
Buffalo & Susquehanna RR

tion, the tram was relocated in the next to the south and east.

A further extension brought the mainline south to Wharton on the East Fork of the Sinnemahoning River and from there east to Hull in 1892. This line was called the Susquehanna Railroad, since the Sinnemahoning flows into the West Branch of the Susquehanna River. Two trams branched off from this line; the first was the Long Hollow, and the second the Hammersley, which logged the last section of timber destined for the Austin mills. After the railroad to Hull had been completed another road called the Cherry Springs Railroad was chartered to build from Hull to Cherry Springs. The major obstacle it had to overcome was the Hogback, a mountainous barrier to the east of Hull. Rejecting a tunnel on the advice of an engineer as too expensive, the Goodyears opted for another switchback. Approaching the west or Greco side of the Hogback, the tracks ascended a 2.5 percent grade through two switchbacks and reached the top of the Hogback where a 130 car wye was located. The place was known thereafter as Cross Fork Junction, since a thirteen-mile branch to Cross Fork left the mainline there. From Cherry Springs yet another railroad, the (first) Buffalo & Susquehanna, continued eastward down two more switchbacks on the Van Heusen side to Galeton near which the Goodyears had bought up timberland along Pine Creek.

On September 7, 1893, these five companies, the Sinnemahoning Valley, the Susquehanna, the Cherry Springs, the Cross Fork, and the Buffalo & Susquehanna, were merged into the (second) Buffalo & Susquehanna. It ran from Keating Summit to Galeton with a branch to Cross Forks, sixty-two miles in all not counting the trams. On this new road the closest station to Buffalo, Keating Summit, was 107 miles away.

Meanwhile to the northeast of Galeton but contemporaneously with the growth of the Goodyear lines, the Addison & Northern Pennsylvania, a three-foot railroad, was being constructed between Addison on the mainline of the Erie eleven miles west of Corning and Galeton, the eastern terminus of the Buffalo & Susquehanna. In the summer of 1882 the Addison & Northern Pennsylvania was incorporated in both New York and Pennsylvania to build a line from Addison to Gaines. (Figure #9.) The ultimate objective of its incorporators was to link up with a large network of three-foot lines in southwestern New York and north central Pennsylvania centering around Bradford, Pennsylvania. Narrow gauge lines had the initial advantage of being cheaper to build. By November of 1882 trains were running between Addison and Westfield, by the summer of 1883 they were running as far as Gaines, and by spring of 1884 the line had been completed to Galeton. The road went bankrupt in 1886 and remained that way for a year when it emerged from reorganization as the Addison & Pennsylvania. An 1889 timetable shows two passenger trains each way daily between Addison and Galeton and one between Addison and Westfield. Unable to compete with or to exchange traffic conveniently with standard gauge lines, the A&P entered bankruptcy a second time in 1892 from which it emerged as a second Addison & Pennsylvania. The born-again company converted to standard gauge, but suffered a serious blow when the Goodyears bought the Clinton sawmill in Galeton which had been the A&P's major customer.

Still very much on the move, the Goodyears opened a Galeton to Wellsville line in 1895 which gave their road two further connections with major railroads: with the Western New York & Pennsylvania at Keating Summit, and with the Erie at Wellsville and Addison. The B&S then arranged the construction of a short line from Galeton to Ansonia on the NYC. Thereafter, shops and the headquarters of the road were moved from Austin to the now more centrally located Galeton. At one point upwards of two hundred men were employed there. In 1898 the B&S leased the component

XII, 10

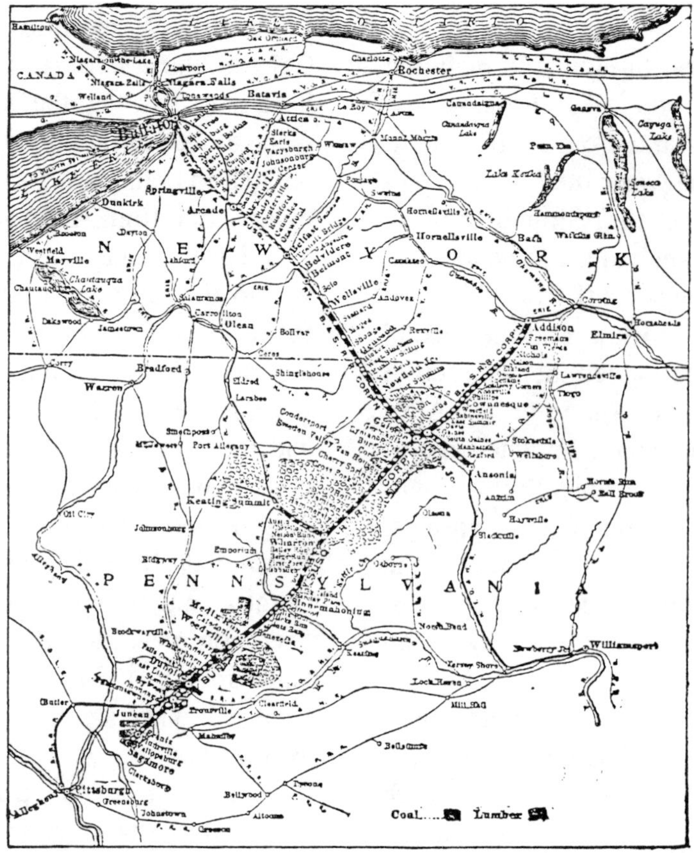

parts of the A&P for twenty-five years. In 1901 the A&P, with the exception of the line from the state line to Addison, was merged with the B&S, a small railroad still, but growing.

The Goodyears' drive for expansion seemed to know no limits. In December, 1901, the Buffalo & Susquehanna Coal and Coke Company was organized, which proceeded to acquire vast tracts of coal lands containing an estimated 50 million tons of bituminous coal in around Du Bois, Pennsylvania, which the Rochester & Pittsburgh had tapped in 1883. The next May the Buffalo & Susquehanna Iron Company was chartered, with William Rogers, the Goodyear brothers, Asher Brown, and Wilson S. Bissell as the only stockholders. Rogers and Brown were already involved in steel making. On the origins of the Buffalo and Susquehanna Steel Company, Josephus N. Larned writes in his 1911 History of Buffalo:

One of Messrs. Rogers, Brown & Co.'s numerous iron manufacturing interests is a plant of two blast furnaces at South Chicago, operated under a corporation known as the Iroquois Iron Company. Messrs. J. J. Albright, Edmund Hayes and S. M. Clement, of Buffalo, who had interests in the company, had never seen its property, until Mr. Rogers invited them to accompany him on one of his visits to it. Mr. Frank H. Goodyear, president of the Buffalo and Susquehanna Railroad Company, tendered the use of his private car to the party and was invited to join it, which he did. What he saw at Chicago gave him ideas of the importance of the furnace plant as a producer of freight for a railroad, which led to negotiations with Mr. Rogers, resulting in the formation of the Buffalo and Susquehanna Iron Company and the building of a pair of blast furnaces in South Buffalo, which are the most modern and the most perfectly equipped of any now existing.

The two furnaces are each 80 feet high and of 20 feet diameter in the bosh. The are located alongside of a canal, 200 feet in width, 23 feet deep, and nearly 3,000 feet long, connecting directly with the outer harbor, so that vessels of the largest size float their cargoes underneath the unloading bridges. The canal was built jointly by the B&S Iron Company, the B&S Railroad Company, and the PRR Company, with each of which roads the furnace plant is connected. [10] (Figure #11.)

The iron company was situated just north of the DL&W Steel Company across the Buffalo city line. It owned mines in the Mesabi Range in Minnesota and in Michigan at Iron Mountain and in the Iron River district. To bring the ore to Buffalo the Buffalo & Susquehanna Steamship company was organized which had two ships on its roster, the *Frank H. Goodyear* and the *S. M. Clement.* In Pennsylvania the iron company owned coal mines and 600 coke ovens at Tyler and Sykesville near Dubois.

It remained only to close the circle, and the Goodyear interest would have a horizontally integrated coal, iron, steel, and transportation empire. Accordingly on November 29, 1902, the (third) Buffalo & Susquehanna Railway Company was incorporated in New York to build a line from Wellsville eighty-five miles northwest to Buffalo. Several routes were under consideration. The first would have been a line north from Wellsville and down the Genesee Valley to Belfast, from there to Arcade where the Buffalo Arcade & Attica would be used as far as Java Center. From there a new line could be constructed to Depew on the DL&W over which running rights would be obtained to Buffalo. In furtherance of this plan, the Goodyears, for $75,000 and a railroad in Pennsylvania, bought the BA&A in 1904 and moved its head office to Buffalo, where Frank Goodyear was elected president. Grading was actually begun on a railroad to Depew but was halted when the scheme was abandoned. The Goodyears, whose ambitions had now moved into the stratosphere, next projected a route from Attica

XII, 11

to Charlotte on Lake Ontario north of Rochester where a coal dock would be built for lake steamers to supply cities on the lake.

The line finally chosen to Buffalo ran north out of Wellsville, down the Genesee Valley to Belfast and across the hills to Arcade, where the grade of the long defunct narrow gauge Springville & Sardinia was followed into Springville. There the line turned northwest along Eighteen Mile Creek to Hamburg where a connection was built to the Erie Railroad's Jamestown branch into Buffalo at a point known briefly as Goodyear Junction. (Figure #10.)

The first train on the B&S from Wellsville ran into the Erie's Buffalo station on December 11, 1906. Shortly thereafter, a four mile section was completed from Goodyear Junction to Blasdell where trackage rights into Buffalo were acquired from the LS&MS, after which B&S passenger trains used the NYC's Exchange Street Station. Later the B&S pushed its own tracks through Lackawanna alongside the other railroads approaching Buffalo from the south. At the Buffalo City Line B&S tracks turned sharply west and headed for the Buffalo & Susquehanna Iron Company's plant along the south bank of the Goodyear Ship Canal. (Figure #11).

In February, 1916, there were two passenger trains each way daily on the B&S between Galeton and Buffalo. (Figure #12.) Three years earlier there had been three. The Keating Summit-Wharton branch had one, and the Ansonia branch two. An attempt had been made to sell the Buffalo-Ansonia route as the first stage in "The New Way" to New York. Actually, it was roundabout and never caught on.

Most patrons to and from Buffalo were from towns north of Wellsville. The road also operated Sunday excursions, especially to Crystal Lake, three miles beyond Arcade. During the Erie County Fair in August B&S trains were crowded with fairgoers from Buffalo and towns in the Boston Valley, since the road ran through the fairgrounds in Hamburg. There were no Pullman cars but a buffet-parlor car operated between Galeton and Buffalo. The morning train to Buffalo picked up milk along the way together with students from nearby towns.

Meanwhile, in another mindless fit of unnecessary reduplication of facilities, the B&S was being pushed south from Wharton to Sinnemahoning (1901) and to Sykesville (1905.) At Medix Run, about twenty-two miles beyond Sinnemahoning, a branch was built to coal lands of the Susquehanna Coal & Coke Company which would produce 1,000 tons of coal daily destined for the B&S Railroad. Eventually the B&S's southern extension deadended at Sagamore, about thirty-five miles northeast of Pittsburgh. There was passenger service of sorts on the 188.8 mile Addison-Sagamore route, but no through trains.

The Buffalo & Susquehanna was, however, primarily a coal road. In 1906 out of a rolling stock of 2,616 cars, 1,874 (over 70%) were coal or coke carriers. The switchbacks between Wharton and Galeton were the weak links in delivering coal from the coalfields of Pennsylvania to Buffalo. The Pittsburgh Shawmut & Northern hauled many B&S coal drags from Weedville, Pennsylvania, to Belvidere, Pennsylvania, but this involved a diversion of revenue to a rival road. The BR&P also extended trackage rights to the B&S for a short distance between its junction with that road and Juneau near the southern end of the line.

The Buffalo & Susquehanna was a financial disaster waiting to happen. The cost of the new line to Buffalo and the extensions toward Pittsburgh had left the road deeply in debt, in a manner reminiscent of the Lehigh Valley's extension to Buffalo a decade previously. Then on May 13, 1907, Frank Goodyear died, leaving an estate valued at $10,522,089.48. The railroad went bankrupt in May, 1910, and a receiver was appointed. Shortly afterward the iron company, the railroad's best customer,

XII, 12

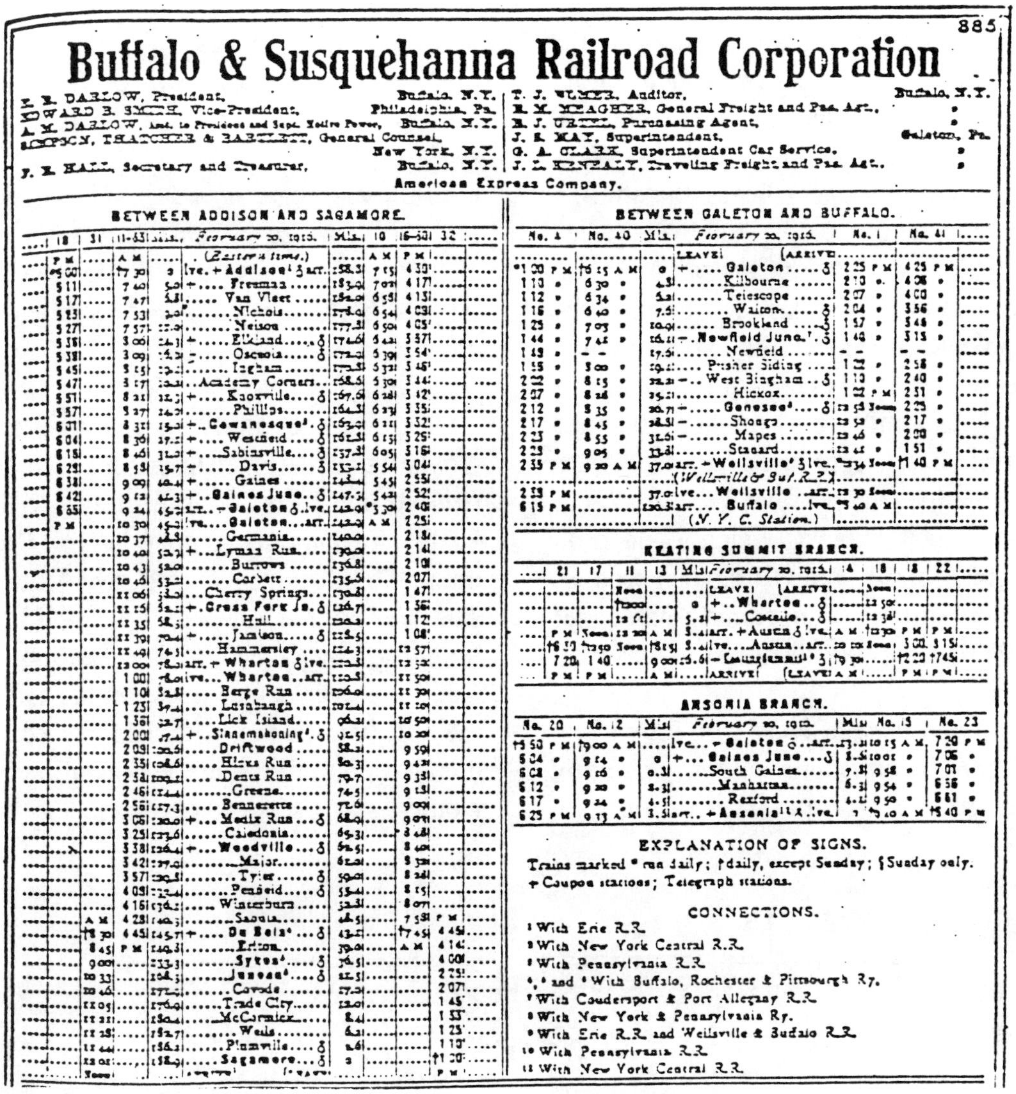

885

Buffalo & Susquehanna Railroad Corporation

F. R. DARLOW, President, Buffalo, N.Y.	T. J. [illegible], Auditor, Buffalo, N.Y.
EDWARD B. SMITH, Vice-President, Philadelphia, Pa.	R. M. MEAGHER, General Freight and Pas. Agt., "
A. M. DARLOW, Asst. to President and Supt. Motive Power, Buffalo, N.Y.	R. J. [illegible], Purchasing Agent, "
SIMPSON, THATCHER & BARTLETT, General Counsel, New York, N.Y.	J. S. MAY, Superintendent, Galeton, Pa.
	G. A. CLARK, Superintendent Car Service, "
F. R. HALL, Secretary and Treasurer, Buffalo, N.Y.	J. L. [illegible], Travelling Freight and Pas. Agt., "

American Express Company.

BETWEEN ADDISON AND SAGAMORE.

18	31	11-63	Mls.	February 20, 1916. (Eastern time.)	Mls.	10	16-30	32
P M		A M				A M	P M	
*5 00		†7 30	0	lve. + Addison[1] § arr.	158.3	7 15	4 30	
5 11		7 40	5.0	+ .... Freeman	153.0	7 07	4 17	
5 17		7 47	[illegible]	.... Van Vleet	[illegible]	6 59	4 13	
5 23		7 53	[illegible]	...... Nichols	[illegible]	6 54	4 03	
5 27		7 57	[illegible]	...... Nelson	[illegible]	6 50	4 05	
5 35		8 00	[illegible]	+ ..... Elkland ....§	[illegible]	6 42	3 57	
5 38		8 09	[illegible]	+ ..... Osceola ....§	[illegible]	6 39	3 54	
5 45		8 15	[illegible]	...... Ingham	[illegible]	6 32	3 45	
5 47		8 17	[illegible]	.. Academy Corners	158.5	6 30	3 44	
5 51		8 21	[illegible]	+ .... Knoxville ....§	[illegible]	6 28	3 42	
5 57		8 27	[illegible]	.... Phillips	[illegible]	6 23	3 35	
6 01		8 31	[illegible]	+ .. Cowanesque[3]. §	[illegible]	6 21	3 32	
6 04		8 36	[illegible]	+ .... Westfield ....§	[illegible]	6 15	3 25	
6 15		8 46	[illegible]	+ ... Sabinsville....§	[illegible]	6 05	3 16	
6 29		8 55	[illegible]	+ ...... Davis......§	[illegible]	5 54	3 04	
6 38		9 00	[illegible]	+ ..... Gaines	[illegible]	5 45	2 55	
6 42		9 12	[illegible]	+ .. Gaines Junc .. §	[illegible]	5 42	2 52	
6 55		9 24	[illegible]	arr. .. Galeton § lve.	[illegible]	*5 30	2 40	
P M		10 30	[illegible]	lve.... Galeton ... arr.	[illegible]	A M	2 25	
		10 37	[illegible]	...... Germania	[illegible]		2 18	
		10 40	[illegible]	+ ... Lyman Run	[illegible]		2 14	
		10 43	[illegible]	...... Burrows	[illegible]		2 10	
		10 46	[illegible]	...... Corbett	[illegible]		2 07	
		11 06	[illegible]	... Cherry Springs	[illegible]		1 47	
		11 15	[illegible]	+ . Cross Fork Jc. §	[illegible]		1 56	
		11 35	[illegible]	.... Hull	[illegible]		1 12	
		11 30	[illegible]	+ ..... Jamison ....§	[illegible]		1 08	
		11 49	[illegible]	..... Hammersley	[illegible]		12 57	
		12 00	[illegible]	arr. + Wharton § lve.	[illegible]		12 [illegible]	
		1 00	[illegible]	lve... Wharton .. arr.	[illegible]		11 50	
		1 10	[illegible]	..... Berge Run	[illegible]		11 30	
		1 23	[illegible]	..... Lorabaugh	[illegible]		11 10	
		1 36	[illegible]	..... Lick Island	[illegible]		10 50	
		2 00	[illegible]	+ .. Sinnemahoning[4]. §	[illegible]		10 30	
		2 09	[illegible]	...... Driftwood	[illegible]		9 59	
		2 35	[illegible]	..... Hicks Run	[illegible]		9 42	
		2 38	[illegible]	.... Dents Run	[illegible]		9 33	
		2 46	[illegible]	.... Greene	74.5		9 15	
		2 56	[illegible]	..... Bennezette	[illegible]		9 00	
		3 06	[illegible]	+ ... Medix Run ... §	[illegible]		9 07	
		3 25	[illegible]	...... Caledonia	[illegible]		8 48	
		3 38	[illegible]	+ ... Weedville ... §	[illegible]		8 40	
		3 42	[illegible]	.... Major	[illegible]		8 30	
		3 57	[illegible]	.... Tyler ..... §	[illegible]		8 24	
		4 09	[illegible]	.... Penfield ..... §	[illegible]		8 15	
		4 16	[illegible]	..... Winterburn	[illegible]		8 07	
	A M	4 28	[illegible]	.... Sabula	[illegible]		7 58	P M
	†8 30	4 45	[illegible]	+ .... Du Bois[5] ... §	[illegible]		†7 45	4 45
	8 45	P M	[illegible]	.... Erlton	[illegible]		A M	4 14
	9 00		[illegible]	.... Sykes[6] ..... §	[illegible]			4 00
	10 33		[illegible]	.... Juneau[6] .... §	[illegible]			2 25
	10 46		[illegible]	.... Cowde	[illegible]			2 07
	11 05		[illegible]	..... Trade City	[illegible]			1 45
	11 21		[illegible]	.... McCormick	[illegible]			1 33
	11 28		[illegible]	.... Wells	[illegible]			1 25
	11 44		[illegible]	...... Plumville ... §	[illegible]			1 10
	12 02		[illegible]	..... Sagamore ... §	0			†1 00
	Noon			ARRIVE LEAVE				P M

BETWEEN GALETON AND BUFFALO.

No. 4	No. 40	Mls.	February 20, 1916.	No. 1	No. 41
			LEAVE (ARRIVE		
*1 00 P M	†6 15 A M	0	+ ..... Galeton ..... §	2 25 P M	4 25 P M
1 10 "	6 30 "	4.3	.... Kilbourne	2 10 "	4 08 "
1 12 "	6 34 "	5.2	.... Telescope	2 07 "	4 00 "
1 16 "	6 40 "	7.5	.... Walton ..... §	2 04 "	3 56 "
1 25 "	7 05 "	10.0	...... Brookland ... §	1 57 "	3 48 "
1 44 "	7 45 "	16.1	+ . Newfield Junc.[7] §	1 40 "	3 15 "
1 49 "	- -	17.5	.... Newfield	- -	- -
1 55 "	8 00 "	19.2	.... Pusher Siding	1 [illegible] "	2 58 "
2 [illegible] "	8 15 "	[illegible]	+ .. West Bingham .. §	1 10 "	2 40 "
2 07 "	8 28 "	25.2	.... Hickox	1 [illegible] P M	2 31 "
2 12 "	8 35 "	30.7	+ ..... Genesee[8] .... §	12 53 Noon	2 25 "
2 17 "	8 45 "	[illegible]	+ ...... Shongo	12 53 "	2 17 "
2 23 "	8 55 "	32.6	+ ...... Mapes	12 46 "	2 00 "
2 29 "	9 05 "	33.8	...... Stannard	12 41 "	1 51 "
2 35 P M	9 20 A M	37.0	arr. + Wellsville[9] § lve.	*12 34 Noon	†1 40 P M
			(Wellsville & Buf. R.R.)		
2 33 P M		37.0	lve... Wellsville .. arr.	12 30 Noon	
6 15 P M		120.8	arr. .... Buffalo .... lve.	*9 40 A M	
			(N. Y. C. Station.)		

KEATING SUMMIT BRANCH.

21	17	11	13	Mls.	February 20, 1916.	14	18	18	22
		Noon			LEAVE (ARRIVE		Noon		
		†12 00		0	+ .. Wharton .. §		12 50		
		12 [illegible]		5.2	+ ... Costello ... §		12 38		
P M	Noon	12 30	A M	8.4	arr. + Austin § lve.	A M	†12 30	P M	P M
†6 30	†12 50	Noon	†8 15	8.4	lve... Austin .. arr.	10 00	Noon	3 00	3 15
7 20	1 40		9 00	[illegible]	+ Keating Summit[10] §	†9 30		†2 20	†7 45
P M	P M		A M		ARRIVE (LEAVE	A M		P M	P M

ANSONIA BRANCH.

No. 20	No. 12	Mls.	February 20, 1916.	Mls.	No. 15	No. 23
†5 50 P M	†9 00 A M		lve... + Galeton § .. arr.	13.2	10 15 A M	7 20 P M
5 04 "	9 14 "	0	+ ... Gaines Junc ... §	8.5	10 02 "	7 06 "
5 08 "	9 16 "	0.3	...... South Gaines	7.8	9 58 "	7 01 "
5 12 "	9 20 "	2.3	.... Manhattan	6.3	9 54 "	6 56 "
5 17 "	9 24 "	4.5	.... Rexford	4.2	9 50 "	6 51 "
5 25 P M	9 33 A M	8.5	arr. .. + Ansonia[11] § lve.	0	*9 40 A M	†5 40 P M

EXPLANATION OF SIGNS.

Trains marked * run daily; † daily, except Sunday; § Sunday only.
+ Coupon stations; Telegraph stations.

CONNECTIONS.

[1] With Erie R.R.
[2] With New York Central R.R.
[3] With Pennsylvania R.R.
[4], [5] and [6] With Buffalo, Rochester & Pittsburgh Ry.
[7] With Coudersport & Port Allegany R.R.
[8] With New York & Pennsylvania Ry.
[9] With Erie R.R. and Wellsville & Buffalo R.R.
[10] With Pennsylvania R.R.
[11] With New York Central R.R.

was merged with the Rogers Brown Iron Company, which had been in attendance at its birth. After the appointment of a receiver, an arrangement was made with the PRR to hand over coal shipments coming north from the coalfields to the PRR at Driftwood to be carried into Buffalo on the former Buffalo New York & Philadelphia. This lifted the B&S out of bankruptcy but removed the only excuse, if there had ever been one, for its existence. The line from Wellsville to Buffalo was sold on September 13, 1915, to a committee of bondholders who could abandon the road and salvage the property. Instead they sold it for about $800,000 to the Susquehanna Finance Corporation, which formed the Wellsville & Buffalo Railroad, incorporated on December 13, 1915. Service continued only until November 16, 1916, when the road gave up the ghost for good. The price of scrap metal was high at the time, and the tracks and some of the engines were sold to Imperial Russia. Because of political unrest there, the shipment was diverted to France. Some say the ship bearing the remains of the B&S was sent to the bottom of the Atlantic by a German U-boat. B&S bridges remained in place until World War II. Its abutments and culverts lasted even longer, and several of its stations survived as private dwellings.

Buffalo Arcade & Attica Update

After the death of Frank Goodyear, the Buffalo Arcade & Attica continued under Buffalo & Susquehanna management until 1913 when Goodyear's widow sold it to W. L. Kann of Pittsburgh. Under his administration two trains ran daily except Sunday between Arcade and Attica. On Sundays one train ran each way to and from the Arcade station of the Pennsylvania Railroad. (Figure #13.) There was a cheese factory at every station along the line, and cheese, milk, hay, lumber, and feed were the principal freight items handled by the road. Its principal shippers were the O'Dell & Eddy Last Block Factory which opened in 1900 and the Merrell-Soule Company, producers of powdered milk. Concerning passenger service at this time, the historian of the road writes:

The track had been in good condition when the Goodyears first took over operation, but by the time Kann got to it the physical property was rapidly disintegrating. Trains were forced to run slower and slower. The passengers made the best they could of the poor situation and a few good jokes resulted. It was reported that on at least one occasion the conductor and brakeman got off a slow moving train to chase some cows off the track. Before long they were so far ahead of the train that they decided to stop and pick some berries. Two hatfuls had been collected before the train caught up with them. [11]

Expenses regularly exceeded revenue. On November 1, 1916, passenger service was cut back to one mixed train each way daily, after Kann had announced that he had lost more than $50,000 since taking over the BA&A. The Wellsville & Buffalo, which had tried and failed to keep the B&S operating, offered Kann that line's spur between the BA&A and the PRR at Arcade. But Kann's son recommended that the line be abandoned. This would create serious problems for business-

XII, 13

BUFFALO, ATTICA & ARCADE RAILROAD COMPANY.

W. L. KANN, President, Farmers Bank Bldg. Pittsburgh, Pa.
W. R. BROWN, Vice-President, 128 Broadway, New York, N.Y.
GANSON DEPEW, Vice-President, Buffalo, N.Y.

R. G. KANN, Sec'y and Treas., Arcade, N.Y.
E. J. BOWEN, Asst. Auditor, "
R. I. CARTWRIGHT, Car Acct., "
A. B. CAMPBELL, Traffic Mgr. and Auditor.
J. L. ELDRIDGE, Gen. Supt., Arcade, N.Y.
General Offices—Arcade, N.Y.

7	5	3	Ms.	*September 12, 1915.*	2	4	6	108
P M	P M	P M	...	(*Erie R.R.*)	P M	A M	P M	....
8 05	9 05	8 05	....	lve....New York....arr.	7 45	7 15	7 45	....
4 55	8 40	4 55	....	lve.....Hornell.....arr.	10 25	7 40	10 42	....
7 22	10 09	7 22	....	........Warsaw........	8 46	5 50	9 41	....
....	9 40	....	....	......Rochester.......	11 10	6 00	....	....
....	11 36	....	....	........Batavia........	9 40	4 05	....	....
8 30	2 20	7 00	....	........Buffalo........	9 35	7 45	9 35	....
A M	P M	A M	....	LEAVE] [ARRIVE	A M	P M	A M	....
§9 20	†3 50	†8 20	0	+......Attica[1]......δ	7 50	3 14	7 50	....
9 32	4 05	8 32	4	.........Sierks.........	7 37	2 59	7 37	....
9 44	4 40	8 44	8	+.....Varysburg.....δ	7 24	2 39	7 24	....
9 57	5 00	8 52	10	+....Johnsonburg....δ	7 18	2 19	7 18	....
10 02	5 25	9 02	13	+.....North Java.....δ	7 07	1 54	7 07	....
10 11	5 45	9 11	17	+....Java Center....δ	6 57	1 30	6 57	....
10 17	5 55	9 17	20	+......Curriers......δ	6 50	1 00	6 50	A M
10 37	6 20	9 37	26	+.Arcade (*Main St.*) ..	†6 30	†12 30	§6 30	11 35
10 40	P M	A M	....	Arcade[2] (*B. & S. Sta.*)	A M	Noon	A M	§11 32
10 47	....	....	....	.Arcade[3] (*P.R.R. Sta.*).	....	....	....	§11 25
A M	....	....	....	ARRIVE] [LEAVE	....	....	....	A M
12 30	....	....	....	... Buffalo (*P. R.R.*) ...	....	....	....	§9 30
Noon	....	....	....	ARRIVE] [LEAVE	....	....	....	A M

† Daily, except Sunday; § Sunday only. + Coupon stations; δ Telegraph stations. American Express Co.

Connections.—[1] With Erie and New York Central R.Rs. [2] With Wellsville & Buffalo R.R. [3] With Pennsylvania R.R.

men along the line, especially the Merrell-Soule Company. These interests tried first to get the PRR, the Erie, or the BR&P to take over the line, but were turned down. Abandonment seemed certain when the railroad entered bankruptcy in March, 1917. However, on May 23, 1917, the Arcade & Attica Railroad was incorporated and stock in it was sold to 365 purchasers up and down the valley - farmers, merchants, businessmen - with an interest in the continuance of the little railroad. A Wellsville & Buffalo salvage crew had arrived at Arcade and was preparing to rip out the connection with the PRR, but at the last moment the new A&A was enabled to negotiate a lease. Freight operations were resumed on June 1, 1917, after seven months of inactivity, and passenger trains began running a few weeks later on a twice daily basis each way between Arcade and Attica.

Southwestern Detours

Just as the Erie, the NYC, and the DL&W in the seventies and eighties had constructed northwestern shortcuts to the International Bridge to bypass the growing congestion in Buffalo, so too the NYC and the LV in the nineties and in the first decade of the twentieth century built detours from their mainlines east of Buffalo to the southwest. (Figure #6.) On June 12, 1895, nine directors (five of them Buffalonians) of the Terminal Railroad of Buffalo secured incorporation of a company to build a line from the mainline of the NYC at Depew to the LS&MS at Blasdell. Two years later - by which time the road was in operation - new directors were chosen, of whom Cornelius Vanderbilt III, grandson of the late Cornelius II, became chairman. Others on the board were William K. Vanderbilt, William H.'s sporting son, who had been vice president of the NYC, Hamilton Twombley, a son-in-law of William H., H. Walter Webb, vice president of the NYC and a Vanderbilt kinsman, and Chauncey Depew, president of the NYC. They concluded a lease of the line to the Central on terms very favorable to themselves. On this line a classification yard was built at Gardenville for freight trains ten year later.

In 1904 a group of Buffalo capitalists headed by the Goodyear brothers planned a 27.7 mile circumferential line, the Buffalo Frontier Terminal Railroad, that would start at Bay View on Lake Erie below Woodlawn Beach and swing around the city, ending on the Niagara River in the City of Tonawanda. (Figure #14.) The argument of its promoters was that "we have long needed a terminal of such non-partisan character." They cited Chicago "which has three such roads and they are a success." "Other cities," they alleged, "in which are belt lines serving the entire public and built for the benefit of no single road, have also profited largely by such service." Existing railroads opposed the scheme, which was turned down at least twice by the New York State Public Service Commission.

Archer thus describes improvements made at this time at the western end of the LV:

Crucial to the LV's ability to cope with the traffic surge during the period prior to World War I was the program of modernizing and expanding existing terminal facilities. Expansion of the Tifft Farm Terminal was imperative in light of the growing volume of Great Lakes and interchange traffic arriving at Buffalo. Wharf frontage was rebuilt, yard trackage was expanded, and a double track terminal line, the Lehigh & Lake Erie Branch, was built in 1907. The ore docks at Tifft Farm were rebuilt to increase their handling capacity, and a 22-foot channel was dredged to permit berthing of larger lake vessels at the ore and coal transfer plants. [12]

Terminals

The turn of the century found Buffalo with scattered and aging terminals. Grandiose plans for a union station in 1888 had died aborning. In answer to civic agitation for bet-

XII, 14

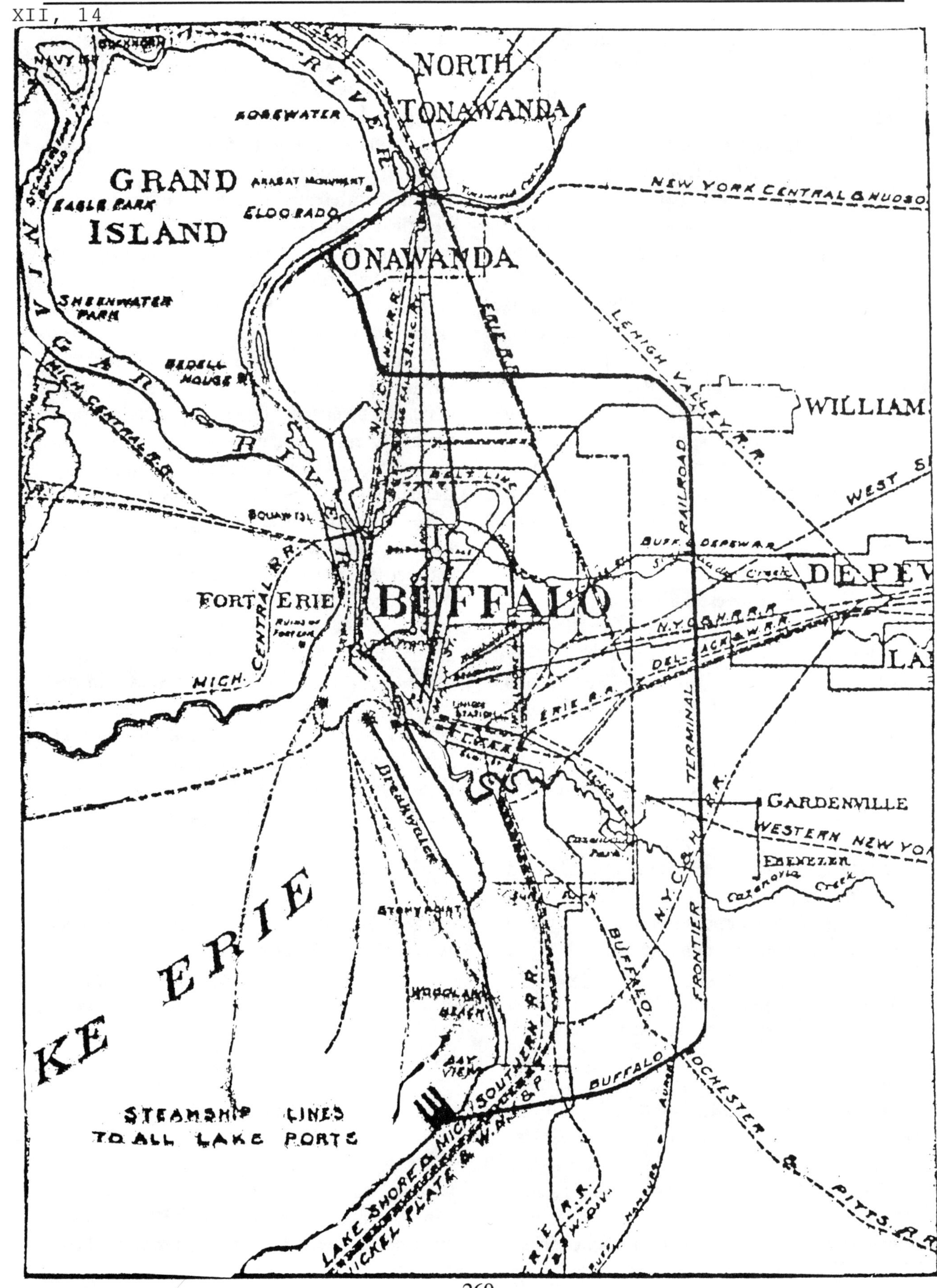
NORTH
TONAWANDA
ROSEWATER
GRAND
ISLAND
EAGLE PARK
ELDORADO
TONAWANDA
SHEENWATER
PARK
BEDELL
HOUSE
NEW YORK CENTRAL & HUDSO
LEHIGH VALLEY R.R.
WILLIAM
RIVER
NIAGARA
MICH. CENTRAL R.R.
BELT LINE
SQUAW ISL.
WEST S
BUFF. & DEPEW R.R.
DEPEW
FORT ERIE
BUFFALO
N.Y.C. & H.R.R.R.
DEL. LACK & W.R.R.
MICH. CENTRAL R.R.
ERIE R.R.
TERMINAL
RAILROAD
GARDENVILLE
WESTERN NEW YO
EBENEZER
Cazenovia Creek
BREAKWATER
STONY POINT
KE ERIE
WOODLAWN
BEACH
BAY
VIEW
FRONTIER
BUFFALO
ROCHESTER & PITTS. R.R.
STEAMSHIP LINES
TO ALL LAKE PORTS
LAKE SHORE & MICH. SOUTHERN R.R.
NICKEL PLATE
ERIE R.R.

ter terminal facilities, the NYC put a second addition on its Exchange Street Station in 1900 and a third in 1901, but the result remained a patched up post-Civil War relic. Cousins takes up the story:

The New York Central's brilliant engineering vice president, William J. Wilgus, a native of Buffalo, published a spectacular union station proposal for the city in the January 6, 1906, Railroad Gazette. The 13 railroads which agreed on the plan, a feat in itself, generated a total of 4,300 daily passenger train movements "past the tower" (the contemporary index of frequency) compared with 5,000 for the old (1871) Grand Central in New York, 4,000 at Boston's South Station, 3,618 at Pennsy's Broad Street station in Philadelphia, and 2,500 at St. Louis Union Station.

The 107-acre [West] Genesee Street site, originally suggested by prominent local architect George Cary, was just west of Niagara Square, hub of the city's radial street plan, and extended to the harbor. An expansive boulevard and park approach fanned out in front of the station on the east. The track plan called for 12 6-car stub-end platform tracks and 20 15-car through tracks, the latter feeding into a vast loop track to allow trains to execute a 360-degree change in direction and return to their main lines. Another imaginative feature of the plan was construction of adjacent steamboat wharves. Finally, the proposal entailed elimination of all grade crossings from downtown north to Fort Porter, with concentration of freight terminal activity in the vacated Exchange Street Station. [Figure #15.]

A city commission, set up to act as a liaison between politicians and merchants of Buffalo and the railroads, endorsed the plan. But Buffalo balked at the cost of closing streets, demolishing structures, and constructing harbor facilities, and without the city's participation the project died. Instead the Exchange Street Station received a fourth addition in 1906 and a fifth and final one in 1907, even as other union stations were proposed for downtown sites at Lafayette Square, Driving Park, and Eagle Street. [13]

The next summer the ultimate in pre-World War I union station plans was presented by representatives of the city, the NYC, and the Erie. The site selected was a 300 acre, mile and a half long tract, which contained the NYC's East Buffalo freight and stockyards, the functions of which were to be transferred to the Gardenville Yards then under construction. It was the same site as was actually chosen for Central Station a decade later on Fillmore Avenue two and a half miles from Exchange Street. To meet the objection that it was too far from Buffalo's business center, plans were included for a surrounding park of 100 acres, opening new and widening existing streets, electrifying the Belt Line, and building a new station on the Terrace where passengers could purchase tickets and check their baggage before boarding connecting trains to the new station. It was also pointed out that construction on the East Side would obviate interference with train movements at Exchange Street. The architecture of the station house was to be the neo-classical, popular throughout America in the wake of the Columbian Exposition in 1893. (Figure #16.)

Downtown businessmen objected to moving the station out of downtown and demanded through the Chamber of Commerce that the new station should be built at Exchange Street. The NYC refused, alleging that there was no room for expansion there. The presidents of the Erie and the DL&W announced that they would not participate in the undertaking, and the LV dropped out after buying the old Hamburg Canal strip just south of its Scott Street Station. In 1911 William H. Fitzpatrick, a prominent Democratic leader and real estate developer, pushed through the legislature a bill creating a Terminal Station Commission, but first the LV and then the DL&W built their own terminals, and America's entry into World War I diverted the public's attention to win-

XII, 15

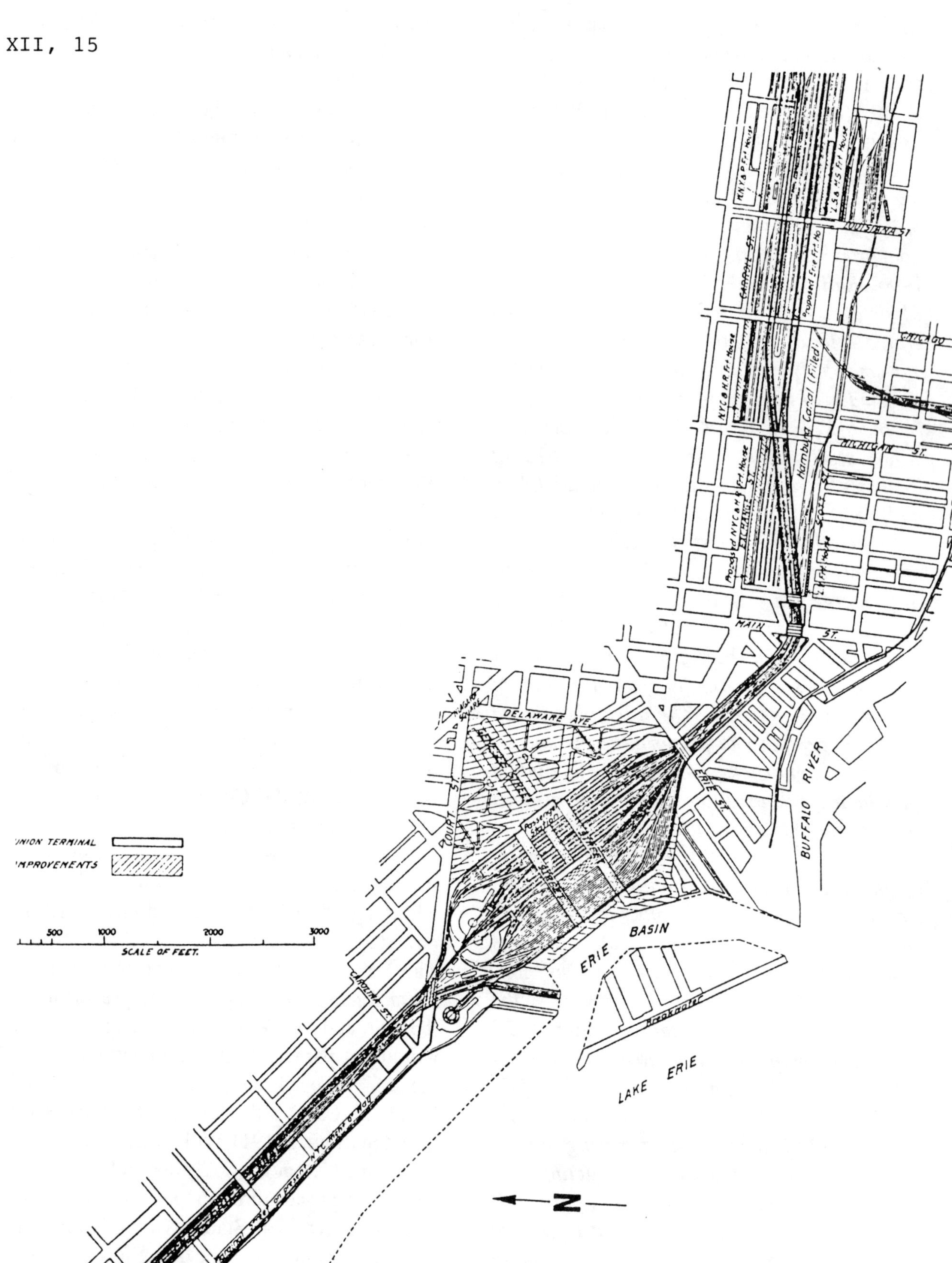
LOUISIANA ST.
CHICAGO
MICHIGAN ST.
Hamburg Canal (Filled)
MAIN ST.
DELAWARE AVE.
ERIE ST.
COURT ST.
BUFFALO RIVER
ERIE BASIN
LAKE ERIE
Breakwater
UNION TERMINAL
IMPROVEMENTS
500 1000 2000 3000
SCALE OF FEET.
N

XII, 16

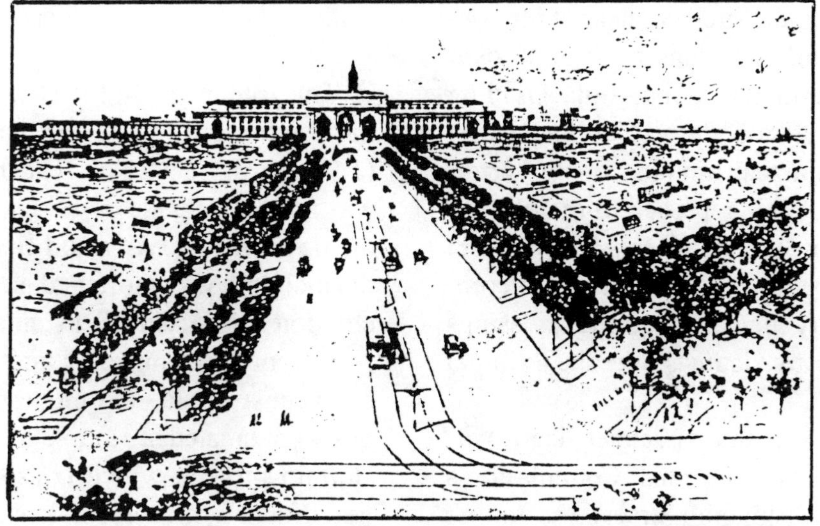

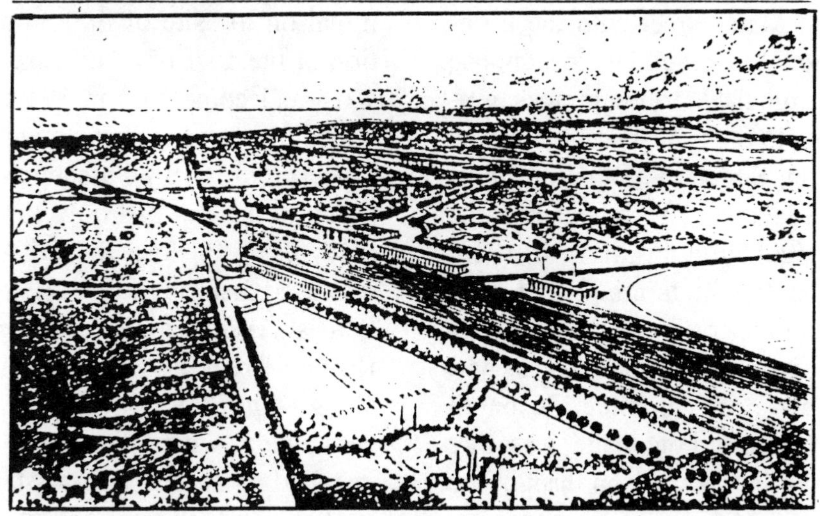

ning the war.

Two months before that event, however, on February 13, 1917, a fire damaged the west tower of the NYC's Exchange Street Station. The time department lost most of its records, and the telegraph system was wiped out temporarily, as were the dispatcher's office and the ticket windows. When the tower was repaired the cupola was not replaced, which gave the station an even more patchwork look than before.

By 1912 the LV had decided to replace its old depot at Scott and Washington Streets with new passenger and freight stations which would cost an estimated $5 million. The City of Buffalo sold the railroad the land (the abandoned Main & Hamburg Canal) for an enlarged terminal, the site was cleared for construction, and building plans were gone over with the city's Terminal Commission. Grading and tracklaying were underway in earnest by 1914 before the actual building of the terminals The double track approach to the old terminal was relocated on the land acquired from the city, and expanded to four tracks. In compliance with city demands, grade crossings were eliminated by viaducts over the terminal approach.

Construction of the passenger depot was complicated by the Terminal Commission's refusal to close Washington Street so as to link the headhouse on Main Street with the trainshed. The solution was to build the headhouse across the street from the terminal tracks, giving patrons access to the trainshed by a tunnel under Washington Street, a deviation from standard terminal layouts. Work began on the passenger and freight buildings in April, 1915. By December the freight terminal and yard were finished and in operation. The passenger terminal which opened August 29, 1916, was designed by New York architect Kenneth Murchison. A box-like colonnade was like that of a notable earlier Murchison design, the DL&W passenger station and offices at Scranton. (Figure #17.)

From the main waiting room extending to the ceiling of the four-story building, travelers walked down a ramp to the tunnel beneath Washington Street emerging at the concourse and train gates. (Figure #18.) The headhouse was a two-story building containing the mail, express, and baggage room. An 842-foot steel and concrete Bush train shed, a design developed by the DL&W and installed at the Scranton Station, protected the terminal's end stub-end tracks. Alas, Archer concludes:

> *Although the new terminal was a vast improvement over its predecessor, the inconvenience for through passengers was unresolved. Since the union station proposal had fallen through, the traveler was left to transfer from one station to another as best he could when making through connections.* [14]

The golden age of the DL&W Railroad was the administration of William H. Truesdale (1899-1925.) Under his leadership the railroad was rebuilt as grade crossings were eliminated on the Morris & Essex and Boonton Divisions, the mainline was shortened eleven miles by the creation of a cutoff in northwestern New Jersey and three miles by another in northeastern Pennsylvania, and modern terminal facilities were created at Hoboken and Buffalo. The Buffalo project, which consisted in the erection of a new, elevated, lakeside passenger terminal on the site of the old ground-level station at the foot of Main Street, was begun in 1914 and completed in 1917. Included were docks for passenger steamers right at the station. (Figure #19.) Passengers changing transportation modes had only to walk a few hundred feet. Besides the DL&W the terminal was used also by the BR&P, the NKP, and the Wabash. With the elevation of all tracks along Buffalo Creek, those which had formerly run along Ohio Street to the freight house and the coal yard were removed. Ramps were installed to nearby freight stations. The long coal dock which went back to the road's earliest days was replaced by a coal dumper.

XII, 17

LEHIGH VALLEY TERMINAL

XII, 18

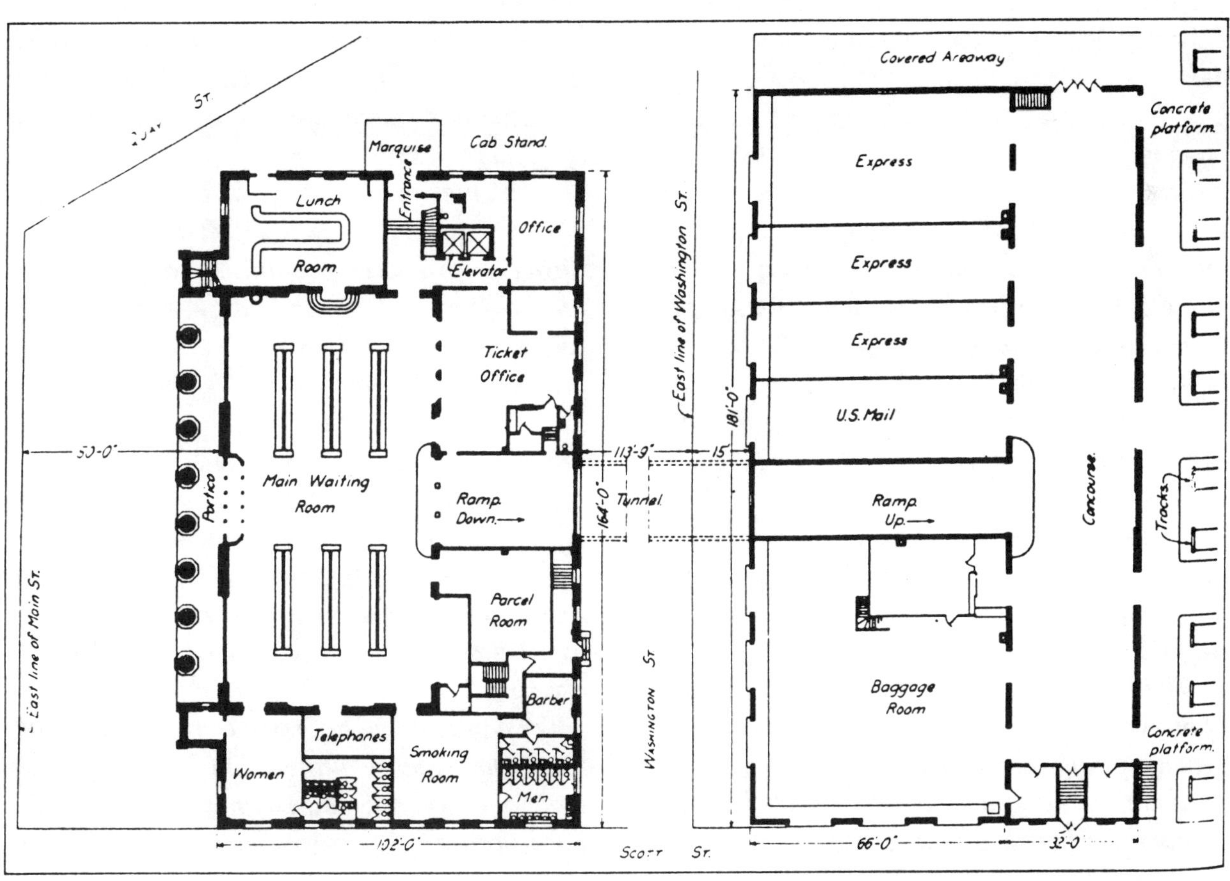
Covered Areaway
Concrete platform
Express
Express
Express
U.S. Mail
Ramp Up
Concourse
Tracks
Baggage Room
Concrete platform
66'-0"
32'-0"
181'-0"
15
113'-9"
Tunnel
East line of Washington St.
Washington St.
Scott St.
Marquise
Cab Stand
Entrance
Lunch Room
Office
Elevator
Ticket Office
Main Waiting Room
Portico
Ramp Down
Parcel Room
Barber
Telephones
Smoking Room
Women
Men
164'-0"
50'-0"
102'-0"
East line of Main St.

XII, 19

(Figure #20.) *The Buffalo Evening News* for February 1, 1917, thus saluted the new terminal:

Trains will begin today to use the new DL&W railway station at Main and Ohio streets. The first train, #15, scheduled to arrive at 1:00 P. M. from New York pulled in on time. The first train leaving is an accommodation, #36 to Groveland, and it goes out at 4:00 this afternoon. The first New York train is #10 leaving at 5:50. The building is spic and span throughout for the opening of business. Passengers will use the Ohio street entrance. A long wide portico protects those going to and from conveyances to the station. Passengers arriving by boat will enter the station from the south side which fronts on the Buffalo river.

The building is three stories high and built of brownstone. There are waiting rooms on the ground floor and on the second floor. The ground floor has one ticket office and checking counter and benches along the sides. A double stairway leads to the second waiting room which is fitted with accommodations for about 200 persons. There are long rows of seats back to back. Shaded lights are on the back of the seats.

Off the waiting room at the north is the women's parlor, finished in soft brown and furnished with wicker furniture. There are rugs on the floor and a writing desk invites to correspondence. In a corresponding corner on the other side of the stairs is a smoking room. The middle of the east side of the waiting room affords entrance to the concourse whence issue is had to the trains. Opening off the waiting room are the customary news stand, telegraph and parcel booths, and restaurant. The restaurant is most complete and besides the usual a la carte service will have a table-de-hote meal at noon and night.

On a mezzanine floor are rooms for the railroad employees, waiting room for immigrants, and room for railroad business mail. On the third floor are various offices, including those

XII, 20

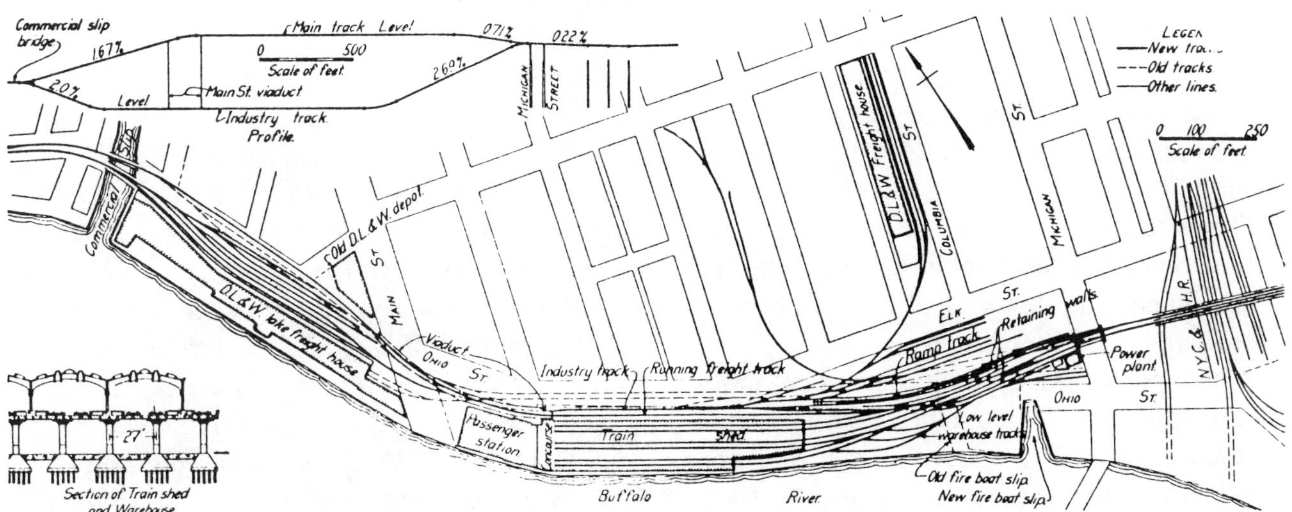

Track Plan Showing the Lackawanna Improvements along the River Front in Buffalo, N. Y.

The new Buffalo station and elevation of tracks in its vicinity required three years of work stretching from 1914 to 1917. Situated at the foot of Main Street, the railroad's station was very accessible to the center of the city. The new terminal also would serve the Buffalo, Rochester, and Pittsburgh Railroad (Baltimore and Ohio), the Nickel Plate Road, the Wabash, and the Great Lakes steamships sailing into Buffalo. All tracks along the Buffalo River were elevated with special ramps down to nearby freight stations. To the left of the map, out of view, is the Great Lakes coal transfer yard. As part of the Buffalo improvement project, the long coal dock, which had served since the railroad was built, was replaced by a coal dumper. The freight house west of the station adjacent to the water was for transfer of freight to and from Great Lakes merchant ships.

of Superintendent Shepard and the train dispatcher. The office of assistant general freight agent C. F. McTague is on the Main street front of the second floor.

Grade Crossing Elimination

In Metropolitan Corridor, John R. Stilgoe writes:

In 1902, the Interstate Commerce Commission recorded that nearly 4,000 people "struck by trains, locomotives, or cars" died instantly or within twenty-four hours of the collisions; another 3,563 suffered injuries. Federal statistics under-reported fatalities and injuries, however, because the commission never adequately defined such terms as persons, persons not trespassing, *and* trespassers. *In fact, the Commission struggled unsuccessfully with defining terms relating to the locations of collisions, and early twentieth-century journalists learned to distrust both government and private industry statistics. Despite warped or incomplete statistics, however, expert observers eventually understood the magnitude of the problem. "Two hundred thousand trespassers have been killed or injured by the railroads of the United States in the past twenty years," wrote one journalist in 1921. Railroad travel became increasingly safer for the passenger but it grew increasingly dangerous for those Americans termed crossing maniacs or trespassers. Each year of the new century saw more fatalities; in 1919 alone, nearly 14,000 persons died after being struck by trains. Railroad and government officials agreed with journalists that a new disease had struck the nation, but no one clearly understood its underlying cause.* [15]

Among the thousands killed, hoboes constituted a large percentage, but no reliable statistics exist concerning their deaths. Children and adults crossing tracks away from proper crossings added to the toll as trains were speeded up. Industrial zones became deathtraps at quitting time, when thousands of factory workers took shortcuts. Several thousand people died between 1900 and 1920 because they climbed over gates, fences, and other barriers erected by the railroads as safety devices. Horses caused thirteen percent of grade-crossing collisions, and matters worsened with the multiplication of automobiles, whose drivers often tried to outrace trains to the crossing. At other times careless motormen drove trolley cars directly into the path of oncoming trains resulting in fearsome carnage.

Eliminating grade crossings produced problems of its own. Dead-ending roads seemed a natural solution, but, as Stilgoe remarks, "When a road ended in a permanently fixed fence, some railroad companies learned, many motorists for reasons not clearly understood simply drove into them, through them, and onto the tracks." Separating track and road by elevating one or the other produced environmental changes which were not universally appreciated. Embankments spoiled views, blighted neighborhoods, and destroyed locations. Opponents referred to them as "Chinese Walls." Railroads soon discovered that even if state or local governments shared half the cost of raising or lowering tracks, tax assessors treated the finished structure as a taxable improvement.

The beginning of systematic grade crossing elimination in Buffalo was the tunnel under Main Street connecting the Exchange Street and Terrace Stations. In the Evening News for December 12, 1951, during another grade crossing and track relocation project in the same area, Harvey K. Elsaesser recalled:

The tunnel built under Main St. at the Terrace in 1896 was just a part of the $5,000,000 plan to eliminate grade crossings. The cut from [West] *Seneca St. to Washington St., including the Main St. tunnel cost $109,155, a mere fraction of the cost today. Back in the 1890s, however the tracks were not moved but merely lowered. The Michigan Ave. viaduct was built at the same time at a cost of $170,840.*

But the marvel of the time was the tunnel under Main St. Robert B. Adam was chairman of the Grade Crossing Commission. The NYC, which footed part of the bill, was controlled by Cornelius Vanderbilt, chairman, and Chauncey M. Depew, president. Until the recent excavation on Main St. their names could be read on the green-coated copper plate on the Main St. Bridge over the tracks.

While men were working in the air on the 910 foot long Michigan Ave. bridge on the other side of Main St., others were burrowing into the ground. They were making a 900 foot cut starting at [West] *Seneca St. and extending in a compound curve to Main St.* [Figure IX, #19] *under which was a beam tunnel extending 195 feet. The walls were constructed of sandstone blocks surmounted by pipe-iron rails. Some of those blocks weighed as much as three or four tons. The tunnel, when completed, was 28 feet wide and had a clearance of 15 feet. Two foot bridges were constructed over the tunnel* [he means over the tracks] *at Franklin St. and at Pearl St.*

As in tunnel construction now, obstacles were encountered. Gas mains had to be relocated. A 10-inch water main had to be built east of Franklin St. Five sewers had to be rebuilt. Telephone conduits had to be lowered. Six fire hydrants had to be changed and a 6-inch water main laid. A major operation was reconstructing the Pearl St. sewer, which had to be lowered as much as 19 feet in one place.

Chief engineer on the job was George E. Mann. He said the entire work of abolishing grade crossing[s] *could be completed in about three years, and that when completed, it was to make Buffalo "a model place from the railroad construction point of view."*

This stage of the project was finished when the Michigan Street Viaduct over the NYC was opened in June, 1896. Construction costs were $265,116.52, of which the railroads paid $228,546 and the city $36,570.52. Awards for lands taken amounted to $157,668.67, of which the railroads paid $105,112.45 and the city $52,556.22. (Figure #21.)

In an article he wrote in 1897 which was published eight years later by the Buffalo Historical Society, Adam ventured a prediction:

When all the work included in the present plan has been completed, it will be possible to travel out Seneca Street from Main Street to the city line, or down Hamburg Street to Elk Street and thence out Elk Street and Abbott Road to the city line without encountering a single railroad track on grade. All the streets which are crossed by the tracks of the New York Central Railroad from Swan to William Streets inclusive will be carried under the railroad, the tracks being raised an average of seven feet above their present elevation.

An editor's footnote contained this information:

In the eight years that have elapsed since Mr. Adam prepared the foregoing history, the work of abolishing the grade crossings has gone on. Since May 22, 1895, thirty-seven structures have been completed, which with the closing of streets have eliminated sixty-five crossings at grade. Five structures are yet to be built to complete the General Plan of the Commission. The cost of completed structures to the spring of 1905 has been as follows: right-of-way work, $500,000 borne by the railroads; construction, $824,697.96 borne by the city, $3,005,555.08 borne by the railroads, a total of $3,830,249.04. Lands bought $292,697.86 by the city, $575, 254.94 by the railroads; a total of $867,952.80. The grand total of cost including right-of-way, construction, and lands bought, is $5,198,201.84, of which the city pays 21.5 percent, amounting to $1,117,391.82, and the railroads 78.5 percent, amounting to $4,080,810.02. To these figures are to be added the consequential damages [i.e., losses sustained by adjacent property holders], *amounting to $2,035,244.91, of which $1,055,101.84 are apportioned to the city and $980,143.07 to the railroads. Including the consequential damages, the total cost of the work to the spring of 1905 has been $7,233,446.75. The estimated cost of the structures to be completed is $233,152.36, of which $60,885.79 is apportioned to the city, and $172,266.57 to the railroads* [for a grand total of $7,466.599.15]. *There have been constructed fifteen viaducts spanning seventeen crossings; eighteen subways under nineteen crossings; and four foot bridges. Twenty-five streets have been closed. By these means seventy grade crossings have been abolished. Three more will be done away with by work now included in the General Plan.*

In a statistical summary prepared by Chief Engineer Edward B. Guthrie in March, 1905, after the foregoing and other data were given, this statement is made: "While insufficient time has elapsed to appreciate the full benefit of this improvement, it is of interest to note the decrease in fatal accidents to others than railway employees at grade crossings in the city, notwithstanding the fact that for the latest period mentioned below some of the structures were not commenced. For thirty-one months in each of the periods there were: From Jan. 1, 1890, to Aug. 1, 1892, fifty-five fatal accidents. From May 1, 1902, to Dec. 1, 1904, (thirty-one months) twenty-four fatal accidents, a difference of thirty-one [a drop of 56%]." [16]

By 1906 neighborhoods along the NYC's Belt Line (Figure VII, #8) had grown to such an extent that a supplementary plan was adopted which called for the abolition of fifty-two more grade crossings. To relieve the situation at Amherst and Austin Streets negotiations had to be carried on with the Erie, the NYC, the DL&W, and the International Bridge Company. A deep depression was necessary to carry Niagara Street under the approach to the company's bridge over the Niagara River. The rest of the Belt Line required twenty bridges.

XII, 21

BUFFALO GRADE CROSSING IMPROVEMENT
1888 to 1905

All structures shown on Map are built to Spring, 1905, except those marked "A" which are yet unfinished.

XII, 22

NEW VIADUCTS OVER NEW YORK CENTRAL BELT LINE: DEWEY, LEROY, JEWETT AND MAIN

Moreover, this line was reconstructed for five miles from Bailey north and west to Delaware Avenue. This involved cuts thirty feet deep extending in some places for over a mile. (Figure #22.)

Of the three more bridges built under this plan, the Chamber of Commerce's *Live Wire* for December, 1910, noted:

Two [bridges] *on Hertel Avenue over the NYC, one on the Niagara Falls line and the other on the Y are on contract. Two crossings on the Belt line between Broadway and Military and ten over the Erie, one at Hertel Avenue and nine between Walden and Delaware under negotiation. Five of the latter also involve the Erie and the DL&W's own belt lines which swung alongside each other northwest across the city to International Bridge.* [Figures VII, #6 and IX, #9.] *Another crossing of the NYC, the DL&W, and the LV at Bailey* [just north of Seneca] *is also under negotiation. . . . Down to 1910 the supplemental plan had cost the city $522,808 and the railroads $1,951,377.* [17]

Worthy of special mention were the six bridges that carried the Erie over Bailey between William and Dingens Streets. (Figure #23.)

XII, 23

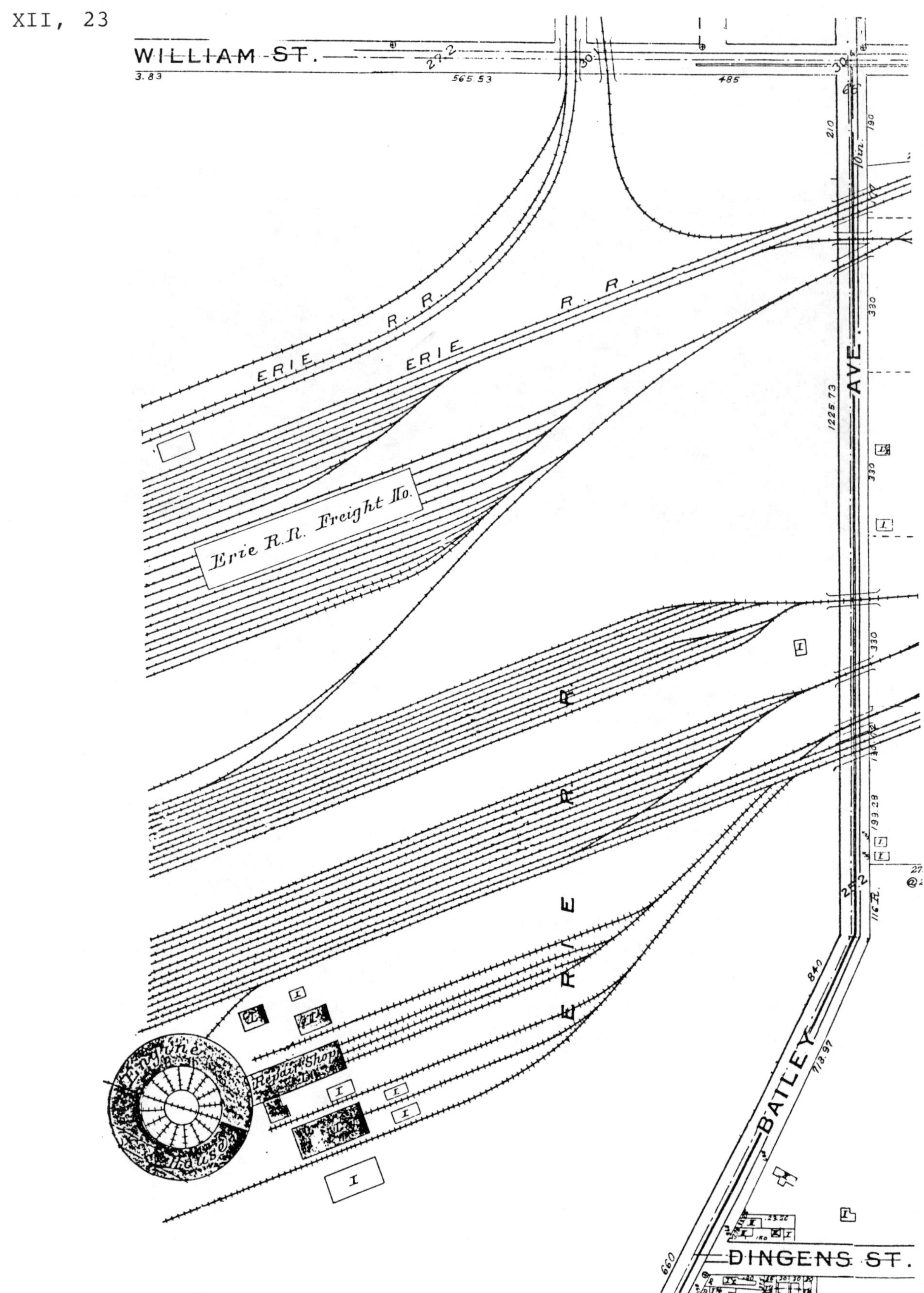
WILLIAM ST.
ERIE R. R.
ERIE R. R.
Erie R.R. Freight Ho.
ERIE R.R.
AVE.
BAILEY
DINGENS ST.
Engine House
Repair Shop

13
Origins Of Decline

It is one of the ironies of history that the years America's railroads reached the summit of their power also witnessed the appearance of rivals and hostile forces that would in the years to come undermine the railroads' strength and prosperity. These adversaries were (1) interurbans, (2) automobiles, trucks, buses, and airplanes, (3) state and federal governments, and (4) unions. The discussion of interurbans which follows is based largely on George W. Hilton and John F. Due's The Electric Interurban Railways in America. On Western New York's interurbans a major source is William R. Gorden's misnamed 90 Years of Buffalo Railways, the text of which is disorganized, though the pictures are excellent.

Interurbans

As railroads owed their origin to the steam engine, streetcars and interurbans owed theirs to the electric engine. By 1880 the technology for electric traction was in place. The necessity for it became urgent during the following decade. The horsecar was still the principal means of public street transport, but it had many drawbacks. Horses were slow, they could be worked only four or five hours a day, their feed bill was expensive, they lasted in service for five years at most, and they created a health problem as well as an aesthetic one on city streets. Moreover, the industry faced the constant danger that its horses would be decimated by an epidemic as had happened in 1872. Battery cars required constant recharging. Cable car lines entailed heavy initial expenses, broke down frequently, and deteriorated rapidly.

Frank J. Sprague, an 1878 graduate of Annapolis who spent five years on active duty almost wholly engaged in electronics, was the father of American electric railways. On leaving the service in 1883 he became an assistant to Thomas A. Edison for work on electric lighting, but left within a year to found the Sprague Electric Railway and Motor Company, which failed to interest the management of New York City's elevated railroads in electrification. Meanwhile, he developed a reliable direct current motor and solved the problem which had bedeviled his predecessors of transmitting motion from the motor to the wheels by mounting his motor between the axle and a spring and securing a sure mesh by having the motor engage with a cogwheel on the axle.

In May, 1887, Sprague received an order for installing his system from the Richmond Union Passenger Railway in the capital of the old Confederacy. Hilton and Due recount the fabulous success story which followed:

His firm was to build about 12 miles of track, a power-house, and 40 double-motored cars. The line included an 8 per cent grade and presented other formidable operating problems. Sprague's installation was a great success from its opening in 1888, and it attracted wide notice. After Henry M. Whitney adopted the Sprague system for his West End Railway of Boston, Sprague received an avalanche of orders; within three years 200 streetcar systems were built or ordered, about half built by Sprague himself and 90 per cent based on Sprague's patents. Few inventions have ever achieved a more rapid and complete acceptance. The superiority of the electric car to the horsecar was obvious from the outset, and by 1893 the cable car was demonstrably inferior except on very heavy grades. By 1902 97 per cent of street railway mileage was electrically operated; only twelve years earlier, 70 per cent of street railways had used animal power. In 1901 there were some 15,000 miles of electric railway in the United States. [1]

Successes in urban settings led to the employment of the electric car in rural and intercity operations. The period 1897 until the first World War was one of almost unparalleled agricultural prosperity, which led farming families to demand easier access to cities. The horse and buggy was limited in range to a few miles, while railroad trains stopped chiefly in towns often miles away from a farmhouse. In New England, electric railways came to rural areas mainly by way of extending city systems outward. Elsewhere interurbans assumed a more durable form. While in cities and towns tracks were laid in the streets, in the country they were laid alongside the highway or on a private right-of-way just like a steam railroad. Speeds almost always exceeded fifteen miles an hour. The two systems were as different as are today extensions of local bus lines and intercity buses. In an attempt to distinguish between streetcars and interurbans, Hilton and Due contend that:

The intercity electric lines actually formed a continuum from suburban operations of city systems to heavy electric railways that interchanged freight with steam railroads and differed from them only in type of motive power. Since some definition is necessary, the term interurban may be applied to railways that shared most or all of the four following characteristics: electric power, primary emphasis on passenger service, equipment that was heavier and faster than city streetcars, and operation on streets in cities but at the sides of highways or on private rights-of-way in rural areas. [2]

The rise and fall of the interurban industry was spread over the seventy year period between 1890 and 1960. But, as a glance at Figure #1 will show, the sharp rise and equally sharp decline of route mileage occurred in the forty years between 1900 and 1940. As Hilton and Due observe:

Few industries have arisen so rapidly or declined so quickly, and no industry of its size has had a worse financial record. The interurbans were a rare example of an industry that never enjoyed a period of prolonged prosperity; accordingly they played out their life cycle in a shorter period than any other important American industry. [3]

The history of the interurbans is a telescoped version of that of steam railroads. (Compare Figure #1 with Figure V, #1.) For both the peak year was 1916. Yet interurbans and railroads were fierce rivals. It was while the interurbans were being built that they first encountered railroad opposition. The two most hostile major railroads were the largest in the Northeast, the PRR and the NYC, which regularly secured injunctions to prevent

FIGURE ONE: Interurban Statistics, 1890-1960

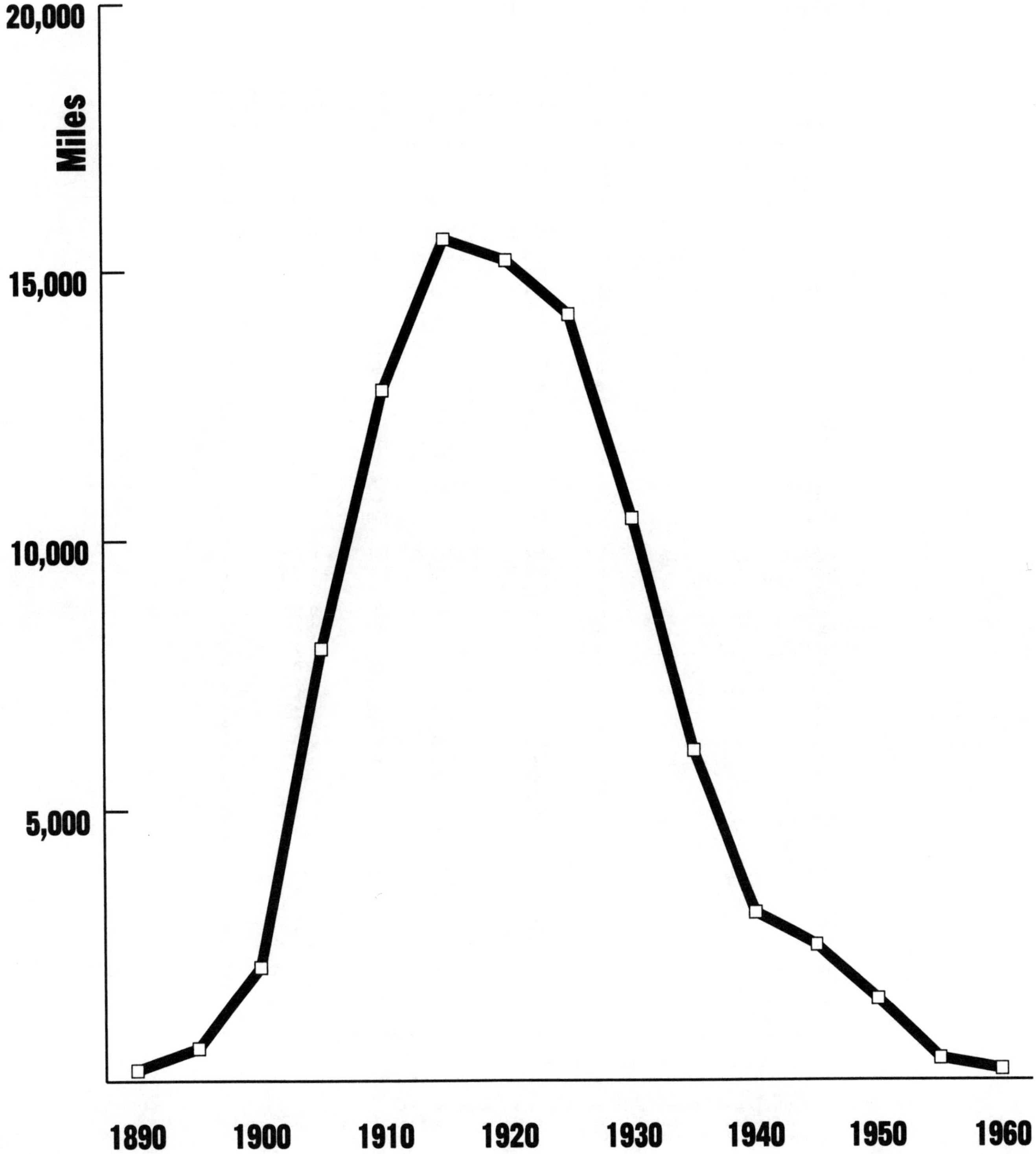

Interurban Mileage (data)
Hilton and Due, *Electric Interurban Railways*, 186-187

Year	Miles built*	Miles abandoned†	Miles in service‡	Operating ratio, %	Rate of return, %	Car orders
1918	52	144	15,470	75	2.7	255
1919	29	70	15,429	76	3.0	128
1920	0	92	15,337	79	3.0	227
1921	13	102	15,248	84	2.1	107
1922	15	237	15,026	81	2.3	128
1923	51	220	14,857	83	2.3	253
1924	51	264	14,644	85	2.2	170
1925	0	302	14,342	87	1.8	177
1926	45	689	13,698	91	1.1	139
1927	34	510	13,222	91	1.1	116
1928	0	914	12,308	90	0.9	53
1929	0	869	11,439	93	0.5	69
1930	0	1,017	10,422	101	−0.5	35
1931	0	1,219	9,203	101	−0.9	40
1932	0	1,303	7,900	115	−1.3	2
1933	0	1,029	6,871	110	−0.8	0
1934	0	548	6,323	106	−0.6	0
1935	0	294	6,029	104	−0.3	0
1936	0	124	5,905	100	0.0	0
1937	0	494	5,411	105	−0.6	0
1938	0	798	4,613	105	−0.7	0
1939	3	902	3,711	101	−0.1	8
1940	0	514	3,197	100	0.0	0
1941	0	505	2,692	97	0.6	10
1942	0	5	2,687	87	3.1	0
1943	0	7	2,680	88	3.0	0
1944	0	0	2,680	87	3.7	0
1945	0	16	2,664	89	3.5	0
1946	0	214	2,450	96	1.1	8
1947	0	316	2,134	99	0.3	0
1948	0	296	1,838	—	—	0
1949	0	83	1,755	—	—	0
1950	0	236	1,519	—	—	0
1951	0	262	1,257	—	—	0
1952	0	240	1,017	—	—	0
1953	0	167	850	—	—	0
1954	0	59	791	—	—	0
1955	0	393	398	—	—	0
1956	0	64	334	—	—	0
1957	0	52	282	—	—	0
1958	0	73	209	—	—	0
1959	0	0	209§	—	—	0

SOURCE: See Fig. 7, p. 190.

The sign — means that figures are not available. After 1947 there is no suitable base for comparison with earlier years.

* This figure does not include line relocations.

† Abandonments consist of discontinuance of all service, or of passenger service only, if the latter occured first.

‡ Miles in service figures consist only of miles in passenger service.

§ Applications to abandon 99 miles of the remaining trackage were before the I.C.C. or state regulatory commissions as of March 1960.

interurbans from crossing their tracks. Outright violence between interurban employees and railroad men was common. Some railroads fought back by establishing cheap local service with steam locomotives and standard passenger cars. A few others instituted local service with McKeen cars which stopped at major highway crossings. Most refused to share their urban stations with interurbans. A handful of railroads even electrified short portions of their lines, an innovation that most dropped quickly. In 1907 the Erie electrified its passenger service between Rochester and Avon (nineteen miles) and on a branch line from Avon to Mount Morris (fifteen miles) for eighteen trains daily. (Figure III, #1.) Electrified service on this line lasted for over twenty-five years.

Besides opposition from railroads, there were other problems interurbans had to contend with. Their flexibility in being able to stop almost anywhere along the line made for a slow schedule. That they had to reach downtown over city streetcar tracks caused a further slowdown. Most steam railroads refused to permit them to share their right-of-way to a downtown terminal, and the cost of acquiring their own right-of-way through legal proceedings would have been prohibitive. In addition, the financing of many interurban lines was inherently unstable, and bankruptcies were numerous even in the prosperous days of the Edwardian era. Writing in 1960, before disenchantment with highways began to set in, Hilton and Due nonetheless conceded some value, however ephemeral, to interurbans:

On land, the interurban was the first major challenge to the railroad passenger train. In 1926, when the interurbans had already passed their peak, they accounted for 11.7 percent of American passenger miles by common carrier, and the railroads 75.2 percent. The rise of the interurban demonstrated that there was a substantial amount of local traffic that could readily be taken away from the railroads. [4]

Locally, Belt Line passenger service, which in its peak years had consisted in twenty-six small trains a day, was abandoned after the First World War, a victim of a one-two punch delivered by street and motor cars. Figure IX, #26 is a 1914 Belt Line timetable, among the last of its genre to be issued.

Figure #2 depicts the interurbans emanating from Buffalo along with some extended streetcar lines. All these routes paralleled existing railroad lines. Clockwise from the Niagara River were five interurbans: (1) the Buffalo & Niagara Falls Electric Railway, (2) the Buffalo & Niagara Falls High Speed Line, (3) the Buffalo Lockport & Olcott Beach, which connected at Lockport with (4) the Buffalo Lockport & Rochester, and (5) the Buffalo and Lake Erie Traction Company. The extended street car lines were: (1) the Buffalo & Williamsville Electric Railway, (2) the Buffalo & Depew Railroad (3) the Buffalo Depew & Lancaster Railway, (4) the Buffalo Gardenville & Ebenezer Railway, and (5) the Hamburg Railway.

The Buffalo & Niagara Falls began operating on September 20, 1895, its construction having taken only 113 days. It was a twenty-mile long double-track line from the Buffalo city line to that of Niagara. Within Buffalo its cars used the tracks of the Buffalo Railway from Court Street to Niagara Street to Tonawanda Street in Lower Black Rock, thence out Amherst Street to Military to the City of Tonawanda where it snaked its way through city streets and crossed the Tonawanda River on the Delaware Avenue Bridge. In North Tonawanda it again worked its way through city streets until at Gratwick it reached the NYC's and Erie's branches to the Falls, both of which it crossed on a trestle. Thence it followed River Road, which in La Salle became Buffalo Avenue, along which it ran into Niagara Falls where, through an agreement with the Niagara Falls & Suspension Bridge Railway, it reached downtown Niagara Falls. The B&NF was an interurban in that it

Figure #2 Electric Railways of Western New York
Gordon, *Buffalo Railways*, 112

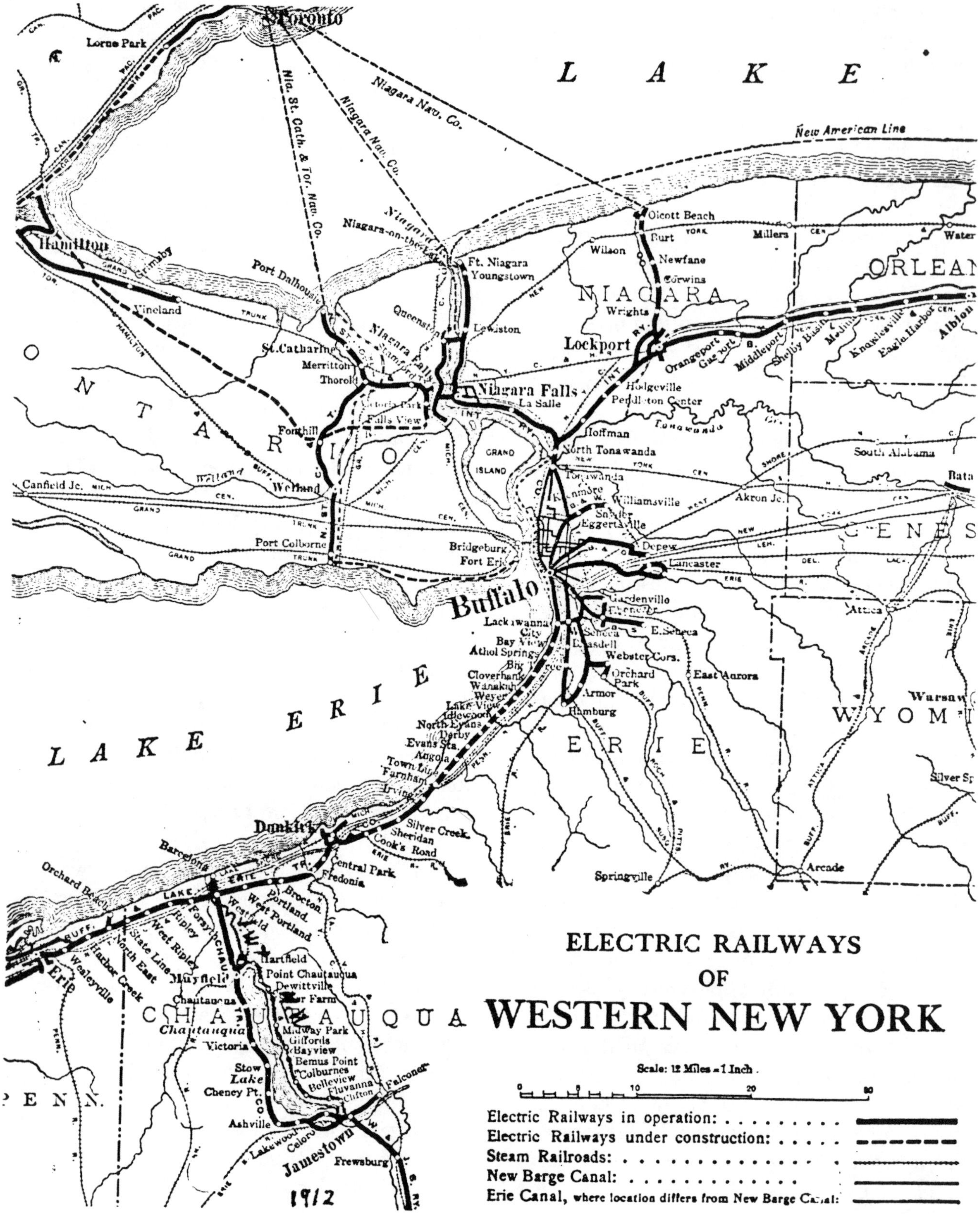

ELECTRIC RAILWAYS
OF
WESTERN NEW YORK

Scale: 12 Miles = 1 Inch.

Electric Railways in operation:
Electric Railways under construction:
Steam Railroads:
New Barge Canal:
Erie Canal, where location differs from New Barge Canal:

1912

connected two cities, but it lacked that other mark of an interurban, a private right-of-way.

In its first year of operation the B&NF carried 662,445 passengers on its thirty-five cars. It ran a car every fifteen minutes from each terminal, and on busy days every seven and a half minutes. The cars did seven and a half miles per hour, including stops, within the city limits of each terminal city, and twenty miles an hour in the open country. Fares were thirty-five cents one way and fifty cents round trip. The steam railroads (the NYC and the Erie) had charged a dollar for a return ticket except on Sundays when it was ninety cents. Because of increased patronage along the line and the resulting frequency of time-consuming stops, an express service was soon inaugurated between the Queen City and the Cataract City whereby cars left Niagara Falls at half hour intervals between 9:00 A. M. and 7:00 P. M. covering the intervening distance in an hour. Arrangements were made to have express cars go around locals at designated points. The 7:00 P. M. departure from Niagara Falls carried theatergoers to Buffalo. Correspondingly, express cars left Buffalo every half hour from 8:30 A. M. to 5:30 P. M. At 11:15 P. M. a theater car departed from Buffalo scheduled to arrive at the Falls at 12:15 A. M. As Gordon remarks, "The neighboring carriers felt the competition," which may have been one of the reasons why the Buffalo & Niagara Falls, though chartered in 1893, could not secure an entrance into the Falls until 1895. Increasing congestion from vehicular traffic made it difficult to adhere to this one hour schedule.

In February, 1902, the Buffalo & Niagara Falls was consolidated with other lines to form the International Railway Com-pany, which thereafter became the dominant force in the electric railroad business (streetcars and interurbans) on the Niagara Frontier. The phenomenal success of the Buffalo-Niagara Falls line explains the decision of the IRC to construct a true interurban between the two cities. To this end, the Frontier Electric Railway was organized in 1907 as a subsidiary of the IRC. Difficulties raised by jurisdictions along the route slowed down progress; and it was not until 1917, just after interurban construction had peaked nationwide, that the IRC put into operation its High Speed Line at a cost of $4,000,000. (For construction photographs of this line see Figure #3.) From Court Street in downtown Buffalo, IRC cars ran on Main Street to a private right-of-way paralleling the Erie Railroad through North Buffalo and the Town and City of Tonawanda to Niagara Falls where it ran from Portage Road along Buffalo Avenue, Erie Avenue, and Falls Street to the terminal. Cars were of the Kuhlman center-entrance variety, capable of sixty miles an hour. Stations north of Main Street were located at Englewood, Elwood, Ellicott Creek, Goundry Street, Division Street, Felton Street, Payne Avenue, Ward Road, La Salle, and 77th Street. The eighty minutes on what was now being called the Old Line was cut to one hour, of which about thirty minutes were spent on Main Street in Buffalo. On this point Gordon writes:

Local service was continued on the old line for about four years, until June 11, 1922, after which it was abandoned, and the High Speed had to take care of local stops between North Tonawanda and the Falls; the running time was increased until it reached seventy-two minutes. While operation on Main Street had always been slow, vehicular traffic congestion increased until it became increasingly so, and part of the twelve minutes added running time was spent there. If even part of the money that was spent for the High Speed had been used to provide a faster entrance into the city, it might have been possible to do as good a job or better with less expenditure of capital. [5]

The Buffalo & Niagara Falls and the High Speed Line exemplify both the strengths and weaknesses of the interurban industry, indicated by Hilton and Due:

Between 1895 and 1902, owing to the open-

Figure #3. Building the High Speed Line
Author's collection

ing of interurbans, traffic on the Lake Shore & Michigan Southern between Cleveland and Painesville fell from 199,292 passengers per year to 28,708, and on the Nickel Plate between Cleveland and Lorain from 42,526 to 9,795. Interurbans had greatest success in attracting traffic from towns ten to forty miles from a major city; they offered service at two-thirds the speed of the railroads, but with at least four to six time the frequency, and at half to two-thirds the fare. The mere fact of this success was enough to stimulate a great deal of uncritical promotion of interurbans. There was little explicit recognition among the interurbans that the industry was attracting the railroad's least profitable passenger traffic: an anonymous official of the Lake Shore & Michigan Southern pointed out that the traffic being lost to the electric lines was barely profitable at best. This realization, however, did little to mollify the hostility with which the railroads viewed the spread of the interurbans. [6]

The Erie's Lockport & Buffalo branch had, despite dogged opposition from the New York Central, gone into operation between North Tonawanda and Lockport in 1879. (Figure VII, #6.) In April, 1898, the Buffalo & Lockport Electric Railway was organized to connect Buffalo and Lockport with a first-class, high-speed electric railway. It proceeded to acquire the trackage and equipment of the Lock City Electric Railway Company, Lockport's streetcar system. In June the Erie Railroad leased to the B&L a portion of its branch between North Tonawanda and Lockport as well as its former Suspension Bridge & Erie Junction line to Main Street in Buffalo whence the tracks of the Buffalo Railway provided access to downtown. As Gordon writes:

Through traffic contracts with the Buffalo Railway Company and the Buffalo-North Tonawanda Electric Railway the [Buffalo & Lockport Railway] *company provided a through line from all parts of Lockport to Buffalo and Niagara Falls. The company did the freight, mail, and express business of the Erie Railroad between Lockport and North Tonawanda. Both the electric cars and the steam trains between Buffalo and Lockport ran directly to the main station of the Erie Railroad at North Tonawanda, and the sight of steam and electric cars, side by side at this point, and doing business through the same train yard was a novel one indeed. . .*

There were six cars on the line between Lockport and Buffalo, making half-hour trips between 6:15 a. m. and 7:15 p. m. The first car left Lockport at 5:15 a. m. and the last at 10:15 p. m. From Buffalo the first car left at 6:30 a. m. and the last at 11:30 p. m. [In Lockport] *the cars switched onto the local line at Transit Road, and ran to East Avenue and Vine Street. A baggage car made three trips daily between 6:20 a. m. and 6:30 p. m.* [7]

An extension of the Buffalo and Lockport was the Lockport & Olcott Beach Railway which opened in the summer of 1900. It was taken over by the IRC in the great merger of 1902 and thereafter operated as the Lockport & Olcott Beach Division. Concerning the Olcott Beach operation Geoff Gerstung writes:

Since trolley lines were built primarily to handle the rush hour crowds of workers going to and from their jobs, street car owners began to dream up ways to entice people to ride the cars that would otherwise be idle on evenings and weekends If a car line could be easily extended to a beach or other attraction, a destination would be developed. Olcott Beach was a natural for such a seasonal business. The trolley company purchased the pine grove along the lake front and developed a park. The large Olcott Beach Hotel was erected at the west end of the park. It featured a fine ballroom, dining room, casino, and 100 rooms for guests. In the park itself a number of attractions were added assuring activities for an enjoyable outing. The Rialto amusement park was across the Lake Road. The beach, wooded park, hotel and amusement area were developed by the railway to generate off-hour traffic. Steamboat service from Toronto brought capacity loads to Olcott and met the railway's dock branch along eighteen Mile Creek also generating trolley revenues . . . In warm weather months thousands rode the electric cars to Olcott Beach. [8]

For many years the 74th Regiment band played for the Saturday night dances. The members of the band rode an open trolley for the thirty-five miles out from Buffalo playing as they passed through towns along the way.

By 1916 the IRC was operating during the season four express fruit trains daily between Buffalo and Olcott and throughout the year it did a lucrative business for way-freight, fast freight, and Wells Fargo shipments between Buffalo and all stations on the division. One-story stations on the line between North Tonawanda and Olcott were at Glenwood Cemetery, Pendelton Center, Burt, Newfane, Wrights, Hoffman, and Corwins. Frame shelters were at Young Street in Tonawanda, and Hinman Road, Railway Street, Hodgeville, Payne Avenue Junction, and Martinsville. In 1916 a brick concrete and steel station was built at Lockport for the Buffalo & Lockport and the Lockport & Olcott Beach divisions of the IRC and the Buffalo Lockport & Rochester. Figure #4 is a 1903 timetable of the IRC's Buffalo, Lockport, and Olcott Beach line.

The Buffalo Lockport & Rochester Railway was chartered on June 22, 1905, as the result of a merger of the Albion & Lockport and the Albion & Rochester, which had both been incorporated on September 2, 1904, and the Albion Electric Railway, which had been incorporated in 1901. Only the AER had done any track laying, 1.7 miles in the village of Albion. The BL&R opened for business between Rochester and Albion (31 miles) on September 4, 1908. The next year it was extended to Lockport, fifty-five miles from

Figure #4 Buffalo-Lockport Line timetable
Gordon, *Buffalo Railways*, 404

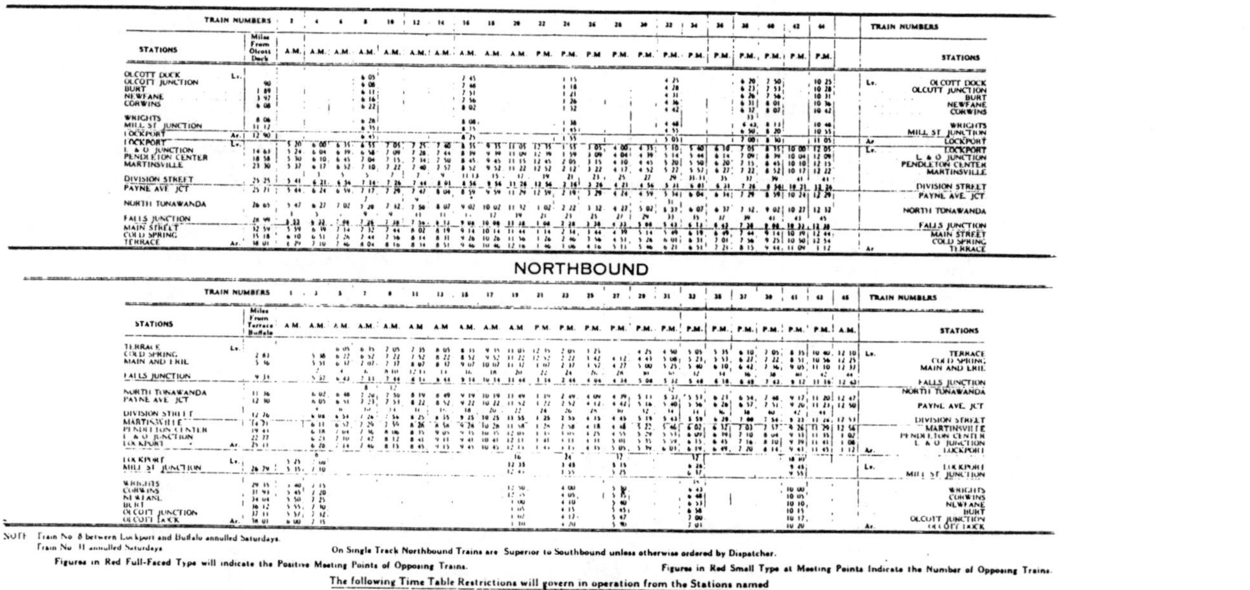

WEEKDAY TIME TABLE NO. 30
Superseding Buffalo, Lockport and Olcott Time Table No. 28
ISSUED FOR THE GUIDANCE OF EMPLOYEES

INTERNATIONAL RAILWAY COMPANY
UNDER MITTEN MANAGEMENT
BUFFALO, LOCKPORT AND OLCOTT DIVISION

EFFECTIVE 5 A.
FEBRUARY 1, 19

SOUTHBOUND

STATIONS		Miles From Olcott Dock	2 A.M.	4 A.M.	6 A.M.	8 A.M.	10 A.M.	12 A.M.	14 A.M.	16 A.M.	18 A.M.	20 A.M.	22 P.M.	24 P.M.	26 P.M.	28 P.M.	30 P.M.	32 P.M.	34 P.M.	36 P.M.	38 P.M.	40 P.M.	42 P.M.	44 P.M.
OLCOTT DOCK	Lv.					6 05				7 45				1 15				4 25			6 20	7 50		10 25
OLCOTT JUNCTION		.90				6 08				7 46				1 18				4 28			6 23	7 53		10 28
BURT		1 89				6 11				7 51				1 21				4 31			6 26	7 56		10 31
NEWFANE		3 97				6 16				7 56				1 26				4 36			6 31	8 01		10 36
CORWINS		6 08				6 22				8 02				1 32				4 42			6 37	8 07		10 42
WRIGHTS		8 06				6 28				8 08				1 38				4 48			6 43	8 13		10 48
MILL ST JUNCTION		11 12				6 35				8 15				1 45				4 55			6 50	8 20		10 55
LOCKPORT	Ar.	12 90				6 45				8 25				1 55				5 05			7 00	8 30		11 05
LOCKPORT	Lv.		5 20	6 00	6 35	6 55	7 05	7 25	7 40	8 35	9 35	11 05	12 35	1 55	3 05	4 00	4 35	5 10	5 40	6 10	7 05	8 35	10 00	12 05
L & O JUNCTION		14 63	5 24	6 04	6 39	6 58	7 09	7 28	7 44	8 39	9 39	11 09	12 39	1 59	3 09	4 04	4 39	5 14	5 44	6 14	7 09	8 39	10 04	12 09
PENDLETON CENTER		18 58	5 30	6 10	6 45	7 04	7 15	7 34	7 50	8 45	9 45	11 15	12 45	2 05	3 15	4 10	4 45	5 20	5 50	6 20	7 15	8 45	10 10	12 15
MARTINSVILLE		21 30	5 37	6 17	6 52	7 10	7 22	7 40	7 57	8 52	9 52	11 22	12 52	2 12	3 22	4 17	4 52	5 27	5 57	6 27	7 22	8 52	10 17	12 22
DIVISION STREET		25 25	5 41	6 21	6 56	7 14	7 26	7 44	8 01	8 56	9 56	11 26	12 56	2 16	3 26	4 21	4 56	5 31	6 01	6 31	7 26	8 56	10 21	12 26
PAYNE AVE JCT		25 71	5 44	6 24	6 59	7 17	7 29	7 47	8 04	8 59	9 59	11 29	12 59	2 19	3 29	4 24	4 59	5 34	6 04	6 34	7 29	8 59	10 24	12 29
NORTH TONAWANDA		26 65	5 47	6 27	7 02	7 20	7 32	7 50	8 07	9 02	10 02	11 32	1 02	2 22	3 32	4 27	5 02	5 37	6 07	6 37	7 32	9 02	10 27	12 32
FALLS JUNCTION		28 99	5 53	6 33	7 08	7 26	7 38	7 56	8 13	9 08	10 08	11 38	1 08	2 28	3 38	4 33	5 08	5 43	6 13	6 43	7 38	9 08	10 33	12 38
MAIN STREET		32 59	5 59	6 39	7 14	7 32	7 44	8 02	8 19	9 14	10 14	11 44	1 14	2 14	3 44	4 39	5 14	5 49	6 19	6 49	7 44	9 14	10 39	12 44
COLD SPRING		35 18	6 10	6 51	7 26	7 44	7 56	8 14	8 31	9 26	10 26	11 56	1 26	2 46	3 56	4 51	5 26	6 01	6 31	7 01	7 56	9 25	10 50	12 54
TERRACE	Ar.	38 01	6 29	7 10	7 46	8 04	8 16	8 34	8 51	9 46	10 46	12 16	1 46	3 06	4 16	5 11	5 46	6 21	6 51	7 21	8 15	9 44	11 09	1 12

NORTHBOUND

STATIONS		Miles From Terrace Buffalo	1 A.M.	3 A.M.	5 A.M.	7 A.M.	9 A.M.	11 A.M.	13 A.M.	15 A.M.	17 A.M.	19 A.M.	21 P.M.	23 P.M.	25 P.M.	27 P.M.	29 P.M.	31 P.M.	33 P.M.	35 P.M.	37 P.M.	39 P.M.	41 P.M.	43 P.M.	45 A.M.
TERRACE	Lv.				6 05	6 35	7 05	7 35	8 05	8 35	9 35	11 05	12 35	2 05	3 25		4 25	4 50	5 05	5 35	6 10	7 05	8 35	10 40	12 10
COLD SPRING		2 83		5 38	6 22	6 52	7 22	7 52	8 22	8 52	9 52	11 22	12 52	2 22	3 42	4 12	4 43	5 08	5 23	5 53	6 27	7 22	8 51	10 56	12 25
MAIN AND ERIE		5 16		5 51	6 37	7 07	7 37	8 07	8 37	9 07	10 07	11 37	1 07	2 37	3 57	4 27	5 00	5 25	5 40	6 10	6 42	7 36	9 05	11 10	12 37
FALLS JUNCTION		9 35		5 57	6 43	7 13	7 44	8 14	8 44	9 14	10 14	11 44	1 14	2 44	4 04	4 34	5 04	5 32	5 48	6 18	6 48	7 43	9 12	11 16	12 43
NORTH TONAWANDA		11 36		6 02	6 48	7 20	7 50	8 19	8 49	9 19	10 19	11 49	1 19	2 49	4 09	4 39	5 11	5 37	5 51	6 21	6 54	7 48	9 17	11 20	12 47
PAYNE AVE JCT		12 30		6 05	6 51	7 23	7 53	8 22	8 52	9 22	10 22	11 52	1 22	2 52	4 12	4 42	5 16	5 40	5 56	6 26	6 57	7 51	9 20	11 23	12 50
DIVISION STREET		12 76		6 08	6 54	7 26	7 56	8 25	8 55	9 25	10 25	11 55	1 25	2 55	4 15	4 45	5 19	5 43	5 59	6 29	7 00	7 54	9 23	11 26	12 53
MARTINSVILLE		14 71		6 11	6 57	7 29	7 59	8 26	8 58	9 26	10 28	11 58	1 28	2 58	4 18	4 48	5 22	5 46	6 02	6 32	7 03	7 57	9 26	11 29	12 56
PENDLETON CENTER		19 41		6 18	7 04	7 36	8 06	8 35	9 05	9 35	10 35	12 05	[illegible]	[illegible]	4 25	4 55	5 29	5 53	6 09	6 39	7 10	8 04	9 33	11 35	1 02
L & O JUNCTION		22 77		6 23	7 10	7 42	8 12	8 41	9 11	9 41	10 41	12 11	1 41	[illegible]	[illegible]	5 01	5 35	5 59	6 15	6 45	7 16	8 10	9 39	11 41	1 08
LOCKPORT	Ar.	25 11		6 26	7 14	7 46	8 15	8 45	9 15	9 45	10 45	12 15	1 45	[illegible]	4 35	5 05	5 39	6 01	6 19	6 49	7 20	8 14	9 41	11 45	1 12
LOCKPORT	Lv.		5 25	7 00								12 35		3 45		5 15			6 26				9 45		
MILL ST JUNCTION		26 79	5 35	7 10								12 41		3 55		5 25			6 37				9 55		
WRIGHTS		29 15	5 40	7 15								12 50		4 00		5 30			6 43				10 00		
CORWINS		31 93	5 45	7 20								12 55		4 05		5 35			6 48				10 05		
NEWFANE		34 04	5 50	7 25								1 00		4 10		5 40			6 53				10 10		
BURT		36 12	5 55	7 30								1 05		4 15		5 45			6 58				10 15		
OLCOTT JUNCTION		37 11	5 57	7 32								1 07		4 17		5 47			7 00				10 17		
OLCOTT DOCK	Ar.	38 01	6 00	7 35								1 10		4 20		5 50			7 01				10 20		

NOTE Train No. 8 between Lockport and Buffalo annulled Saturdays.
Train No. 11 annulled Saturdays.

On Single Track Northbound Trains are Superior to Southbound unless otherwise ordered by Dispatcher.

Figures in Red Full-Faced Type will indicate the Positive Meeting Points of Opposing Trains.

Figures in Red Small Type at Meeting Points Indicate the Number of Opposing Trains.

The following Time Table Restrictions will govern in operation from the Stations named

MAIN STREET No train or section of a train will move northbound without calling Dispatcher.
NIAGARA FALLS JUNCTION No train or section of a train will move northbound without a clearance card or a train order issued at Niagara Falls Junction by Dispatcher.
DIVISION STREET, END D. T. No train or section of a train will move southbound without a clearance card issued at Division Street, by Dispatcher.
LOCKPORT, END D. T. No train or section of a train will move northbound or southbound without a clearance card issued at Lockport, by Dispatcher.
OLCOTT BEACH No train or section of a train will move southbound without a clearance card or train order issued by Dispatcher.
MILL STREET JUNCTION No train or section of a train will move northbound or southbound without clearance card or train order issued by Dispatcher at Lockport.

M. L. CAMPBELL,
Operating Manager

Rochester, paralleling the New York Central's Falls Road. The project had gone bankrupt during construction and was completed by Toronto interests as part of a projected high-speed Rochester-Toronto route. Consequently it was exceptionally well built with seventy pound rail and crushed rock ballast, and equipped with heavy high-speed, multiple unit cars. The link with Toronto was never built. By agreement with the IRC, BL&R cars ran to Olcott and to Buffalo between 1914 and 1919, but for the rest of the line's existence a change at Lockport was necessary. Electric railway developments in northern Erie and southern Niagara County had made North Tonawanda a hub of steam, street, and interurban railroads. (Figure #5)

Southeast from the Lockport line in Figure #2 was the Buffalo & Williamsville Electric Railway, a suburban single track route which ran from the end of the Buffalo Railway's Main Street line at the Buffalo-Amherst boundary for four and a half miles along Main Street through Eggertsville and Williamsville to Transit Road. It was chartered in 1891 and began operations on April 4, 1893. An undated timetable, undoubtedly from the little line's glory days, shows cars leaving Williamsville every twenty minutes from 5:40 to 8:30 A. M. and City Line every twenty minutes from 6:00 until 8:30 A.M. Thereafter, cars followed each other every half-hour each way until 5:00 P. M. when a twelve minute headway between cars was established until 7:30 when they proceeded in both directions at half-hour intervals until midnight. While most cars only went as far as Williamsville, fourteen cars a day went to and from Transit Road. In fiscal year ending June 30, 1904 the line carried 427,604 passengers and showed a surplus of $4,498.

At the turn of the century, Depew, some twelve miles from Buffalo, was a village of about 2,200. Its two major employers were the NYC and the Union Car Company. The Buffalo & Depew Railway was incorporated in 1897. It ran east from a connection with the terminus of the Buffalo Railway's Genesee Street line at Pine Ridge Road to Depew on a private-right-of-way (now George Urban Boulevard) to Transit Road, where it turned south and then east, threading its way through village streets to the end of the line at Burlington Avenue and Ellicott Street. When completed in 1901, it had 7.25 miles of double track, five of which was private right-of-way, with an additional half mile along Pine Ridge Road to service the cemeteries. A safety feature that many electric railroads lacked was the fact that the B&D crossed no steam railroad at grade. Management had visions of extending the line to Batavia and even Rochester, but the completion of the Buffalo Lockport & Rochester in 1909 forced the abandonment of this project.

South from the Buffalo & Depew was the Buffalo Bellevue & Lancaster Electric Railroad which began operations between Lancaster and the Buffalo-Cheektowaga line in April, 1893. A special attraction during the summer was Bellevue Park, a mecca for picnickers, where the electric line crossed Cayuga Creek. By 1894 a newer and more direct line was in place. It began at the terminus of the Buffalo Railway's Broadway line, turned south on Atlantic Avenue for about four hundred feet, and then struck eastward on its own right-of-way to Union Road, along which it ran before turning again east and heading straight for Lancaster. In 1897 the BB&L was taken over by Buffalo Railway, which was in turn merged into the IRC in 1902. The Lancaster line ended in a loop. As explained by Gordon, "the first car would go by way of Depew and return from the south end of Lancaster with the next car going through the south end of Lancaster and returning by way of Depew." After the merger, Lancaster cars ran through to Buffalo on Broadway, terminating at Main and Clinton Streets. The schedule at the turn of the century was a car every twenty-two minutes from 6:00 A. M. to 9:00 P. M.

To the south of the BB&L was the Buffalo

Figure #5. North Tonawanda, a steam and electric railway hub
ibid., 472

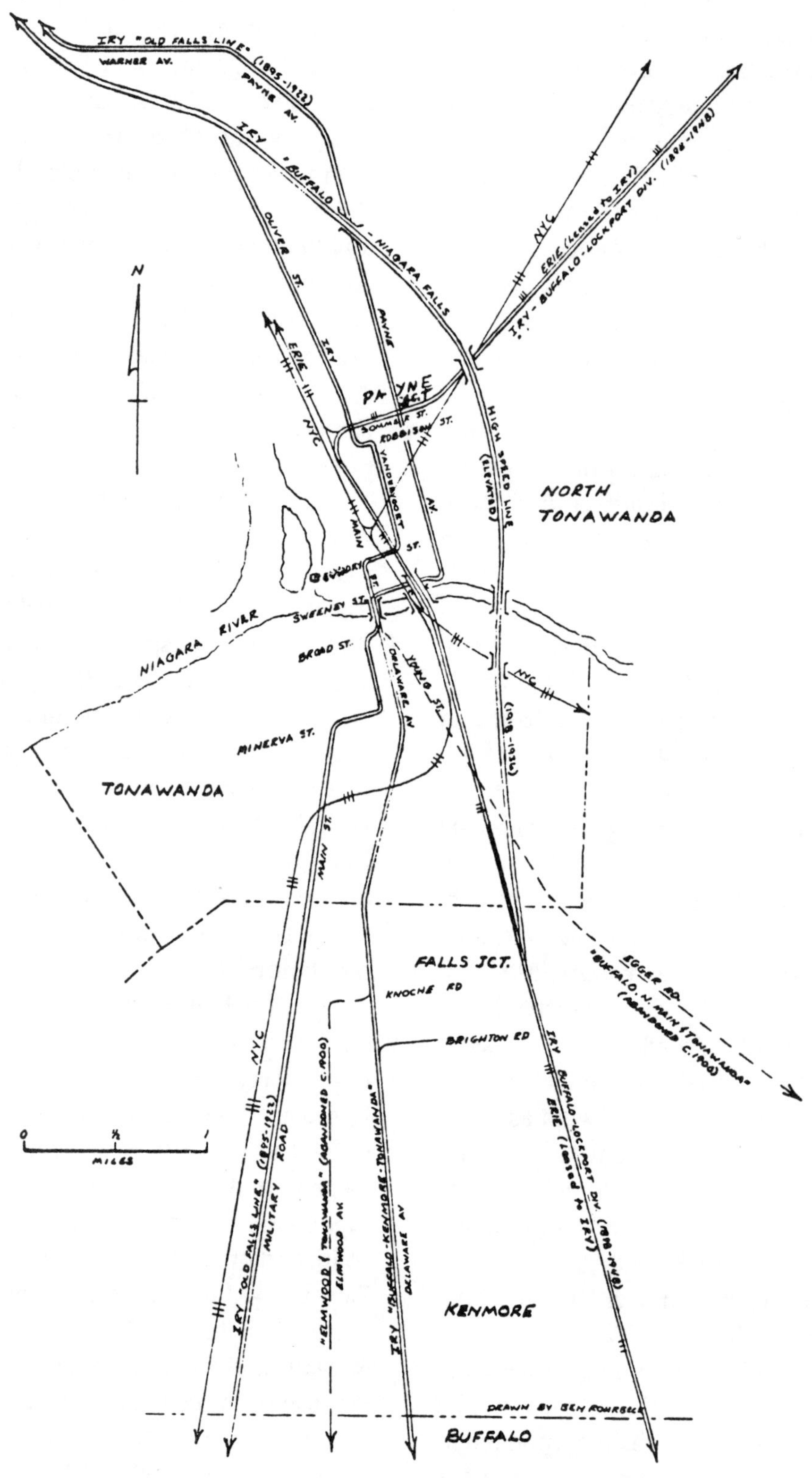

Gardenville & Ebenezer which started operations on April 18, 1896. It ran from a connection with the Buffalo Railway's Seneca Street line at the Buffalo-West Seneca boundary. From there it turned northeast along Burch Street and ran north for 1.75 miles to Winchester Avenue (later Indian Church Road), on which it ran east for two miles to Gardenville where it turned south on Union Road for 5.75 miles to Ebenezer on Cazenovia Creek. Cars were operated between 5:25 A. M and 9:45 P. M. on a headway of forty minutes during winter, thirty during summer, and fifteen on Sundays and holidays. On weekends the last run was at midnight. The BG&E serviced two popular picnic grounds, Island Park in Gardenville and Lein's Park in Ebenezer. By 1906 at the latest an alternate line was in place which ran straight out Seneca Street to Ebenezer.

South of the BG&E was the Buffalo Hamburg & Aurora which opened for business on October 5, 1899. Its point of departure from Buffalo was the same as that of the BG&E, Seneca Street and the city line, whence it ran south along the city line on a private right-of-way (later Onondaga Street) through Cazenovia Park to Dorrance Avenue, where it turned west to Abbott Road and down Abbott through Windom to Armor. There it turned southwest along Clark Street past the Erie County Fairgrounds into the Village of Hamburg, running along Buffalo Street to the terminal on Main Street. On "Buffalo Day at the Fair" fifteen to twenty cars would be lined up at the fairgrounds to handle the crowds from the city. The mainline to Hamburg was eleven miles long. At Webster's Corners Road south of Windom, at a place called Orchard Park Junction, a four mile long branch line led to Orchard Park. Hopes were entertained for an extension to East Aurora - as indicated by the corporate title - but this was never built. In 1904 the BG&E and the BH&A were merged into the Buffalo Southern. Yet a third suburban line departed from Seneca Street and the city line, the Hamburg Railway, which had commenced operations in 1897 as a two and a half mile single track line from Ridge Road and South Park Avenue in West Seneca (soon to become Lackawanna) to Blasdell along a thoroughfare aptly named Electric Avenue. In 1901 it was extended south to the Village of Hamburg, thus providing the most direct route thence to Buffalo.

The last of the electric lines out of Buffalo was the Buffalo & Lake Erie Traction Company, the outgrowth of the Erie, Pennsylvania, streetcar system which had thrust out a line to North East and then, under the aegis of the Lake Erie Short Line, crossed into New York State. By 1906 its cars were covering the thirty-five miles from Erie to Westfield. Meanwhile, from the opposite direction, in a manner reminiscent of the construction from both ends of the Union Pacific-Central Pacific Railroads, the Buffalo Dunkirk & Western, chartered in 1903, was being built southwest along the shores of Lake Erie. By contrast with the line out of Erie, which consisted mostly of roadside trackage and which when it entered towns ran down the middle of the street, the BD&W was an authentic interurban. It reached its Buffalo terminal adjoining the Hotel Lafayette on Lafayette Square over the tracks of a leased streetcar line, the Buffalo & Lackawanna Traction Company, incorporated in 1906, which ran out to Lackawanna on Louisiana Street and, after crossing Buffalo Creek, ran along the Hamburg Turnpike past the steel plant to Woodlawn. Here cars transferred to the B&LE's double-track private right-of-way, which paralleled on the west the Lake Shore Division of the NYC to Farnham, where it ran under the tracks of NYC, the NKP, and the PRR and proceeded southwest alongside the railroads to Westfield. The BL&E then absorbed the lines beyond Westfield and opened for business along its entire line on January 1, 1909. It operated into Buffalo on its own leased trackage, the IRC having acquired all the other city lines. This facilitated operations since the Erie-Buffalo cars were not obliged to compete with local trolleys. Elsewhere operating conditions were not so felicitous. As Gordon writes about Dunkirk:

The through limiteds joined the Dunkirk-Fredonia local cars on a meandering route through the twin cities. At one point in Dunkirk where the tracks went north to Lake Erie, the limiteds were farther from Fredonia and their ultimate goal of Erie than when they entered the city. [9]

In addition to the Lackawanna Traction Company, the B&L also acquired the Hamburg Railway, a connection between the two being supplied by a line along Ridge Road in Lackawanna. Gordon describes the history of the B&LE during the second decade of the twentieth century:

Except for the terminal cities, the only substantial community served was Dunkirk, with its 20,000 citizens and famed as the home of the American Locomotive Works. The south shore of Lake Erie is fertile for only a few miles inland and is justly famed for its grapes, garden crops, and general farming. But once you are south of the verdant shoreline the land is rough and poor. The only important feeder to the B&LE was at Westfield, where passenger and freight traffic from Jamestown and the Lake Chautauqua resorts transferred from two lines, the Jamestown and Lake Erie and the Chautauqua Traction Company. The former was leased by the B&LE from 1906 to 1915, when it was returned to its bondholders and became the long-lived electric Jamestown Westfield & Northwestern [JW&NW -Jesus walked and no wonder!] *Peak of B&LE operations was about 1914 when with its subsidiary lines it brought in over $17 million in fares and operated 4.6 million car miles and hauled 15,000 tons of freight, using 200 cars of all types. Through Buffalo-Erie service had steam competition plus the growing motor traffic over roads which had been fully paved between the two cities by 1920. Relatively light traffic was originated by small towns and cities along the line, and the JW&NW feeder at Westfield was of a resort nature and specially susceptible to the motor car. In 1915 the B&LE went into ten years of receivership.* [10]

Automobiles

Highway transportation had won such an apparently crushing victory over the railroad by the 1960s that it was difficult to realize that for almost thirty years after the first horseless carriage was exhibited at the Chicago World's Fair in 1893 the role of the automobile in American life was still evolving. As Martin writes in <u>Enterprise Denied</u>:

By 1910, to be sure, automobile manufacturing was a prominent industry. Railroads were hauling thousands of the machines, no longer a rich man's toy, to all parts of the nation. No category of finished manufactured goods added more to the railroads' traffic burden in these years. Until after World War I the railroads looked upon the automobile as an almost pure blessing. Since the dawn of the railroad age, the lack of a practical road vehicle to bridge the gap between farm and depot had been one of the major irritants of American life, and when one became available farmers turned out to be the first mass market for cars. Henry Ford transformed the problem from one of vehicles to one of roads. After 1910 the chorus of complaints grew rapidly into the good roads movement, of which the railroads were a highly vocal sponsor. Rails and motors had, if anything, a symbiotic relationship before about 1916. Present-day notions of their antagonistic relationship are not applicable to their history before World War I. [11]

To this day a popular type of auto is called a station wagon. For an illustration of the positive relationship between the auto and rural stations see the picture of the Albion station in Figure XVI, #2.

Statistics on the growth of automobiles to 1920, however, gave the railroads cause for concern. They had contributed to unleashing a Frankenstein. As Spencer Miller wrote in Highways in Our National Life:

From 1895 to 1904 the number of automobiles in the U. S. increased from four experimental cars to 55,290 in actual use - including 700 trucks. The rate of increase of both passenger automobiles and trucks from that time on was enormous. By 1910 there were in use 468,500 registered motor vehicles of which 10,123 were motor trucks. By 1920 there were 9,239,161 registered motor vehicles of which 1,1107,639 were trucks and buses. [Figure #6.] [12]

Two other authors in an article on railroads and highways in the same work observed that railroads had long been interested in the improvement of feeder roads, adding that:

. . . in 1901 the first "Good Roads" trains were inaugurated, with the cooperation of railroad officials and manufacturers of road machinery. The Illinois Central Railroad ran such a train in that year between Chicago and New Orleans at an estimated cost of from 40 to 50 thousand dollars for a three month period. In the same year, "Good Roads" trains were operated also by the Lake Shore and Michigan Southern and by the Southern Railway. Later, such trains were run by other railroads, and the railroads continued to encourage the improvement of public highways. By 1916, however, highways and highway traffic were beginning to have an effect on the movement of persons and goods from city to city, over short distances, as well as locally. Both private automobiles and trucks were increasing their radii of operation, and the bus was making its appearance. Highway transportation for inter-city traffic, although at that time in its infancy, was destined to grow increasingly important with the years. [13]

An unfortunate development from the railroad point of view in this growth was the fact that that less than ten percent of highway user payments were spent on urban roads. Rural roads were the chief beneficiaries of the system and it was these roads, once they were pushed beyond the country station, that facilitated intercity motor vehicle transportation. This was also highly unfair to cities since almost one half of the revenues received from motor-fuel taxes and vehicle-license fees was derived from traffic using urban streets. The result after 1916 was an increasing congestion in urban traffic.

Progressive Strangulation

By the end of the 1880s, as a result of the extensive railroad construction of that decade, America's railroad network was, as has been noted above, substantially in place. The railroads converted fifty-four different times Americans observed into four time zones. Rate adjustment would prove more difficult. As canals before them, railroads discovered that if they were to move heavy commodities which sold cheaply they had to grant low rates. Thus rates for coal, wheat, livestock, and metals were lower than those for groceries, furniture, or clothes. Furthermore, terminal costs were the same for local and transcontinental shipments, which made it impossible to determine rates by a simple weight-mileage formula. Also, on through long-distance traffic it was best to carry full cargoes both ways, since hauling empty cars hundreds of miles was costly. Finally, railroads had a high fixed investment in roadbeds, rolling stock, and stations, to say nothing of interest on their bonds. These costs continued whether any business was done or not, a situation which led freight and passenger agents to reduce rates to get any business at all. As a result, railroads resorted to a pricing system which consisted, according to disgruntled shippers, in "charging all the traffic will bear." A more nuanced description would be "charging no more than the article will bear," since above that point the shipper

Figure #6. Surfaced road mileage, 1793-1925
Labatut and Lane, *Highways*, 78

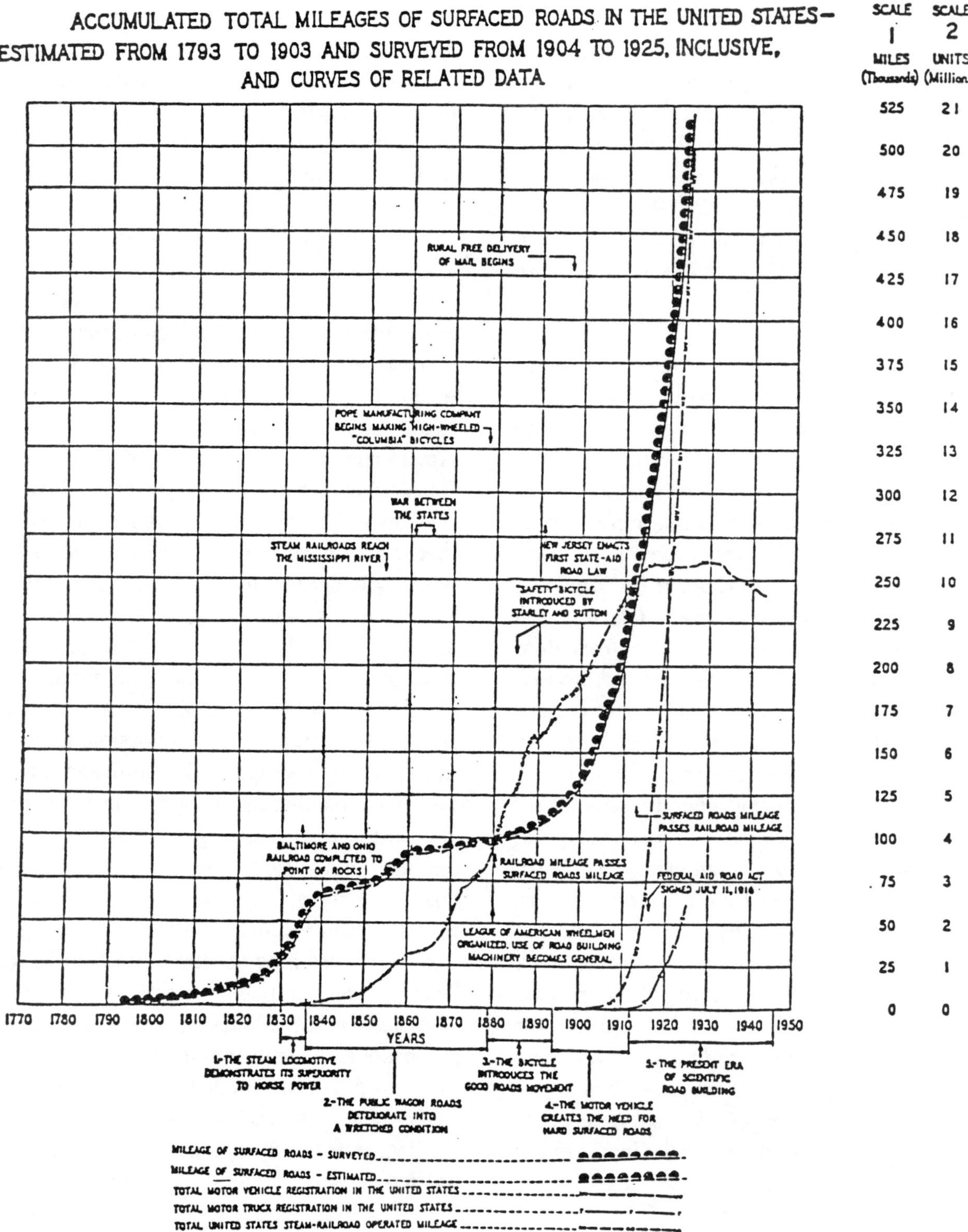

would not ship, and railroads would be putting themselves and their customers out of business.

While economically rational where monopoly prevailed, value-of-service (to the passenger or shipper) pricing became irrational and self-destructive where competition existed. That railroads competed in some places and were monopolies in others made rational rates difficult to establish. By the mid-1880s two or more competing railroads served most cities, while one road served most rural sections. The fiercest rivalry was in Trunk Line territory, handling long-haul through traffic between Chicago-Saint Louis and the major northeastern seaports, the battleground of the Grand Trunk, NYC, Erie, PRR, and B&O. Sporadic rate-cutting culminated in the disastrous 1876-1877 rate war when eastbound first class freight rates were slashed by eighty-five percent and westbound rates by two-thirds. Moreover, to increase freight and to stabilize costs for large shippers, railroads rebated up to half of published rates to companies guaranteeing big and steady shipments.

To maintain rates under these conditions, railroads formed pools and assigned to member roads an agreed upon part of the traffic. The Iowa Pool (between the Chicago Burlington & Quincy, the Chicago & Northwestern, and the Chicago Rock Island & Pacific), which lasted from 1870 to 1885, allowed member roads to retain forty-five percent of passenger income and half of freight income while equally dividing the income from the remainder, meanwhile eschewing rate-cutting. (Figure #7.) In 1877, following the rate war, the NYC, the PRR, the Erie, and the B&O formed a pool administered by the Eastern Trunk Line Executive Committee; Western roads formed the Western Executive Committee; and Albert Fink chaired the Joint Executive Committee which administered the arrangement by enforcing pooling rates and dividing traffic and receipts among member roads. But though they helped stabilize rates,

Figure #7. Iowa Pool Roads, 1873
Grodinsky, *Continental Railway Strategy*, 86-87

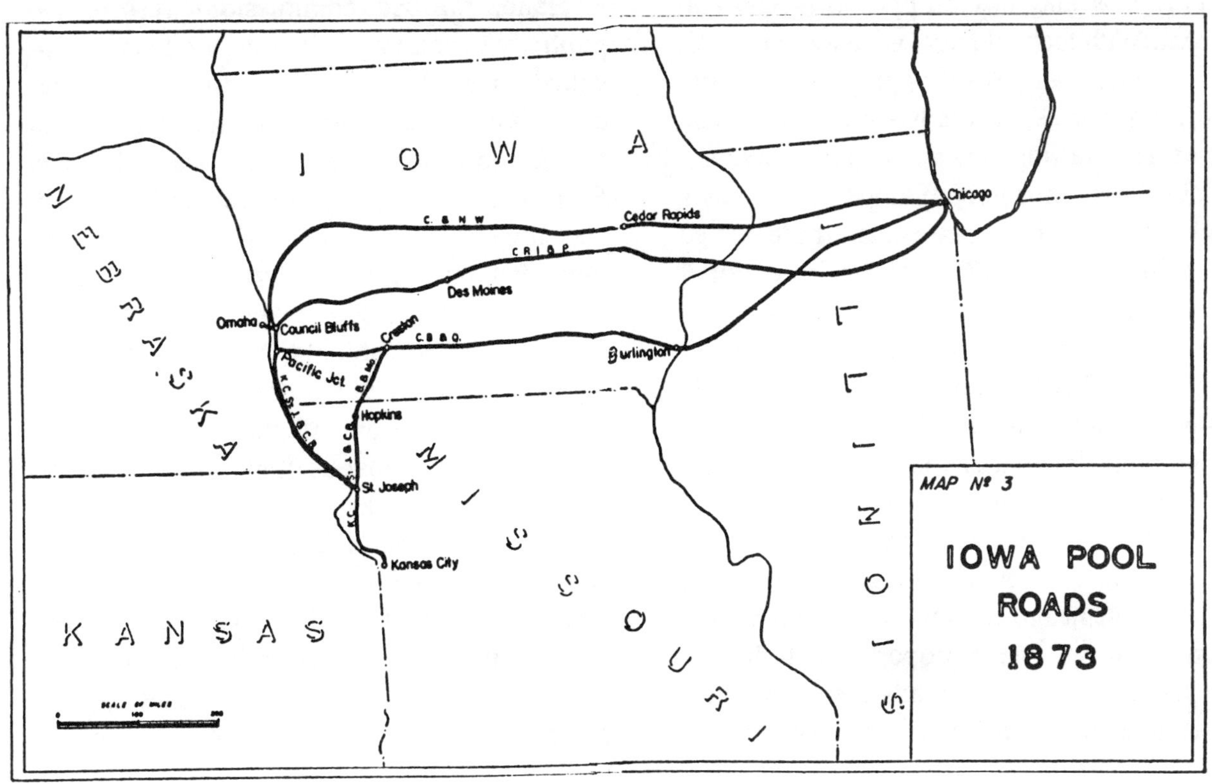

most pools were unstable. Individual roads cheated by keeping more than their share of revenue, and the courts refused to enforce agreements.

Railroad management preferred consolidation to pools. Mighty railroads like the PRR and the NYC had built their systems by leasing feeder and competing lines. In the twenty years before 1873 many short lines combined end-to-end to form trunk lines, and during the succeeding two decades these trunk lines acquired feeder lines and became giant systems. Railroad executives alone or through their companies frequently neutralized a troublesome road by acquiring stock control. Personal holdings and interlocking directorships got around recently enacted state legislation prohibiting railroads from buying competing properties. During the 1880s, restrictions on combinations began to disappear. The consolidation movement peaked during a sixteen month period in 1899-1900 when a sixth of the nation's rail mileage was absorbed by other lines.

Nonetheless, from 1865 to 1885 freight rates, outpacing the deflation which characterized the '70s and '80s, dropped as much as 50 percent. With technological advances and with fuel and steel rail costs dropping more rapidly than freight rates, railroads were able to sustain these falling rates, which, however, remained discriminatory. Shippers served by a single road paid higher rates than those served by competing roads. The PRR, with its Pittsburgh-Lake Erie monopoly, charged Carnegie's steel company proportionately higher freight rates than those paid by his rivals, while competing railroads gave John D. Rockefeller rebates and drawbacks (part of his competitors' payments!) for his Cleveland-based Standard Oil Company. The PRR charged more to ship grain from Chicago to Pittsburgh than from Chicago to New York, and everywhere local rates were proportionately higher than through rates. Railroads destroyed businesses and stunted regions. Thus discriminatory rates on Minneapolis flour ruined New York State millers, while rates on Chicago-bound Iowa grain and livestock starved Iowa towns on the Mississippi.

Although many shippers opposed discrimination, they could not agree on how to eliminate it. Moreover, railroads appeared more prosperous than they were, since their total costs were greater than their operating costs indicated. Some opinion makers favored nationalization, others wanted stabilized pools, and still others wanted to consolidate all roads into a few privately controlled systems. Others, rejecting these solutions, called for government regulation compelling roads to compete. But competition had introduced discriminatory rates in the first place. Regulation, some railroad executives hoped, could also stabilize rates and reduce competition by promoting pools.

By 1860, four states had established railroad commissions to see that a railroad's charter was complied with, to enforce safety regulations, or to prevent rate and service discrimination. Between the end of the Civil War and 1887, their number grew rapidly. In New England, railroad commissions resorted to publicity to achieve their ends, while in the so-called Granger states of the Midwest stronger commissions determined maximum rates and forbade discrimination on the basis of place. Railroads challenged state regulation which was upheld in the early 1870s by state and lower federal courts. In 1876 the United States Supreme Court upheld state regulation in *Munn v. Illinois,* holding that when "one devotes his property to a use in which the public has an interest, he, in effect, grants to the public an interest in that use; and must submit to be controlled by the public for the common good, to the extent of the interest he has thus created." Moreover, "common carriers exercise a sort of public office, and have duties to perform in which the public is interested. . . . Their business is therefore 'affected with a public interest.' " These common carriers could, accordingly, "charge only a reasonable sum." Courts could determine these reasonable rates, it was decided, until state legislatures acted, and, absent federal legislation, state legislatures could regulate even interstate railroads. However, conflicting state laws frequently produced confusion, and railroads tried to recoup money lost on regulated local traffic by raising unregulated through rates. In 1886 the Supreme Court's *Wabash Railroad v. Illinois* decision denied the right of Illinois to regulate interstate rates between points in Illinois and New York, concluding that if interstate commerce were to be regulated it must be by "general principles, which demand that it should be done by the Congress of the United States under the commerce clause of the Constitution."

Farmers, merchants, and independent oil producers had secured the enactment of state laws regulating rates and creating commissions to enforce them. By 1878, however, Granger laws in Minnesota, Wisconsin and Iowa had been repealed. Limiting rates limited profits and discouraged construction of new railroads in the offending states. Congressman John H. Reagan of Texas sponsored a bill in 1878 which prohibited pooling, rebates, and discrimination, required that railroads post rate schedules, and looked to the courts for enforcement. It passed the House but was defeated in the Senate, which in those days performed its Hamilton-envisioned role of protecting property. With the disintegration of pools in the early 1880s and the return of cutthroat competition, some railroad officials accepted the principle of federal regulation, but not Reagan's bill. They favored a bill proposed by Senator Shelby M. Cullom of Illinois which also outlawed rebates and called for reasonable and publicized rates, but did not outlaw pooling, had a more flexible long-short-haul clause, and provided for a commission which conceivably could enforce pools. In January, 1885, the House again passed the Reagan bill. while next month the Senate approved the Cullom bill, but Congress adjourned before reaching an agreement. For some, the Wabash decision made federal legislation necessary since it created a twilight zone, in which states could not, and the federal government did not regulate railroads. Managers from both houses compromised. Reagan antagonized Grangers by accepting a commission and disappointed railroad management by outlawing pooling and stiffening Cullom's long-short-haul clause.

In February, 1887, President Cleveland signed the Interstate Commerce Act, which created a five-man commission appointed by the president, outlawed pools and rate discrimination, whether by special rates, rebates, drawbacks, or long-short-haul discrimination "under substantially similar circumstances and conditions" - and demanded that rates be "reasonable and just" and published. The commission was empowered to investigate interstate railroads, secure testimony and documentation, and issue orders. If a railroad ignored the ICC's orders, the commission had to take the matter to the appropriate federal circuit court, with the aid of the Attorney General and federal district attorneys, for determination which, could include damages and criminal penalties. The commission's findings were to be deemed *prima facie* evidence as to the facts in the case in subsequent judicial proceedings. However, the carriers could disregard the commission's orders until these were upheld by the courts.

Shortly after the law went into effect over a thousand complaints and questions swamped the ICC. The most vexing problem concerned section 4, the long-short-haul clause. Long-short-haul discrimination was common in the South, where competing water transportation often forced low rates. Pending an investigation, the ICC temporarily suspended section 4 for roads south of the Ohio and east of the Mississippi. On May 18, 1887, the ICC ruled that no general exceptions would be made, and that exceptional cases would be established by investigation. One month later in its key

Louisville & Nashville decision, the ICC declared that railroads - not the ICC - would have to decide initially whether the "circumstances and conditions" of their long-short-haul traffic were sufficiently dissimilar to justify charging less for a long haul than for a short one. For guidelines, the ICC stated that exceptions to Section 4 were justified only when competing either with unregulated traffic (water transport or foreign carriers, e.g. Canada's Grand Trunk) or in "rare and peculiar cases." If a railroad decided upon rate discrimination and was challenged, it would have to prove that circumstances warranted discrimination or suffer the consequences, a $5,000 fine. While railroad men were happy with this decision, it also benefited many shippers who would be hurt by a rigid application of Section 4. Where competition from water routes and Canadian railroads existed, strict adherence would raise, not lower, both long-haul and short-haul rates by diverting through-traffic revenue to unregulated competitors. (The roads would have to raise the long haul in order to also raise the short haul which was the only traffic they would now get.) As might be expected, some railroads judged that in their case competition even with a regulated railroad constituted that "rare and peculiar" circumstance which justified their adopting a long-short-haul discrimination, so in 1892 the ICC ruled that carriers themselves could no longer decide exceptions when competing with other regulated railroads since they were rendering the exceptional ruling meaningless. Thereafter for a time, Section 4 did have an effect, and railroads did lower short-distance rates.

Restraint by the federal courts on the presumed powers of the ICC was not long in developing. In *Kentucky & Indiana Bridge* (1889) a federal circuit court rejected the ICC's decision as binding and ordered that the facts in the case be reconsidered by a court of law, which the ICC most definitely was not. A year later the Supreme Court in *Chicago Milwaukee & St. Paul Ry. Co. v. Minnesota* ruled that the attempt of the state's Railroad Commission to set rates with absolute finality violated the due process clause of the Fourteenth Amendment. As a dissenting justice noted, this overturned *Munn v. Illinois*. It also meant that the ICC's determination on the reasonableness of rates could always be appealed to the courts, which seems to have been the intent of the law anyway. The chairman of the ICC suggested that Congress institute a procedure of "administrative due process of law," but Congress declined. In 1892 the Supreme Court upheld a shipper who, citing the 5th Amendment, had refused in 1890 to testify whether he had received rebates on interstate grain shipments. Congress responded with the 1893 Compulsory Testimony Act (compelling testimony before the commission but prohibiting prosecution on the basis of that testimony), which the Supreme Court upheld in 1896. In the interim, the commission had to be satisfied with voluntary testimony for six years. Nevertheless, during its first seven years, due both to prosperity and the reasonably effective action of the ICC, discrimination, which destroyed both stability and profits, was on the decline, published trunk-line rates on long-distance grain shipments attained a relative stability, and trunk line net receipts and stock prices rose.

When the ICC, enforcing the provisions of the ICA, outlawed rebates, carriers continued the large shipper's advantage by reducing carload rates without reducing less-than-carload rates. The justification for this discrimination had been that railroads could handle a full carload (with one destination and one bill of lading, loaded and unloaded at one time and place) more cheaply than a carload comprising more than one shipment. Understandably, the commission agreed with this reasoning, but refused to permit extreme rate differences. However, it repeatedly refused lower rates, equally justifiable from the railroads' point of view, for entire trainloads, predecessors of today's unit trains.

A severe economic panic which devastated the railroad industry occurred in 1893. In May, the Philadelphia & Reading failed, followed, as already noted, by four other major railroads. Together these five systems controlled more than 21,000 miles of track. By the end of June, 1894, more than 40,818 miles and one-fourth of the capitalization of American railroads were in the hands of receivers. The Hoogenbooms write in A History of the ICC:

Desperately needing revenue, railroads abandoned their cartel agreements, slashed rates, and offered rebates to attract traffic. Any inclination railroad officials may have had to obey the ICC or their own traffic associations was stopped by the depression. Even the consolidation movement (aided by the reorganization of the bankrupt lines by bankers, such as J. P. Morgan) failed to halt falling rates and sharp competition. The depression brought decline to the ICC both by encouraging competing railroads to defy it and by keeping politicians so preoccupied that they ignored it. [14]

Then at the end of its first decade, the ICC had its wings clipped by the Supreme Court. Assuming that it could set the reasonable and just rates the ICA had called for, the commission for almost a decade had decided on replacements for rates it found unreasonable. In 1897, however, in the *Maximum Freight Rate* case the court flatly declared that the act had not granted the commission the right to set rates, as indeed it had not. That same year, moreover, the court destroyed the ICA's section 4 which outlawed long-short-haul discrimination. In the *Alabama Midland* case, the ICC had insisted that regulated railroad competition was no justification for lower westbound freight rates to Montgomery than to Troy, which on the Alabama Midland Railway was fifty-two miles east of Montgomery and without competing rail facilities. The court accepted the railroad's contention that railroad competition created dissimilarities between Troy and Montgomery justifying an exception to section 4. On this case Albro Martin comments:

Troy demanded a lower rate than Montgomery under the long-short-haul clause of the Interstate Commerce Act. They did not get it because Montgomery got its stuff from the east by two or three more direct lines and the Supreme Court in the Alabama Midland *case (1897) interpreted the "substantially similar circumstances and conditions" clause of Section Four of the Act to include railroad competition. What Troy wanted, of course, was dirt-cheap rail transportation below Montgomery's rate, which was already determined by strong competition. Distance had nothing to do with it, except that a local lawyer, offering his services to the town fathers, could make a good prima facie case for it, until a high-priced railroad lawyer got through with him. Long-short-haul "discrimination" was a very big bone, however, constantly dug up by small-town "boosterism," and men chewed on it for years thereafter.* [15]

Finally, it was in 1897 in the *Trans-Missouri* case that the court ruled that rate and tonnage agreements among railroads violated the Sherman Antitrust Act. The ICC had accepted cartel agreements of railroad traffic associations, which set rates and tonnage but did not apportion freight; from 1887 to 1893 - years of reasonably strong ICC regulation and effective cartelization of trunk line railroads - rates remained relatively stable and railroads relatively prosperous. Most of these agreements, however, broke down in the depression following the panic of 1893. In the spring of 1895, after experiencing the most extensive rate disruption since the passage of the ICA, trunk line railroads formed the Joint Traffic Association, which the ICC opposed, since in dividing traffic it violated the ICA's anti-pooling section 5. However, because of these violations, stable grain rates were maintained throughout 1896. The Joint Traffic Association - very similar to the Trans-Missouri Rate Association - was dissolved by the Supreme Court in October 1898, not because it violated the ICA, but because it violated the Sherman Antitrust Act. The court came down on the side of regulating railroads by fostering competition rather than through ICC rules or traffic associations. Ironically the *Trans-Missouri* and *Joint Traffic* decisions encouraged the railroads to eliminate competition through consolidation, a movement which went into high gear at the end of the century, as prosperity returned and rates rose sharply.

The Panic of 1893, however, did more than enable the railroads to ignore the ICC, whose ability to meddle with their concerns had been noticeably restricted. As Martin writes in Enterprise Denied:

No understanding of the history of American railroads from 1896 to World War I is possible for him who perceives them as they were before the nineties depression: overbuilt, financially undernourished, divided into hundreds of poorly integrated corporate entities, and ridden by rate wars which reduced the profits of the best-situated roads drastically and drove the weaker ones to the wall of bankruptcy. That was the "railroad problem" in the nineteenth century, but the depression of the 1890s changed all that. Not that the great "shake-out" which brought strength out of weakness via financial reorganization and consolidation was the spontaneous result of the Panic of 1893. It had been gathering momentum for at least a decade, but it accelerated sharply after massive defaulting on bonds removed old managements from one railroad after another. The trustees of these bonds, which were usually secured by first mortgages on the physical assets of the railroads, were banks. The heads of these institutions thus found themselves more and more involved in railroad affairs, and it was perhaps inevitable that after 1893 they would never be far from the day-to-day management of many of the lines. Thus there grew up the legend that sensible management policies based on what was good for the roads and the territories which they served, were replaced by "banker control," which was ignorant, incompetent, and interested only in "speculative" gain. That the bankers (a catch-all term for anyone who had made a fortune in financial dealings) were in the great majority of cases competent judges of railroad properties and their problems, frequently combining in one persona the equally indispensable skills of financial analyst and operating expert, has been little appreciated. [16]

Clues to the achievements of the railroads during the Progressive Era were as available to their friends as to their foes, and it was a tragedy for the nation as well as for the railroads that these clues were not made the basis of a sound national railroad policy. As Martin writes:

It is a simple matter to demonstrate that remarkable strides were made in the production of transportation with relatively less and less labor, a significant contribution in those inflationary years. In 1910 American railroads produced about 125% more transportation "units" (passenger plus freight) than in 1898, with only about 93% more labor. By 1914 the two measures had diverged even more: transportation was 155% above 1898; labor, only 95%. Clearly, the wartime burden could not have been carried in 1916-18, a period of critical labor shortage, without these gains. The impressive gains in intensity of utilization of the basic railroad plant which were made possible by the rebuilding programs are dramatized by the fact that whereas in 1898 an average mile of railroad route produced 618,000 ton-miles of freight, in 1910 it produced 954,000, and in 1913, 1,245,000. The exhilarating way that the bigger cars and the beefier locomotives paid off is easy to see: in

1900 an average freight train hauled only 271 tons of payload. By 1910 it had been transformed into a longer train of heavier cars, hauling 380 tons; and by 1915 the average tonnage was 474. In 1898 the old-fashioned locomotives of America's railroads had scurried 5.5 billion miles on their appointed freight rounds; by 1910, despite a burden 125% higher, locomotives traveled only 7.2 billion miles. Most amazing of all, however, were the figures for 1914. Although tonnage had continued to climb, the total mileage run by locomotives had actually decreased since 1910. [17]

The community of interest movement, promoted by Cassatt in the East and Edward H. Harriman in the West, was dealt a crippling blow by the Supreme Court's 1904 decision in *Northern Securities Company v. United States.* James J. Hill, the Empire Builder, controlled his personal creation, the Great Northern, and, as he thought, the Northern Pacific. Since neither road had access over its own rails to Chicago, Hill's roads secured control of the Chicago Burlington & Quincy, which brought them into conflict with Harriman, the master railroader of the age. To gain control of the Burlington he attempted to wrest the Northern Pacific from Hill. Harriman had been a Wall Street stockbroker whose interest in railroads began in 1881 when he took over, rebuilt, and sold at a profit a small railroad in upstate New York to the Pennsylvania. His next objective was the Illinois Central, whose board he joined in 1883. Within a few years, having abandoned the brokerage business, he became vice-president of the IC whose lines he expanded and whose facilities he improved, as a result of which the IC weathered the Panic of 1893. In 1898 he took over the Union Pacific, just emerging from bankruptcy, which then went no further west than Ogden, Utah. In short order he added to it the Oregon Short Line and the Oregon Railway and Navigation Company which gave the UP an outlet on the Pacific at Portland, Oregon, and rivalry with the Hill lines in the Northwest. In 1901 Harriman bought the Southern Pacific (New Orleans to Los Angeles and San Francisco) and shortly afterwards the Central Pacific (Ogden to San Francisco) and the San Pedro Los Angeles & Salt Lake.

To snatch the Burlington away from Hill, Harriman had to secure control of the Northern Pacific, joint owner with the Great Northern of the Burlington. It was a case of buying the mare to get the colt. This precipitated the Northern Pacific Panic of May 9, 1901, when shorts, unable to pick up Northern Pacific stock at any price since Hill's and Harriman's brokers had nailed down most of it, bid up the price from 320 to 550, to 700 and finally to 1,000. Meanwhile other stocks plummeted five to ten points at a time as shorts liquidated their holdings to finance their Northern Pacific purchases. Hill eked out a victory, but the two protagonists took steps to prevent this happening again and to introduce stability into the railroad picture in the Northwest. As Richard Overton writes in The Burlington Route:

The sequel to Harriman's attempt to control the Northern Pacific was the formation by Hill of the Northern Securities Company. Its purpose was to provide a single holding company for the Great Northern and the Northern Pacific and through them the Burlington in such a way that future attacks would be unable to split control. A holding company would also provide a medium whereby Harriman could be represented without holding directly the stocks of either of the Northern Lines or of the Burlington. The Northern Securities Corporation, therefore, was incorporated in New Jersey on November 12, 1901, with capitalization of $400 million. On the board were fifteen directors, six representing the Northern Pacific, four the Great Northern, three (including Harriman) the Union Pacific, and two of no particular affiliation. Hill was unanimously elected president and all holders of Great Northern and Northern Pacific stock were invited to exchange their shares for shares of

Northern Securities Company. Eventually about 76% of Great Northern and 96% of Northern Pacific stockholders, including Harriman [$82 million worth], *surrendered their shares for those of the new company.* [18]

The sequel took place three years later, as caustically narrated by Maury Klein in his Union Pacific:

On March 14, 1904, the Supreme Court by a five to four vote ordered the Northern Securities dissolved. Justice John M. Harlan's majority opinion argued that any combination with the power to restrain trade was illegal even though it had not actually used that power. No case better illustrated the confused attitudes of Americans toward the new corporate giants that had become so significant a part of their economic life. Northern Securities had not yet done anything, but it might, and what might it do? It would promote "monopoly" by restraining "competition." The fact that this might be the most desirable state of the rail industry never entered their thinking. Competition was good, monopoly evil, and concentrations of power a menace regardless of their purpose. Or so most Americans believed.

Great cases like hard cases make bad law," wrote Oliver Wendell Holmes in his dissent. He was only half correct. Certainly the decision was bad law in that it pointed Americans in the opposite direction from where their economic life was tending. But Northern Securities *proved not so much a great case as a loud one. "The nearer one gets to the core of the matter," sneered one analyst, "the more narrow and inconsequential is the item of fact and law that is found to be settled." Not one major element of the decision endured except as a bad example. The railroads torn asunder in 1904 finally got back together again in 1970. The "rule of reason" urged in vain by Justice David J. Brewer was embraced by the Court in 1911. Through a series of acts Congress soon replaced competition among roads with a strait- jacket of regulation, including the power to set rates.* [19]

More briefly, Martin writes in Railroads Triumphant that "in a five-to-four decision the Court decided that the theoretical presence of great economic power was sufficient to require that it be given up." Actually, the Hill-Morgan interests retreated to an ad hoc method of keeping control of these three roads which dominated the Midwest and the Northwest as an informal syndicate from 1904 to 1970 when, as Martin notes above, they were formally merged into the Burlington Northern.

Had William McKinley not been assassinated in Buffalo in September 1901, the nation might have been spared the nearly two terms in the White House of the government activist, Theodore Roosevelt, an artful politician who preached principle as he understood it and practiced compromise. As the Hoogenbooms write: "The *Northern Securities* case also notified railroads that their power to regulate themselves was limited, that the federal government could dissolve them and other trusts and that Roosevelt as president wielded enormous economic and political power." Victorious Western and Southern politicians, many of them crass populists or, as Martin styles them, "archaic progressives," took to the hustings calling for stricter federal regulation of the railroads. Roosevelt heard the call and to cheering Western and Southern audiences denounced railroads for their hostility to federal rate regulation since its defeat would bring demands for nationalization. Among his "malefactors of great wealth" he included Edward Harriman.

Still, it was at the urging of the railroads themselves that the Elkins Anti-Rebating Act was passed in 1903. As explained by I. L Sharfman, the historian of the ICC, this law:

. . . made the published tariff, filed with the Commission, the standard of lawfulness; and every departure therefrom, whether or not a different rate was charged for a like and con-

temporaneous service, was declared to be a misdemeanor punishable by penalties provided in the Act. In other words, general rate-cutting as well as special rates, drawbacks, or other concessions, was made unlawful: the mere fact that a lower or different rate is charged than that specified in the published tariff was to constitute a criminal violation of the statute. The maximum fine for such violations was increased fourfold (from $5,000 to $20,000). . . Contrary to the situation prevailing prior to the enactment, the prescribed penalties were made applicable to the railroad corporations themselves as well as to the carriers' agents directly involved in the discriminatory conduct, thereby removing the immunity which had previously extended to the principal and real beneficiary of these unlawful transactions; and shippers soliciting or receiving any rebate or other concession from the published tariff were made equally punishable with the carriers or their agents who offered or granted such special terms . . . Finally jurisdiction was conferred on the United States circuit courts to restrain by injunction any deviation from the published rates. [20]

The railroads still retained the basic free enterprise right of determining the charges for their services. Under Roosevelt and his successor, William Howard Taft, that would all be changed. The first step in this process was the Hepburn Bill which passed the House in February, 1906, 346-7, and, with only three negative votes, the Senate on May 18th. The powers the bill conferred on the ICC were ominous since it could now upon complaint and after full hearing replace an existing rate with a just-and-reasonable maximum which was binding on promulgation, a flat rejection of the doctrine in *Kentucky & Indiana Bridge* and the *Minnesota Rate* case. The courts were to compel obedience, and the railroads must obey or contest the decision in court; and instead of subjecting the commission's decisions to a broad judicial review they were declared final and not subject to review as to their substance (i. e., as to the specific maximum rate orders). Hepburn was the deathknell of free enterprise on American railroads. The Senate had fought to the bitter end to maintain full court review against the House's concept of the independent regulatory commission but failed. The mix of executive, legislative, and judicial powers conferred on the ICC an awesome maximum rate-making power which would prove to be the power to destroy. At the very time when railroads needed to raise huge amounts of money to cope with growing demand and new forms of competition, their ability to do so was being eroded since their charges were now subject to politically appointed bureaucrats highly responsive to public opinion which had been aroused against the railroads by populist politicians and sensation-mongering journalists. There were some dissenters, however. Off the record, Judge Holmes asserted in 1910:

I don't disguise my belief that the Sherman Act is a humbug based on economic ignorance and incompetence, and my disbelief that the Interstate Commerce Commission is a body fit to be entrusted with rate making . . . The Commission naturally is always trying to extend its power . . . However, I am so skeptical as to our knowledge of the goodness or badness of laws that I have no practical criticism except what the crowd wants. Personally, I bet that the crowd, if it knew more, wouldn't want what it wants. [21]

It was also in 1906 that TR's Attorney General, Charles Joseph Bonaparte, Napoleon's grandnephew, declared war against the PRR's community of interest, the most stabilizing influence in the railroad industry. To head off certain defeat, President Cassatt announced that the PRR was divesting itself of its controlling interest in the B&O, the Norfolk & Western, and the Chesapeake & Ohio. Bonaparte also took on Harriman by instituting suit early in 1907 seeking to dissolve the

UP-SP tie and to challenge the UP's 80 percent control of the Illinois Central. Break-up of the UP-SP was achieved four years after Harriman's death. Soon thereafter intrusive government attorneys attempted to strip the CP's Oakland-Ogden route from the SP and to hand it over to the UP. The matter was settled in the SP's favor in 1923, but the episode cost the company uncounted money and lost opportunities.

Martin's judgment on the impact of progressive legislation on the railroad industry is devastating:

It has been estimated that $5.6 billion of capital that might have gone into a continuation of the remarkable technological transformation of the railroads from 1897 to 1907 went elsewhere. But the great tragedy of this failure of human beings intelligently to order their economic environment lies in the long term effects on the railroad system as an enterprise. American railroads literally never got over the shock which archaic Progressivism's cruel repudiation of their leadership produced. It was not that the country had lost a few billions in railroad investment. What was lost was something much more precious, the spirit of enterprise which had produced such remarkable results from 1897 to 1907 and which had seemed then to stand on the threshold of even greater accomplishments. [22]

Labor's Growing Muscle

On yet another front, labor, the condition of the railroad industry was deteriorating. As Martin points out:

Nothing the railroads bought, however - not rails, nor crosswise, nor coal, nor rolling stock, nor even investors' confidence - even when lumped together, came anywhere near equaling human labor as an input to the nation's transportation mechanism. Nineteen-seven, in many ways the best year the railroads ever had, saw 1,700,000 men (and a few women) working on or for the railroads. Out of a total expense bill of $1.7 billion, workers received $1.1 billion, or 64% of the total. In 1898 the labor share was 65%, in the very good year of 1910 it was 61%, and by 1914 it was back up to 64%. From these simple figures two conclusions may be drawn: the significant increase in productivity during the past decade was being absorbed, in large measure, by increases in money wages, preventing any reduction in relative labor costs; and the constant upward pressure on wage rates as unions became more effective in pressing the workers' demands absolutely necessitated further investment in better plant and equipment if labor costs were not to outstrip gains in productivity. As long as the railroads could keep the two factors in balance, and maintain profits, they were reasonably sure that the flow of new capital would be maintained. But it was dangerous to assume that labor would key its demands to actual gains in productivity (as dangerous then as now), for the rising cost of living was a guarantee of unrest. Railroad management and labor, in short, were on a treadmill in these years, and the strain showed clearly after 1907. [23]

The success of railroad workers in obtaining wage raises did not guarantee labor peace in the industry in the long run because the men never won any increases in real wages during the Progressive era. Their real wages never rose above the 1890-1899 average between 1896 and 1914. In fact they sank to 6 percent below that average in 1907. Not until the large increase awarded by the government during World War I did railroad workers achieve any improvement in their standard of living. As a result the question of wages hung like a black cloud over the industry during these years. Still, there were no nationwide strikes, and though there were walkouts on individual lines, the need to move the vast amounts of goods piling up in freight yards even during normal delays led to quick settlements or replacement of the strikers. The more prosperous and enlightened roads tried to anticipate demands for raises before 1907. Cassatt announced a 10 percent raise for 100,000 employees in 1902. That same year conductors and trainmen on Western lines formed the Western Association and demanded better working conditions and higher wages. Railroads had come to favor arbitration because they could not afford a shutdown in the face of capacity traffic and because arbitrators were generally favorable to the roads.

Moreover, the prosperity of the railroads before 1908 made them willing to pass some of their profits along to the workers in a time of rising consumer prices. In November 1906 the PRR came out with another 10% wage increase. The Western Association demanded a 15 percent increase and the establishment of the eight-hour day. The carriers offered 10.5% but refused to discuss working conditions which were still considered management's prerogative to determine. Chairman Margin A. Knapp of the ICC, mediating under the Erdman Act of 1898, secured a 10 percent raise but no reduction in the workday for men working ten hours. However he persuaded the roads to reduce the maximum day from twelve to ten hours with no reduction in wages, which meant that these men, who were for the most part engaged in local freight service, received a 20 percent raise. This is what Buffalo's switchmen had struck for unsuccessfully in 1892.

In 1907 an Eastern association of conductors and trainmen was formed and two years later one in the South. In 1908 the Brotherhood of Locomotive Firemen and Engineers also formed regional bargaining units. As a result, by 1910 the railroad unions could close down America's entire transportation network, although such concerted action would not become a real threat until 1916. Raises of 25-50 percent were obtained for the poorly paid conductors and trainmen in the south in 1910, and the PRR accepted an arbitration award the brotherhoods had obtained against the B&O and were demanding be made general. From this time forward, demands of one kind or another were almost continuously before the railroads. Thus the railroads, which in 1906 had lost the power to determine their charges, were by 1910 rapidly losing the power to determine what they would pay for labor, their largest expense.

The Power to Destroy

"Did the passage of the Hepburn Act, the movement to apply the anti-trust laws to the railroads, the hostility of state leg- isolators, the rising demands of increasingly powerful labor unions," Martin asks rhetorically, "reduce the railroads' ability to bid for capital resources in a market which was growing ever tighter?" To no one's surprise he answers in the affirmative, but points out that the so-called smart money on Wall Street was slow to perceive the big change in the railroad's position. It was not until 1912 when their federally induced plight became obvious that a really sharp cutback in new investment occurred.

One danger signal was the roads' increasing reliance on outside financing (stocks and bonds) rather than on retained earnings. This they did by turning to foreign investors, by emphasizing new forms of financing like equipment trusts, and by paying a steadily rising price for the money they raised. Dividends were maintained up to 1910 when they averaged 5.4 percent, thus encouraging continued investment, but after the shattering events of 1910 and 1911 - soon to be narrated - it was a different ballgame. Retained earnings after 1907 never reached the 1904-1907 level. In 1911 the railroads plowed back the smallest sum since 1898, and 1912 was worse despite the fact that dividends on stocks that still paid such things had fallen from those of 1910. (Figure #8.)

From 1907 to 1914 the deficiency in capital flow into the railroads, on the basis of pre-1907 relationships, totaled $5.6 billion. In

Figure #8. Deficiency of Net Investment, 1898-1915
Martin, *Enterprise Denied,* 131

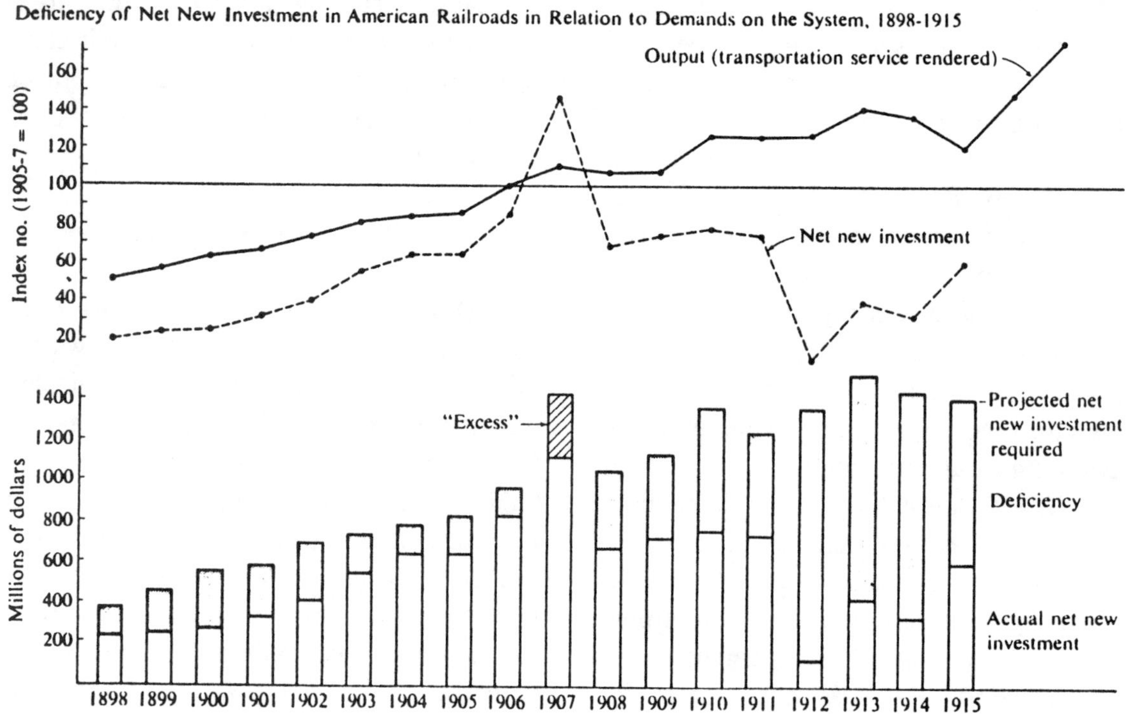

early 1907 railroads had attained a peak of prosperity and confronted a national economy demanding services in excess of anything projected in the boom years after 1897. A rapidly expanding technology promised to keep down the operating ratio, that hallowed measure of operating results which had been rising so disturbingly. Tradition held that it was never to go above 66 percent if adequate profits were to be realized, and that is where it stood for railroads as a whole on June 30, 1910. But no one expected it to stay there unless some way out of the cost-price squeeze was not discovered. Unfortunately it rose to 68.6 in 1911, to 69.3 in 1912, and, despite a 10 percent increase in traffic in 1913, it stood at 69.4. In the very bad year of 1914 it went through the ceiling at 72.2.

It was obvious to railroad men by 1909 that rates had to be raised. The answer seemed to be a general increase in rates which had been frozen at the 1906 level, which was not much above the depression levels of the 1890s. According to the Hepburn Act, the roads could raise their rates as high as they wished, subject to investigation by the ICC after the increase and an investigation which would ensue only on complaint of an affected shipper. In April, 1910, twenty-four railroads west of the Mississippi jointly filed with the ICC general rate hikes on 200 commodities throughout their territories. The Eastern roads were less brave and filed general rate increases as individual roads. The increases, under the Hepburn Act, would become effective within thirty days, and could then be challenged, rate by rate, by shippers or other interested parties before the ICC. An astronomical number of individual rates was involved in these increases affecting tens of thousands of classifications and shippers. The times were not propitious, since public opinion was almost solidly against a general increase in railroad rates, and friends of the railroads in Congress were now few. Muckraking journalists had succeeded in identifying railroad presidents as robber barons.

The House had gone over to the enemies of the roads in 1905, and the Senate was taking on a radical complexion where the railroads - and much else about economic life - were concerned. Leading exponents of this kind of thinking were Senators Robert M. La Follette of Wisconsin and Albert B. Cummins of Iowa, professional railroad bashers. Moreover, intellectuals and other shapers of the public mind, the "chattering classes" generally, had turned against the concept of laissez faire, and were condemning big business because it destroyed competition. They looked to government to reestablish that earlier and presumably happier world whose existence was an article of faith for all but the most questioning minds. In the face of what evidence there was, these ideologues never doubted that government regulation would work. They preferred to worry instead about the potential for domination contained in the growth of big business.

Just when the new tariffs were to take effect, George W. Wickersham, President Taft's attorney general, obtained an order from a federal judge enjoining the railroads from implementing them, pending the outcome of a suit charging the roads with conspiracy to violate the Sherman Anti-Trust Act. The day the antitrust suit was filed, the Supreme Court in the *Missouri River and Denver* rate cases upheld the constitutionality of the Hepburn Act. A week later Eastern and Western railroad executives meeting with Taft and Wickersham agreed to withdraw their rate application until a new railroad bill then before Congress should become law. This was the Mann-Elkins Bill, which was enacted on June 18, 1910, the product of the kind of Progressivism represented by Deliver and LaFollete. This bill, which Martin calls a "killer," gave the ICC authority to initiate rate reductions where it felt they were warranted and to suspend new rates for ten months while the commission investigated their reasonableness, the burden of proving reasonableness being placed squarely on the railroads. By way of rubbing salt into the wound, the law required that railroads establish the reasonableness not merely of the increases but of the old rates themselves, many of which antedated 1887. Whereas the bill as authored by Senator Stephen Elkins of West Virginia would have legalized pooling, as passed it required that the application of the antitrust law to railroads not be compromised.

It was under the lethal provisions of Mann-Elkins that the railroads' request for rate increases were handled. Representing shippers' groups was Louis D. Brandeis, who succeeded in portraying his clients as the people battling the interests. (Actually, both sides, shippers and transportation companies, were interests.) The commission, which was stacked against the railroads anyway, regarded its task as that of keeping down rates, and insisted that it could not take cognizance of the fact that railroad profitability was down, that railroad securities were selling at a discount, and that railroads needed money to finance the improvements which increasing traffic was making necessary. Relying on figures for 1910, which had been a good year but not typical of the years since 1907, the commission early in 1911 denied the roads their increase. It declined on principle to grant general increases, insisting that each and every rate must be shown to be reasonable. Railroad lawyers searched the decision in vain for clues as to what the commission would consider proof of reasonableness of rates in the future. With the announcement of the commission's decision, Martin writes:

. . . reports of retrenchments began to pour in. The Central cut its dividend from six dollars to five. The Harriman roads were reported to be economizing. Chairman Elbert Gary of U. S. Steel agonized publicly that the railroads, which usually bought about a third of his output, were now taking only 7 to 8 per cent. Investors began to doubt that the railroads would ever get an increase. They almost turned out to be right. [24]

Two years later, in May, 1913, the Eastern

railroads made a second attempt to have their rates raised and met a second denial. By 1913 it appeared that economic depression, which had struck in 1873 and twenty years later in 1893, was preparing for a third regular appearance. Physical business activity which had been at an all-time high in January was down 13 percent a year later. Factory employment had dropped 7 percent by year's end and pig iron production - a critical item for railroads - had fallen by a third. Net income of the nation's railroads was down 35 percent. Moreover, public opinion, at least in some quarters in the East, was coming to realize that in the face of some of the worst inflation the western world had ever experienced, that of 1897-1913, it was self-defeating to hold railroads to rates some of which went back thirty years. The roads were asking for tariff changes which averaged only about 5%, which would generate barely $50 million. This was a mere token of what they really wanted and needed, but they were trying to get the commission to admit that rates could be raised en bloc (which was to admit that the commission had a creative administrative function to perform) and that it was abandoning what Martin terms "the uncompromising enforcement of the Act of 1910, that unworkable piece of legislation which caused most of the trouble."

Hearings did not get off the ground until November, when President Daniel Willard of the B&O showed the commissioners how the roads east of Buffalo and Pittsburgh had fared in the three years since 1910. Net additions to property (investment) totaled $660 million. After making this investment, the railroads in the fiscal year ending mid-1913 showed a gain in gross revenues of $187 million, a rise in operating costs of $203 million, and therefore a net profit $16 million below 1910. An award just made by a board of arbitration would give conductors and trainmen in the territory $6 million more a year.

Brandeis, who had trashed the railroad's case in 1910, was special counsel to the commission, which must have given the railroad presidents pause. A string of railroad witnesses showed that increased productivity had not resulted in increased profitability because the price of materials and labor had risen steadily while railroad rates had not. Coal was 7.7 percent higher than in 1910, wages 9.02 percent. The commission turned down the Eastern railroads and granted a five percent raise to Midwestern roads with such important exceptions (e.g., coal) as to be almost worthless. The decision was announced on July 29, 1914, fourteen months after the railroads had made their request and on the eve of the outbreak of World War I.

The first six months of that war were dark days for America's railroads and their customers, as European demand for cotton and wheat dried up and sources of vital raw materials for American technology were closed off. By the end of 1914 rail freight volume was off 20 percent. The roads serving the seaports of the Northeast were particularly hard hit. On August 29, 1914, the Eastern roads requested a rehearing of their case by the commission. In November the third denial came down. Brandeis argued against a general increase because, he claimed, the whole rate structure was unreasonable. He told railroad presidents, who had been understandably proud of the increase in productivity their roads had achieved, to try scientific management instead of asking for rate increases.

As if the ICC was not a heavy enough millstone around the railroads' neck, their executives during the Progressive era had to cope with hostile states. There the worst clashes took place over taxation and valuation, but dozens of other bills were aimed at railroads calling for the creation of commissions, employers' liability, labor rights, full-crew requirements, train size restrictions, and mandated crossing eliminations and other improvements which did not increase the roads' profitability. In 1887 eighteen of the twenty-six state railroad commissions were only advisory, but by 1903 there were thirty state commissions, twenty of them of the strong variety, i. e., regulatory agencies claiming the power to prescribe rates.

Adamson Act

Dissatisfied with the raises the engineers and trainmen had won through arbitration in 1912 and 1913 respectively, leaders of the four railroad brotherhoods determined in December, 1915, to employ their ultimate weapon against management, a nationwide strike in the fall of 1916 when the heavy seasonal traffic would be further burdened by demand for war goods by Britain and France and by President Woodrow Wilson's Preparedness program. Overshadowing the conflict, the first attempt at collective bargaining across the entire industry, was the growing likelihood of American involvement in the European war, to which the president's own policies were leading. What the brotherhoods wanted was an eight-hour day and time-and-a-half for overtime. At the time the only limitation on a day's work on the railroads was a 1907 federal law limiting a worker to sixteen hours in a twenty-four hour period. Most railroad men worked the standard ten-hour day, with differing arrangements for overtime. In practice an over-the-road man's workday was determined by the run to which he was assigned. Some seniors on crack passenger trains worked much less than ten hours, while others, especially those on local freights, which were frequently sidetracked for higher class trains, had difficulty completing their runs in only ten hours. (The average freight train at the time traveled only ten miles an hour or a hundred miles a day.) Therefore, while an eight hour law, even without time-and-a-half for overtime, would not establish an eight hour work period, it would result in a big wage increase, since an essential of the eight hour movement was the requirement that wages for the shorter day be the same as formerly for ten hours. With time-and-a-half, which the unions were also calling for, the increase would be even greater. If a trainman had earned $2.50 a day, an eight hour day with overtime would involve a fifty cent or 20 percent raise for a ten hour day; with time and a half for the same kind of day it would involve a seventy-five cent or 30 percent raise. Such a raise would mean a drastic curtailment of improvement programs on even the most successful lines and bankruptcy for weaker lines. Gathered in New York early in 1916, representatives of the Eastern roads voted to present a united front to the opposition. In response, all the brotherhoods refused to submit their demands to arbitration and voted for a strike at any time if the railroads did not surrender completely. Taking their cue from the progressives in Congress and from the ICC, the unions argued that the railroads were perfectly able to grant labor's demands without increasing their rates.

In a final vote in mid-August 1916, 94 percent of the union delegates voted for a strike that could begin immediately, but held off when Wilson requested the contestants to come to Washington. This was bad news for the railroad executives, since Wilson was up for reelection in November and could be expected to side with labor, a formidable voting bloc. On August 14th the President listened to the head of the conductors present the unions' position and in the afternoon to that of the railroads. However, the president warned the executives that they would have to make most of the concessions. They were to grant the eight hour day and leave the demand for time and a half to arbitration. As far as higher rates were concerned, that was up to the ICC and he could promise nothing.

The next day Wilson relented somewhat and in separate conferences with labor and management continued his insistence that the eight hour day be adopted, but told the unions to drop their demand for time-and-a-half. The union leaders agreed, subject to ratification by over 600 chairmen of railroad locals. All the representatives of the railroads rejected Wilson's offer. The scarcely impartial President then called the 600-odd local labor leaders to Washington, where he invited them to the White House and asked them to go along with his compromise plan. A meeting of the national labor leaders with the 600 from the provinces was adjourned without having reached a decision. Pursuing his pro-labor policy further, Wilson next summoned the presidents of thirty of the largest railroads to Washington. On August 18 the 600 representatives of railroad labor marched to the White House and announced their acceptance of the president's compromise. A few minutes later thirty railroad presidents were ushered into the same room. None was asked to be seated. Wilson made a dramatic entrance, treated his guests coldly and told them that if they went along with his compromise he would try to get the ICC to grant rate relief, provided the eight hour commission recommended it. Before staging an equally dramatic exit, he pointed his finger at the railroad presidents and pontificated: "If a strike comes, the public will know where the responsibility rests. It will not be upon me" - a completely gratuitous assertion. The next day sixty-three more railroad presidents were summoned to Washington. When they arrived on August 21st, they joined their fellows in opposition to Wilson's plan, which they characterized as a cynical grab for a 20% wage raise that would cost the railroads $50 million a year. His refusal to call for arbitration was "inconceivable in a democracy like ours," they cried. Twenty years before, railroad managers would have spurned the idea of an outside party determining wage scales; now they were grasping at partial arbitration as at a straw. It was on this occasion that the minister's uptight son in the White House exclaimed bitterly, "I pray God to forgive you, I never can," and left the room. The next day a delegation of presidents went to the White House and told Wilson that they would cooperate if he would submit at least the overtime demand to arbitration and would guarantee a rate increase. That night Wilson asked the presidents of four major roads to come to the White House immediately, where he told them he was considering a definite promise of a rate increase.

However, he could not deliver on such a promise, and the presidents knew it. It would involve Congress, where enemies of the railroads were still powerful, disowning its own creation, the ICC. Congressional leaders had told Wilson that the most they could do was to create two new seats on the commission, the occupants of which in concert with the existing minority just might create a majority which would see things from the railroad viewpoint. But suppose Wilson was not reelected?

In the meantime the presidents changed their tactics, offering to accept the eight-hour day but demanding arbitration of ten hours pay for eight hours of work. This involved a wholesale rejection of the unions' demands, and no labor leader took the move seriously. On the 25th the union leaders, whose sessions had become more and more rebellious, gave Wilson a seventy-two-hour ultimatum, reminding him that they had $15 million in their strike fund. The following day Senator Francis Newlands, chairman of the Interstate Commerce Committee, warned Wilson that the senate would debate the proposal to reorganize the ICC for at least a month.

On August 28th a group of brotherhood leaders admitted that a strike order had gone out for September 4th. They claimed that the locals had taken matters into their own hands. On the 29th Wilson personally delivered a special message to Congress. He demanded that it enact a law requiring the establishment of the eight hour day with undiminished pay (a compromise in as much as time-and-a-half was not mentioned but a rejection of the railroad executives' last offer), a commission to assess the impact of the law, and the enlargement of the ICC by two members. What he got was the Adamson Act, passed by Congress two days before the nationwide strike was to take place. After January 1, 1917, eight hours was to be the basic workday on the railroads, with the added provision that "the compensation of railway employees subject to this Act for a standard eight-hour workday shall not be reduced below the present standard day's wage." The railroad managers refused to accept the Adamson Act and immediately instituted proceedings to test its constitutionality. In mid-November the unions announced that they would strike on January 1, 1917, if the law had not been put into effect by then, regardless of what the Supreme Court might do in the meanwhile. When the railroads threatened to apply for an injunction against the strike, however, and then agreed to make benefits retroactive to January 1, 1917, if the court decision went against them, the brotherhoods rescinded their strike threat. Then as war clouds lengthened, the brotherhoods on March 12th announced that a strike would be called for the 17th. They feared that once the nation was at war, they would not be able to call a strike. The strike never came off because it was not necessary. On March 19, 1917, the Supreme Court by a 5-4 decision ruled that the Adamson Act was constitutional. The swing vote came from Brandeis, Wilson's most recent appointment to the court and a long-standing enemy of the nation's railroads. The majority, in an extremely loose interpretation of the Commerce Clause, rationalized that it gave Congress not only the power to fix conditions of employment but, "in an emergency arising from a nation-wide dispute over wages," the power to fix wages as well, as long as the law was not confiscatory.

Klein's comment on this sad development in American railroad history bears repetition:

A historic turning point had been reached in both government-business relations and labor negotiations, and its influence would reach deep into the twentieth century. Wilson saw the Adamson Act as imperfect but necessary to avert a strike that would have amounted to a national calamity. "All here recognized that the strike would be the greatest catastrophe that ever befell our country," wrote a southern [Democratic] *congressman. "Another thing," he added, "if the strike had not been averted, the present Administration would have been destroyed."*

But the price had been high. What some people saw as a protective umbrella of government influence struck others as a spreading web. To avoid the strike congress had snatched from the railroads control over the wages paid workers, which was by far the largest single factor in the cost of operations. By 1916, then, the government had taken over both sides of the ledger, income and expenses, and the mechanisms for regulating one were in no way coordinated with those for adjusting the other. Ahead lay even more drastic controls, but they served merely to confirm what had already taken place by 1916; the railroads could still manage their affairs but they could no longer manage their destinies. [25]

Appearing in March, 1917, before the Newlands Committee, a joint committee of the Interstate Commerce Committees of both houses of Congress, Julius Kruttschnit, chairman of the Southern Pacific, asserted that railroad executives were finding their job harder to perform because of the deteriorating loyalty and efficiency of labor. "Labor no longer looks to the carrier, to its employer, as being in charge of its wages and destiny, but elsewhere. It looks to the state legislatures and to Washington." No authority, no responsibility is what the "Von Moltke of Transportation" was telling the nation's lawmakers. Sumner Schlichter's laboristic society had come of age.

14
World War I And Its Sequel

Congestion

In 1915 there were 300,000 more freight cars than loadings, but in 1916 surpluses were turned into shortages as English and French orders began to produce traffic congestion on eastern trunk lines. As war exports increased, conditions reached the critical stage. The winter of 1916-1917 proved to be the worst within living memory. In the wake of threats by union leaders of a nationwide strike, biased prodding from a president avid for reelection, the continuing unresponsiveness of the ICC to the needs of a troubled industry whose profit margins were disappearing rapidly, and the ritualistic bashing by intellectuals, journalists, and "archaic progressives," came record-breaking snowstorms and abnormally low temperatures. Instead of falling off once the coal yards, warehouses, and grain elevators of Northeastern cities had been filled, freight shipments desperately needed by the Allies kept growing. Then terror struck when Germany announced the resumption of unrestricted submarine warfare, effective February 1, 1917. Merchant ships loaded with cargo stayed in port, afraid to venture into the North Atlantic, and the arrival of empty bottoms into which thousands of dockside freight cars could be unloaded soon ceased completely. Martin thus describes the situation in New York Harbor in early February, 1917:

"Cars, cars everywhere, and not a ship to load," reported an amazed observer. Along the Hudson River docks hundreds of car floats were tied up, loaded to capacity with railroad cars which, temporarily at least, had reached the end of their journey. Railroad yards abutting the piers were so packed with cars that hardly an unobstructed track remained on which the switch engines could maneuver. For miles up the Palisades, loaded cars were strung out along the tracks of the New York Central's West Shore Division. Nowhere were the familiar sights of smoking funnels and white plumes of exhaust steam to be seen. In the Pennsylvania Railroad's Jersey City yards idlers stared incredulously as a giant wrecking crane stretched its powerful arm out over two adjoining tracks, grasped a boxcar, swung it clear of its fellows, and placed it down on the only unobstructed track in sight. [1]

The ports of Boston, Philadelphia, and Baltimore experienced similar congestion as freight cars loaded with grain or manufactures from the interior were sent east without any assurance of ocean shipping space. Cars with low-priority goods blocked the piers, and those with high-priority items sat in the yards or were sidetracked miles from the seacoast. Coal and fuel prices skyrocketed, and the specter of urban riots loomed on the horizon. Responses available to the railroads were limited since pooling or any kind of collusion was forbidden by both the Interstate Commerce and Sherman Anti-Trust Acts, which enjoined competition while what was needed was cooperation.

At the suggestion of the Wilson administration, America's railroads on April ll, 1917, five days after America entered the war, formed the Railroad's War Board to operate America's railroads as if they were "a continental railway system." But pooling was still illegal, railroad officials could not easily adopt new traffic strategies, government agencies competed with each other in obtaining priority treatment, and the War Board could not enforce its directives. As Walker D. Hines, later director-general of the railroads, wrote in his account of his stewardship:

This effort of the railroads at unification was entirely voluntary. No form of guaranty was provided by the Government to protect any railroad company against any loss it might sustain as a result of low rates or high costs or as an incident to being put at a disadvantage in the process of unification through diversion of its traffic or car supply or transfer of its locomotives for the benefit of other lines. [2]

In addition, because government action had denied a healthy profitability to the industry, a shortage of motive power had plagued the railroads for several years, and despite the Adamson Act, railroad men were throwing over their jobs in order to go to work for war industries at higher wages and under better working conditions.

Therefore in March, 1917, the railroads had petitioned the ICC for an across-the-board rate increase of 15%. This time opposition from shippers was almost non-existent. They favored anything that promised improved service. Incredibly, the commissioners turned the railroads down. "Everything," Martin writes, "that might justify immediately higher earnings, even the war itself, seemed to the Commission to be a temporary phenomenon, and 'it would be unfair,' said [Commissioner] McChord, 'to burden the public with a big rate increase as a war measure.' " By the time the railroads applied for a rehearing in the fall of 1917, though volume for eastern railroads had shot up by $123 million, net profit was down $57 million. Many roads were on the brink of bankruptcy. In November the Railroad's War Board announced a pooling arrangement east of Pittsburgh, only to be told by Wilson's Attorney General that the Interstate Commerce and Sherman Antitrust Acts had not been repealed. Finally seeing the light, the ICC passed the buck to Congress, with the recommendation that the railroads be freed from anti-pooling and antitrust laws. The commission also recommended effective unified operation, either private or public. The same recommendation was made by Senator Francis G. Newlands' Joint Committee on Interstate Commerce.

United States Railroad Administration

Three days after Christmas, Wilson issued a proclamation taking control of the railroads in the name of the people of the United States. Now that the government was responsible for the railroads, it began to view their government-caused problems in a more sympathetic light. Unified efficient transportation was what Hill and Harriman had sought to promote, only to have their efforts go for naught by a government that had listened too closely to the roads' enemies. Wilson appointed his son-in-law, William Gibbs McAdoo, Director General of the unified national railroad system. McAdoo's chief advisors and administrators were to be railroad executives. The president was authorized to make agreements guaranteeing each railroad compensation based on its average net operating income for the three years ending June 30, 1917. The railroads were to be returned to private control twenty-one months after the conclusion of peace. It was like renting a furnished house with a guarantee of payment for damages at the termination of the lease. The government assumed responsibility for all expenses of operations including maintenance and taxes.

On the impact of the United States Railroad Administration Klein writes:

USRA created what one ICC commissioner called a "mild revolution in transportation." For most of the century shippers had dominated transportation policy through their influence with the ICC and Congress. During this brief interlude their dominance waned as USRA took command of both operating and regulatory functions. It transformed the railroads into an efficient system by doing what individual carriers could never do: bypass the ICC, ignore the anti-trust and antipooling statutes, and brush aside the interference of state commissions. The ICC had for two decades specialized in negative policy, but negativism could not make the railroads run as a unified system or respond effectively to an emergency.

Under the RA the roads could do things never before possible. They could pool equipment, share terminals, yards, depots, and other facilities, repair cars and engines in the nearest shop, create joint agencies, consolidate shipments, standardize design, curtail marginal service, and eliminate such abuses as cross-hauling. And they could raise rates. In May 1918 McAdoo issued an order hiking freight rates about 28 percent and passenger fares about 18 percent. Ironically, the freight increase came to just about what the railroads had sought in their last three supplications to the ICC. With the ICC dropped into limbo by the takeover, shippers lost their usual forum for complaint. "There was not even any formal consultation with the ICC," said [Walker D.] *Hines with a smile. "There was no consultation with the State commissions."* [3]

Estimates on the success of the USRA depended upon the formulae by which the estimators wished to determine postwar legislation. While all parties had to admit that the tie-up was broken and that some savings had resulted under federal control, many pointed out the increase in railroad employment and the huge deficit piled up - $900 million - when federal control ended. Defenders of the Administration claimed that employment had risen because of the eight hour workday imposed by the Adamson Act. The deficit could be seen as the result of denying rate increases in the interest of controlling inflation or simply as inevitable in war. Facilitating the movement of troops and war goods often conflicted with considerations of efficiency. The judgment of later, more dispassionate historians is that the overall gains that were effected were at best moderate.

Buffalo's Railroads on War Time

Erie County's contribution of men to the armed services was proportionately less than it had been during the Civil War, which is not to be wondered at since the Civil War lasted more than twice as long. In all, 170,763 men registered for the draft, but only 18,982 reached training camps. The inductees marched to the various stations on their way to camp but in dribs and drabs. Propaganda was extremely active during the war and provoked much flag waving and hatred for the Hun, but the enthusiasm that greeted the departing (and returning) troops seems to have been less than during the extremely short and quickly successful Spanish-American War.

As a major railroad center, Buffalo did not escape severe congestion of freight cars and sporadic shortages of material vital to the war effort and food for domestic consumption and for export. At the end of January, 1917, before America's entry into the war in April, the railroads placed an embargo on coal shipments to Buffalo because the yards here and across the river in Canada were bulging with cars that could not be moved. As a result, several industrial plants in Black Rock had only a few days' coal on hand and were in danger of being shut down. The local superintendent of the Grand Trunk stated that "since the outbreak of the war traffic has increased enormously because of coal shipments and shipments of munitions of war and raw materials for their manufacture." He added that "the best of our men, mechanics especially, are at the front." On February 12, 1917, the *News* claimed that the situation was one of the worst in the industrial history of Buffalo. The elevators were filled with grain that could not be shipped, and one plant at Lockport had been forced to shut down because of delayed shipments of coal. Supplies of newsprint had dwindled to such a point that publishers were forced to shrink the size of their papers by eliminating features and pictorials, but not news and advertisements. However, with the coming of warmer weather the log jam began to break up, and by February 17th, the NYC had moved out about 2,000 loaded westbound freight cars that had tied up its Buffalo yards.

After Congress declared war, local railroads began to lop off passenger trains to release crews for work on freight trains as well as to conserve fuel. Several of these roads began hiring women as dispatchers, porters, station agents, and car cleaners. At the Erie car shops and yards, women received the same pay as men for similar work, twenty cents an hour. The LV sent a demonstration train on tour across the state to teach women how to can fruits and vegetables in order to relieve the growing shortage of these commodities. Railroad spokesmen pleaded with shippers to unload boxcars quickly to free them up for further use. The number of non-performing freight cars had dropped from 148,627 on May 1, 1917, to 33,776 in August. The War Board claimed that railroads had provided fifteen to twenty percent more freight service than during the same period in 1916 with the same amount of equipment. However, the nation braced for the upcoming winter of 1917-1918. The DL&W eliminated twenty-four trains out of Hoboken, but none out of Buffalo. Overall, the PRR discontinued 102 daily passenger trains. Ominously, trucks stepped into the breach with their greater flexibility. In fact, Buffalo was becoming the center for a number of radiating motor truck lines delivering freight to relieve the congestion on the railroads.

The winter of 1917-1918 added to the wartime problems of Buffalo's railroads. The December 12, 1917, *Morning Express* carried this report of winter's first big storm:

The downfall here was the heaviest in the country. Buffalo streets are blanketed under 17 inches of snow. There are drifts four to six feet high in some of the parkways. The temperature here was the lowest in the country. It was from 6 to 4 below yesterday; it will be zero or below today. Tomorrow may be just as cold and that is not encouraging with the gas low in the burners and coal hard to get at any price.

The gale howled over the housetops and whistled through the chinks in the windows at 72 miles per hour. Last night the wind died down to a bitterly cold 50 miles per hour gushiness. At 11:00 o'clock the snow began to come down afresh that threatened a repetition today of yesterday's trolley delays, intensified because of 1,000 workmen who must be carried to the factories in the city.

The railroads entering and leaving the city are congested now more than at any time in the past three years. Freight is being moved as much as possible with trains stalled everywhere in the yards for miles on every side of the city. One train was 18 hours late in leaving Buffalo. It couldn't get through the yards. Trains from the West and the East are from 2 to

10 hours late in arriving. All day yesterday passengers looked through the little holes they had rubbed in the frosted windows at the storm howling outside. They sat there for hours waiting for the train to move into the city anywhere within reach of the few trolley cars that the International was able to run during the early afternoon.

The Buffalo River rose six and one half feet above its normal level. The little supply tugs which provision the freighters were lifted upon the docks in several places along the water front. Some of them were capsized. The Erie Canal broke its banks at International Bridge and Bird Island which was inundated. Three houses were crushed by the waters and carried away.

Things were to get worse. In his annual report for 1918 Alfred H. Smith, Regional Director for the Eastern Region (he was also president of the NYC from 1914 to 1924), described the unprecedented winter of 1918:

During January and the early part of February the weather conditions in the eastern territory were the most severe ever recorded. With abnormally low temperatures, ranging from 5 degrees to 30 degrees below zero, accompanied by high winds, reaching a velocity of 70 miles per hour, blizzards of snow and sleet following one another with such frequency that recovery from one was not possible before another was upon us, with yards buried deep in snow and ice, main tracks blocked, passenger trains abandoned and freight traffic practically paralyzed, the railroad forces struggled to keep going the flow of food, munitions and fuel so vitally essential to the successful conduct of the war and to the communities in the eastern territory dependent thereon.

The Railroad Administration ordered hundreds of passenger trains to be abandoned nationwide to ease the movement of freight trains, especially those carrying coal to Eastern cities. The LV cut its through passenger service between Buffalo and Jersey City to two through trains a day, the NYWS&B dropped two trains between Buffalo and Weehawken, and the NYC removed eleven passenger trains between Buffalo and Niagara Falls to release additional motive power to move freight trains. Extra cars were added to the seven surviving trains. Frenzied headlines in the *Morning Express* for January 9, 1918, screamed: "Buffalo robbed of needed coal supply. Garfield orders railroads to rush shipments of fuel to New England. All of interior of state faces coal famine. Buffalo chief sufferer. City will be paralyzed if mandate is obeyed. All industries to shut doors with City left helpless to fight fire." Harry A. Garfield, son of former President James A. Garfield and president of Williams College, had been named Fuel Administrator by McAdoo. Garfield followed this with an order closing all factories for five days to save thirty million tons of coal. The January 18 *Express* estimated that this order would idle 60,000 workers in Buffalo and its environs. Exceptions were made in the case of ship and airplane building plants and those manufacturing explosives. Pierce Arrow and Lackawanna and Donner Steel were affected. These forced closings were followed by the institution of heatless Mondays for industrial and commercial businesses, with the same exceptions. Curtiss Airplane on Elmwood Avenue remained open as did Lackawanna Bridge and Kellogg Structural Steel which turned out steel plate for the merchant marine. Coal production for January 1918 was one third what it had been in January 1917. The problem was getting empty coal cars to carry the product of the mines to market.

Coal for domestic consumption was also in short supply. The *Express* reported that:

The crowd of 1,500 persons who besieged the office of the fuel administrator in the Prudential building yesterday [January 17] *proved that the people see little hope for a better coal supply in the closing of factories and stores. It was the greatest rush the local fuel officials have dealt with, and they confessed they were swamped.*

Women fainted in the halls and were carried into other offices for medical attention. There were babies in the crowd and they added their wails to the hubbub. Some stood in line for hours and finally gave up in despair of ever getting into the fuel office.

The heatless Mondays order was finally rescinded on February 13th. On that day the *Express* announced:

RAILROAD TRAFFIC IS NEARLY NORMAL: More coal arrived in Buffalo yesterday; more general freight was moved, and many more empty boxcars were released than on any other day since the first week of December. The mild weather enabled the railroad to make vast strides in clearing terminals here. Potatoes dropped two cents a peck, because of improved shipping conditions. Railroad men are confident that one or two more days of open weather will double the movement of freight and remove any possibility of further serious congestion in Western New York this winter.

It was estimated by New York Central railroad officials that between 150 and 175 cars of hard and soft coal for Buffalo had arrived during the day. From 300 to 350 cars passed through bound east. Canada shipments were normal, about 100 cars.

Nearly 400 empty boxcars were sent west to bring back wheat. In general it was a good day for the railroads.

The bituminous situation is better than last week. Nearly 200 cars of soft coal were in the railroad yards yesterday morning, and the supply was distributed to manufacturers. More than that number of cars arrived yesterday, it was estimated.

As during the previous year, conditions improved with the coming of spring and with the decline of the U-boat menace. As an historian of the war noted, “For the last quarter of 1917 the destruction of tonnage was little more than half that of April-June, and throughout 1918 the curve of decline though slow was steady.” Another historian points out that while “the convoy of June, 1917, had been hastened for moral effect and did not represent the start of the flow [of men and materiel], by the end of July, 1918, a host of twenty-two divisions had arrived with two more disembarking.” By Armistice Day, November 11, 1918, 2,086,000 American troops had been transported across the Atlantic, fifty-six percent on British ships. The Kaiser’s gamble that England and France would have been defeated long before America could make a significant military contribution to an Allied victory had been lost.

It was almost five months after the declaration of war against Germany before any of the young men who had registered for the draft in June left Buffalo for training camp. The September 4, 1917, *Express* reported that “last night Buffalo sent her first contingent to the National Army.” An even hundred inductees were involved, forty going on the LV, the rest on the DL&W, all on regularly scheduled trains. The destination was Wrightstown, New Jersey, the station for Camp Dix, on the Pennsylvania & Atlantic Railroad, a connection of the PRR. “Not since Buffalo sent her boys to the front in 1898,” the paper reported, “has Main Street seen such a display of patriotism” marked by “the cheers and the blazing red fires, the blaring of the 74th Regiment band, and the cannonade of bursting bombs.” The parade had formed up at City Hall, and the young men were escorted to their respective stations by units of police and firemen and the home defense guards. Crowds reportedly “swarmed the new LV Station which never before held such a crowd as jammed into its doors.” No sleeping cars were available so the boys “settled down for the long trip in the cramped quarters of a day coach.” More departures were scheduled on the 4th and on the 7th. The object was to have five percent of those registered for the draft across the country inducted and dispatched to training camp. A large scale departure for training camp took place at the end of February, 1918, as reported by the *Express*:

There was crisp winter weather for the departure last night of the last 600 draft recruits for the National Army. The weather was in pleasant contrast with the rain and the mud of Monday night when the 1,000 selected men from the local divisions [draft board designations] *started for Camp Upton at Yaphank, L. I. But the weather conditions which permitted an enthusiastic, cheering parade along Main Street didn't bring any added comforts to the women who hurried to the Lehigh and the Lackawanna stations last night to say a last good bye. The boys got away safely in much better order than did the 1,000 who splashed in the mud and rain of the yards of Michigan, Carroll and Exchange Streets. The young men will detrain near Camp Upton some time this morning.*

Buffalo's quota in the first draft has now been completed. Several months ago the city sent away about 2,800 young men. That was the first call under the draft and there were scenes of wild confusion and the disorder that grief puts in a crowd where mothers and sisters are weeping, apparently inconsolably and the boys themselves had lost heart at the sight. The newer spirit of the day - the calmer resignation of parents and relatives, the happier eager air of the young men for the service under the colors now that the war has worn out its weary first year - was apparent at the leave taking of these last 1,600.

More soldiers were needed, however, and a second draft call went out. On Tuesday, April 2, 1918, 250 entrained for Camp Dix on the Erie and the PRR, the next day 290 left on the NYC, and on Thursday 176 on the LV. It was none too soon since on March 21th the Germans, enjoying numerical superiority on the Western Front, finally launched their long expected and feared spring offensive along a fifty mile front along the Somme, the objective of which, like that of Hitler's commanders twenty-six years later in the Battle of the Bulge, was to reach the Channel ports. American casualties would soon increase, and departures of troops for training camps and for the front would become routine. There was no general civic farewell for some of these later departures, and tears and sobs often equaled the cheers. (Figure #1.) Local railroad stations, yards, and sidings were also used to promote the sale of war bonds. (Figure #2.)

Because of competition from streetcars, passenger service on the Belt Line had dwindled by 1914 to two daily commuter trains morning and evening. (Figure XVI, #3.) However, with thousands working at plants along the Belt Line, especially at the Curtiss factory at Elmwood Avenue, the Belt Line took on a renewed importance, especially after a January 24 fire at the IRC's Forest Avenue carbarns had destroyed fifty trolleys. Officials of the NYC were unhappy with this development since operating morning and evening rush hour trains was a money-losing proposition, and increased use of the double tracked Belt Line would hinder setting out and picking up freight cars along the route. The NYC compromised and on March 12 agreed to run two fifteen-car commuter trains in the morning and two in the evening between Genesee Street and Elmwood Avenue with intermediate stops at West Ferry, Northland, and Main Street.

Overall, the war experience seems to have been unfortunate for the nation's railroads. Revenues were way up, but so were expenses. The USRA raised wages 41.8 percent, this in addition to the havoc caused by passage of the Adamson Act. Rehor calls the period a "monumental episode of confusion" for an already ailing industry. Archer notes how, despite a brief flush of prosperity, the heavy wartime traffic caused a deterioration of the LV's physical plant, a process the government did noth-

Figure #1. Author's collection

Figure #2. Author's collection

ing to reverse. President Truesdale of the DL&W, Taber writes, "was exceedingly unhappy over the policies and practices of the government and its administration of the Lackawanna, for he saw its [i. e., the government's] inefficiency, waste, and the deterioration of his beloved railroad." The policy of the federal government before and immediately after the war was another step in the decline of the American railroad industry.

The Transportation Act of 1920

With the Armistice, McAdoo and Hines recommended either that the government extend the USRA for several years to see how unified operation would work in peacetime or return them at once to private hands to relieve the uncertainty of their status. The railroad brotherhoods endorsed the Plumb Plan which called for the government to buy the railroads for $18 billion and to run the resulting public corporation through a board of directors representing labor, the public, and management. The ICC would continue as before with its rate-making powers unimpaired. Profits would be split equally by the federal government and the employees. Profit-sharing, it was alleged, would stimulate efficiency and cost-cutting. Samuel Gompers, president of the American Federation of Labor, to which the shopmen's unions belonged, feared the Plumb Plan would drive them into the operating brotherhoods, and so he opposed it. Though the plan was popular with intellectuals and rank-and-file railroad workers, the president of the Brotherhood of Railroad Trainmen came out against it. Moreover, the socialism it represented was unpopular in the United States, especially during the year of the Red Scare. Robert S. Lovett, president of the Union Pacific, denounced the plan as an attempt to "Russianize the American railroad industry."

Albert B. Cummins, Republican from Iowa and chairman of the Interstate Commerce Committee, sponsored a bill which passed the Senate and which would have abolished much of the prewar bargaining power exercised by labor unions and shippers. Cummins, a progressive who had seen the light, believed that ICC regulation had been sheerly negative and repressive, and observed that, while some railroads were profitable, others were not. This made it impossible to set rates uniformly. The solution was a mandatory sectional consolidation of weak and strong lines. Consolidation had to be mandatory; otherwise the profitable lines would never assume the deficits of roads either in bankruptcy or hovering on the brink. The federal government would guarantee minimum earnings and place profits over 6% on investment in a fund to be administered by both the carriers and the government which would cushion the industry against economic depression and promote improvements. A Transportation Board would be created which would clip the wings of the nay-saying ICC and would take a broader view of what was being called "the Railroad Problem." Strikes would be outlawed by mandatory arbitration of labor disputes. Needless to say, labor unions on the left and executives of profitable railroads on the right for different reasons opposed the Cummins Plan.

The lower house, however, came up with its own plan, sponsored by Representative John J. Esch which, as Klein writes, "was a classic exercise in time-warp politics. It sought to restore the *status quo ante bellum,* with the roads run privately under strict ICC regulation." Even worse, it provided for federal regulation of new issues of railroad stocks and bonds and gave the ICC the power to approve and regulate railroad extensions and abandonments. Moreover, it deferred action on rationalization and stabilization by entrusting the ICC with the task of supervising mergers, pooling, and traffic agreements.

A compromise, the Esch-Cummins Bill, passed both houses in February, 1920, and was signed into law by President Wilson, now incapacitated by a stroke, on February 28, the day before federal control was to end. Like all compromises it pleased no one, but was more Esch than Cummins. In deference to the railroads, the ICC could set minimum as well as maximum rates to insure adequate earnings (thus introducing a certain flexibility into the rate-making picture.) But it also included the one feature of the Cummins Bill that the roads disliked the most, the prescription of a supposedly fair return of 5.5 to 6 percent on the physical value of the railroad's property. Half of total net earnings above that figure would be placed in a fund to pay for interest, dividends, and rentals. The other half would be "recaptured" by the government for loans to weaker railroads. The consolidation principle remained but was merely voluntary. The ICC was instructed to draw up a plan for regional consolidation but in such a way as to preserve competition. A Railroad Labor Board was created, but its findings were not binding since strikes were not outlawed. In the area of service the authority of the ICC was notably increased. It could order adequate transportation service even to the extent of prescribing the construction of new lines. No carrier could extend or abandon lines or passenger service or combine with another road without ICC approval. The latter power would often be abused by preventing the elimination of superfluous mileage. But roads were also allowed to pool or combine if this improved service and did not restrain competition, of which, of course, the ICC was to be the judge. The commission, moreover, was authorized to revise intrastate rates set by state railroad commissions which discouraged interstate traffic. As a kind of severance pay, the government guaranteed earnings for six months at the rate of half the annual compensation each road had received during the war.

Klein's judgment of Esch-Cummins is extremely negative:

In one stroke the Transportation Act of 1920 closed one era in railroad history and opened another, the character of which no one could yet foresee. The takeover had ended, yet in a sense the takeover was now complete. Outright federal control had been relinquished, but the carriers found themselves more in the control of Washington than ever before. Not for another half century would they regain from the government some control over their destinies. The enlarged role of government in their affairs troubled most rail executives. [4]

A similar judgment is rendered by William R. Doezema in his study of Ralph Budd, president of the Great Northern:

American railroads faced an uncertain, even a grim future in the early 1920s. First there was the fight to return them to private ownership over the bitter opposition of the labor unions that had fared handsomely under government control. But after that fight was finally won on March 1, 1920, indemnity payments from the government, representing wartime deferrals of maintenance to roadbed, motive power and rolling stock, hardly covered the real deterioration of the nation's main transportation system. Finally the ICC, which had repressed all efforts to raise rates even modestly during the inflationary decades before World War I, was given still more powers by the Transportation Act of 1920. It was soon apparent that the ICC was going to determine national transportation regulatory policy by regulating in favor of the growth of "competitive modes" of transportation - that is, the nascent trucking industry. Worst of all, it must have seemed to the new president of a major railroad, the ICC had been given a mandate by the Transportation Act to recast the American railroad network by "consolidation" into a limited number of systems. [5]

Statistics gathered by Julius Kruttschnitt, president of the Southern Pacific, reveal at a glance what had happened to the railroads during the first two decades of the twentieth century. They demonstrate that the decline of the railroad cannot be attributed solely to the rise of trucks, buses, and cars:

Between 1900 and 1917 wholesale prices rose 120 percent while freight rates declined 1 percent. By July 1920 both wholesale prices and railroad wages were 240 percent higher than in 1900; freight rates had risen only 30 percent. An increase granted in September 1920 pushed rates up to 74 percent, and prices had fallen to 180 percent higher than 1900; but the gap was still huge. [6]

The provision of Esch-Cummins on which the senator had placed such store and which called for the "recapture" by the government of earnings above 6 percent quickly became a dead letter. Although it was approved by the Supreme Court - opponents had rightly claimed that it amounted to confiscation - controversies over the valuation to be placed on railroad property and legerdemain by railroad accountants to bury excess (of 6 percent) profits in other categories kept the fund low. Between 1920 and 1931 railroads reported excess profits of $23 million. The ICC (which now had over two thousand employees) claimed the amount was over $300 million. Litigation tied up what money actually reached the fund, and the provision was finally repealed in 1939. The grand consolidation plan called for by Esch-Cummins met a similar fate. The Hoogenbooms write in their history of the ICC:

In May 1920 the ICC began work on consolidation and in August 1921 the commission announced its tentative plan consolidating railroads into nineteen competitive systems. The ICC plan modified - by eliminating two systems - the plan prepared for the commission by William Z. Ripley, professor of economics at Harvard and one of the nation's leading transportation experts. Although the ICC did not elaborate on its plan, it published Ripley's maps and explanations. Over the next two years, while transportation conditions improved, the commission held extensive hearings and discovered not only hostility to specific groupings in its plan but strong feeling that consolidations were neither necessary nor desirable. Above all, railroads, particularly strong ones, wished to plan their own consolidations. [7]

Consolidation had to be voluntary, and in every case strong railroads objected to being saddled with weak ones with poor managers, claiming that this had the effect of penalizing strong lines for being efficient. Moreover, the ICC was uncomfortable with its mission to promote consolidation and on several occasions sought to be relieved of this obligation. This left the railroads to plan their own consolidations, if any, subject to ICC approval. In 1924 a proposal was submitted to the commission to create four major trunk lines in the Northeast and Middlewest: the NYC, the PRR, the B&O, and the Van Sweringen roads (the NKP, the Pere Marquette, the Erie, and the Chesapeake & Ohio). Each proposed trunk line would acquire its share of the other railroads in the Northeast, exclusive of New England. Both the Van Sweringen brothers and the NYC expressed interest in the LV.

The next year, Leonor F. Loree, president of the Delaware & Hudson and flush with cash for filling his road's security file, got into the act by calling for another eastern trunk line system which would have had a major impact upon Buffalo. As narrated by the historian of the D&H:

[Loree] *opened fire with his so-called "Fifth-Trunk Line" in 1925 when he submitted a plan to the ICC while it was still considering the general "four system" plan of railroad consolidation. His line would consist of the BR&P, D&H, LV, Wheeling & Lake Erie, and Wabash, together with a proposed* [283 mile] *low grade line through central Pennsylvania* [from Easton on the LV to Pittsburgh] *to be known as the New York Pittsburgh & Chicago. The new line would be 50 miles shorter than any route from New York to Chicago and 30 miles closer to St. Louis. Stretching from the Canadian border to southern Pennsylvania and from the Atlantic to the Mississippi, the transportation empire thus created would encompass the whole tonnage producing area of the industrial heartland of the nation.*

Loree's plan never jelled because of government opposition, one of his pet peeves, nor did the ICC's own plan. The BR&P refused to extend a lease negotiated by the D&H in 1924 and be completely Loreeized, while the NYC and NKP gained control of the Wheeling & Lake Erie, a key road in Loree's trunk line plan. His foray into the market in an effort to bring off his amalgamation plan obtained for him virtual control of the LV and the Wabash. When he sold these interests to the PRR for $63 million, a tidy $22 million profit was netted for the D&H. Money from the sale was invested in 595,000 shares of NYC in 1932, giving the 840 mile D&H over 10% control and the largest single ownership in the 11,000 mile giant. [8]

The ICC's grand consolidation plan appeared in December, 1929. By then, America's railroads had other problems to solve.

Tonawanda Turnout

The NYC's line to the Falls ran dangerously down Tonawanda's Main Street. (Figure #3.) Construction of a two mile detour began in July, 1917, beginning at Franklin Street. The route curved east through Gastown and crossed the Erie Canal by a bascule lift bridge into North Tonawanda. The project involved elevating the roadbed with half a million cubic yards of fill, eliminating thirteen grade crossings, erecting eleven bridges, and transferring the passenger station to North State Street (now Roosevelt Avenue). (Figure XVI, #2.) Shortages of men and materials caused by the war delayed opening of the turnout until June 19, 1922.

Figure #3. Tonawanda detour (drawn in by author)
Century *Atlas of Greater Buffalo*, 1915, III, Plate #7

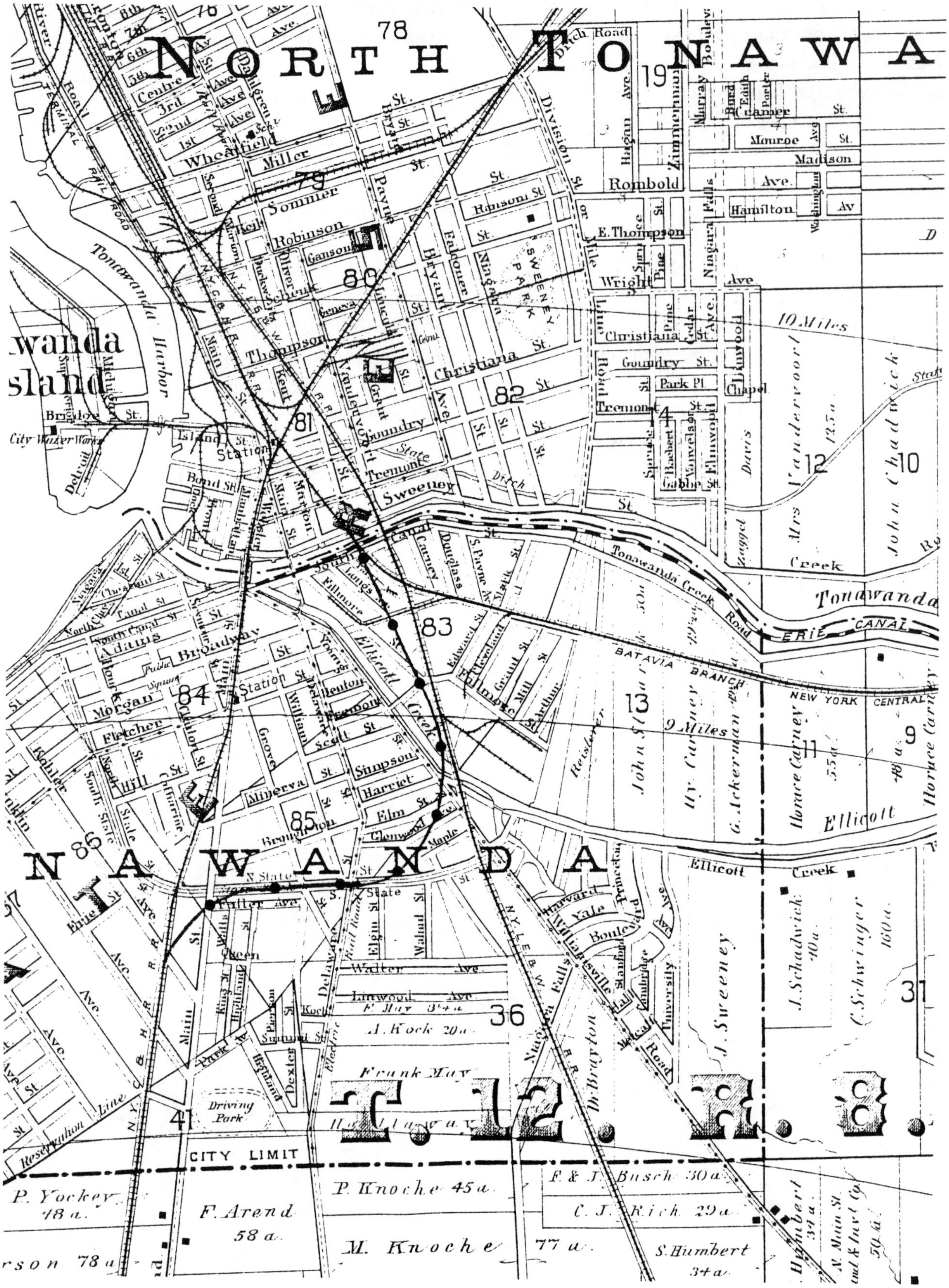

15
"The Railroads That Served Buffalo:" 1927

The popular impression that the 1920s were a prosperous decade is inaccurate. Following an unusual period of postwar business activity which lasted from late 1918 until January, 1920, a brief depression set in which bottomed out in the summer of 1921 and continued until the end of 1922. Moreover, the agricultural regions of the South, Midwest, and Mountain States did not share in the good times that followed, nor did the railroads. The authors of American Economic History observe:

A survey of railroad statistics during the 1920s gives conclusive evidence of the weakened position of the railroads. While investment in rolling stock and other equipment substantially increased, and associated technological advances reduced total employment from 2 million in 1920 to 1.7 million in 1929, the burden of taxation grew heavier, freight revenue stagnated, and passenger traffic declined by one third. [Figure XI, #10.] *The cause of this decline was obviously the rapid development of privately owned automobiles, motor buses, and trucks. Although domestic airplanes were carrying more than 400,000 passengers by 1930, competition from this source was not yet significant. It was obvious that motor transportation was enjoying temporary advantages during the 1920s because of the low burden of taxation under which it operated and the lack of efficient regulation, but these advantages to some extent disappeared in the 1930s.*

In spite of this new competition, the low 4.3 percent average return on investment for Class I railroads over the period 1921-1927, and the impending long-run stagnation of the industry, many were deceived by the large profits of the favored roads. Optimism was also fostered by a substantial investment performance. In the eight years 1920-1927, Class I railways and their subsidiaries spent over $5 billion for extensions, additions, and improvements. Until the depression that began in 1929 there was a steady increase in total track mileage, although "first-track" mileage barely held its own. [1]

Moreover, the provisions of the Transportation Act of 1920 which authorized the ICC to plan for the consolidation of the nation's railroads into not less than twenty nor more than thirty-five systems and to see to it that the roads received a fair return on capital were never implemented. As was later pointed out:

None of the big roads wanted to take on deficit-ridden smaller ones except in cases where extraordinary tax benefits might result. None of the rail executives wanted to merge themselves out of well-paying positions. Nor would the brotherhoods support mergers if the jobs of union members where threatened. [2]

In 1927 the Manufacturers & Traders-Peoples Trust Company put out a booklet about Buffalo's railroads in the preface to which Lewis S. Harriman, president of the bank, reminded his readers:

The thirteen trunk lines in Buffalo provide employment for 22,000 persons in this district, with a payroll of about $35,000,000 yearly. And they pay millions of dollars to the city and county every year in taxes." [3]

This chapter is based largely on this booklet which emphasizes freight service, since passenger service is covered elsewhere. For an overview of Buffalo's freight yards see Figure #1.

New York Central

Buffalo, according to Patrick E. ("Pull Eighty Cars") Crowley, president of the NYC, "is today at the very heart of the greater NYC system. As a traffic producing center, it ranks second only to New York and Cleveland. It stands ahead of Chicago." The system he was speaking of was the New York Central Railroad, which had come into existence December 23, 1914, as the result of a merger of the NYC&HRR, the LS&MS, and nine subsidiaries. The new system controlled 5,600 miles of line. It had taken two years to bring about the merger with the LS&MS, three-fourths of whose bondholders had to agree to the plan. LS&MS stockholders got five shares of the new stock in exchange for one LS&MS share, while holders of NYC&HRR stock received new stock on a mere one-for-one basis. The merger had proved such a harrowing experience for management that it was decided not to go through the same thing with the Big Four and the MC. These would have to be content with a continuation of their leases. Ninety-nine year leases were concluded with both in 1930.

The NYC's Buffalo Division, an area fifteen miles wide east and west and twenty-two miles north and south, had 250 miles of mainline track, 550 miles of sidings, and more than 3,500 switches and frogs (crossovers). No less than 350 industries, some requiring an average daily movement of one hundred cars in and out, were serviced by this division, which also operated five major classification yards where trains were put together and broken up. "Cars standing idle in yards were a graphic representation of the inefficiencies of railroad freight operations and explain why car mileage and productivity were so abysmally low," observes John H. White, Jr. in The American Railroad Freight Car. He adds that "travel time between terminals was generally good; getting out of the terminal was the problem. . . . [Moreover,] cars were more likely to be damaged during switching operations than in any other phase of their normal life," - an illustration of the truth that terminal costs were a major part of overall operating costs.

White's observations on running a railroad during the nineteenth century bear repetition here. Some of the problems continued into the twentieth:

The operation of trains, especially in the wood era, was a wearisome thing. There was so much that could go wrong. The weather was forever acting up with a succession of storms, floods, and blizzards. Once winter's ice and snow abated, the spring rains sent streams over their banks. Bridge abutments were scoured loose, track roadbeds were washed out or made spongy. Even when the weather was more benign, the physical plant would break down. Because of uncertain metallurgy, bad design, or indifferent maintenance, things mechanical kept breaking. Rails

Figure 1, Buffalo's freight yards

Courier-Express, October 17, 1954

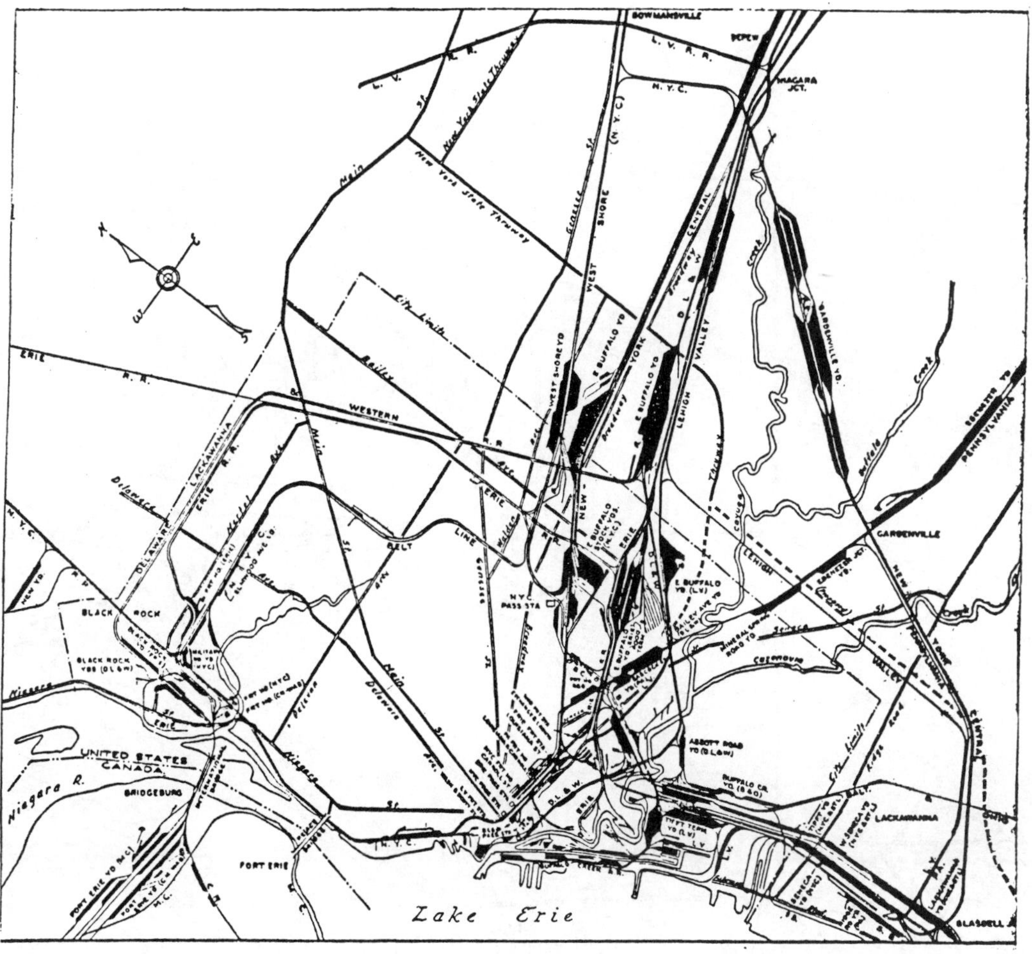

and rail joints, axles, wheels, and tires would crack from time to time. Springs and bolts would snap. Wooden parts, such as ties and car frames, failed through dry rot. . . . So the reasons go on about why trains ran late or not at all, and why the job of moving large tonnage's over the immature railroads of the last century was such a terrible ordeal. [4]

The NYC's Gardenville Yard in Cheektowaga (Figure #2) on the Terminal Railroad of Buffalo, a shortcut from the mainline at Depew to the LS&MS at the Lackawanna-Hamburg line (Figure XII, #6), had eighty-five miles of track able to handle 5,000 cars daily. Adjoining the yards was a thirty-four stall roundhouse, a repair shop for freight cars in transit, and facilities for icing refrigerator cars. Cars destined for points east and west of Buffalo were handled at Gardenville. Cars to and from Buffalo were marshaled at the so-called East Buffalo Yards, which were located mostly in Cheektowaga next to the mainline directly north of Broadway. There were 125 miles of track here and two roundhouses with a capacity of sixty-seven engines. To the west and inside Buffalo were 105 acres of stockyards on William Street where livestock was brought in from American and Canadian points for sale and distribution

Figure #2. NYC's Gardenville yards

Reinstein, *Cheektowaga Atlas*, 1948

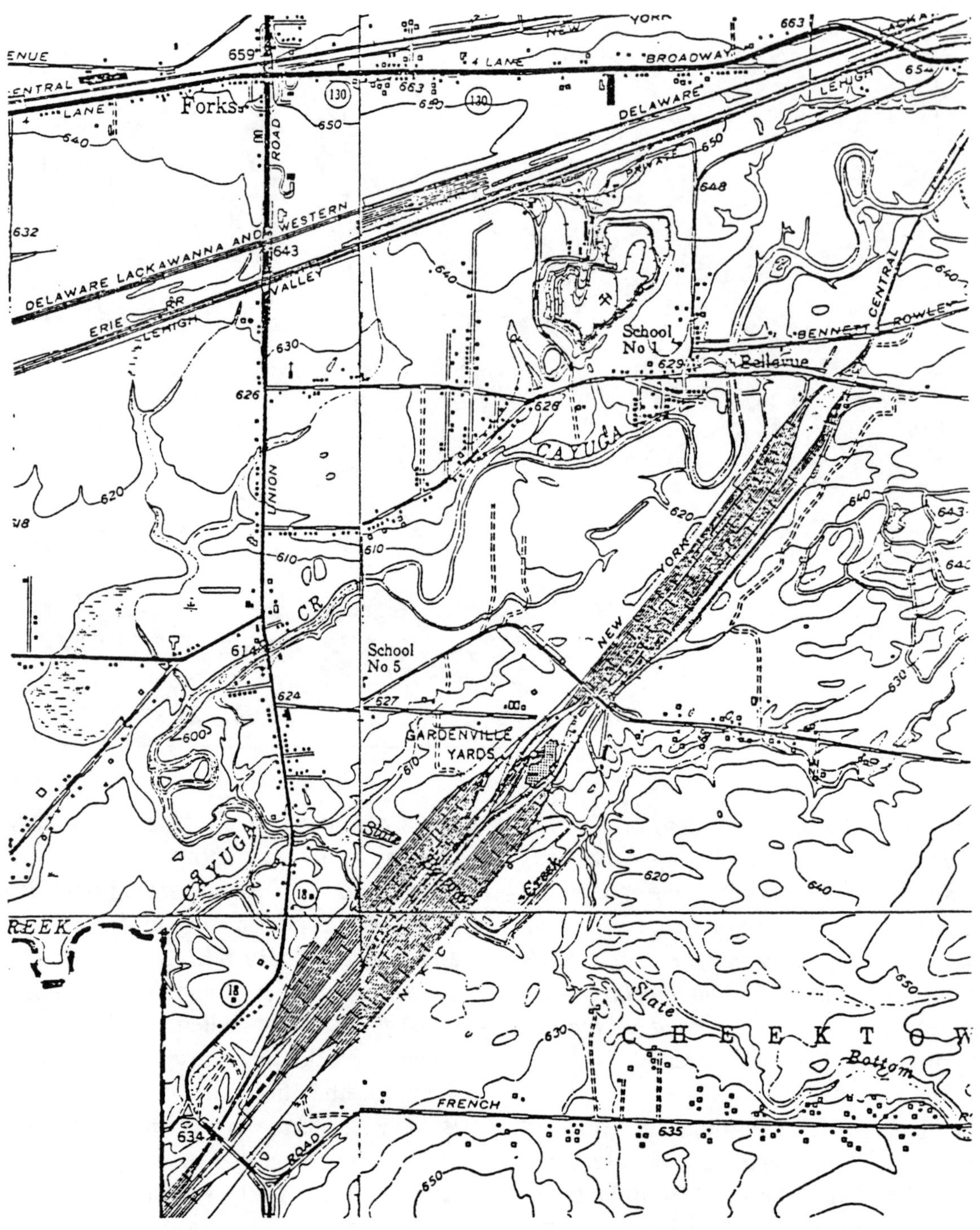

to the East. Despite the growth of traffic in dressed meat, much of the East's meat supply was still shipped on the hoof. Cattle, hogs, and sheep passed through these yards which, though open to the public, were located entirely on NYC property. No matter what road a livestock shipment came in or went out on, it had to pass through the NYC's yards. As a result, most of this traffic, after feeding and resting, moved eastward over the NYC. (Figure #3.) In 1925, 297,024,000 head of cattle, 1,226,440 sheep, 1,831,063 hogs, 291,483 calves, and 18,364 sheep had been processed through these yards. Dunn claims in his History of Erie County that "as late as 1920 the livestock market in Buffalo was among the half dozen largest of its kind in the world, handling more sheep than any other in the United States and ranking second in trade in horses."

South of Buffalo were the Seneca Yards in Lackawanna west of South Park along the LS&MS. (Figure XII, #7.) Its forty-two miles of track could discharge 1,600 cars a day and collected and distributed Buffalo traffic to and from the West. The Black Rock yards with seven miles of track lay northeast of the corner of Amherst and Tonawanda Streets and along the approaches to International Bridge. (Figure #4.) Here, cars originating in the vicinity were marshaled and interchanged with

Figure #3. NYC's and Erie's East Buffalo yards and William Street stockyards

Atlas of Buffalo, 1884, Plate 30

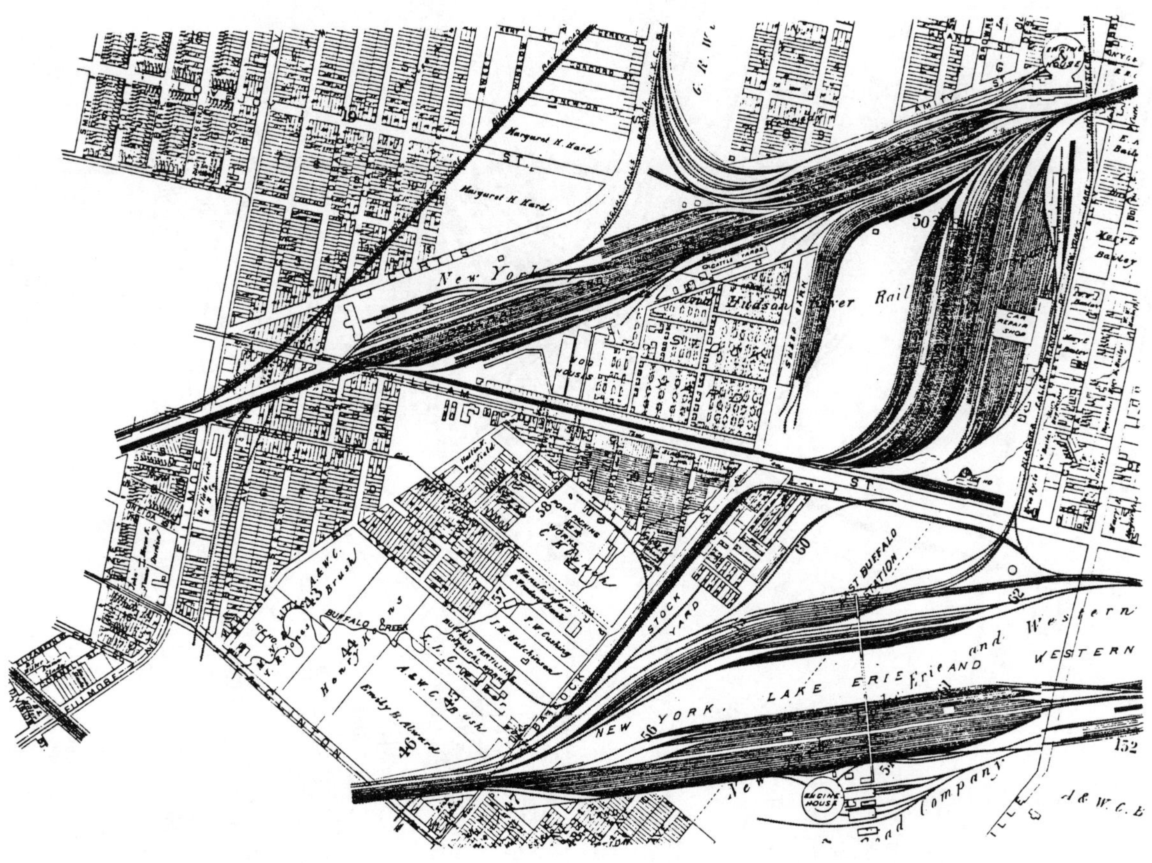

Figure #4. NYC's and Erie's Black Rock yards and approaches to International Bridge

Hydrographic Harbor and Railroad Chart of Buffalo 1907

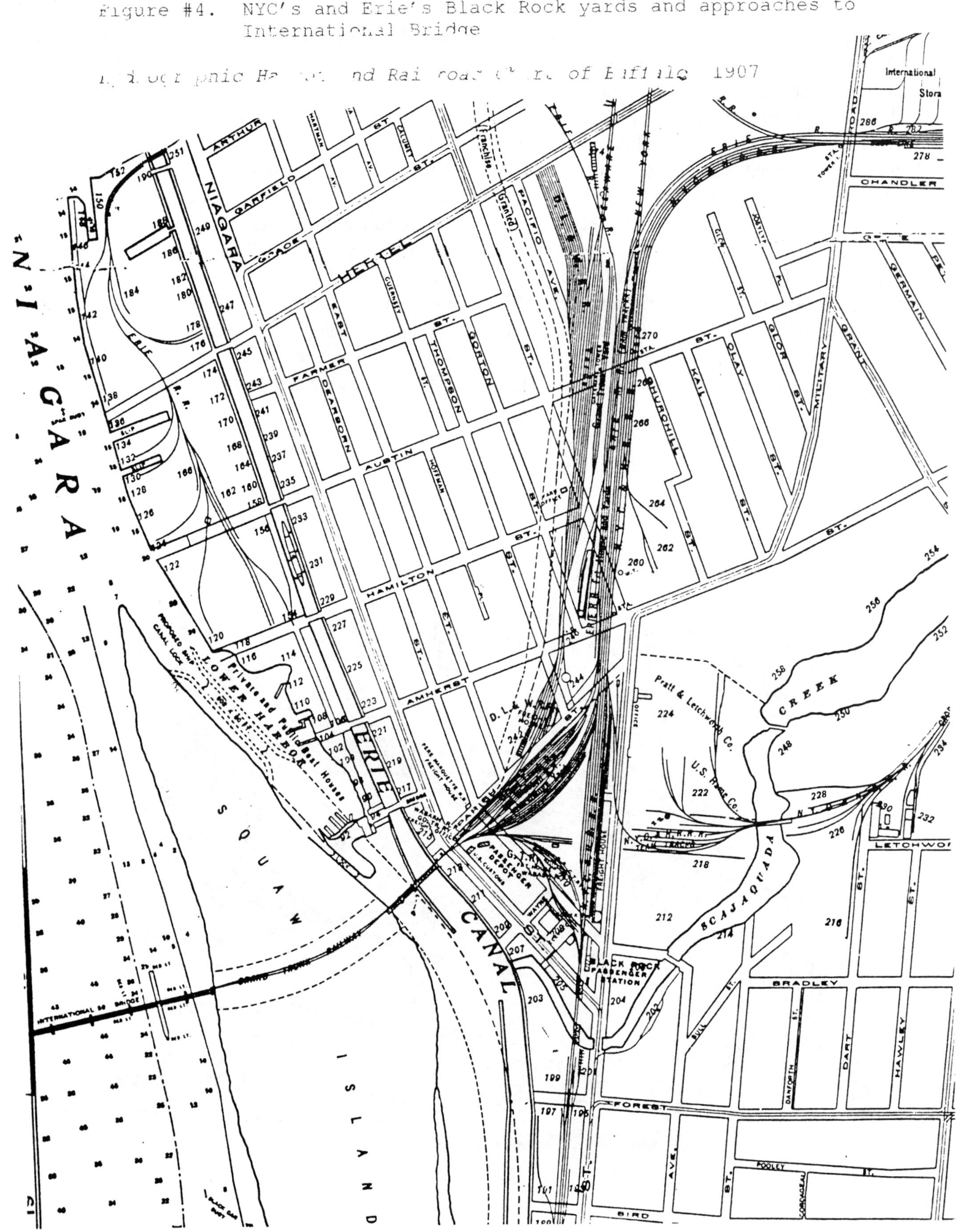

the belt lines of both the Erie and DL&W. At Suspension Bridge on the western end of the Falls Road the NYC operated a yard with forty miles of trackage which could handle 2,000 cars a day. (Figure #5.) There also was a roundhouse with stalls for twenty-seven locomotives. The Depew shops embraced ten buildings on a forty acre tract and could repair thirty-eight locomotives at a time. In March, 1931, the NYC shut these shops down, alleging that they were obsolete, and transferred the work to modern shops at West Albany and Avis, Pennsylvania, a move which threw nearly 700 men out of work. They were invited to seek employment at either of these two plants, but as the March 14, 1931, Times, commenting on the village's "Industrial Death Watch" observed, workers there "feared the 'invasion' from Depew might reduce their hours of labor, and were none too friendly toward the visitors, many of whom hold seniority rights."

Freight stations for shippers of both carload and less-than-carload-lots (LCL) were maintained by the NYC at Carroll Street, a block north of Exchange Street, between Michigan and Chicago (273 car capacity), the former LS&MS freight house on Louisiana Street below Exchange (186 cars), Erie Street on the site of the former Buffalo & Niagara Falls depot (43 cars), at Ohio and Moore Streets in the First Ward (200 cars), and at Tonawanda and Dearborn Streets in Black Rock (44 cars). When his shipment arrived, a consignee would be informed to get down to the freight house and pick it up. The lack of door-to-door transit from producer to consumer for LCL shipments was inherent in the nature of the railroad as opposed to the trucking industry. On the subject of LCL White remarks:

These were smallish shipments weighing 50 to 100 pounds each. They were too big for express or the U. S. mails, but they were too many and too small to work well in the normal boxcar mode of operation that was the basis of the railroad business. It was a complex, labor-intensive, and costly business. The sorting and handling of so many small crates, boxes, casks, parcels, bags, and carboys, all going to different places and consignees, could be nothing but trouble. Yet these small shipments were vital to industry and home alike. A hot-water heater would likely go LCL, as would repair parts or replacement mining gear. . . Special yards and transfer houses were established to unscramble and rationalize the LCL traffic. Long, low sheds with eight to ten tracks sorted boxes and bags from two hundred to five hundred cars a day. [5]

A very different judgment on LCL has been rendered by Charles W. Bohi's "When LCL Meant Fast Freight" in Trains:

Defined as "freight in one car from more than one shipper or destined to more than one receiver," LCL shipments were sometimes termed "merchandise" or "package" traffic. Although a cut below the more valuable express shipments that commanded premium rates and usually moved on passenger trains, the LCL business could be lucrative. This was because of its high freight classification and because a minimum price was charged for each package regardless of weight. In 1932, for example, rail LCL traffic constituted only 2.4 percent of the freight tonnage but generated more than 10 percent of the revenue.

To handle this important revenue source, the carriers usually moved package freight in boxcars that operated between specific points on regular schedules and were hauled by designated trains. When traffic warranted, of course, more than one boxcar could be used to protect a particular schedule. In 1932 there were 8,793 schedules between city pairs that had at least two regularly operated package cars linking them. Additional cities were linked by single schedules.

In communities where volume justified it, a separate freight station was employed to handle the packages. If there was enough traffic whole carloads of merchandise could be loaded for a specific community. In the 1920s

Figure #5. NYC's Niagara Falls yards

Atlas of the Vicinity of Buffalo, 1893, Plate 4

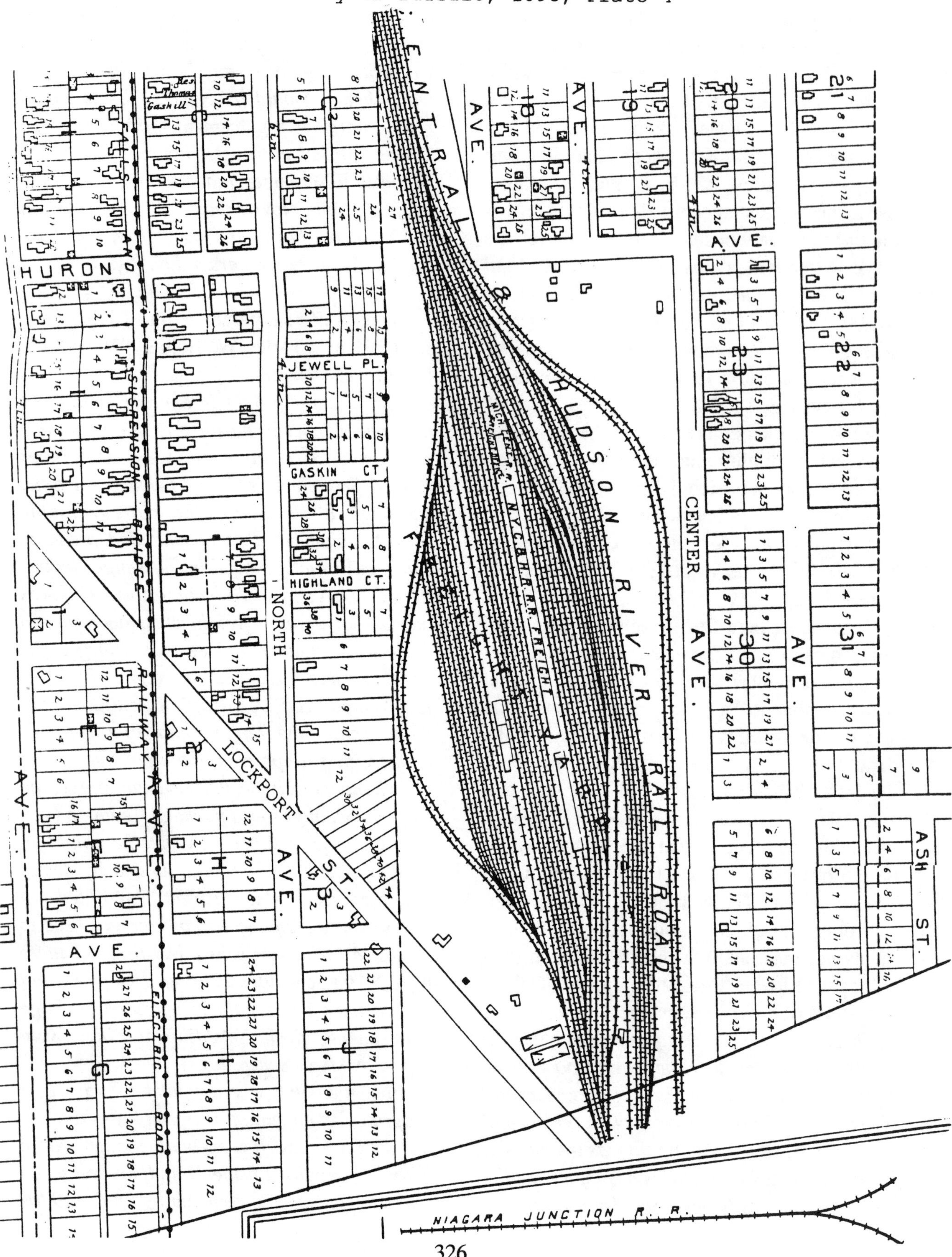

and 1930s, even branchline points might receive several carloads of LCL a day. In smaller communities, which usually received more merchandise than they dispatched, package cars - often called "way cars" and placed next to the engine or caboose - would be unloaded into a combination station that served both freight and passengers. Even as late as the 1950s I recall watching a Chicago & Great Western conductor and depot agent unload LCL from cars labeled "System Merchandise Service Only" in a rural Iowa town. The LCL business to country points was so important that standard depot designs commonly provided half or more of the floor space for freight storage.

However, later in his article Bohi admitted that:

. . . as efficient as this system might seem, by late 1920s railway LCL was in trouble. In 1934 a federal study concluded that by the early 1930s, "highway transportation [of merchandise was] *relatively more economical than rail transport for all distances." By 1932 the greater speed, door-to-door service, and cheaper rates offered by truckers had reduced rail LCL to 15.23 million tons, 34 percent of its 1923 peak of 44.38 million tons, a larger drop than could be explained by the Depression and less than half of the 32.26 million tons moved by trucks.*

Not only was traffic being lost to trucks. The federal study found that by 1932 each ton of LCL "failed to bear [its] *full proportion of total operating expenses and taxes by $1.13." Yet, the study argued that the merchandise traffic was worth fighting for because revenues exceeded the direct costs of providing the service by nearly $5 per ton, producing "about $73 million" in net income for the railroads.* [6]

The most important of the NYC's freight houses was on Ohio Street, with a frontage of 2,200 feet on the Buffalo River, where package and carload shipments in and out of lake steamers to and from the West were handled. (Figure #6.) At the Carroll Street station, a block north of Exchange Street, a crane transfered containers between freight cars and trucks. Some fresh meat shipments were handled here. At the Louisiana Street freight house of the former LS&MS three blocks away (Figure #7), in-bound merchandise from the west and the greater part of the city's carload shipments of fresh fruits and vegetables were handled. Because of its location, the Erie Street Station of the quondam B&NF was largely occupied with MC business, as was also true of the Black Rock station. The NYC also maintained an ore dock for transferring ore from lake steamers to gondola cars on the west bank of the City Ship Canal, called accordingly the West Shore Ore Dock. (Figure #6.) On Erie Basin at the foot of Georgia Street was located the Philadelphia & Reading Lake Coal Trestle for supplying lake carriers with coal. Coal was the single most important item carried by America's railroads, but this was not the case with the NYC. On Curtiss Street in the heart of Polonia on what was soon to become the site of Central Terminal was located the NYC's express station, a large, modern facility with a capacity of 187 cars. The floor area of the freight house was 60,000 square feet. Express was carried on regularly scheduled passenger trains as was the mail, but the NYC also ran solid express and mail trains, the latter of which were handled at a mail terminal at Clinton Street, halfway between Curtiss and Exchange Street. Along the fifteen mile long Belt Line (Figure VII, #8) were located 350 industries, many of which had their own sidings. This made trips to the freight houses unnecessary. Some of these plants required an average daily movement of one hundred cars in and out. In 1926 alone sidings were laid to thirty-five industries newly established in Buffalo.

Statistics for the NYC's freight business during the 1920s stagger the imagination.

Figure #6

Inner Harbor

Hydrographic Chart

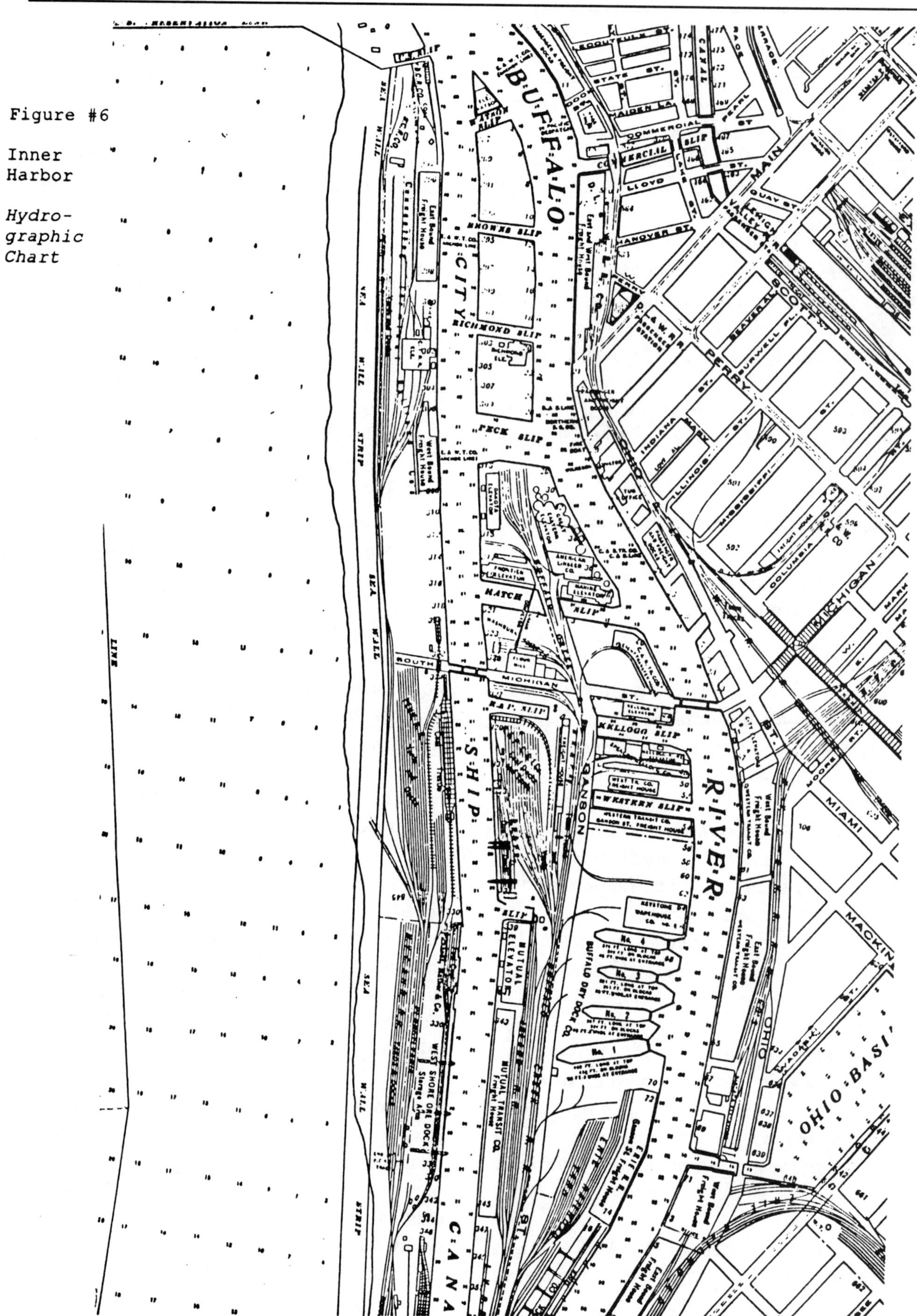

Figure #7. Freight houses, NYC, Erie, PRR, *Atlas of Buffalo*, 1915, II, Plate 34

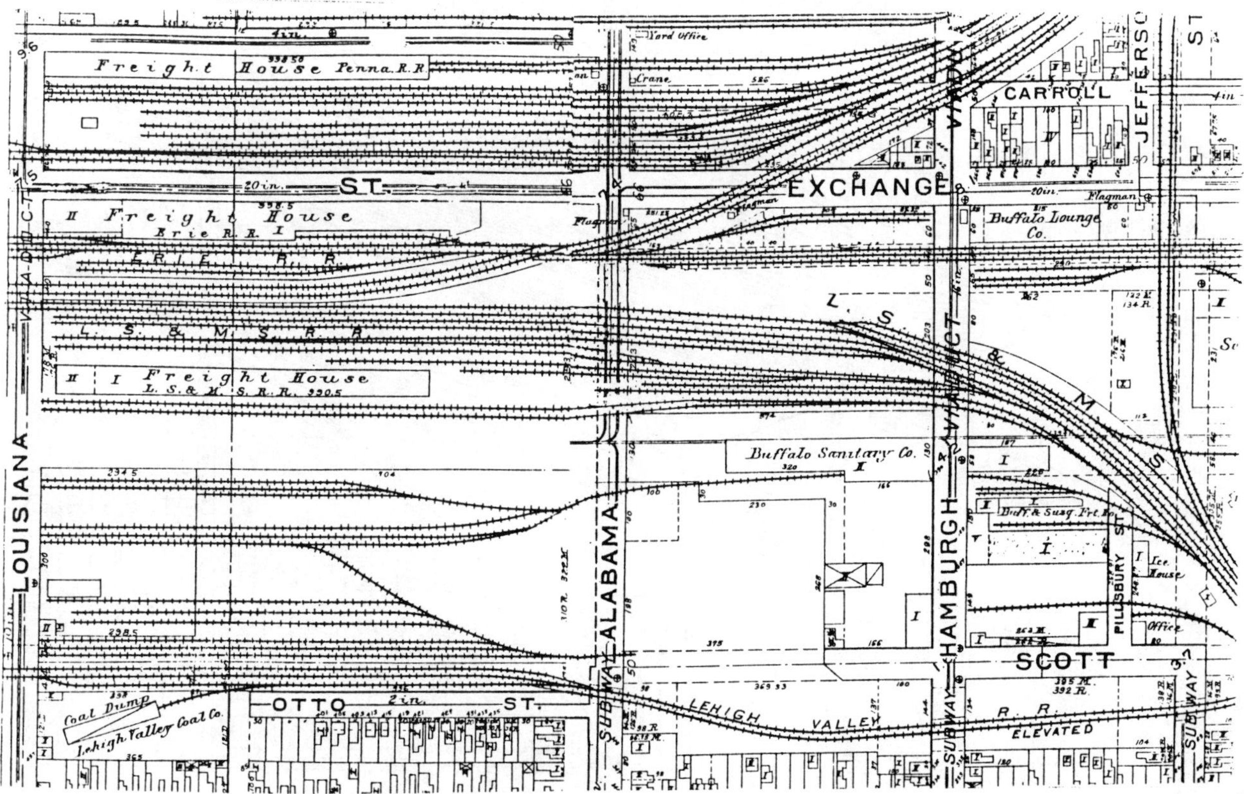

During 1925 the railroad moved 714,765 loaded eastbound cars through the Niagara Frontier. Westbound it moved 181,011 loaded cars and 357,500 empties. Figures were not available for eastbound empties, since the bulk of freight traffic on the NYC traveled east so that there were relatively few eastbound empties. On the Niagara Frontier in 1926 the NYC employed approximately 10,000 people at a payroll close to $15 million.

Though it was acquired by Vanderbilt interests almost immediately after its completion in 1885, the NYWS&B had been built as a competitor of the NYC. Hence it had its own yards, shop and three roundhouses northeast of the corner of Broadway and Bailey. At the northeast corner of that intersection were the shops of the Pullman Company, which had bought out the previous tenant, the Wagner Palace Car Company, in 1899. (Figure XI, #2.) In its heyday, according to the *News* for July 24, 1958, Buffalo's Pullman plant was the second largest in the country, with nearly a thousand employees, among them tinsmiths, machinists, carbody builders, upholsterers, and seamstresses. Most of the bedding throughout the system was laundered at Buffalo.

Delaware Lackawanna & Western

Following the NYC on the Niagara Frontier in the mid-1920s, but at a great remove in terms of work force and payroll, was the DL&W, with three thousand employees who received an annual compensation of $4,500,000. It had, however, considerably less route mileage than the sprawling Erie. The DL&W's principal freight yard was in Sloan, just across the Buffalo city line at the junction point of the road's lines to Black Rock and to downtown Buffalo. (Figure #8; see also Figure IX, #9.) Hence it was known as the East Buffalo Yard. It was half a mile long and had a capacity of 4,406 cars. Its large transfer platform handled and consolidated LCL shipments for points east and west. Facilities were pro-

Figure #8. DL&W's Sloan yards and shops, *ibid.*, II, Plate 12

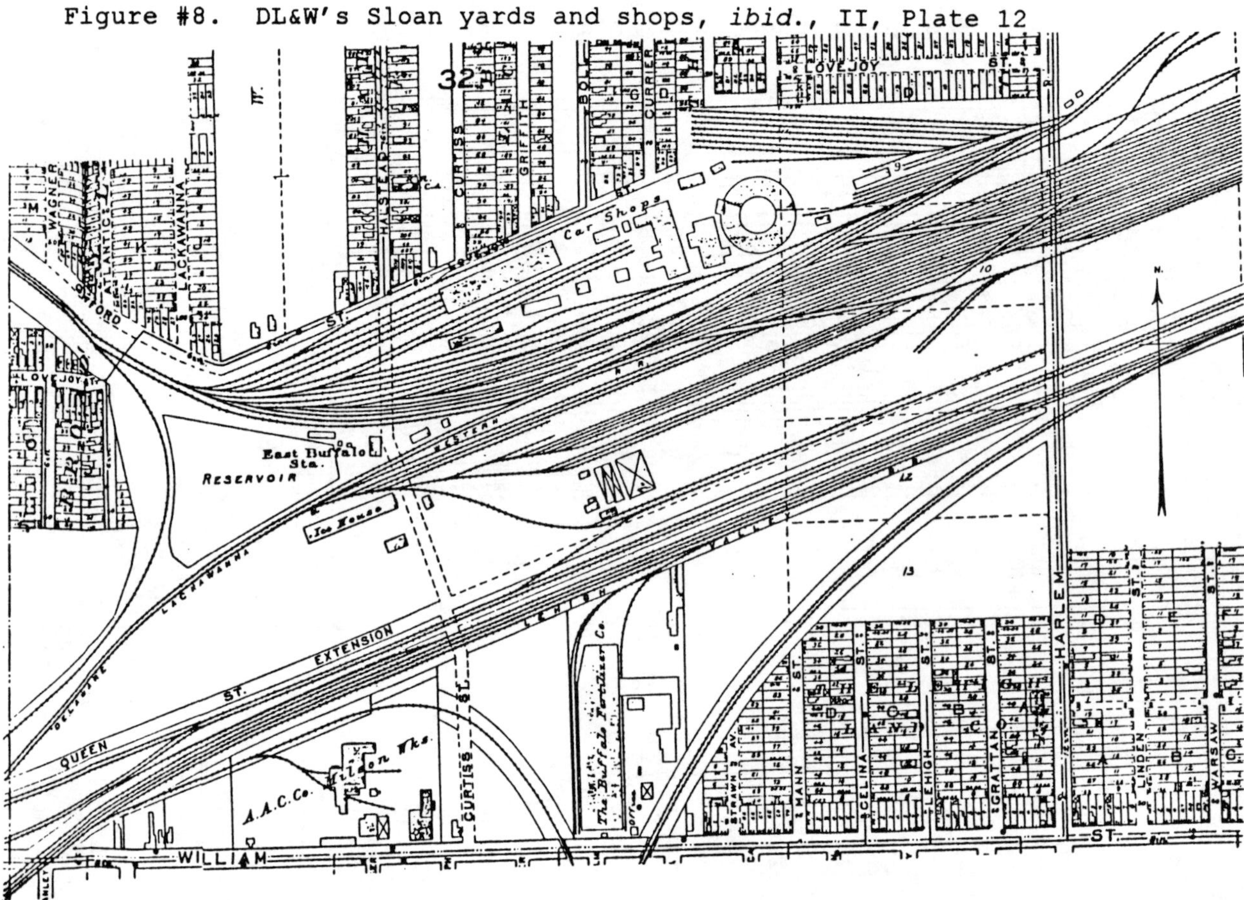

vided for icing perishables and feeding and resting livestock, and a huge reservoir, in which employees of the railroad were permitted to fish, assured a constant supply of water for thirsty locomotives. In 1926 the DL&W forwarded from East Buffalo 266,368 carloads of eastbound freight and 196,196 carloads of westbound freight. Total eastbound livestock movement amounted to 8,104 cars. That same year eastbound traffic from East Buffalo included 10,000 cars of flour milled in Buffalo and 6,300 cars of iron and steel products. LCL merchandise handled through the transfer averaged 10,000 tons monthly. In addition, sixty through merchandise cars were made up there daily. At Black Rock the Lackawanna had a new freight house, two team tracks for the delivery of carload freight, and a ten ton electric pillar crane and concrete platform with a ramp for unloading automobiles for distribution to local car dealers. Along with the Erie and the NYC, the DL&W maintained an already mentioned classification yard at Black Rock (Figure #4), which enabled the road to interchange not only with these two roads, but also with the MC, the Canadian National, the Pere Marquette, and the Wabash.

The DL&W, however, was primarily an anthracite road. For the importance of this commodity to the road in the years 1899-1960, see Figure #9. For delivery of coal up the Great Lakes a coal dock trestle had been built in 1882 and replaced in 1916-1917 when the new passenger station was built. At the foot of Erie Street was a coal dumper where cars were lifted, turned onto their sides, and dumped into the hold of colliers. This dumper had a capacity of 10,000 tons daily or 3,000,000 a year. In 1883 the Lackawanna had built a mile long coal trestle east of Sloan in Cheektowaga. (Figure IX, #13.) Two-hundred car trains loaded with coal entered the enclosed trestle on an incline to an elevation at which the cars would open up their bottoms and eject their contents to the ground for haulage by retail coal dealers for home consumption. Rebuilt in

Figure #9. DL&W freight traffic, 1899-1960, Taber, *DL&W in the 20th Century*, 239

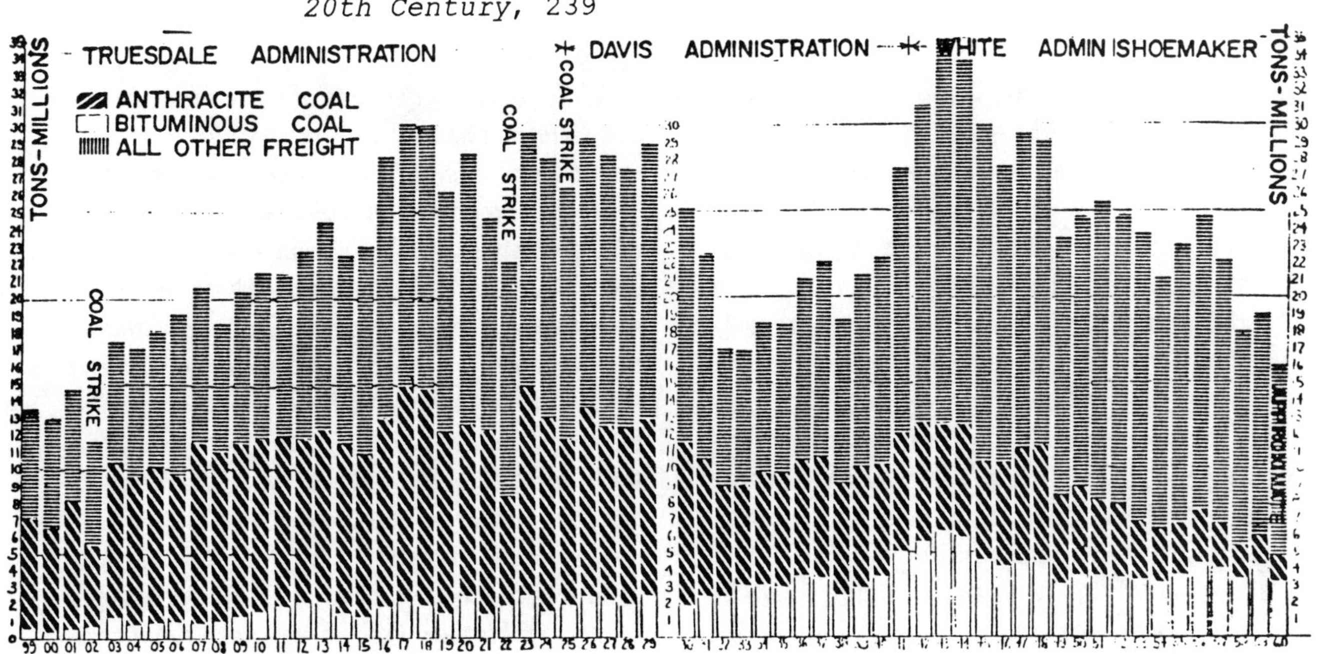

1910 after a fire, the coal trestle burned again ten years later and was razed.

Erie Railroad

The third largest railroad operation in Buffalo in the mid-1920s was that of the Erie with 200 miles of track, 2,500 employees, and an annual payroll of $4,000,000. Besides its mainline, the Erie had branches in Western New York to International Bridge, Suspension Bridge, Lockport, and Jamestown. (Figure III, #1.) It maintained a classification yard and a forty stall roundhouse in East Buffalo between Clinton and William Street where thirty-five engines were engaged daily in switching operations. (Figure #3) A second Erie classification yard for interchange with lines coming over Suspension Bridge from Canada was located at Black Rock. It had a capacity of 325 cars and was serviced by a dozen switch engines. (Figure #4.) Within Buffalo's city limits were six freight houses located at Louisiana Street, East Buffalo, the Waterfront, East Ferry Street, Main Street, and Black Rock. (Figures #3, #4, #6, #7.) The Erie had grown up like Topsy, and there was something topsyish about the disposition of its freight houses around the city in comparison with its competitor, the more rationally planned DL&W.

The 1927 booklet on Buffalo's railroads describes the activity at the first of these freight houses:

Louisiana street [at Exchange Street (Figure #6)] *is the principal Erie station in Buffalo at which carload freight is received and delivered. The inbound freight house is 40 x 476 feet; outbound freight house, 40 x 461 feet. In connection with the freight house a transfer platform, 680 feet long, is worked jointly. Through combined operation solid merchandise cars* [LCL] *are here made up direct for the principal Erie points as well as many points on connecting lines, including Canada and New England. The schedule of LCL move-*

ment at this station contemplates 55 cars daily. Serving the station are team tracks at three locations, namely, Louisiana street, Hamburg street and Smith [better Alabama] *street. These tracks have a total of seven sidings with a capacity of 91 cars for handling carload station freight inbound. An electric crane of 35 tons capacity handles heavy material.* [7]

The misnamed Buffalo Lake station, actually located on the Buffalo River between Louisiana and Ohio Streets on the southeasternmost point of the First Ward north of the Hamburg Turnpike Bridge (Figure #7), handled interchange with lake steamers and neighboring industries. Here too was an elevator through which flour from lake vessels was transferred to Erie boxcars for the East. The floor space of this two story structure was 520 feet on each side and was served by three tracks with a thirty-three car capacity. Directly across the river on Ganson Street on the Island was a concrete fireproof warehouse 125 x 675 feet with a capacity of 10,000 tons for storing lake freight and serviced by three sidings with space for thirty-two cars; on the opposite and eastern bank of the canal were coal docks with a dumping capacity of 280 cars daily. The Erie, with its two branches into northeastern Pennsylvania, was the third largest carrier of hard coal into Buffalo for local consumption and transshipment up the lakes. The other two were the LV and the DL&W. Access to these docks was by way of the Buffalo Creek Railroad, joint lessees of which since 1890 were the Erie and the LV.

Attached to the Erie's major classification yards in East Buffalo between William and Clinton Streets was the road's East Buffalo freight house approached from Babcock Street (Figure #3), where interchange was made with the NKP, NYC, PRR, LV, DL&W, and BR&P trunk lines and two connecting terminal lines, the Buffalo Creek and the South Buffalo. On the Erie's line to International Bridge (Figure VII, #7), freight houses with team tracks could be found at East Ferry and Main Streets and on Amherst Street in Black Rock. There were also team tracks at Kensington Avenue.

Paul Carleton writes in The Erie Railroad Story:

Aside from its early use of the six foot gauge, the Erie of old had one particular drawback which was eventually turned into an asset. With the exception of Youngstown, Ohio, the old girl missed most revenue (road freight) generating areas in the east. Once the Erie's management restored this Chicago-through-the-woods-to-New York railroad to relative health early in this century, one fact became clear: once the track was in good condition, with no Philadelphia, Altoona. Pittsburgh, or for that matter no Albany or Buffalo areas of congestion to slow down the freight for days or even weeks [there was no reason] *why a reefer of perishables or you name it could not get from Chicago to New York mighty fast on our subject road. Of course, the cartel arrangements perpetuated by the Interstate Commerce Commission would see to it that the Erie never got a larger share of ordinary cargo, but those fast perishable movements became a trademark of sorts for many years.* [8]

Pennsylvania Railroad

The mighty PRR (nationwide it had 200,000 employees and paid a million dollars a day in wages) was represented in Buffalo by two lines. One, the former Buffalo New York & Philadelphia, branched off from the Philadelphia & Erie at Emporium Junction; the other, the former Buffalo Corry & Pittsburgh, left the mainline at Pittsburgh. (Figure XI, #4.) The PRR had eight miles of trackage on the Island, exclusive of three miles of sidings to various industries. (Figure #6.) On the thirty-three acre Burrow's Lot Yard on the south end of the Island, just east of the Hamburg Turnpike at the first loop of the Buffalo River, the PRR serviced these grain and milling firms: Marine Elevator, Cargill Electric

Elevator, Dellwood Grain Elevator, Marine Grain Elevator, American Elevator, Russell Miller Milling, Francis Perrott Malting, and International Milling & Flour. In addition, there were sidings for Kelly Island Lime & Transport and Pierce & Stevens Chemical. Over on the west bank of the City Ship Canal was the huge Connecting Terminal Elevator, owned by the PRR and leased by the Lake Elevator Company. It had a storage capacity of a million bushels of grain. During 1926 the PRR shipped east from Buffalo 10,684 cars of flour, and brought in from the Lakes 7,951 carloads of grain.

Directly north of the Union Ship Canal in the southwest corner of Buffalo on the lakefront was a giant ore dock, successor to the Goodyears' defunct Buffalo & Susquehanna operation, 1,000 feet long and sixty-five feet wide, and built by the PRR. The canal was twenty-two feet deep at the dock which enabled it to handle any lake boat. Dock and yards embraced 232 acres, over a third of a square mile, fifty-five percent of which was used for dock and storage facilities, with a capacity in pit and field of over 700,000 tons and track space for over 1,000 freight cars. Giant mechanical unloaders transferred 1,600,000 tons of ore from lake steamers to freight cars in 1926. At the entrance to the Union Ship Canal was the Great Lakes Portland Cement Company's plant with a daily output of 7,000 barrels of cement which began operations in 1927.

The PRR's major classification yard, engine house, and shops were located at Ebenezer in West Seneca along the former Buffalo New York & Philadelphia just east of Harlem Road and south of the NYC's Gardenville yards. Eight receiving tracks could hold 700 cars. These yards had a natural gravity hump over which 253,351 cars were shunted during 1926. The PRR also maintained yards on the peninsula between the lake and the Ship Canal and on the former LS&MS on Babcock Street. Fast regularly scheduled freight trains in and out of Buffalo were known as the *Bison*, the *Blue Goose*, the *Flying Cloud*, the *Crackerjack*, the *Excelsior*, and the *Purple Eagle*. It is not recorded that any other Buffalo freight trains bore proper names. The Buffalo Division's general repair shops were located at Olean.

The PRR's Buffalo freight house was on Louisiana Street between Seneca and Exchange Street, the site of the former Buffalo, New York & Philadelphia station. (Figure #7.) During 1926 288,222 cars of LCL and carload freight were handled at this station, whose house tracks could accommodate 127 cars. Adjacent to the freight station were the Alabama Street team track yards for the delivery of perishable and other carload commodities. The yard could hold 185 cars in transit and 80 in storage. During 1926, 3,539 cars of perishable freight were unloaded at this point. The yard boasted a forty ton electric crane, three tracks wide, under which eight cars of heavy freight could be unloaded. For the convenience of patrons on the outlying districts of Buffalo, team tracks for the delivery and reception of freight were provided at Fillmore Avenue. The volume of freight traffic handled by the Buffalo Division during 1926 was 1,442,725,352 tons. That year this division had 2,070 employees with an annual payroll of $3.8 million.

Lehigh Valley

In terms of the number of workers employed locally the next railroad after the PRR was the LV with 1,700 who collectively earned an annual salary of $3 million. The LV's local property tax bill was $435,000. Its Buffalo freight house adjoined the passenger terminal at Washington and Scott Streets. Twenty through freight trains in and out of Buffalo each day serviced by thirty-two switching crews were the LV's contribution to the city's railroad action. The following is from the treatment of the LV freight business in Buffalo in the 1927 booklet:

At the Scott street freight station last year the LV received 41,867 tons of freight and forwarded 42,887 tons in less-than-carload lots. The carload freight handled in the team tracks in the Scott street freight yard amounted to 24,259 tons. The less-than-carload freight required the use of 9,547 cars while 1,668 cars were necessary to handle the carload freight. In 1926 the carload business handled from the industries which have side track facilities on the LV in Buffalo amounted to 27,976 cars.

Outbound, the principal commodities handled by the LV are grain, flour and mill products, iron and steel, livestock, merchandise, perishable products and manufactured articles. Inbound the principal commodities are coal, cement, iron and steel products, brick and clay products, and perishable freight.

The principal freight terminal of the LV, on its western end, comprising 742 acres fronting on Lake Erie, is located in the Tifft Farm section of Buffalo. [Figures IX, #1 and #2.] *The Canadian pool grain elevator, Buffalo's first lake front elevator, is located on this site. The largest single cargo of grain ever brought to Buffalo was recently unloaded at this elevator. Tifft Farm is connected with the main line of the LV through* [the Buffalo Creek Railroad and by] *a branch, the Lehigh & Lake Erie, which makes possible the handling of freight received from and delivered to western connections without moving it through the Buffalo terminal proper.* [Figure XII, #6.]

At Tifft Farm are two large freight houses for the handling of lake shipments, one having a capacity of 7,500 tons and the other 13,000 tons, a coal dock and mechanical car unloader capable of transferring 1,000 tons of coal per hour from cars to steamers for points on the Great Lakes, a dock for the transfer of ore from lake steamers to cars, an automobile unloading platform and other modern freight handling facilities. Steamers operating between Buffalo and Chicago and Milwaukee, as well as Lake Superior ports, interchange package freight at the LV docks [at Tifft Farm], *cooperating with the LV in forming an important route for the handling of east and westbound through lake-and-rail traffic. Rail and water freight is interchanged with steamers for Cleveland, Detroit, and other ports.*

LV freight service to New York is expeditiously handled. Freight loaded at Buffalo in the afternoon arrives in New York the second morning; less-than-carload shipments frequently receiving the same fast service as carloads. Coal arriving at Buffalo over the LV is shipped from the road's coal docks [at Tifft Farm] *to the northwest. It is unloaded from cars at the rate of thirty cars an hour at less than two cents a ton, the fastest and cheapest transfer in Buffalo. Approximately one million tons were transported last year by the LV for lake shipment from Buffalo. About 21,000 cars were used to carry this coal. The ore shipments handled by the LV in 1926 amounted to 45,000 tons in 850 cars; the pig iron, 12,300 tons in 306 cars.* [9]

New York Chicago & Saint Louis

During the thirty-four years that the NYC controlled the NKP (1882-1916), strenuous efforts were made to give the impression that it was really an independent line, lest the vague provisions of the Sherman Anti-Trust Act against combinations in restraint of trade or commerce between the states be invoked to set aside the arrangement. But in comparison with the sums spent on upgrading and locating new industries along the route of LS&MS, the NKP was permitted to slip into a decidedly second-rate status with increasingly obsolete facilities. In 1916 two Cleveland real estate developers, the brothers Oris Paxton and Mantis James Van Sweringen, were induced by the NYC management, anxious to avoid prosecution by the Wilson administration under the terms of the recently passed Clayton Anti-Trust Act which ostensibly strengthened the Sherman Act, to purchase the NKP. The

NYC was anxious to keep the NKP out of the hands of the DL&W, which had wanted to acquire the NKP (a move which would have given the NYC real competition for the New York-Buffalo-Chicago traffic) and had the means to do so. Moreover, the PRR was bidding for the NKP since its possession would have given the Standard Railroad of the World the means to compete with the NYC in the industrial heartland of America along the southern shores of Lake Erie and in northern Ohio and Indiana. The NYC-PRR community of interest prescribed by J. P. Morgan and promoted by Alexander Cassatt had become a thing of the past.

The Van Sweringens had started as developers of Shaker Heights, a Cleveland suburb, moved thence into Cleveland interurbans, and thence into the NKP. NYC management reasoned that the Vans, as the brothers were called, would prove more cooperative than either the DL&W or the PRR. The Vans chose as president of their road John Bernet, a NYC vice president, who thoroughly upgraded the NKP's trackage and motive power so that, as noted by The Historical Guide to North American Railroads, "by 1925 the road had doubled its freight tonnage and average speed, halved its fuel consumption per ton mile, and led all U. S. roads in car miles per day." As the NKP's chronicler, John H. Rehor, wrote: "Entertaining no illusions about competing with his late employer for the passenger trade, Bernet's plans were built around the NKP's freight business." In 1922 the Vans acquired the Lake Erie & Western, which gave the NKP access in the rich agricultural lands of central Illinois, and the Toledo Saint Louis & Western which finally presented the New York Chicago & Saint Louis with an outlet to its third titular city, the Gateway to the Golden West. It was the first notable railroad consolidation since the infamous *Northern Securities* decision in 1904 and it was in the spirit of the Transportation Act of 1920, which had called for precisely this type of activity.

Whoever wrote up the NKP for the 1927 booklet had very little to say about the road's freight activity in Buffalo beyond stating that "the Nickel Plate's facilities at Buffalo include the Blasdell, Lackawanna, and West Seneca storage tracks with a total capacity of 564 cars; the Tifft yard [north of Tifft Street] for eastbound freight and the Abbott Road yard [between Seneca Street and Abbott Road just east of Selkirk Street] for westbound freight, accommodating respectively 967 and 470 cars." The problem with this laconic statement is that by 1927 the so-called West Seneca yard was in Lackawanna. The writer added that "Buffalo carload freight and merchandise is received and delivered at the Louisiana street station *[sic]* which is operated by the NKP and the NYC as a joint operation," which suggests that most of the road's freight business in Buffalo consisted in interchange of through freight. There were about 700 NKP workers in and around Buffalo in 1927 earning $1.2 million annually.

Buffalo Rochester & Pittsburgh

The BR&P was a well-run hauler of soft coal from the mines of Western Pennsylvania to the Great Lakes cities of Rochester and Buffalo, most of which was destined to ports further up the lakes or to Canadian ports on Lake Ontario. On the return trip coal cars carried iron ore to furnaces at Punxsutawney and Du Bois in Pennsylvania, thus producing a payload on both legs of the trip. Since ore weighed four times as much as coal, train crews, as Paul Pietrak, the road's historian, put it, "were instructed to run ore trains easy and not too fast." The ore business was short-lived, however, since the iron furnaces were gone by the mid-1920s. The BR&P did not penetrate very far into Buffalo but terminated at Buffalo Creek Junction on the south bank of the creek whence it reached its installations in the city via the Buffalo Creek Railroad. The BR&P had freight houses and team tracks at

Ganson Street on the Island (Figures #6 and #10)) and at the southeast corner of Fillmore and Clinton Avenues. About 285 Western New Yorkers worked for this railroad whose annual salary bill came to half a million.

The Ganson Street freight house, according to the account in the 1927 booklet:

. . . is 504 feet long with a track capacity of 46 cars. Adjacent to the freight house is a team track delivery with a total of 1,000 feet of trackage served by an electric crane of 30,000 pounds capacity. The Fillmore avenue freight station serves the east side of the city and has team track facilities for 35 cars. Adjacent to the Ganson street freight house is an 844-foot ore dock equipped with two Hulett steam unloading machines with a capacity each of 400 tons of ore per hour. Another dock for lake vessel transshipment has a 700 foot frontage on Buffalo Creek [actually the Ship Canal], *over which pulpwood, pig iron, structural steel and other commodities are handled to and from water line carriers.* [10]

To this Pietrak adds:

Besides coal and iron ore, the railroad had some on-the-line business on its Buffalo Branch. Added to the normal lumber yards, feedmills and general freight that would generate at the small towns along this branch, the BR&P served a number of brick yards. These were located at Orchard Park, Loveland and at Jewettville. They are all but a memory today, the only one still standing is the yard at Jewettville. [11]

The BR&P's marshaling yard was just south of Tifft Street for interchange with the NYC, PRR, NKP, Erie, and South Buffalo. Pietrak recalls that:

At the north end of the Tifft Street yard the BR&P had its roundhouse and turntable. The roundhouse had eight stalls and minor repair work was conducted there. [The main shops were at Du Bois.] *There was also a coal tower and sand house as well as small offices for the engine dispatcher and crews but no train dis-*

Figure #10. The Buffalo Creek on the Island; Ganson Street, Ron Dukarm collection

patcher as that was handled in Salamanca. Just about on any given day during the 1920s, if one should happen into the BR&P's yards at Tifft Street, one could see at least five or six engines at work or being serviced at this terminal. [12]

A Greek Revival freight house on the west side of Moore Street from Miami to Elk had been built for the NYC in the 1860s, but at the turn of the century was owned by the BR&P. When the DL&W was put through to the foot of Main Street in the 80s, its abutment cut this building in half. By 1927, however, the BR&P had also abandoned it.

Canadian National

The fact of vast distances determined much of Canada's railroad history, a concise account of which from the 1860s to the 1920s is provided by D. D. G. Kerr:

Land grants and other aid from all levels of government were largely responsible for the rapid progress in railway building after Confederation [in 1864.] *Total mileage in 1867 was 2,278; in 1900, 17,657; in 1914, 30,797; and in 1931, 42,280. The main line of the first transcontinental, the Canadian Pacific Railway, was completed in November 1885. Encouraged by the flood-tide of migration to the West in the 1890s and 1900s, a railway boom took place which covered the prairies with a network of feeder lines and resulted in the emergence of two more transcontinental systems. The first, the Grand Trunk Pacific between Prince Rupert and Winnipeg, a subsidiary of the Grand Trunk, was intended to be operated in conjunction with the National Transcontinental built by the federal government from Winnipeg to Moncton, N.B. The second, the Canadian Northern from Vancouver to Montreal, was built and pieced together by William Mackenzie and Donald Mann. Both lines were in serious difficulty by 1917 due partly to overbuilding and partly to the outbreak of the First World War which occurred as they were being completed and delayed further immigration and western development. Accordingly, in the period 1917-1923 it became necessary for the federal government to take over the Canadian Northern, the Grand Trunk Pacific, and the Grand Trunk and consolidate them along with the government-built National Transcontinental, Intercolonial* [Quebec to Halifax via Riviere-du-Loup] *and Prince Edward Island Railways to form the Canadian National Railways system. The Hudson Bay Railway, completed in 1929, was later added to this. The Canadian Pacific Railway and some smaller companies remained independent. (Figure #11.)* [13]

Overbuilding, which had marked railroad construction on the Niagara Peninsula, was to be characteristic of Canada as a whole.

Though the Canadian National owned no trackage in Buffalo, its city freight terminal, known as Buffalo-River Street, was located on River Street between Erie and Genesee Street with dockage on Erie Basin Canal Slip #1, on the southwest side and Slip #2 on the northwest Side. It was convenient to the Elk Street Market, wholesale house, public storage warehouses and general jobbing districts. Freight house #1, on the east side of River Street, was used for outbound LCL which was loaded onto through cars for western United States and Canada. Freight house #2, on the west side of River Street, was for inbound LCL destined for local delivery and connecting eastbound railroads. It was equipped with a derrick and a ramp for autos and trucks from Detroit. A resident U. S. customs official speeded up the release of bonded goods. The Black Rock freight house on Niagara and Parrish Streets at the eastern end of the International Bridge (Figure #3.) owned by the Canadian National was similarly equipped, and also boasted a forty ton Gantry electric crane for heavy articles. Across the bridge in Fort Erie there were forty miles of switching tracks for classifica-

Figure #11. Railroads of Canada

Kerr, *Historical Atlas of Canada*, 64-65

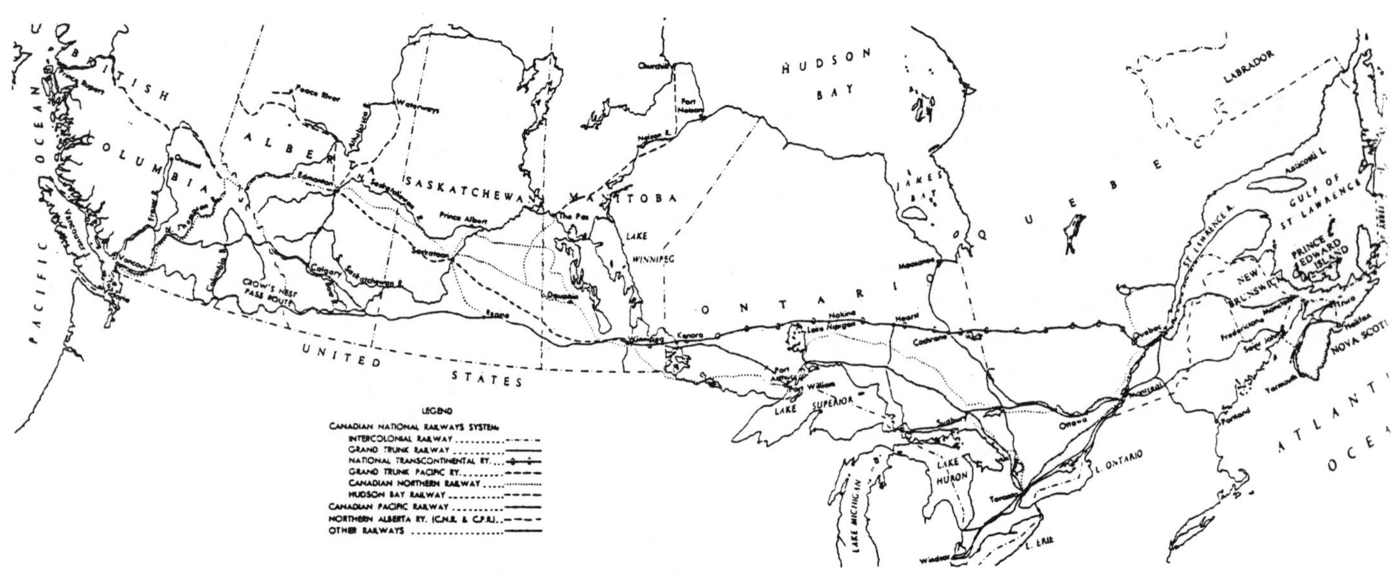

tion purposes, a roundhouse and a freight house. A large staff of Canadian and American customs inspectors were stationed at both ends of the bridge, which was also used by the MC, Wabash, and Pere Marquette. At Black Rock the CN interchanged directly with the DL&W, the Erie, the NYC, and the PRR. Interchange with Buffalo's other railroads was by way of the NYC's Belt Line. Over 700,000 cars passed over International Bridge annually. In 1926 the CN employed 480 persons in the Buffalo-Fort Erie district, most of them on the Canadian side, with an annual payroll of about $820,000.

Wabash

Wabash tracks did not come within two hundred miles of Buffalo but by an agreement effective March 1, 1898, the Wabash was granted the use of Grand Trunk tracks between Windsor, Ontario, opposite the Wabash's eastern terminal at Detroit, and Black Rock via Glencoe and Saint Thomas, 228.4 miles, and between Welland Junction and Suspension Bridge via Allanburg Junction. These running rights totaled 245.9 miles. Included also was a car-ferry service between Detroit and Windsor on the Detroit River. The Wabash serviced both Chicago and Saint Louis, but its main asset was its direct line from Detroit to Kansas City on the Missouri River, bypassing both Chicago and Saint Louis. All that the writer of the article on the Wabash had to say about the road's freight activity in Buffalo in 1927 was:

The Wabash specializes in fast freight service through Buffalo to all points east, and westward to the north and south Pacific coast, as well as the entire territory south and west of Saint Louis and Kansas City. There are two freight terminals in Buffalo, one located at Exchange and Larkin streets and the other at Black Rock. . . The Wabash provides employment for 147 persons in this territory with an annual payroll approximating $271,160. [14]

In Buffalo the Wabash trains operated over the

Erie's tracks and both Black Rock and Larkin Street yards were shared jointly with the Erie.

Pere Marquette

The Pere Marquette was the result of a 1900 consolidation of three lines in Michigan built to serve the state's lumber industry which by that time was being logged out. By 1904 the new creation had acquired from the LS&MS trackage rights to Chicago and from the MC rights from Saint Thomas to International Bridge. The PM's classification yards on the Niagara Frontier were at Lawson, Ontario, near the western end of International Bridge. The road's presence in Buffalo was a shadowy affair. On its area personnel, the author of the road's 1927 description wrote:

By virtue of the contract with the New York Central and the Lackawanna for the handling of freight at Buffalo and Black Rock, the staff of the Pere Marquette at Black Rock is necessarily small. It consists of an agent, two chief clerks, a clerk, a stenographer-clerk and a telegraph operator. The staff at Suspension Bridge is a more extended one, consisting of an agent, an assistant agent, a night chief clerk, three yard clerks, and an office staff of seven. [15]

South Buffalo Railway

An account of the South Buffalo Railway, like the Buffalo Creek essentially a terminal railroad, is contained in Chapter XI. Its *raison d'etre,* the Lackawanna Steel Company, was taken over by Bethlehem Steel in 1922. Though it had only 108 miles of track, chiefly sidings within the steel plant itself, the South Buffalo in 1926 had thirty locomotives, 700 employees, and an annual payroll of $1,250,000. Its average annual tonnage was about 5,100,000 tons. Freight originating on the line included iron and steel products, coke and its by-products, and cement.

Buffalo Creek

The Buffalo Creek had no freight houses, car shops, or passenger stations, though its locomotives were serviced at a modern roundhouse (Figure #12) with a machine shop attached. Its mainline extended 4.08 miles from its junction with the NYC in East Buffalo near the intersection of William and Fillmore to a point between City Ship Canal and Buffalo Creek, 700 feet north of South Michigan Avenue. The Beach Branch ran from this mainline east of the Hamburg Turnpike .82 miles to a point between the canal and the lake where it connected with the West Shore dock terminal of the NYC and the beach tracks of the PRR. (Figures #6, #10 and IX #1.) A second branch left the main line just north of its bridge over Abbott Road and ran east for .87 miles along what was once Prenatt Street. With the exception of the Prenatt Street branch, the entire route was double, and in busier sections triple and quadruple tracked. Including sidings, the BC operated thirty-eight miles of tracks. The BC had 250 employees and met an annual payroll of about $400,000.

Niagara Junction

Similar to the BC in function but with a novel twist was the Niagara Junction Railroad in Niagara Falls. The novelty was electric motive power. Western New York was at the cutting edge of the development of this new source of power at the end of the nineteenth century. As Dunn explains:

Once Jacob Schoellkopf had gained a foothold in Niagara Falls as owner of the hydraulic canal which he bought in 1878, events began to more steadily toward the full employment of this tremendous source of power. Late in 1896 energy began to flow from huge generators at the Falls to Buffalo and its streetcars. At the time this now commonplace transaction was anything but ordinary, indeed, it was the first movement of massive power to

Figure #12. Railroad employment on the Niagara Frontier in 1926

Railroads that Serve Buffalo, passim

Road	Employees	Annual Salaries
Buffalo Creek	250	$400,000
Bufalo Rochester & Pittsburgh	258	$500,000
Delaware Lackawanna & Western	3,000	$4,500,000
Erie	2,500	$4,000,000
Canadian National	480	$820,000
Lehigh Valley	1,700	$3,000,000
New York Central	10,000	$15,000,000
New York Chicago & St. Louis	700	$1,250,000
Pennsylvania	2,070	$3,800,000
Pere Marquette	13	$20,000
South Buffalo	700	$1,200,000
Wabash	147	$271,160
	21,845	$34,791,160

a distant place of employment to be achieved anywhere in the world. In fact the story is of the wildest chance-taking or of the completest faith, as one regards the technicians of our age, for the people who decided to harness the power of Niagara Falls at enormous expense had no clear idea as to how it was to be transmitted to Buffalo where its abundance might be used, when they began to construct the immense works needed to produce it. Engineers employed by the company ransacked Europe and America for the answers and in the nick of time found that the mystery of alternating current had been penetrated, so that it was available as the media for economical transmission of power. Not only had the problems of power for Buffalo industry been solved, but the electric age had begun in earnest. [16]

Abundant electric power, Dunn adds, "made possible entirely new processes, chiefly in producing chemicals," which explains the growth around Niagara Falls of chemical plants and other industries. Such industries had to be serviced. George Drury writes:

The Niagara Junction was established in 1892 as a subsidiary of the Niagara Falls Power Co. which was seeking to increase its business by attracting industry to the area.

The new railroad connected the industrial area of Niagara Falls with the New York Central and the Erie. The line was electrified in 1913 - a logical enough move for a road owned by an electric power company. The road's freight business prospered. [17]

Employment and Valuation

Based on figures given above, in 1926 the Niagara Frontier's railroads had 21,832 employees who received a total annual compensation of $34,791,000. That year the total United States railroad work force was 1,822,000, so that 1.19% of all American railroad workers lived here. The average salary of a Buffalo area railroad worker in 1926 was $1,593, compared with the United States average for steam railroad workers that year of $1,566. The percentage of railroad households in the area was 12.23 percent, assuming one railroad worker per family and a 1930 average population per household of 4.11. This figure does not include Pullman Car porters, Railway Express and Railway Post Office employees, or suppliers of specialized services to the railroads. e. g., icing refrigerator cars in transit or selling newspapers at stations, manufacturing railroad cars and equipment, and handling the railroads' legal affairs, all of which might well boost the total percentage involved with the railroads to 20%. (Figure #12.) In the 1920s the New York Stock Exchange listed dividends not in dollars and cents but as "rate of dividend," that is the percentage of the stock quotation on any given day represented by the dividend. On June 29, 1926, the BR&P was paying 4 percent of 79 ($3.16); the Erie nothing, though quoted at 35; the DL&W 7 percent of 144 ($10.08); the Lehigh was not listed on the NYSE on this date; the Nickel Plate 11 percent of 68 ($7.48); the NYC 7 percent of 131.5 ($9.20); the PRR 3 percent of 52.75 ($1.82); the Pere Marquette 8 percent of 95.5 ($7.64); and the Wabash nothing. Thirty-nine months later at the beginning of the month the crash occurred, but, before the balloon burst, the Erie and the Wabash were still paying nothing on their common, though the former was now being quoted at 90.75 and the latter at 71. The BR&P was paying 4 percent of 100 ($4.00); the DL&W 7 percent of 162 ($11.34); the LV 3.5 percent of 95.5 ($3.34); the Nickel Plate 6 percent of 187.5 ($11.25); the NYC 8 percent of 253 ($20.24); the PRR 4 percent of 109 ($4.36); and the Pere Marquette 8 percent of 245 ($19.60.)

16
Buffalo's Passenger Service From The Turn Of The Century To World War II

"The Train a century ahead of its time!" proclaimed the New York Central System, introducing the 20th Century Limited *in 1902. Speeding the 960 mile "Water Level" Route connecting New York and Chicago in just 20 hours, the Central's all-Pullman extra-fare deluxe symbolized for many contemporaries the lure of the railroad passenger train. Only the rich could afford to ride the Central's new train or its competitor, the Pennsylvania Railroad's* Broadway Limited, *but all Americans could watch for free these and other crack limited of the day speed through their towns and villages "exactly on the advertised." Farmer and city dweller alike witnessed in these trains an impressive display of engineering achievement, controlled power, and, above all, hope. For years after the debut of the* 20th Century, *Americans continued to look to the railroads " for a peek at the future. As one historian described it, the express train of the age "represented the promise of industrial development; an efficient, electrically lit, uniformly shaped and colored unit." Such hope lingered after the railroad decline began at the end of the Progressive Era, providing a comforting vision for millions.* [1]

So writes Donald Itzkoff in Off the Track. The *20th Century*, however, was only the icing on the cake. As Martin writes:

The two decades before World War I were the golden age of the railroad passenger train in America, for those years were the last period of great prosperity before the automobile and the airplane. Except for a relatively small volume of lake and coastal travel by boat, the railroads had it all, from the traveling salesman who was making his way through his territory in ten and twenty mile hops, to the well-to-do family setting out in Pullman drawing-room comfort for a tour of the great American West. These years are unique in the history of railroad travel, not just in the rate of growth (although that was spectacular, nearly tripling between 1896 and 1916), but also in the relationship between freight and passenger business. Almost since the beginning of the railroad age, passenger traffic had been falling relative to freight, although there had been a time in the 1880s when freight rate wars made passenger business somewhat more profitable. Passenger miles per 100 freight ton-miles were at their lowest point in history in 1900 (11.3), but by 1908 this ratio had risen to 13.32. Only after 1911 did freight traffic regain its steeper trend. Pullman journeys, reflecting the good times, shot upward in an unbroken line, from 5 million in 1900 to 26 million 1914. [2]

Martin, of whom a reviewer said, "He likes trains," lovingly recounted in Enterprise Denied how at the end of summer vacation on September 4, 1910, the NYC's *Adirondack Express* ran in sixteen sections at five minute intervals transporting 12,500 people from the North Country to the chaos of Grand Central Station, then under construction. Meanwhile, across town at Penn Station, the *Seashore* from Atlantic City arrived in nine sections, many with eight to eleven heavy new all-steel coaches holding eighty-eight passengers each. In all, that memorable day in September during the Presidency of William Howard Taft set the record for long-distance passenger travel to Manhattan with over 200,000 arrivals.

On the local railroad scene during the years surrounding the turn of the century the Vanderbilt lines had in 1895, in concert with the Canadian Pacific, completed the Toronto Hamilton & Buffalo; next year the LV opened its branch from Depew to Tonawanda, which provided a shortcut for Canadian-American freight interchange and passenger connections with the Falls via the NYC and with Toronto and Chicago via the Grand Trunk. The PRR took over the financially troubled and physically deteriorated WNY&P in 1901 and proceeded to pump millions of dollars into plant improvements. The next year Lackawanna Steel's South Buffalo Railway, linking the mill on the lake with Buffalo's major railroads, commenced operations.

"In the first years of the twentieth century," John H. White writes, "the railroad industry came to accept steel as the preferable material for passenger car construction." White divides the history of metallic passenger cars into four major periods: experimentation (1845-1902), introduction (1902-1910), full production (1910-1930), and streamlining. "Fewer improvements," he noted, "have been longer heralded or slower in coming than the metallic passenger car." Wooden cars were weak, likely to splinter, and highly combustible. Nevertheless, they were cheap, light, and serviceable, while even the best metallic cars proved far heavier and more costly than the traditional wooden coach. The first commercially successful steel cars were 300 built by the American Car and Foundry in time for the opening of New York City's Interborough Rapid Transit subway in 1904. President Cassatt promoted steel cars on the PRR in connection with tunneling under the Hudson and East Rivers because of the dangers that would result from wooden cars burning underground.

1903

The backbone of the NYC's westbound through passenger service in 1903 consisted in eleven daily trains, ten running between New York and Chicago (six with Boston sections) and a single train to Chicago from Boston only. At Buffalo five of these eleven trains were split into MC and LS&MS sections. The five sections that were routed through Canada went on to Chicago. One express train ended its run in Buffalo, and of the two that originated there, one proceeded to Chicago on the LS&MS and the other on the MC. Of the ten New York to Chicago trains (five that had been split and five that had not been) that ran along the lakeshore route, four went to Chicago only, while the rest carried through cars for Chicago and/or Saint Louis, Cincinnati, and Pittsburgh. Three New York-Chicago trains carried sleepers or parlor cars for Toronto on the TH&B. The NYWS&B, a lessor of the NYC, ran three westbound trains from New York (Weehawken) and Boston to Chicago and Saint Louis in conjunction with the Wabash across Ontario and Michigan: the *Continental Limited*, the *Chicago & Saint Louis Limited*, and the *Pacific Express*. These trains arrived at the NYC's Exchange Street Station but departed from the Erie Station. A fourth NYWS&B express, the *National Limited*, terminated at Suspension Bridge. NYWS&B's former Boston connection, the Fitchburg Railroad, had been taken over by the Boston & Maine in 1900 after the NYC had leased the parallel Boston & Albany. The westbound *Empire State Express* terminated at Buffalo, and the MC's Chicago-bound American Express and the LS&MS's *Buffalo & Pittsburgh Express* originated there. Three of the New York-Chicago trains required the payment of extra fare: the *North Shore Limited* (the pride of the MC), the *Lake Shore Limited* (the pride of the LS&MS), and the *Southwestern Limited.* A fourth, the *20th Century Limited,* did not come into Exchange Street but, after stopping at East Buffalo to change engines and crews, took the Compromise Track west. This crack train of the NYC carried no passengers for any point east of Chicago. While the other expresses took between twenty-two and twenty-seven hours to reach Chicago, the *20th Century* in 1903 did it in twenty hours. Harlow tells the early history of this famous train:

The Central's executives remembered what the Exposition Flyer *had done in 1893, and in 1895 they ran a test train from Chicago to Buffalo, 525 miles, at 65.07 miles an hour. They had new locomotives known as Central Atlantics which could accomplish the speed. When the first* Century *left New York on June 15, 1902, it carried only three Pullman sleepers, a buffet and a diner, but* [George H.] *Daniels* [general passenger agent] *had given it also a barber shop, valet, maids, stenographer, electric lights with current generated from the axle, then a comparatively new thing. Even the* Lake Shore Limited *had to get along with lights from a dynamo in the baggage car. The* Century *served a* table d'hôte *meal for a dollar. There were only twenty-seven passengers on the first trip. One of them was John W. (Bet-a-Million) Gates, the steel and oil tycoon, who told reporters at Grand Central Station that the train "makes Chicago a suburb of New York." Interviewed as he stepped off in Chicago, the diplomat beamed at the scribes over his cigar and said, "It makes New York a suburb of Chicago."*

Those Atlantics which drew the first train cost between $15,000 and $16,000, and the whole train $115,000. Twenty years later, someone remarked that the cost of the cars had more than doubled and of the locomotive had almost quadrupled. Today [1947] *one Pullman costs as much as that whole train of 1902. One five car train could do the business then, but in recent years there have been times when the* Century *had to run in six or seven sections of twelve to fourteen cars each. Just one of those sections, at present-day prices, may now represent an outlay of nearly two million dollars!*

Running time and locomotive power also show the trend. In 1905, with new equipment, the time was lowered to eighteen hours o meet the competition from the PRR which that year came out with the Broadway Limited *which took eighteen hours between Jersey City and Chicago and in 1910 would open Penn Station on 34th Street* [in Manhattan.] *But it was difficult to make this schedule practical, and for several years the time wavered back and forth between eighteen and nineteen and one-half hours. Finally, in 1912, both gave up and went back to twenty hours.* [3]

Fifteen eastbound through trains arrived at Buffalo from the west on a weekday in 1903, ten with cars for New York and eight for Boston. These trains were made up of cars from four MC trains from Chicago and one from Grand Rapids, and from ten LS&MS trains, seven of which carried cars from Chicago, three from Saint Louis, two from Cincinnati, and two from Pittsburgh. A final arrival originated in Cleveland. The LS&MS's *Pittsburgh-Buffalo Express* terminated in Buffalo. There were four extra-fare eastbound trains but, with the exception of the *20th Century Limited* (which like its westbound companion did not stop for passengers in

Buffalo), luxurious appointments rather than speed seem to have been the basis for the added expense. The *Lake Shore Limited*, an extra fare train, took twenty-six and a half hours to complete its run.

There were fifteen eastbound departures from Buffalo on the NYC with cars for Boston (8) and New York (12). Thirteen of these were continuations of arrivals from the west and two, the *Empire State Express* and the *Buffalo Special*, originated in Buffalo. Toronto was considered west of Buffalo by the NYC and three of its eastbound trains to New York carried through cars from the TH&B to Gotham.

The NYWS&B-Wabash ran three eastbound expresses from Chicago-Saint Louis through Buffalo to New York-Boston, the *Continental Limited*, the *New York Express*, and the *Atlantic Express*. These trains arrived at the NYC's station and left from the Erie's. A fourth NYWS&B train to New York, the *National Limited*, originated in Niagara Falls; a fifth, #18, also originated there but was an all-coach train. Reversing the process used with westbounds, these NYWS&B eastbounds arrived at the Erie Station and left from Exchange Street.

The BR&P and the PRR, successor to the WNY&P, also operated long distance trains out of the NYC's Exchange Street Station in 1903. The BR&P ran a day and a night train in each direction between Buffalo and Pittsburgh. On the BR&P's passenger service at this time the historian of the road writes:

The inauguration of through service over the BR&P to Pittsburgh caused some minor excitement in Rochester. In a newspaper report dated October 6, 1899, it was stated that "new coaches were on display at the depot, and that "the new cars were worth attention and were plush. The train will be one of the handsomest running in this part of the country. This new train is a full vestibule train of four cars, a combination baggage express and mail, a day coach, a coach fitted with reclining chairs and a buffet car. The new train will leave Rochester at 9 a.m. and arrive in Pittsburgh at 6:30 p.m."

October 10, 1899, at 9 a.m. sharp the Pittsburgh bound train left Rochester's West Avenue Station for its 330 mile trip. According to the schedule the southbound train was called the Pittsburgh Mail and Express *and the northbound train leaving was called the* Buffalo Rochester Mail and Express. *There was also a night train that left Rochester called the* Pittsburgh Night Express. *The northbound night train out of Pittsburgh was, of course, called the* Buffalo Rochester Night Express. *Later this north-south service was known as the* Great Lakes Express *and the* Pittsburgh Flyer.

At first these trains were pulled by handsome Brooks Ten Wheelers purchased especially for the job. They were referred to as the "Big Engines" by the men of the BR&P since they were much larger than the standard passenger 4-4-0 type used up to this time. These new 4-6-0 locomotives were the pride of the railroad.

Up to the turn of the century the 4-6-0 and the lighter 4-4-0 types were adequate to handle the passenger trains of the BR&P. Then in 1901 the railroad purchased what was called the Atlantic type or 4-4-2 passenger engine. There were a total of 15 Atlantic type locomotives purchased between 1901 and 1909. They were graceful looking engines with large driving wheels and built for speed, but speed was not the only requirement of the BR&P. With the coming of the steel passenger car, the company looked to heavier, more powerful locomotives. In 1912 the BR&P purchased the 4-6-2 or Pacific type engine. These beautiful engines hauled the passenger trains over the BR&P and later the B&O right up to the end of passenger service in the mid 1950s.

The BR&P Railway was shaped on a map like a giant "Y" and East Salamanca was the spot where the train out of Buffalo and the Rochester train met. [Figure IX, #15.] *The Rochester train arrived slightly ahead and discharged its through passengers and baggage and when the Buffalo train arrived, people boarded these coaches for the continued trip south. Meanwhile the Rochester train, loaded only with people going to Salamanca, departed for the Main Street Station. While the Rochester train headed for downtown Salamanca, a fresh engine coupled onto the Buffalo train and it left for Pittsburgh. The Rochester train meanwhile would discharge its passengers, then back out of the downtown station into the East Salamanca yard to await the trip back to Rochester which was later in the day. Extra coaches were kept on a siding in back of the East Salamanca depot in case the combined patronage of both trains could not fit on the Buffalo train bound for Pittsburgh. While the coaches of the Rochester train were laying over in East Salamanca during the winter, they were hooked up with a steam line that lay just south of the East Salamanca depot. This kept the coaches warm until they were coupled to the engine for the return trip to Rochester. On the night train, the sleeper on the Rochester section was uncoupled and gently moved and coupled on to the Buffalo train for the balance of the trip to Pittsburgh.*

In Buffalo the company used the NYC's Howard Street depot on the Belt Line at first, then later the Exchange Street Station. The trains were run over the Buffalo Creek Railway to William Street, the engine was then cut off and the coaches were moved to Exchange Street by a NYC switch engine consuming thirty extra minutes per train. This practice was later dropped. [4]

Now that the mighty PRR was a presence on the Niagara Frontier, passenger service on the two routes of the quondam WNY&P, now the Buffalo and Allegheny Valley Division, was improved. Within this larger division the line to Pittsburgh was christened the Chautauqua Division, since it ran through Chautauqua County, and the line to Emporium became the Buffalo Division. On the Buffalo Division, the former BNY&P, long distance passenger service during the first decade of the twentieth century consisted in a day and a night train each way between Philadelphia-Washington and Buffalo, the dividing point being Harrisburg. In addition to through coaches, the day trains carried a "Pullman Broiler Buffet Parlor Car" between Philadelphia-Washington and Buffalo and the night trains "Pullman Buffet Sleeping Cars" between the same points. Meals were served in the coaches from the Pullman buffets. The Chautauqua Division also ran a day and a night train similarly equipped each way between Buffalo and Pittsburgh. On the subject of buffet cars White writes:

The buffet car served drinks and snacks and might consist entirely of a closet-like kitchen and a serving bar. The remainder of the car was devoted to parlor or sleeping space. On the other hand, the cafe car might be a true half diner, that is, a small kitchen and dining room serving cooked meals, but without the variety or grandeur of a full restaurant car. Cafes were useful both on express trains whose runs were too short to serve many full-course dinners and on less well patronized first-class trains that had to offer proper if somewhat limited food service. [5]

The Erie ran the same three through trains each way between Jersey City and Buffalo that it had ten years before. With one exception, the thirty-six mile an hour eastbound night train, *New York Special*, Erie through trains were slower than in the 1890s, ten years before. After describing the Erie of the early nineties as a "woebegone property," the author of the article on Frederick D. Underwood in Railroads in the Age of Regulation, 1900-1980 wrote:

After a history marked by financial upheavals, the Erie had fallen upon hard times. J. P. Morgan had reorganized it in 1895, but the property was still physically decrepit, financially weak, and low in public esteem. Morgan offered the presidency to

Underwood [then Vice-President of the B&O]. *During the next quarter of a century (1901-1926) Underwood made dramatic improvements to the Erie and kept the railroad afloat.*

Underwood is chiefly remembered for his physical rehabilitation of the Erie. The Graham cutoff, which required a mile-long tunnel and the high Moodna Viaduct, added miles but provided a low-grade freight line near Middletown. A second cutoff reduced grades on a section of line in western New York. Still another cutoff near the New York-Pennsylvania line reduced grades in that area. Much double track was installed, a new route through Bergen Hill in northern New Jersey was constructed, new and more powerful locomotives were added to the roster, shops were consolidated and rebuilt, and terminals were improved.

Under Underwood's regime, Erie freight traffic almost doubled to over 9 million ton-miles in 1926. Annual revenues rose from $40, million to over $118 million, while operating costs fell because of longer and heavier trains. Over $174 million was spent on improvements, and the Erie wound up with more low-grade trackage than any other eastern trunk line except the NYC. [6]

Be it noted, however, that all these improvements were aimed at making the Erie a better freight handler. Edward Hungerford relates this story about Underwood in Men of Erie:

In those years No. 1 and No. 2 were the prides of the Erie. They ran between Jersey City and Buffalo, at a comfortable rate of speed, and were well equipped, even to observation cars. But one day, the unpredictable Fred Underwood took a hatred to them and, despite much protest, ordered them off the line. The protest continued, and eventually Underwood had them restored, but not as No. 1 and No. 2. This time they were 1000 and 1001 and were operated between Jersey City and Jamestown, not Buffalo. [7]

Retaining them at all was probably for the sake of public relations.

The DL&W ran five trains daily each way between Buffalo and Hoboken, Table #1

The Lackawanna's passenger service to Buffalo had already surpassed that of the much older Erie. Numbers Five, Seven, and Fifteen left sleepers at Buffalo Junction near Buffalo Creek, where the DL&W intersected the NKP, for trains of that road to take to Chicago, and at its junction with the Erie at William Street in Sloan cars were left to be brought into the Erie Station for transfer to the Wabash for Chicago. Eastbound Numbers Two, Six, and Eight picked up NKP sleepers at the same point for delivery to Hoboken, and Number Twelve received from the Erie Wabash sleepers from Saint Louis. On this subject the historian of the DL&W writes:

By 1899 the basic passenger service had been established. During the Truesdale era [William H. Truesdale, president, 1899-1925, the golden age of the road] *little was changed, either in the way of additional trains, major rescheduling, or faster speed. His efforts were directed at merely filling the trains, and with the* Phoebe Snow *advertising campaign, this was eminently successful. Train No. 15 carried considerable mail and express business; No. 9 carried sleepers for Buffalo, Ithaca, Oswego, and Utica and a buffet library car; No. 7* [along with its companion No. 8] *had the slowest schedule as it performed considerable local work. Train No. 3, which in the late nineties had been renamed the* Queen City Special, *was the only named train and now carried its original name,* Lackawanna Limited. *Due to the heavy suburban traffic on the Morristown line and that it was only single track west of Morristown, only train No. 5 ran through Newark.*

Eastbound service was comparable to the westbound. No. 6 covered the 410 miles from Buffalo in 9 hours 49 minutes which was almost an hour faster than the next fastest train, No. 10. After the opening of the New Jersey

Table #1

	Westbound Arrivals			Eastbound Departures		
AM		lv. Hoboken	mph		arr. Hoboken	mph
1:45	#5	2:00p	34			
2:45				#2	3:17p	35
7:00	#7	6:30p	32			
	Chicago Vestibuled Express					
7:45	#9	9:10p	38			
9:30				#6	7:19p	41
				Lackawanna Limited		
PM						
1:00	#15	2:30a	41			
5:30				#8	6:30a	31
7:55	#3	10:15a	38			
	Lackawanna Limited					
8:45				#12	7:30a	38
11:30				#14	10:35a	36
				The Owl		

[1911] *and Nicholson* [1915] *Cut-Offs, trains were speeded up east of Scranton, but there was no appreciable change to Binghamton, and west of there the runs were slowed so that the trip to Buffalo, now only 396 miles, still took the same time in 1916 and 1926 as it did in 1902. As three New York Central Directors sat on the Lackawanna's Board, they were not anxious to see the Lackawanna capture any significant number of Central passengers to Syracuse particularly after 1917 when the new Buffalo Station was completed.* [An illustration of the evils of interlocking directorships.] *At the foot of Main Street, less than a mile from the center of the city, it was far more convenient than the NYC station.* [This was true only after the opening of Central Station on the East Side in 1929.] *The combination of both cleaner and faster trains than the NYC would have induced many New Yorkers to use the Lackawanna.* [8]

For a 1900 menu of the Lackawanna Railroad see Figure #1.

The LV operated four express trains between Buffalo and Jersey City-Philadelphia in 1903, the break off point being Bethlehem. With the opening of the Depew & Tonawanda in 1896 to a connection with the NYC's ex-Canandaigua & Niagara Falls line and Suspension Bridge, LV through cars could

Figure #1. Taber, DL&W in the 20th Century, 157

- 1900 -

Menu.

Soups.

Beef, 20c. Tomato, 20c.

Baked Beans, 20c.

Meats.

Roast Beef, 50c. Fricassee Chicken, 50c.
Ham and Eggs, 40c. Roast Lamb, 50c.
With Potatoes, Bread and Butter.

Vegetables.

Sliced Tomatoes, 15c. Green Peas, 15c.
Mashed Potatoes, 10c.
Fried Potatoes, 10c. Celery, 15c.
Green Corn, 10c.

Cold Meats.

Sliced Tongue, 35c.
Boiled Ham, 35c. Chicken, 40c.
With Bread and Butter.

Sardines, 30c. Olives, 10c. Pickles, 10c.

Bread and Butter, 10c.
Parker House Rolls, 10c. Banquet Crackers, 10c.

Eggs.

Boiled, 15c.
Poached, 20c. With Toast, 25c.
Ham and Eggs, 40c. Fried Eggs, 20c.
Omelette, 25c.

Sandwiches.

Ham, 15c. Tongue, 15c. Chicken, 25c.
Roast Beef, 15c.

Tea, Coffee, Etc.

Tea, 10c. Coffee, 10c. Milk, 5c.
Iced Tea, 10c. Cocoa, 10c.

Sliced Oranges, 15c. Assorted Cake, 10c.
Bananas, 10c. Fig Preserves, 20c.
Apple Pie, 10c. Berry Pie, 10c.
Plum Pudding, 25c. McLaren's Cheese, 15c.
To order.................... Berries, 20c.

Cooked to Order.

Porter House Steak, 75c. Sirloin Steak, 60c.
Omelette with Ham, 45c. Spring Lamb Chops, 45c.
.... Fish, 40c.
Broiled Spring Chicken, 60c.

Potatoes, bread and butter included with orders under this head.

Apollinaris, 25c. Imported Ginger Ale, 25c.
Lemonade, 10c.

Cigars.

Imported, 15c. Domestic, 10c.

Extras.

No order issued for less than 25c. each person.
Any inattention to duty on this car please report to
W. HANLEY, Scranton, Pa.

now reach Toronto and Chicago via the Grand Trunk. Lehigh Valley #3, the westbound *Chicago Vestibule Express*, arrived at Buffalo at eight in the morning and immediately pulled out again for Suspension Bridge, Toronto, and Chicago. Number Five, the *Buffalo Train*, pulled in to Main Street two hours later and immediately headed out again for Toronto as the *Toronto Express*. After a five hour wait, passengers for Chicago could take a connecting train with Pullmans to Suspension Bridge and Chicago on GT #5. *The Day Express* arrived at 7:50 P. M. but its westbound connection went only as far as Niagara Falls. The last westbound, the *Black Diamond*, the pride and joy of the road, carried Pullmans destined for the Grand Trunk's *Buffalo & Chicago Express* via Suspension Bridge.

Eastbound there was a slight variation, as #8, the *Detroit & New York Express*, arrived at Suspension Bridge at 3:40 A. M. and bypassed Buffalo on the Depew & Tonawanda. Grand Trunk #4, the *LV Express*, arrived in Buffalo from Chicago at 8:20: A. M. and immediately departed for Depew and the east as the LV's *New York & Philadelphia Vestibule-Express*. Whether the sleepers from Chicago were left at Depew or brought into Buffalo and out again can only be surmised. Grand Trunk #6, the *Buffalo Express*, arrived at Buffalo via the LV at 3:05 P.M. but dead-ended there. An unnamed LV #20 left for Jersey City at 7:00 P.M., and the final eastbound of the day, the *Philadelphia & New York Express*, which had originated in Chicago as Grand Trunk #2, left for Philadelphia and New York at 9:30 P. M. The fastest LV train to Jersey City, the *Black Diamond*, averaged forty miles an hour and the slowest, the *Buffalo Train*, thirty-two. The LV also ran a train to and from Toronto unconnected with any of its through trains. Since Canadian engines did not meet American appliance and safety standards, GT trains east of Suspension Bridge were pulled by LV engines and manned by LV crews and hence are considered LV trains.

William T. Greenberg and Frederick A. Kramer write in The Handsomest Trains in the World:

The significant part of the western routing on the Grand Trunk was its service to Toronto, reached by branching around the head of Lake Ontario at Hamilton and turning back to the northeast. The Niagara Falls Toronto distance was 82 miles, with Hamilton at the halfway mark. Until commercial airlines usurped this business more than half a century later, the LV offered the preferred service to Toronto from New York City and, by connection with the Reading at Bethlehem, from Philadelphia and points south. [9]

J. Pierpont Morgan had taken control of the LV and also of the DL&W, the Reading, the Erie, and the Central Railroad of New Jersey, all of them anthracite roads, as part of a master plan which dovetailed with Alexander Cassatt's community of interest between the NYC and the PRR, the objective being to stabilize rates and profits and eliminate ruinous competition in the railroad and coal business. This objective was never realized because of President Theodore Roosevelt's hostility to rail combinations manifested in his Attorney General's successful prosecution of the Northern Securities Company in 1904. But Morgan's program of increasing the road's operating efficiency and traffic volume put the Lehigh in the black, and by 1904 it resumed dividend payments. Archer narrates an unintended by-product of this program:

In the autumn of 1910 track crews had relaid the mainline through Manchester, N. Y. with new 90-lb. rails. What they did not know at the time was that one of the new rails, laid just west of the deck bridge spanning Canandaigua Outlet, was riddled with transverse fissures. On the morning of August 25, 1911, passenger train No. 4 left Buffalo, running 40 minutes behind schedule. After adding cars at Rochester Junction, the train carried a consist of 14 cars double-headed by locomotives No. 1804 and No. 2476. Heading east toward Geneva, No. 4 slowed to a speed of 25 miles an hour as it approached Manchester Yard. Nearing the east throat of the yard with a clear signal block ahead, the train began to accelerate. As they came to the Canandaigua Outlet bridge, the locomotives hit the defective rail, which began to disintegrate under the pounding of the driving wheels. By the time the sixth car of the train struck the rail, it shattered, derailing all of the cars behind and spilling two of them off the bridge into the stream below. Twenty-three persons were killed outright, most of them in the wooden coaches that fell into the water. The casualty list totaled 29 killed and 62 injured, making this the worst LV passenger disaster since the infamous collision at Mud Run, Pa. in 1888. [10]

Greenberg and Kramer note that:

. . . during the period 1891-1913 when the LV was using the PRR's terminal in Jersey City, passenger traffic grew until it stabilized at between four and five million riders annually. To handle this level of ridership, all-steel equipment was introduced. A large order for coaches was placed with Pullman in 1911 and as the cars were delivered in 1912, both wooden and steel cars were on the roster. All told, 522 pieces of passenger train equipment were

active, but scrapping reduced the number of wooden cars, leaving only 442 pieces by the end of 1913. [11]

The NYC operated numerous locals in 1903, especially on its Niagara Falls and Lockport branches, despite inroads by the burgeoning interurbans. There were eighteen daily arrivals and an equal number of departures between Exchange Street and Suspension Bridge or Lewiston and one round trip to North Tonawanda. Three of the Lewiston trains continued on the Rome Watertown & Ogdensburg to Waterport, Oswego, and Massena Springs. There were ten trains from and nine to Lockport daily. The ex-Canandaigua & Niagara Falls was serviced by a single train each way between North Tonawanda and Batavia. The MC operated a single round trip daily (morning departure, afternoon return) between Buffalo and Niagara-on-the Lake via International Bridge. Also crossing this bridge were two MC locals from and one to Detroit. Eastbound on the NYC's mainline there were seven locals, two to Syracuse, two to Rochester, one to Fairport, one to Batavia, and one to Grimesville just beyond Depew. Five locals traversed this route westbound, two from Syracuse, and one each from Fairport, Batavia, and Grimesville. The LS&MS operated only two accommodations each way daily, one to and from Westfield, the other to and from Erie, as well as a local to Toledo. Interurban competition was partly responsible for this sparse service since by 1903 the Buffalo Dunkirk & Western interurban (after 1909 the Buffalo & Lake Erie Traction Company) was in operation. The NYWS&B operated two locals each way between Buffalo and Lyons, New York, one pair of which terminated at East Buffalo. Besides carrying passengers, accommodations did a great deal of mail and express business. It should be reemphasized that many trains on all lines billed as expresses made numerous local stops.

Non-Vanderbilt railroads also did a considerable local passenger business in Western New York in 1903. The Erie had ceded its Lockport passenger business to the Buffalo & Lockport Electric Railway in 1898. A notation on the Erie's 1903 timetable stated: "North Tonawanda to Martinsville, Hoffman, Pendelton Center, Hodgeville and Lockport (13 miles). Electric cars to and from Lockport and intermediate points will connect with all Niagara Falls Branch trains at North Tonawanda." IRC cars left Main and Court Streets in Buffalo "every 30 minutes at 5 and 35 minutes past the hour, 6:05 a.m. to 11:35 p. m." which was much more frequent service than the Erie had ever provided. But the Erie continued to run varnish on its line to Suspension Bridge (four westbound and five eastbound) and on the ex-Buffalo & Jamestown. Only two and of the eastbound and only three of the westbound trains on the Falls branch were true locals, stopping as they did at Walden Avenue, Kensington, Main Street, North Tonawanda, and La Salle. The others were express train connections to and from the Falls that made fewer stops. Five locals on the Jamestown line ran to Jamestown and one only as far as Dayton. The same distribution held for arrivals in Buffalo. The 7:05 P. M. arrival in Buffalo from Jamestown carried a sleeper from Chicago from the Atlantic Express. On the Hornell line there were two Attica round trips, the Castile round trip and the Hornell round trip.

Back at the NYC's Exchange Street Station the PRR ran three trains daily on its Buffalo Division to and from East Aurora (thirty-five minutes) and one to and from Olean (an hour and a half). Moreover, the PRR's two round trips to Emporium made almost all the local stops on their 121 mile trip. On the Chautauqua Division a commuter train arrived from Brocton at 8:20 in the morning and left for Brocton at 5:25 P. M. In addition, one train each way stopped at every station along the 138 mile run to Oil City, Pennsylvania. From

Exchange Street the Grand Trunk ran two trains each way daily to and from Saint Thomas and Goderich via the International Bridge on the ex-Buffalo & Lake Huron which crossed the Niagara at International Bridge and serviced points along the north shore of Lake Erie - Erie Beach, Crescent Beach, Rosehill, Windmill Point, Point Abino, Sherks, and Lorraine - where many Buffalonians had summer cottages. Travelers could also reach Saint Catherines and Port Dalhousie via the GT but only by first taking the NYC's Niagara Falls line to Suspension Bridge. Also at Exchange Street the BR&P ran two Bradford-Buffalo trains each way daily and one Springville-Buffalo and return. (For representative local stations see Figure #2.)

The DL&W operated two round trip locals, one Buffalo-Groveland, the other Buffalo-Scranton. In addition, the 5.92 mile long Lackawanna Steel Company's South Buffalo Railway ran four commuter trains each way on work days for its employees out of Lackawanna Station through the First Ward and Lackawanna. From its nearby station on Scott and Main Streets the LV operated two Sayre-Buffalo locals and one eastbound to Wilkes Barre.

By 1903 there were 143 arrivals and 154 departures at Buffalo's four terminals, for a grand total of 297 train movements daily, exclusive of the NYC's Belt Line. Two hundred and eleven of these took place at the NYC's Exchange Street Station (167 NYC, 24 PRR, 10 BR&P, 6 NKP, 4 GT), thirty-eight at the Erie Station (30 Erie, 8 Wabash), twenty-two at the DL&W's (14 DL&W, 8 SB), and twenty-six at the LV's. Buffalo's railroads were operating 145 long distance passenger trains with sleepers, diners, or parlor cars, and 152 locals and trains that went longer distances but without dining or sleeping cars. The total of 297 daily passenger train movements was thirty-seven or 14 percent greater than the 260 ten years before, this despite inroads being made in the local business by interurbans. Through trains were longer, carried more passengers, and were increasingly the major source of the railroads' passenger receipts. Trains were also getting heavier, hence the need of bigger motive power. Americans (4-4-0s) had yielded to Atlantics (4-4-2s), which in turn would give way to Pacifics (4-6-2s). More drivers obviously made for greater tractive effort, and the rear truck was added to support a larger firebox area. The Pacific was to be the standard passenger engine on American railroads for the next three decades. One hundred and sixty-seven of the total daily passenger trains operations (57 percent) were conducted by the NYC or its affiliates. The Erie came second with thirty or 10 percent of the total, but both the DL&W and the LV ran more New York-Buffalo expresses (eight each) than the older Erie (six). The Erie operated locals on its branches to Jamestown and Suspension Bridge, as well as on the mainline to Hornell.

The lineup of passenger train movements (arrivals and departures) at Buffalo in 1903 was as in Table #2.

1916

1916 was the peak year for railroad size in the United States, 254,251 miles. Decline set in thereafter, though at first it was hardly noticeable. Ten years later there were still 249,138 miles of American railroad lines. Through an exchange of stock the LS&MS and the New York Central & Hudson River Railroad had been merged into a greater New York Central in December, 1914, and operated as a single company. (Thereafter the LS&MS no longer received separate listing in the *Official Guide*.) The Big Four and the MC were not included in the merger and their shareholders had to be content with leases.

Locally, the Buffalo & Susquehanna ran its first passenger train into the NYC's Exchange Street Station on December 11, 1906. The new NYC fielded an awesome line of seventeen express trains from New York and/or Boston

Table #2

Road	Expresses	Locals	Total
NYC	(26)	(17)	(43)
LS&MS	(23)	(6)	(29)
MC	(11)	(5)	(16)
TH&B	(6)	-	(6)
NYWS&B	(10)	4	(14)
B&L	-	(19)	(19)
B&NF	-	(38)	(38)
C&NF	-	(2)	(2)
Vanderbilt Lines	76	91	167
B&NYC	(6)	(8)	(14)
SB&EJ	(1)	(5)	(6)
B&J	(9)	(1)	(10)
Erie	16	14	30
BNY&P	(4)	(12)	(16)
BC&P	(4)	(4)	(8)
Pennsylvania	8	16	24
BR&P	4	6	10
DL&W	10	4	14
SBRY	-	8	8
NKP	-	6	6
mainline	(9)	(5)	(14)
D&T	(8)	(4)	(12)
LV	17	9	26
GT	-	4	4
Wabash	-	8	8
Total	145	152	297

Figure #2. Western New York Stations

Albion, NYC, Ron Dukarm

Black Rock, NYC, <u>Courier-Express</u> files, SCNYAB

Farnham, LS&MS, WNYHI

Lake View, LS&MS, Ron Dukarm

North Tonawanda, NYC, Historical Society of the Tonawandas

Medina, NYC, (taken by author, 1995)

Elmwood Avenue, Buffalo, NYC, Ron Dukarm

Lake View, PRR, author's collection

Derby, LS&MS, WNYHI

Silver Creek, LS&MS, WNYHI

Athol Springs, LS&MS, Ron Dukarm

Union Station, Lockport, Ron Dukarm

Niagara Falls, Erie, WNYHI

Suspension Bridge, Erie, Ron Dukarm

Kensington Ave., Buffalo, Ron Dukarm

Hamburg, Erie, Ron Dukarm

Alden, Erie, Ron Dukarm

North Collins, Erie, WNYHI

East Buffalo, Erie, (front) Ron Dukarm

East Buffalo, Erie, (rear) Ron Dukarm

La Salle, Erie, WNYHI

Walden Ave., Erie, Ron Dukarm

Blasdell, B&S, Ron Dukarm

Blasdell, PRR, Ron Dukarm

North Tonawanda, Erie, Ron Dukarm

Main Street, Buffalo, Erie, Ron Dukarm

Depew, DL&W, Ron Dukarm

Springville, BR&P, WNYHI

Tonawanda, NYC, (old) taken by author, 1995

Tonawanda, NYC, (new) taken by author, 1995

North Boston, B&S, WNYHI

across New York State and on to Toronto, Chicago, Pittsburgh, Cincinnati, and Saint Louis in 1916. Westbound these were (and most had eastbound companions) Table #3.

Some of the same overall routes were also serviced by the NYC's lessor, the NYWS&B, at the Exchange Street Station, in conjunction with the Boston & Maine to the east and the Wabash and NKP to the west Table #3A.

All the NYC's through trains charged extra fare. The *Southwestern, Lake Shore, Cleveland,* and *20th Century Limiteds* did not stop for passengers at Exchange Street but by-passed the station on the Compromise *Track. The Lake Shore, Wolverine, Cleveland, Boston & Buffalo Special*, and *20th Century* carried Pullman passengers only. In addition, the *Buffalonian*, an 8:20 A. M. arrival from New York, and #57 from Albany, which sported a parlor car, terminated in Buffalo; and the Chicago-bound *Pacific Express* on both the LS&MS and the MC originated in Buffalo. Eastbound, the NYC likewise operated seventeen through trains from west of Buffalo to New York, and two, the aptly named *New Yorker* and *Metropolitan*, which originated in Buffalo. The eastbound LS&MS *Pittsburgh-Buffalo Special* and *Cleveland-Buffalo Special* terminated in Buffalo.

Pennsylvania Station in Manhattan had been opened in 1910, and the NYC's third Grand Central Station in 1913. Both hosted only electric trains since, as a result of a rear-end collision in the smoke-filled Park Avenue tunnel in 1902, the legislature had banned steam engines in the tunnel after July 1, 1908. It is unfortunate that a plan for a union station for all the roads serving New York City, briefly bruited at the time the PRR was planning its new terminal, was not implemented, but such a scheme had faltered even in Buffalo. When the railroads should have been burying their differences in the face of growing outside

Table #3

arrival		train	from	destination
A. M.				
1:25	#7	*Westerner*	NY	Chicago 6:00p LS Pittsburgh 2:10p P&LE
2:05	#11	*Southwestern Ltd.*	NY	Saint Louis 6:50p
3:00	#17	*Wolverine*	NY	Chicago 3:00p MC
3:20	#13	*B&A Wolverine*	Boston	Chicago 4:30p MC
3:40	#19	*Lake Shore Ltd.*	NY	Chicago 5:00p LS
4:00	#21	*Cleveland Ltd.*	NY	Chicago 6:00p LS Pittsburgh 2:10p P&LE Toronto 8:43a TH&B
6:15	#23	*Western Exp.*	NY	Chicago 10:00p LS Chicago 10:50p MC
6:30	#49	*Buffalo & Boston Special*	Boston	Chicago 10:00p LS Chicago 10:50p MC
7:15	#29	*Canadian*	NY	Chicago 10:00p LS Toronto 11:28a TH&B
9:55	#59	*Western NY Exp.*	NY-Boston	Toronto 1:33p TH&B
PM				
1:10	#45	*Albany & Buffalo Exp.*	NY-Boston	Chicago 2:00p LS St. Louis 8:30a Big 4
5:30	#51	*Empire State Exp.*	NY	Cleveland 9:30p LS Pittsburgh 11:05p P&LE Toronto 4:36p TH&B
7:30	#3	*Fast Mail*	NY	Chicago 8:30a LS
8:15	#1	*Mohawk*	NY-Boston	Chicago 9:00a MC Chicago 9:15 LS
10:55	#9	*Fast Mail*	NY	Chicago 11:43a LS Chicago 1:15p MC
11:44	#25	*20th Century Ltd.*	NY-Boston	Chicago 10:45a LS
11:45	#41	*No. Forty One*	NY-Boston	Chicago 12:50p LS Pittsburgh 7:30a P&LE

Table #3A

AM				
1:35	#15	*Continental Ltd.*	NY-Boston	Chicago 5:55p St. Louis 9:1:15p
6:55	#3	*Chicago Exp.*	NY-Boston	Chicago 10:50p St. Louis 8:58a
PM				
8:15	#21	*West Shore Ltd.*	NY	Chicago 1:50p St. Louis 3:55p

competition from the auto, they were still competing with each other as usual. Community of interest had its limits.

By 1916 express passenger service on the Erie to Buffalo had deteriorated. Westbound, a night express from Jersey City arrived at seven in the morning and a day express at eight in the evening. That was all there was, though a local from Hornell arrived at noon with passengers from the east from a mainline Chicago express. The same diminished arrangements held eastbound in 1916 by which date the Wabash was no longer operating out of the Erie Station. Ten years before there had been three bona fide Buffalo-Jersey City expresses both ways. The fastest through train on the Erie averaged only thirty-nine miles an hour between Jersey City and Buffalo, while the NYC's fastest, the *20th Century*, did forty-eight between New York and Chicago. By arrangement with the NKP, the Wabash, and the MC, the DL&W ran three through trains westbound and eastbound between Hoboken and Chicago. Two further westbound through trains from Hoboken ended at Buffalo as a single train after consolidation at Scranton, and two eastbound Buffalo-Hoboken trains carried a good deal of mail and express in addition to sleepers and diners.

The LV had lost its lease at the PRR's Exchange Place terminal in Jersey City in 1913 and moved to the Central Railroad of New Jersey's Communipaw station in the same city. In connection with the Philadelphia & Reading, the LV ran five westbound trains (and five eastbound) daily to Buffalo from Jersey City/Philadelphia: the *New York & Chicago Express*, arriving at 12:58 A. M., the *Chicago Toronto Express*, at 6:45 A. M., the Cornellian at 7:55 A. M., the *Black Diamond*, at 7:55 P. M., and the *Philadelphia & Buffalo Day Express*, at 8:15 P. M. The first three of these trains carried through cars for Toronto and/or Chicago via the Grand Trunk, which were uncoupled at Depew on the LV's Depew & Tonawanda branch to Suspension Bridge, while those scheduled for Buffalo were run into the city on the mainline. Eastbound, the process was reversed for the three corresponding through trains. A sixth Chicago to New York/Philadelphia LV express ran from Suspension Bridge to Depew, completely bypassing Buffalo. The PRR's two Pittsburgh to Buffalo express trains on the Allegheny Division were prosaically christened the *Buffalo Day Express* and the *Buffalo Night Express*, while their opposite numbers were called the *Pittsburgh Day Express* and the *Pittsburgh Night Express*. The Buffalo Division (Buffalo to Emporium) operated three round trips daily between Buffalo and Washington (and Philadelphia). All these through PRR trains carried Pullmans and/or restaurant cars depending on the time of day. The Pittsburgh run took eight hours and the Washington run thirteen.

Between its termini the BR&P ran two through trains each way daily, the excellent service on which is proudly described by Pietrak:

The high standards of the BR&P were largely due to the efforts of William T. Noonan. During the years he was president, the railroad reached its peak. These were the golden years, 1910 until the Great Depression. Under Noonan everything had to be spit and polish, and while the NYC's highly publicized passenger trains seemed to be a standard of excellence, the BR&P would not be outdone for a railroad of its size.

"Safety and Service," an expression of the BR&P characterized on it emblems, not only exemplified freight traffic but it also set the norm in the railway's passenger business. The road was one of the pioneers in the use of all-steel coaches. These heavy cars were equipped with every known comfort. The company operated Cafe and Parlor-Observation cars on the four straight-through trains between the Tri-Cities. These cars were manned by their own crew and though this extra service was expensive, the BR&P took pride in providing every convenience and comfort for its patrons.

The railway even had a Dining Car Commissary Agent who would pick the markets where only the best food could be ordered, a far cry from today's [1992] coin operated food dispensers. To insure freshness, a large quantity of these provisions came from points along the main line. For example, butter was purchased at Warsaw because it was known to be of superior quality. Beef came from Salamanca because the local butcher knew just the cuts and how to prepare steaks the way dining car patrons seemed to like best. Poultry came from specialized farms and eggs were guaranteed fresh or not accepted. All provisions were shipped to the Commissary Store at East Salamanca. On the trains themselves specially selected cooks, waiters, and porters assumed responsibility to carry out the company's service banner, something they did with pride. This pride was instilled into every employee, not only the trainmen, but the sectionmen and trackwalkers as well.

Art is the gracious, kindly, generous beautiful way of doing things. Mr. Noonan knew this well and applied it to the BR&P. Flowerbeds, lawns, shade trees, graciously winding roadways, cleanliness, and order are all essentially artistic. It was said by Elbert Hubbard [the Sage of East Aurora who was lost at sea in 1915] *that "the next time you ride over the BR&P just go into the observation car and take a seat on the rear platform and note the artistic quality of the scene that will meet you. Ballast is lined up in straight lines, not scattered, grass is cut, weeds removed, no litter of any kind." There were hired gardeners assigned to various sections of the railroad to make the rounds of the depots to tend lawns and flower beds.*

All depots were inspected periodically. This was done at times by the general manager in a special train. Windows were to be clean, rooms swept out and lanterns were to be full of oil. No matter how busy a station agent was selling tickets or making out train orders, he was required to put on his full uniform, coat and cap, to meet an oncoming train. [12]

The most frequently used of the NYC's Buffalo routes for locals was the former Buffalo & Niagara Falls, which every weekday in 1916 handled twenty-five westbound trains to Suspension Bridge, seven of which continued 5.3 miles further to Lewiston. Moreover, two of the MC westbound express trains carried passengers to North Tonawanda and Niagara Falls. Weather permitting, all but one of the Lewiston trains made connections with lake steamers to Niagara-on-the-Lake and Toronto. The Toronto boat took an hour and ten minutes. A similar service was maintained eastbound with eighteen locals from the Falls and eight from Lewiston. Six Niagara Falls-Buffalo locals exchanged cars with the former Rome Watertown & Ogdensburg at Niagara Falls. Service on the Niagara Falls Division had increased substantially since 1903 despite competition from the IRC line to Niagara Falls which took eighty minutes between the two cities until the opening of the High Speed Line in 1918. NYC locals took on the average one hour.

The next most used of the NYC's Western New York lines by locals was the Lockport branch, over which five trains ran each way daily. Lockport was a smaller city than the Falls, and the IRC line to Lockport, unlike that to Niagara Falls, ran on its own right-of-way. Three locals arrived daily on the NYC's mainline from Rochester while two returned to Rochester and a third to Syracuse. Small towns between Buffalo and Rochester on the NYWS&B were served by a morning and an evening round trip. The ex-Canandaigua & Niagara Falls ran two round trips between Buffalo and Batavia, twice the number operated in 1903. The NYWS&B featured arrivals of locals from the Flower City at 9:00 A. M. and 8:20 P. M., and departures at 6:10 A. M. and 5:36 P. M. The former LS&MS, which continued to be called that long after its 1913 merger with the NYC, ran two locals each way, one in the morning and one in the evening, between Buffalo and Erie. The MC operated one local each way between Buffalo and Detroit, both versions of which averaged nineteen miles an hour, taking thirteen hours to cross the Ontario Peninsula. These were mail and express runs with a passenger coach for those who wished to ride for only a few stops. Of the six trains between Buffalo and Toronto on the TH&B, five had sleepers, parlor cars, or dining cars depending on the time of day for the three hour trip. The sleepers were through cars while the parlor and dining cars were attached or uncoupled at Buffalo. One train each way, however, carried only coaches, made numerous stops, and between Suspension Bridge and Buffalo was part of the MC's Detroit local.

Tenants who operated locals from the NYC's Exchange Street Station in 1916 were the PRR, the BR&P, the Grand Trunk, and the Buffalo & Wellsville (successor to the ill-starred Buffalo & Susquehanna), which was to abandon its Galeton-Buffalo extension in November, 1916. On its line to Emporium the PRR operated two round trips to Emporium, two to Arcade, and one only as far as East Aurora. The Arcade runs, arriving as they did at Buffalo at 7:50 and 8:40 A. M. and departing at 5:25 and 6:15 P. M., were commuter trains. On the Pittsburgh line, which paralleled the LS&MS and the NKP from Buffalo to Brocton, Dunkirk and small towns in Erie and Chautauqua County were serviced by a daily round trip to Oil City, Pennsylvania. The BR&P ran a round trip daily to Punxsutawney, another to Bradford, and a third only as far as Springville. In 1910 the BR&P had ordered a motor car from the McKeen Motor Car Company for its train to Le Roy, outside Rochester. It looked like a streetcar, was powered by a direct drive marine type gasoline engine with chain and sprocket, and was called the Comet. The idea was to save money by eliminating the need for a fireman. In 1911 a second motor car was ordered, this time from General Electric. Promptly named the *Meteor,* its engine drove a generator which produced electricity to turn the wheels. Both cars suffered frequent breakdowns and by 1917 had been sold as the BR&P went back to conventional steam power. The Grand Trunk operated two round trips daily to Stratford and Goderich. However, an advertised round trip to Merritton and a one-way to Port Dalhousie consisted merely of GT cars attached to trains on the NYC's Niagara Falls Branch to Suspension Bridge.

The Buffalo & Susquehanna had entered bankruptcy back in 1910 and had been operated since by receivers as explained in Chapter XI. As an expedient, the Buffalo & Wellsville was formed to operate the Buffalo-Wellsville section, a state of things which lasted only until November, 1917, when it was sold for scrap. Just before the end, the B&W operated two round trips daily on its eighty-nine miles between Wellsville and Buffalo. One of the two trains went on to Galeton. The Buffalo extension of the B&S had lasted exactly ten years. "Last in, first out" would become a rule for American railroads.

At the Erie Railroad's nearby station there were two daily round trips on the Hornell line to Attica, two to Castile, and two all the way to Hornell. (Fr. James P. Sweeney S. J., a former president of Canisius, was a student at the college in 1916 and came in from Attica, his hometown, on the train which arrived in Buffalo at 8:08 A. M.) There were five round trips daily on the Jamestown line. The westbound train on this line which left Buffalo at 12:55 P. M. carried through coaches for Chicago. The Niagara Falls line was down to one round trip daily for the convenience of passengers on the east and westbound *Night Express*. The DL&W operated a round trip to Scranton daily and another to Groveland. The LV ran two round trips to Toronto daily in addition to the Toronto sections of its through Jersey City-Buffalo expresses.

There were 291 passenger train movements (145 westbound, 146 eastbound) on any given week in Buffalo in 1916. (To keep these figures in perspective it should be noted that soon after Penn Station in New York was opened in 1910 it was handling 750 trains a day coming in under both the Hudson and the East River.) Locals accounted for 140 of Buffalo's 291 train movements and express trains 151. There had been almost the same number of express trains in 1903 (139), but then there had been 161 locals. It was the steam railroad local that first fell before the interurban and the auto. A rare Buffalo Belt Line timetable for 1914 (Figure #3) shows four trains circling the city daily clockwise from Exchange Street to Exchange Street. This should be compared with an 1885 timetable of the same line (Figure IX. #25), which shows twenty-five trains making the circuit every weekday. After 1900 construction of surface roads began to skyrocket, (Figure XIII, #6) and 1916 was the peak year for electric railroad mileage (Figure XIII, #1.) Passenger service on the Belt Line was becoming a casualty of the streetcar.

The lineup of passenger train movements at Buffalo in 1916 appears in Table #4.

1926

"At the height of its operation in the 1920s," writes Peter T. Maiken in Night Trains: The Pullman System in the Golden Years of American Rail Travel, "the Pullman system welcomed to its berths and rooms more than 50,000 people nightly, a traveling contingent

Figure #3. Empire State Express, February, 1987

BUFFALO BELT LINE

NEW YORK CENTRAL LINES

Schedule of June 28, 1914

Leave Buffalo, Exchange St., Via William St., East Ferry St. and Black Rock.

	STATIONS	01 Ex. Sun.	05 Ex. Sun.	07 Ex. Sun.	09 Ex. Sun.
		AM	AM	PM	PM
Lv	Exchange St. Sta.	.....	6 10	4 40	5 40
"	Exchange Street	.....	.....	.....	5 43
"	Clinton Street	.....	6 15	4 45	5 45
"	William Street	5 25	6 18	4 48	5 48
"	Broadway	5 29	6 22	4 51	5 51
"	Genesee Street	5 31	[illegible]	4 53	5 53
"	East Ferry Street	5 33	6 29	4 55	5 55
"	Northland Avenue	.....	6 31	.....	5 57
"	Main Street	.....	6 33	5 00	6 00
"	Central Park	.....	6 38	5 03	6 03
"	Elmwood Avenue	5 46	6 47	5 12	6 13
"	Military Road	5 48	6 49	5 14	6 15
"	Amherst Street	5 51	6 53	5 18	6 20
"	Black Rock	5 53	6 55	5 20	6 23
"	Potomac Avenue	5 55	6 57	5 21	.....
"	Ferry Street	5 57	6 59	5 24	6 27
"	Terrace	6 04	7 04	5 31	6 35
Ar	Exchange St. Sta.	6 03	7 10	5 35	6 38
		AM	AM	PM	PM

BUFFALO BELT LINE TRAINS DO NOT CARRY BAGGAGE

Table #4

Road	Expresses	Locals	Total
NYC	(38)	(6)	(44)
LS&MS	(30)	(4)	(34)
MC	(12)	(2)	(14)
TH&B	(10)	(2)	(12)
NYWS&B	(6)	(2)	(8)
B&NF	-	(51)	(51)
B&L	-	(10)	(10)
C&NF	-	(4)	(4)
New York Central	96	81	177
B&NYC	(4)	(12)	(16)
SB&EJ	-	(2)	(2)
B&J	-	(10)	(10)
Erie	4	24	28
BNY&P	(6)	(10)	(16)
BC&P	(4)	(2)	(6)
PRR	10	12	22
BR&P	4	6	10
DL&W	9	4	13
NKP	6	-	6
mainline	(11)		(11)
D&T	(7)	(5)	(12)
LV	18	5	23
B&W	-	4	4
GT	-	4	4
Wabash	4	-	4
Total	151	140	291

that would have filled Chicago's Hilton Hotel and Towers once the world's largest inn twenty times over." The NYC fleet of express trains from New York and/or Boston through Buffalo to points west had risen from seventeen in 1916 to twenty by 1926, and some of these were faster than they had been a decade earlier. The *Southwestern Limited* averaged forty-seven miles an hour between New York and Buffalo and forty-six between Buffalo and Saint Louis; the *Genesee* on the MC did fifty miles an hour between Buffalo and Detroit; the westbound *20th Century* did forty-eight miles an hour between New York and Buffalo and forty-nine between Buffalo and Chicago; while the *Empire State Express* did forty-nine miles an hour between New York and Buffalo and fifty between Buffalo and Detroit. Most express trains, however, were slower than this. Because of Buffalo's location between New York City and Chicago, most express trains between these two cities passed through Buffalo late in the evening or in the wee hours of the morning which enabled Pullman passengers to break the journey of twenty hours or more by sleeping. Between 10:40 P. M. and 4:07 A. M. *Number 41*, the *Ohio State Limited*, the *20th Century Limited*, the *Southwestern Limited*, the *Westerner*, the *Wolverine*, the *New England Wolverine*, the *Lake Shore Limited*, the *Detroiter*, and the *Cleveland Limited*, passed through Buffalo, ten of the twenty westbound through trains.

There were twenty-nine eastbound arrivals of NYC trains at the twelve track Exchange Street Station, where an average of 3,500 tickets were sold daily, and only eighteen departures. One reason for the difference is that LS, MS, and TH&B arrivals were often merged into a single departure on the mainline to New York and/or Boston. Three of the twenty-nine terminated at Buffalo. In addition, three more trains, and these were among the fastest, bypassed the station on the Compromise Track. No eastbound expresses originated at Buffalo, another reason for the preponderance of arrivals over departures.

"Just like the *Century*" was how the NYC advertised the posh *"Southwestern Limited* all-Pullman Saint Louis New York Boston." Its club car boasted "Barber, Bath, Valet, Stock Reports, Sporting Events, Newspapers, Magazines, Stationery;" its observation car had a "Maid, Stenographer, Telephones at Terminals, Ladies' Lounge and Bath, Magazines, Newspapers, Stationery." Unfortunately, all-steel cars were not proof against human error. At 3:36 on the cold, clear morning of January 12, 1919, train #17, the westbound *Southwestern Limited*, rammed the rear Pullman of the second section of #11, the *Wolverine*, which was standing in the South Byron station seven miles east of Batavia. The *Wolverine* was a Pullman-passenger only train, equipped with all-steel cars. As the engine hit the last car at full speed, the second car left the tracks and crashed into the center of the rear car, ripping off the roof and reducing berths and seats to a tangled pile of debris. No passenger in the rear car escaped death or injury. Automatic signals were working and were set against #11, though the engineer and fireman denied it. A flagman on #17 had placed a red fuse on the track only to see #11 pass over it and crash. A fireman on a nearby freight engine saw the flagman go back and wave his red lantern at #11 only to be ignored. As soon as officials of the railroad learned of the accident, they assembled a relief train at Batavia with every available doctor. The death toll was twenty-two, all of them passengers in the rear Pullman.

The NYWS&B no longer ran its former three round-trip through trains between Weehawken and Buffalo. Its arrangement with the Boston & Maine and the Wabash had been a casualty of federal control during World War I. Its luxury service in 1927 was limited to six trains with parlor cars between New York and Albany. In addition to the NYC's through trains, two westbound expresses terminated in Buffalo, the *Buffalonian* and the *Buffalo Express*; and four, the *Buffalo-Chicago*

Special, the *Forest City Special* to Cleveland, and the *Empire Limited* and the *Pittsburgh Special* to Pittsburgh, originated in Buffalo. A bewildering amount of shuffling of through cars both east and westbound took place at Buffalo on the NYC because it was the point where the original mainline divided into the LS&MS, the MC, and the TH&B.

The PRR, still a tenant at the NYC station, operated the same two Buffalo-Pittsburgh round trips and the same three Buffalo-Philadelphia-Washington round trips in 1926 that it had in 1916. Now, however, one of its round trips to Washington bore the impressive name *Dominion Express* and carried appropriate through cars to Toronto in cooperation with the TH&B and the MC. The BR&P's two night and day round trips between Buffalo and Pittsburgh, however, had been working out of the DL&W's new station at the foot of Main Street since its completion in 1917.

Through passenger service between Jersey City and Buffalo on the Erie, the Cinderella of Buffalo's railroads, consisted merely of through cars cut off or coupled on to one of the road's two Jersey City-Chicago round trip trains (eastbound the *New York Scenic Express* and the *Atlantic Express* and westbound the *Chicago Express* and the *Pacific Express*) at Hornell. Clearly, Underwood's Erie was not competing with Buffalo's other railroads for through Buffalo-New York passenger business. Unlike the DL&W and the LV, it never really got over the fact that its Buffalo Division deadended at the Niagara River. Most of the Erie's stations, including its terminals at Buffalo and Jersey City, dated from the nineteenth century. The Erie merely skirted the hard coal fields which had made the rival DL&W rich. It generated little on-line traffic, a fact which made it dependent on western connections for traffic. A major problem was inherited debt going back to the days of Drew, Fisk, and Gould, which successive reorganizations had never fully wrung out. It was saddled with brutal taxes and money-losing commuter operations in northern New Jersey, and with costly terminal and literage expenses in New York harbor. Nevertheless, Richard Saunders puts a benign interpretation on the saga of the Scarlet Woman of Wall Street:

The Erie never competed for the passenger traffic of the eastern cities but provided a gracious service that was proper for the small cities and towns along its line. In freight, it specialized in high-speed merchandise and perishable traffic. It may have been the quintessential American railroad, a railroader's railroad - double track, heavy rail, long trains, and high speed. Through much of its history, it may have enjoyed more genuine affection from the people it served and the people who worked for it than any other American railroad ever has. [13]

From its new terminal at the foot of Main Street the DL&W operated five through trains each way between Buffalo and Hoboken, as it had in 1903. Westbound, two of these, the *Whitelight Limited* and the *Lackawanna Limited*, terminated at Buffalo; the other three, the *Chicago Limite*d, the *Buffalo Special*, and the *Buffalo Mail*, exchanged through cars, including Pullmans, with the NKP. The *Chicago Limited* also interchanged Chicago sleepers with the Wabash. Corresponding service was provided eastbound. The Wabash operated two express trains each way between Buffalo's DL&W station and Chicago, one of which carried Pullmans to Saint Louis.

From 1882 to 1916 the NKP languished under the control of the NYC which had no intention of permitting it to become a serious competitor of the LS&MS. By 1916, the historian of the road writes, "the NKP had fallen into almost total obscurity." That year it was sold to the Van Sweringen brothers who knew little about railroad operations and so chose John J. Bernet as president. Born and raised in Farnham, Bernet started there as station agent and worked his way up the ladder on the LS&MS until he was made resident Vice-

President of the NYC and the MC at Chicago. Rehor thus describes service on the NKP after 1916:

During the early years of the Bernet regime there were marked reductions in passenger service. This was due to the fact that what money was available was earmarked for freight equipment and physical improvements. In March 1917 the road quit the Erie's Buffalo depot and moved into the Lackawanna's new passenger terminal at the foot of Main Street. At the same time, the last joint operation with the West Shore the Boston-Chicago sleeper service was discontinued. On January 12, 1918, by USRA edict, trains 3 and 4 made their "last" runs. On the same date most of the through car operation with Lackawanna was also discontinued. Through New York-Chicago sleepers were left only on trains 1 and 2 respectively, operated in conjunction with DL&W trains 4 and 5.

On June 6, 1920, trains 3 and 4 were restored to the schedule but, as during the first decade of operation, they were run only between Cleveland and Chicago. . . . Trains 3 and 4 were restored to their prewar express schedules on April 30, 1922, and assigned sleeper equipment. Some of the through arrangements with the DL&W were restored on the other trains, including the Scranton-Cleveland sleeper on trains l and 2. [14]

Bernet became president of the Erie, now part of the Van Sweringen empire along with the Chesapeake & Ohio, in 1927. The next president of the NKP was Walter Ross, former president of the Toledo Peoria & Western, another Van Sweringen line. On this development Rehor writes:

Back in the early 1900s when the Clover Leaf was fighting to hold its own against the overwhelming competition of the Wabash, Walter Ross established his road's reputation for comfort, convenience and courtesy. The "Comfortable Way," as Ross styled the Clover Leaf, could not outrun the Wabash flyers, but it could and did try harder to please. The overnight trains enjoyed many years of popularity simply because they offered convenient departures and arrivals and provided a pleasant, comfortable way to travel. If the NYC had speed and frequency of operation out of reach, the NKP could score in many other areas. Cars could be cleaner and more comfortable, food could be prepared better and served faster, and employees could be more congenial and helpful. The NKP could afford to concentrate on the needs of Cleveland and lesser cities even more so than its competitors.

For many years the railroads operating between New York and Chicago had agreed to charge an excess fare on any train scheduled to run between those cities in less than 28 hours, and for each hour under that time the charge amounted to $1.20. It was stipulated that the failure to meet the schedule entitled the passenger to a proportional refund of excess fare. This agreement tended to discourage improvement on the NKP-DL&W schedules, since the fare differential was an important attraction of the service offered by these roads. Hence the premier trains, Nos. 2 and 3, were still operated in 1927 in conjunction with the DL&W on the 28 hour schedules of 1897. No. 3 made the best time between Buffalo and Chicago. 14 hours 40 minutes, despite the fact that it made 29 scheduled and 12 conditional stops and could be halted anywhere else for passengers transferring from the DL&W.

The four new Hudson's *[4-6-4s] went into service on the 407 mile Conneaut-Chicago run and were normally assigned to trains 1, 2, 5, and 6. While the last two had the poorest Buffalo connections and worked locally east of Cleveland, their overnight schedules between Cleveland and Chicago were growing in popularity. Nos. 1 and 2 offered convenient daytime service between Cleveland and Chicago as well as through New York and Scranton sleeping cars. In June 1927 the NKP bought a pair of new 30-chair car dining cars and assigned them to these trains west of Cleveland. The*

Pullman-built cars featured fully carpeted floors and unusually spacious pantry and kitchen areas, the railroad having insisted on the latter feature as a means of expediting table service. The 84-ton diners were 81 feet long and rode on six-wheel Commonwealth cast-steel trucks.

The scope of Rose's strategy was revealed by sweeping changes put into effect on Sunday, February 19, 1928. New York-Chicago and Cleveland-Chicago service was sharply improved, and a number of new trains were added to the timetable. New No. 8 left Cleveland's West 25th Station at 6 p.m. and made a 4 1/2-hour run to Buffalo where it connected with DL&W No. 14, the White Light Limited. *The dining car assigned to No. 8 was dropped at Buffalo, but the coaches and a 12-section, drawing-room Pullman ran through to Hoboken, arriving there at 9:35 a.m. Connecting Hudson River ferries docked at Manhattan 17 minutes later. This excess-fare train was intended to compete with NYC No. 4, the all-Pullman* Cleveland Limited, *which also departed from Cleveland at 6 p.m. and was due into Grand Central Station at 8:05 a.m. No. 8 made regular stops only at Ashtabula, Conneaut, and Erie, but could be flagged at Painesville and Dunkirk.*

In competition with the westbound Cleveland Limited, *NYC No. 21, the DL&W put on the new* Western Special, *No. 7, which left Hoboken at 6:00 p.m. and connected with NKP No. 1 at Buffalo. The latter was scheduled to arrive at Cleveland at 8:55 a.m. and Chicago at 4:50 p.m. Overall running time of less than 24 hours represented a 4 hour reduction over that of the old combination with DL&W 5. The schedule could have been cut even more but the NKP elected to hold back No. 1's Buffalo departure in order to utilize the engine that brought No. 2 into that city at 2:30 a.m. Refurbished 12-1 sleepers* [twelve open sections and a single drawing-room], St. Elmo, St. Cloud, St. Angele, St. Collins, *and* St. Leon *were assigned to these trains and the Cleveland-Hoboken run. In addition to the sleepers and roller bearing diners, Nos. 1 and 2 handled the plush parlor-observation cars,* Mountainburg *and* Monte Carlo *between Chicago and Conneaut.*

The Buffalo-Chicago schedules of trains 5 and 6 were also tightened up. No. 5 now made its run in 14 1/2 hours and departed from Cleveland at 11:30 p. m. the same time as NYC 89, the all-Pullman Forest City, *which stopped only at Toledo, Elkhart, and Englewood. The NKP train still pulled into La Salle Street at the convenient hour of 7:30 a.m. 15 minutes behind the* Forest City. *Eastbound, NYC 90 left Chicago at 11:30 p.m., 10 minutes after the departure of NKP 6, and arrived at Cleveland at 7:40 a.m. No. 6, running on a new 13 hour 50 minute schedule, had an 8:35 a.m. Cleveland arrival and carried Pullmans for that city, Buffalo, and New York.* [15]

The success of Ross's new and improved "Nickel Plate-Lackawanna Scenic Line" forced the NYC to improve its own service into and out of Cleveland with new 8 section lounge-buffet cars and faster schedules on its *Ohio State Limited* and Cleveland Limited beginning on April 28, 1929. Rehor continues:

Though the NKP and DL&W made no changes in their competing service between those cities, [Cleveland and New York] *they did add a pair of crack new trains the same day between New York and Chicago. NKP No. 4 experienced a startling transition from a Chicago-Cleveland accommodation to a new-excess-fare train, the* NKP Limited, *operated in connection with DL&W 6, the* Lackawanna Limited. *The west-bound* NKP Limited, *No. 4 now ran between Buffalo and Chicago in 13 hours but still competed with NYC 89 west of Cleveland. This train with DL&W 3 offered a 9:37 a.m. New York departure and 23-hour service to Chicago. Four 12-1 Pullmans, the* Bijou, Anbury, Imola, *and* Planter, *were assigned to the pool and the* NKP Limited *were also graced by a pair of Pullman club-*

cars, the Barnegat *and* Bellfontaine. [For an advertisement of the *Nickel Plate Limited* see Figure #4.] [16]

The April 28, 1929 timetable represented the all-time high-point of NKP passenger service, which also proved to be extremely profitable for a time. Although local passenger business continued to fall off resulting in the abandonment of passenger service over 10 percent of the line, NKP passenger receipts for that year were 17 percent higher than two years before. When the NYC responded by coming up with combination lounge-buffet cars for its trains, NKP ordered four *Hudsons* (4-6-4s), state of the art passenger engines, from Lima Locomotive Company and thirty-four all-steel cars from Pullman, including eight new 80-ton passenger coaches, three 84-ton cafe parlor cars, eight mail-baggage cars,

Figure #4. Rehor, Nickel Plate, 212

eight sleepers of the latest design, and two sun parlor observation cars. The sun parlor cars were richly carpeted and equipped with table lamps, deep-seated armchairs, and lounge.

After the Panic of 1893 the LV came under the control of J. P. Morgan interests until 1902 when it regained financial independence. "The Lehigh Valley," writes Saunders, "prospered in the Morgan years and achieved a kind of golden age in the 1920s as a well-engineered, well-maintained railroad, the first in the country to lay its entire double tracked mainline with 136-lb. rail. The railroad was a gritty symbol of the golden days of heavy industry in the northeast." It operated five through trains daily between Buffalo and New York-Philadelphia in 1926. Effective September 15, 1918, the USRA rerouted most of the LV's scheduled trains via Penn Station in order to centralize passenger traffic in and out of the city. This arrangement continued after the war down to the end of LV passenger service. The Erie and DL&W were not affected by this ruling, possibly because their North Jersey local trains were too numerous for even Penn Station to handle. Three of these LV round trips also had Toronto sections and Chicago sections. Westbound, these sections were cut off at Depew; eastbound the trains from Toronto transferred New York cars to the train from Buffalo at Depew and then proceeded into Buffalo. The trains that had only a Buffalo section were known as the *Black Diamond* and the *Star*. One LV Toronto train originated in and another terminated at Buffalo. They both carried buffet-parlor cars and a Montreal sleeper. Another such set carried only coaches and parlor cars but at Hamilton took on (or let off) a Chicago sleeper. The LV's partner in the Toronto operation was now the Canadian National. (See Chapter XV, "Canadian National.") Chicago cars were handed over to either the MC or the Canadian National.

On the LV's express passenger service at this time Greenberg and Kramer make these observations:

Even with hindsight it cannot be said that management should have interpreted the annual decline in passenger business during the late 1920s as permanent and adjusted their plans accordingly. On the matter of main line passenger operations, for example, there were no changes to the basic operating pattern of five trains each way between New York and Buffalo. The Black Diamond, New Yorker, Toronto, LV Limited, *and* Star, *furnished through service. Schedules were frequently adjusted, but with little effect on patronage.*

The market for New York-Buffalo passenger service was crowded. Three other railroads competed with the LV for this traffic: the NYC, the Erie, and the DL&W. The DL&W had the shortest mileage at 396, the Erie was next at 425, and the NYC was third with 438. The LV came in last at 448, about one-sixth longer than the DL&W and, although both roads had routes that penetrated the mountains of Pennsylvania, the DL&W had marvelously re-engineered its line during its Concrete Era of construction. The NYC, though nearly as long as the LV, made excellent time as a result of its famous "Water Level Route."

The upshot was that the LV's fastest schedules were slower than its competitors, a matter of eleven hours instead of ten. Running times for the DL&W and the Erie included a slow start caused by the ferry connections to Manhattan. Here was one of the LV's service strengths; it left from midtown New York. So too did the NYC, but access to Manhattan and mountain scenery kept the LV in contention despite its longer running times to Buffalo.

The long distance service to Chicago owed its persistent life more to terminal-to-point and point-to-point travel than to patronage of through passengers. The GT route was nearly a hundred miles longer than the PRR's and the MC route wasn't much better. In the late 20s, both the PRR's Broadway Limited *and the NYC's* 20th Century Limited *were scheduled for twenty hours. These were their best offerings and they slugged it out for the cream of the traffic. Their ordinary name trains took 22 or 23 hours, making these the targets for the LV's passenger sales force. It was nevertheless, a difficult job to sell through travel because the LV's running times were 25 hours on the best train via the MC and 27 hours over the GT.* [17]

By 1926 Buffalo's local service had been considerably curtailed. The NYC ran twenty-four locals between Buffalo and Niagara Falls in 1926, down nineteen from 1916. Lewiston no longer enjoyed passenger service to Buffalo. On the NYC mainline two round trip locals ran between Buffalo and Rochester. Longer local service westbound consisted in one train daily to Syracuse and one to Albany. Eastbound there was a local to Syracuse and another to Poughkeepsie. The NYWS&B ran two trains each way between Buffalo and Rochester, one pair in the morning, the other in the evening. Service on the Peanut was back to a single daily train each way from Buffalo to Batavia. Another single train each way ran between Buffalo and Erie on the LS&MS. A local on the MC took thirteen hours to cover the 252 miles between Detroit and Buffalo via Fort Erie stopping at every station along the way. Westbound the MC's single local ran only as far as Saint Thomas. These locals were primarily mail and express runs.

The PRR provided East Aurora with commuter service by way of two morning trains from Arcade and two late afternoon trains to Arcade. On this same line which ran through Olean the PRR also operated two round trips to Emporium Junction on the PRR's Philadelphia & Erie. Local service on the PRR's Pittsburgh line consisted of one train a day each way between Buffalo and Oil City. More than a thousand passengers a day traveled over the PRR at Buffalo in 1926. The Erie also ran a morning local commuter train on the Jamestown line which came in from Gowanda at 8:02 and left for Jamestown at 5:05 and for Gowanda at 6:06 in the evening. There were four other locals from Jamestown and two to Jamestown, bringing the daily total on this division to eight. On the line to Hornell there was a round trip to Attica and another that went on to Hornell. Yielding to competition from the IRC's "Buffalo-Niagara Falls High Speed Line" which paralleled the Erie from North Tonawanda to Main Street in Buffalo and had commenced operations on June 9, 1918, the Erie abandoned all passenger service on its branch to Suspension Bridge. It was estimated that in 1926 approximately 718,000 passengers passed through the Erie's Buffalo station, of whom 108,000 were commuters. On the basis of 312 workdays in a year this comes to 346 passengers daily. The Stillwell passenger coach, standard for the Erie at the time, carried eighty-eight passengers. This meant that four coaches, if full, could have carried the Erie's daily commuter load in Buffalo.

The DL&W operated a daily round trip between Buffalo and Groveland, an eastbound to Bath, and a westbound from Scranton. From the same station the BR&P ran two daily locals between Buffalo and Springville, and one each way to Bradford and another to Punxsutawney. The morning train from and the afternoon train to Springville were commuter runs. The only locals on the LV were #129 from and #130 to Sayre. The Canadian National's timetable listed two round trips daily between Buffalo and Hamilton, but this was simply a case of the NYC's Niagara Falls branch carrying Hamilton cars for exchange at Suspension Bridge. However, a daily train each way on the former Buffalo & Lake Huron continued service of sorts to residents, permanent and summertime, of the Canadian shore of Lake Erie. The lineup of Buffalo's passenger trains (arrivals and departures) in 1926 appears in Table #5.

1933

The stock market crash of September, 1929, ushered in the depression decade of the 1930s

Table #5

Road	Expresses	Locals	Total
NYC	(40)	(8)	(48)
LS&MS	(30)	(2)	(32)
MC	(17)	(2)	(19)
TH&B	(12)		(12)
NYWS&B		(4)	(4)
B&NF		(24)	(24)
C&NF		(2)	(2)
New York Central	99	42	141
B&NYC	(4)	(6)	(10)
SB&EJ		(2)	(2)
B&J		(8)	(8)
Erie	4	16	20
B&NYP	(6)	(8)	(14)
BC&P	(4)	(2)	(6)
Pennsylvania	10	10	20
BR&P	4	6	10
DL&W	10	4	14
NKP	6		6
mainline	(10)	(2)	(12)
D&T	(10)		(10)
LV	20	2	22
Wabash	4		4
Total	157	82	239

wherein double-digit unemployment, which bottomed at 24.9 percent in 1933, lasted until 1941, the year America entered World War II. Railroads, given their enormous fixed charges, outmoded work rules, and federal and state bias in favor of highway transport, were particularly vulnerable. As the Hoogenbooms write in their history of the ICC:

For American railroads the depression brought disaster. Tonnage and revenues were halved from 1929 to 1932. In 1929 railroads carried 1,419 million tons of freight for $4,899 million; in 1932 they carried 679 million tons for $2,485 million. Passenger revenue declined even more rapidly than did freight receipts from $1,305 million in 1920 to $876 million in 1929, to $378 million in 1932, to $330 million in 1933. Even though from 1929 to 1932 railroads countered by nearly halving their operating expenses and reducing their dividends by almost three-quarters, their taxes fell less than a third and their interest on bonds rose from $581 million to $591 million. American railroads' $977 million net income in 1929 had dropped by 1932 to a $122 million loss, and during these years their miles in receivership rose from 5,703 to 22,545. Only once during the war year 1942 did net income surpass the 1919 figure, and despite generous government aid during the 1930s, bankrupt-

cies multiplied until in 1939 receivers operated over 77,013 railroad miles [32.7 percent]. [18]

America's railroads were in trouble long before the depression which only made their situation worse, much worse, as the Hoogenbooms note:

By 1929 railroads had lost their virtual monopoly on freight and passenger service. While railroads languished during the Great Depression, the federal government liberally subsidized their motor-driven competitors with massive spending on roads, bridges, and airports. Since railroads had already encountered a decade of increasing competition, their problems were compounded. With competition decimating passenger receipts, railroads became increasingly dependent on freight revenue and allowed passenger equipment and service to erode. Rail-passenger revenue which approximated a third of rail freight revenue before 1920, was down to a fourth in the early twenties, a fifth in the late twenties, an eighth in the thirties, and a ninth in 1941.

Peaking at 57,451 in 1924, railroad passenger cars in service dropped by 1941 to 38,334. Partly responsible for railroad decline and profiting from it, trucks increased their registrations which were less than 100,000 in 1914, increased to over 1.1 million in 1920, over 3.5 million in 1929, and 5.2 million in 1941. Cutting into railroad profits, buses increased their registrations from 34,000 in 1929 to 120,000 in 1941, while automobile registrations grew from 1.2 million in 1913, to 8.1 million in 1920, to 23.1 million in 1929, and to 29.6 million in 1941. Although 1929 was the first year airline passengers topped 100,000, they reached 476,041 in 1932 and almost 3.5 million in 1941. [19]

By 1933 the seat of NYC's Buffalo passenger operations had been located for four years at the magnificent Central Terminal on the East Side where, it will be recalled from the section on terminals in Chapter XI, the railroad had wished to place a union station back in 1907. Downtown businessmen objected, the LV and the DL&W went their own way, and World War I intervened. In 1922 plans were drawn up for an office building and station for local trains at Exchange Street with another station just east of the Compromise Track at Clinton Street for through trains. Patrick E. Crowley, president of the New York Central, placed new stations for Buffalo and Cleveland at the top of his agenda, along with an office building behind Grand Central and the Castleton cutoff near Albany. He wanted nothing to do with the two station projects. As Cousins writes in an article in *Trains*, which has already been cited and upon which much of what follows is based:

New York Central (including Boston and Albany and Ohio Central but excluding subsidiaries Big Four and Michigan Central) carried 69 million passengers a year (the head count would go to 72.3 million in 1929). NYC counted on passengers and related mail and express revenues for $122 million, vs. $240 million from freight in 1925; and passenger train-miles handily exceeded freight (38.1 million to 27.8 million). NYC stock that year hit a high of 137 1/2 and would peak at 265 1/2 in 1929 (before plummeting to a low of 8 3/4 in 1932). The time was ripe for a first class passenger station. [20]

By June, 1925, the city and the railroad and the Grade Crossing and Terminal Station Commission signed an agreement for a new station on a seventy acre site east of Fillmore Avenue in a working class Polish neighborhood, where to complete the site it was necessary to acquire 150 houses. (Figure #5.) How the city and the railroad were able to agree on a location that had caused such wrangling Cousins regards as a mystery but he hints at an influential role played by William H. Fitzpatrick, a local realtor and a power in the Democratic party. Operations would no longer

Figure #5. Site of Buffalo Central Terminal

Cousins, Trains, 28

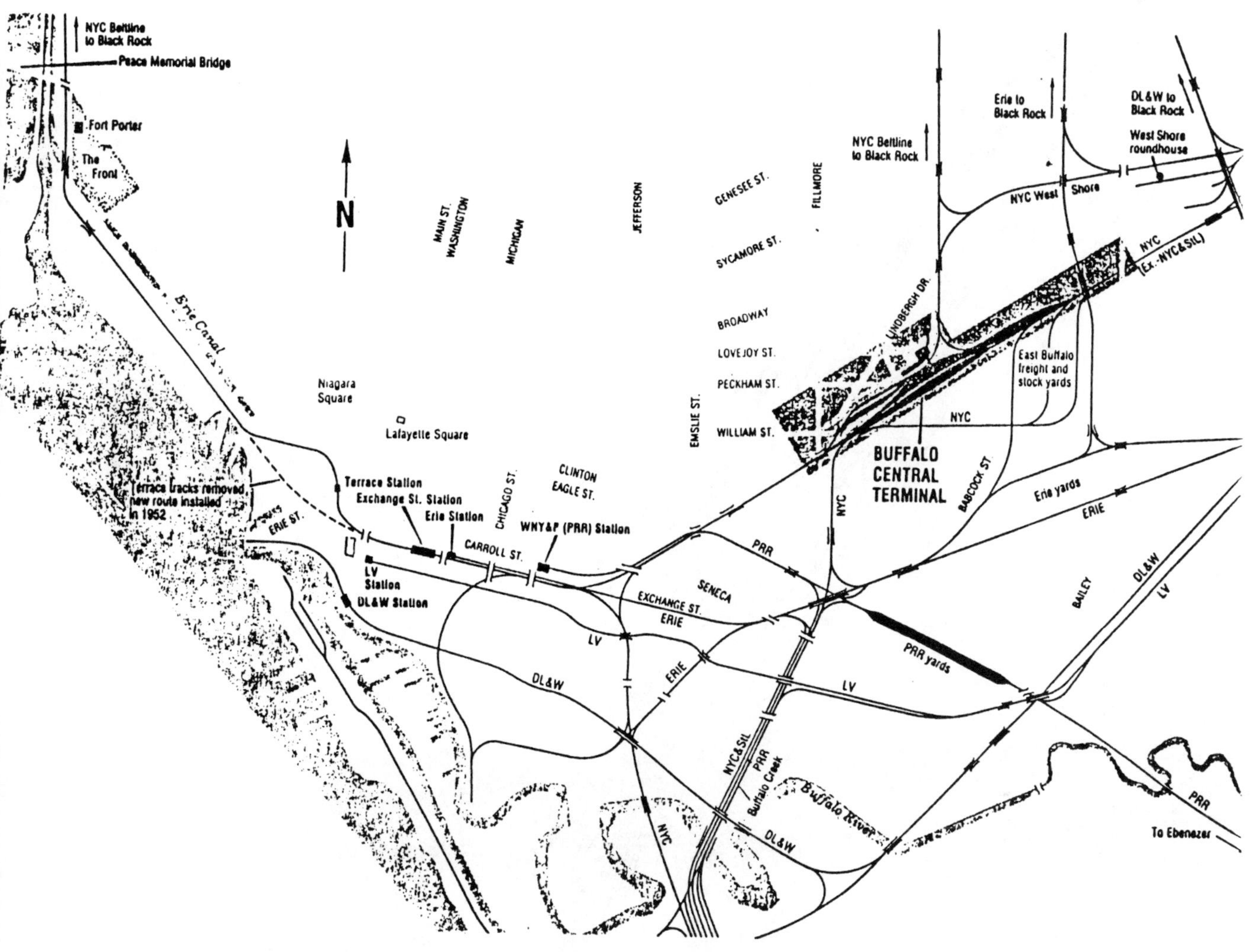

be cramped as they had been at Exchange Street, and LS&MS trains would not have to back in and out of the station. Penn Station in New York had pulled the shopping center of the city up to 34th Street, and Crowley may have had similar dreams for Buffalo. A supplemental agreement promised that plans would be submitted for a new downtown station by the end of 1926 and that the Terrace tracks would be removed. The $9 million estimate for these two projects may explain why the agreement was not honored.

A storm sewer system was built to relieve water buildup on the mostly hard clay East Side site which drained poorly, thirty miles of track were relocated, and Peckham and Lovejoy Streets (the latter renamed Paderewski in honor of the great Polish concert pianist and president of Poland in 1919) were widened. (Figure #6.) The former right-of-way of the NYWS&B was leveled and a 100 foot wide road was laid upon it named after Charles E. Lindbergh, the famed aviator. Architects of the building were Alfred Fellheimer and Steward Wagner, who had been profoundly influenced by the Finish architect, Eliel Saarinen. Their creation was "an enormous passenger train support complex" dominated by a 271 foot high 80 foot square seventeen story station/ office building from which

Figure #6. <u>Ibid.</u>, 28-29

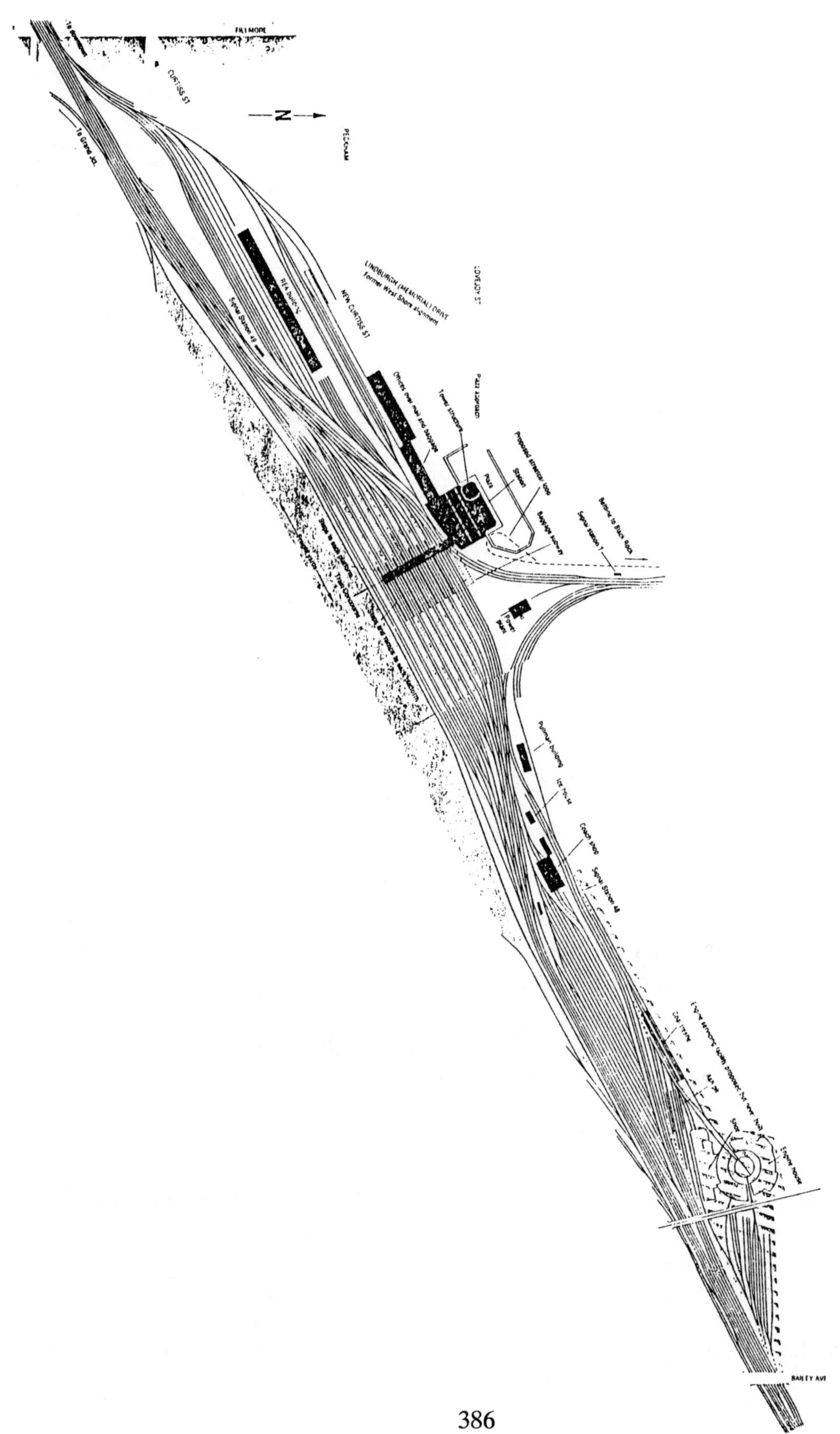

extended a 450 foot long train concourse over the tracks and a 362 foot long baggage and mail wing. (Figure #7.) Cousins' description is detailed:

The Terminal's grandest room was the 225 foot long, 66 foot wide passenger concourse [Figure #8], with a height of 58 1/2 feet from floor to vaulted ceiling and 63 1/2 feet at the domed sections over balconies at either end. Art Deco details were continued throughout: ornamental meal finials in fleur-de-lis *patterns; carved marble finials reminiscent of papyrus leaves, lights faceted like crystals, as concerned with geometry as illumination; and terrazzo floor designs in four shades of marble. . . The overwhelming volume was given human scale by a central information booth and clock kiosk reminiscent of the Golden Clock in GCT.*

The high arched tile ceilings became one with the walls as this material continued in an unbroken line, stopping 15 feet above floor level before changing to a more easily maintained marble. . . To the outbound passenger's right were the beautiful bronze grillages and marble ticket counters of 18 ticket windows, manned by 46 employees with phone connections to 22 Pullman reservationists. From the ticket windows one had a short walk to the baggage checkroom with its clever spiral-chute connection to the track level baggage room. The adjacent waiting room had a Spanish stucco finish throughout, differentiating it from other major areas where tile was employed. Its high and arched ceiling flattened out at the upper portion, which was painted sky blue with rendered clouds and indirect lighting to create the impression of being opened to the outdoors.

Accessible from the waiting room was a woman's room patterned after the most opulent theaters. Decorative panels done in an American Indian-like pattern of red, gold, green, black, and gray were placed regularly along ivory-colored walls. Low modern furniture was used throughout. Divans were done

Figure #7. Buffalo Central Terminal

Courier-Express files, SCNYAB

Figure #8. Central Terminal Concourse, <u>ibid</u>.

in salmon-red leather with gold buttons and had dark, Macassar wood legs. End tables had black marble tops. Four desks in Macassar wood and black marble were provided.

Across the passenger concourse and opposite the waiting room was a 100 foot, 10 inch long, 56 foot deep combination coffee shop/lunch room/dining room restaurant seating 250 persons. The theme was an interlocking series of trapezoids in red, green, black, and ivory, decorated with a continuous soffit that contained interior lighting shining up on a blue, 21 foot high ceiling. Double U-shaped lunch counters had black Carrara glass tops. A black and gold colored marble wainscot ran continuously along the side walls, and silver and bronze ornamental grill work created the half walls which separated the restaurant into its three sections. [21]

The train concourse was a 44 foot wide, 450 foot long hallway with seven stairways descending to trackside, each stairway equipped with a bulletin board indicating departure time and destination of the train below. Platforms were covered by open air butterfly sheds made of steel columns with pre-cast concrete roofs. Train movements were controlled by two signal towers, one at either end of the approaches to the station. To the west of the station was the American Railway Express Company's depot, which occupied two floors serviced by 5,000 feet of covered platforms, the largest facility of its kind in the world. To the east was the power plant whose three coal-fired boilers fed by automatic stokers consumed six tons of coal an hour. To the east of the power house were a Pullman service building, a coach repair shop, and an 11 track coach yard with a 100 car capacity. A projected round house was never built. The complex was designed to handle 3,200 passengers an hour in anticipation of

Buffalo's population reaching 1.5 million. It never did.

Bands, bunting, flags, and speechifying marked the opening of the Buffalo Central terminal on Saturday, June 22, 1929, the high-point of which was a noon-time lunch served in the passenger concourse for 2,200 people, hosted by the Chamber of Commerce and catered by the Statler and Buffalo hotels, the largest such affair ever held in the city. After lunch a huge crowd followed Crowley and other officials down to a platform to watch the 2:10 departure of the eastbound *Empire State Express*. Among those present was Charlie Hogan of Engine #999 fame. At midnight, 200 daily trains began using the Terminal.

From then on it was all downhill. Cousins observes that "between 1929 and 1933 operating revenues of the NYC fell 52 per cent and net skidded almost 80 per cent. In the same period annual passenger revenues declined from $131 million to $53.2 million." It quickly became apparent that the road had over-built in Buffalo. Several trains to and from the east, among them the *Empire State Express,* continued to originate and terminate at Exchange Street. Cousins writes about this station:

This was clearly an effort by the NYC to ameliorate irate feelings over its failure to build a new downtown station as promised back in 1925. The NYC's annual reports had continually assured the city the matter was under study, as in 1926: "Negotiations are progressing with the City of Buffalo for a downtown station in the vicinity of Main and Washington Streets and for the removal of the existing tracks from the surface of the Terrace and Church Street by relocation of the company's roadway in the abandoned Erie Canal bed." [Figure #9, an architect's drawing of a 1922 downtown station proposal.]

The Buffalo Evening News *caustically stated that "of course, we are not entirely through with the talk, for the downtown station problem is still to be settled. We hope that the period of talk is about at an end." NYC's true feelings about a downtown station were revealed by the engineer in charge of the Central terminal project, William F. Jordan: "I might say that there will be a downtown station that will take care of commuters. Its location has not been determined, but Buffalo has little of that kind of business, and it is growing less and less." By the early 1930s, major trains had ceased to use Exchange Street; it served only daily commuters.* [22]

A writer for *Truth* in August, 1931, described the Exchange Street scene after the captains and the kings had departed:

The new center of decay will amaze anyone who has not yet noticed it. Instead of the hurrying throngs of people keeping the old doors of the station aswing, the place is deserted. Three-fourths of the old waiting room has been partitioned off and closed. Two trains a day, possibly four, stop there. Rails are rusting and weeds are growing on all but the two main tracks which run through the old [station] to connect the Terrace and Falls lines with the new terminal.

Across the street the famous dining room which made a fortune for Duncan McLeod is given over to cobwebs and rats. Westward on the same side of Exchange, for half a block, the single or two-story shacks are abandoned or torn down. At the west end of this long stretch the old Matthews-Northrop building has just fallen before the wreckers. North from the old station, at the end of Wells street, the famous old Broezel has recently closed its doors. [23]

The NYC's Exchange Street Station was demolished in November, 1935, though platforms remained for the dwindling number of commuters on the NYC and the PRR. Crowley resigned as president of the road in 1931, amid rumors that his decision to build Central Terminal away from downtown had led to his leaving office. Nevertheless, he remained a director until 1940. His career was in the best traditions of Horatio Alger. He was

Figure #9. Proposed downtown NYC station

Courier-Express, July 14, 1922

Imposing New York Central structure to be located at Washington and Exchange streets. Suburban and local trains will enter it from the main station in Clinton street. It will be the terminal for all except through trains.

born in Cattaraugus, New York, in 1864, the son of the station agent for the Erie Railroad there. At age thirteen he started selling papers, fruit and candy aboard trains. At eighteen he became station agent for the Erie at Custer, Pennsylvania, and rose through the ranks to become dispatcher at Buffalo. He left the Erie in 1889 to take a similar position at Oswego on the Rome Watertown & Ogdensburg shortly before it was taken over by the Central. He became chief dispatcher and train manager for the RW&O. During his forty-two years with the Central he rose from trainmaster through divisional superintendent, general superintendent, assistant general manager, general manager, assistant vice president and vice president. During the First World War he was named Federal Manager of the New York Central. In 1924 he was elected president of the New York Central His decision to place the station out in East Buffalo was the first in a series of moves like locating the University of Buffalo in Amherst and Rich Stadium in Orchard Park, and the building of shopping malls in suburbia that contributed to urban sprawl and the decline of downtown Buffalo.

It was in March, 1933, that Franklin D. Roosevelt was inaugurated. Five days later the Hundred Days began, during which Congress enacted a spate of legislation known as the First New Deal, at the heart of which was the National Industrial Recovery Act and the Agricultural Adjustment Act. At this point, the New Deal's basic solution to the Depression was based on the "strange assumption," as Albro Martin calls it, "that what a nation of people with empty pockets needed was high prices." In the years ahead, federal involvement in the nation's economy was to reach unprecedented levels. The passenger train picture in Buffalo in 1933 reflected national trends downward. Table #6

Passenger service, measured by the number of train movements, was down by seventy-two runs (30 percent) since 1926. The decline was even sharper in the case of locals, down thirty-five (42 percent), than in that of express trains which were down thirty-five or 26 percent. Yet, though the demise of the local (except for commuter trains in metropolitan areas) was at hand, some railroads tried to reverse the decline of long distance trains by increased speed, streamlining, and air conditioning. At an average speed of fifty-four miles an hour the *20th Century* now covered the distance between Chicago and New York in seventeen hours and forty-five minutes, two hours and forty-five minutes faster than in 1926 when it was the fastest train on the road. A new train, *Commodore Vanderbilt,* took only an hour longer. *Lake Shore Limited* made the same run in three hours less than in the mid-'20s. Half an hour was shaved off the running time of the *Empire State Express* between New York and Buffalo, bringing it down to a flat eight hours, while the time of the fastest NYC train to Saint Louis, *Southwestern Limited,* was cut by an hour and forty-three minutes. While railroads could not compete with airlines in terms of speed, they tried to make up for this in comfort, at least on luxury trains, and in the mid-'30s the railroads' slogan, "From Downtown to Downtown," meant more than it would later. In order to attract patrons with less money during the Depression the NYC introduced a train between New York and Buffalo, *Day Coach De Luxe,* with a parlor car and an observation car attached to add a touch of class. Though an express, it made numerous stops on its nine hour and fifty minute run. The PRR cut off an average of two hours on its Buffalo-Washington runs, but the other railroads that served Buffalo made little effort to go along with a speedup that did not apply even to most NYC expresses.

Though the number of NYC locals on the Buffalo scene was halved between 1916 and 1926 that of expresses actually increased. These trains were longer and frequently ran in several sections. Moreover they were heavier as steel cars became the standard consist for

Table #6

Road	Expresses	Locals	Total
NYC	(35)	(3)	(38)
LS&MS	(26)	(2)	(28)
MC	(10)	(1)	(11)
TH&B	(8)	(2)	(10)
B&NF	-	(17)	(17)
B&L	-	(3)	(3)
New York Central	79	28	107
B&NYC	(4)	(2)	(6)
B&J	-	(8)	(8)
Erie Railroad	4	10	14
BNY&P	(6)	(2)	(8)
BC&P	(4)	-	(4)
Pennsylvania	10	2	12
B&O	4	4	8
DL&W	7	1	8
NKP	6	-	6
LV	(8)	-	(8)
D&T	(4)	(2)	(6)
LV	12	2	14
Grand Total	122	47	169

through trains. As Staufer and May observe in their study of NYC motive power:

The tremendous surge in the railroad's passenger business in the mid-1920s was a bit much for the road's K3 Pacifics *[4-6-2s]. The K5s* [another class of *Pacifics] didn't quite solve the problem, and as a result never graduated to the main line. Nine cars were about the limit for a K3 which resulted in many name trains being operated in multiple sections as a regular practice. A new and improved passenger engine capable of handling 12 to 14 heavyweight Pullmans at consistent high running speeds was the requisite placed before the Equipment Engineering Dept. and its chief, Paul W. Kiefer. They were up to the task given them to create a locomotive with greater starting effort, a corresponding increase in boiler capacity to provide the needed cylinder horsepower with maximum output at higher speeds, all this within the prescribed weight limitations, bridge-loads, and within the then existing clearances. To provide for the increased boiler and firebox size, and to spread the resultant increased weight over more axles, the designers created the first 4-6-4. There followed an order for one sample locomotive, No. 5200, Class J1a.*

If ever there was a locomotive class that received more publicity from the time it rolled out of ALCO's plant than the NYC's J1 Hudson, it has escaped the eyes of the writers. It was a natural for a railroad that had long ago learned the value of publicity from the master, George H. Daniels, who gave them the 999, Empire State Express, *and* 20th Century. *The 5200 and its brethren were the features of four successive railroad calendars that adorned walls throughout the world. J1s were used in newspaper advertising to sell everything from overalls to automobiles. Lionel, the toy train manufacturer, marketed several versions in the toy field and untold numbers of small boys knew* Hudsons *when they knew little else. And how many railroads used their locomotives to advertise their passenger train service? The* Hudson *was as handsome a machine as ever rode the rails at the head end of a string of varnish, and the NYC had plenty such strings to show them off. In later years there may have been faster and more efficient machines but none ever encompassed all these features in one package as did the J1s. When they were new and kept clean, with their shorter original stacks and clean running boards, they were a cameraman's delight, both professional and railfan.* [Figure #10.] [24]

In all, 275 *Hudsons* were ordered by the NYC, and they supplied the motive power for the road's name trains throughout the 1930s. Ten of them, engines 5445-5454, were to become the most famous streamlined steam locomotives in the world. They were designed by the famous industrial designer, Henry Dreyfuss, for the all-streamlined new 1938 *20th Century Limited*, which did the 960 miles between New York and Chicago in 960 minutes. They were painted light gray with a dark gray band on the tender. Drivers and nose crescent were painted silver and cylinder heads were natural aluminum. Staufer and May call them "that perfect balance of looks, function, and class." (Figure #11.) Newspaper coverage of the maiden run of the NYC's streamlined edition of the *Empire State Express* (Figure

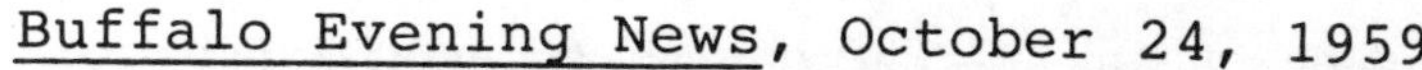
Figure #10. NYC 4-6-4, Class J 1b, Alco, 1927

Buffalo Evening News, October 24, 1959

Figure #11, NYC 4-6-4, Class J 3a, Alco, 1939
Ibid., September 16, 1962

#12) was pushed off the front page by the bombing of Pearl Harbor on December 7, 1941.

Streamlining and lightweight cars, innovations that first appeared in the 1930s, were in the popular mind merely aspects of the same thing. Streamlining was a new idea which appealed to the public with its connotation of bullet-like speed. As White writes: "What had been an obscure technological term in aerodynamics was made into a household word through an astute publicity campaign mounted by several railroad traffic departments." From an engineering viewpoint streamlining was little more than "a dramatic gesture aimed at the public." The real change that occurred during the 1930s was in car construction. With the coming of the steel car in the first decade of the twentieth century, over-all train weight increased. Eighty ton coaches, often referred to as "battleships," and ninety ton diners, were becoming common. Aluminum was tried but found wanting because of its tendency to corrode, especially when joined to steel frames, although about a thousand aluminum cars were actually built. When Edward G. Budd, a Philadelphia automotive parts manufacturer, developed a method of welding stainless steel, the possibility of lightweight passengers cars became a reality. The astounding success of the Burlington Zephyr (west wind), a three car stainless steel motor train in 1934, marked Budd's successful entry into the passenger car business. Budd's first full-size passenger car weighed forty-two tons. However, stainless steel was the most expensive material ever used for passenger car construction. This made their acquisition difficult for perennially strapped railroads like the Erie and the LV.

Streamlining was skin, or as White prefers, tin deep, a mere cosmetic improvement. The same was not true, he adds, of a contemporary and far more substantial development. "How to balance the conflicting requirements for a large volume of clean, pure air, without drafts, while maintaining a comfortable temperature

Figure #12. NYC 4-6-4, Class J, 3a, Alco, 1937

Buffalo Evening News library

on cold days was a problem that was never resolved until the advent of air conditioning." Sixty people crowded into a relatively small space, or Pullman passengers, especially those in upper berths, frequently found train travel offensive and stifling because of cinders, dust, and smoke from outside, and bad breath and stale air from within. Vents, transoms, clerestories, and fans were tried, yet each solution seemed to generate new problems. The B&O first successfully tested air conditioning aboard one of its coaches in 1929, a refrigeration unit made by Willis Carrier, and by 1931 the road had over 100 air-conditioned cars in service and several air-conditioned name trains. A full page ad in the 1933 *Official Guide* declared:

It's Always Springtime on the [Chesapeake & Ohio's] George Washington, *the World's Finest Air-Conditioned Train. Clean, fresh, circulating air in every car throughout the entire trip, day and night, no drafts, dust, dirt, restful lounge cars with radio and every comfort, restaurant cars serving delicious meals at moderate prices, beautiful Colonial interiors, and many conveniences entirely new to railroad travel. The* George Washington *has justly been called The Most Wonderful Train in the World.* [25]

However, air-conditioning was expensive, and a unit weighed about 7.5 tons, which worked against the movement afoot to produce lighter cars. No railroad was as enthusiastic in promoting air-conditioning than the Pullman Company. The new development seemed to offer a luxury that would reverse Pullman's declining business at a cost much less than building new cars. White details the results:

In 1936 there were 5,800 air-conditioned passenger cars running in this country, about 40 percent of them Pullman owned. One year later the company had 3,300 air conditioned cars, on which it had spent 25.5 million dollars. Before World War II Pullman had all but completed its air conditioning program; only its oldest cars lacked the new equipment. [26]

At the end of the decade, 12,204 passenger cars were air-conditioned out of a total of 45,000 cars. This proportion is even better than it appears since among the 45,000 are included baggage and express cars.

In 1933 the Erie ran the same number of round trip express trains (two) between Jersey City and Buffalo as it had in 1926, which as then were merely through cars cut off or coupled on to the *Erie Limited* and the *Lake Cities* at Hornell. As usual, the Erie's through trains did a good deal of on-line business and hence their speed was no greater than it had been in 1916. No longer did locals on the Erie's Niagara Falls branch provide a connection between the expresses and Suspension Bridge. Local service had shrunk to a daily round trip to Attica and two to Jamestown. On August 4, 1935, the Erie abandoned its Exchange Street station and became a tenant of the LV. The Erie station was torn down in December, 1936. On the occasion of the abandonment a reporter for the *Courier Express* reminisced:

The passing of the Erie station just about completes the exodus from Exchange Street begun a few year ago when the NYC completed its new terminal in East Buffalo. At present, Central commuter trains utilize the old Exchange Street station, but the company now is seeking discontinuance of the station. If this request is granted, Exchange Street as a railroad center will fade into obscurity. The Erie station was built in 1875. It was of brick construction and replaced a wooden structure which had served for nearly twenty years before. During its construction divisional offices were housed in the old Continental Hotel across the street.

Old timers undoubtedly will remember the Continental as one of the leading hostelries of Buffalo. It shared this renown with the Mansion House which stood for half a century at Exchange and Main streets and the Tifft House farther up Main Street on the site of the present William Hengerer Building.

About 35 years ago, thousands of Buffalonians crowded the Erie station every weekend for the popular excursions to Portage, Rock City, Kinzua Bridge, Gowanda, and Alden. In those days it was a common sight to see trains of twelve to fourteen coaches loaded with members of social clubs and church societies bound for these nearby resorts. The excursions were usually run on Sundays and in the early morning hours thousands laden with picnic baskets would arrive by horse and buggy and streetcars at the Exchange Street station. The Erie depot reached its height of popularity during the Pan-American exposition in 1901. That year also marked Exchange Street's zenith of activity. In fact, so great was he rush of activity that the facilities at the station had to be enlarged. The old train shed was razed, new platforms built, and three butterfly canopies constructed over the six tracks.

Every arriving train disgorged crowds of passengers who moved up Exchange Street toward Main, and merchants along the way did a thriving business. Popular hotels along the way were Dunc McLeod's, the old Broezel House, the Arlington, and the Mansion House. [Actually the best way to the Exposition was on the NYC's Belt Line.]

On September 25, 1938, fifty two years of commuter service on the Jamestown line ended as Erie Railroad #517 pulled out of the LV station at 5.29 P. M. for its last run to Gowanda with 100 passengers aboard, not its usual handful. A lady from Water Valley who had been riding the train for thirty-two years was designated by the other regulars to present a ring to the stationmaster in commemoration of the event. A bus line called the Hamburg Railway Company stepped into the breach with an express bus during rush hours between Eden-Hamburg and Buffalo. Passenger service on this line was now down to a single daily round trip between Buffalo and Jamestown.

The PRR ran three through round trips to Washington-Philadelphia (two of them with Toronto cars) and two to Pittsburgh as it had in the previous decade, but there were no locals on the Pittsburgh line and only a single round trip on the Washington line to Olean. Throwing in the towel, the PRR substituted two bus round trips Olean-Buffalo. However, day expresses on the Pittsburgh line made several local stops in Erie and Chautauqua Counties.

At the beginning of 1933 through service on the DL&W consisted of five westbound and four eastbound trains, as had been the case in 1916. Six of these trains carried Hoboken-Chicago sleepers with the help of the NKP. But on May 15, 1933, Numbers 9 and 10 were discontinued. Local service, never extensive, had dwindled to a single slow train from Scranton. When John M. Davis succeeded Truesdale as president of the DL&W in 1926, he quickly became aware of the need to speed up schedules to meet automobile and bus competition. Number 5, *Chicago Limited*, had its New York-Buffalo time reduced by ninety minutes, Number 7, *Western Special*, was speeded up by three hours, Number 9, *Whitelight Special*, by an hour, and Number 3, *Lackawanna Limited*, by twenty minutes. The same was done for their corresponding eastbound runs. However, the DL&W still failed to outpace the NYC or even the LV for that matter, whose New York to Buffalo mileage was twelve miles longer.

Now operating out of the DL&W station was the B&O. Drury explains how America's oldest common carrier came to acquire the BR&P:

After the ICC merger plan of the 1920s was published, both Delaware & Hudson and B&O petitioned for control of the BR&P: the ICC approved B&O's application in 1930. Meanwhile the BR&P was sold to the Van Sweringen brothers (who owned the NKP and controlled the C&O) in 1928. B&O still wanted the BR&P, and the Van Sweringens wanted the Wheeling & Lake Erie, in which the B&O held a minority interest. They traded, and on January 1, 1932, B&O acquired the BR&P [and what was left of the Buffalo and Susquehanna in Pennsylvania.] [27]

The B&O wanted the BR&P and the B&S as links in a new short freight line which with low grades between Chicago and New York. This route was projected to run east from Chicago over the mainline of the B&O to New Castle, Pennsylvania, whence it would use the B&O's branch to Butler, the BR&P to Du Bois, and the B&S to Sinnemahoning. From there the B&O would build a wholly new line to the Reading at Williamsport and would secure entry to New York Harbor on the Central Railroad of New Jersey, both of which railroads were already controlled by the B&O. (Figure #13.) The time for this sort of thing had passed. It is obvious that the B&O was not seeking primarily an entry into Buffalo by its acquisition of the BR&P, but that is what it got. The B&O continued to maintain the BR&P's day train (with an observation-dining car) and its night train (with Pullmans) between Rochester-Buffalo and Pittsburgh. The night trains were true limiteds, making few stops. The day trains, however, stopped at Orchard Park, West Falls, Colden, Glenwood, East Concord, Springville, and West Valley. None of these set any speed records. There were also two round trip locals, one to Springville and the other to DuBois.

The LV had cut its five through trains each way of the 1920s to four by 1933. One originated in Buffalo and another terminated here. The rest carried through cars via Suspension Bridge for Toronto via the CN and for Chicago via the CN and the MC. No local trains were operated by the LV, though three connections on the D&T stopped at Williamsville and North Tonawanda.

A major development on the local railroad scene during the late thirties and early forties was the extension outward from Buffalo of grade crossing elimination, made necessary by

Figure #13. B&O plans for the future
Pietrak, BR&P, 102

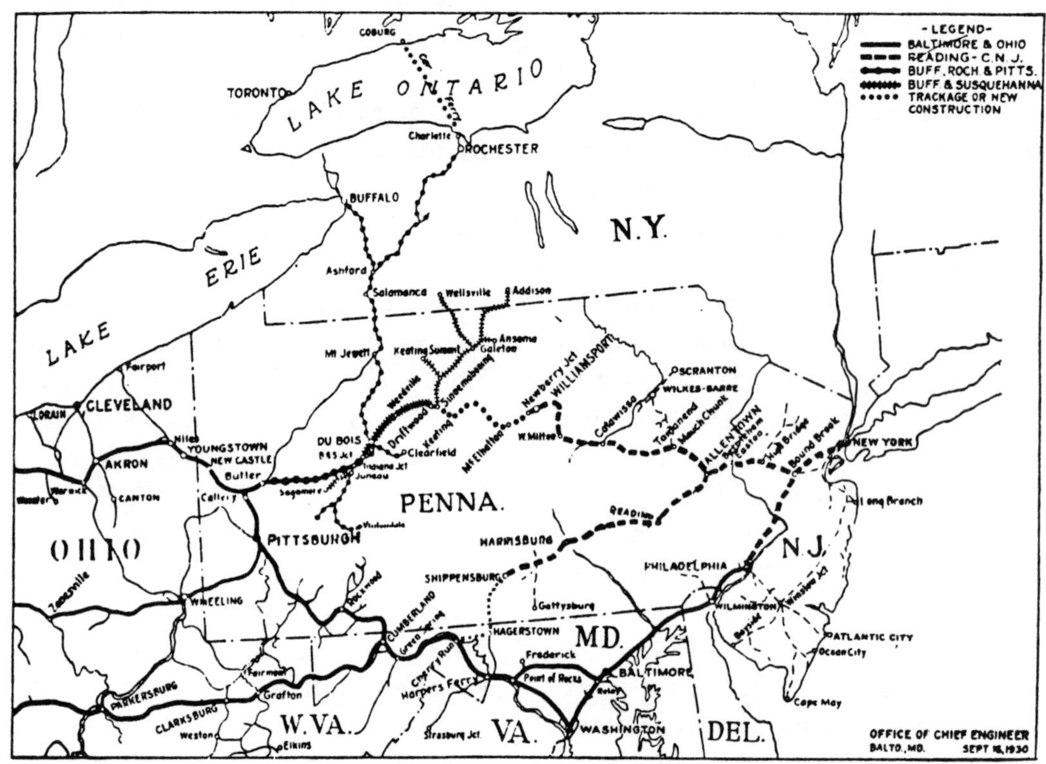

suburban growth, which, in turn, was fueled by the greatly increased number of cars on the road. Automobile registration, which in 1933, the low-point of the Depression, was 20,675,275, increased to 29,813,718 by 1941, when the United States entered World War II. By a law passed by the New York legislature in 1928 the Public Service Commission was given authority to determine where grade crossings needed to be eliminated. Outside New York, Buffalo, and Syracuse, costs were to be borne "forty percentum by the state, ten percentum by the county or counties in which the crossing is located, and fifty percentum by the railroad corporation or corporations affected thereby." In the summer of 1938, the million dollar Tifft Street bridge over the NYC, PRR, B&O, NKP, the South Buffalo, and the Erie was completed (Figure #14), as were three bridges carrying six tracks of the NYC, three of the Erie, and two each of the DL&W and LV over Transit Road in Depew at a cost of half a million dollars. The bridge which carried the Niagara Falls branch of the NYC over Sheridan Drive that year cost $750,000. The November 11, 1941 *Buffalo Evening News* contained this report:

The dedication today of the overpass spanning the NYC and the PRR tracks in the Orchard Park Road, West Seneca, at a cost of $175,000, marked completion of the 13th grade-crossing elimination in the Buffalo district in the last three years. The cost of the 13 jobs was $6 million. Listed in the Public Service Commission's files as Case 5993, the Orchard Park overpass was first ordered eliminated Oct. 1, 1930, but the actual construction work did not start until ten years later. Elimination of the grade crossing removes another serious traffic hazard from Western New York. There have been many deaths recorded there, the last occurring Oct. 23, 1940. According to a survey by the Buffalo office of the State Highway Department, four other projects costing $700,000 are under construction while 18 more estimated at $12 mil-

Figure #14. Tifft Street Viaduct

<u>Buffalo Evening News</u>, January 7, 1936

How Viaduct Will Eliminate Crossings

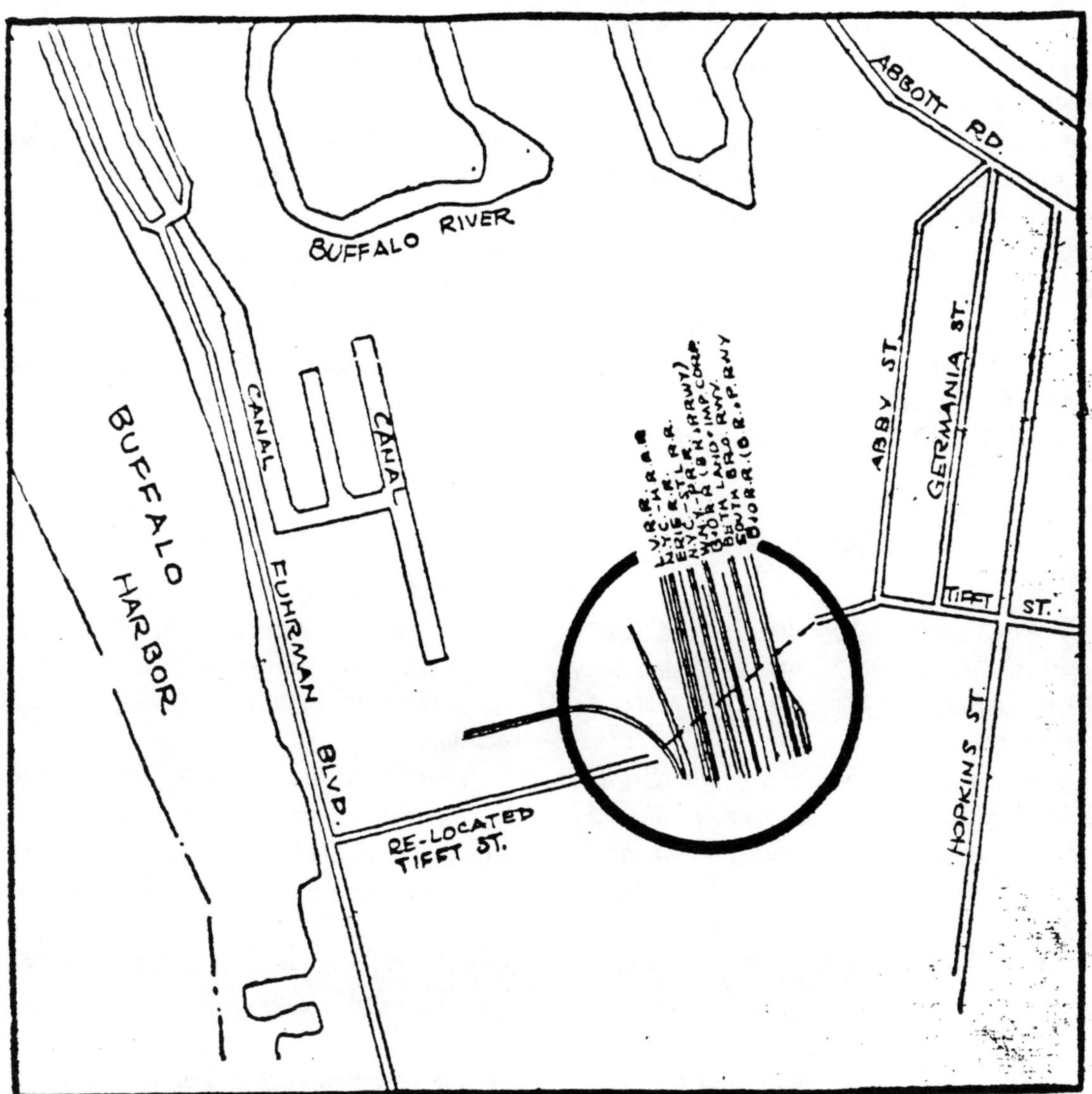

This is the manner in which the new Tifft street viaduct will eliminate grade crossings over the tracks of railroads entering Buffalo. Tifft street will be relocated so it will cross the tracks at an angle by means of the viaduct and will intercept Fuhrmann boulevard, formerly the Harbor turnpike, at a point to the south of the present interception. Construction of the viaduct is expected to begin next Summer and will take a year to complete.

lion are planned for the district, comprising Erie, Niagara, Chautauqua and Cattaraugus Counties.

Still under construction are Transit Road, Bowmansville, NYC West Shore $175,000; Goodyear-Miller Ave., NYC $350,000; Lakewood, Erie, $185,000; Devil's Hole, Niagara Falls, NYC, $42,206. The projects open to traffic in addition to the Orchard Park Road overpass follow: Union Road, Williamsville, LV, $125,000; Union Road-Walden Avenue, NYC, $350,000; Union Road, Cheektowaga, DL&W-Erie-LV, $380,000, Center Road, NYC-PRR $150,000; Ridge Road, Lackawanna, LV, $125,000; Alden-Crittenden Road, LV, $75,000; Alden Village, Erie, $205,000; Jamison Road, Elma, PRR, $205,000; Camp Road, Hamburg, Erie, $205,000; Irving, NYC-PRR-NKP, $700,000; Dunkirk, PRR-NKP, $700,000; Dunkirk, NYC-Erie $3,000,000.

1943

Stephen B. Goddard in his The Epic Struggle Between Road and Rail in the American Century aptly sums up fifty years of railroad history:

As America approached mid-century, railroads had reaped a bitter harvest of ruinous over-regulation, uninspired management, and public hostility. The highwaymen's carefully orchestrated plan to win passengers and freight away from the rails had borne abundant fruit. The idea that railroads represented America's past, and cars and trucks its future, had by 1940 become deeply entrenched in the American psyche. During the Second World War, a shaft of sunlight would break through the clouds that railroads had lived under for several decades, while discord broke the highwaymen's ranks for the first time. But the rails would face their biggest challenge when post-war prosperity led to car-fever. [28]

Highwaymen is Goddard's shorthand for what he calls the "highway-motor complex," which for him is similar to President Eisenhower's "military-industrial complex," an unholy alliance. The highway complex was an informal association of engineers, automakers, roadbuilders, tire and cement and steelmakers, and the oil industry, which transformed America and not for the better. Goddard notes:

The plight of the railroads at the advent of World War I had been too little capacity and too much business; a generation later the reverse was true. Urged by the ICC to over-invest, the lines had added 15,000 steam locomotives and 850,000 freight cars in the 1920s and 1930s, but motor competition had left many lying idle on rail sidings. The Depression and competition had forced the industry to cut costs and boost efficiency, leaving it lean but with excess capacity to absorb large numbers of soldiers, tanks, and supplies. [29]

The highway-motor complex had confidently expected an avalanche of business and orders for new vehicles as a result of the war. They were to be disappointed, as Goddard recalls:

Then quite unpredictably, these prospects plummeted. In the early days of World War II Japan seized Southeast Asian rubber plantations, and in the Atlantic, German U-boats sank coastal oil tankers bound for American shores. Before long, Washington was strictly rationing rubber and gasoline, and imposing a thirty-five mile-an-hour speed limit to conserve both commodities. The shortages caused automobile and trucking production to screech to a halt, as Detroit retooled its production lines to produce planes, tanks, and ships. At the same time, coal-fired steam railroads surged to the fore. By the war's end they would move 97% of war-time passengers and 90% of its freight, posting profit margins they had not seen since early in the century. For the first time in decades, the highwaymen felt unappre-

ciated. . .

Technology and geography smiled on the railroads as well. Advances in traffic-control systems, larger railcars, and more powerful locomotives allowed the rails to move half again as much freight as in the World War I with nearly a third fewer locomotives and a quarter fewer freight cars. In World War I railcars had shipped passengers and material across the country to East Coast ports and returned home unprofitably empty. Now their westbound backhauls sped toward California ports, where Far East shipments padded their earnings. . . Americans smiled on the rails as a friend of the public. But mighty lines such as the NYC and Southern Pacific would soon find that their oasis of prosperity was only a mirage, built as it was on a temporary crisis. [30]

It was to be the American railroads' finest hour. As H. Roger Grant writes in Death of an American Railroad:

Railroads handled eighty-three percent of all military freight between 1941 and 1944, and they moved 91 percent of all military freight within the country and 98 percent of all military personnel. Freight traffic measured in ton-miles, soared from 373 billion in 1940 to 737 billion in 1944 (the industry would not pass the latter record until 1966). [Figure #15.] *Passenger traffic, expressed in revenue passenger miles, skyrocketed from 223 billion in 1940 to 95 billion in 1944, and that peak would never again be equaled.* [Figure XI, #10.] [31]

There was an underside, however, to this wartime prosperity. Many, whose first and only experience with train travel was with some very inferior passenger equipment the railroads were forced to utilize to meet wartime demands, resolved never to take a train again when other options became possible. As experienced railroad employees were drafted into the services, less well trained men took

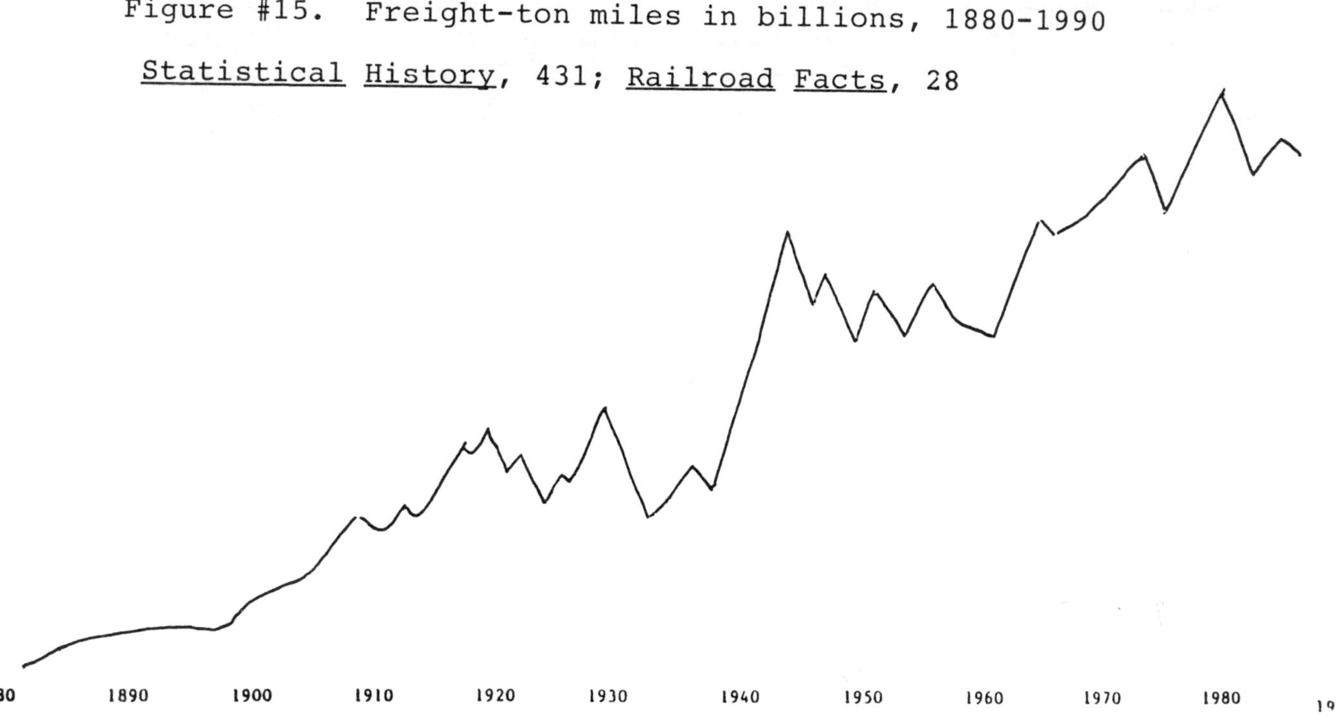

Figure #15. Freight-ton miles in billions, 1880-1990

Statistical History, 431; Railroad Facts, 28

their places with dire results for safety. Table #7 shows railroad fatalities, 1940-1946.

The eighty-three killed in 1940 was out of line with previous peacetime passenger fatalities due to the wreck of the NYC's *Lake Shore Limited* with 250 passengers aboard at Little Falls, New York, on Saturday, April 20, 1940, at 11:35 P. M. The *New York Times* called it "one of the most stupendous and disastrous wrecks in Eastern railroad history." The sharpest curve on the system was located there, with a speed limit of forty-five miles an hour. Instead the engineer, running fifteen minutes late, hit the curve at fifty-nine miles an hour. The locomotive jumped the track, headed into a rock wall, and exploded. The nine cars following, six Pullmans, two day coaches, and a diner, were derailed and piled up behind. One day coach and three Pullmans at the rear of the train stayed on the tracks. Ghastly sights greeted the rescuers. In the first two Pullmans were found mostly mangled bodies; in the next two were most of the injured. By noon the next day the death count was thirty, including the engineer, and the list of wounded reached one hundred. A black porter in the fourth car behind the engine broke a rear window and lowered to safety sixteen of the occupants including women and children. Only one of the revenue-paying passengers killed was from Buffalo. The record for American railroads looked very bad that year when compared with that of regularly scheduled airlines, which finished the year with no fatalities.

Train movements of expresses, though not of locals, showed a decided growth in 1943 over the previous decade. See Table #8.

NYC schedules were speeded up for several through trains, though how often these schedules were met during the hectic war years is uncertain. Back in 1912 the PRR and the NYC had agreed on twenty hours between New York and Chicago on their crack trains, the *20th Century* and the *Broadway Limited.* The NYC's historian continues their story:

But the public was crying, "Faster! Faster!" and the engine designers were doing what they could. The Hudson *or 5200 series of locomotives was produced, and in 1932 the* Century *again became an eighteen-hour train. Three years later this was cut to sixteen hours and thirty minutes. Then in '37 the* super-Hudsons *appeared, and a new* 20th Century *sped over the rails in sixteen hours, or a little better than a mile a minute for the whole 961 mile course. World War II threw such a tremendous burden on the railroads that fast trains had to give*

Table #7

	Passengers		Employees	
	killed	injured	killed	injured
1940	83	2,597	583	18,350
1941	48	3,009	807	25,866
1942	122	3,501	1,005	36,032
1943	278	5,166	1,072	46,971
1944	267	4,854	1,087	48,613
1945	156	4,840	972	48,632
1946	128	4,714	738	39,472 [32]

Table #8

Railroad	Expresses	Locals	Total
NYC	(52)	(1)	(53)
LS&MS	(40)	-	(40)
MC	(13)	(2)	(15)
B&NF	-	(13)	(13)
TH&B	(6)	(2)	(8)
New York Central	111	18	129
B&NYC	(6)	-	(6)
B&J	-	(2)	(2)
Erie Railroad	6	2	8
BNY&P	(4)	(2)	(6)
BC&P	(2)	-	(2)
Pennsylvania	6	2	8
B&O	4	2	6
DL&W	8	-	8
NKP	4	-	4
mainline	(7)	-	(7)
D&T	(2)	-	(2)
LV	9	-	9
Grand Total	148	24	172

ground to more prosaic traffic, and the Century *during the war became a slower vehicle, but in the spring of 1946 it went back to sixteen hours again.* [33]

The speed of the NYC's other through trains and the express trains of Buffalo's other railroads was much the same as it had been a decade earlier. An ominous disclaimer appeared in the NYC's timetables in 1943: "Air-conditioned equipment is assigned as far as possible but the right is reserved to employ non air-conditioned cars as necessitated by volume of traffic or emergencies." With 111 daily express train movements, the NYC in 1943 was up thirty-two or 40 percent compared with 1933. To all extents and purposes its local business was down to thirteen locals between Buffalo and Niagara Falls.

"For the duration," as the expression at the time was, the Erie added another train and now had three each way between Jersey City and Buffalo. However, these trains were really locals consisting merely of coaches which made connections with the mainline at Hornell. Moreover, as noted above, the Erie's trains now terminated at the LV's station. A single round trip between Buffalo and Jamestown was all that remained of the Erie's once extensive local traffic on that line. The

PRR's passenger service on the Pittsburgh line was down to one night train each way with sleepers. On the Philadelphia-Washington line there was a night train with Pullmans each way still called the *Dominion Express* which, however, no longer carried Toronto sleepers. There was also a *Washington & Philadelphia Day Express* eastbound and a *Buffalo Day Express* westbound, both with parlor and dining cars. This line also ran a commuter train between Buffalo and Olean which arrived at 8:55 in the morning and left at 4:50 in the afternoon. The B&O also ran two round trips between Buffalo and Pittsburgh. Its night trains no longer provided sleepers, but the day train carried a buffet-lounge car. There was also a local, actually a mail train with a passenger coach attached, which made every stop between Buffalo and Du Bois, averaging twenty-eight miles per hour.

The DL&W, the B&O's landlord at the foot of Main Street, featured four round trip through trains a day between Buffalo and Hoboken, two of which enjoyed a Chicago connection via the NKP. The westbound *Chicagoan* reached its ultimate destination via the MC, but it had no eastbound companion. On the DL&W's passenger service at this time Taber writes:

World War II saw the DL&W in a good position to handle the increased passenger business caused by gas rationing. All the seasonal equipment now saw use more than just a few days each year. While the PRR and the NYC trains were jammed to Chicago, the DL&W-NKP was still a pleasant ride. While passengers stood in the aisle on the NYC from New York to Buffalo, New Yorkers, who knew better, went over to Hoboken and got window seats for their somewhat slower, but more dependable trip to Buffalo. [34]

There was one occasion, however, on which the Buffalo run proved anything but dependable. At 5:22 P. M., August 30, 1943, the *Lackawanna Limited* with more than 500 passengers aboard, some of them volunteers to upstate harvest areas, side-swiped a local freight at Wayland, New York. As Taber tells the story:

The freight had gone into the clear after doing some switching. The engineer believing he could get in another move before No. 3 arrived (it had left Bath 26 miles away 20 minutes late) pulled up to the switch fouling the main line. Engine 1151, pulling eleven cars had a scheduled time of 27 minutes for the distance, but had made up four or five minutes and was hitting 80 when she rounded a curve and saw No. 1248 fouling the mainline. With the brakes in emergency, 1151 tore off the cylinder of the freight engine and both derailed. No. 3 slithered to a stop with escaping steam from the still open throttle of 1248 pouring through broken coach windows. Twenty-six passengers in the car were killed from the steam. [35]

The *New York Times* reported that rescue workers from Wayland and surrounding towns laboring in a roped-off area under the glare of floodlights and the beams from the headlights of parked automobiles searched the wreckage that night to make sure that all bodies had been accounted for. A passenger from Kenmore describing the "awful gruesome sight," said, "The man sitting next to me and the woman sitting ahead were both killed. Glass and steam filled the car. The people were paralyzed with fear, and outside a woman knelt alongside the wreckage repeating the Lord's Prayer."

The LV operated four westbound express trains to Buffalo from New York-Philadelphia, and three eastbound. One pair christened the *Maple Leaf* carried Toronto cars on the D&T. However the LV no longer carried through cars to Chicago. Along with Buffalo's other railroads on July 15, 1945, the LV dropped all sleeping cars from the *Maple Leaf* and the *Star* in accordance with an Office of Defense Transportation directive prohibiting the use of

Pullmans on runs under 450 miles. This hit Buffalo's major railroads hard since the New York-Buffalo mileage was 396 on the DL&W, 424 on the Erie, 435 on the NYC, and 447 on the LV. On the PRR Buffalo to Pittsburgh was 270 and Buffalo to Washington was 435 miles. New York and Boston to Chicago runs were not affected.

The war in Europe had ended on May 8, 1945, and millions of GIs were anxious to get home. Complaints were aired that prisoners of war were being transported in Pullmans while American soldiers were forced to ride on substandard day coaches. Moreover military leaders were gearing up for an invasion of Japan which, it was estimated, would require a huge force given the tenacious defense which the Japanese had offered Americans at Imo Jima from February to March (4,189 Americans killed) and at Okinawa from March to June (11,260 Americans killed). The need to transport millions of soldiers from Europe to the Pacific was not stressed in the publicity surrounding the ODT's directive. The July 7 *New York Times* announced:

Parlor car facilities will not be affected by the order, according to DOT spokesmen, who estimated that it would mean the withdrawal of 895 sleeping cars from regular use, leaving civilians with a "rock-bottom" number of about 3,000 cars which are to be continued in service on the long runs. The 895 cars are to be assigned to the Army to augment the number available for the exclusive use of military personnel, giving the armed forces the use of about 66% of the sleeping cars in the United States.

Action was made necessary according to Col. J. Monroe Johnson, ODT Director, by the unexpectedly heavy arrival of troops from Europe, "well in advance of the schedule originally announced by the War Department. Arrivals in June were one-third greater than had been anticipated. It now appears that July arrivals will be greater than originally expected. In fact, July may be the biggest month of the whole program for arrivals from Europe. As troops go across the Pacific in increasing numbers there may have to be further withdrawals of sleeping cars for their use, perhaps within the next month."

It was explained by officials of the agency that the objective of the order was solely to obtain more sleepers for the redeployment of the armed forces and not to ration travel or impede it any more than was necessary.

Two days after the directive concerning Pullmans went into effect the director of DOT ordered all coaches, combination cars, and express and baggage cars owned by the railroads pooled for the immediate use of the military. The order involved about 30,000 cars. Explaining his action the director said: "Our men are coming back from Europe faster than we expected. Fifty thousand more men than were actually scheduled to arrive from Europe in June actually reached our home ports in that month." Though dramatic, this new directive merely formalized a procedure that had been in effect for some time.

Responding to the edict on Pullmans, the NYC withdrew 159 Pullmans from its lines. Schedules were altered for four trains on which coaches and parlor cars were substituted for sleepers, but service on other long-distance trains including the *20th Century*, the *Commodore Vanderbilt*, and the *Southwestern Limited* remained as before. *The Montreal Limited*, a night train between New York and Montreal operated in cooperation with the Delaware & Hudson, was canceled. The *Genesee*, a night train between New York and Buffalo, was rescheduled to offer coach and parlor car service on trains leaving Grand Central at 3:45 P. M. and Buffalo at 4:00 P. M. (Figure #16.) No sleepers would henceforth be included on trains between New York and Albany, Utica, Syracuse, Rochester, Buffalo, Lake Placid, Massena, Ogdensburg, Oswego, Malone, Watertown, Boston, Worcester, and Burlington. On July 15, sleeping car space

Figure #16. New York Times, July 18, 1945

New Late Afternoon Schedule

"The Genesee"

to BUFFALO

Albany, Utica,
Syracuse and Rochester

•

To help meet business travel needs due to the discontinuance of sleeping cars on runs of 450 miles or less, under Office of Defense Transportation Order No. 53, *The Genesee*, formerly leaving New York at 11:45 P.M., now leaves at 3:45 P.M. daily.

•

Parlor Car, Coaches and Dining Car

Lv. New York (Grand Central Terminal)	3:45 P.M.
Lv. Harmon	4:36 P.M.
Ar. Albany	6:25 P.M.
Ar. Utica	8:09 P.M.
Ar. Syracuse	9:05 P.M.
Ar. Rochester	10:31 P.M.
Ar. Buffalo	11:45 P.M.

Returning "The Genesee" leaves Buffalo at 4:00 P.M. daily, arriving Grand Central Terminal 12:10 A.M. making the same intermediate stops.

Consult your local agent for other important Time Table changes

NEW YORK CENTRAL

sufficient to accommodate 20,000 persons nightly were transferred to exclusive military use when the railroads handed over to the government 485 Pullman cars.

The day after the Pullman decree took effect the first atomic bomb was exploded at Alamogordo, New Mexico. A bomb was dropped on Hiroshima on August 6 and on Nagasaki on the 9th. The Japanese government surrendered on the 15th, and plans for an invasion were dropped.

As of September 16th, all major restrictions on railroad passenger travel, except the ban on short haul sleeper service was eliminated. Pullmans were needed for several months to bring the boys home. Finally on January 18, 1946, the ODT announced that the ban on civilian use of Pullman cars for trips of less than 450 miles would begin to be lifted on February 15th, when the minimum distance would be reduced to 351 miles. On March 15th this would be lowered to 250 miles, and on March 15th restrictions would be lifted altogether.

Troop movements which reached their peak in December were rapidly decreasing and by March 1 the army would have 1,200 new troop sleepers ready for use.

World War II was over.

17
Postwar Meltdown

Indian Summer

The difference between the situations facing railroads in Europe and in America on the morrow of VJ Day has been cogently set forth by Stephen Goddard. Looking upon railroads as a means of quickly bringing up troops and supplies to the front, European governments, surrounded as they were by hostile neighbors, had nationalized their railroads even before the war. The wholesale destruction inflicted upon the continent's roads and rails by allied bombing had made immediate use impossible. Europe's rebuilders had a clean slate to start with which enabled them to rectify past mistakes in railroad policy. Since governments now owned and operated the railroads, it made sense not to encourage their highway-motor car complexes to undermine the railroads as had happened in the United States.

The fears of American economists that war's end and demobilization would produce a postwar depression were quickly dissipated as the second half of 1945 witnessed the take-off of the biggest spending spree in the nation's history fueled by pent up demand and massive wartime forced savings. Veterans married in droves and bought up houses in Long Island's Levitttown at $6,990 apiece. And Levittown was no isolated phenomenon. Detroit, which moved in step with the home building industry, turned out 2.1 million cars in 1946. Two years later auto production doubled again. Washington's Bureau of Public Roads, its coffers bulging with $624 million unspent, anxiously awaited word to start laying asphalt and concrete. However, the word did not come from President Harry Truman's government, which awarded priority to housing for returning GIs. Moreover, postwar inflation was driving up the price of road building materials and urban rights-of-way. State governments had almost as much as the federal government to spend on roads. So they sprang impatiently into the gap and began building major limited access highways themselves, which destroyed established urban neighborhoods and enabled middle-class commuters to speed to their homes in the sprawling new suburbs unstopped by traffic lights.

Though the honeymoon would not last, the nation's railroads were in excellent fiscal shape at war's end. Their executives, therefore, decided to fight the highway-motor complex, despite the fact that it was being subsidized by the government, for passengers' dollars. Huge sums were spent on lightweight streamlined luxury trains. In a burst of what was to prove unjustified optimism the NYC's historian wrote in 1947:

The Empire State Express *has become a glittering steel projectile in which there are day coaches of a luxury that would startle even the insatiable George H. Daniels, with a seat reserved for your own particular use, though at no extra cost. Leaving New York at 9 A. M., it speeds to Buffalo, splits there into two parts which flash away to Detroit and Cleveland, landing passengers at each place in time to sleep in hotel or home. At the other end of the road, a similar flyer, the* Mercury, *performs the same service between Chicago, Detroit and Cleveland.*

But the Century *and the* Empire *are by no means the NYC's only show trains. There are shoals of them; the* Commodore Vanderbilt, *for example, a seventeen-hour, all-Pullman, New York-Chicago speedster, which does not make a station stop between New York and Toledo, Ohio, and but for the Century's dominance, would be a world marvel. No less than thirty-five named trains streak to and from each way daily over the New York-Chicago course or parts of it, some diverging to St. Louis; while others ply between Cleveland and St. Louis, Cleveland, and Cincinnati and Chicago. All are air conditioned, of course; that has long since become an ordinary but expensive requisite of fast train travel, and all are equipped with the latest types of mellow yet adequate lighting.*

Early in 1946, the Central announced a $56,000,000 order for new passenger cars, 720 of them, to be distributed among 52 trains, including the Century, *which is to be completely rehabilitated. There will be greater luxury than ever before, including public address and telephone equipment, for announcing stations, calling attention to points of interest by the way, car-to-car and train-to-train communication, etc. . . . The summer of 1946 saw the inauguration of through sleeping car service to greater distances than ever before; New York to California; New York to Mexico.* [1]

One could leave New York at 11:00 P. M. on March 31 on the *Iroquois* and arrive at San Francisco at 9:20 A.M. April 4 on the *Overland Limited,* operated jointly by the Chicago & Northwestern and the Union Pacific. Similar service to Los Angeles was available on the NYC's *20th Century* and the Santa Fe's *Chief.* The DL&W, flush with wartime profits, announced the expenditure of $5,000,000 to equip all its Hoboken-Buffalo passenger trains with completely modernized air-conditioned, streamlined cars. In the fall of 1949 the *Lackawanna Limited* was renamed *Phoebe Snow* and received a wholly new diesel-pulled consist. (Figure #1.) For a time at least these trains were money-makers. After all, travelers can't sleep overnight and dine in style in a Ford. For a postwar pile-up of the streamlined NYC *Ohio State Limited,* see Figure #2.

It was love's labor lost, as the drift to the auto became a landslide. In his study of the decline of the intercity passenger train, Donald M. Itzkoff writes:

It soon became apparent that the railroads would have to begin the postwar years with a handicap: no new equipment. As a result of strikes in the key supply industries of copper, steel, coal, and electrical equipment, plus shortages of critical parts, uneven production in the years after World War II led to poorly balanced inventories, stalled assembly lines, rising costs, and ruptured customer relations. These bottlenecks hit railroad equipment manufacturers particularly hard. Practically a national scandal because of the wear of the war years, the railroads needed additional locomotives and new rolling stock, and had 2682 passenger coaches alone on order. According to reliable estimates, the railroad equipment industry possessed a production capacity in excess of 4000 cars per year. By the third quarter of 1946, the equipment man-

Figure #1. Phoebe Snow, Taber, DL&W in the 20th Century, 4

Figure #2. Wreck of the Cleveland Limited, Buffalo Evening News, December 29, 1965

ufacturers had delivered only 285 new coaches to the railroads. In Philadelphia, the Budd Company had targeted production of 9000 passenger coaches, but finished only 60 of them by September of that year. At Pullman Co., Inc., a shortage of electrical components such as lighting fixtures, transformers, and generators held up over 90 nearly completed passenger cars worth $7.5 million. Unable to replace worn-out coaches and aging steamers with stainless-steel streamliners and brand new diesel-electric locomotives, the railroad industry failed to cash in on the anticipated postwar boom. By the time the equipment backlog eased in the late 1940s, the air lines had already carved out a solid market share with war surplus DC-3s. Detroit too mobilized to introduce its post-war models. Beaten at the staring gate, the railroads would never catch up. [2]

Railroad passenger losses rose five times from 1946 to 1953. Thirty percent of passenger rail trackage was abandoned from 1947 to 1957. The 112,000 miles left were down nearly 85,000 miles since that category began to be reported to the ICC in 1941. According to Itzkoff, by 1949 "red ink in the rail passenger business reached $649 million. Losses in passengers wiped out almost half of freight net revenue, the main source of railroad income."

Railroaders knew that their only salvation lay with freight, which had traditionally made up for passenger train losses. But truckers could haggle with shippers and reach an agreement with them with a handshake. As common carriers, truckers could be regulated by the state, according to the doctrine in *Munn v. Illinois*. But many trucking companies which were really common carriers masquerading as contract carriers to a limited number of firms successfully evaded state regulation with the blessing of the Supreme Court in the mid-1920s. The Motor Carriers Act of 1935 regulated the rates of only that one-fifth of trucking companies deemed common carriers. Railroads, on the other hand, had to get ICC permission to modify their charges which might take months or even years, by which time the entire situation might have changed. Several dozen railroads initiated overnight service of up to 450 miles for the lucrative less-than-carload trade. It was another love's labor lost. The bottom had fallen out of the LCL business by 1965. When truckers came up with highway racks each carrying five new cars from Detroit to the dealers the railroads, whose boxcars could carry four cars at most and were clumsy to load, watched another major customer depart. By 1958 less than ten percent of new cars were shipped by rail. Handcuffed by unbelievable regulations, freight lines ended up by default with long-distance, low-profit bulk shipments like ore, coal, and grain.

Dieselization

The most noticeable development on the railroad front immediately after World War II was dieselization, a process that was completed by the mid-1950s, by which time even coal roads like the Norfolk & Western and the Chesapeake & Ohio had given up on the steam engine. This rapid change in railroad motive power has been described by Maury Klein in the American Heritage of Invention & Technology:

The diesel engine, invented and patented by Rudolf Diesel in 1893, employs internal combustion to convert liquid fuel into mechanical energy far more cheaply and efficiently than a steam engine. Early diesels were stationary engines, but by 1910 Germany and Britain had installed diesels in submarines. The first diesel-engine to pull a passenger train was manufactured in 1921. Railroads, the oldest, largest, and most tradition-bound industry in America, were slow to make use of this new technology since they had so much capital tied up in the steam engine. By the 1920s, however, the steam locomotive was nearing the limit of its capabilities. Under attack by autos, trucks, buses, airplanes, barges, and pipelines, railroads needed to cut costs. Developments in electrical technology had made it possible to adapt the constant-speed diesel to the variable speed requirements of a locomotive (the so-called diesel is actually a diesel-electric) and strong light-weight alloys were making possible diesel engines small enough to be installed in a locomotive.

Klein compares the two power sources with special reference to railroads:

The steam locomotive could not be easily started up but first had to get up a head of steam. Even then its speed was difficult to regulate smoothly. Stopping was also difficult and wore out brake shoes quickly. A steam engine could run only a hundred miles or so without stopping for fuel and water. On grades it could not use full speed efficiently and often required helper engines [each of which required a two-man crew]. Heavy engines were hard on rails, especially on curves, and required costly maintenance. The shopwork on steam locomotives was intense, difficult and time-consuming. Most new parts had to be custom-made in the shop.

The diesel offered striking improvements in absolutely every area. It started and stopped on command and could maintain whatever speed was needed for peak efficiency. It required no stops for water and could run for five or six hundred miles between fuelings. Low axle loadings, uniform wheel torques, and freedom from "pounding" made diesels easier on rails and allowed them to take curves at higher speeds. On grades full power was available at any track speed, and engines could be doubled to increase power without the use of helpers. Many functions such as oiling, which had been done manually on steam power, could be performed automatically. The diesel could handle heavier trains at higher average speeds. At terminals it turned around quickly, required far less servicing, and used standardized parts. Mechanical advances during the 1920s raised the thermal efficiency of steam locomotives - the portion of the energy in their fuel that they could make useful - from about 5 percent to 10 percent. Impressive as this achievement was, it paled before the 33 to 40 percent level of the diesel. "For all the romance that surrounds it," wrote one authority, "the steam locomotive was a relatively primitive form of converter." [3]

In the mid-1930s the Burlington and the Union Pacific developed diesel-hauled streamliners that shortened the run between Chicago and the Pacific Coast by a whole day; and in 1941 the Santa Fe made the newspapers by sending a freight train pulled by a giant 5,400 horsepower diesel engine from Chicago to Los Angeles. Steam engines on this run had needed thirty-five stops for water and fuel and nine engine changes. The diesel required only five stops. World War II brought diesel production to a halt, but after 1946 the diesel swept all before it. In 1941 there were 41,911 steam engines and only 1,517 diesels on the rosters of American railroads. By 1961 there were 30,123 diesels and 210 steamers in service. Without economies produced by dieselization, the railroads would have been even less able than they were to cope with the dead hand of ICC regulation, subsidized highway transportation, and labor union obstinacy.

Unfortunately, savings made possible by dieselization were negated by labor union intransigence. As Itzkoff explains it:

With broad federal protection, the more than two dozen railway labor unions extracted lucrative concessions from management. Interdivisional and interseniority district rules limited not only the runs to which train crews could be assigned but also the regions in which they could operate. Mileage restrictions and constructive payment allowances forced management to compensate operating employees by the number of miles traveled per shift.

Since a "basic day" equaled the average distance attained in 1919 (approximately 100 miles for engineers and 150 for conductors), train crews routinely received overtime pay for exceeding old standards with new equipment. States imposed full-crew laws. Craft jurisdictional lines and job protection clauses hampered efficiency in the repair shops. Rail labor impeded the introduction of new technology such as diesel locomotives, centralized traffic control, maintenance of way machinery, automatic freight yards, and computerization. Even relatively inoffensive restrictions like full-crew laws forced railroad management to run longer trains in order to save money, thus resulting in increased delays, slower speeds, and poorer service to disenchanted customers. [4]

Terrace Relocation

The long simmering dispute between the city and the NYC over relocation of street level trackage on the Terrace boiled over after the end of World War II. As noted in a 1946 decision of the Supreme Court, Appellate Division, Fourth Department:

In the year 1896 as result of the work of the Grade Crossing and Terminal Station Commission of the City of Buffalo, the crossing of Main Street and the route of part of the line across the Terrace was sunk into a tunnel partly covered and partly uncovered; arising out of the tunnel to street grade in the Terrace the railroad lines and tracks turn west from the Terrace into Church Street, and from Church Street along the lake and waterfront toward the northern part of the City known as "Black Rock" and toward Niagara Falls [Figure IX, #24]. . . In 1925 the New York Central entered into a contract with the Grade Crossing and Terminal Station Commission of the City of Buffalo, now succeeded by the Public Service Commission (L. 1946, c. 902), which contract provided for the elimination of the tracks in the Terrace, the construction of a new passenger station in East Buffalo, some two miles from the then location of the main station, and for the construction at the expense of the railroad company (appellant herein) of a new downtown station [on the site of the Exchange Street Station]. . . .

After the execution of this contract, the new main station was erected at East Buffalo, but neither the elimination of the Terrace tracks nor the construction of the new downtown station was performed. The crossings along the Terrace and Church Street have long been regarded as dangerous and in 1929 proceedings were begun which resulted in the first order of the Commission covering the "Terrace Elimination Project." In 1940 the Commission issued a revised order determining the method of elimination to be followed and directed the railroad company to submit plans. These plans were submitted in 1941 and were approved by the Commission on September 23, 1941. Revised plans were submitted by the railroad company in 1944 and 1945. Both of these plans, those of 1941 and of 1944-45, showed as projected in connection with the elimination the construction of a new station and a new signal system as now ordered. The 1941 plans contained no notations which could be regarded as expressing the thought of the railroad as to who should bear the expense of construction of station and of signal system, but on the revised plans of 1944-45, evidently with reference to the questions now involved, the railroad company noted on such revised plans the following: "All work shown in this plan is necessary for the elimination of grade crossings," "no railroad improvements," "no railroad improvements except increased weight of rails, if any." [5]

Since 1925, Section 14 of Article 7 of the State Constitution had required the state to provide 50 percent and the railroad 50 percent of the cost of grade crossing eliminations ordered by the Public Service Commission.

This was changed in 1938 as explained by Peter Galie in his guide to the New York State Constitution:

Prior constitutional amendments had brought little progress toward the elimination of railroad grade crossings, either because the railroads were financially unable or were simply unwilling to bear their costs of the elimination. Those costs had been set at 50 percent. This section, which some referred to as the railroad relief amendment, was based on the assumption that the railroads could not pay the 50 percent. It required the state to bear the cost of all projects begun after January 1, 1939, except that the state was permitted to seek reimbursement, not to exceed 15 percent of the expense involved, for improvements that resulted in a net benefit to the railroads. [6]

The NYC argued that the new station and signal system were essential parts of the grade crossing elimination project and that therefore the state should pay the whole cost for both. The argument was a strong one since relocating the tracks away from the Terrace Station made it and the old signal system useless. The engineer for the Grade Crossing and Terminal Commission told the *Buffalo Evening News* that "the Central is not so much concerned with the extra price for betterments, but is afraid that a precedent will be established which will affect its costs in other projected grade-crossing eliminations in the state." The state argued that the station and the signaling system were not part of grade-crossing elimination and that for the state to pay for these improvements was against Section 8, Article 7 of the Constitution which prohibited the state from giving or loaning money in aid of any individual, association, or corporation.

The Appellate Division ruled against the NYC which took its case to the Court of Appeals. On March 18, 1948, the Court dismissed the appeal and ordered "the matter remitted to the Appellate Division with directions to dismiss the appeal taken to that court" which was declared "without jurisdiction to review the order of the commission because the order did not affect a substantial right of the appellant." The state's highest court called for "a hearing de novo with respect to the extent to which the plans include railroad improvements and the nature and cost thereof." The matter was not brought before the courts again, and a groundbreaking ceremony was held on November 16, 1949, with Governor Thomas E. Dewey in the stellar role. A past president of Buffalo's Chamber of Commerce rashly predicted that "this event will rank in historical significance with the opening of the Erie Canal in 1825, the completion of the first through railroad connection in 1843, and the bringing of electrical energy from Niagara Falls to Buffalo in 1896."

Buffalo Business for November, 1950, reported the project as 40 percent completed. The general contract amounted to $4,112,571. In addition, the NYC was spending about a million dollars on tracks and signals and a further $124,715 on a new Exchange Street Station. Evidently, the railroad had failed to force the state to pay for this construction. The 1896 tunnel under Main Street had to be entirely rebuilt. The new tunnel, called Tunnel A, extended from the east side of Main Street to the west side of Pearl Street and came closer to Memorial Auditorium than its predecessor. Tunnel B further north carried the tracks under Erie Street and Perry Boulevard. The new station, located on the south side of Exchange Street slightly east of the end of Ellicott, was fifty-five feet long and fifty feet wide. Vehicles reached it on a forty foot wide roadway curving in from Exchange Street. Between the station and the two tracks on the south side of the station was a platform one hundred feet long and twelve feet wide for westbound passengers, extending west to the Washington Street Bridge. An eastbound platform of the same size was reached by stairs and an overhead pedestrian bridge over the tracks. A 1951 photograph (Figure #3) shows that track relocation was contemporaneous with construction by the Buffalo Municipal Housing Authority of a slum clearance project known as Dante Place, which had been planned before the war but, like the relocation project, could not begin until afterwards. Groundbreaking ceremonies were held on October 10, 1950. As a result of these two projects, the geography of the area south of Erie Street and west of Main Street was completely changed.

"A long civic struggle ended today as the first train traveled the relocated NYC tracks and a new downtown passenger station was opened to the public," announced the August 8, 1952, News. About a hundred persons, including Buffalo railroad officials, civic dignitaries, and representatives of the State Department of Public Works were on hand for the ceremony. Mayor Joseph Mruck cut the red, white, and blue ribbon stretched across the station doorway and fatuously proclaimed, "This is another important milestone of civic progress in the history of Buffalo." Herman Hopf, an employee of the railroad for fifty-two years, who had been station agent at the Terrace Station since 1937, took over at Exchange Street. The first train to use what the mayor had called "this beautiful new building which will enhance the architectural beauty of the area" was the 12:30 P. M. TH&B train from Toronto.

The New York State Thruway

The long-standing hostility of governments, state and federal, toward the railroads reached new heights in the decade or so immediately after World War II. Even before the war was over, Governor Thomas E. Dewey, on January 31, 1945, proposed to the legislature a New York-Buffalo toll road, a project which had been suggested by his predecessor, Herbert H. Lehman, but delayed by the war. A year later, on July 11, 1946, Dewey turned the first spadeful of earth for this 486 mile long superhigh-

Figure #3. *Ibid.*, December 1, 1951

Figure #4. *Courier-Express*, April 15, 1958

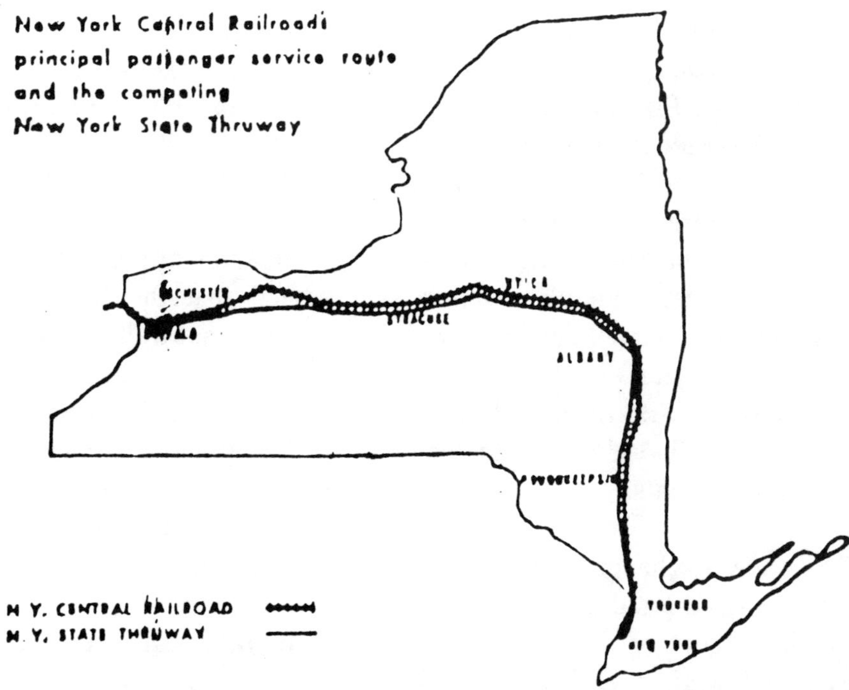

Thruway, New York Central run parallel

way to be completed in 1950 through the Hudson and Mohawk Valleys to Lake Erie, paralleling the NYC all the way. (Figure #4.) Along this concrete ribbon, cars would speed at seventy miles an hour, which must have seemed like motorists' heaven to residents of a state whose speed limit at the time was fifty. Estimated cost was $202 million.

Both the price tag and the completion date proved excessively optimistic. By the summer of 1950 at the time of the outbreak of the Korean War only sixteen miles had been completed, twenty-four were under contract, and 200 were in the planning and survey state. The soaring price of materials and labor had deterred contractors from entering agreements they might live to regret. Creation of a Thruway Authority in 1950 with the right to issue bonds on the credit of the state moved construction along. Finally, the New York State Thruway was opened along its entire length from near the Bronx-Westchester line to Buffalo on December 15, 1955. By this time costs had risen to $962 million, twice the estimate as late as 1951. The most expensive item was the Tappan Zee Bridge across the lower Hudson at $65 million. The second most expensive section, after the New England Section in Westchester County, was the Niagara Spur at the Buffalo end of the Thruway which cost $4,310,000. In October, 1954, the Thruway Authority paid $6.95 million for the Lehigh Valley's 4.25 mile spur into downtown Buffalo. The Authority agreed to preserve rail service for all but two customers of the railroad and to buy those two out. The chairman of the Authority claimed that an alternate route would have taken a year longer, involved extensive property damage, and forced the eviction of from 600 to 1,000 homeowners.

The LV spent $1.45 million of what it had received for its Buffalo extension to built a combination passenger station and divisional office building at its East Side yards at Dingens and South Ogden Streets on the outskirts of the city, another small step in the decline of downtown Buffalo. Moving into either the DL&W or the NYC stations had been an option, but the rent asked by both roads was too high. Land not needed for the Thruway on Washington Street was sold by the Authority to the News for its main office and plant. Former LV land on Main Street across from Memorial Auditorium was sold to the state for the state office building. The new LV terminal consisted of a brick and glass station, an LCL freight house, canopied dead-end terminal tracks, and facilities for servicing engines and passenger cars. (Figure #5.) It was opened on August 11, 1955 and remained in service less than six years.

The NYC's new Exchange Street Station which had been opened amid such hoopla in 1952 was another victim of the extension of the Thruway into downtown Buffalo in 1959. The pedestrian bridge over the tracks and the platform and canopy on the east-bound side were knocked down to make way for an approach to the elevated highway. Arguing that the property around the station was "so severed by bridges, ramps, approaches, that it is worth less from a real estate standpoint," the NYC asked Buffalo's Board of Assessors to reduce by $1 million its valuation on the tract bounded by Washington, Main, Exchange, and Scott Streets. Though it had originally been a twenty-four hour operation, the little station by now was closed on weekends and open on weekdays only from 9:00 A. M. to 6:00 P. M.

In September, 1958, the NYC received permission from the ICC to eliminate six name trains, the most drastic reduction of passenger service yet made by the company. The fact that the number of passengers carried by the NYC had dropped thirty-three percent since the opening of the Thruway and forty-seven percent since the opening of the Massachusetts Pike (Figure #6) convinced the ICC, which often gave too much consideration to complainants, that this step was necessary. Once proud names bit the dust. The *20th Century* was consolidated with the Commodore *Vanderbilt*, the *5th Avenue Special* with the *Cleveland Limited*, and the *Ohio State Limited* with the *Knickerbocker*. The road had lost $52 million in 1957, a $1 million a week. On January 25, 1958, Robert Young, depressed by the NYC's deteriorating condition, committed suicide.

Readers of the September 12, 1959, *News* learned that the NYC would eliminate six more name trains, including four serving Buffalo, when Eastern Standard Time went into effect on October 26. Elimination was once again by way of consolidation. Forthcoming amalgamations were the *Chicagoan* with the *Tuscarora*, and the *Upstate Special* with the *Hendrick Hudson*.

The Interstate Defense Highway System

As if the harm done to the railroads by the state's highway building program was not enough, the federal government began to get into the act. Dwight D. Eisenhower had been impressed by the military as well as civilian potential of Adolph Hitler's *Autobahnen*. He wanted something similar for America to be built under federal auspices because it was a national project. It would also create jobs, identify a national highway system with himself, and answer his critics who were complaining that he was a do-nothing president. In 1955 he called upon Congress to provide the staggering sum of $5 billion annually for ten years for an interstate superhighway system to be financed by bond issues backed by increases in gas and tire taxes. His bill passed in the Senate but failed in the House where the Democrats favored higher taxes on the trucking industry rather than bonds.

Next year, however, the measure passed because of the creation of a diversion-proof (for over twenty years anyway) Highway Trust Fund, what Goddard calls "the political version of a perpetual motion machine." Federal

Figure #5. LV's Dingens Street Station, <u>Courier-Express</u>, August 3, 1955; floor plan, Archer, <u>Lehigh Valley</u>, 268-269

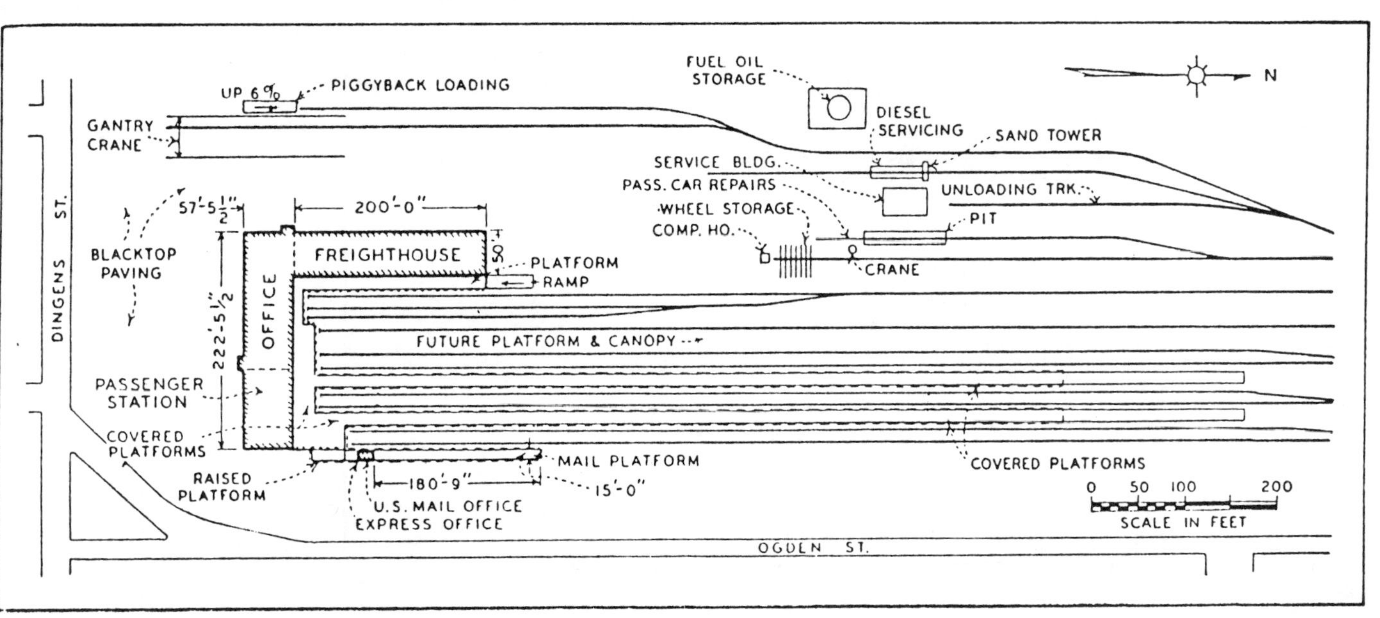

Figure #6. NYC passenger revenue in millions of dollars. Courier-Express, April 15, 1958

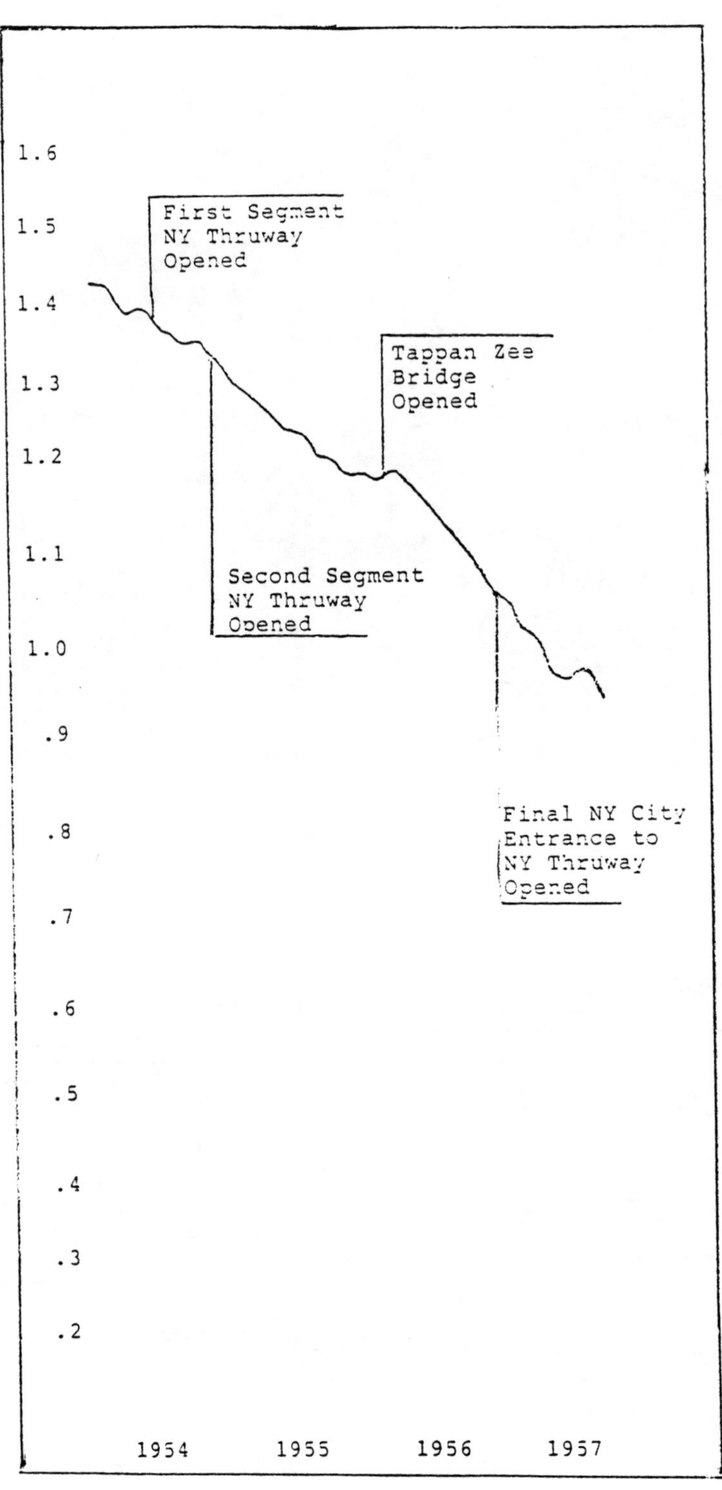

taxes on gasoline and truck tires would be funneled into a fund from which the program's directors could appropriate money for superhighway construction without further congressional authorization. The federal government provided overall planning and contributed ninety percent of the cost. Individual states were to provide the rest. The 42,500 mile system (Figure #7) was ninety-three percent complete by the end of 1978, and its total cost, due to inflation and design change, had risen to $100 billion. Forgetting that as far as intercity transport was concerned it was railroads, not trucks, that had won World War II, Congress called its creation "The National System of Interstate and Defense Highways." What the Thruway had done for New York State's railroads, the Interstate System would do for those of the nation. In the discussions which had led up to both projects almost no attention was paid to their impact on the nation's railroads. Helen Leavitt in <u>Superhighway-Superhoax</u> called it "the largest single public works project ever undertaken by man."

We're Still Number Two

Ernest E. Momberger, manager of the transportation department of the Buffalo Chamber of Commerce, defended Buffalo's oft reiterated claim to being the largest railroad center in the United States after Chicago in the November 10, 1954, *Courier Express*. He readily conceded that, measured by the number of carriers serving each city, Buffalo was surpassed by Saint Louis, Kansas City, and Minneapolis. "Measured by the quantity or origin and destination [of] freight and passengers," he also awarded the palm to several other cities. But by the "true yardstick of greatness," which was "the volume of freight and passenger traffic that moves from, to and through the Niagara Frontier," Buffalo was clearly Number One. He insisted that Buffalo's "location astride the general east-west flow of commerce and of international

Figure #7. Interstate Defense Highway System

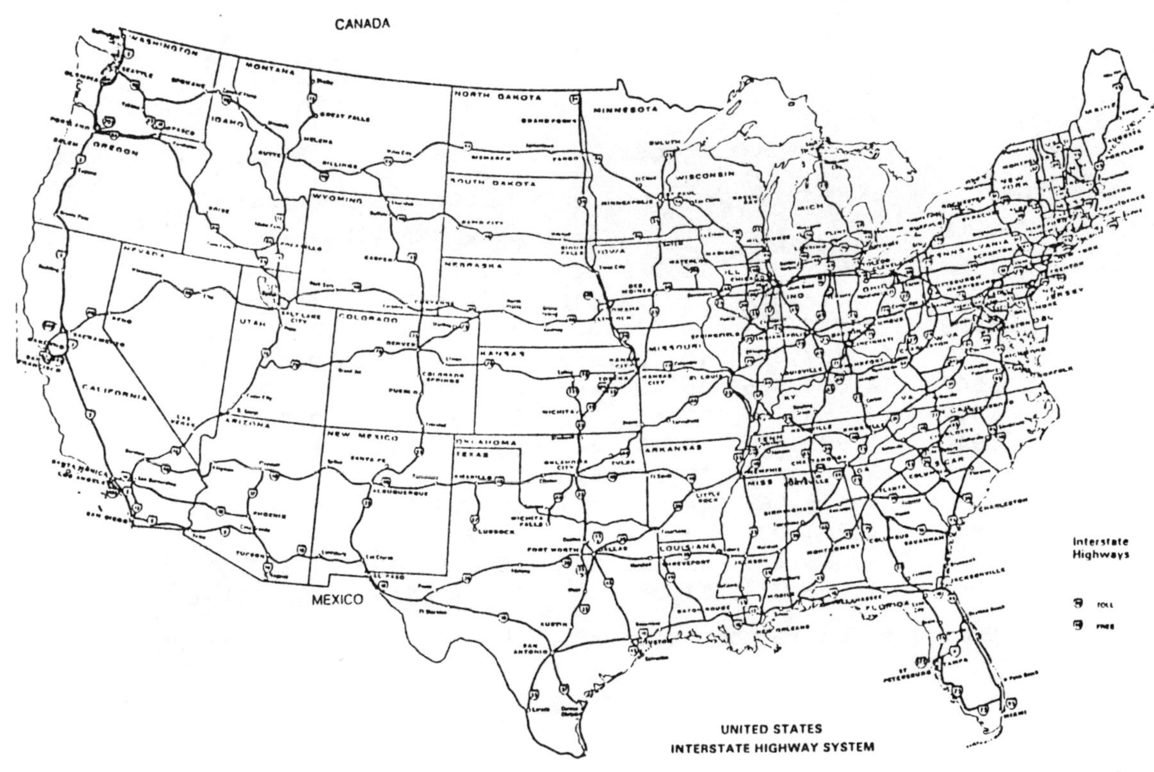

trade between industrial Canada and the United States" supported Buffalo's claim to second place and "spikes the boasts of the pretenders." He pointed out that "commerce crossing the Ohio, Missouri, Mississippi and Potomac Rivers is divided among a number of cities, and there is no convincing proof that the volume which passes through any one crossing can equal anywhere that of the Buffalo-Niagara Falls gateway." Momberger provided tonnage figures of inbound and outbound rail commerce and of water commerce from 1941 to 1953. Water commerce was not segregated into in and out bound, but he added that "receipts of waterborne commerce predominate over shipments by a large margin because of the heavy inbound movement of raw materials for the steel plants, grain for elevators and flour mills, and coal for generating electric power and other purposes." "The end product of these raw materials," he said, "make up a substantial part of the outbound tonnage of the railroads." The peak year for waterborne commerce in tonnage was 1941 and for combined rail shipments was 1944. (Table #9.)

But what Momberger added about trucks did not bode well for the railroads:

No tonnage figures of truck transportation in and out of Buffalo ever have been tabulated and it would be difficult to estimate the volume. It is substantial, and the impact of that form of transportation has fallen almost 100 percent on the railroads. In 1953 railroads hauled 52.5 percent of the ton miles of commercial freight traffic in the county. In 1930 they hauled 75 per cent and in 1944 69.4 percent. Comparable figures for truck transportation show 3.9 percent in 1930 and 17.1 in 1953. Oil pipe lines also show an increase in ton-mile volume from 5.4 per cent of the total in 1930 to 14.5 per cent in 1953.

Buffalo Passenger Train Service, 1945-1970

The effect of these hostile developments on

Table #9

Year	Railroads in	out	total	Water combined
1953	14,204,560	11,326,051	25,530,611*	22,008,987
1952	14,217,972	11,322,119	25,540,091	19,383,974
1951	14,113,836	11,563,046	25,676,882	21,950,718
1950	12,706,697	9,924,878	22,631,575	20,375,224
1949	11,487,095	10,181,552	21,668,647	19,799,895
1948	14,594,635	10,496,893	25,091,528	20,257,130
1947	14,363,077	11,867,663	26,230,740	20,005,372
1946	12,889,072	10,107,449	23,996,521	16,150,366
1945	13,765,835	13,965,415	27,731,250	23,127,699
1944	14,435,063	14,588,312	29,023,375	23,360,759
1943	14,794,037	13,924,397	28,718,434	21,718,917
1942	14,026,195	12,222,907	26,249,102	23,312,501
1941	11,696,278	11,055,070	22,751,348	24,338,876

[* indicates where Momberger's arithmetic has been corrected.]

the nation's passenger service can be seen in Figure XI, #10. The 1945 figure of 897,384,000 miles can be ignored since the war lasted until August of that year. From 794,824,000 miles in 1946 the count dropped to 440,770,000 in 1954 and 304,000,000 in 1967. This decline fed on itself, as Itzkoff observes:

Attempting to save money, railroads downgraded service. Paper headrests on the back of coach seats replaced cotton ones. Window washing on many runs at halfway points ended, as did the vacuuming of coach interiors en route. Running water for drinking and lavatories disappeared. Management discontinued coach attendant service on lesser trains, and the courtesy of railway employees declined. Once prestigious flyers added coaches to the consist for the first time. Other trains dropped chair cars, lounge cars, and observation cars. Adding insult to injury, fares continued to increase as well. [7]

Diners lost money, as always, because of the labor-intensive nature of the service, which required a crew twice as large as a restaurant in order to serve a given number of people. When wages for cooks doubled and for waiters tripled from the late 1930s to the postwar period, the increased costs hurt the railroads badly. As one dining car executive commented, "The fewer people we can manage to feed on a railroad dining car, the lower our losses are." Deficits in the diners reached nearly $30 million in 1957, despite such cost-cutting measures as the introduction of paper napkins and tablecloths, the elimination of finger bowls, doilies, and silver flatware, and substantial reductions in waiter service. Passengers objected to automatic vending machines, club-type grill cars, and worst of all, the cafeteria car.

This decline was, of course, mirrored locally. Total train movements in Buffalo dropped from 172 in 1943, (this was a war-time figure and several of the trains listed for that year often ran in multiple sections) to 124 in 1954, and to 67 in 1967, by which time only the NYC (65) and the Erie-Lackawanna (2) were running any trains at all, the PRR, LV, B&O, and NKP having dropped out of the picture completely, and the Erie and the DL&W having merged to form the Erie-Lackawanna. Table #10.

At about 10:00 P. M. on March 3, 1953, several thirty-five foot lengths of eighteen inch iron pipe which had been improperly secured fell from a gondola car on an eastbound Pittsburgh-Buffalo freight two miles east of Conneaut, Ohio. One pipe bent the north section of the westbound passenger (inside) track over which a few moments later a westbound passenger train, #5, doing eighty miles an hour, passed and was derailed. At that very moment, #5 was passing a westbound Buffalo-Chicago freight. The derailment of the locomotive of #5 threw it into the westbound freight, fifteen cars of which were derailed as were eleven cars on the passenger train. Before warning flares could be put out, eastbound #12, the *Southwest Limited*, likewise doing eighty miles an hour, piled into the wreckage of the two trains. About 400 persons were involved in this triple train wreck in which twenty-two died, two from Buffalo, and 150 were injured, five from Erie County. Casualties would have been much higher if wooden cars had been involved. Forty-nine passengers and 343 employees were killed in 1953 on America's railroads.

President Perlman of the NYC had some bad news for the New York Society of Security Analysts according to the financial editor of the News in October, 1954. Whereas Perlman's road currently had four to six tracks on its Buffalo-New York main-line, this abundant capacity, which went back to the days of Cornelius Vanderbilt and his son William H., would soon be cut to two tracks to save money. The move, which the president described as "a modernization program," would force all freight and passenger trains to use single east and westbound tracks. Centralized Train

Table #10

1954

Railroad	Expresses	Locals	Total
NYC	(37)	-	(37)
LS&MS	(32)	-	(32)
MC	(11)	-	(11)
B&NF	-	(10)	(10)
TH&B	(8)	-	(8)
New York Central	88	10	98
PRR	4	-	4
B&O	-	2	
DL&W	8	-	8
NKP	4	-	4
LV	(6)	-	(6)
D&T	(2)	-	(2)
Lehigh Valley	8	-	8
Grand Total	112	12	124

1967

Road	Expresses	Locals	Total
NYC	(20)	-	(20)
LS&MS	(32)	-	(32)
MC	(11)	-	(11)
TH&B	(2)	-	(2)
New York Central	65	-	65
Erie-Lackawanna	2	-	2
Grand Total	67	-	67

Control (CTC) was a method of dispatching trains developed in the 1920s which enabled a single dispatcher to set signals and switches electronically in order to utilize track more efficiently and so operate with less trackage. On the occasion of the opening of a $6,238,460 electronic control system for two tracks on the NYC between Buffalo and Cleveland, the *New York Times* for January 16, 1957, explained how CTC worked:

The installation, the longest of its type in the world, permits full control of train movements on the line from remote points through a series of electronic devices. It will enable the road to abandon two tracks without losing any track capacity. Trains moving over the double track system can operate in either direction on either track at high speeds while under constant observation and control of the dispatcher located at Erie, the mid-way point on the division. Two dispatchers seated at huge control panels at Erie direct the traffic over the entire 163-mile stretch.

With CTC, freight trains can travel at sixty miles per hour instead of the usual thirty. Cross-overs from one track to another have been installed every seven miles to allow dispatchers to move trains when they meet from one track to another as frequently as necessary. Under the old system, dispatchers could only cross over trains every twenty miles. Dispatchers will be able to run fast express trains around slower freights or give preference to the roads "name" passenger trains.

Mr. Perlman said that safeguards installed in the system provided the Central with the "world's safest stretch of traffic." He said a leverman could not throw a wrong switch and an engineer could not fail to obey a signal without the train coming to an automatic stop.

What the president failed to mention was that four tracks worked better in the case of stalled trains and derailments or that cutting trackage in half would reduce maintenance and lower property valuation for purposes of taxation. Eliminating two tracks was one step in the NYC's economy drive made necessary by its declining passenger and freight business. NYC officials in Buffalo pointed out that the NYWS&B had cut back from two tracks to one in the 1930s to save money. NYC's 1954 loadings were lower than in the depths of the Depression in 1933.

Other Perlman economy moves were closing the diesel servicing depot in East Buffalo, built only recently at a cost of $3 million, and slimming down the work force in Buffalo from about 700 to 100. Overall, Perlman said in November, 1954, pointing to the "great duplication of facilities on the railroad," that the NYC's payroll has been slashed by 27,000 employees during the last year, 14,500 of these in the last three months. "Central's supervisory echelons," he explained redundantly, "are needlessly overstaffed." Attempting to end on a high note, the president said, "We hope to look to a black figure on passenger operations when we get high speed lightweight trains on the railroad." The NYC's experience with lightweight trains during the '50s and '60s was to prove universally disastrous. (Figure #8.) Well might Perlman spread gloom. In 1955, the year after he became president, the company's stock plunged from 49 1/2 to 15 1/2.

Another economy move was construction of the $10 million Frontier Yard announced by L. W. Horning, Vice-President of personnel, on March 6, 1956. As reported the next day in the *Courier Express*:

In disclosing cost of the project, Horning said the completed yard will be the most modern in the nation. "We will be able to save from 14 to 20 hours time on every freight car moving through the Buffalo district," Horning declared. He said that when the plan was first discussed more than a year ago, NYC engineers traveled all over the country studying every available modern phase of classification yard systems. The planned Buffalo yard will eliminate every mistake encountered in other centers studied, he said.

Figure #8. Two failures: the Aerotrain (1956) and a gas-turbine trainset (1967). Author's collection

The new center, to combine seven yards used to switch cars and make up trains, will occupy 170 acres of NYC-owned land north of the main tracks and extending eastward from a point one mile east of Central Terminal to Harlem Rd. Three groups of receiving and departure tracks will be located as follows: one east of and in line with the classification yard, one on the yard's north side, and the third on the south side. The 27 tracks will have a combined capacity of 2,760 freight cars.

Fifteen receiving and departure tracks, with a capacity of 1,380 cars, will be used to receive trains for switching. The yard is designed to receive and switch 2,000 to 3,000 cars daily. Drafts of cars for switching will be moved to the crest of a hump either by straight shoves from the east receiving tracks, or by pullbacks from the north and south receiving tracks. The car retarding (car speed control) and switching system will be electronically controlled. Adequate communication will be furnished by talkback speakers, yard radios, communicating signals and telephones.

The yard will include an 85-car capacity repair facility for 24-hour operation to eliminate or curtail car delays. A 60-pen stockyard, served by required chutes, is provided in the old West Shore yard area. There will also be an 18-car servicing platform for in-transit hogs. West Shore tracks are rearranged to provide a 250-car capacity cleaning yard to prepare cars for feed, flour and grain loadings.

Sixty-three tracks are provided in seven 9-track groups with lengths varying from 30 to 70 cars, except that each of the three north tracks has 120-car capacity for the makeup of eastbound and westbound trains. Total capacity of the classification yard tracks will be 3,110 cars. A 2-story building with tower, located at the hump, will house control panel and machines for tower operations. Control panel and equipment for automatic switching machine will be in this building, as well as room for hump crews, hump clerks and car inspectors.

Another 2-story retarder building with tower will contain offices for yard officials, automatic retarding system controls and equipment, and communication and signal shop space. A third 2-story building with tower at the west end will house crew facilities and a 59-room YMCA and cafeteria.

Frontier Yard was opened a year later on March 14, 1957. In an article entitled "The Shuffle at Buffalo is Done Electronically Now" the *New York Times* reported Perlman's prophecy at the dedication that the new facility "would enable the Central to move freight through Buffalo in a quarter of the time previously taken." The yard, which replaced eight outmoded yards, including the one at Gardenville, "is so efficient," the president claimed, "that it will save shippers 223,000 car days a year." He expected it to reduce the road's operating expenses by $4.5 million annually and thus pay for itself in slightly more than two years. Frontier, which was adjacent to the NYC's mainline over which an average of sixty-seven freight trains arrived in Buffalo daily, was the first of the NYC's electronic yards, but the company had two more under construction, one at Elkhart, Indiana, and another at Youngstown, Ohio, at a total cost of $20 million. Clearly Perlman was willing to spend money to save money.

Some major improvement in the service rendered local businesses by the NYC and Buffalo's other railroads was clearly indicated. A few days after the dedication of the Frontier Yard, the Buffalo Corn Exchange, representing all the area feed, grain, and flour milling industries, charged in a letter to the presidents of the ten railroads entering Buffalo, as reprinted in the *Courier Express*, that freight service on all of them was very bad. This was a flat denial of Perlman's assertion at the ceremony that his road was "absolutely current" in handling freight cars. The members of the Exchange said, on the contrary, that "loaded grain cars that should have been moved promptly have set in one particular railroad's yard [the new NYC yard] for a week at a time." Electronic controls, it was pointed out, "can never be a cure-all for service problems of the railroads." The letter continued in a somewhat garbled fashion:

It cannot be denied that the service in the Buffalo terminal is in the worst shape than ever in the memory of the members of the Exchange. Loaded cars billed to a destination on one railroad have ended up weeks later at a destination on another railroad. There have been instances where cars loaded at a plant on the NYC for a direct-line haul to destination on that railroad [would] have made better time by loading the cars to the destination via other carriers.

Even the handling of paperwork by the railroads was "confused and delayed to the extent that our members are severely hampered. For our members to trace a car has become an insurmountable task." The missive concluded in very strong language that "the effects of these conditions are far-reaching. Customers of our members in the East are constantly complaining about the delays in deliveries which has almost caused shutdowns in their plants."

The NYC had eighteen Beeliners, some of which had gone into local service on the Buffalo Niagara Falls run in September 1951. Beeliner was the popular name for an RDC (Rail-Diesel Car), a self-propelled stainless steel passenger car which the Budd Company, originally an automotive parts manufacturer, came out with in 1949. (Figure #9.) White calls the Beeliner "one of the most popular and successful rail cars ever produced in the United States." Almost 400 were built between 1949 and 1962. They were built for operation by a two man-crew which should have made them much cheaper than a conventional steam passenger train. "Unfortunately," Itzkoff remarks, "the RDC never realized its economic potential, partially because railway labor

Figure #9. Canadian National Beeliner, Buffalo Evening News, October 17, 1970

insisted on adding a brakeman, a fireman (to watch for signals), and sometimes even a flagman to the original two-man-crew." Thus it was that in May, 1959, the Public Service Commission gave permission for local passenger service on this run to be abandoned. The NYC had lost $111,247 on the five round trips daily between Buffalo and Niagara Falls in 1957 and $74,070 the first six months of 1958. Beeliners seated eighty passengers but were now being used by as few as seven riders per trip. Since the through trains crossed state lines, leave to abandon them had to be sought from the ICC. The Niagara Falls trains, however, and the *Empire State Express*, which at this time was downgraded to a local, came under the jurisdiction of New York's Public Service Commission. A through train each way between Niagara Falls and New York continued to provide Buffalo with train service to the Falls until March 1961 when that too was abandoned.

A description of the activity, or rather the lack of activity, at NYC's Central Terminal appeared in the October 28, 1962, *Courier-Express:*

The terminal's huge main concourse and waiting room have become empty caverns except for brief intervals in late afternoon and late evening. The terminal once had 18 ticket windows - some of them open 24 hours a day. Now there are only four windows, and rarely are more than one or two in use. Even those one or two are closed from 1 to 7 each morning. There once were 50 redcaps. Now there is one - or sometimes two.

There once were 38 public booths, with a cashier and two attendants on duty day and night. Now there are perhaps 20 booths, and the cashier and attendants have vanished. The information booth in the center of the main concourse was converted into a cigar stand - and now it is closed.

The station's drug store has been converted into a novelty shop. The flower shop, the haberdashery, the fruit stand, and the soda fountain are gone. The restaurant coffee shop and lounge remain - but they serve only a fraction of their capacity of 250 persons. The restaurant and nearby magazine stand are the only concession facilities still manned 24 hours a day. The terminal tower, once almost fully occupied, now stands nearly vacant. Only a few tenants are scattered among the many floors.

By 1948 the Erie's passenger service in Western New York was down to two single round trips. One on the ex-Buffalo & Southwestern arrived from Jamestown at 11:15 in the morning and left at 5:10 in the afternoon. The other on the former Attica & Buffalo came in from Hornell at 7:55 A. M. and left at 5:35 P. M. Only the Hornell train, which a reporter called a Beeliner, could have been considered a commuter train. The last run on the Jamestown line was in February, 1950. With the last run of the Hornell train on February 10, 1951, ninety-nine years of passenger service to Buffalo on this route came to an end. Actually, the Erie owned no Beeliners, but rather eighteen gas-electrics which had been built between 1926 and 1931 for local passenger service especially in Northern New Jersey.

The last run of the PRR's commuter service between Olean and Buffalo was described in the January 24, 1948 News. Listed in the timetable as Numbers 990 (southbound) and 991 (north-bound), it was known to its patrons as "The Jerk." It left Olean at 6:20 A. M. and arrived at Exchange Street at 8:35; the return trip left Exchange Street at 5:35 P. M. and was scheduled into Olean at 8:10. The Jerk made every stop along the way. The reporter waxed nostalgic:

Time was when the Pennsy had 750 regular commuters and was running nine commuter specials a day in each direction. The Jerk is the last of them. Other railroads went in for commuter trains in a big way too, and the scramble to catch the trains in the morning and evening rush hours was not entirely unlike today's mob scenes on the Long Island and Jersey trains out of New York. But all that began to die out in the 1920s.

It's quite an event, "taking this train away from us," laments Christian Schopper, Supreme Court chief crier, who has been riding the commuter specials in from East Aurora and out again in the evenings for 34 years. "Some of these fellows on this train I may never see again, people I've been seeing every day all these years."

There's an air of informality on a commuter train that never has a chance to show up on any other train. The conductor and brakemen call passengers by their first names and passengers return the familiarity. A lot of them sit in the same seat every day.

Take Joseph A. Pempsell, an employee of Adam, Meldrum, & Anderson for 62 years who has been riding the Pennsy's commuter trains since 1910. He's the oldest rider on the Jerk, and he puts it this way: "I've been drifting into the same seat every day for years just like an old cow that finds its own stall. Some times, people who didn't know that would beat me to it and the conductor would tap them on the shoulder and say, 'I wouldn't sit there if I were you. Kinda drafty there. Take a seat back here away from the door.'"

Friday morning, when the Jerk stopped as usual at 8:30 in a vacant Exchange St. lot where the old Exchange St. Station once stood, passengers hopped out of the two aged cars - one of them also carries the baggage, and gas lights would look appropriate in either of them. There was a brief and touching ceremony. Gifts were presented to their old friends, Conductor John Corrigan of Olean and Charles H. Greatwood who doubles in brass as brakeman and baggageman. Mr. Greatwood who lives at 692 Abbott Rd., has been riding the commuters since 1909.

There have been just enough incidents through the years to break the Jerk's monotony. There was that day after New Years three years ago for instance when the big storm stalled the little train and it didn't get to Buffalo until 5:50 that evening. Then there was March 3, last year. But let Chris Schopper tell about that.

"I remember the day because it was my birthday. We pulled out of Buffalo at 5:50 and ran into a snowbank just south of Elma Depot. The train was there for three days and we were on it all night. Another train came out from Buffalo the next morning and took us back. When we got off that morning, the Jerk was covered with snow and looked like one big snowbank."

There have been other remembered events, though not quite so strenuous. Just about a year ago, the engine became uncoupled from the cars. The engineer breezed into East Aurora that night without knowing he'd left his cars a mile behind. The Jerk has jumped the tracks a few times, disrupting the inevitable card games, and once years ago, it collided head on with a freight train, telescoping the two head-end baggage cars.

The reporter also threw light on the contemporary state of Buffalo's commuter service:

Western New Yorkers cling to their commuter trains with a death grip. Ask the Pennsy which has been battling for more than 15 years to scrap the Jerk. They've taken their case to the Public Service Commission three times and up to now have been out-battled by Jerk riders. "The railroad always comes around with figures on how much money it loses," says Mr. Schopper. "No doubt it does lose money. But I feel they make it up on freight and other business they pick up at points along our line. If the Jerk was the only thing the Pennsy had, I wouldn't say a word about the railroad dropping it."

Or ask the Baltimore & Ohio about commuter trains. After one of the innumerable coal strikes during which the railroads had to suspend many of their passenger trains, B&O

conveniently forgot to put back the commuter train that runs down through Orchard Park, Springville, Ellicottville, Salamanca and Bradford to Dubois. The howl that went up was deafening and the B&O lost no time restoring its service. So the railroad still has its commuter train that leaves Buffalo at 6 P. M. and another that arrives at 11 A. M. B&O also makes its Pittsburgh-Buffalo train, in here at 7:30 A.M., a local from Salamanca to Buffalo.

The NYC has no commuter trains but sells commutation tickets on the basis of 54 trips a month to and from points within a radius of 50 miles.

From April 4-16, 1958, there appeared in the Courier Express a series of four articles headlined "RAILROADS SEE DOOM AHEAD" about Buffalo's railroads, "a vital key to the Niagara Frontier's industrial greatness." They were said to "face a bleak future unless someone keeps them from rushing into bank-ruptcy." Local railroaders laid the blame on "outmoded government regulations complicated by too burdensome taxes compared with their competitors." In addition, eastern railroads were seen as "harassed by short hauls and mounting passenger deficits." To substantiate the charge about high taxes a list was appended of Buffalo's "Top 10 Taxpayers in 1957." Table #11.

To lower "their backbreaking tax load," some roads were reported trying to sell passenger stations and other real estate holdings. Many of the NYC's 500 stations, including the ill-placed Central Terminal, were for sale. Selling unused passenger stations went back some time. In 1952 the NYC had sold its Getzville Station on the Peanut to the proprietor of a local tavern who paid $600 (much more than he had paid the railroad) to move the structure a thousand yards south on Campbell Road. He told a reporter for the *News*, "I knew I had something here. You couldn't replace the lumber for $2,000. Where most houses have two-by-fours, I have two by sixes and the floor joists are two-by-twelves - all full sized, too." The new owner intended to shorten the eaves, install the usual conveniences, and enclose the clapboard exterior of the 52 foot long, 16 foot wide, 25 foot high station with "conservative brick."

On the subject of government regulation, the first of the *Courier's* articles made these points:

Railroad men claim they are the victims of regulations made necessary when the rails

Table #11

	Name	Assessment	Taxes Paid
1.	New York Central	$38,865,575	$1,426,638
2.	New York Telephone Co.	$38,069,805	$1,397,428
3.	Niagara Mohawk Power Co.	$32,220,160	$1,182,705
4.	DL&W Railroad	$13,124,365	$ 481,756
5.	Iroquois Gas Co.	$10,465,705	$ 383,834
6.	Erie Railroad	$10,399,595	$ 381,737
7.	Allied Chemical & Dye	$ 7,392,780	$ 271,366
8.	Pennsylvania Railroad	$ 7,373,059	$ 270,644
9.	Republic Steel	$ 6,500,000	$ 238,595
10.	Socony Mobile Oil Co.	$ 4,048,990	$ 148,626

were a giant monopoly with the power to make or break communities. But their monopoly has ended and the great maze of regulatory rules remains to haunt them. What rankles with many Buffalo railroads is that they are regulated much more than other forms of transportation. Railroads often seek higher rates to meet steadily rising operating costs, but there are times when they want to lower their rates to a figure below that of a competitor. Yet the railroads often are blocked from lowering their rates by the ICC. Even when a decision is made, it is often based by ICC law on how it affects a competing form of transportation rather than whether the rate covers cost plus a reasonable profit. George Alpert, president of the New Haven Railroad, said in Buffalo recently that railroads must get help immediately from this sort of discrimination or many of them will go broke.

Discrimination against railroads and favoritism toward other forms of transportation were particularly galling to railroad executives and in the long run were highly injurious to the nation's economy. Government regulation lay lightly on the trucking industry as a whole, railroad officials complained to the *Courier's* reporter, and governments generously provided trucks with cheap right of ways.

Buffalo's railroaders say that if their industry were losing business to more efficient forms of transportation, they'd have little to gripe about. That's the way things are supposed to be in a free, competitive market. What does burn them up is that they often have to retreat in the face of less efficient competition because of government subsidies. John P. Kiley, president of the Milwaukee Road, said in Chicago recently that as long as a teaspoon of diesel fuel in a locomotive can carry a ton of freight one mile the railroads hold all the trumps. This is seven times the efficiency of any truck. But government regulations have canceled out much of this advantage.

On the other hand, it's estimated that 65% of intercity highway freight trailers have no regulation. And only about 10% of river and canal traffic is under ICC control. The railroad competition comes from trucks, boats, and airplanes. Railroaders quickly point out that trucks are provided with publicly-owned highways, boats benefit from millions spent by the federal government to improve waterways, and airlines get millions from government-provided airports and navigational aids. As for truck competition railroad men say licenses and fees paid by truckers are a drop in the bucket compared with the free roads they get.

Truckers are making sharp inroads into railroad freight business. In 1946 there were 13,377 carloads of fruits and vegetables brought into the region. Almost all of it was by rail. In 1957, however, only 9,689 carloads were brought in by rail, and the equivalent of 5,335 carloads were brought in by truck.

The airlines were another form of competition which bene-fited from government largess. In 1956-1957 the NYC paid the city $372,474 in taxes on the Central Terminal complex which it had built at a cost of $14 million and continued to maintain. Meanwhile:

Buffalo Airport, built with Buffalo and WPA funds, gives airlines a free terminal on which virtually no taxes are paid. . . . The airlines pay the Port Authority a landing fee totaling $170,000. They also pay combined rental of about $70,000, But railmen are quick to say that the air lines have no maintenance costs. These are borne by the Port Authority. Furthermore, the federal government pays for airport signal equipment while the railroads foot the bill for their own signals.

Meanwhile, railroad passenger and freight traffic is falling off in Buffalo, while air traffic is on the increase. The dollar volume of passenger tickets at Central Terminal dropped from $3,434,691 in 1947 to $2,589,002 in 1957, a decline of $845,669. NYC revenue freight cars loaded or received in the Buffalo *region declined from 22,340 in March, 1956, to 16,237 in March, 1958.*

On the other hand, figures supplied by the airlines show inbound passenger traffic rose from 192,827 in 1947 to 749,373 last year. Air express and freight figures also rose sharply. In 1953, the earliest figures available show in and out total of 19,003,472 pounds. In 1957 the in and out total was up to 26,927,570 pounds.

Like the NYC earlier, Erie Lackawanna, whose rise and fall will be chronicled in the next chapter, invested heavily in a classification yard which, it was hoped, would speed freight handling and cut operating costs. Bison Yard, similar to the Frontier Yard six-tenths of a mile to the northwest, promised to save $3 million annually and was described in the July 21, 1961, *News*:

The Erie-Lackawanna Railroad has started to let contracts for its big $7.5 million electronic freight classification yard at Buffalo, and has set the end of 1962 as target date for completion. All contracts will be let in the next six months, President Milton G. McInnes said in Cleveland. Preliminary clearing for the 3000-car-a-day capacity yard already is under way.

This project, biggest improvement planned following the merger last fall of the Erie Railroad and the Delaware Lackawanna & Western, is "designed to speed delivery of freight through the important Buffalo gateway," Mr. McInnes said.

The new yard will consolidate freight car classification work now done at the old Erie yard near Clinton St. and Bailey Ave. and the present Erie-Lackawanna yard north of William St. in Sloan, site of the new "push-button" facility. [Figures XV, #3 and #8.] *The project will extend from Buffalo city line at William St. north easterly through the village of Sloan and Town of Cheektowaga to a point 1.3 miles east of Union Rd. The main body of the yard will lie between Harlem Rd. and the New York State Thruway. At its widest area it will have 72 tracks.* [Figure #10.] *Following com- pletion of the new yard, the old Erie yard in East Buffalo will be vacated and may be made available for industrial sites.*

The classification yard itself will have 49 tracks, each about a mile long, fanning out from six lead tracks coming off the main hump track. Diesel engines will shove the freight cars over a hump, where they will roll downhill by gravity, through a series of electronically-controlled retarders that automatically control the cars' speed. Other trackage in the yard will include 8 eastbound receiving tracks, 3 westbound receiving tracks, 3 departure tracks, and 2 running tracks. Operations will be conducted from a four-story towered building near the hump.

Videograph, a camera-type television system, will record and check each freight car as it passes scanning devices. A giant electronic track scale will weigh freight cars and automatically record them while they're moving. At least 80 private-line dial telephones will be installed, in addition to teletype and radio systems.

Carmen and locomotive crews will have pocket-size radio receivers and transmitters for instant communication. Six networks of loudspeaker inter-communications systems will have a total of 170 "talk-back" speakers. Floodlights on 17 towers will illuminate the yard at night. The 210 switches in yard tracks will have electrically operated switch heaters to melt ice and snow.

The sequel, as narrated by H. Rogers Grant, to this pronouncement was less than upbeat:

Shortly after work started in 1961 the company felt even better about this multimillion dollar project. The NKP agreed to participate; it would pay half the cost of the land and betterments. The NKP concluded that this commitment served its best interests: it needed to upgrade its terminal operations in Buffalo, and there existed the real chance that if the

Figure #10. Erie-Lackawanna's Bison Yard. Ibid., July 21, 1961

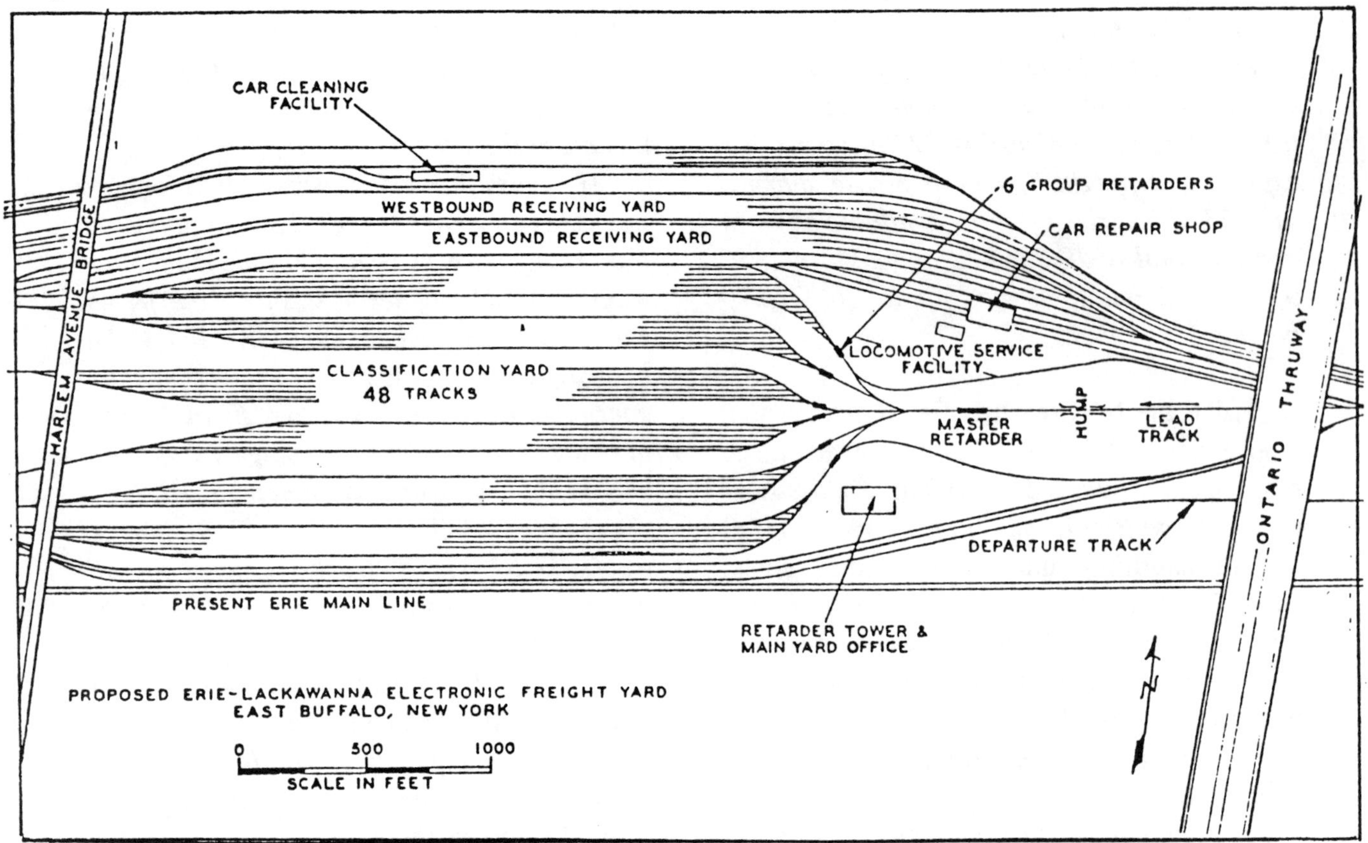

ICC approved the contemplated merger between the NKP, the N&W, and Wabash, it would add the "feeble" Erie-Lackawanna. Not only did the NKP provide needed financial support, but it brought in the Wabash as a rent-paying tenant. Yet Bison failed to be the "good thing that we expected." Construction of this 3,000 cars-a-day facility was not completed until July, 1963, and joint operations did not begin because of work-rule disputes with several brotherhoods. [8]

Rehor tells the story from the NKP point of view:

Early in 1963 E-L, C&O [which in 1947 had merged with Pere Marquette which had running rights over the MC from Saint Thomas, Ontario to Suspension Bridge and over the NYC from there to Buffalo], *and Wabash began using Bison Yard, and Nickel Plate was expected to join them in July. Nickel Plate men supervised operations but the road never did run its trains into Bison because of EL labor opposition. Ironically, the Nickel Plate's $7.5 million investment and a double-track access route* [5.44 miles of PRR main track from Blasdell to the former Erie mainline near Fillmore Avenue in Buffalo which the NKP had bought from the PRR in 1963] *to the yard served only to provide substantial aid to three of its toughest competitors.* [9]

For nighttime activity at the Bison Yard in 1963 see Figure #11.

But the E-L continued to downgrade its passenger service. On November 28, 1962, along with the NKP, E-L moved its Buffalo passenger operations to a remodeled freight office on Clinton and Babcock Streets, abandoning its once magnificent terminal at the foot of Main Street which thereafter rapidly deteriorated. As noted by Itzkoff:

In order to discontinue the Phoebe Snow *between Hoboken and Chicago The Erie-Lackawanna added two hours to the running time between Hoboken and Buffalo; unnecessarily split the train into two separate sections*

Figure #11. Bison Yard at night. Ibid., April 23, 1973

which ran simultaneously, adding $128,000 per year to the "deficit;" abandoned the main station in Buffalo and replaced it with a "tin shanty" in the East Buffalo freight yards; and finally eliminated the Buffalo branch connection altogether. [10]

The once splendid station at the foot of Main Street quickly became a ruin. For a view of its interior as it was in better days and as it had become by 1970 see Figure #12. The headhouse was subsequently demolished, but the train shed was retained to serve as a carbarn for the Niagara Frontier Transit Authority's Main Street subway cars. (Figure #13.)

Early in his tenure of office, however, William White president of E-L from 1963 to 1967, reactivated the tavern-observation cars from the abandoned *Phoebe* and assigned them to the road's premier train between Buffalo and Chicago, which, however, no longer ran through Buffalo but on the former Erie's ex-Atlantic & Great Western mainline to Chicago. This rejuvenation lasted only two years and the famous name train made its last run on November 27, 1966. Thereafter only one train, *The Lake Cities*, made the 977.8 mile run between Hoboken and Chicago. At Hornell this train was met by one round trip a day train between Buffalo and Hornell, consisting of a single coach and on some days an express car which the ICC insisted be operated until May 1969. This arrangement had made money because of a government mail subsidy which was going to be withdrawn, but the ICC examiner ruled this "a future possibility which could not be considered in this case." At Hornell the Buffalo cars were coupled onto ex-Erie mainline trains to New York. The last mainline passenger trains on the line, the east and west bound *Lake Cities*, which came no closer to Buffalo than Hornell, were discontinued on January 4, 1970.

The LV had not imitated most other major eastern railroads by acquiring new lightweight streamlined passenger cars after the war.

Figure #12. Interior of Lackawanna Terminal. Courier-Express, October 5, 1962; Buffalo Evening News, October 27, 1979

Figure #13. NFTA carbarns. Ibid., March 21, 1990

Riders had to be content with a 1952-1953 remodeling of the aging prewar fleet and the magnificent scenery that could be seen from daylight trains. The contrast was sharp between the obsolescent consist of the *Black Diamond*, once the pride of the LV, and DL&W's sleek new *Phoebe Snow*. However, the financial history of the LV during the Eisenhower Era duplicated that of the DL&W. As Archer writes:

The company's fluctuating financial performance in the immediate post-war period had stabilized somewhat by the early 1950s. Net income, despite declining tonnage, managed to remain fairly steady, due in large part to the operating economies of the diesel locomotive and also to a successfully negotiated shipping rate hike. The second half of the decade proved to be a far different story. Between 1956 (the last year the LV would ever show a profit) and 1958, total operating revenues fell approximately $14 million, an alarming slide of 20% in just three years. The resulting delicit in net railway operating income for 1958 alone was a staggering $3.36 million. The sudden drop in operating revenues was precipitated by three critical factors that were sapping the road's financial health: the ever more competitive inter-city trucking industry, the ongoing decline in anthracite production and shipping, and the escalating losses from passenger operations. [11]

It is understandable, therefore, that the LV became the first Class I railroad to abandon Buffalo passenger service completely. Late in 1958 the road had requested permission from the ICC to do this but received merely half a loaf. Numbers Four and Nine, the daylight *Black Diamond* between New York and Buffalo, made their last runs on May 11, 1959. But management was required to continue operating the nighttime *Maple Leaf* for one more year, the maximum time limit permitted the ICC by a recent law. The commission said that "there appears to be a substantial public use of and need for the continued operation of all the trains involved in this proceeding." Employing a ponderous double negative, the commission stated that it was "unable to find, however, that the continued operation of all such trains would not unduly burden interstate or foreign commerce." So the LV was ordered to continue for a year the operation of a pair of trains between New York and Lehighton, Pennsylvania, and Numbers Four and Seven, the *Maple Leaf* between New York and Buffalo. On the occasion of the LV's request to discontinue, Mayor Frank Sedita of Buffalo told a reporter from the *News,* "I'm sympathetic to the plight of railroads that are losing money. On the other hand, I cannot condone abolition of Lehigh Valley service into Buffalo." Sentiments like this should have earned His Honor the next appointment to the ICC. One year stretched into two until finally on the morning of February 4, 1961, the westbound *Maple Leaf* crept into Dingens Street over three hours late. Slowed down by snowdrifts, its eastbound companion, Number Eight, running eight hours late, made it only to Pennsylvania Station in Newark. Abandonment of the *Maple Leaf* insured the demise of the Reading's sleeping car service from Philadelphia to Buffalo and Toronto via Bethlehem and the Depew & Tonawanda.

Itzkoff explains the thinking behind the changed federal policy concerning passenger train discontinuance:

When accelerating deterioration finally forced hearings on "The Problems of the Railroads" in 1958, Congress chose to save the freight business by allowing the railroad industry to abandon the passenger train. The new section 13A of the Transportation Act of 1958 consolidated discontinuance proceedings under the ICC, forcing the Commission to allow railroad exit petitions unless it found the service in question to be "required by the public convenience and necessity." The ICC mandate proved a difficult test indeed. Encouraged, the railroads submitted thousands of dis-

continuance requests, and systematically, the passenger train network began to disintegrate. In many cases the destruction was deliberate. By 1968, only a third of the 1,500 daily trains running a decade before still survived. [12]

To halt and reverse the gradual disappearance of the intercity passenger train, Anthony Haswell, a Chicago attorney, founded the National Association of Railway Passengers (NARP) in 1967. Two years before, Haswell had petitioned the ICC to investigate the adequacy of railroad passenger service. When the Commission finally got around to denying his petition, Haswell organized NARP, which by 1970 had 5,000 members and a annual budget of $100,000. During its first three years, NARP had forced several railroads to keep operating passenger trains, won a favorable decision from the Supreme Court on the right of the public to appeal train abandonments, and secured the introduction of several bills in Congress setting up minimum standards of passenger train service. However, it was upon the ICC that Haswell focused his efforts to preserve and improve the nation's passenger trains.

The result was a report by ICC Examiner John Messer which accused the Southern Pacific, a notorious offender in the eyes of NARP, for deliberately sabotaging its *Sunset Limited*, a 2,033 mile train from New Orleans to Los Angeles. According to Messer, railroads were quasi-public corporations that were obliged to provide transportation "upon reasonable request." The Commission sat on the Southern Pacific case for well over three years while 249 intercity passenger trains were discontinued. When, in September, 1969, the Commission finally ruled that it had no jurisdiction in the case, the death of the American passenger train seemed at hand.

Congress was the only hope now for train preservationists. A federally financed High Speed Ground Transportation Act (HSGTA) had been signed by President Lyndon Johnson in 1965. There were numerous voters along the corridor. This act led to the creation of the Northeast Corridor Metroliner Service. Stuart Saunders, chairman of the PRR, promised his cooperation in providing two-and-a-half hour service between New York City and Washington (226.5 miles) by 1967. The PRR was committed to purchase fifty electrically powered self-propelled Metroliners from Budd. These trains would be capable of speeds up to 170 miles an hour. Technical problems bedeviled the project so that Metroliners did not start running until January, 1969, on a three hour schedule. Public response was encouraging, and during the first year the number of passengers rose from 509,000 in 1968 to 730,000 in 1969. However, because of inferior roadbed, the New York-Washington ride was bumpy, and the PRR's overhead electrification was dated and failed to supply the motors properly. On only twenty-one miles of track could the Metroliners be operated at top speed; forty percent of the cars were in the repair shop on any given day; engineers and trainmen had to be paid a full day's pay for four-and-a half hours work. Hence by 1970 the Penn Central had invested over $57 million in the project while the federal government had only contributed $2 million. That year the only non-stop Metroliner was discontinued and the schedule had become only fifty minutes faster than conventional service had been.

Disappointed by the failure of the Metroliner to live up to its billing, supporters of the passenger train turned again to Congress, whose members had come to realize that the demise of all such service would be highly unpopular back home. Numerous bills were introduced in Congress during 1969 calling for the continuation of intercity passenger trains through federal aid and subsidies for day-to-day operation. The *New York Times* in December, 1969, observed that "the most advanced distillation" of these plans called for federal capital and operating subsidies of $409 million over four years. The Secretary of

Transportation would designate certain routes for subsidies. Congress, however, wanted more of a say about what trains were continued and what trains were terminated. Moreover, no routes longer than 300 miles were to be subsidized. Deadlock between different factions in Washington seemed to have set in, and railroads were stepping up their petitions to the ICC to abandon what runs still survived. Then in June came the bankruptcy of Penn Central which had serviced eighty percent of industrial America and three-quarters of the nation's passenger trains. PC had posted losses of $100 million in 1969 alone, and its demise led many economists to predict the collapse of other major railroads.

The stage was being set for Amtrak, a government takeover of the nation's railroads that would enable them to get out of the passenger business entirely.

18
Merger Mania

During the 19th century, America's railroads, e. g., the PRR and the NYC, had grown through mergers. Mergers of large systems into communities of interest through lease and stock ownership had produced seven great but informal combinations by 1906: (1) the New England system, dominated by the New York New Haven & Hartford and including the Boston & Maine; (2) the eastern trunk lines, dominated by the NYC and the PRR; (3) the southern system, created out of chaos by J. P. Morgan; (4) Jim Hill's roads in the northwest, the major lines of which were the Great Northern, the Northern Pacific, and the Burlington; (5) Edward H. Harriman's system, based on the Illinois Central, the Union Pacific and the Southern Pacific; (6) Jay Gould's empire, which had been inherited by his son George, consisting of the Wabash, the Missouri Pacific, the Texas & Pacific, and some other lines; and (7) most ephemeral of all and not all that great, the Rock Island and Saint Louis-San Francisco. Taken together, these systems accounted for the greater part of the nation's railroad mileage and even more of its haulage.

However, the drive toward consolidation was upset by the decision in the Northern Securities case in 1904 which broke up the holding company Hill and Harriman had created to bring order to the railroad scene in the Northwest. Almost a half century would pass before mergers again became acceptable, despite the encouragement theoretically given them by the Transportation Act of 1920. The ICC was given oversight over mergers and abandonments and routinely rejected them on the grounds that they inhibited competition. The ICC was also sensitive to the complaints of on-line shippers, patrons, and their congressmen.

CSX

From the 1960s to the 1980s, however, mergers and bankruptcies would drastically alter the railroad situation on the Niagara Frontier, extinguishing companies that had been household names and eliminating miles of trackage. (Figure #1.) In 1937 Robert R. Young, a flashy financier who had gotten out of the stock market before the 1929 Crash, purchased 47% of the stock of the late Van Sweringen brothers' Alleghany Corporation, a holding company which controlled the Chesapeake & Ohio Railroad, a prosperous

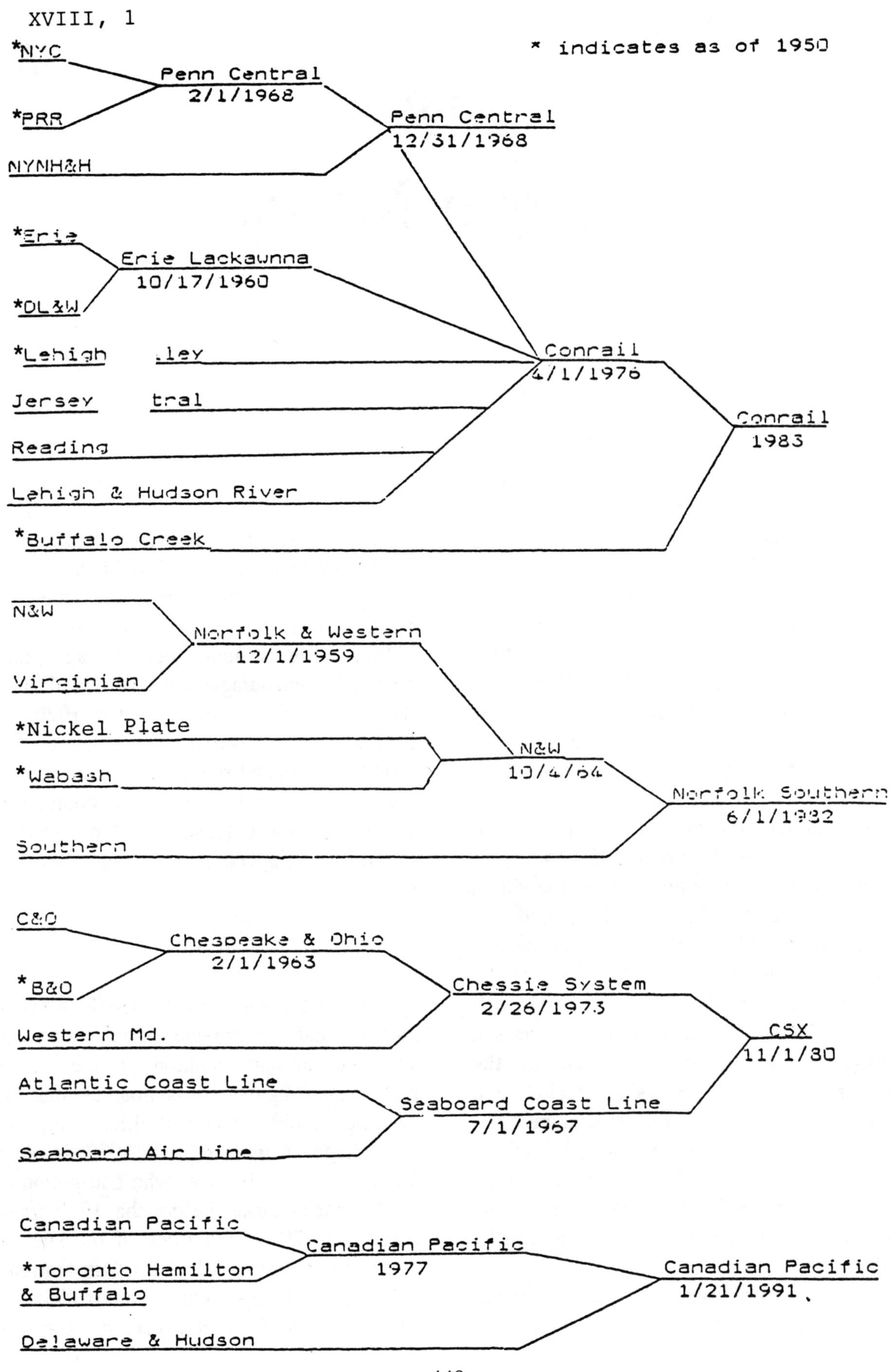
XVIII, 1
* indicates as of 1950
*NYC
*PRR
Penn Central
2/1/1968
NYNH&H
Penn Central
12/31/1968
*Erie
*DL&W
Erie Lackawnna
10/17/1960
*Lehigh .ley
Jersey tral
Reading
Lehigh & Hudson River
Conrail
4/1/1976
*Buffalo Creek
Conrail
1983
N&W
Virginian
Norfolk & Western
12/1/1959
*Nickel Plate
*Wabash
N&W
10/4/64
Southern
Norfolk Southern
6/1/1982
C&O
*B&O
Chesapeake & Ohio
2/1/1963
Western Md.
Chessie System
2/26/1973
Atlantic Coast Line
Seaboard Air Line
Seaboard Coast Line
7/1/1967
CSX
11/1/80
Canadian Pacific
*Toronto Hamilton
& Buffalo
Canadian Pacific
1977
Delaware & Hudson
Canadian Pacific
1/21/1991

soft coal carrier. He became chairman of the C&O in 1943 and in 1947 merged it with the Pere Marquette, a road with numerous lines in southern Michigan which enjoyed running rights over the MC from Saint Thomas, Ontario, to Suspension Bridge and from there on the NYC to Buffalo. In this way, C&O gained access to Buffalo. (See Chapter XV, "Pere Marquette.") The PM provided its dominant partner with western connections and merchandise traffic to diversify its freight business. Young sold the C&O to Cyrus Eaton in 1954 and left to become chairman of the NYC, installing Alfred E. Perlman as president. Perlman, who had had phenomenal success in revitalizing the Denver & Rio Grande Western, managed briefly to improve the NYC's finances by ruthless retrenchment of services and abandonment of branches, but the recession of 1957-1958 and construction of the New York State Thruway hurt the NYC badly.

The ICC, Itzkoff observed, "favored the merger movement, having decided in 1959 that as long as a choice of transport mode remained, the elimination of inter-railroad rivalry could not be construed as the elimination of competition." Eaton merged the C&O with the B&O in 1963. Perlman had wanted the B&O for the NYC, but the B&O's stockholders preferred to exchange their stock with the C&O which was paying dividends of $4.00 a share. For a few years, the C&O/B&O were operated as separate roads. This avoided many of the problems later experienced by the ill-fated Penn Central. The C&O now had a second route to Buffalo via the ex-BR&P which the B&O had acquired in 1932. The Western Maryland entered the fold in 1968 through a takeover by the C&O/B&O until 1973, when the Chessie System was incorporated to own the three railroads, C&O, B&O, and WM. (Chessie was the name of a cat which had been the C&O's logo.) Thereafter, much WM trackage and facilities were abandoned.

When Conrail, which will be discussed later, was being put together out of the wreckage of the Northeast's railroads, C&O sought to enlarge its system by buying 2,200 miles of Erie Lackawanna and Reading lines between Buffalo and Philadelphia for $54 million, knowing full well that half a billion dollars would be required for repairs and equipment. This would have been in keeping with Congress's intention to preserve a viable alternate to Conrail for Eastern shippers. What made C&O back off was the ICC's insistence that employees would have to work in accordance with EL and Reading contracts. As quoted in *Trains* for September, 1988, the chairman of C&O explained that "taking over the labor practices and agreements which contributed to the bankruptcy of the acquired lines would have resulted in our assuming a loss operation." With C&O out of the picture, the path taken by the ICC was, as will be seen, to create an expanded Delaware & Hudson which proved to be a largely symbolic gesture.

The C&O was not through with mergers. The Atlantic Coast Line and the Seaboard Air Line had been given permission by the ICC to merge at the end of 1963. It was the first time that two prosperous competing lines were permitted to do so. The commissioners had belatedly come to recognize that competition among railroads was not as important as competition with other forms of transportation, and that railroads were entitled to a fair return on investment. The principal argument for merger was the elimination of duplicate lines and facilities. The merger went into effect in 1967 under the corporate title of the Seaboard Coast Line Railroad. In 1980 the Chessie Lines merged with Seaboard Coast Line. The result was called CSX, the holding company for the former C&O, B&O, WM, ACL, and the Louisville & Nashville. The L&N had been owned by the ACL since 1902 but had been operated independently until 1982 when it was merged into Seaboard Coast Line, which continued as a subsidiary of CSX. CSX was now a huge railroad operation with 27,000 miles in twenty-two states, 70,000 employees, and assets in excess of $7.5 billion. (Figure #2.) The ninety-six mile Rochester branch of the ex-B&O from Ashford to Rochester was sold to Genesee & Wyoming Industries in 1985 and commenced operations on July 21, 1986, as the Rochester & Southern, with rights over the Chessie System from Ashford, the junction with the Buffalo branch, to Salamanca. The 340 mile ex-B&O from Buffalo to a point north of Pittsburgh was also sold to Genesee & Wyoming and to AWP, parent of a Pennsylvania coal road, on July 19, 1988. This was very nearly a resurrection of the BR&P which had been absorbed by the B&O in 1932. Now CSX's only access to Buffalo was via the former Pere Marquette's running rights over what was now Conrail, across the Ontario Peninsula.

N&W-NKP-Wabash

A second series of mergers to impact on the Buffalo railroad scene began in 1962 when the Norfolk & Western merged with the Virginian. Like the C&O, these were soft coal carrying roads. In 1925 the ICC had refused to permit the N&W to lease the Virginian, but times had changed. Galvanized by the C&O's overtures to the B&O, the N&W initiated discussions with the NKP in 1960. There was no physical connection between the two but the N&W planned to buy the 111 mile long PRR branch from Columbus, Ohio, on the N&W to Bellevue on the NKP for $27 million. In addition, the N&W proposed to lease the Wabash for fifty years with an eventual exchange of stock between the two roads. A third participant in the merger was the Pittsburgh & West Virginia, successor to George Gould's unhappy Wabash Pittsburgh Terminal. Opposition from E-L, which had contemplated a marriage with the NKP itself, was headed off by agreeing to negotiate E-L's eventual inclusion in N&W and by promoting NKP's access to the new Bison Yard in Buffalo. By a 10-1 vote the ICC approved the N&W-NKP merger in June 1964. By then the proposal to unite NYC and PRR had been revived and the B&O-C&O merger appeared set. The ICC wished to provide strong competition in former trunk line territory for what was perceived as the immensely powerful Penn Central, then in the planning stage. The PRR was required to divest itself of its N&W and Wabash stock. When NYC and PRR were planning their merger it was clear that the ICC would not permit them to include Wabash. PC was big enough already. The most logical place for Wabash to go, it seemed, was with N&W. The NW-NKP merger and the lease of the Wabash took effect on October 16, 1964. The N&W now had two lines into Buffalo, the Wabash's running rights over the Canadian National and the former Nickel Plate. N&W began buying the PRR's stock in the Wabash and by 1980 owned it almost completely.

XVIII, 2

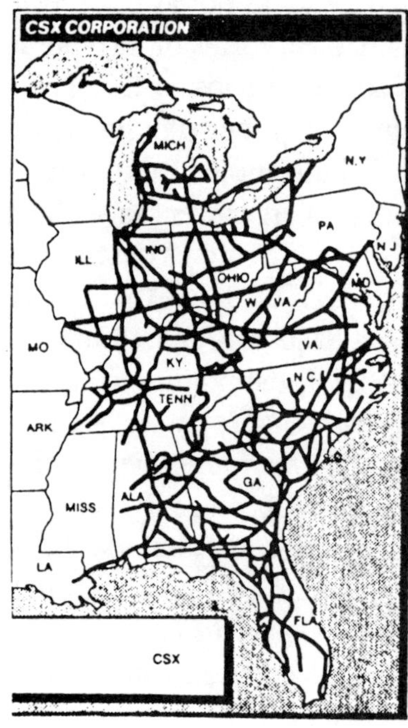

Erie Lackawanna

Less enduring than the above mergers but exercising far greater impact on the economy of Western New York was the 1962 consolidation of the Erie and the DL&W into the Erie-Lackawanna. Much of the DL&W's mainline between Hoboken and Buffalo and particularly between Binghamton and Buffalo paralleled that of the Erie. (Figure IX, #6.) With the financial crunch experienced by both lines and by many other of the nation's railroads in the late 1950s, officials of both companies wanted to shed excess capacity and reduce operating expenses. A small step in this direction was combining their freight houses in Binghamton and Elmira which produced some savings. A year later, the Erie routed its long-distance passenger and off-rush-hour local trains from its decrepit station on Pavonia Avenue in Jersey City to the relatively newer DL&W terminal in Hoboken, less than a mile to the north. By March, 1957, the Pavonia station had been shut down completely. Abandonment of seventy-five miles of DL&W trackage between Binghamton and Gibson, New York (two miles east of Corning), and routing DL&W trains over the parallel Erie tracks went into effect on August 31, 1958. Erie trackage was chosen over that of the better engineered DL&W because more customers were located on the Erie.

Corporate merger had been discussed informally by presidents of both lines in 1954. Since 1940 the Erie had worried that the DL&W would merge with the NKP. They had long exchanged through passenger and freight cars. Though the DL&W had been put into excellent physical shape during the Truesdale administration (1899-1925), it was clearly on the skids physically and fiscally by the mid-1950s. During the depression gross revenues had dropped from $81 million in 1929 to $43 million in 1933. Prosperity returned during the war years under the administration of William White who became president in 1941. When he resigned in 1952, the DL&W held 15% of the NKP's outstanding stock. Then the bottom began to fall out. Hard coal revenues on the quondam "Road of Anthracite" fell sharply from $10.3 million in 1952 to $5.1 million in 1977. (Figure XV, #9.) Confiscatory New Jersey taxes, outrageous labor practices known as featherbedding mandated by state and federal governments, a commuter service in New Jersey losing $3 million a year, loss of export grain and container business after the opening of the Saint Lawrence Seaway through its entire length in 1959, and the appearance of superhighways financed by state legislatures and Congress which amounted to subsidies for truck and bus lines were strangling the DL&W and other northeastern railroads and not slowly.

Perry Shoemaker, White's successor and the last president of the DL&W, was forced to liquidate his company's NKP holdings in 1958 to replace a Hackensack River Bridge condemned by army engineers. By this time, hopes for a union with the NKP had been dashed. NKP stockholders wanted nothing to do with the DL&W because of the New Jersey tax situation and the growing losses on its commuter service. Those stockholders gladly entertained offers from the prosperous N&W, a merger which, as already noted, was achieved in 1964 along with the Wabash. In desperation the shaky DL&W turned to the Weary Erie.

Before this happened, however, a third party entered the picture, the Delaware & Hudson. Its president, William White, formerly of the DL&W, had surrendered the helm of the NYC after only two years to Robert Young who had sold his C&O holdings and set out to gain control of the NYC. White lost the bitter proxy fight to Young in 1954. White had more stockholders behind him but Young had more stocks. The D&H was a bridge line from Wilkes Barre via Binghamton to Albany and to Rouses Point on the Canadian border with a direct connection to Montreal. It operated no commuter trains and at the time was in very good financial shape. In 1955 its net gain after taxes was $9,897,374, that of the Erie (which was three times as big) was $7,897,354, while the DL&W had lost a million dollars.

A firm of transportation consultants recommended the triple merger in July, 1958, but by then White had begun to have second thoughts. He broke off discussions with the Erie and the DL&W in April, 1959. The 1958 recession had hurt both roads badly, and White was upset on learning that the DL&W had liquidated its NKP holdings. This left the original two to go it alone, without the D&H. An exchange of stock in a new company, the Erie-Lackawanna, was arranged on the basis of 65 for Erie and 35 for DL&W stockholders. The smaller and weaker road could not dictate a 50-50 ratio. An acerbic writer for *Trains* described the merger as a case of "a man with a leaky boat lending a hand to a swimmer in shark infested waters." By this time the books of both companies were awash in red ink. The DL&W had losses of $3.9 million in 1958 and $4.3 million in 1959; the Erie lost $3.6 million in 1958 and $5.6 in 1959.

This was not a case merely of two rust belt railroads going under. Nationally many railroads were in awful shape at the end of 1950s, as they kept losing business to subsidized competitors: airlines, barges, buses, pipe lines, and trucks. Obtuse unions blessed with tunnel vision refused to change archaic work rules and permit the railroads to derive the full advantage they might have from dieselization and other technological improvements. Iron and steel producers moved away from traditional northeastern centers like Cleveland, Youngstown, Pittsburgh, and Lackawanna. Increased imports of foreign steel and the use of substitute materials hurt railroads in the area. The ICC moved with snail-paced, nitpicking slowness in allowing railroads to abandon losing branches, runs, and stations. Cutbacks on maintenance was causing serious deterioration of roadbed and equipment and consequent customer dissatisfaction.

Stock and bondholders gave overwhelming support to the merger at a meeting in New York on September 22, 1959. ICC hearings in Buffalo at the Hotel Buffalo, the original Statler, began a week later. Spokesmen for the prospective road repeated the findings of the transportation consulting firm and stressed that the merger would be in the public interest. Most shippers agreed that better service would result from a merger. Hearings shifted to Washington where other railroads sought traffic concessions from E-L to safeguard their own interests which would have negated the advantages sought from the merger. The ICC's chief emissary had no difficulty in rejecting these self-seeking demands; but he was less successful dealing with the equally selfish demand of the Railway Labor Executives' Association which had determined to resist an expected outbreak of mergers unless the roads made extraordinary concessions to employees. The RLEA insisted that every job on the existing roads be frozen on the new road for four years. This would have eliminated one of the major benefits expected from the merger. On September 13, 1960, the ICC approved the merger effective October 17, 1960. The RLEA appeared in federal court demanding that the merger be postponed until the employee protection issue could be settled. The court ruled against the association but ordered E-L not to abolish any jobs or transfer any workers until further hearings took place, which dampened the enthusiasm of the officials of the two roads for unification. Their new creation would operate 3,031 route miles, the twelfth largest railroad system in the nation. (Figure #3.)

The Supreme Court finally resolved the employment dispute in favor of E-L on June 12, 1961, which meant that eight months had gone by after the merger before progress could be made on consolidating personnel, facilities, and functions. The second track on the former DL&W mainline from Corning to Buffalo was torn up, as were four miles of the Lackawanna's Black Rock branch from Genesee Street to Delaware Avenue in Buffalo. Unfortunately, no detailed pre-merger planning had been done so that the attempt to fuse two companies whose procedures on every level had been completely different resulted in disaster.

XVIII, 3

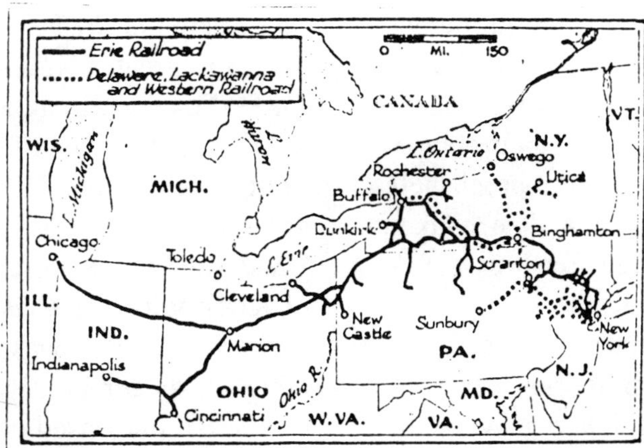

Featherbedding was costing the company $7 million annually during the early 1960s. On this issue the railroad industry finally won in the Supreme Court in 1963, but state full-crew laws took longer to repeal, and E-L operated through mostly full-crew law states. Corporate losses were $26 million in 1961 and $16 million in 1962. That year long-term debt stood at $322 million. Management of the new enterprise was largely in the hands of former Erie officials, some of whom, including the president, were simply incompetent. Morale among employees, especially those from the better run and maintained DL&W, deteriorated. Customer service frequently became surly.

A renaissance of sorts occurred during the administration of President White who agreed to become chairman of the board and chief executive officer of the E-L in June, 1963. He dropped the hyphen from the corporate logo, terminated unfit officials, extended the maturities of a major bond issue by five years, secured loans to upgrade the property, cut the work force by several thousand, improved the car repair shops at Meadville, rehabilitated the freight car fleet, got rid of some passenger trains, induced New Jersey to subsidize what commuter service remained, overcame the state's unfair taxing policies, and got permission to retire the aged Hudson River ferry boat fleet. His company lost $17 million in 1963, which was reduced to $8 million in 1964, and in 1965 actually made a profit of $3.2 million, which was nearly doubled in 1966. White also continued to look for a strong merger partner. The object of his desires was a merger with N&W which was not destined to come off in the way White, who succumbed to a heart attack on the job on April 6, 1967, envisioned. The year he died E-L lost $ 8.7 million.

Penn Central

The taste of their victory over William White in the Great Proxy Fight of 1954 quickly turned to ashes for Young and Perlman when they learned that the road, control of which they had won, was insolvent. It was much more passenger-oriented than Perlman had realized, and passenger trains were losers. Its freight tracks were in bad repair and signaled for only thirty miles an hour, unlike those of the NKP which was a well maintained fast freight line. A 1955-1957 economic upturn enabled the NYC to stave off bankruptcy, while Young wasted time and $12 experimenting with a string of high-speed futuristic streamliners all of which proved to be lemons.

Railroads across the land were especially

hard hit by the Eisenhower Recession of 1957-1958 which seriously curtailed the production of durable goods. Young and Perlman agreed that the way to salvation lay through merger. The question was with whom. On November 1, 1957, Young and James M. Symes, chairman of the PRR, announced that their companies intended to merge. This was a bombshell, since throughout the industry it had been taken for granted that Trunk Line Territory's two biggest roads would become the magnets for the formation of two distinct mega-systems, rather than merging and smothering everyone else. Young may have regretted leaving the C&O, for he shot himself to death on January 5, 1958, at his winter home in Palm Beach.

Perlman, now in complete control of the NYC, began dismantling its passenger service and upgrading its freight carrying potential. CTC was extended to all main lines, electronic classification yards were built not only at Buffalo but also at Elkhart, Indiana, Indianapolis, Cleveland, and Youngstown. The redundant NYWS&B was abandoned west of Albany as was most of the RW&O, the Peanut, and numerous other rural branches and stations. With Young's death, whatever zeal Perlman might have felt for union with the PRR noticeably cooled. He was angry with Symes when the PRR-controlled N&W took over the Virginian, which had been a friendly supplier of soft coal traffic to the NYC. Perlman broke off discussions with the PRR on January 8, 1959, and sent out feelers to the C&O's president, Walter Tuohy, two weeks later. The problem here was that though the NYC was a larger road, the C&O was richer. In a merger, which set of managers was going to run the railroad? On March 18, 1960, Perlman received more bad news when the N&W announced its forthcoming merger with the Wabash and the NKP. Both these roads were members of the PRR financial family, so the demarche indicated the PRR's intention of securing control of the NKP, the NYC's chief competitor for traffic west of Buffalo. Perlman called upon Tuohy again who told him that the C&O and the B&O were merging since the B&O needed some place to go and could help the C&O strengthen its position vis-a-vis the greater N&W. Yet more bad news for Perlman was that the NYC did not fit in the C&O's plans. There followed a second Great Proxy Fight, that of 1960, between the NYC and the C&O for the B&O. As noted above, B&O stockholders preferred the an exchange of stock with the C&O rather than with the shaky NYC. This was the last chance for creating a truly competitive railroad system in the Northeast, one based on the PRR, the other on the NYC. Defeated, Perlman was forced to reopen negotiations with the PRR.

After years of backing and filling, the ICC finally approved the merger of the PRR and the NYC on April 29, 1966, (Figure #4.) but it appended to the agreement two fatal provisions. The first was lifetime job protection for employees. The second was that Penn Central had to take over the New York New Haven & Hartford, which had entered bankruptcy in the summer of 1961, a victim of short hauls, high terminal costs, the demise of heavy industry in New England, excessive branch line and commuter service, and bad not to say crooked management. The theory behind the merger which produced PC was that enough duplicate lines and facilities could be eliminated to make this hybrid profitable. (Figure XII, #4.) The disastrous outcome is described in <u>Railroads in the Age of Regulation</u> which shows that the lesson of the E-L merger had not been taken to heart:

The decision to merge the two companies' operations at once, without preparation, was probably [Stuart] *Saunders'* [president of the PRR], *not Perlman's because Saunders believed that it was essential to achieve instantly the savings that merger was supposed to produce. Perlman was the man who had to carry out the orders. The urgency was so great that no time was taken to retrain employees or make the necessary physical changes to connect the two railroads properly. The operating*

XVIII, 4

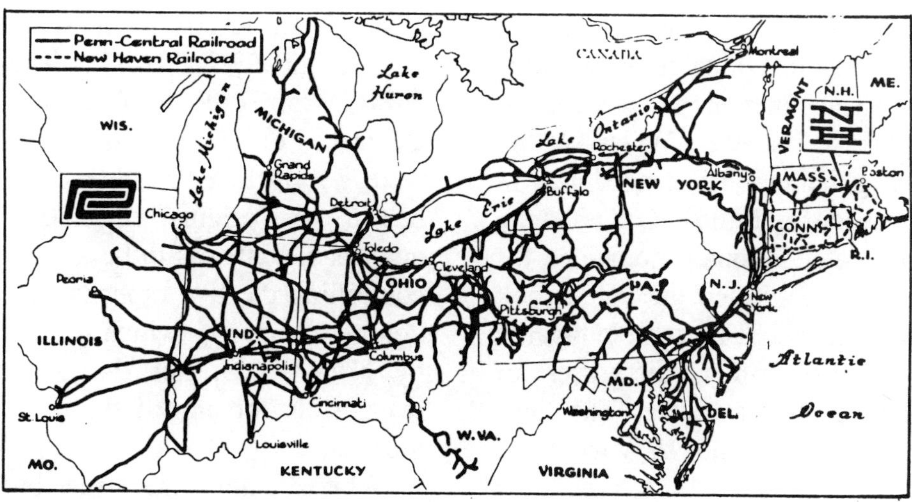

breakdown was nearly total and brought the railroad to paralysis by early 1970, with shippers deserting in droves to other railroads or other forms of transportation because the service was so bad. The debacle was worst at two key points - Big Four Yard at Indianapolis, where traffic from all over the Midwest was gathered and cars were pre-blocked (grouped for common destinations) for dispatch eastward, and at Selkirk Yard near Albany, where trains from the West were broken down for delivery to points on the East Coast. At Big Four, the problem seems to have been largely a failure to instruct crews in the myriad of new routings and new operating procedures they would use. At Selkirk, the failure was in not completing the expansion of the yard before a crush of new traffic fell in on it, making it impossible to either classify the trains or complete the yard.

All over the system, untrained crews mixed up paper work and sent it to the wrong place. Shipments and paper work became separated, until whole trains of "no-bills" (cars with no paperwork and thus unknown destinations) were dispatched over the line to get them out of one yardmaster's yard and into someone else's. Accountants, equally untrained, failed to bill some customers and continued to dun customers who had paid because the payment had been entered in the wrong accounts. The latter mistake brought mountains of ill will. [1]

Even the personalities of the Red Team (ex-PRR managers) and the Green Team (ex-NYC) clashed. Perlman felt himself a Jewish technician who loved trains forced to deal with WASP aristocrats who cared more about their investments and country clubs.

By 1970 the railroad, one of whose directors was Seymour H. Knox of Buffalo, president of Marine Midland Bank, one of PC's many creditors, was losing a million dollars a day and had no place to go to get money. At a stormy meeting on June 8, 1970, the directors fired the company's top executives and thirteen days later declared bankruptcy. It was the biggest business failure in America up to then. Thereafter, no further credit was available from private investors and the road continued to get worse.

Dereco

President White's tenure at EL aimed chiefly at ending continuing deficits. In this he was moderately successful, but he realized from the beginning that long term recovery demanded a strong merger partner and so fixed his sights on N&W. When N&W-NKP merger negotiations had begun back in 1961, N&W agreed that if the ICC blessed the union, it would enter serious negotiations for the inclusion of E-L. When the union took place in October, 1964, N&W was told that the commission would superintend the process of including E-L in the larger system. The commission also indicated that the N&W would be permitted to absorb the ailing Boston & Maine and the D&H. Even before this, however, White began to fear the effects of the proposed merger of the NYC and the PRR. He could not foresee what a disaster it would be. Therefore he opposed the merger unless EL were itself included. If, however, N&W was willing to take EL into its fold, EL would then support PC.

At this point the plot began to thicken when on August 31, 1965, the N&W announced that it would seek a merger with another profitable coal hauler, the C&O, already engorged by the recent acquisition of B&O. Such a giant could easily take in orphans like EL, the D&H whose glory days were ending, and the B&M. But there was more to it than that. The C&O had inherited from the B&O a large position in the Reading, another anthracite road with a large commuter deficit. The Reading, for its part, controlled the Jersey Central, yet again another anthracite road with yet another hefty commuter deficit. The ICC, it was felt, would sanction a N&W-C&O merger if this huge combination would include in the union these five orphans. The purpose of all this ICC tinkering was to make it unnecessary for the federal government to be forced to take over these roads, also known as weak sisters, and nationalize them. Free enterprise was being compromised in the name of free enterprise.

For the solvent N&W and C&O the problem was how to avoid being dragged down by a gaggle of losers. The solution was Dereco (originally DERJCO). The D stood for D&H, E for EL, R for Reading, JC for Jersey Central. For some reason B&M's initials were not included. Dereco was settled on because the original suggestion was unpronounceable. It was to be a holding company controlling the five orphans. But neither the holding company, which would be controlled by N&W-C&O, nor the parent would be responsible for any of the operating companies' debts.

White did not want Dereco but rather direct inclusion in the present N&W and so petitioned the ICC. Fearing EL's huge debt the N&W wanted nothing of EL under White's terms and asked the ICC to approve the N&W-C&O merger before discussing inclusion of the five orphans. In December 1966 the ICC authorized the creation of Dereco which was obliged to take over D&H and EL and permitted to take over B&M. The ICC believed that N&W-C&O-Dereco would provide competition in the northeast for PC, the creation of which had been approved by the ICC in April, 1966. In April 1968 Dereco took control of EL. John P. Fishwick, as senior vice president of N&W and president of Dereco, became chairman of EL and president of D&H, when it joined Dereco in June. These were the only two subsidiaries Dereco would ever have. B&M stockholders refused the invitation to join Dereco, as did those of the CNJ and Reading.

Fishwick felt that he was being exiled to Siberia since doing anything with EL was almost impossible. It had posted a net loss of $8.7 in 1967. The company earned $4.5 million in 1968 and $1.6 million in 1969. Then a series of blows fell which led to bankruptcy. Losses in 1970 reached $7 million. The economy of the Northeast, where there was too much trackage anyway, was deteriorating badly, PC had cut interchanges with EL and D&H in favor of its own enlarged lines, calculations of settlements made with labor unions at the time of the merger were unrealistic, the Post Office's cancellation of Railway Postal Service on most intercity trains was the last straw for through passenger trains in America. The Jersey Central had gone bankrupt in 1967 and the ICC ordered the N&W and the C&O as the price of approving their merger to help the Jersey Central, the Reading, and the B&M remain operational.

This plus the bankruptcy of PC in 1971, which shook the financial community badly, troubles C&O was having with B&O's finances, the declining demand for coal, and disputes as to who would head up the unified company led N&W and C&O to withdraw their merger petition in 1971. Moreover the national economy was in trouble. As Grant writes in Death of an American Railroad, from which much of the present treatment of EL and Dereco is taken:

The economics of the early 1970s were unsettling. Near the close of the Lyndon B. Johnson administration severe economic winds began to buffet the nation and they continued unrelentingly through much of Richard Nixon's presidency. The escalation of government expenditures, most of all for the Vietnam Conflict, boosted interest charges, increased inflation, and caused growing pessimism in business and financial circles. An indication of the malaise was the change in the prime rate, that is, the rate banks charge their best customers. It stood at 6% in January 1968, but climbed to 8.5% eighteen months later, and reached 9% by 1970. The impact of limiting or even eliminating access to credit for marginal borrowers became known as a "credit crunch," and would strike again in the mid-1970s. Moreover, workers responded to the higher costs of living by demanding pay hikes, and this produced inflationary wage increases. [2]

The impact of mandated wage increases upon railroad finances can be seen in Figure #5 which shows that though railroad employment dropped from 675,000 in 1963 to 525,000 in 1973, wages, exclusive of payroll taxes and health benefits, rose from $4.6 to $7.25 billion during the same period.

Erie Lackawanna survived but just barely into mid-1972 when a one-two punch delivered by federal regulators and the elements knocked the railroad down for the count. A federal pay board ordered major pay raises early in 1972, and the ICC refused to grant the carriers a four percent rise in freight rates, a decision which the road's last president estimated would cost EL $3 million annually. Banks responded by refusing loans at any manageable rate. Then in June, Hurricane Agnes struck with three days of constant rain through the valleys of the Allegheny, Chemung, Genesee, and Susquehanna Rivers. One hundred and eighteen people died and property damages exceeded $1.5 billion. Parts of the mainline, up to 4,000 feet long and fifteen feet deep, for a distance of 200 miles between Hornell and Owego were washed out. The ancient 818-foot long 235 foot high Portage Viaduct across the Genesee River in Letchworth Park was destroyed. Total cost to EL, consisting in damage to plant and loss of revenue was upwards of $11 million.

The N&W had had it with EL, which was forced to petition for reorganization on June 26, 1972. N&W had not wasted money on EL, but then it had not milked Dereco after the classical pattern for holding companies. Until the decline of its on-line freight revenues at the time of the EL bankruptcy, the D&H showed a profit which was loaned to EL rather than being skimmed off for N&W. But by the same token, N&W did not lavish money on EL, which it had only accepted in order to promote its merger with C&O. In an analogous case, C&O had pumped $232 million into B&O and so saved it. N&W declined to do this for EL.

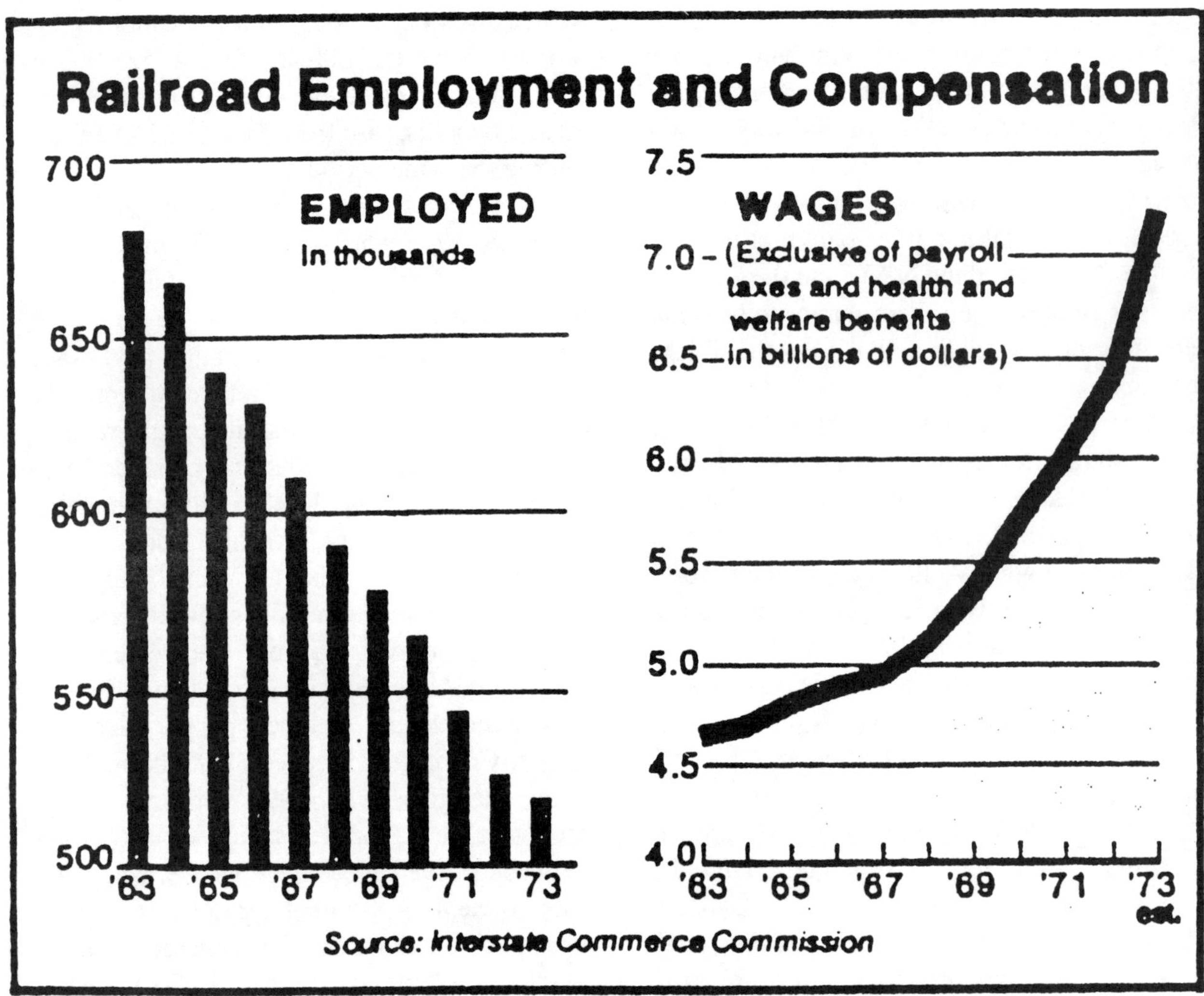

Conrail

It was primarily the catastrophic bankruptcy of Penn Central in June 1970, itself a dramatic instance of the battered finances and physical plant of the northeastern railroad industry as a whole, that led to the formation of Conrail in April 1976. Mergers had not solved the railroad problem because financially strong roads had refused to be saddled with weak ones, a repeat of their performance subsequent to the Transportation Act of 1920. The three railroads that made up PC, the NYC, PRR, and NYNH&H, were essential to the economy of the region but, because of conditions endemic to that region compounded by bad management and government meddling, they were among the most troubled.

After the Great Bankruptcy, with losses continuing to run about $3.3 million a month and no hope of help from the private sector, PC trains ran only by grace of huge infusions of federal funds. Moreover, insistent creditors could not be put off forever despite the vital importance to the region of continued operation of the railroad. The bankruptcy judge, John Fullen, explored the possibility of selling sections of the line to solvent roads but found no takers. Liquidation, another alternative, would mean the end of rail service throughout the northeast with resultant industrial shutdowns, loss of jobs, incomes, investments, and property values. The chickens of overregulation were coming home to roost with a vengeance. Early in 1973, with the court, creditors, politicians, and businessmen at loggerheads, and with branches of the federal government, the judiciary, Congress, and the administration pursuing diverse solutions (Senator Vance Hartke of Indiana had sponsored a bill providing for nationalization), Judge Fullam threatened to begin liquidation proceedings unless a practicable plan of reorganization was presented to him by the end of June.

The plan eventually adopted was in its essentials that drawn up by Frank E. Barnett, a brilliant Union Pacific lawyer. UP, like other western railroads, was appalled by the specter of not being able to forward traffic to the Northeast and to the North Atlantic coast. Baronet's plan embodied in the Regional Rail Reorganization (3R) Act enacted at the end of 1973 provided for the creation of a United States Railway Administration, a nonprofit corporation under the Department of Transportation with directors nominated by the president from a wide spectrum of interests including labor, creditors, shippers, sound railroads, and the government. This corporation would make loans or loan guarantees to the railroads and formulate a plan for a final system which would emerge after a thoroughgoing elimination of branch lines. The United States Department of Transportation would release a massive study on February 1, 1974, showing that 15,575 of 61,575 miles of rail lines in seventeen states in the North East and Middle West were unprofitable or redundant and should be abandoned or consolidated. Once the USSR's plan had been accepted, the slimmed down system would be taken over and operated by the Consolidated Rail Corporation (Conrail), a private company whose stock would be issued to creditors of the bankrupt roads. As long as more than half of Conrail's credit consisted in loans made or guaranteed by the government, the government would select the majority of the directors.

Conrail commenced operations on April 1, 1976, six years after the PC's bankruptcy. Besides PC, it had taken over five other bankrupt northeastern roads: the Jersey Central, the Lehigh Valley, Erie Lackawanna, the Reading, and the Lehigh & Hudson River. (Figure #6.) The Washington-Boston Corridor was sold for $85 million to Amtrak which later acquired the PRR's former Broadway mainline from Philadelphia to Harrisburg, Conrail retaining trackage rights for limited freight service. Corporate headquarters were to be at Philadelphia as those of PC had been, an indication that the new creation was basically PC redivivum.

Conrail was a failure, at least at first. New management did a creditable job of restoring the property, but this did not produce profits. The decline of heavy industry in the Northeast only speeded up after Conrail's appearance. Officials were as unable to get a handle on things as PC officials before them. Five years and billions of federal dollars later, the system was still losing a quarter of a billion a year.

Things had no where to go but up. In a final settlement with creditors Washington picked up most of Conrail's stock. In 1971, the year after PC's bankruptcy, Congress had created the National Rail Passenger Corporation (trade name Amtrak) to run what was left of the nation's intercity passenger trains, a limited operation whose losses would be made good by the federal government. This got all railroads, not just those in the Northeast, out of the losing business of running through passenger trains. The real turnaround in Conrail's fortunes, however, came with the appearance in 1980 of L. Stanley Crane as chairman and chief executive officer. Crane had earned his spurs in the engineering department of the Southern Railway of which he became vice president. He also had a two-year tour of duty

XVIII, 6

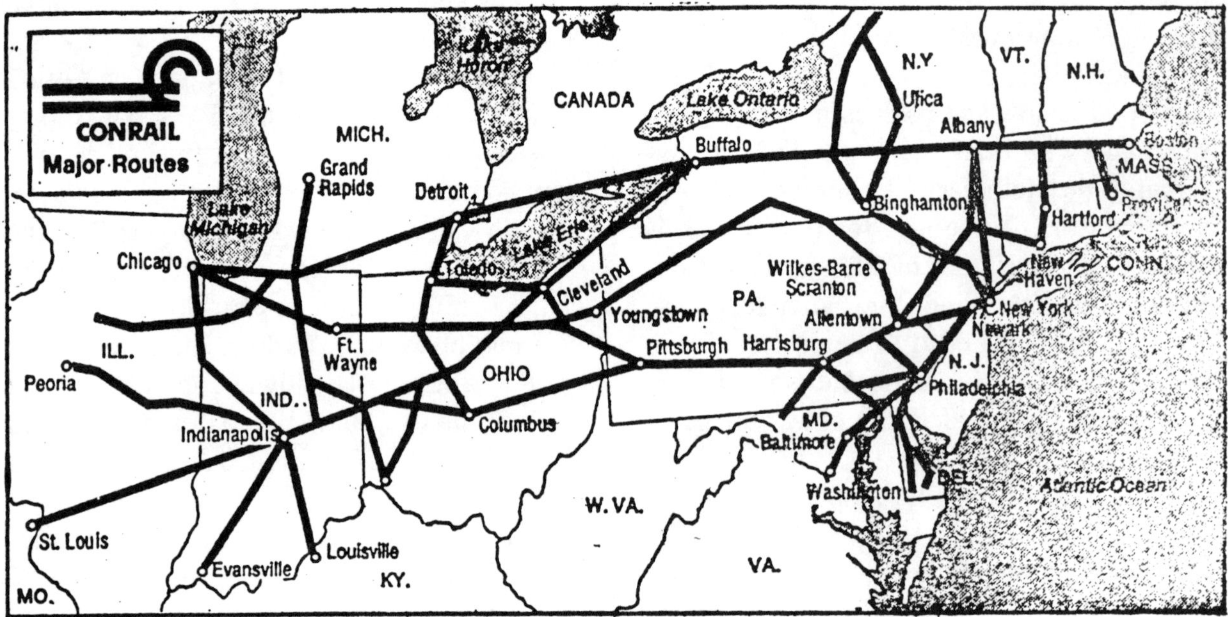

as director of industrial engineering on the PRR. His path to success was eased by passage of the Northeast Rail Reorganization Act of 1981 which let Conrail drop all commuter service, another perennial loser. Most of these runs were taken over by state authorities. This law also allowed Conrail to phase out thousands of nonessential jobs, and to abandon thousands more miles of unessential track. At the same time the railroad unions agreed not to seek raises until economic conditions improved. "Conrail unions," in an astounding *volte-face* reported by the May 6, 1981, New York Times, "join with administration to forgo some $229 million in wages and benefits a year in an attempt to make the system profitable and head off [Ronald Reagan's] administration attempt to break it up and sell it." By the end of Crane's first year, Conrail showed a slight profit. Then more black ink appeared. Net income rose from $38 million in 1981 to $500 million in 1984 and, despite an economic downturn in 1985, net in 1986 was $442 million. Employment had been reduced from 95,000 at the time of Conrail's creation to less than 40,000 in 1986. It was during Crane's administration that Conrail in 1983 gained control of the Buffalo Creek Railroad.

The climate in which Crane operated was immeasurably improved by the passage in 1980 of the Staggers Act which went a long way toward getting the ICC out of the rate regulation business. This invites the surmise that under these changed circumstances railroads might have made it earlier. The genesis of Staggers is narrated in a lively manner by Goddard:

When Congress put trucking under the ICC's thumb in 1935, it actually exempted most of the industry - fleets owned by shippers, truckers working for only a few customers, and for-hire carriers hauling fruits and vegetables. During the 1940s and 1950s, the ICC, fearing withering rate wars that would harm truckers, blocked railways from cutting rates to lure shippers away from trucks. But no one was protecting the railroads whose profits continued to erode. A trucker hauling fresh produce, for example, could change his rates to reflect a banner crop or a drought by making a phone call. His rail competitor had to apply for a rate change to the ICC, then go through hearings and deliberations over months or years, by which time the market conditions might have changed several time. It was scarcely surprising that by the late 1970s truckers carried the lion's share of the nation's fresh fruit and vegetables.

In 1976, prodded by Congress, the ICC began to ease its grip on both railroads and truckers. The Commission let truckers take detours up to 20 percent of the length of their trips. This important change meant that owner-operators could truck lumber from Butte to Seattle, then carry a backhaul to a city near Butte without ICC permission. One-way trips covered costs, but back hauls generated profit. Word spread fast through the truck stops and the number of independents seeking to join the industry doubled between 1975 and 1980.

President Jimmy Carter campaigned to deregulate transportation across the board. Recognizing the need for public support, the president started with the airlines, feeling that Americans could identify with air travel more easily than freight handling. Carter pushed his deregulation bill through Congress in 1978 and turned his attention to the railroads. But unlike his predecessors, Carter attacked with both barrels, seeking reform legislation while also pledging to "pack the ICC with fervent deregulators." [3]

The irony here was that Democrat Carter showed himself more friendly to big business, at least railroads, than Republican Eisenhower whose 1956 Federal Highway Act hastened the demise of the railroads that had helped him so much in winning his war. Goddard continues:

Carter delivered on his promise, and soon railroads - for the first time in nearly a century - could haul produce in new refrigerated cars, on any terms they wished, and thus compete head-to-head with the truckers. The ICC also let the railways abandon unprofitable lines it had earlier demanded they keep. A Gerald Ford appointee to the ICC went so far as to say that the ICC should stop running the railroads altogether. Clearly, events were building toward an election-year denouement on Capitol Hill

As Carter campaigned for reelection in 1980, the beginnings of deregulation had proved popular with the American public, which looked forward to the low fares they expected price competition to bring. Senator Ted Kennedy, challenging Carter for his party's nomination, adopted more deregulation as one of his main campaign themes. Looking over his shoulder, the president flogged Congress to adopt major bills to remove the shackles from both trucking and the railroads in time for the election. [4]

The desired legislation was sponsored by Representative Harley Staggers of West Virginia. His task was made easier by the worsening condition of Conrail which was costing a million dollars a day in operating subsidies, something the public would not tolerate much longer. Goddard explains the overall thrust of the Staggers Act:

The ICC had historically been an officious aunt to the road and rail industries, not content to simply drive them to the ball but demanding to dance with them as well. Now Congress told her to simply sit on the sidelines and chaperone. The Staggers bill that Carter signed in October 1980 just before losing the presidential election to Ronald Reagan, let railroads cancel unprofitable services or routes and set their own rates within limits. Congress then evened the rules through a companion measure called the Motor Carrier Act, letting for-hire truckers do the same. Truckers seeking to run between two cities were free to do so, unless existing carriers could prove their competition would be damaging. Despite having existed side-by-side for nearly a century, road and rail had never been allowed to compete within the free marketplace. Clearly a new day had dawned.

The Grangers had demanded that the ICC control railroad monopolies, but the railways had not had a monopoly in most areas since the 1920s; in that sense the Staggers bill was fifty years late. Now for the first time in nearly a century, a railroad could set its own terms with a shipper, without ICC interference, as long as others could bid on the publicly posted rate. From that point on, regulators would step in only to stave off cutthroat competition or to prevent monopolies. Piggybacking and Big John hopper cars had made railroads more competitive, so the ICC freed piggybacking entirely from regulation. [5]

The Act of 1981 had set a deadline of 1984 for transfer of Conrail to the private sector. Ronald Reagan was president, and the gospel of free enterprise was once again the ruling orthodoxy. Not that there were no objections raised to the sale. The federal government and taxpayers, some urged, should be compensated for the more than $7 billion they had pumped into the system since the Great Bankruptcy of 1970. In the spirit of the Progressives in the opening decades of the century, others argued that the government should keep control of Conrail which could serve as a yardstick to measure the validity of requests by the rest of the railroad industry for rate hikes and other concessions. A third group feared the contemporary trend of business managers to make a quick profit and get out. The Reagan administration, however, strongly supported privatization.

Norfolk Southern

Norfolk Southern had come into existence in 1982 as the result of a merger between N&W and Southern Railway. (Figure #7.) Together the two companies, which competed at very few points, employed 43,000 workers. In 1980 their combined sales were $2.9 billion. The combination overlapped CSX at many

XVIII, 7

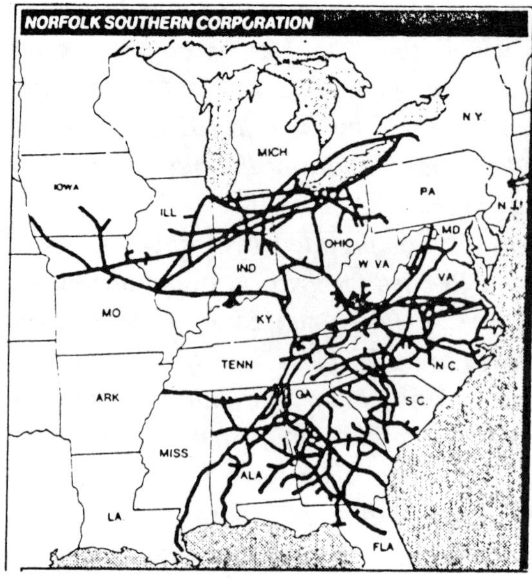

points and was created in order to compete with that system. In terms of mileage, NS was America's fourth largest railroad behind the Burlington Northern, CSX, and Conrail. CSX, however, had more track and better access to Northeastern markets like Pittsburgh and New York City. Possession of Conrail would enable NS to overcome this advantage; hence it offered $1.9 billion for Conrail, a ridiculously low figure in the judgment of Albro Martin and of the Congressional Budget Office which came up with the figure of $3.5 billion. NS's bid, however, was supported by Elizabeth Dole, Secretary of Transportation. She wanted Conrail to have a partner with deep pockets. Other bidders were Alleghany Corporation, employees of the railroad, and executives including Crane himself. The solution adopted by Congress was public sale of the government's 85 percent of Conrail's stock. The other 15 percent was held by present and past employees. On March 26, 1987, a hundred years after the passage of the Interstate Commerce Act, 58.75 million shares of Conrail, the largest single offering in New York Stock Exchange history, went on the market. The opening bid that day was $31.50 a share, which at $1.65 billion was $250 million below

Norfolk Southern's offer. It was estimated that Goldman Sachs, which arranged the sale, received $80 million for its trouble.

Norfolk Southern, however, was a presence on the Niagara Frontier through N&W's merger 1964 merger with the NKP and the Wabash. In an editorial entitled "Bison Yard Revived," in a supplement to a Kalmbach Publishing Company flyer, Bill Stephen updates NS activity here:

Bison Yard, formerly Erie Lackawanna's major facility in Buffalo, N.Y., was a vacant sea of rail and grass in 1984 when William "Skip" Stigall, a Norfolk Southern senior terminal trainmaster, arrived in town. Shortly afterward, Conrail and NS ripped up the tracks, shared the spoils, and split the co-owned yard's property. NS retreated to its small Buffalo Junction yard, except for five "seldom filled" spurs used for intermodal [rail-truck coordinated service] *and auto unloading. Conrail emphasized Frontier Yard, a large former New York Central facility on the Chicago-New York mainline.*

Now Stigall is overseeing a $20 million Bison expansion that will enable the yard to handle Norfolk Southern's ballooning intermodal, auto, and lumber traffic, plus Road Railer [an intermodal container with dual flanged wheels and rubber tires but no flat car] business of subsidiary Triple Crown Services. NS broke ground for the project in late October 1992. When construction is done in early 1994, NS will utilize all 105 acres of its property, compared with 25 acres prior to expansion.

The new traffic that NS has generated since 1988 has clogged Bison - especially the 1992 jumps of 36 percent more overall traffic and 140% more intermodal business. Stigall attributes that growth to an aggressive NS sales staff, the railroads' new customer-driven service, the US-Canada free trade agreement, and Conrail closing its intermodal terminal in favor of a hub in Syracuse, 160 miles east.

Traffic at Bison has risen steadily since November 1988, when NS began Triple Crown service in Buffalo and added one track to accommodate the Road Railers. In March 1992, a local lumber distributor began a rail-truck transfer operation at Bison. Also in March, NS added two temporary tracks for piggyback service two weeks after Conrail closed its intermodal activity.

"The business came a lot faster than we expected," Stigall says. "We needed track space a year ago." Relief is on the way. The new Bison will contain a longer, 4-track intermodal and Triple Crown facility with an overhead crane; larger, 5-track auto unloading center; 2 tracks for lumber unloading; and 10 switching and storage tracks.

NS plans to begin dedicated intermodal service between Buffalo, Chicago, and Kansas City once the yard is complete, and expects its intermodal business to double. NS, which hired 33 employees in the past year to bring its Buffalo force to 80, operates 12 to 14 trains in and out of the city on its former Nickel Plate and Wabash lines. "There are more trains in the wings," Stigall says. "I haven't seen a recession at this end of the railroad."

Despite the NS revival, Stigall says the yard "will never be what it once was." That's for sure - at its peak Bison handled up to 100 trains a day from EL, Norfolk & Western, and Chesapeake and Ohio. Built in 1963 by EL and Nickel Plate, the yard was a victim of Conrail's surplus trackage in Buffalo. While a return to the yard's glory days is out of the question, Bison's reversal of fortune is an interesting twist to the usual fate of abandoned yards. [6]

The D&H (Canadian Pacific) Comes to Buffalo

The Delaware & Hudson appeared first on the transportation scene as a canal which was completed in 1823 to carry hard coal from Honesdale, Pennsylvania, to Kingston on the Hudson River. (Figure I, #1.) A gravity railroad with stationary engines brought the coal cars over the mountain to Honesdale from the mines at Carbondale. It was over a section of this railroad that the first commercial steam locomotive in America, the Stourbridge Lion, ran in 1828. By October 28, 1870, the D&H had completed a direct line from the mines at Carbondale, bypassing the gravity railroad and the canal, to Nineveh near Binghamton on the Albany & Susquehanna which had been completed between the state capital and Binghamton the last day of 1868. In 1870 D&H leased the Albany & Susquehanna. D&H was a coal company and was seeking markets for its product. Later it leased the 181 mile long Albany to Whitehall Rensselaer & Saratoga which placed it at the head of Lake Champlain. In 1875, as the New York & Canada, it reached Rouses Point on the international border with a direct connection to Montreal. With the decline of anthracite, the Montreal-Albany part of the D&H became its main source of revenue, chiefly from paper and pulp shipments from on-line and Canadian mills. Nevertheless, together with the section southwest of Albany, the D&H continued to function as a bridge line between eastern Canada/New England and the Erie and DL&W at Binghamton.

In 1964, as noted above, as a condition of the merger of the N&W, the NKP, and the Wabash, the N&W had to include EL in its system and was encouraged to take over the Boston & Maine and the Delaware & Hudson. The reasoning was that the merged N&W-NKP-Wabash would be prosperous enough to take over these ailing lines (the B&M, which connected with the D&H at Mechanicville just north of Albany, was being called the "Busted and Maimed") and that competition had to be created to face the impending arrival of PC for which permission had first been asked of the ICC in 1962. To meet this requirement and at the same time to protect itself from being dragged down by unprofitable partners, N&W in 1966 created Dereco, which acquired control of EL and D&H in 1968, as noted above. Hurricane Agnes in 1972, which finished off EL, severely damaged D&H. When Dereco, fronting for N&W, arranged almost immediately afterwards the bankruptcy of EL, D&H stood alone with the assistance of federal loans ($70 million) and a subsidy from New York for maintenance and rolling stock ($67 million), but it was no match for PC, bad as that misbegotten construct turned out to be. EL entered Conrail in 1976 but D&H remained independent. The creation of Conrail threatened the D&H bridge line business since Conrail would long-haul its own lines wherever possible. "To assure competitive rail service in the Northeast," the ICC insisted that the D&H be given trackage rights over Conrail to Buffalo via the former EL, to Philadelphia and Newark via the former LV and Reading, and to Alexandria, Virginia, on the ex-PRR's Northern Central. (Figure #8.) These trackage rights produced roundabout routes and were more trouble to the D&H than a help. Interchange fell from 10.7 million tons in 1973 to 6.4 million in 1982. D&H's operating ratio went above 100 in 1978, and thereafter the road posted losses. In 1982 Timothy Mellon's Guilford Transportation Industries took D&H off Dereco's hands for a token half million dollars and joined it to the Maine Central, which Mellon had bought in 1981, and to the Boston & Maine, which he acquired a year later.

Mellon was trying to create a viable railroad system in post-heavy industry New England, but was blocked by a federal arbitrator's June 11, 1988, decision requiring Mellon to reinstate original MC and B&M labor agreements. This decision was followed five days later by the D&H's bankruptcy. The ICC designated as operator of the D&H Delaware Otsego which did the job through its subsidiary, New York Susquehanna & Western.

Delaware Otsego dates from 1966, when several businessmen and railfans began running excursions over a section of NYC's abandoned Ulster & Delaware branch near

XVIII, 8

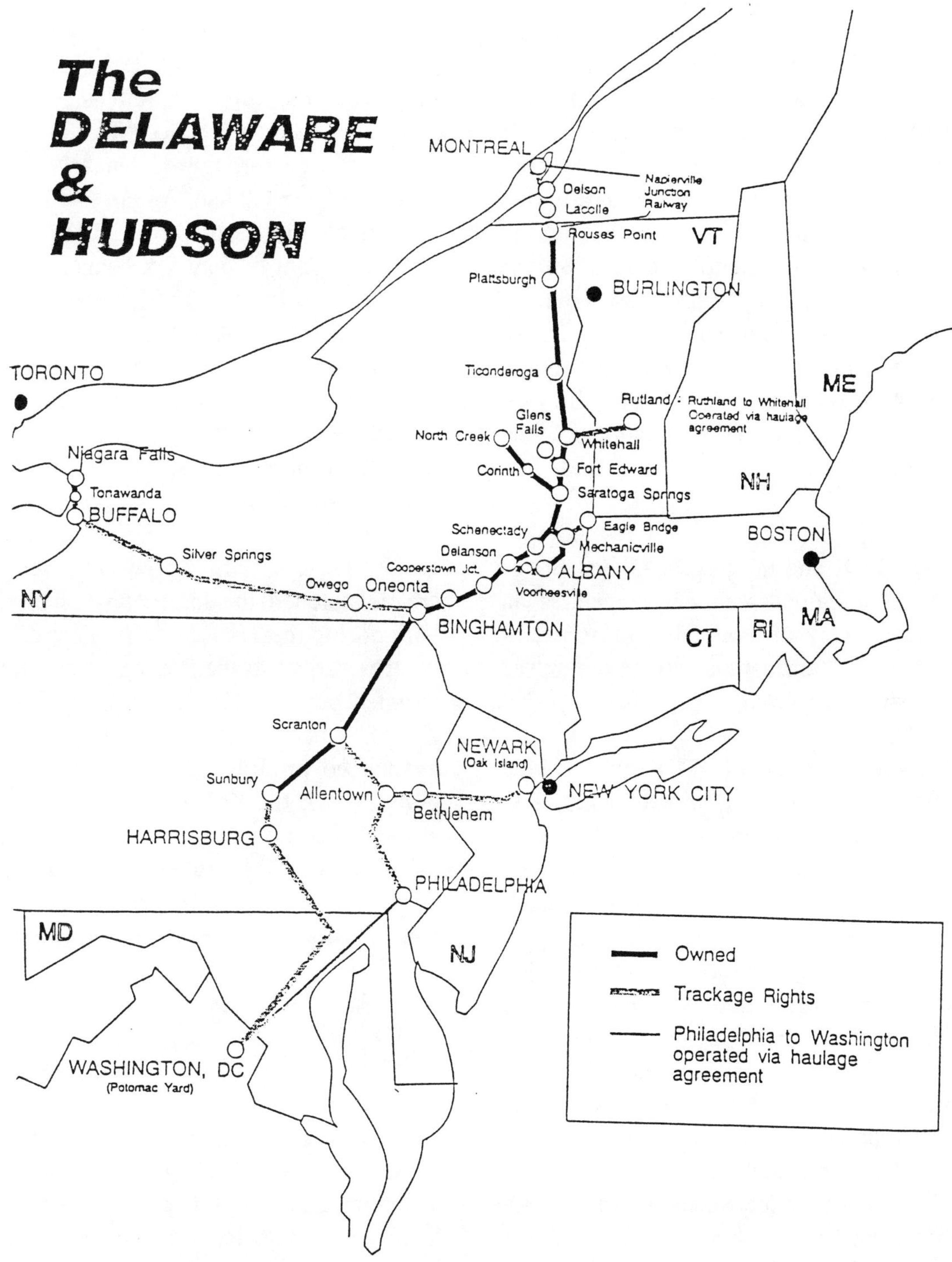
The DELAWARE & HUDSON
MONTREAL
Napierville Junction Railway
Delson
Lacolle
Rouses Point
VT
Plattsburgh
BURLINGTON
TORONTO
Ticonderoga
ME
Rutland
Ruthland to Whitehall Operated via haulage agreement
Glens Falls
North Creek
Whitehall
Corinth
Fort Edward
NH
Niagara Falls
Tonawanda
BUFFALO
Saratoga Springs
Eagle Bridge
Mechanicville
Schenectady
Delanson
BOSTON
Silver Springs
Cooperstown Jct.
ALBANY
Owego
Oneonta
Voorheesville
NY
BINGHAMTON
CT
RI
MA
Scranton
NEWARK
(Oak Island)
Sunbury
Allentown
NEW YORK CITY
Bethlehem
HARRISBURG
PHILADELPHIA
MD
NJ
Owned
Trackage Rights
Philadelphia to Washington operated via haulage agreement
WASHINGTON, DC
(Potomac Yard)

Oneonta, New York. Later the company operated the Fonda Johnstown & Gloversville and the ex-Erie's Honesdale, Pennsylvania, branch. In 1980 through a subsidiary the DO bought the bankrupt New York Susquehanna & Western which at the time ran from Little Ferry near the Hudson River to Butler, New Jersey. This was extended by rehabilitating the NYS&W's abandoned mainline twenty-five miles to Sparta Junction where DO had bought a thirteen-mile segment of the ex-Lehigh & Hudson River from Conrail in 1982. From Warwick to Campbell Hall on the ex-Erie line to Binghamton the NYS&W had trackage rights from Conrail. Beginning in 1986 the NYS&W began hauling double-stack container trains over this route to Sea-Land terminal at Little Ferry in conjunction with the D&H (after 1990 read CP) and CSX as the Chicago-Little Ferry portion of a transcontinental service from Tacoma, Washington, and Los Angeles.

Sea-Land Service, a wholly owned subsidiary of CSX and the largest United States flag container-shipping concern, operates an extensive network of terminals and a fleet of eighty-three container ships serving a hundred ports in seventy countries. Containers on Flat Cars (COFC) are a great improvement over Trailers on Flat cars (TOFC) and enabled trains to function as land ships that began to put a serious dent in the trucking business. Though COFC is operated in conjunction with trucks, the railroad collects for the longer haul. Though DO/NYS&W and D&H/CP were promoted as providing an alternate Conrail, much of their route from Buffalo to Little Ferry was actually owned by Conrail. One reason for DO's success was the fact that its trains were operated by two or three-man crews rather than the four which Conrail and other larger railroads were obliged to employ.

Avid to penetrate the Northeast, the mighty Canadian Pacific, which already owned the Soo Line in the upper Midwest and had purchased Penn Central's interest in the Toronto Hamilton & Buffalo in 1977, agreed with the trustee in May, 1990, to pay $25 million to the D&H's creditors in order to take control of the bankrupt line, this despite failing to secure an arrangement with Conrail for the running rights to Hagerstown, Maryland, and connections with CSX. The ICC approved the merger on October 2, at which time CP announced that it planned to spend $18 million a year improving the rundown line and to acquire sixty-two locomotives costing $37 million. The sale went through on January 21, 1991, by which time CP and Conrail had reached an agreement that assured the D&H of trackage rights on Conrail between Niagara Falls and Buffalo and into Philadelphia and Newark. The arrangement also included an option for CP to buy what was now called Conrail's Southern Tier line, the old Erie main between Buffalo and Binghamton on which CP had inherited running rights from the D&H. The D&H also abandoned its steep mainline between Scranton and Binghamton in favor of the ex-DL&W's fifty-eight mile mainline, which included the famed Nicholson Cutoff, built during the Truesdale administration.

The sequel to the Southern Tier story was narrated by Scott Hartley in the March, 1993, *Trains*. In a surprise turnaround, Conrail announced on July 2, 1992, that it was not going to sell the line to CP but was going to spend $7 million upgrading it. Conrail plans called for converting the double track road to single track with CTC and passing tracks which with track repair would restore the route to a fifty mile an hour maximum speed limit. Overhead clearances were to be replaced to handle double-stack containers for the CP which interchanged with the NYS&W at Binghamton.

For years there had been too many NY-Buffalo railroads. Then after the war came abandonments. Much of the DL&W west of Binghamton had been abandoned during EL days except from Binghamton to Vestal (seven miles), from Painted Post to Bath (nineteen miles), from Griegsville to North Alexander (twenty- two miles), and from Depew to East Buffalo (five miles.) Conrail had abandoned most of the NYWS&B west of Albany by the early 1970s and pulled up LV tracks west of Waverly. NY-Buffalo Conrail freight trains used the NYWS&B to Albany and what was now called the Water Level Route (the original NYC) to Buffalo. Ex-PC lines were in better shape and had none of the EL's tough grades in Pennsylvania.

However, as part of an agreement with the New York Department of Transportation, which underwrote reconstruction of the Southern Tier line in the late 1970s to help the economy of the area, Conrail had promised to run one through train in each direction every weekday on the Southern Tier until 1988. The D&H, now under the CP's wing, ran three regularly scheduled freight trains in each direction daily over the Southern Tier in addition to several intermodal trains and frequent coal and grain extras. The D&H's running rights over the Southern Tier provided a bridge linking CN, CP, and NS at Buffalo with the former parent Guilford Industries near Albany. CP trains with CP equipment and crews could now run through from Toronto through Buffalo to Newark, Philadelphia, and Washington. Though CP decided to exercise its option to purchase the 204 miles of Southern Tier between Buffalo and Binghamton, Conrail called the deal off on July 2, alleging CP's repeated efforts to change the terms of the deal, which CP authorities denied. Soon after Conrail decided to hold on to the Southern Tier, it added a pair of freight trains, one of which carried autos from Detroit to North Jersey and empties back. Not included in Conrail's renewed interest in the Southern Tier was the old Erie mainline to Chicago west of Hornell now called the Meadville line, more than half of which was abandoned. Fifty-one miles were retained from Jamestown to Olean where a junction was made with the PRR's Buffalo-Harrisburg line (originally the Buffalo New York and Philadelphia.)

A July, 1992, article in *Trains* describes present day D&H traffic patterns:

D&H runs daily intermodal service between Philadelphia and Montreal, Toronto, and Chicago. Train #557 departs Philadelphia for Binghamton, where Montreal-bound train #553 splits off. After adding boxcar traffic from Guilford and stack cars from Susquehanna, train #557 continues on to Buffalo, Niagara Falls, and Toronto. Cars for Chicago are put on CP train #505 out of Toronto; from Detroit, #505 operates west to Chicago over CSX. In the New York area, D&H plans to renew service over Conrail trackage over the former Lehigh Valley between Allentown, Pa., and Newark. CP Rail has spent nearly $1 million improving the [Newark] *Terminal.* [7]

The Demise of the Lehigh

The PRR and the Wabash had held forty-four percent of the LV's stock since the late 1920s. But in the interests of promoting competition the ICC had blocked the PRR from voting any of its LV stock. By the late 1950s, however, the LV began piling up huge deficits due to ruinous taxation, the growth of intercity trucking, the continuing decline of the anthracite business, and spiraling losses in the passenger business. (The last named of these problems was solved with the termination of passenger service in February, 1961.) The LV's last year of profitability was 1956. Between then and 1958 operating revenues fell $14 million. In a move designed to safeguard the value of its holdings, the PRR on April 11, 1962, took over the LV through an exchange of stock. Despite opposition from the EL and the NYC, the ICC blessed the union because the LV could no longer survive under independence management. In 1962 it was to lose more than $8 million. Next year the PRR tried to sell the LV to the C&O but the offer was rejected. As Archer remarks, the LV lived out the rest of "the decade in a state of limbo, concerning itself in a near desperate struggle for mere survival." No large scale infusions of cash could be expected from the now ailing PRR. Branch lines were lopped off, mainline maintenance was deferred, and some coordination of trackage was effected with a former rival, the Jersey Central. When the merger of PRR and NYC was approved by the ICC in 1966, it was with the understanding that the LV was to be offered to either the C&O or the N&W. If neither wanted the sick unto death LV (as turned out to be the case), it was to become part of Penn Central. There it remained, piling up deficits. Losses for 1969 had been $5.2 million with $2.5 million in red ink for the first quarter of 1970. Unable to meet interest and principal on its government guaranteed loans, the LV petitioned for a bankruptcy which would enable it to continue operating while trustees attempted to set its finances in order. They gave it their best try, but it was not enough and on June 7, 1973, they petitioned the Federal District Court in Philadelphia to terminate all service. A survey of the road's traffic patterns showed that though it operated 950 miles of trackage, nine-tenths of its freight business was carried on 165 miles of it. Congress provided $250 million in emergency funds to tide the LV over, pending the creation of Conrail. The United States Railroad Administration determined that of the three major trunk line carriers, PC, EL, and LV, the LV carried the least traffic and was not worth saving. With additional federal cash the LV staggered through 1975. On April 1, 1976, what was left of a once great railroad was taken over by Conrail and the LV's 130 year old history came to an end. For a time Conrail operated a short distance of the ex-Depew & Tonawanda from Niagara Junction to Williamsville and an equally short distance of the old mainline from Pittsburgh and Lehigh Junction to Batavia, but these were speedily abandoned.

With the abandonment of the Lehigh and much of the former Lackawanna, what had once been grade crossing elimination was itself extensively dismantled. Numerous bridges over Buffalo streets on the Erie and the Lackawanna's branches to International Bridge were removed, as were those on the Lehigh's mainline over William Street near Ogden and the Lehigh's branch to Tonawanda over Sheridan Drive. (Figures #9 and #10.)

Amtrak

The Rail Passenger Service Act (Railpax) which President Richard M. Nixon signed at the end of October, 1971, was emergency legislation aimed at saving the railroad industry by relieving it of increasingly unacceptable losses from the operation of intercity passenger trains. At the time, twenty percent of America's railroads were in bankruptcy or on the brink thereof. Railpax provided for a formative period of ninety days. During the first thirty the Secretary of Transportation, John A. Volpe, was to select routes for preservation; during the second thirty days the ICC, railroads, unions, and state public service commissions were to comment on proposals in the act and on the routes selected; during the third thirty days Volpe was to draw up a final report. Route selection presented the hardest choices, but other thorny issues had also to be dealt with. Fewer trains would mean fewer jobs, and the unions wanted job protection. Minimum track standards had to be maintained for fast passenger trains by railroads which were getting out of the passenger business but whose lines were to be used by Railpax. Financial arrangements had to be made for leasing terminals and constructing scaled down stations elsewhere.

The corporation created by Railpax was to be superintended by fifteen directors, eight designated by the administration, four by preferred stockholders, and three by the railroads. The federal government was the preferred stockholder, and the stock which represented

XVIII, 9

XVIII, 10

federal operating and capital payments made to the company totaled $8.1 billion by 1993. The arrangement gave taxpayers a senior claim on the corporation's assets in the event of a dissolution. The government was obliged to extend $40 million in grants and another $100 million in guaranteed loans. Two hundred million dollars more was expected from participating roads. The railroads could either refuse to join, in which case they had to keep their passenger trains running as of October 30, 1970, for five years, or they could join up (i. e., opt out of the passenger train business) by paying cash or contributing acceptable equipment. The exit fee was set at half of their fully distributed passenger losses for 1969. Participating railroads would operate what trains were left, but would be reimbursed for their services.

Vole's plan called for the 366 intercity passenger trains still running to be cut down drastically to 50. The routes centered around New York and Chicago and served Seattle, San Francisco, and Los Angeles in the West, Houston, New Orleans, and Miami in the South, Detroit, Saint Louis, and Cincinnati in the Midwest, and Buffalo, Washington, and Boston in the East. Bowing to criticism, Volpe raised the number of trains to 184, linking 114 cities along 21 basic routes. (Figure #11.) Maine, New Hampshire, Vermont, Arkansas, South Dakota, and Wyoming were left with no passenger service. Representatives of these states denounced the plan bitterly as did the press generally which looked on it as too stingy as regards the pubic and too generous to the railroads. Railpax supporters countered that the populous Northeast Corridor would be the first order of business with high speed trains supplanting air-shuttle by the mid 1970s.

With no locomotives, cars, stations, yards, or repair shops, Amtrak began service on May 1, 1971. The name was substituted for Railpax since by that time any word with rail in it generated a negative public reaction. Roger Lewis, Amtrak's first president, picked his team of top administrators from aviation. They spent money on image building while the infrastructure continued to deteriorate. Moreover, personnel and equipment remained as before, with the government picking up the tab for operating losses, a procedure which undermined any attempt to maintain quality and keep costs low. The summer of 1971 found Lewis at Congress's door begging for an additional $173 million to keep Amtrak running until 1973. Contracting roads failed to maintain equipment and roadbed, and dispatchers frequently and illegally gave freight trains priority over passenger trains shunting the latter on to sidetracks. The Arab oil boycott of 1973-1974 spurred a sizable increase in ridership on the Northeast Corridor, but when the embargo was lifted the traveling public returned to the highway.

On the subject of Amtrak's early rolling stock Mike Schafer writes in All Aboard Amtrak:

But clues of a new regime began to appear in short order, and nowhere was this more evident than in the realm of equipment, which Amtrak began to acquire in autumn 1971 from member railroads following a period of selection that began before Amtrak even started operations. With 20 member railroads, Amtrak had a rainbow of rolling stock and motive power to choose from - some 3,000 passenger cars and hundreds of locomotives.

Of course, the newborn corporation hardly needed all 3,000 cars to protect the spindly network of services that survived past May 1, 1971, so it set about picking the best of the lot - narrowing it down to some 1,200 cars and 300 locomotives. The new pool resulted in what many Amtrak watchers and passenger-train aficionados were anxiously awaiting: Amtrak's short lived era as a rolling artist' palette. Well into the summer of '71, cars and locomotives were being re-deployed throughout the US. In particular, equipment of Western roads, which in general had a history of meticulous maintenance, migrated east-

XVIII, 11

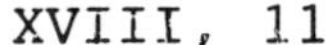

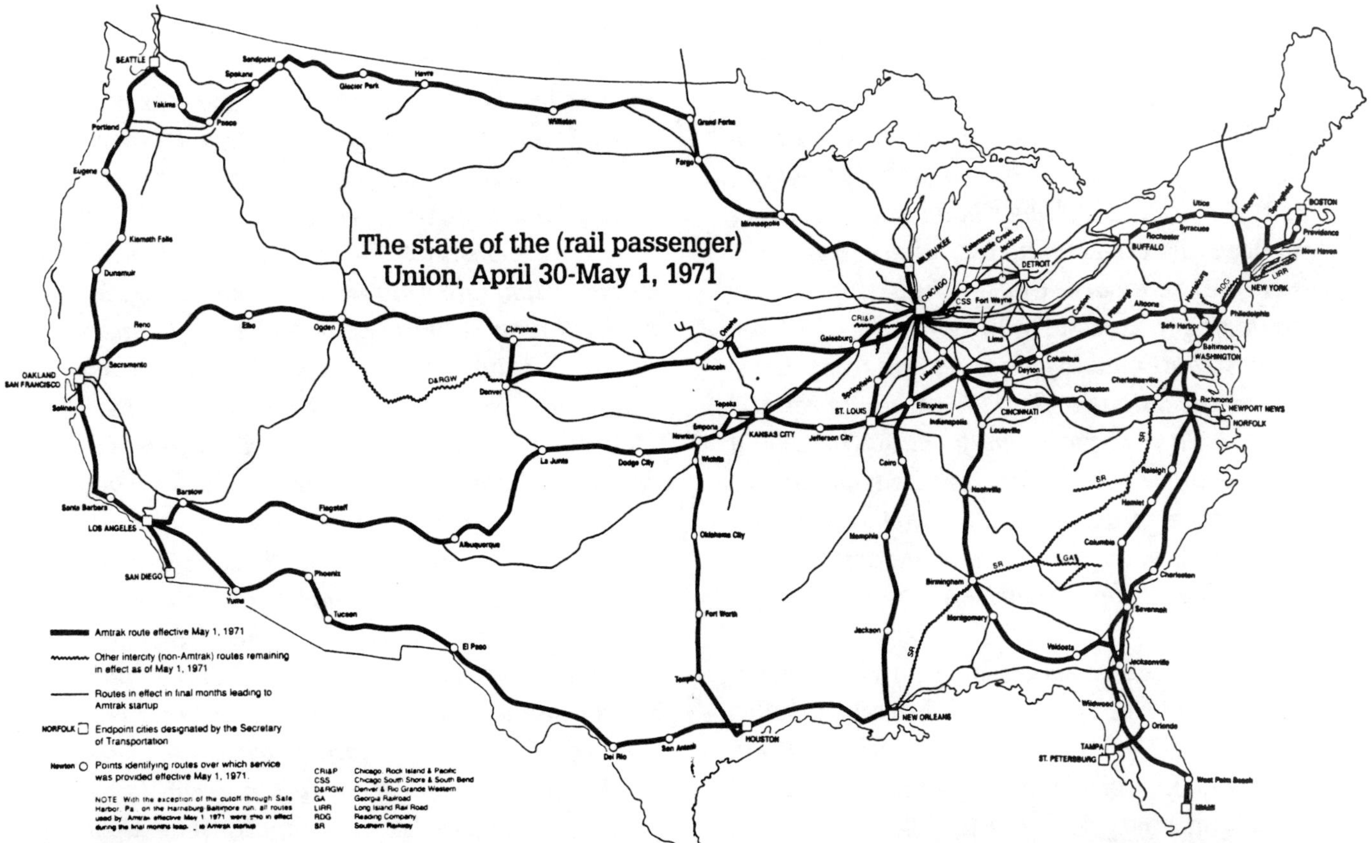
The state of the (rail passenger) Union, April 30-May 1, 1971
SEATTLE
Portland
Eugene
Klamath Falls
Dunsmuir
Reno
Sacramento
OAKLAND
SAN FRANCISCO
Ogden
Cheyenne
Denver
D&RGW
Omaha
Lincoln
Topeka
KANSAS CITY
ST. LOUIS
Jefferson City
Newton
Wichita
La Junta
Dodge City
Barstow
Flagstaff
Albuquerque
Santa Barbara
LOS ANGELES
SAN DIEGO
Yuma
Phoenix
Tucson
El Paso
Oklahoma City
Fort Worth
Temple
Del Rio
San Antonio
HOUSTON
NEW ORLEANS
Jackson
Memphis
Cairo
Birmingham
Montgomery
Nashville
Louisville
Indianapolis
Effingham
Springfield
Galesburg
CRI&P
CHICAGO
MILWAUKEE
Minneapolis
Fargo
Grand Forks
Williston
Havre
Glacier Park
Sandpoint
Spokane
Yakima
Pasco
DETROIT
CSS
Fort Wayne
Lima
Dayton
Columbus
CINCINNATI
Charleston
Pittsburgh
Altoona
Harrisburg
Safe Harbor
Philadelphia
Baltimore
WASHINGTON
Richmond
NEWPORT NEWS
NORFOLK
Raleigh
Hamlet
Columbia
Charleston
Savannah
Jacksonville
Valdosta
Wildwood
Orlando
TAMPA
ST. PETERSBURG
West Palm Beach
MIAMI
BUFFALO
Rochester
Syracuse
Utica
Albany
Springfield
BOSTON
Providence
New Haven
NEW YORK
RDG
LIRR
SR
GA
Amtrak route effective May 1, 1971
Other intercity (non-Amtrak) routes remaining in effect as of May 1, 1971
Routes in effect in final months leading to Amtrak startup
NORFOLK Endpoint cities designated by the Secretary of Transportation
Newton Points identifying routes over which service was provided effective May 1, 1971.
NOTE With the exception of the cutoff through Safe Harbor, Pa. on the Harrisburg Baltimore run, all routes used by Amtrak effective May 1, 1971 were also in effect during the final months lead... to Amtrak startup
CRI&P Chicago, Rock Island & Pacific
CSS Chicago South Shore & South Bend
D&RGW Denver & Rio Grande Western
GA Georgia Railroad
LIRR Long Island Rail Road
RDG Reading Company
SR Southern Railway

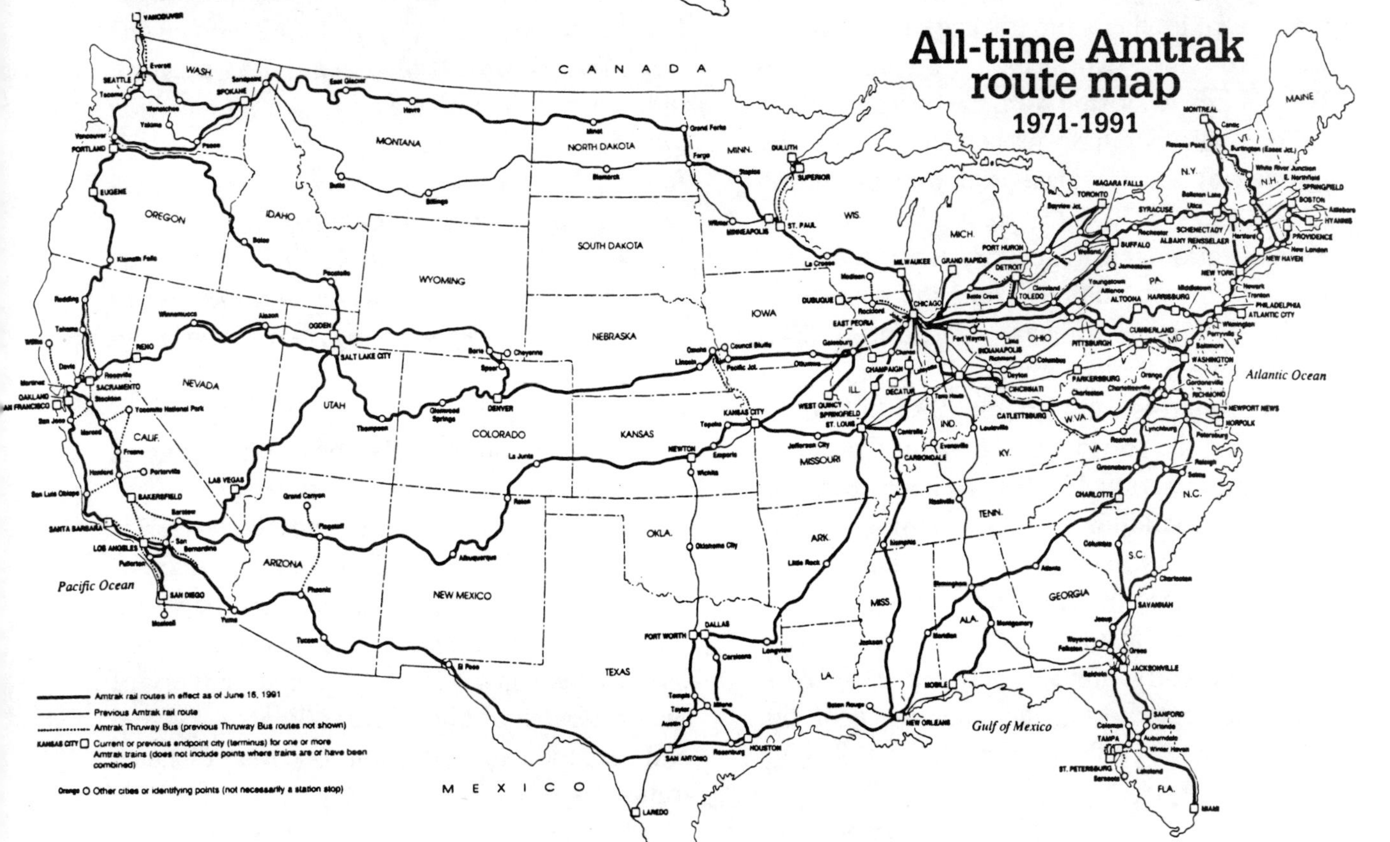
All-time Amtrak route map
1971-1991
CANADA
MEXICO
Pacific Ocean
Atlantic Ocean
Gulf of Mexico
VANCOUVER
WASH.
SEATTLE
Tacoma
Everett
SPOKANE
Sandpoint
East Glacier
Havre
Minot
Grand Forks
MONTANA
NORTH DAKOTA
SOUTH DAKOTA
MINN.
DULUTH
SUPERIOR
ST. PAUL
MINNEAPOLIS
WIS.
MICH.
PORTLAND
EUGENE
OREGON
IDAHO
WYOMING
NEBRASKA
IOWA
OGDEN
SALT LAKE CITY
NEVADA
RENO
SACRAMENTO
OAKLAND
SAN FRANCISCO
CALIF.
UTAH
COLORADO
DENVER
KANSAS
KANSAS CITY
NEWTON
LAS VEGAS
BAKERSFIELD
LOS ANGELES
SAN DIEGO
ARIZONA
NEW MEXICO
OKLA.
TEXAS
FORT WORTH
DALLAS
HOUSTON
SAN ANTONIO
LAREDO
El Paso
Phoenix
Tucson
Yuma
MISSOURI
ARK.
MISS.
ALA.
LA.
NEW ORLEANS
MOBILE
ILL.
CHICAGO
MILWAUKEE
ST. LOUIS
IND.
KY.
TENN.
OHIO
TOLEDO
DETROIT
PA.
PITTSBURGH
HARRISBURG
PHILADELPHIA
ATLANTIC CITY
W.VA.
VA.
RICHMOND
NEWPORT NEWS
NORFOLK
WASHINGTON
N.C.
CHARLOTTE
S.C.
SAVANNAH
GEORGIA
JACKSONVILLE
SANFORD
TAMPA
ST. PETERSBURG
FLA.
MIAMI
N.Y.
NIAGARA FALLS
TORONTO
SYRACUSE
SCHENECTADY
ALBANY RENSSELAER
BUFFALO
NEW YORK
NEW HAVEN
PROVIDENCE
BOSTON
SPRINGFIELD
MONTREAL
VT.
N.H.
MAINE
Amtrak rail routes in effect as of June 16, 1991
Previous Amtrak rail route
Amtrak Thruway Bus (previous Thruway Bus routes not shown)
KANSAS CITY Current or previous endpoint city (terminus) for one or more Amtrak trains (does not include points where trains are or have been combined)
Orange Other cities or identifying points (not necessarily a station stop)

ward. Shabby Penn Central cars that had tumbled along in Broadway Limited *service were largely replaced by Union Pacific rolling stock, while former Burlington* Zephyr *cars began showing up on the Northeast Corridor.*

The shuffling worked better on paper than in practice. It didn't matter how well-maintained a Santa Fe sleeper had been: if it experienced an air-conditioner failure while on, say the Seaboard Coast Line, it probably couldn't get fixed right away - to the SCL carman, steam-injection air-conditioning systems, somewhat unique to Santa Fe, were "foreign." As a result, equipment malfunctions became a sore point, ranking third (behind haphazard reservation procedures and often indifferent personnel) in the list of customer complaints in the early months of Amtrak. [8]

Under Lewis' successor, Paul H. Reistrup, an Illinois Central executive, federal subsidies rose from $278 million in 1975 to $570 million in 1977. Losses continued to mount. and service worsened. Reistrup did, however, manage to acquire the entire trackage and right-of-way to the Northeast Corridor from Washington to Boston from the bankrupt PC in 1976. This purchase was made possible by passage of the Regional Rail Reorganization (3-R) Act in 1973 and the Railroad Revitalization and Regulatory Reform Act (4-R) in 1976. In addition came the passage in 1977 of the Northeast Corridor (NEC) Improvement Project, a nine-year program for which Congress came up with $2.5 billion for improving the corridor by upgrading track and signaling to permit 125 mile an hour operation and for rebuilding terminal facilities. The objective was to achieve regular, dependable, and fast service of three hours and forty minutes between Boston and New York and two hours and forty minutes between New York and Washington. On the importance of the NEC, Frank N. Wilner writes in his 1994 The Amtrak Story:

Today on the Northeast Corridor between Washington D.C. and New York 125-mph Metroliners whisk a passenger between those endpoint cities in two hours, 40 minutes; and compete for space with more than 100 other Amtrak trains, almost 200 New Jersey Transit trains, more than 150 Southeastern Pennsylvania Transit Authority trains, some 36 State of Maryland (MARC) commuter trains, and dozens of Conrail freights and Amtrak work trains. Eliminate Amtrak and commuter agencies will require the same public funds to operate, maintain, and renew the Northeast Corridor. Eliminate Amtrak and its more than 10 million northeast Corridor passengers will require infinitely more expensive new highway lanes and new airport runways.

Privatize Amtrak's Northeast Corridor trains and profits will not be available to cross-subsidize upkeep of the Northeast Corridor, nor money-losing long-distance passenger services Amtrak provides at the direction of Congress. Amtrak trains between Washington DC and New York currently produce $145 million more annually than their long-term costs, and by decade's end, when New York-Boston transit times are reduced, that service is projected to earn $40 million annually more than long-term costs. . . . Indeed, Amtrak's success in corralling 43 percent of all commercial air-rail travelers between Washington and New York has reduced environmental costs and eliminated the need for even more expensive new highways and airports. [9]

Shortly after the acquisition of the Northeast Corridor, Amtrak began taking delivery of the new F40PH (Full width cowl, 40-series engine, Passenger, Headend power) locomotive, which was destined to become the workhorse on the lines outside the corridor. Nineteen seventy-six also saw the delivery of the first batch of bilevel Superliners for cheap and dependable operation on long-distance trains.

Former Secretary of Transportation Alan

Boyd became third president of Amtrak in 1979. Realizing that despite the expenditure of millions, Amtrak was still a second class operation, he completed the job of acquiring new engines and cars including 150 Amfleet II cars for service on Eastern long-hauls and the new AEM7, considered by many to be the world's most successful electric locomotive, for service on the Metroliners. They were worthy successors to the PRR's superb GG1s of happy memory which first appeared in 1934 and continued in service, some of them until 1982.

Amtrak carried 19.9 million passengers in 1982. However, its financial picture was spotty. Seventy percent of the line's passengers traveled on the Northeast Corridor. This section alone covered costs. Overall, Amtrak accounted for less than two percent of all intercity travel in the United States. Table #12

Ronald Reagan's budget director, David Stockman, wanted to reduce Amtrak's subsidy drastically in the interests of balancing the national budget. Drew Lewis, the new secretary of the Department of Transportation, called Amtrak "an economic disaster," asserting that "it had grown like Topsy." Congress usually frustrated sizable reductions in Amtrak's subsidy, though in 1982 several Amtrak trains were discontinued in an economy move. Table #13

Schafer's book which appeared in 1991, the twentieth anniversary of Amtrak, was very laudatory of the leadership of W. Graham Claytor and positive about the company's accomplishments and future. Claytor had been chairman of the Southern Railway and president of Amtrak, 1982-1993. Wilner was even more optimistic. Therefore, it must have come as a shock to friends of the railroad to read an article in the April 6, 1995, *Wall Street Journal* entitled "Down and Dirty." The company, it

Table #12

Year	Route (000)	Stations	Intercity Passengers (millions)	Passenger Miles (billions)
1972	23	440	16.6	3.0
1973	22	451	16.9	3.8
1974	24	473	18.2	4.3
1975	26	484	17.4	3.9
1976	26	495	18.2	4.2
1977	26	524	19.2	4.3
1978	26	543	18.9	4.0
1979	27	573	21.4	4.9
1980	24	525	21.2	4.6
1981	24	525	20.6	4.8
1982	23	506	20.6	4.8
1983	24	497	19.0	4.2
1984	24	497	19.0	4.2
1985	24	503	20.8	4.8
1986	24	491	20.3	5.0
1987	24	487	20.4	5.2
1988	24	498	21.5	5.2
1989	24	504	21.4	5.9
1990	24	526	22.2	6.1
1991	25	523	22.0	6.3
1992	25	524	21.3	6.1
1993	25	535	22.1	6.2 (10)

Table #13

Year		Revenues (millions)	Expenses (millions)	Rev./Exp. Ratio
1966		$1017.6	$1417.2	
1967		877.7	1362.8	
1968		685.8	1171.8	
1969		638.2	1102.0	
1970		585.7	1062.5	
1971		100.9	192.5	0.52
1972		162.6	310.1	0.53
1973	(Jan-Jun)*	89.2	168.0	0.54
1974		240.1	438.2	0.57
1975		246.4	559.8	0.47
1976		268.0	674.3	0.42
1976	(Jul-Sep)*	79.4	202.5	0.43
1977		415.5	945.3	0.48
1978		433.3	1010.6	0.47
1979		496.3	1113.2	0.49
1980		558.8	1275.7	0.48
1981		612.2	1442.5	0.48
1982		630.7	1401.4	0.53
1983		664.4	1469.4	0.54
1984		758.8	1522.1	0.56
1985		825.8	1600.1	0.58
1986		861.4	1563.5	0.62
1987		973.5	1672.0	0.65
1988		1106.7	1757.1	0.69
1989		1269.1	1934.5	0.72
1990		1308.4	2011.8	0.72
1991		1359.4	2080.5	0.79
1992		1324.8	2036.6	0.79
1993		1403.0	2134.0	0.80 [11]

appears, was "struggling to close a $200 million budget deficit this year and cope with years of neglect that may cost more than $4 billion to fix." Differing explanations were offered for Amtrak's troubles:

Cheap air fares, of course, stole many customers. But Amtrak was also hamstrung by a chronic lack of capital to maintain its trains and stations, and by costly union work rules. What's more Amtrak executives painted a far rosier picture than was justified so they could keep federal subsidies flowing, according to the General Accounting Office, the investigative arm of Congress. [12]

Scheduled for elimination was a big stretch of the *New York Chicago Broadway Limited* while the *City of New Orleans* would no longer run seven days a week. Passengers' complaints include aged passenger cars, rude crew members, and dirty bathrooms. At the company's huge repair shops in Beech Grove, Indiana, "leaking roofs, crumbling walls and wobbly track slow production and raise costs."

During the Reagan years the government limited capital appropriations for new trains and facilities, a policy which led to a badly deteriorating liquidity. The result was a 1993 drop in on-time performance of long-distance trains due to mechanical breakdowns and floods in the Midwest. Ridership peaked in 1991 and has since fallen off. Several well-publicized wrecks including that of the *Sunset Limited* in Alabama in which forty-two passengers died after a barge hit a railroad bridge created a negative picture of train travel. Meanwhile, the *Journal*, noted:

Amtrak's labor productivity gains, brisk in the 1980s, have slackened. Amtrak estimates union work rules and manning levels cost it an extra $60 million a year. Just attaching a passenger car to a locomotive at Amtrak's Sunnyside yard in New York requires a conductor to open the coupler, a carman to connect air hoses and an electrician to plug in electrical cables

In addition, a resurgence of freight shipping on the nation's rails is causing lengthy delays to Amtrak trains that share freight tracks. Mr. [Thomas] *Downs* [Amtrak's chairman and president] *has pressured railroaders to improve by sending out public-relations statements identifying carriers with the worst on-time handling of Amtrak passenger trains. "They like to point the finger at the freight railroads and gloss over their own shortcomings," responds a vice president of Southern Pacific Lines who insists that Amtrak is "not paying its fair share" for use of the tracks.* [13]

Friends of the American long-distance passenger train undoubtedly hope that the last word on the subject will not reflect the opinion of Representative Bud Shuster, Republican from Pennsylvania, who heads the congressional committee that oversees Amtrak. "The American people are choosing to fly and not ride the train" he told the *Journal.* "People want to get places quickly. That's why the car replaced the horse."

Amtrak's Buffalo-New York service as of May 1, 1971, consisted in three all-coach trains each way. They were scheduled to cover the distance in seven and a half hours. Of this period Schafer writes:

Until Amtrak there remained three Chicago-Buffalo-New York trains on the well-populated ex-NYC route, so the absence of service west of Buffalo effective with Amtrak stunned rail advocates. Fortunately, this major shortcoming (necessitated by woefully inadequate start-up funding for Amtrak) was remedied when, only 10 days after Amtrak's birth, a through Chicago-Cleveland-Buffalo-New York train was established by some of the states it served (Illinois, Ohio and New York). The Lake Shore *- as it became known on Nov. 14, 1971 - was doomed for lack of cooperation between the states and was discontinued on Jan. 6, 1972.*

What the states could not accomplish on their own, Congress did in 1975 by mandating that Amtrak make the Chicago-Cleveland-New York/Boston an experimental route. Amtrak built upon service patterns established by the erstwhile New England States *and the* 20th Century Limited *and borrowing a name used by New York Central predecessor railroads for a similar run dating from the turn of the century, on Oct. 31, 1975, unveiled the new* Lake Shore Limited. *And nobody has looked back since then.* [14]

On New York-Toronto service, Schafer adds:

In pre-Amtrak days, this international route was a joint effort between New York Central, Toronto Hamilton & Buffalo, and Canadian Pacific. Trains connected at Buffalo, and until 1970 there was through sleeper service.

Today's service is an extension of what in earlier Amtrak days had been a New York-Buffalo corridor train. After Amtrak started, TH&B-CP continued to operate a Budd RDC [Beeliner] *between Toronto and Buffalo, where connection was made to Amtrak's* Empire State Express *(later renamed* Niagara Rainbow). *On April 26, 1961, this arrangement was supplanted by a new through New York-Toronto train, the* Maple Leaf, *jointly operated by Amtrak and VIA Rail Canada. The TH&B train was dropped and the new train began operating through Niagara Falls and on VIA's Canadian National route to Hamilton.* [15]

Buffalo's Exchange Street station was reopened on October 29, 1977. Central Terminal was abandoned as of October 28, 1979, and the main station of Amtrak in the Buffalo area was moved to Depew. As was the case with its NYC predecessor, Amtrak's *Lake Shore Limited* bypasses Buffalo, stopping at Depew.

Conrail has been far more successful, operationally and financially, than Amtrak. Table #14

South Buffalo Railway

In the Summer of 1985 *Business and Society Review* John Strohmeyer described the demise of a once thriving heavy industry in Western New York:

Lackawanna, New York, is a city without a pulse. It was severely stricken in October, 1983, when Bethlehem Steel "pulled the plug" on steelmaking in this one-industry town. An estimated 7,300 well-paying jobs in this city of 21,700 went down the drain and the ripple effect took many others with them in one of the largest single industrial shutdowns in the nation.

Table #14

Conrail: Annual Report, 1993

PLANT AND EQUIPMENT	
Miles operated	11,831
Miles of road owned	10,017
Freight cars in service	62,700
Locomotives in service	2,134
Net investment, as reported	$6,379,402,000
Net investment, revenue adequacy	$5,361,981,000
FINANCIAL	
Operating revenue	$3,349,562,000
Operating expenses	$2,771,531,000
Net railway operating income	$353,613,000
Return on shareholders' equity	5.97%
Return on investment, revenue adequacy	6.99%
Total capital expenditures	$623,525,000
TRAFFIC	
Carloads originated	2,426,547
Tons originated	126,261,988
Ton-miles	86,953,372,000
EMPLOYMENT	
Total compensation	$,1,022,994,000
Average number of employees	24,728
Hours paid for	60,298,000 [16]

Three generations of Lackawanna families had poured steel here for a great cross-section of American industry since 1900. Bethlehem steel acquired Lackawanna Iron and Steel Co., the parent company, in 1922 and by the 1960s it expanded the annual steel making capacity there to more than 5.72 million net tons. Lackawanna became the third largest steel producer in the world with a work force of 21,000. Company brochures say the annual payroll during the peak years reached $120 million.

Today the plant lies ghost-like on the shore of Lake Erie. It is an industrial corpse, a cannibalized complex of lifeless smokestacks, black buildings, motionless and empty rails. The only sign of life is at the far end where plumes of steam rise from the coke works. Only a bar mill and the galvanizing and cold strip mills across Highway No. 5 still turn out steel products, from semifinished steel shipped in from Johnstown, Pennsylvania, and Burns Harbor, Indiana. The plant's total work force is down to 1,300 and rumors abound that it may soon shrink some more. [17]

The construction by Bethlehem of a new, integrated steel plant at Burns Harbor in the 1960s initiated worries about the future of the Lackawanna plant. The situation grew more ominous with the increase of foreign imports and competition from non-union mills. Lackawanna lost more than $100 million for Bethlehem in 1981. The advantage derived from accessibility to the Great Lakes and the Saint Lawrence Seaway was no longer what it had been. The expense in replacing old facilities was deemed excessive. Management believed that the city of Lackawanna had been gouging the company for years. At one time Bethlehem paid seventy-three percent of the city's property taxes. Moreover, the plant had a notorious record of labor hostility. More labor grievances were filed in Lackawanna than in all of Bethlehem's other plants combined. Long established work rules inhibited productivity.

Yet though the South Buffalo Railroad had come to Western New York with the steel plant, the road survived the shutdown and continued to carry coal to the coke ovens and to service the Ford Stamping Plant. Figure #12 dramatically illustrates the relationship between the railroad and the mill.

Somerset Railroad

In November, 1983, the Somerset Railroad was opened to operate unit coal trains to the West Somerset power plant on Lake Ontario of its parent, the New York State Electric and Gas Company. Its route north from a connection with the ex-NYC's Falls Road at Lockport was largely that of the defunct interurban, the Buffalo Lockport & Olcott Beach. At first the plan had been to reactivate the ex-Rome Watertown & Ogdensburg from Niagara Falls to Somerset, but homeowners along the route objected to hundred-car coal trains rumbling past their property. Hence the route change. Conrail has operated the Somerset from the beginning.

Conrail-CSX

As this book went to press, this announcment appeared on page one of the October 16, 1996, *New York Times:*

Conrail Inc., the freight railroad that dominates the Northeast, said yesterday that it had agreed to merge with the CSX Corporation, a far larger railroad that blankets the Southeast, Middle Atlantic and eastern Midwest, to create one of the nation's largest transportation companies. [Figure #13.]

The merger, valued at $8.4 billion would be the biggest yet in the cascade of deals that has been combining railroads since the industry was deregulated in the 1980's, and it would

XVIII, 12

Figure 13. Proposed merger of Conrail and CSX, *New York Times*, October 16, 1996

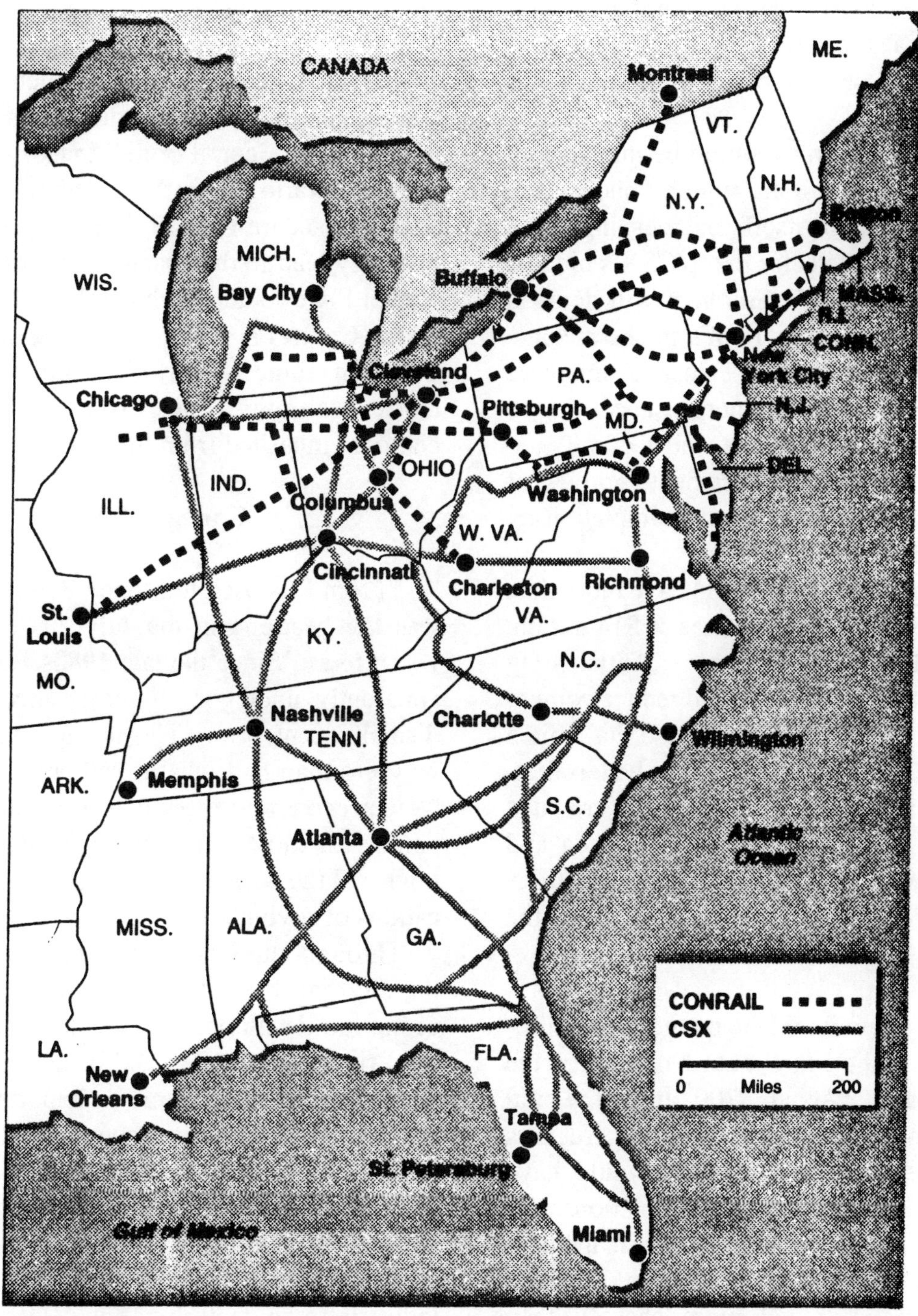

leave most of the nation east of the Mississippi with just two big railroads that carry only freight.

Conrail and CSX have routes extending nearly 30,000 miles, with nearly 54,000 miles of track, from Boston to New Orleans and from Chicago to Miami. The combined company would also control CSX's Sea-Land container shipping subsidiary and its inland barge company.

Its only major rival would be the Norfolk Southern Corporation, which had often expressed interest itself in merging with Conrail and might yet try to top CSX's bid. At the very least, Norfolk Southern will demand to run its trains over its rival's tracks in some areas that would otherwise lose competitive freight service under the merger, according to Wall Street analysts. CSX and Conrail said they expected to seek government approval of the merger early next year and complete it by the end of 1997.

The merged company would have more than 50,000 employees and revenues of $14 billion, based on 1995's performance. Anticipating criticism that the merger would reduce competition, CSX and Conrail contended that united they could offer many shippers a better alternative to trucking, especially on the crowded highways from the Northeast to Florida and other Southern states. The trucking industry is roughly a $300 billion industry, 10 times the size of the American railroads

CSX and Conrail said the merger would produce $550 million in annual benefits for the new company. About $200 million would come from taking business from truckers because the combined railroads would have shorter routes to important destinations and would offer more efficient traffic management to allow the shipping of cars, grain, coal and other goods faster and more cheaply than today. The other $350 million would come from savings on equipment, reductions in duplicated services and other efficiencies. "Work force reductions would be the smallest part of it," said [David M.] LeVan, Conrail's chairman. He said that it was too soon to tell where those reductions would be made and that he expected them to be short-term because the merged railroad's growth would eventually led to more hiring.

Locally CSX owns no trackage but inherited from the Pere Marquette, which had been taken over by the C&O, running rights over the Michigan Central from Windsor and Sarnia across Ontario to Buffalo. Should Norfolk Southern secure Conrail, however, this would probably lead to the abandonment of NS's ex-Nickel Plate route which parallels the ex-New York Central's Lake Shore & Michigan Southern route. Norfolk Southern already enjoys running rights over the Canadian National inherited from the Wabash.

Epilogue [18]

"From Rust Belt to Money Belt in Buffalo" was the headline in the July 20, 1990, *New York Times*. Since the late 1980s Buffalo had apparently undergone a renaissance from its dismal recent past. The unemployment rate was less than half what it had been in the late 1970s; economic growth in the suburbs was among the most vigorous in the nation; downtown and the waterfront were giving clear indications of revival.

Throughout much of the nineteenth century the city had benefited by world and national economic developments. With the arrival of the Erie Canal in 1825 and of the railroads in the 1840s Buffalo became an important break-bulk port of the frontier economy. It was for a time the largest inland port and water-based distribution point in the national economy. As the economy shifted in the late nineteenth century from an extractive-mercantile mode to an industrial-manufacturing one, Buffalo again benefited because of its situation on the Great Lakes and as the hub of a great railroad network. During World War II 225,000, about 47 percent of the local workforce, were employed in war related industries. However by mid-century signs were appearing that Western New York was failing to benefit by the third round of economic restructuring, the shift in the global economy from centralized heavy manufacturing to dispersed modes of production and a post-industrial service economy. The end of the war saw the closing of the Columbus, Ohio-based Curtiss-Wright Aircraft Plant, which at its peak had 40,000 employees. A decade later the local DuPont plant moved to Ohio, and new divisions of Allied Chemical and Hooker Chemical opened elsewhere. The Saint Lawrence Seaway was opened in 1959. Six years later American Shipbuilders closed, along with five of the nation's largest grain millers. Things got worse in the 1970s with closings of steel, auto, and chemical plants including Bethlehem Steel, already noted, Republic Steel, and component manufacturing plants at Ford and General Motors, resulting in further loss of almost 25,000 jobs. Only growth in the service sector, especially health services, retailing, and education prevented the region from suffering a serious overall employment downturn. Service industries, moreover, do not pay the salaries heavy industry did.

Economic restructuring was completed by 1980. Whereas in 1950 four of the top five local employers were engaged in manufacturing and construction, by 1980 four of the top five were service-related. The process continued throughout the decade. Figure #14 indicates the employment statistics of the Buffalo area's top dozen employers in 1995.

The service economy has become the primary employer in a region whose 1995 unemployment rate stood at 6 percent. While the automobile industry is the chief source of manufacturing jobs, the major employer is the public, not the private sector. Of the dozen top employers in Western New York in 1994 only two are engaged in heavy industry, and those are two General Motors divisions manufacturing automotive components. (Figure #14.) The automotive business is extremely vulnerable to fluctuations in demand, which makes Buffalo's future in manufacturing highly problematical. Seven of the top twelve employers are government operated, one is a health care provider, one is a supermarket chain with a high percentage of part-time employees, and there is only one bank, despite the highly touted growth of local financial firms.

Since heavy industry and America's railroads have always enjoyed a symbiotic relation, and since freight revenues have regularly constituted the major source of railroad profits, the deindustrialization of Buffalo sketched here seems ominous for the future of its railroads. A comparison of Figure #14 with Figure #15 will illustrate better than any words why so many of the area's classification yards (Figure 15, #1) have disappeared, why there are no freight houses and few sidings leading to plants and warehouses (see Chapter 8), and why the mainline of the New York Central & Hudson River Railroad which boasted four tracks since the halcyon days of William H. Vanderbilt (see Chapter 9, "Update on the Central") is down to one, enough to handle unit trains and those carrying intermodal freight non- stop through Buffalo east and west bound. Some local business remains, but a pale reflection of what once was. As an observer of Buffalo's railroad scene for fifty years recently expressed it, "Computer chips are not shipped in boxcars."

Commuter trains have made a comeback in metropolitan areas like New York, Philadelphia, Baltimore, and Chicago, but Buffalo's railroads never did an extensive commuter business, and today as a result of urban sprawl its downtown is no longer a magnet for office workers and shoppers. Besides, commuter trains need to be subsidized by local or state governments. Historian Edwin J. Perkins wrote an article on the future of long distance passenger trains in America in the *Buffalo News* for October 20, 1996 titled "If Amtrak is

Figure 14. Buffalo's top twelve employers, 1993, *The Top 25: A Supplement of [Buffalo] Business First* (Charlotte, NC: American City Business Journals, 1995), p. 32

WNY's Largest Employers

Ranked by number of full-time employees in Western New York

Rank	Company	Full-time employees in WNY	Business description / Parent company	Local CEO/manager / Personnel director / Purchasing director	Year founded in WNY
1	**State of New York*** 65 Court St. Buffalo, N.Y. 14202 847-7110	26,200	State government State of New York, Albany	Mario Cuomo Virginia Apuzzo Robert Adams	1788
2	**United States of America*** 111 W. Huron St. Buffalo, N.Y. 14202 846-4020	10,840	Federal government United States of America, Washington D.C.	Bill Clinton James King Roger Johnson	1787
3	**Erie County*** 95 Franklin St. Buffalo, N.Y. 14202 858-6300	6,844	County government —	Dennis Gorski Richard Slisz Joseph Heleniak	1821
4	**Harrison Division of General Motors Corp.** 200 Upper Mountain Road Lockport, N.Y. 14094 439-2011	6,800	Manufacturer of radiators and heat exchangers General Motors Corp., Detroit	Paul Tosch Janet Weatherbe Jerome Piecuch	1910
5	**Buffalo City School District** 712 City Hall Buffalo, N.Y. 14202 851-3570	6,410	Public school district —	Albert Thompson Richard Hitzges Jack Sperrazza	1838
6	**University at Buffalo** Buffalo, N.Y. 14260 645-2000	5,050	State university State University of New York, Albany	William Greiner Ellen McNamara Judith Miller	1846
7	**U.S. Postal Service** 1200 William St. Buffalo, N.Y. 14202 846-2400	4,450	Mail delivery and related services U.S. Postal Service, Washington D.C.	John Rapp, William McComb John Baker Margaret Cio	1804
8	**Powertrain Group of General Motors Corp.** P.O. Box 21 Buffalo, N.Y. 14240 879-5220	4,300	Manufacturer of car and boat engines General Motors Corp., Detroit	Donald Rust Gay Tosch Clayton Martin	1937
9	**Marine Midland Bank** One Marine Midland Center Buffalo, N.Y. 14203 841-2424	4,122	Commercial bank Hongkong & Shanghai Banking Corp., Great Britain	Brian Keating Nancy Johnston —	1850
10	**Tops Markets Inc.** 6363 Main St. Williamsville, N.Y. 14221 635-5000	3,783	Supermarket retailer Royal Ahold nv, The Netherlands	Lawrence Castellani John Dobinski Don Keller	1962
11	**City of Buffalo** 65 Niagara Square Buffalo, N.Y. 14202 851-4200	3,480	City government —	Anthony Masiello Sharon Comerford Ronald Carnevale	1832
12	**Buffalo General Hospital** 100 High St. Buffalo, N.Y. 14240 845-5600	3,039	Hospital General Care Corp., Buffalo	John Friedlander Neal Wixson Robert Nusall	1855

Figure 15. Top ten lucrative commodities, *Trains*, March, 1994, 19

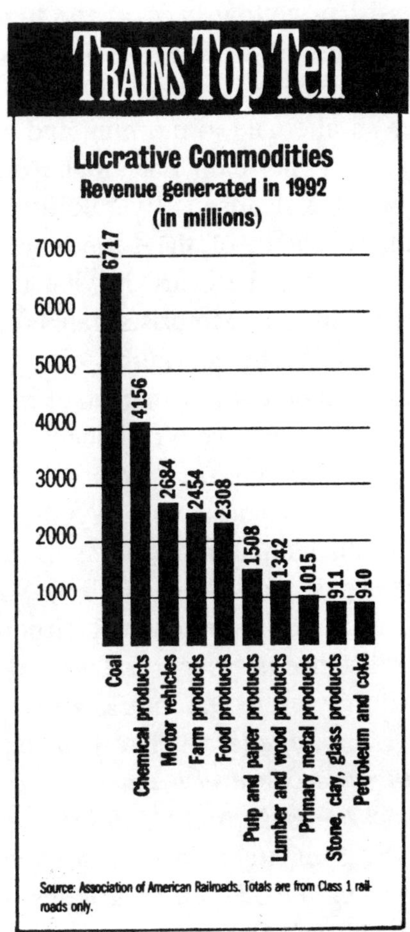

to flourish, it needs to be repackaged." His strictures are difficult to dispute, though many rail fans will try to do so anyway.

It's time for the United States to stop Amtrak's annual agony of budget deficits and the amputation of one or two long-distance trains with low ridership.

We should recognize that the United States has no substantial public stake in long-haul passenger trains. Instead, let's focus public attention and financing on the places where trains fill an important niche in the transportation spectrum and find a better way to finance and operate recreational trains.

The only compelling case to be made for public financing and possible subsidy of rail service is in high-seed, short-haul train service. In dense urban areas, fast intercity trains can significantly reduce the demands that would otherwise be placed on highways and airports. In those cases, money spent on track improvements and train operations may well buy more transportation capacity than the same amount of public money spent on airports or highways.

Amtrak should concentrate its efforts and funds on developing such routes and on train technology to improve speed and reliability. And because short-haul services are essentially regional, regional financing may be more appropriate than national.

But long haul trains that run once a day or less and average around 40 mph? Forget them. Use of the classical economic arguments about "transportation linkages" to justify continual long-haul Amtrak service is a joke. If you believe there's a public need for subsidized transportation to small communities, buses can provide that service at a fraction of the cost of trains.

This doesn't mean we should abandon long-haul trains, however. Let's recognize that long-haul trains are really sightseeing excursions and land cruises, and that there's a demand for both.

The best way to satisfy that demand without public subsidy - and without mixing politics into route and schedule decisions - is to turn the operation of those trains over to people who know something about that business. That means cruise lines, sightseeing porters and tour companies.

Slow speed - the bane of Amtrak's long-haul trains - really doesn't matter to a land cruise. What's most important is to schedule the trips for daylight runs through the most scenic areas. It's also important to market such trips as tours, with fly-one-way, train-the-other, destination-stay and other attractive packages.

Private operators might well develop another rail market, too: overnight "hotel trains" running between cities that are 300 to 400 miles apart. I well remember when I was in elementary school my father's business trips on over-night sleepers from our hometown of Chicago to Louisville, Omaha, St. Louis and other Midwestern cities.

Given the cost of a room in a business hotel, such overnight sleeper trains might well find a good market. The only major innovation required for today's travelers would be shower facilities - either on the trains or in the major stations. Who could design, run and market such trains most successfully? Obviously, the big hotel companies.

As with land cruises, speed isn't important to a hotel train, as least at the shorter end of the distance range. All that really matters is that the train leave after the end of the usual business day and arrive the next morning in time for another full business day. Average speeds under 35 mph would be perfectly adequate for many such runs.

Large cities within a 300 to 400 mile radius of Buffalo include New York, Baltimore, Washington, Detroit, Richmond, Cincinnati, Providence, and Montreal. The huge metropolis of Chicago, 454 air-miles away, could easily be slipped into this charmed overnight circle.

An argument could be made, however, that Perkins' restructuring of Amtrak goes too far. Why should 300 to 400 mile train trips be limited to nighttime? Lawyers, for example, could get in eight or nine daytime hours amid pleasant surroundings while preparing arguments for next day's cases in distant cities. Travelers visiting friends or relatives in these cities cold read, rest, or enjoy the scenery without the need to stay at a hotel on arrival and freed from the harassment incidental to driving. For those really intent on relaxation there is always the friendly lounge car.

Americans must learn to consume less if the nation is to survive and prosper in the next century. The largest single element in the nation's burgeoning imbalance of payments is imported petroleum. The bill for the romance with the automobile and the open highway has become excessive. Railroads are not only the cheapest way to transport many categories of freight long distances but if properly managed could assist in getting cars off the highways. Though much of Buffalo's rail network is gone, much remains. Updated Budliners might yet offer an alternate to morning and evening traffic jams. The main line of the old New York Central & Hudson River Railroad runs under the sidewalk of the former Memorial Auditorium near the heart of what is left of downtown Buffalo. Motorists trapped in traffic tie-ups with engines idling after Buffalo Bills' games should know that a half mile spur from Rich Stadium would connect with the Buffalo & Pittsburgh, the former BR&P, now operated by the Genesee and Wyoming Railroad. The abandoned right-of-way of the West Shore goes past the Walden Galleria Mall and the Greater Buffalo International Airport.

Long distance passenger trains need not be limited to forty mph. O.S. Nock writes:

With the Japanese Hikari *or lightning trains, there is one every quarter of an hour from Tokyo to Osaka, from 06.00 in the morning till 21.00 at night, in each direction, all alike covering the 517 km (320 miles) in 3 hr 10 min inclusive of two intermediate stops. A similar procession is traveling from Osaka to Tokyo at the same time. . . . In total contrast to the geography of the old Hokaido line, the new one is carried on an alignment such that a speed of 210 km/h (130 mph) can be sustained for practically the entire distance. The track is carried on viaducts high above the towns, across valleys, over rivers, through mountains - directly through or over any natural obstacle. All* Hikari *are exactly alike, and have seating for 1.400 passengers. In Japan there are no classes as such, though one can pay a small supplement to travel in '"green cars,'"which provide greater comfort. This however is only relative, because Japanese passenger trains, whether on the* Shinkansen *or elsewhere are very comfortable.* [19]

Less speedy but covering a linger distance was the *Mistral* of the French National Railways, which did the 536 miles between Paris and Marseilles, with stops at Dijon, Lyon, Valence, and Avignon, in 6 hours and 50 minutes - an average of 75 1/2 mph. And this was twenty years ago.

ABBREVIATIONS

A&A	Arcade & Attica
A&AV	Attica & Allegany Valley
APB	Attica & Buffalo
ACL	Atlantic Coast Line
AG&MM	Avon Genesee & Mount Morris
A&GW	Atlantic & Great Western
A&GWNY	Atlantic & Great Western of New York
A&GWO	Atlantic & Great Western of Ohio
A&H	Attica & Hornellsville
A&NP	Addison & Northern Pennsylvania
AM	Alabama Midland
A&P	Addison & Pennsylvania
A&R	Auburn & Rochester
A&S	Albany & Susquehanna
A&S	Auburn & Syracuse
AV	Allegany Valley
B&O	Baltimore & Ohio
B&A	Boston & Albany
BA&A	Buffalo Arcade & Attica
BB&G	Buffalo Brantford & Goderich
BB&P	Buffalo Bradford & Pittsburgh
BC	Buffalo Creek
BC&P	Buffalo Corry & Pittsburgh
B&CV	Buffalo & Cohocton Valley
BD	Belvidere Delaware
BE&C	Buffalo Eldred & Cuba
B&E	Buffalo & Erie
G&G	Buffalo & Geneva
BHT&W	Boston Hoosac Tunnel & Western
B&J	Buffalo & Jamestown
B&LH	Buffalo & Lake Huron
B&L	Buffalo & Lockport
B&LO	Buffalo & Lake Ontario
B&M	Boston & Maine
B&NYC	Buffalo & New York City
BNY&P	Buffalo New York & Philadelphia
B&NF	Buffalo & Niagara Falls
B&R	Buffalo & Rochester
BP&W	Buffalo Pittsburgh & Western
BR&P	Buffalo Rochester & Pittsburgh
BR&U	Black River & Utica
B&S	Baltimore & Susquehanna
B&S	Buffalo & Susquehanna
B&SL	Buffalo & State Line
B&SW	Buffalo & Southwestern
B&W	Buffalo & Wellsville
B&W	Buffalo & Washington
C	Chemung
C&A	Chicago & Alton
CaSo	Canada Southern
CB&Q	Chicago Burlington & Quincy
CC&C	Cleveland Cincinnati & Chicago

CC&C	Cleveland Columbus & Cincinnati
CC&I	Columbus Chicago & Indiana Central
CCC&StL	Cleveland Cincinnati Chicago & Saint Louis
C&E	Canandaigua & Elmira
CF	Cross Forks
CG	Cobb's Gap
C&GW	Chicago & Great Western
CH&D	Cleveland Hamilton & Dayton
CL	Chautauqua Lake
C&M	Cleveland & Mahoning
CN	Canadian National
C&NW	Chicago & Northwestern
C&NF	Canandaigua & Niagara Falls
C&O	Chesapeake & Ohio
Conrail	Consolidated Rail
CP	Canadian Pacific
CP&A	Cleveland Painsville & Ashtabula
CRI&P	Chicago Rock Island & Pacific
CRRNJ	Central Railroad of New Jersey
CS	Cherry Springs
CSX	
C&T	Cleveland & Toledo
C&X	Columbus & Xenia
D&CG	Delaware & Cobb's Gap
D&H	Delaware & Hudson
DL&W	Delaware Lackawanna & Western
D&RGW	Denver & Rio Grande Western
D&SJ	Detroit & Saint Joseph
D&T	Depew & Tonawanda
EI	Erie International
EJ&C	Elmira Jeffersonville & Canandaigua
EL	Erie Lackawanna
E&NE	Erie & North East
E&NYC	Erie & New York City
F	Fitchburg
FESH&W	Fort Erie Snake Hill & Western
FJ&G	Fonda Johnstown & Gloversville
F&W	Franklin & Warren
GT	Grand Trunk
GVC	Genesee Valley Canal
G&W	Genesee & Wyoming
GTW	Grand Trunk Western
GW	Great Western
HR	Hudson River
IB&W	Indiana Bloomington & Western
I&GN	International & Great Northern
JC&A	Jersey City & Albany
KP	Kansas Pacific
L&B	Lockport & Buffalo
LG	Liggett's Gap
L&HR	Lehigh & Hudson River
LM	Little Miami
LN	Louisville & Nashville
L&NF	Lockport & Niagara Falls

LOS	Lake Ontario Shore
LS	Lake Shore
LS&MS	Lake Shore & Michigan Southern
LV	Lehigh Valley
L&W	Lackawanna & Western
M	Meadville
M&E	Morris & Essex
MC	Michigan Central
MG	Manassas Gap
M&H	Mohawk & Hudson
MoPac	Missouri Pacific
MS	Michigan Southern
MS&NI	Michigan Southern & Northern Indiana
N	Northern
NA&S	New Albany & Salem
NC	Northern Central
NI	Northern Indiana
NJ	Niagara Junction
NP	Northern Pacific
NR	North River
NS	Norfolk Southern
N&W	Norfolk & Western
NYC	New York Central
NYC&HR	New York Central & Hudson River
NYC&StL	New York Chicago & Saint Louis
NY&E	New York & Erie
NY&H	New York & Harlem
NYL&W	New York Lackawanna & Western
NYNH&H	New York New Haven & Hartford
NYO&W	New York Ontario & Western
NYPANO	New York Pennsylvania & Ohio
NYP&C	New York Pittsburgh & Chicago
NYS&W	New York Susquehanna & Western
NYWS&B	New York West Shore & Buffalo
NYWS&C	New York West Shore & Chicago
OC	Oil City
O&M	Ohio & Mississippi
P	Panhandle
PC	Penn Central
P&E	Philadelphia & Erie
PFW&C	Pittsburgh Fort Wayne & Chicago
P&LE	Pittsburgh & Lake Erie
PM	Pere Marquette
PRR	Pennsylvania Railroad
P&R	Patterson & Ramapo
P&R	Philadelphia & Reading
PS&N	Pittsburgh Shawmut & Northern
P&W	Potsdam & Watertown
R	Rutland
R&D	Richmond & Danville
R&GV	Rochester & Genesee Valley
RL&NF	Rochester Lockport & Niagara Falls
RW&O	Rome Watertown & Ogdensburg
S	Somerset (New York)

S	Susquehanna (Pennsylvania)
SAL	Seaboard Air Line
SB	South Buffalo
SB&EJ	Suspension Bridge & Erie Junction
SB&NY	Syracuse Binghamton & New York
SCL	Seaboard Coast Line
S&E	Sunbury & Erie
S&N	Syracuse & Northern
SP	Southern Pacific
SP	South Pennsylvania
SPLA&SL	San Pedro Los Angeles & Salt Lake
StIM&S	Saint Louis Iron Mountain & Southern
StLKC&N	Saint Louis Kansas City & Northern
StL&SW	Saint Louis & Southwestern
SV	Sinnemahoning Valley
T	Tonawanda
TAA&NM	Toledo Ann Arbor & Noorth Michigan
TP	Texas & Pacific
TP&W	Toledo Peoria & Western
T&G	Troy & Greenbush
TN&C	Toledo Norwalk & Cleveland
TV&C	Tonawanda Valley & Cuba
UP	Union Pacific
U&S	Utica & Schenectady
U&S	Utica & Syracuse
V	Virginian
VC	Vermont Central
V&C	Vermont & Canada
W	Warren (New Jersey)
W	Western (Massachusetts)
W&A	Western & Atlantic
W&B	Wellsville & Buffalo
W&E	Williamsport & Elmira
W&LE	Wheeling & Lake Erie
WM	Western Maryland
WNY&P	Western New York & Pennsylvania
W&R	Watertown & Rome
WStL&P	Wabash Saint Louis & Pacific

ENDNOTES

Chapter 1. Beginnings

1. Oswald S. Nock, *Railways Then and Now: A World History* (New York: Crown Publishers, 1975), 7.

2. Albro Martin, *Railroads Triumphant: The Growth, Rejection, and Rebirth of a Vital American Force* (New York: Oxford University Press, 1992), 81.

3. Gerald G. Eggert, *Railroad Labor Disputes: The Beginnings of Federal Strike Policy* (Ann Arbor: University of Michigan Press, 1967), 2-3.

4. Ronald E. Shaw, *Canals for a Nation: The Canal Era in the United States, 1790-1860* (Lexington, Ky.: University of Kentucky Press, 1990), 47.

Chapter 2. Before the Central Was

1. *Buffalo Journal and General Advertiser*, September 7, 1831.

2. Garnet R. Cousins, "A Station Too Late, Too Far," *Trains*, 45 (September, 1985), 20.

3. Henry W. Hill, ed., *Municipality of Buffalo, New York: A History, 1720-1923* (New York: Lewis Historical Publishing Co., 1923), 1:271.

4. Michael Chevalier, *Histoire et Description des Voies de Communication aux Etats-Unis* (Paris: C. Gosselin, 1840), 1: 275, in Arthur J. Gibbons, "Some Legal Origins of Two Great Railroad Systems on the Niagara Frontier from 1825-1935," Masters Thesis, Canisius College, 1951, 15.

5. Raymond F. Yates, "The Old Lockport & Niagara Falls Strap Railroad," *Occasional Contributions of the Niagara County Historical Society*, 4 (June, 1950), 29.

6. *Ibid.*, 31-32.

Chapter 3. New York & Erie Railroad

1. Maury Klein, *The Life and Legend of Jay Gould* (Baltimore: Johns Hopkins University Press, 1986), 77.

2. Benjamin F. Taylor, *The World on Wheels and Other Sketches* (Chicago: S. C. Griggs & Company, 1874), 148-149.

3. Edward H. Mott, *Between the Ocean and the Lakes: The Story of Erie* (New York: John S. Collins, 1901), 362.

4. *Ibid.*, 361.

5. *Ibid.*

6. *Ibid.*, 362.

7. Robert L. Gunnarson, *The Story of the Northern Central Railroad* (Sykesville, Maryland: Greenberg Publishing Co., 1991), 8.

8. *Ibid.*, 138.

9. *Ibid.*

Chapter 4. Consolidation: The Birth of the New York Central

1. John Stover, *Iron Road to the West: American Railroads in the 1850s* (New York: Columbia University Press, 1978), 46-47.

2. Edward Hungerford, *Men and Iron: The History of the New York Central* (New York: Thomas Y. Crowell Co., 1938), 81.

3. *Ibid.*, 112.

Chapter 5. Rails East and West

1. Stover, 24.

2. John N. Jackson and John Burtniak, *Railways in the Niagara Peninsula: Their Development, Progress and Community Significance* (Bellville, Ontario: Mika Publishing Co., 1978), 39.

3. *Ibid.*, 138.

4. *Ibid.*, 142.

5. G. R. Stevens, *History of the Canadian National Railways* (New York: Macmillan, 1973), 129.

6. *Ibid.*

7. Jackson and Burtniak, 94.

Chapter 6. The Civil War

1. George Edgar Turner, *Victory Rode the Rails: The Strategic Place of Railroads in the Civil War* (New York: Bobbs-Merrill Co., 1953), *passim.* Martin, *Railroads Triumphant*, 368-369.

2. John T. Horton, *History of Northwestern New York; Erie, Niagara, Wyoming, Genesee, and Orleans County* (New York: Lewis Historical Publishing Co., 1947), 1:186.

3. H. Perry Smith, *History of Buffalo and Erie County* (Syracuse: D. Mason & Co., 1884), 1:240.

4. Carl Sandburg, *Abraham Lincoln: The War Years* (New York: Harcourt & Brace, 1939), 4:401.

Chapter 7. Gilded Age Railroading

1. Horton, 1:218.

2. Gunnarson, 45.

3. George H. Burgess and Miles C. Kennedy, *Centennial History of the Pennsylvania Railroad Company* (Philadelphia: Pennsylvania Railroad Company, 1949), 482-483.

4. Alvin F. Harlow, *The Road of the Century: The Story of the New York Central* (New York: Macmillan, 1947), 191-192.

5. Mott, 140.

6. *Ibid.*, 363-364

7. Edward Hungerford, *Men of Erie: A Story of Human Effort* (New York: Random House, 1946), 185-186.

8. John S. Gorden, *The Scarlet Woman of Wall Street* (New York: Weidenfeld and Nicholson, 1988), 125.

9. Klein, *Jay Gould*, 94.

10. Grodinsky, Julius, *Jay Gould: His Business Career* (Philadelphia: University of Pennsylvania Press, 1957), 65.

11. Jackson and Burtniak, 152-153.

12. William R. Gordon, *90 years of Buffalo Railways, 1860-1950* (np: 1970), 333.

13. Mott, "Men of Note in Erie Towns."

14. Harlow, 235.

Chapter 8. The Great Railroad Strike of 1877

1. Walter Licht, *Working for the Railroad: The Organization of Work in the Nineteenth Century* (Princeton: Princeton University Press, 1983), 126.

2. R. V. Bruce, *1877: Year of Violence* (New York: Bobbs-Merrill, 1959), for treatment of strikes throughout the United States except for Hornellsville and Buffalo.

3. Mott, *passim.*

4. The following version of the strike in Buffalo is an abridgment of the accounts in the *Buffalo Morning Express* fleshed out from the *Buffalo City Directory* for 1877 and 1878 and the 1872 *Atlas of the City of Buffalo*. No attempt has been made to alter the viewpoint of the editor of the *Express*, James N. Matthews, or to comment on it.

5. Licht, 232.

6. Bruce, 201.

7. Harlow, 303-304.

Chapter 9. Railroading in the '80s and Early 90s

1. Robert F. Archer, *A History of the Lehigh Valley Railroad* (Forest Park, Illinois: Heimberger House Publishing Company, 1977), 139.

2. Martin, *Railroads Triumphant*, 167.

3. Grodinsky, *Jay Gould*, 221-222.

4. Thomas Taber, *The Lackawanna Railroad in the Nineteenth Century* (Muncy, Pennsylvania: Thomas Taber, 1977), 258.

5. *Ibid.*, 266.

6. John H. Rehor, *The Nickel Plate Story* (Waukesha, Wisconsin: Kalmbach Publishing Company, 1965), 13-14.

7. *Ibid.*, 40.

8. This section is based chiefly on Paul Pietrak, *The Buffalo Rochester & Pittsburgh Railway* (Rochester: S. R. Ames Enterprises, 1992).

9. Horton, 1:218.

10. Howard Fleming, *Narrow Gauge Railways in America* (Canton, Ohio: Railhead Publications, 1983), preface.

11. This section is based on Harlow, *Road of the Century,* Chapter 14, 319-340, and Albro Martin, "Crisis of Rugged Individualism: The West Shore-South Pennsylvania Railroad Affair, 1880-1885," *Pennsylvania Magazine of History and Biography*, 93 (April, 1967), 218-243.

12. Harlow, 326.

13. Oneta M. Baker, *History of the Town of Clarence* (Clarence Center, New York: Oneta M. Baker, 1983), 169.

14. H. Roger Grant and Charles W. Bohi, *The Country Station in America* (Sioux Falls, South Dakota: Center for Western Studies, Augustana College, 1988), 36.

15. Horton, 2:298.

16. Linus Ormsby, "Landscaping, waterline replace tracks," *On Campus: Faculty and Staff Newsletter, Niagara University*, 24:3 (November, 1990), 1,6.

17. Hungerford, *New York Central*, 297-298, 301-302.

18. Cousins, "A Station Too Late," 22.

19. Robert B. Adam, "History of the Abolition of Railroad Grade Crossings in the City of Buffalo," *Publications of the Buffalo Historical Society,* 8 (1905), 213-214.

20. Edward A. Lewis, *Arcade & Attica Railroad* (Arcade, New York: The Baggage Car, 1972), 27

21. Jackson and Burtniak, 116.

22. Walter S. Dunn, *History of Erie County, 1870-1970* (Buffalo: Buffalo and Erie County Historical Society, 1972), 49.

Chapter 10. Buffalo Switchmen's Strike of 1892

1. *Laws of New York*, 1892, chapter 711.

2. Horton, 1:326.

3. *Laws of New York*, 1887, chapter 63.

4. Horton, 1:327.

5., Lindsey Allotment, *The Pullman Strike: Story of a Unique Experiment and of a Great Labor Upheaval* (Chicago: University of Chicago Press, 1942), 263.

6. Martin, *Railroads Triumphant*, 313.

7. Altmont, 267.

Chapter 11. Buffalo's Passenger Service in the 19th Century

1. Alvin Staufer and Edward L. May, *New York Central's Later Power, 1910-1968* (Medina, Ohio: Alvin F. Staufer, 1981), 324,

2. Hungerford, *New York Central*, 246-247.

3. John H. White, Jr., *The American Railway Passenger Car* (Baltimore: Johns Hopkins Press, 1978), 1:317.

4. Hungerford, *New York Central*, 244-245.

5. Robert C. Reed, *Train Wrecks: A Pictorial History of Accidents on the Main Line* (New York: Bonanza Books, 1968), 26-27.

6. White, *Passenger Car*, 1:312-313.

7. Grodinsky, *Jay Gould*, 87

8. Reginald C. McGrane, "Ingalls, Melville Ezra," *Dictionary of American Biography,* ed. Dumas Malone (New York: Scribner's Sons, 1932), 9:466

9. White, *Passenger Car*, 1:320.

10. *Ibid.*, 2:551.

11. *Ibid.*, 2:563.

12. Harold U. Faulkner, *Politics, Reform and Expansion, 1890-1900* (New York: Harper & Brothers, 1959), 141-142.

13. White, *Passenger Car,* 1:447.

14. Archer, 152-154.

15. James E. Kranefeld, "The Number that Became a Train," *National Railway Bulletin*, 58 (1993), #1, 5-8.

16. Alvin F. Staufer, *New York Central's Early Power, 1831-1916* (np. Alvin F. Staufer, 1967), 74.

17. *Ibid.*, 63.

18. Taber, *Lackawanna in the 19th Century*, 269.

Chapter 12. Triumph

1. Frank Mogavero, "Military Activity in Buffalo during the Spanish American War," Masters Thesis, Canisius College, 1946, p. 28.

2. Jackson and Burtniak, 111-112.

3. Burgess and Kennedy, 486.

4. Joseph R. Daughen and Peter Binzen, *The Wreck of the Penn Central* (Boston: Little Brown Co. 1971), 90-91.

5. Dunn, *Erie County, 32.*

6. Thomas E. Leary and Eizabeth Sholes, *From Fire to Rust: Technology and Work at the Lackawanna Steel Plant, 1899-1983* (Buffalo: Buffalo and Erie County Historical Society, 1987), 9.

7. Horton, 1:359.

8. Leary and Sholes, 39.

9. Paul Pietrak, *The History of the Buffalo & Susquehanna* (North Boston, New York: Paul Pietrak, 1967), passim.

10. Josephus N. Larned, *History of Buffalo* (New York: Progress of the Empire State Co., 1911), 1:277-278.

11. Lewis, 27.

12. Archer, 183.

13. Cousins, “A Station Too Late,” 23.

14. Archer, 184.

15. John R. Stilgoe, *Metropolitan Corridor: Railroads and the American Scene* (Westford, Massachusetts: Yale University Press, 1983), 167.

16. Adam, 253-254.

17. *Live Wire*, December, 1910

Chapter 13. Origins of Decline

1. George W. Hilton and John F. Due, *The Electric Interurban Railways in America* (Stanford, California: Stanford University Press, 1964), 7.

2. *Ibid.*, 8-9.

3. *Ibid.*, 3.

4. *Ibid.*, 118.

5. Gordon, *Buffalo Railways*, 372.

6. Hilton and Due, 15.

7. Gordon, *Buffalo Railways*, 334.

8. Geoff Gerstung, "By Trolley to Olcott," *Empire State Express,* December, 1995, 4.

9. Gordon, *Ibid.*, 457.

10. *Ibid.*, 457-458.

11. Albro Martin, *Enterprise Denied: Origins of the Decline of American Railroads,* (New York: Columbia University Press, 1971), 9.

12. Spencer Miller, Jr., "History of the Modern Highway in the United States," in Jean Labatut and Wheaton J. Lane, eds., *Highways in Our National Life* (Princeton: Princeton University Press, 1950), 95-96.

13. Albert C. Rose, "The Highway from the Railroad to the Automobile," *ibid.*, 227-228.

14. Ari and Olive Hoogenboom, *A History of the ICC: From Panacea to Palliative* (New York: W. W. Norton, 1976), 34.

15. Martin, *Railroads Triumphant*, 328.

16. Martin, *Enterprise Denied*, 17-18.

17. *Ibid.*, 94.

18. Richard C. Overton: *Burlington Route: A History of the Burlington Lines* (New York: Alfred A. Knopf, 1965), 262.

19. Maury Klein, *Union Pacific: The Rebirth, 1894-1969*, (New York: Doubleday, 1989), 148.

20. I. L. Sharfman, *The Interstate Commerce Commission: A Study in Administrative Law and Procedure* (New York: The Commonwealth Fund, 1931), 36-37.

21. Martin, *Railroads Triumphant*, 339.

22. Martin, *Enterprise Denied*, 361.

23. *Ibid.*, 124.

24. *Ibid.*, 230.

25. Klein, *Union Pacific*: *The Rebirth*, 218.

Chapter 14. World War I and its Sequel

1. Martin, *Enterprise Denied*, 335-336.

2. Walker D. Hines, *War History of American Railroads* (New Haven: Yale University Press, 1928), 12.

3. Klein, *Union Pacific: The Rebirth*, 228.

4. *Ibid.*, 239.

5. William R. Doezema, "Ralph Budd," *Railroads in the Age of Regulation* (New York: Facts on File Publications, 1988), 58.

6. Klein, *Union Pacific: The Rebirth*, 241.

7. Hoogenboom, 106.

8. Jim Shaughnessy, *Delaware & Hudson* (San Diego: Howell-North Books, 1982), 307-309

Chapter 15. "The Railroads that Serve Buffalo"

1. Harold U. Faulkner *et al.*, *American Economic History* (New York: Harper & Row, 1976), 340.

2. Daughen and Binzen, 45.

3. *Railroads that Serve Buffalo* (Buffalo: Manufacturers and Traders-Peoples Trust Co., 1927), 5.

4. John H. White, Jr., *The American Railroad Freight Car from the Wood-Car Era to the Coming of Steel* (Baltimore: Johns Hopkins University Press, 1993), 89.

5. *Ibid.*, 34.

6. Charles W. Bohi, "When LCL Meant Fast Freight," *Trains*, 53 (August, 1993), 59-60, 62.

7. *Railroads that Serve*, 22-23.

8. Paul Carlton, *The Erie Railroad Story* (Dunnellon, Florida: D. Carleton Railbooks, 1988), 7.

9. *Railroads that Serve*, 35-39.

10. *Ibid.*, 10-11.

11. Pietrak, *Buffalo Rochester & Pittsburgh*, 66.

12. *Ibid.*, 65

13. D. G. G. Kerr, ed., *A Historical Atlas of Canada* (Toronto: Thomas Nelson & Sons, 1960), 64.

14. *Railroads that Serve*, 78-79.

15. *Ibid.*, 70-71.

16. Dunn, *Erie County*, 31.

17. George Drury, *Historical Guide to North American Railroads* (Waukesha, Wisconsin: Kalmbach Publishing Co., 1985), 232.

Chapter 16. Buffalo's Passenger Service from the Turn of the Century to World War II

1. Donald M. Itzkoff, *Off the Track: The Decline of the Inter-City Passenger Train in the United States* (Westport, Connecticut: Greenwood Press, 1985), 7.

2. Martin, *Enterprise Denied*, 23.

3. Harlow, 413-414.

4. *Pietrak, Buffalo Rochester & Pittsburgh*, 130-135.

5. White, *Passenger Car*, 331-333.

6. James N. J. Henwood, "Frederick D. Underwood," *Railroads in the Age of Regulation*, 442-443.

7. Hungerford, *Men of Erie*, 237-238.

8. Thomas Taber, The Delaware *Lackawanna & Western Railroad in the Twentieth Century: The Route of the Phoebe Snow* (Muncey, Pennsylvania: Thomas T. Townsend III, 1980*)*, 153-154.

9. William T. Greenberg and Frederick A. Kramer, *The Handsomest Trains in the World: Passenger Service on the Lehigh Valley Railroad* (New York: Quadrant Press, 1978), 44.

10. Archer, 180.

11. Greenberg and Kramer, 45.

12. Pietrak, *Buffalo Rochester & Pittsburgh*, 128-130.

13. Richard Saunders, "Erie Railroad," *Railroads in the Age of Regulation*, 137.

14. Rehor, 76.

15. *Ibid.*, 206-209.

16. *Ibid.*, 210.

17. Greenberg and Kramer, 59.

18. Ari and Olive Hoogenboom, *ICC*, 119-120.

19. *Ibid.*, 120-121.

20. Cousins, "A Station Too Far," 24-25.

21. *Ibid.*, 29-30.

22. Cousins, "Dedication to Dethronement," *Trains*, 45 (October, 1985), 44.

23. Anon., *Truth*, (August, 1931), 41.

24. Staufer and May, *New York Central's Later Power*, 183-184.

25. *The Official Guide of the Railways and Steam Navigation Lines of the United States, Puerto Rico, Canada, Mexico and Cuba* (New York, National Railway Publication, 1933), 66 (April, 1933), 454.

26. White, *Passenger Car*, 1:409.

27. Drury, *Historical Guide*, 45-46.

28. Stephen B. Goddard, *Getting There: The Epic Struggle between Road and Rail in the American Century* (New York: Basic Books, 1994), 164-165.

29. *Ibid.*, 165.

30. *Ibid.*, 166-167.

31. H. Roger Grant, *Erie Lackawanna: Death of an American Railroad* (Stanford: University of California Press, 1994), 34.

32. *Statistical History*, 437

33. Harlow, 414.

34. Taber, *Lackawanna in the Twentieth Century*, 168.

35. *Ibid.*, 123.

Chapter 17. Postwar Meltdown

1. Harlow, 421-422.

2. Itzkoff, 26.

3. Maury Klein, "The Diesel Revolution," *American Heritage of Invention & Technology*, 6 (Winter, 1991), 16-17.

4. Itzkoff, 50.

5. *64th New York Supplement, 2nd.* 764, 766 (4th Department, 1946), Appeal Dismissed; 297 NY 274.

6. Peter Galie, *The New York State Constitution: A Reference Guide* (New York: Greenwood Press, 1991), 179.

7. Itzkoff, 37-38.

8. Grant, 117-118.

9. Rehor, 382.

10. Itzkoff, 83.

11. Archer, 273.

12. Itzkoff, 81.

Chapter 18. Merger Mania

1. Richard Saunders, "Alfred E. Perlman," *Railroads in the Age of Regulation*, 346-347.

2. Grant, 172.

3. Goddard, 231-232.

4. *Ibid.*, 232-233.

5. *Ibid.*, 233.

6. Bill Stephens, "Bison Yard Revived," Kalmbach Publishing Co., nd.), np.

7. Bill Stephens, "Delaware & Hudson Thrives under CP Rail," *Trains,* 52 (July, 1992), 26.

8. Mike Schafer, *All Aboard Amtrak* (Piscataway, New Jersey: Railpace Co., 1991), 17.

9. Frank N. Wilner, *The Amtrak Story* (Omaha, Nebraska: Simmons-Boardman Books, Inc., 1994), 83-84.

10. *Ibid.,* 90.

11. *Ibid.*, 89.

12. Daniel Machalaba, "Down and Dirty," *Wall Street Journal,* April 6, 1995, A1, 6.

13. *Ibid.*

14. Schafer, 116-117.

15. *Ibid.*, 142.

16. Economics and Finance Department, Association of American Railroads, *Railroad Facts,* Washington, Association of American Railroads, 1994.

17. John Strohmeyer, "The Agonizing Ordeal of a One Company Town," *Business and Society Review,* 45, (Summer, 1985), 45.

18. Data on Buffalo's deindustrialization and economic restructuring are from "Buffalo Change & Community: A Symposium," *Buffalo Law Review*, Vol. 39 (Spring, 1991) n. 2, pp, 313-383.

19. O. S. Nock, *Encyclopedia of Railways* (London: Octopus Books Ltd., 1977), 236

Bibliography

Almont, Lindsey. *The Pullman Strike: Story of a Unique Experiment and of a Great Labor Upheaval.* Chicago: University of Chicago Press, 1942.

Archer, Robert F. *A History of the Lehigh Valley Railroad.* Forest Park Illinois: Hamberger House Publishing Company, 1977.

Baker, Oneta M. *History of the Town of Clarence.* Clarence Center, New York: Oneta M. Baker, 1983

Bruce, R. V. *1877: Year of Violence.* New York: Bobbs-Merrill, 1959.

Bryan, Kieth L., ed. *Railroads in the Age of Regulation, 1900- 1980. Encyclopedia of American Business History & Biography Series.* New York: Facts on File Publication, 1988.

Burgess, George H., and Miles C. Kennedy. *Centennial History of the Pennsylvania Railroad Company.* Philadelphia: Pennsylvania Railroad Company, 1949.

Carlton, Paul. *The Erie Railroad Story.* Dunnelton, Florida: D. Carlton Railbooks, 1988.

Daughen, Joseph R., and Peter Binzen.*The Wreck of the Penn Central.* Boston: Little Brown Company, 1971

Drury, George. *Historical Guide to North American Railroads.* Waukesha, Wisconsin: Kalmbach Publishing Company, 1985

Dunn, Walter S. *History of Erie County, 1870-1970.* Buffalo: Buffalo and Erie County Historical Society, 1972.

Eggert, Gerald G. *Railroad Labor Disputes: The Beginnings of Federal Strike Policy.* Ann Arbor, Michigan: University of Michigan Press, 1967.

Faulkner, Harold U. *Politics, Reform and Expansion, 1890-1900.* New York: Harper & Brothers, 1959.

Faulkner, Harold U. *et al. American Economic History.* New York: Harper & Row, 1876

Fleming, Howard. *Narrow Gauge Railways in America.* Canton, Ohio: Railhead Publishing Company, 1965.

Frey, Robert L. *Railroads in the Nineteenth Century. Encyclopedia of American Business History and Biography Series.* New York: Facts on File Publication, 1988.

Galie, Peter. *The New York State Constitution: A Reference Guide.* New York: Greenwood Press, 1991.

Goddard, Stephen B. *Getting There: The Epic Strugle between Road and Rail in the American Century.* New York: Basic Books, 1994.

Gordon, John S. *The Scarlet Woman of Wall Street: Jay Gould, Jim Fiske, Cornelius Vanderbilt, the Erie Railway Wars, and the Birth of Wall Street.* New York: Weidenfield & Nicholson, 1988.

Gordon, William. *90 Years of Buffalo Railways, 1860-1950.* np:1970.

Grant, H. Roger. *Erie Lackawanna: Death of an AmericanRailroad.* Stanford: Stanford University Press, 1994.

Grant, H. Roger and Charles Bohi. *The Country Railroad Stationin America.* Sioux Falls, South Dakota: Center for Western Studies, Augustana College, 1988.

Greenberg, William T., and Frederick A. Kramer. *The Handsomest Trains in the World: Passenger Service on the Lehigh Valley Railroad.* New York: Quadrant Press, 1978.

Grodinsky, Julius. *Transcontinental Railway Strategy, 1869-1893: A Study of Businessmen.* Philadelphia: University of Pennsylvania Press, 1962.

Grodinsky, Julius. *Jay Gould: His Business Career.* Philadelphia: University of Pennsylvania Press, 1957.

Gunnarson, Robert L. *The Story of the Northern Central Railroad.* Sykesville, Maryland: Greenberg Publishing Company, 1991.

Harlow, Alvin F. *The Road of the Century: The Story of the New York Central.* New York: Macmillan, 1947.

Hill, Henry W., ed. *Municipality of Buffalo, New York: A History, 1720-1920.* New York: Lewis Historical Publishing Company, 1923. 4 vols.

Hilton, George W., and John F. Due. *The Electric Interurban Railways in America.* Stanford, California: Stanford University Press, 1964.

Hines, Walker D. *War History of American Railroads.* New Haven: Yale University Press, 1928.

Hoogenboom, Ari and Olive. *A History of the ICC: From Panacea to Palliative.* New York: W. W. Norton, 1976.

Horton, John T. *History of Northwestern New York: Erie, Niagara, Wyoming, Genesee, and Orleans County.* Lewis Historical Publishing Company, 1947. 3 vols.

Hungerford, Edward. *Men of Erie: A Story of Human Effort.* New York: Random House, 1946.

Hungerford, Edward. *Men and Iron: The History of the New York Central.* New York: Thomas Y. Crowell Company, 1938.

Itzkoff, Donald M. *Off the Track: The Decline of the Inter-City Passenger Train in the United States.* Westport, Connecticut: Greenwood Press, 1985.

Jackson, John N., and John Burtniak. *Railways in the Niagara Peninsula: Their Development, Progress and Community Significance.* Bellville, Ontario: Mika Publishing Company, 1978.

Kerr, D. G. G. *A Historical Atlas of Canada*. Toronto: Thomas Nelson & Sons, 1960.

Klein, Maury. *The Life and Legend of Jay Gould.* Baltimore; Johns Hopkins University Press, 1986.

Klein, Maury. *Union Pacific: The Rebirth*, 1894-1969. New York: Doubleday, 1989.

Labatut, Jean, and Wheaton J. Lane. eds. *Highways in Our National Life.* Princeton: Princeton University Press, 1950.

Larned, Josephus N. *History of Buffalo*. New York: Progress of the Empire State Company, 1911.

Leary, Thomas E., and Elizabeth Sholes. *From Fire to Rust: Technology and Work at the Lackawanna Steel Plant, 1899-1983.* Buffalo: Buffalo and Erie County Historical Society, 1987.

Leavitt, Helen. *Superhighway-Superhoax.* Garden City, New York: Doubleday, 1970.

Lewis, Edward. *Arcade & Attica Railroad.* Arcade, New York: The Baggage Car, 1972.

Licht, Walter. *Working for the Railroad: The Organization of Work in the Nineteenth Century*. Princeton: Princeton University Press, 1983.

Maiken, Peter T. *Night Trains: The Pullman System in the Golden Years of American Rail Travel.* Chicago: Lakme Press, 1989.

Martin, Albro. *Enterprise Denied: Origins of the Decline of American Railroads.* New York: Columbia University Press, 1971

Martin, Albro. *Railroads Triumphant: The Growth, Rejection and Rebirth of a Vital American Force.* New York: Oxford University Press, 11992.

Mott, Edward H. *Between the Ocean and the Lakes: The Story of Erie.* New York: John S. Collins, 1901.

Nock, Oswald S. *Railways Then and Now: A World History*. New York: Crown Publishers, 1975.

Overton, Richard C. *Burlington Route: A History of the Burlington Lines*. New York: Alfred A. Knopf, 1965.

Pietrak, Paul. *The Buffalo Rochester & Pittsburgh Railway.Rochester, New York*: S. R. Ames Enterprises, 1992.

Pietrak, Paul. *History of the Buffalo & Susquehanna. North Boston:* Paul Pietrak, 1967.

Railroad Facts. Washington, District of Columbia: Office of Information and Public Affairs, Association of American Railroads, 1994.

Railroads that Serve Buffalo. Buffalo: Manufacturers & Traders-Peoples Trust Company, 1927.

Reed, Robert C. *Train Wrecks: A Pictorial History of Accidents on the Main Line.* New York: Bonanza Books, 1969.

Rehor, John H. *The Nickel Plate Story.* Waukesha, Wisconsin: Kalmbach Publishing Company, 1965.

Sandburg, Carl. *Abraham Lincoln: The War Years.* New York: Harcourt & Brace, 1939. 4 vols.

Schafer, Mike. *All aboard Amtrak.* Piscataway, New Jersey: Railpace Company, 1991.

Schmuckler, Nathan, and Marcus Edward, eds. *Inflation through the Ages: Economic, Social, Psychological, and Historical Aspects.* New York: Brooklyn College Press, 1983.

Schnapper, Morris B. *American Labor: A Political and Social History.* Washington, District of Columbia: Public Affairs Press, 1975.

Severance, Frank H. "Picture Book of Earlier Buffalo,"*Publications of the Buffalo Historical Society.* Buffalo: Buffalo Historical Society, 1912, 8 (1912).

Sharfman, I. L. *The Interstate Commerce Commission: A Study in Administrative Law and Procedure.* New York: The commonwealth Fund, 1931. 5 vols.

Shaughnessy, Jim. *Delaware & Hudson.* San Diego: Howell-North Books, 1982.

Shaw, Ronald E. *Canals for a Nation: The Canal Era in the United States, 1790-1860.* Lexington, Kentucky, University of Kentucky Press, 1990.

Smith, H. Perry. *History of Buffalo and Erie County.* Syracuse: D. Mason & Company, 1884. 2 vols.

Staufer, Alvin. *New York Central's Early Power, 1831-1916.* United States: Alvin F. Staufer, 1967.

Staufer, Alvin. and Edward L. May. *New York Central's Later Power, 1910-1968.* Medina, Ohio: Alvin F. Staufer, 1981.

Statistical History of the United States from Colonial Times to the Present. Stamford, Connecticut: Fairfield Publishers, 1965.

Stevens, G. R. *Metropolitan Corridor: Railroads and the American Scene.* Westford, Massachusetts: Yale University Press, 1983.

Stover, John. *Iron Road to the West: American Railroads in the 1850s.* New York: Columbia University Press, 1978.

Taber, Thomas. *The Lackawanna Railroad in the Nineteenth Century.* Muncy, Pennsylvania: Thomas Taber, 1977.

Taber, Thonas. *The Delaware Lackawanna & Western Railroad in the Twentieth Century: The Route of the Phoebe Snow*. Muncy, Pennsylvania: Thomas Townsend Taber III, 1980.

Taylor, Benjamin F. *The World on Wheels and Other Sketches*. Chicago: S. C. Grills & Company, 1874.

Taylor, George Rogers, and Irene Neu. *The American Railway Network, 1861-1890.* Cambridge, Harvard University Press,1956.

Turner, George Edgar. *Victory Rode the Rails: The Strategic Place of Railroads in the Civil War*. New York: Bobbs-Merrill, 1953.

Westing, Frederick. *Erie Power: Steam and Diesel Locomotives of the Erie Railroad from 1840 to 1970*. Medina, Ohio: Alvin F. Staufer, 1970.

White, John H. *The American Railroad Freight Car from the Wood-Car Era to the Coming of Steel*. Baltimore: Johns Hopkins Press, 1993.

White, John H.. *The American Railway Passenger Car*. Baltimore: Johns Hopkins Press, 1978. 2 vols.

Wilner, Frank N. *The Amtrak Story*. Omaha, Nebraska: Simmons-Boardman Books, 1994.

Local Atlases

Brown, Joseph, P., ed. *Atlas of the City of Buffalo, New York*. Philadelphia: American Atlas Company, 1894. 3 vols.

Century Atlas Company. *The Century Atlas of Greater Buffalo*. Philadelphia: Century Atlas Company, 1915. 3 vols.

Hopkins, Griffith Morgan. *Atlas of the City of Buffalo, Erie County, New York.* Philadelphia: G. M. Hopkins Company, 1872.

Hopkins, Griffith Morgan. *Atlas of the City of Buffalo, New York.* Philadelphia: G. M. Hopkins Company, 1884.

Hopkins, Griffith Morgan. *Atlas of the Vicinities of the Cities of Niagara Falls, North Tonawanda and Buffalo, New York*. Philadelphia: G. M. Hopkins Company, 1893.

Rayback, Robert J., ed. *Richards Atlas of New York State*. Phoenix, New York: Frank E. Richards, 1957-1959.

Reinstein, Julia Boyer. Town of Cheektowaga Historical Atlas. Cheektowaga, New York: Cheektowaga Town Board, 1975

Articles

Adam, Robert B. "History of the Abolition of Railroad grade Crossings in the City of Buffalo," *Publications of the Buffalo Historical Society*, 8 (1905), 153-254.

Bohi, Charles W. "When LCL Meant Fast Freight," *Trains*, 53 (August, 1993), 58-66.

Cousins, Garnet R. "Beacon at Mile 435.9," *Trains*, 45 (September, 1985), 20-33; (October, 1985), 40-49.

"Elimination of Grade Crossings," *The Live Wire*, 1:1 (November, 1910), 61-64.

Kerr, Al. "On Track," *Empire State Express* (Publication of the National Railway Historical Society, Buffalo Chapter), February, 1987, 2; October 1987, 3-4.

Klein, Maury, "The Diesel Revolution," *American Heritage of Invention & Technology,* 6:3 (Winter, 1991), 16-22.

McGrane, Reginald C. "Ingalls, Melville," *Dictionary of American Biography,* (22 vols., New York: Scribner's Sons, 1928-1944), 9:466.

"Railway Celebration, Buffalo," *Frank Leslie's Illustrated Newspaper,* 1, (April 26, 1856).

Stephens, Bill. "Delaware & Hudson Thrives under CP Rail,"*Trains*, 52 (July, 1992), 24-26.

Strohmeyer, John "The Agonizing Ordeal of a One Company Town,"*Business and Society Review*, 45 (Summer, 1985), 45-49.

Yates, Raymond F. "The Old Lockport and Niagara Falls Strap Railroad," *Occasional Contributions of the Niagara County Historical Society*. Niagara County Historical Society, 4 (1950), 3-35.

Unbound Maps

Emslie, P. E., and T. H. Kirk. *New Subdivision Map of the City of Buffalo, Showing all the Canal and Harbor Improvements, Buildings, etc.* Buffalo: Jewett & Thomas Company, 1850.

Hydrographic Harbor and Railroad Chart of Buffalo. Buffalo: Charles Green & Company, 1907.

Newspapers

Courier-Express, 1926-1982.

Buffalo Courier, 1847-1926.

Buffalo [Morning] Express, 1846-1926

Buffalo [Evening] News, 1851-

LIST OF FIGURES

NAME INDEX

SUBJECT INDEX

MISCELLANEOUS INDEX

Cincinnati Express, 208, 219